JACK R. MEREDITH
University of Cincinnati

THOMAS E. GIBBS
Mentor Systems

THE MANAGEMENT OF OPERATIONS

2nd EDITION

JOHN WILEY & SONS
New York Chichester Brisbane Toronto Singapore

Cover photograph by **Reginald Wickham**

Library of Congress Cataloging in Publication Data

Meredith, Jack R.
  The management of operations.

  (Wiley series in management, ISSN 0271-6046)
  Includes bibliographies and index.
  1. Production management.   I. Gibbs, Thomas E.
II. Title. III. Series.
TS155.M39 1984   658.5   83-10627
ISBN 0-471-09940-6

Printed in the United States of America

10 9 8 7 6 5 4 3 2

TO CAROL AND JUDI

ABOUT THE AUTHORS

JACK MEREDITH received his undergraduate degrees in engineering and mathematics from Oregon State University. He obtained his MBA and his Ph.D. in business administration from the University of California, Berkeley, with a major in production management. He has held positions with Ampex, Hewlett-Packard, TRW, and Douglas Aircraft Company and possesses extensive service sector experience through grants, consulting, research, and executive seminars.

Currently Associate Professor of Production/Operations Management and Director of Operations Management at the University of Cincinnati, he is also editor of *The Operations Management Review* and a reviewer for the *Journal of Operations Management, Decision Sciences, Management Science, American Journal of Public Health,* and *Operations Research.* He has written articles for *Operations Research, Management Science, Computers and Industrial Engineering, Health Care Systems,* and *American Journal of Public Health* and is the author of *Fundamentals of Management Science* (with E. Turban) and *The Hospital Game.* Professor Meredith's research interests include new technology/computer applications to production and managerial control systems. He is a member of TIMS, AIDS, AIIE, APICS and a Vice-President of the new Operations Management Association (OMA).

THOMAS E. GIBBS is President of Mentor Systems, a computer/software company specializing in minicomputer applications. He has served as Assistant Professor of Accounting at the University of Kentucky, as Assistant Professor of Health Care Administration at Florida International University, and as Adjunct Professor of Public Administration in the NOVA University "Fly a Prof" Program.

He received his Ph.D. from the University of Cincinnati. He has consulted with numerous small businesses, governmental units, and health care organizations regarding information system development, computer selection, and software design. He has also served as Editor of *MAS Communication,* the newsletter of the Management Advisory Services Section of the American Accounting Association, and Chairman of the Section. He is the author of more than 30 articles, some of which have appeared in *The Journal of Systems Management, The Accounting Review,* and *The Internal Auditor.*

PREFACE

A tremendous amount of change has occurred in the field of "operations" since the first edition of this book was published in 1980.

- Productivity has become a major focus of attention.
- Quality has become recognized as being imperative to compete successfully.
- Worldwide competition in foreign markets, and even the domestic marketplace, has intensified almost into a war.
- Automated manufacturing techniques such as computerized information systems, robotics, computer-aided-manufacturing (CAM), and automatic-storage/retrieval systems (AS/RS) have become widely familiar.
- Computers, both mini and personal (micro) size, have invaded organizations and homes alike.

All of these developments relate directly to the area of operations. The operations manager's responsibility is knowing how to economically produce a desired product or service and get it to the recipient when it is needed—whether the recipient is a customer, a patient, a client, a passenger, or a student. Operations is concerned with how to produce—economically, competitively, with quality, with new technology, and with results. This is the subject of this book.

In conjunction with the increased external focus on the operations function in organizations, there have been a significant number of developments within the field of operations itself. First, there are the new journals in the field: the *Journal of Operations Management*, the *Operations Management Review*, and the *International Journal of Operations and Production Management*. Then, in 1981 the Operations Management Association (OMA) was founded to join her sister societies in the functional areas of business: FMA (finance) and AMA (marketing).

Meanwhile, the increasing pressure of the American Assembly of Collegiate Schools of Business (AACSB) on colleges to recognize the importance of the operations function and include this material in their curricula created as great an academic awareness of the operations function as has developed in industry. Demand for operations management faculty in relation to the supply is currently twice that of accounting and is paralleled only by the demand for computer/information systems faculty.

This shortage of operations faculty has been a major focus of the revision of this text. In many schools the "production" or "operations" course is necessarily taught by an instructor whose major field is allied but does not lie directly in the operations area, such as general management or management science. In other schools, teaching assistants must, of necessity, carry a greater burden of the instructional load than for other courses. The instructor's manual for this text was written particularly with these situations in mind. In addition, the text itself has been revised to clarify the basic structure and conceptual foundations of the field, not only to help students new to the area but also to aid instructors from allied fields.

The main characteristics of this book reflect the concerns expressed above.

1. *A Generic Framework.* We still find that very few texts provide a "generic" perspective for viewing the operations of every kind of organization in terms of an integrated, logical structure. We have thus maintained the well-received generic view of operations that was developed in the first edition. For example, the terms "organization" and "recipient" are used in place of the more limiting "company" and "customer," respectively. Specificity is attained through numerous examples: farms, hospitals, banks, libraries, factories, schools, funeral homes, insurance firms, and fire departments.

2. *A Design Approach.* In this edition we have kept the planning focus we had previously but simplified it from the first edition to stress the *strategic* role of operations. In many contemporary texts the operations function is viewed by definition as a low-level managerial activity. We feel that operations has a critical strategic role to play in organizations and approach the entire field from this point of view. The four parts of the book reflect this perspective.

Part I: Strategic Operations
Part II: Tactical Operations
Part III: Detailed Operations
Part IV: Operations Control

We believe that, in addition to helping the student understand *why* the operations are designed as they are, as well as *how* they are designed, this approach is superior to others in giving a more *integrated* view of the organization and is thus inherently more generic.

3. *A Functional Orientation.* We focus on the operations functions under discussion and not on the quantitative or behavioral techniques that are available to aid in addressing and analyzing those functions. More complex solution methodologies, such as Monte Carlo simulation and solution approaches to linear programming, are placed in chapter appendices, though the topics are discussed where appropriate in the chapters. Also included in chapter appendices, when appropriate, are discussions of the interface with other business areas such as finance and personnel.

4. *An Introductory Level.* The stress in the book is on the basic concepts of operations. Realistic examples, current illustrations, detailed explanations, and even, on occasion, relevant cartoons are used to help convey these concepts. Learning aids are employed, additionally, to further enhance the learning process. In this edition, for example, the *Key Learning Points* in the chapter summary are tied one-to-one to the *Learning Objectives* at the beginning of each chapter.

Key Terms listed at the end of each chapter are set in boldface in the text. These terms, plus additional comments, are highlighted in the margin notes throughout the chapters. *Review Questions* at the chapter end help the student check whether he or she noted the critical points. And *Discussion Questions* probe conceptual tangents and deeper issues raised by the chapter discussion. In many chapters some highly relevant *Readings* are included to demonstrate the timeliness and practical significance of the topics.

Of particular importance are the end-of-chapter *Problems*, which facilitate the grasp of the chapter topics. On average, the number of problems has been increased 150 percent in this edition and two levels are identified. First, there are *Practice Problems* that are straightforward applications of the material in the text. There are usually both "number" and "word" problems from which to choose, and the problem types follow the same order as the chapter development. Then there are *More Complex Problems*, which combine data or methodologies, extend the chapter discussion into new realms, require solutions in reverse, or are just plain hard.

Cases are also included to help the student understand the application of concepts. Theory is one thing; application is often something else, as students typically learn on their first job. These brief cases are meant to ease that transition and to give a realistic perspective to students' learning. Last, there is a simple workbook available to accompany this text and provide the student with guidance about how and what to study.

We particularly thank those who contributed so greatly to this revision—Allen Kartchner, Matthew Liberatore, Leonidas Charalambides, Jill Ann Kammermeyer, John Ettie, and Henry Owen, III—as well as those who helped guide the development of the first edition—Elwood Buffa, Samuel Seward, Michael Maggard, Edward Heard, Steve Bolander, James Cox, and especially our ever-available critic, counselor, and sounding board, Carol Meredith.

JACK R. MEREDITH
THOMAS E. GIBBS

CONTENTS

II
TACTICAL OPERATIONS
DESIGNING THE TRANSFORMATION PROCESS

THE MANAGEMENT OF OPERATIONS

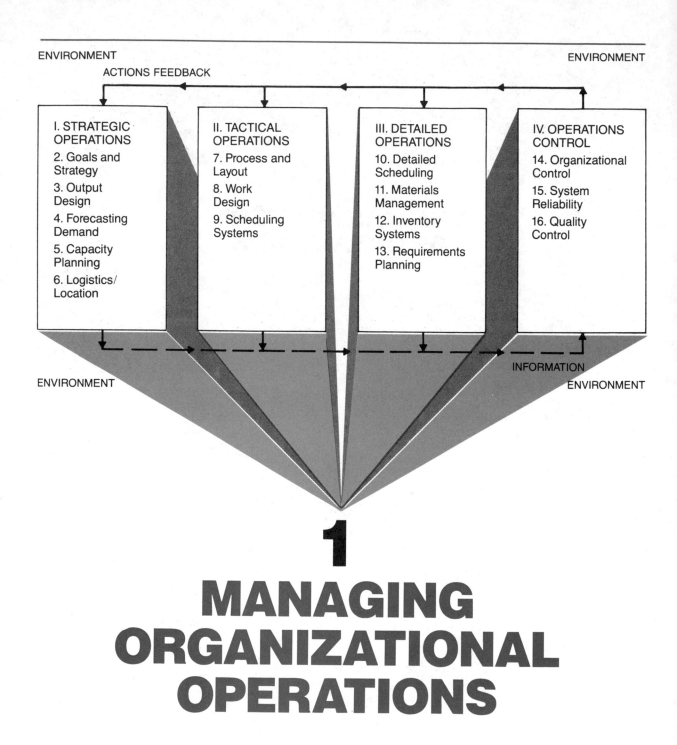

ENVIRONMENT   ENVIRONMENT

ACTIONS FEEDBACK

I. STRATEGIC OPERATIONS	II. TACTICAL OPERATIONS	III. DETAILED OPERATIONS	IV. OPERATIONS CONTROL
2. Goals and Strategy	7. Process and Layout	10. Detailed Scheduling	14. Organizational Control
3. Output Design	8. Work Design	11. Materials Management	15. System Reliability
4. Forecasting Demand	9. Scheduling Systems	12. Inventory Systems	16. Quality Control
5. Capacity Planning		13. Requirements Planning	
6. Logistics/ Location			

ENVIRONMENT   INFORMATION
                                                       ENVIRONMENT

1
MANAGING ORGANIZATIONAL OPERATIONS

1

LEARNING OBJECTIVES

By the completion of this chapter the student should

- Know what process the operations function entails.
- Be aware of the importance of operations to organizations.
- Understand the major ways in which value is added to entities.
- Better appreciate the distinction between products and services.
- Realize the significance and role of the transformation process in the operations system.
- Comprehend the distinction between the common descriptive approach to operations and this text's design approach.
- Appreciate the purpose of organizations for man and the need for, and nature of, management.
- Understand the monitoring and feedback control process.
- Have a feel for the long and detailed history of operations management and its role in contemporary society.
- Be aware of the growth of services in our economy.
- Better understand the interfaces and differences between operations and other allied business and nonbusiness areas, and be familiar with the types of operations job titles.
- Be especially familiar with the conceptual scheme we will follow in the text.

In the late 1970s and early 1980s American industry received a traumatic shock. Americans seemed to prefer foreign goods over American-made products, even, in some cases, when the foreign goods were considerably more expensive. What happened to this once-proud industry, the "showcase of the world" only a few decades earlier?

In this book we will look at some of the reasons for this profound change and how it may possibly be turned around. It is a story of how a major functional business area was, and in many cases still is, virtually ignored for 25 years. It involves an area known as "operations," which is typically responsible for 80 percent of both the physical and human resources in almost every organization. And it illustrates what can happen to a country's "quality-image" and "productivity" when a major business area is given inadequate attention in its industries, business schools, and society in general.

Our discussion will touch on many topics you have probably read or heard about before: "quality circles," "kanban," robots, computers, "CAD/CAM." But to begin, let us go back in time to some simpler organizations than we see today to better understand what "operations" is all about and to clarify some terminology we will use throughout the text.

1.1 THE OPERATIONS FUNCTION

Consider for a moment one of our ancestors of long ago, sitting on the ground in front of his cave with a sharp stone in one hand hitting a piece of obsidian. With each stroke a small splinter of obsidian broke off. As our ancestor kept carefully chipping away, a spear point, or perhaps an arrowhead or axe, gradually took shape. By gathering more such obsidian stones and spending many hours chipping at them, he could form many such spear points and trade them to other cave dwellers for food, animal pelts, or something else he valued.

Adding value. What this ancestor of ours was doing, and what we still do in our mammoth corporations of today, was *adding value* to some object, and then either using it himself or trading it to another for something else he valued. This process is termed the *operations* function and is the heart—indeed, the very reason for being—of every organization. Since we will be using this term throughout the text let us formally define it again.

> **Operations** is the process of changing inputs into outputs and thereby adding value to some entity; this constitutes the primary function of virtually every organization.

The Value-Added Process

Physically, sensually, or psychologically altering an entity. Let us widen the scope of our thinking now and consider *how* value can be added to an entity. There are four major ways.

1. Alter. Something can be changed structurally, such as our ancestor was doing. That would be a *physical* change and this process is basic to our manufacturing industries where goods are cut, stamped, formed, assembled, and so on. We then go out and buy the shirt, or computer, or whatever the good is. But it need not be a separate object or entity; it may, for example, be *us* that is altered. We may get our hair cut, for example. Or our appendix removed.

But other, more subtle, alterations may also have value for us. *Sensual* alterations, such as heat when we are cold, or music, or beauty may be highly valued on certain occasions. Beyond this, even *psychological* alterations can have value, such as the feeling of worth from obtaining a college degree or the feeling of friendship from a long-distance phone call.

2. Transport. An entity, again including ourselves, may have more value if located somewhere other than where it currently is. We may appreciate things being brought to us, such as flowers, or removed from us, such as garbage, or mosquitos.

3. Store. The value of an entity may be enhanced for us if it is kept in a protected environment for some period of time. Some examples are Christmas presents kept on layaway, our pet remaining at a kennel while we go on vacation, or ourselves staying in a motel.

4. Inspect. Last, an entity may be more valued because we better understand its properties. This may apply to something we own, plan to use, are considering purchasing, or, again, even ourselves. Medical exams, elevator certifications, purchase guarantees, and so on fall into this category.

Four major ways to add value.

Thus we see that value may be added to an entity in a number of different ways. The entity may be changed directly, in space, in time, or even just in our mental image of it.

Products and Services

A product or a service?

In the preceding discussion we distinguished between changes made to ourselves and changes made to a separate physical entity. Traditionally we have classified the former as a "service" and the latter as a "product." But this classification may be more confusing than helpful. For example, the transportation, storage, or even refinishing of a desk we own is really more a service we are purchasing than a product; indeed, we already own the product! Or suppose a dentist makes a set of false teeth for us. Is this a product or a service? What about a filling? What if he pulls the tooth instead?

You see the confusion? Let's take another example. You want a load of sand for your child's sandbox. Your neighbor, whose yard is entirely sand, is digging a large hole in which to plant a tree. You negotiate with your neighbor to have him shovel the sand from the hole into your sandbox for $10. Is this a product or a service?

Sasser [20] avoids this ambiguity by adopting the point of view that any physical entity accompanying a transformation that adds value is a **facilitating good** (the desk, the false teeth, the filling, the sand). In many cases, of course, there may be *no* facilitating good and, in this text, we will refer to these cases as being "pure services."

The advantage of this interpretation is that *every* transformation that

A facilitating good solves the ambiguity.

adds value is simply a service, either with or without facilitating goods! If you buy a piece of lumber, you have not purchased a product, you have purchased a bundle of services, many of them embodied in a facilitating good: a tree-cutting service, a sawing-planing mill service, a transportation service, a storage service, and perhaps even an advertising service that told you where lumber was on sale that day. Sasser refers to these services as a bundle of "benefits," some of which are tangible (the sawed length of lumber, the type of tree) and others of which are intangible (courteous sales clerks, a convenient location, payment by charge card). Some services may, of course, even be negative, such as an audit of your tax return.

Tangible and intangible benefits.

> **Services** are bundles of benefits, some of which may be tangible and others intangible, and they may be accompanied by a facilitating good or goods.

Firms often run into major difficulties when they ignore this aspect of their operations. They may think of themselves as only "a lumberyard" and not as providing a bundle of services. They may even recognize that they have to include certain tangible services (such as cutting lumber to the length desired by the customer) but ignore the intangible services (charge sales, having a sufficient number of clerks).

In this text we will adopt the point of view that all value-adding transformations (i.e., operations) are services, and there may or may not be a set of accompanying facilitating goods. With this definition in mind, let us now proceed to further widen our horizons and consider the transformation process itself.

The Transformation Process

Let us review the procedure our caveman used to make his spear points. He took a number of "inputs" from his environment, transformed them in a special way that added value to them, and wound up with an "output," in this case a spear point. This process is illustrated in Figure 1.1. Each of the four elements in Figure 1.1 will now be considered in more detail.

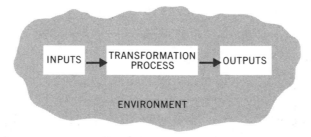

Figure 1.1 The traditional descriptive approach to operations.

I. Inputs. The set of inputs used in operations is more complex than might be supposed, even in our simple caveman example. There, the obvious inputs were the obsidian, the hard, sharp stone to chip the obsidian with, and the labor of the caveman. However, the caveman needed "facilities" in which to work: light to see, shelter from rain, a workplace to support the obsidian, and so on. Another very important input was "knowledge" of how to make the spear point. Others without this knowledge could not transform the obsidian into an entity with value. And let us not forget the last input that is always mandatory—sufficient "time" to accomplish the operations. It is, indeed, quite frequent that the operations function fails in its task because it cannot complete the transformation process within the required time limit.

By and large, these are the same types of inputs we use in our operations today. The only possible additions might be labor-saving "machines" and "supplies" to aid in more complex transformation processes. Supplies are distinguished from raw materials by the fact that they are not usually a part of the final output. Oil, paper clips, pens, tape, and other such items are commonly classified as supplies because they only aid in producing the output.

II. Transformation Process. From our earlier discussion of services it should be clear that the transformation process is also not as straightforward as might be supposed. Part of the difficulty is that the "value added" is in the eye of the beholder. A spear point may be seen as almost equally valuable by all cave dwellers, but Mrs. Van Pelt's new $100 hair design may be viewed by some as an atrocity; and if Mrs. Van Pelt views it as such herself, there is going to be severe trouble at the hairdresser's.

Second, as we pointed out earlier, the transformation process is really producing an entire set of services, only part of which may be tangibly embodied in a facilitating good. The production of the intangible services must not be ignored in the operations.

There are a number of important characteristics of the transformation process which need to be identified:

1. Efficiency. This is usually measured as the output per unit input. The problem in trying to compare different transformation processes, of course, is in choosing good measures for outputs and inputs. In a store it might be dollars of sales per square foot. In a maternity suite it might be deliveries per hour. For our caveman, and for operations in general, it is usually called **productivity** and measured in units of output per manhour. For pure services, defining the units of output is often difficult, but in this case it is simply the number of spear points per hour of work. If our caveman is inefficient, then the work going into the spear points could have been better spent doing something else (such as growing food or trapping animals).

2. Effectiveness. Where efficiency is known as "doing the thing right," effectiveness is known as "doing the right thing." That is, is the right set of outputs being produced? If our caveman is making spear points for himself, then we assume he is being effective (though they may not work as he wishes when he goes to use them, in which case he was *not* effective). But if he was

Inputs of knowledge and time also.

Value is in the eye of the beholder.

Characteristics of the transformation process.

producing an output to trade with other cavemen and they didn't value spear points, then the transformation process was ineffective.

   3. Quality. The output may not work well or last long, in which case we say it is of poor quality. For example, a spear point of sandstone may be made much faster but will become dull very quickly also.

   4. Lead Time. How quickly can the output be produced? If a custom output is desired, or a totally new output, the lead time refers to the time needed to produce the first unit of this different output.

   5. Flexibility. Can the transformation process be used to produce other, different outputs? How easily? How fast? Will the process work for arrowheads? For ax heads?

   All of the above characteristics will, in some way, be reflected in each of the many activities that occur during the transformation process, most of which are usually noted as topics in their own right. We will just identify these activities here since they constitute the major portion of this text. Their major characteristics will then be discussed when we describe each activity in detail.

Some major operations topics.

- *Capacity planning:* Determining when and how much facilities, equipment, and labor to have available.
- *Facility location:* Determining where to locate production, storage, and other major facilities.
- *Transformation process design:* Determining the layout and physical flow aspects of the transformation activities.
- *Work design:* Determining the best way to use labor in the process. This includes motion study, workplace layout, and environmental conditions.
- *Scheduling:* Determining when each activity or task in the transformation process is to be done and where all the inputs should be.
- *Materials management:* Determining the amounts of materials to be located in particular points at particular times.
- *Quality control:* Determining how quality standards are to be developed and maintained.
- *Reliability and maintenance:* Determining how the proper performance of both the output and the transformation process itself are to be maintained.

   III. Outputs. The output bundle of tangible and intangible service benefits resulting from the application of the transformation process to the inputs has been discussed at length already. Suffice it to say that the recipient of the outputs may not value each of the elements of the bundle in the same manner as the producer of the outputs.

   IV. Environment. The environment plays a number of complex roles in the operations function. It provides the inputs, limitations on the transformation process, and the recipients of the outputs. As we will note later, it is extremely important to continually monitor the environment to be immediately aware of any changes affecting our operations function. This would include the political, organizational, geographical, legal, economic, and other such environments in which the operations function is embedded. Specifically, the "environment" is considered to consist of those elements that *affect* the operations function but cannot be controlled *within* it.

Environment affects but cannot be controlled.

The four elements of Figure 1.1 represent what is known as a "system."

> A **system** is a purposeful collection of people, objects, and procedures for operating within an environment.

Levels of systems.

It should be noted that the environment of one system may itself be part of another system, such as the Federal Reserve System, or society. Thus we recognize the fact that there exist *levels* of systems, each embedded within a larger system. Note also that systems are not merely arbitrary groupings but are goal directed or purposeful collections.

1.2 THE DESIGN APPROACH TO OPERATIONS

The design approach versus the descriptive approach.

We adopt in this text what we will term a **design approach** to operations management rather than the more commonly used *descriptive approach* illustrated in Figure 1.1. The difference is primarily one of direction or focus. The descriptive approach is similar to a plant tour. It starts with some *inputs*, such as people, lumber, hardware, facilities, and machines; proceeds through a number of *transformation activities*, such as sawing, sanding, nailing, and painting; and ends with an *output* such as a table. However, the person on tour (you, the student) frequently does not see *why* the process performs as it does or what might happen if inputs or activities changed. Why is pine used instead of oak? Why is it not glued together instead of nailed? Although the descriptive perspective is easy to visualize, it is a *static* view of operations. If certain inputs are no longer available, this static approach offers no insight into the required alterations in the operations to accommodate the change.

A static view.

A dynamic view.

The design approach of Figure 1.2 presents a more *dynamic* view of the operations system and allows for the necessity of constant operations redesign because of change. The design approach is, in essence, one of sequential planning of an operations system, including the planning of change. It starts with the organization and its *goals* operating in some *environment*, identifies a number of potential organizational *outputs* that would generate returns (typically, money) from that *environment*, and considers all of the possible *transformation processes*, and then the *inputs*, that could produce those outputs. Hence, rather than a *single* system of operations being identified, a *complex* of many diverse possibilities is included. "Should it be cast or machined, and, if cast, from iron or aluminum?" The design task is to select among these possibilities those that most effectively meet the organization's goals.

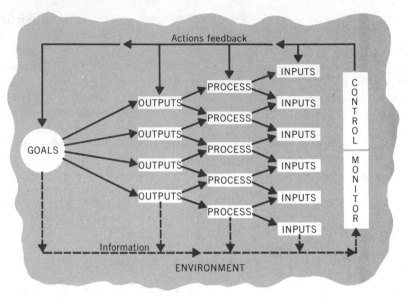

Figure 1.2   The design approach to the operations system.

The inherently
iterative nature of
operations design.

The elimination and selection of the various possible outputs, processes, and so forth is an *iterative* procedure. This means that the operations design is repetitive and cyclical in nature, as illustrated in Figure 1.3, since the outputs depend on the organization's goals and what input resources are available, and the inputs, in turn, depend on the transformation process and what outputs are needed. Each stage of the operation must be reconsidered and improved in a repetitive manner. Furthermore, each stage of the system must be designed with all the other stages in mind at the same time. This is termed the *systems approach*.

But a one-time choice is not sufficient. Sometimes operations do not proceed according to plan, so they need to be **monitored** and if significant

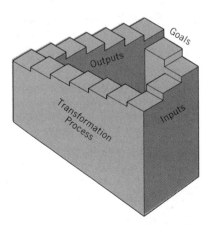

Figure 1.3   The iterative nature of operations design.

The importance of the environment.

differences are noted, **control** is exercised to bring activities back within plan. And, since both the internal and external environments of the organization are constantly changing (sales fall off, materials do not arrive, workers quit), continuous monitoring of these environments is also necessary. These functions, too, must be designed from the start. The purpose of monitoring and control, then, is to sense changes in the subsystems and their environments, plus the external environment, and vary the selection of operations alternatives to meet those changes.

Let us now look a bit deeper into the additional elements of the operations system introduced in Figure 1.2. First, we will consider the organization and its goals operating within some environment. We will also address here the task of managing such organizations. Then we will look more closely at the monitoring and control aspects of the operations system, including the actions feedback process.

Organizations and Their Management

Humans learned early in their evolution that cooperation with their fellow humans was the only way to achieve many important desires that one cannot achieve alone—desires for special foods, certain belongings, acceptance and fellowship, safety, and so on. The instruments for such cooperation to achieve these desires are **organizations,** which, broadly defined, are groups of elements structured by policies, either explicit or implied, to guide the members of a group in their activities. Typical productive organizations are easily envisioned, from Viking explorers to the Aztec Indian nation to modern international businesses. But children's play groups and ''TGIF'' parties are also organizations for satisfying human desires, only the duration is limited and the needs are slightly different.

Why humans form organizations.

Humans are social animals. We automatically form outselves into social groups such as families, tribes, sororities, and clubs. It is no wonder, then, that faced with certain needs and desires, people have learned to organize to satisfy them. But humans are also rational beings and will only become members of organizations if doing so contributes, in some way, to their own personal goals. We join churches and civic organizations, become members of sailing clubs and baseball teams, and accept employment in businesses or other organizations because these activities help us achieve our own needs and desires.

Throughout history people have formed organizations to satisfy individual or collective goals and disbanded or left those organizations when they were no longer of use or when organizational goals conflicted with personal goals. As civilization advanced from a family-centered farming economy to a handicraft-trading economy,* people began to recognize the advantages of specializaton and trade. Rather than produce all of its own goods and services, a family could often produce, with less total effort, an excess of a commodity for which it had a special advantage and trade the excess with others for

*Made by hand, that is, before mass production.

Development of an
interdependent
economy.

desired commodities. Trade thus bound families closer together in cooperation since each family became more dependent on the others' commodities. As people making compatible commodities naturally began working with each other, the informal handicraft organizations evolved into the craft guilds of the Middle Ages and then into factories.

Coordination is one
function of
management.

Any group endeavor requires **management** if it is to be effective in attaining its goals. Coordination of effort is the key to group success, and management performs this activity, among others. Even in ancient times management's role was noted occasionally, as illustrated by this biblical report of adept materials management.

> Let Pharaoh do this, and let him appoint officers over the land, and take up the fifth part of the land of Egypt in the seven plenteous years. And let them gather all the food of those good years that come, and lay up corn under the hand of Pharaoh, and let them keep food in the cities. And that food shall be for store to the land against the seven years of famine, which shall be in the land of Egypt; that the land perish not through the famine [*Genesis* 41:34–36].

The new
institution of
management.

We also know [13, pp. 78–81] that the early Egyptian, Chinese, and Greek scholars conversed at length regarding managment and administration. The need in early times for management becomes obvious when one considers such projects as the pyramids, the Great Wall of China, and the wars of Alexander. Nevertheless, the *function* of management received little recognition in these early times, and reports of notable achievements in management were the exception rather than the rule. As the early handicraft system evolved into craft guilds and then factories, however, the role of management as a necessary function gained new importance and recognition. Peter Drucker, an outstanding management scholar of today, has commented that

> The emergence of management as an essential, a distinct and a leading institution is a pivotal event in social history. Rarely, if ever, has a new basic institution, a new leading group, emerged as fast as has management since the turn of this century. Rarely in human history has a new institution proven indispensable so quickly; and even less often has a new institution arrived with so little opposition, so little disturbance, so little controversy. . . . Management, which is the organ of society specifically charged with making resources productive, that is, with the responsibility for organized economic advance, therefore, reflects the basic spirit of the modern age. It is, in fact, indispensable—and this explains why, once begotten, it grew so fast and with so little opposition [8, pp. 3,4].

The nature of
management.

Whether an organization is a church, grocery store, government agency, or baseball team, management must take place. Managers who operate in each of these organizations may face completely different environments, may require different technical skills or knowledge, may be confronted with different problems, and may have different scopes of authority, power, or influence, but each one of them will carry on similar basic managerial functions.

But just what *is* management? Many have defined management, as the "B.C." cartoon in Figure 1.4, to be the process of "making decisions." This, in turn, has generated the perception of management as an "analytical" function, for which *mathematical* analysis would be particulary appropriate.

(Reprinted by permission of Johnny Hart and Field Enterprises, Inc.)

Figure 1.4   The management process.

The analysis function.   **Analysis** is the process of breaking a system down into its basic parts and examining them. By careful analysis of the parts, a better understanding of the whole may be obtained and, thus, better decisions as well. This is the primary focus of the majority of this text.

However, Starr points out that

Management is a synthesizing function. Therefore, mathematical analysis is used, not produced by the manager. He employs analysis for descriptive purposes so that he may better diagnose and prescribe for the system's performance [22, p. vi].

The synthesis
function.

Synthesis is the creative, insightful process that results in new products and inventions, new techniques, and many discoveries. The synthesizing function of management is the act of combining various parts to produce a complex whole, such as people, machines, and material to produce a table. Sasser [19] even maintains that our whole society has now passed from an age of analysis into a new age—one of synthesis. An elegant comparison of analysis and synthesis was made by Sir Arthur Eddington, a physicist.

> We often think that when we have completed our study of *one* we know all about *two*, because "two" is "one and one." We forget that we still have to make a study of "and." [10, p. 103]

Thus, the manager's task is composed of both analysis and synthesis. The former is used as a foundation that allows the manager to perform the latter, the creative aspect of management. We address the synthesis aspect of operations in the first part of this text when we deal with goals and strategies.

Monitoring and Feedback Control

The process of monitoring and feedback control illustrated earlier in Figure 1.2 is used extensively in the control of systems, including management systems, and will be encountered throughout this text. Let us briefly develop the concept at this point so the reader will understand better the reasoning behind it.

Is there a
significant change?

In essence, the monitoring process must tell the manager when a "significant" change has occurred in either the operations system itself (the inputs, the transformation process, or the outputs), the internal environment (the organization and its goals), or the external environment (which may affect the operations system, the demand for the output, or the organization itself and its goals). If the changes are *not* significant then no control actions are initiated. But if the changes are significant, management must intercede and take corrective control, called **feedback,** which alters the inputs, the transformation process, the outputs, or, on occasion, even the organization's goals themselves.

The role of the
comparator and
effector.

The most widely used example of a monitoring and feedback control system is the common thermostat. Figure 1.5 illustrates graphically the design of a heater's thermostat. Note that there is a monitoring device that senses the actual temperature, a system for reporting the temperature to the *comparator*, which compares the actual temperature with the predetermined desired temperature, a decision maker with a decision rule, and an *effector* for control. The decision maker considers the information submitted by the comparator and, using the decision rule, adjusts the effector (heater). A typical decision rule for a thermostat might be of the following form:

If (actual temperature − desired) exceeds 3 degrees, turn heat off.
If (desired temperature − actual) exceeds 2 degrees, turn heat on.

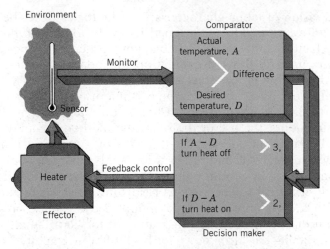

Figure 1.5 Thermostat monitor/control system.

One example of a mechanized, *nonfeedback* process involves food packaging. Many supermarket meat counters use label-applying machines to weigh, print, and affix price labels on packaged meats. Anyone watching this machine at work would notice that it continues "applying" labels even after the packages of meat are all labeled; thus feedback does not occur and this would not be considered a monitoring and feedback control system.

Labeling machines.

1.3 THE HISTORY OF OPERATIONS MANAGEMENT

The field of operations management has evolved in a very short span of time, historically speaking. Its roots, however, go back to the Industrial Revolution, which started in the 1770s with the following important developments.

- The "division of labor" concept, espoused by Adam Smith.
- The steam engine, invented by James Watt.
- The "interchangeable parts" concept, developed by Eli Whitney.

Adam Smith is given much of the credit for the theoretical development of the economics of modern production. In his book, *The Wealth of Nations* [21], he pointed out that where workers are organized to produce large quantities of an item the labor required should be divided into discrete tasks. He believed that this "division of labor" would produce several benefits.

The division of labor.

- Workers who continually performed the same task would acquire greater skill at that task.
- Time would be saved that is normally lost in switching from one task to another.
- A worker's increased concentration on the same task frequently would lead to the development of special tools and techniques for easier or faster accomplishment of that task.

Benefits of a division of labor.

The division-of-labor characteristic of factories described by Adam Smith over 200 years ago has continued its evolution and refinement all the way to the factories, hospitals, schools, governmental agencies, stores, libraries, restaurants, and other organizations of today. Of course, we now are concerned that this process has gone too far and taken away the workers' pride in their work and sense of accomplishment.

In 1832 a mathematician, Charles Babbage, extended Smith's work by recommending the use of the scientific method for analyzing factory problems. In particular, he suggested the use of time study, unit costing, research and development, economic location analysis, bonus payments, and pay on the basis of skill requirements. This latter recommendation was an outgrowth of Smith's observations regarding the specialization of labor. That is, with a division of labor, payment need be made only for the requisite amount of skill needed in a task and not for "craftsman" skills for all operations. Babbage is also known for his "difference engine" and his "analytical engine," the forerunners of today's computer. (The former was never completed, however, due to a lack of tooling technology, and financial backing was withdrawn for the latter by the Chancellor of the Exchequer because it was believed to be "indefinitely expensive.")

The first computer.

However, almost half a century passed after Babbage before anyone addressed the problem of managing factories. In 1878, a U.S. national tennis champion turned his attention to the factories and began a movement that eventually earned him a reputation as "the father of scientific management." His name was Frederick Winslow Taylor. In that year, Taylor began working for the Midvale Steel Company whose president, William Sellers, was an advocate of experimentation in factory methods. Taylor adopted some of Sellers' ideas, and many other factory management ideas of common knowledge, and organized them to form a unique philosophy of management.

Taylor's philosophy.

Briefly, Taylor's philosophy was that successful management was not the result of applying individual management "techniques" to the job but rather of a comprehensive approach to business operations. He believed that improved efficiency in a business could be obtained by

1. Using managers as work *planners* by gathering traditional knowledge about the work and reducing it to standardized procedures for the workers.

2. Methodically *selecting, training,* and *developing* each worker on an individual basis.

3. Striving for *cooperation* between management and the workers to simultaneously obtain both maximum production and high workers' wages.

4. *Dividing* the work between management and the workers so each is working on what they are most proficient in doing.

Although Taylor added a number of his own contributions to the field, his most significant accomplishment was the massive amount of attention he focused on the field of management through his own determination and zeal. Taylor described his new management philosophy in a book, *The Principles of Scientific Management*, published in 1911 [23]. This event, more than any other, can be considered as the beginning of the field of operations management.

The origin of operations management.

The colleagues, contemporaries, and followers of Taylor were many and included the following people.

1911: Frank Gilbreth. Frank Gilbreth is considered by many to be the "father of motion study." He stressed the applications of principles of motion economy to the most minute details of tasks in an attempt to identify the "one best way" of performing a given task. He also developed the well-known motion study technique involving the use of "therbligs" and *chronocyclegraphs.*

Therbligs.

1911: Lillian Gilbreth. Lillian Gilbreth is known not only for her work with her husband but also for her human relations work in the field. Her book, *The Psychology of Management,* is one of the earliest works concerning the human factor in business organizations. From her studies dealing with worker fatigue and psychology she has gained the title of the "first lady of management."

Psychology.

1913: Henry Ford. Henry Ford utilized Eli Whitney's idea of interchangeable parts and a continuous workflow concept he saw in Switzerland to bring "mass production" to large-scale industry. He arranged the work stations into an assembly "line" with a moving belt for the parts, each worker performing a specialized task on the parts as they went by. Ford is also known for his concern for the human element in production, with his early "sociological departments" being the framework for today's personnel departments.

The assembly line.

1913: Henry Gantt. Henry Gantt's best known contribution to management is the charting system he developed for scheduling production. However, he also developed some original incentive pay systems and emphasized the importance of worker psychology in areas such as morale.

The Gantt chart.

1913: Harrington Emerson. Harrington Emerson took Taylor's ideas and applied them to the organization *structure* with an emphasis on the firm's objectives. He emphasized, in a set of organizational "principles" that he developed, the use of experts in organizations to improve organizational efficiency.

Organization structure.

1931: H. F. Dodge, H. G. Romig, and W. Shewhart. H. F. Dodge, H. G. Romig, and W. Shewhart were co-workers at Bell Telephone Laboratories. Together they developed the procedure of "sampling inspection" for the control of quality. To aid in this process they published statistical sampling tables, now in extensive use, which utilized statistical inference and probability theory.

Sampling inspection.

1933: G. Elton Mayo. G. Elton Mayo is best known for his studies at Western Electric's Hawthorne Plant where he emphasized the human and social factors in work. The stress on human relations in management for so many years following this study gave birth to the term the "human

The Hawthorne studies.

relations school" of management thinking. Mayo felt that "scientific management" often emphasized technical skills at the expense of adaptive skills.

1935: L. H. C. Tippett. L. H. C. Tippett is known for his work in statistical sampling theory. His studies, although not fully utilized until much later, provided industry with a method for determining standards for work times, idle times, and other such work activities.

Work standards.

With so much attention being devoted to the management of factories, this special area of management came to be known by the 1950s as "manufacturing management" (other terms such as "industrial management" and "factory management" were used synonymously). The pace of development is illustrated graphically in Figure 1.6.

Early names.

The central concern to many in manufacturing management was increased productivity. And it was, rightly, of concern to our entire society. Increased productivity meant that less human labor was required to produce a given product, which in turn increased the available quantity and decreased the cost of many products. In this country, factories and the "industrial machine" meant increases in the standard of living and availability

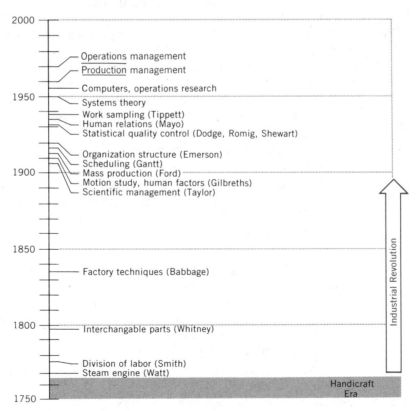

Figure 1.6 The history of operations management.

of consumer goods unheard of in most parts of the world. However, in some instances it also meant pollution, dehumanization of the workplace, and boredom due to repetitive, meaningless tasks.

Some disadvantages.

The 1950s saw the development of systems theory, operations research, and the computer, each of which furthered the cause of manufacturing management. Systems theory emphasized the interrelationships existing in problems and pointed out the futility of considering problems in a vacuum.

OM in the 1950s.

Operations research (also generally known as "management science") is the application of the scientific method to study and devise solutions to managerial problems. Employing a decision focus, the systems approach, and mathematical models, operations research has helped solve allocation, scheduling, planning, processing, inventory, layout, control, and location problems.

Operations research.

In addition, the computer allowed the fast and relatively inexpensive development of management information, expedited the solution of operations research models that were heretofore too large for manual solution, provided support for business functions (such as payroll, general and cost accounting, and customer billing), and formed a basis for automation.

In the late 1950s scholars and researchers in the field began to generalize the problems and techniques of manufacturing management to other productive organizations as well, such as petroleum and chemical processors and wholesalers, and the name for the field evolved into "production management." The intent of this term was to stress the fact that the field had become a "functional management discipline" in itself and not just a set of manufacturing techniques. In the late 1960s the field expanded even further, this time into the *service sector* of the economy. Since the word "production" seemed to connote "product" organizations, the more general term "operations" was substituted to emphasize the **generic** (or general) basis of the field. This transition from "production" to "operations" is still occurring today. Because it is likely to become an increasingly important area of management, the next section is devoted to a closer look at this continuing growth of services in our economy.

Emergence of "production management."

"Operations management" to include services.

The Emergence and Growth of the Service Sector

With the increased standard of living resulting from increased factory productivity came changes in the needs and demands of the population. A person could use just so many pairs of shoes, so many easy chairs, and so many cars. Rather than spend their income on more goods, people decided to take in a movie, eat out more often, pay someone else to clean their house or cut their lawn, improve their education or health, and take advantage of many other types of services.

The growth of services.

Figures 1.7 and 1.8 dramatically illustrate that, since 1950, services have been rapidly increasing as a proportion of both *expenditures* for personal consumption and *employers* of the workforce. Note that less than 25 percent of the workforce is now employed in manufacturing.

In addition to the growth in "private sector" services, there has been a

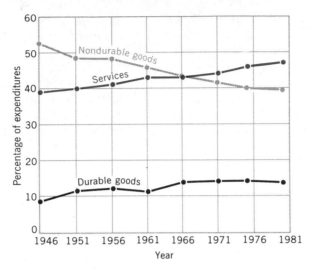

Figure 1.7 Percentage of personal consumption expenditures for goods and services. (*Source:* Economic Report of the President, 1981.)

The growth of public services.

significant increase in public (government) sector services such as fire protection, welfare, and defense, as indicated in Figure 1.8.

Although there has clearly been a marked increase in the demand for services, one reason for the tremendous growth in service sector employment has been a negative one, namely, its lack of productivity growth. The inefficiency of services is evidenced by the constant and often bitter criticism of the post office, the railroads, the health care system, public schools, and many other such systems.

The lack of service productivity.

Only in recent years have service sector organizations received the same attention from researchers as had been paid to manufacturers. Many of the concepts and ideas developed for the manufacturing sector can be modified and applied to service industries. For example, the problems of school bus routing, fire and rescue station facility location, and health center scheduling and layout have been addressed with modifications of manufacturing management methods with encouraging results. But we are only now viewing the tip of the iceberg. There are still numerous problems of design, improvement, and development of systems of welfare, health delivery, criminal justice, solid waste disposal, pollution control, urban renewal, and land use, which are ripe for the application of operations management methods.

Redirecting attention.

1.4 THE OPERATIONS MANAGER

Following the rapid development of the operations function from the 1920s through the 1950s, America agreed with John Kenneth Galbraith when he proclaimed, "We have solved the problem of production." As America turned

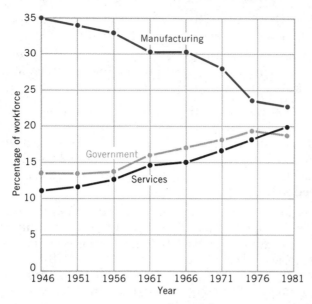

Figure 1.8 Percentage of workforce employed in manufacturing, services, and government. (*Source:* Economic Report of the President, 1981.)

its attention from operations to marketing for increasing demand, and to finance, for bankrolling acquisitions, the Japanese and Europeans were intensely studying "the problem of production." The rest is now history.

The resurgence of operations management in business school curricula has confused many students who were unaware of its earlier existence. It thus may be worthwhile to briefly identify interfaces to contrast operations with other business areas, and even some nonbusiness areas that may appear similar. To conclude this explanation we will note some of the many positions and careers available in the field of operations.

- *Marketing:* The marketing function of business is oriented toward matching the organization's strengths and abilities to the needs of the marketplace. Marketing has many important interfaces with operations, as we will see throughout the chapters of this book. The two major points of contact occur at the front and rear of the operations system. At the front, marketing is usually heavily involved in new product/service design and development and in forecasting demand for the firm's outputs. At the end of the operations system, marketing is involved in the process of distributing the output to the recipient.

- *Finance:* The finance function in business is responsible for obtaining and conserving scarce funds to operate the firm. As such, there are a number of points of interface with operations, which is responsible for managing 70 to 80 percent of the physical resources of the firm. Major points of contact are thus during capital asset (equipment, facilities)

Interfaces with other fields.

acquisition and inventory policy determination (particularly, stocking levels, where significant capital is tied up).

- *Accounting:* Accounting, overseen by the firm's controller, is responsible for maintaining control of the firm's assets. Major interfaces with operations occur in these areas:

    - *Budgeting:* This is the process of allocating the firm's funds among the competing segments of the business.
    - *Cost reporting:* Here, operations reports asset usage to accounting.
    - *Variance reporting:* A part of the control function, variance reports identify deviations from plan that may require corrective feedback actions.

- *Personnel/organizational behavior:* Personnel is responsible for obtaining (and sometimes releasing) properly skilled labor and management for the organization when needed. Labor is sometimes divided into two categories: line and staff. Line has historically consisted of those workers and managers directly responsible for operations, whereas staff has consisted of those who support the line. In many contemporary organizations the personnel department is being renamed "human resources" to more accurately reflect its function.

    Another contemporary phenomenon is the appearance of "organizational behavior" in many business schools' curricula. Whereas operations, marketing, finance, and personnel are basic functional areas of business (accounting is a "support area"), organizational behavior (OB) is what might be termed a "tool area" that, like mathematics, can be used in every business function. OB is concerned with both individual behavior and the behavior of groups and, as such, is a critically important subject for operations, which is often responsible, again, for 70 to 80 percent of the organization's human resources.

- *Management science/quantitative analysis:* Many businesses and colleges have a department referred to as management science, operations research, or quantitative analysis (or methods). This was described earlier under the term "operations research." Like OB, this is an important tool area. But, because of the increased use of these quantitative procedures for operations problems during the last two decades, the operations management function frequently came to be seen as simply applications of certain mathematical techniques used in these areas. Operations management now uses a more balanced approach to solving operations problems, but the heavily quantitative image of the field still seems to remain. In fact, the field of operations is quite concerned with its past lack of attention to the human element and is attempting to employ more OB tools in its search for realistic solutions to operations problems.

- *General management:* The subject of "management" is, like the tool areas, a generic one because all the business functions are concerned with management: operations management, personnel management,

Personnel to human resources.

OB—a tool area.

Another tool area.

An outdated quantitative image.

marketing management, and financial management. In many schools 10 years ago, both OB and operations management had small offerings and were housed in the management department. Both have largely outgrown this arrangement these days, and if either is still housed there, their offerings often overshadow those of general management itself.

- *Industrial engineering:* Last to be considered is another area often confused with operations, namely, industrial engineering (IE). This confusion occurs because many of the topics of interest to operations (such as materials control, layout, scheduling, work design) were set up by industrial engineers. The critical difference, however, is that IE is an *engineering* function and operations is a *management* function.

IE engineers; OM manages.

What this means in practice is that engineering *sets up* many transformation activities and operations' task is to *manage* them—when workers call in sick, when machines break down, and when materials don't arrive. Many firms, of course, tie the two areas together in their organization with all engineering heads reporting to the operations vice-president.

This situation is related to another, unfortunate, practice. Because engineering sets up the transformation activities, top managers often assume engineers are equally adept at *managing* them. Some engineers do make good managers, but no more so than any other segment of the population. As a matter of fact, it is probably true the *best* engineers make *poor* managers—they simply have more interest in engineering than in dealing with people plus machines plus policies and procedures, and so on.

Careers in Operations

The titles of the operations manager.

Regardless of the type of organization considered, there will always be someone in charge of the operations function. This person may be more difficult to recognize in nonmanufacturing organizations, but there is an operations manager nonetheless. He or she may be called the city manager, chief administrator, director, dean, or commissioner, depending on the institution within which he or she functions, but the essential role of managing the operations is still the same.

Figure 1.9 lists some of the many positions and careers in operations management and describes the general duties of each. There is more title variability in the service industries but the activity/problem focus is much the same as what is listed in the figure.

1.5 OVERVIEW OF THE BOOK

Although it is important to bear in mind that the design of the operations is iterative in reality, for ease of discussion and comprehension we will follow each stage of the operations design sequentially in this text, as illustrated

Level	Title	Description
Upper	Vice-President of Operations Chief Administrator Director of Manufacturing Executive Vice-President Chief Operating Officer Commissioner Secretary General	Responsible for overall planning, coordination, policy, budgeting, and control of operations.
Middle	Plant Superintendent Branch Manager Plant Manager Manufacturing Manager Operations Manager City Manager Dean	Responsible for planning, directing, and controlling the operations within their area or facility. Must plan for asset replacement, personnel adustments, materials flows, budget adherence, and so on.
Lower	Department Manager Foreman Supervisor Group Leader Assistant Superintendent Line Manager	Responsible for work flow, job completion, on-time delivery, resource coordination, and motivation of the workforce.
Staff	Production Scheduler Materials Manager Quality Control Manager Systems Analyst Purchasing Agent Maintenance Manager Stores Manager	Responsible for individual areas of support to line operations. Includes planning, monitoring, and controlling materials, information, facilities, and other items and elements relevant to the area of responsibility.

Figure 1.9   Careers in operations management.

in Figure 1.10. To give perspective to these topics, it is well to have some foreknowledge of the entire process so that the details of each topic can be integrated into the perception of the whole process. (This is referred to as a *holistic* view.)

A holistic view.

Our logic follows the "design approach" explained earlier and illustrated in Figure 1.2. Briefly, the organization designs a **strategy** to achieve its goals, and this strategy then dictates the design and implementation of its operations. The control stage completes the cycle through feedback so as to iterate, if necessary, on the original strategy.

A strategy to achieve its goals.

Part I: Strategic Operations—Goals, Outputs, and Facilities

In this first part of the text, we look at the "strategic" aspects of operations. In Chapter 2 we examine the crucial role of operations in setting the organization's overall strategy, or "business plan" as it is sometimes called, to

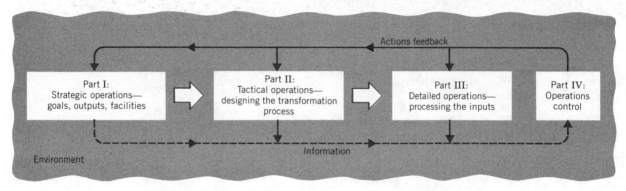

Figure 1.10 The basic flow of the design approach to operations.

achieve its goals. It is here that operations, marketing, finance, and engineering come together to develop the strategy that will guide the organization through the future. This includes the nature of ongoing and future products/services the organization will offer and the size and location of the facilities to house the operations that will produce them.

Chapter 3 outlines the roles of R&D (research and development), operations, and marketing in the selection of the outputs, and Chapter 4 describes methods to forecast their demand. In Chapter 5 we describe how the organization attains both the long- and short-term capacity required to meet marketplace demand. Last, Chapter 6 treats the issue of locating the facilities to best obtain the needed inputs and distribute the outputs to the recipients.

Part II: Tactical Operations— Designing the Transformation Process

Tactics to implement the strategy.
In the second part of the text we consider the task of *implementing* the strategic plan. This process, known as **tactical operations,** is concerned with designing the transformation process, the workplace activities, and the scheduling process that brings all elements of the transformation process together. In Chapter 7 we describe the varieties of transformation processes available and how they are laid out in the facility. Placing the worker in this process is then the subject of Chapter 8, Work Design for Productivity. Last, the design of the aggregate scheduling system, which considers short-term capacity alternatives and ties all the inputs together to be transformed into outputs, is examined in Chapter 9.

Part III: Detailed Operations—Processing the Inputs

Executing the tactics.
In the third part of the text we address the *execution* of the tactical systems designed in Part II. First, we consider the process of "detailed" (virtually minute by minute) scheduling of workers, machines, and materials in Chapter 10. A closer look at the critical topic of the flow of materials is then provided in Chapters 11, 12, and 13. The general subject of materials sys-

tems, including warehousing and materials handling, is discussed in Chapter 11. Chapter 12 follows with a detailed examination of the nature and types of inventory systems, especially for independent demand materials; Chapter 13 then treats materials requirements planning (MRP) systems for the dependent demand case.

Part IV: Operations Control

Maintaining the system.

The final part of the text addresses the monitoring and feedback control function of the operations system. The general concepts of monitoring and control are discussed in Chapter 14 and some specific techniques are presented. These concepts are then applied in Chapter 15 to maintaining the proper functioning of the overall operations system. Chapter 16 completes the control discussion with a treatment of the topic of quality control, including acceptance sampling and process control.

The text concludes with a brief epilogue discussing the future challenges and opportunities facing operations management.

1.6 SUMMARY AND KEY LEARNING POINTS

This chapter has described the central role of operations management to every organization and identified the key aspects and some typical careers in the field. The chapter also laid out the unique approach we will be taking in this text in our discussion of the many topics in this field. The key learning points have been

- The operations function is the process of adding value to some entity.
- Operations is the central function of virtually every organization.
- Value is primarily added to entities by changing them directly, in space, in time, or in our minds.
- All organizations produce services, which are tangible and intangible benefits, but they may be accompanied by a facilitating good, typically known as a "product."
- The transformation process is the heart of the operations function. Its most important characteristics are its efficiency, effectiveness, quality, lead time, and flexibility, and it embodies a full range of activities that are operations subtopics in their own right.
- The design approach to the operations system begins with the organization and its goals, operating in some environment. These goals lead to a number of possible outputs, which could be produced by a set of alternative processes using a variety of alternative inputs. The system and its environment is monitored to ensure that results conform to plan and, if not, that corrective feedback actions are taken.
- Organizations are the natural result of human cooperation to gain results that would be singularly impossible otherwise. Such organizations require

management, a decision-making function requiring both analysis and synthesis, to succeed in achieving their goals.

- A monitoring and feedback control system compares collected information and measurements with a standard to determine if a significant difference exists. If so, corrective feedback actions are then initiated to bring the system under control.

- Operations management has had a long and turbulent history, most recently incorporating the tools of systems theory, operations research, and the computer to aid in its function.

- The service sector of our economy has grown dramatically in the last three decades to the point that manufacturing, for example, now constitutes less than 25 percent of national employment.

- Operations has many interfaces, and its functions are sometimes confused with those of marketing, finance, accounting, personnel/organizational behavior, management science/quantitative analysis, general management, and even industrial engineering. Operations careers span every organization and every level from vice-president to supervisor.

- We follow the design approach to operations in this text, grouping the set of topics into strategic operations, tactical operations, detailed operations, and operations control.

1.7 KEY TERMS

operations (p. 4)

services (p. 6)

facilitating goods (p. 5)

transformation process (p. 7)

efficiency (p. 7)

productivity (p. 7)

effectiveness (p. 7)

quality (p. 8)

generic (p. 19)

lead time (p. 8)

flexibility (p. 8)

design approach (p. 9)

inputs (p. 7)

outputs (p. 8)

environment (p. 8)

system (p. 9)

management (p. 12)

organizations (p. 11)

analysis (p. 13)

synthesis (p. 14)

monitor (p. 10)

feedback (p. 14)

control (p. 11)

operations research (p. 19)

strategy (p. 24)

tactical operations (p. 25)

1.8 REVIEW AND DISCUSSION QUESTIONS

1. Since value is always in the mind of the beholder anyway, how does altering a product differ from advertising or guarantees in terms of added value?

2. What is the operations function in a trucking firm? An advertising agency? A loan institution?

3. How does the concept of a facilitating good clarify the distinction between products and services?

4. Name the tangible and intangible benefits of purchasing an antique. Of going to the theater.

5. Look through the text's table of contents to identify other subtopics of operations management involved in the transformation process besides those listed in Section 1.1.

6. What proportion of time do you think managers spend on synthesis as opposed to analysis in their decision making?

7. Identify some common monitoring systems. Some control systems. Do all control methods use feedback?

8. Name some careers you might entertain in the "service area." In the "production area." Would any of the operations careers appeal to you?

9. Why haven't the "tools" of organizational behavior and general management been as fully utilized in operations as has management science?

10. Contrast strategic and tactical operations. Tactical and detailed operations.

11. Frequently, successful organizations lose sight of their original goals and strive to grow for growth's sake alone. What do you imagine might eventually happen to such an organization?

12. For what reason is it so hard to increase productivity in the service sector?

13. Why is it important for the operations manager to know about other functional areas such as finance, marketing, and personnel?

14. Identify some operations management positions such as those in Figure 1.9 in an organization you are familiar with.

15. Contrast the descriptive and design approaches to operations management.

16. Give some examples of the iterative nature of the design of operations.

17. What are the services embodied in the following products: piped-in water to your house, *Popular Science* magazine, a restaurant meal, a bank loan?

18. Why do you think the field of management took so long to develop?

1.9 REFERENCES AND BIBLIOGRAPHY

1. Andrew, C. G. et al., "The Critical Importance of Production and Operations Management," *Academy of Management Review*, 7:143–147 (1982).

2. Babbage, Charles, *On the Economy of Machinery and Manufacturers*, 4th ed., London: Charles Knight, 1835.

3. Buffa, E. S., "Research in Operations Management," *Journal of Operations Management*, 1:1–7 (1980).

4. Burch, E. E., and Henry, W. R., "Production Management Is Alive and Well," *Academy of Management Journal*, 17:144–419 (1974).

5. Chase, R. B., "A Classification and Evaluation of Research in Operations Management," *Journal of Operations Management*, 1:9–14 (1980).

6. Churchman, C. W., *The Systems Approach*, New York: Dell, 1968.

7. Drake, A. W., Keeney, R. L., and Morse, P. M., ed., *Analysis of Public Systems*, Cambridge, MA: MIT Press, 1972.

8. Drucker, Peter F., *The Practice of Management*, New York: Harper & Row, 1954.

9. Easton, A., *Complex Managerial Decisions Involving Multiple Objectives*, New York: Wiley, 1973.

10. Eddington, Sir Arthur, *The Nature of the Physical World*, Ann Arbor, MI: University of Michigan Press, 1958.

11. Ginzberg, E., "The Service Sector of the U.S. Economy," *Scientific American*, 244:48–55 (March 1981).

12. Hayes, R. H., and Abernathy, W. J., "Managing Our Way to Economic Decline," *Harvard Business Review*, 58:67–77 (July–Aug. 1980).

13. Lepawsky, A., *Administration*, New York: Knopf, 1949.

14. Levitt, T., "Industrialization of Service," *Harvard Business Review*, 54:63–74 (1976).

15. Lubar, R., "Rediscovering the Factory," *Fortune*, 13 July 1981.

16. Miller, J. G. et al., "Production/Operations Management: Agenda for the '80s," *Decision Sciences*, 12:547–576 (Oct. 1981).

17. Moran, William T., "Marketing-Production Interaction," in M. K. Starr, *Production Management*, 2nd ed., Englewood Cliffs, NJ: Prentice-Hall, 1972.

18. Morey, Russell, "Operations Management in Selected Non-Manufacturing Organizations,"

Academy of Management Journal, 19:120–124 (1976).

19. Sasser, W. Earl, "Age of Synthesis," *Harvard Business Review*, 40:36–40 (1962).

20. Sasser, W. Earl et al., *Management of Service Operations: Text, Cases, and Readings*, Boston: Allyn and Bacon, 1978.

21. Smith, Adam, *An Inquiry into the Nature and Causes of the Wealth of Nations*, London: A. Strahan and T. Cadell, 1776.

22. Starr, M. K., *Production Management*, 2nd ed., Englewood Cliffs, NJ: Prentice-Hall, 1972.

23. Taylor, Frederick W., *The Principles of Scientific Management*, New York: Harper & Row, 1911.

24. Wren, Daniel A., *The Evolution of Management Thought*, rev. ed., New York: Wiley, 1979.

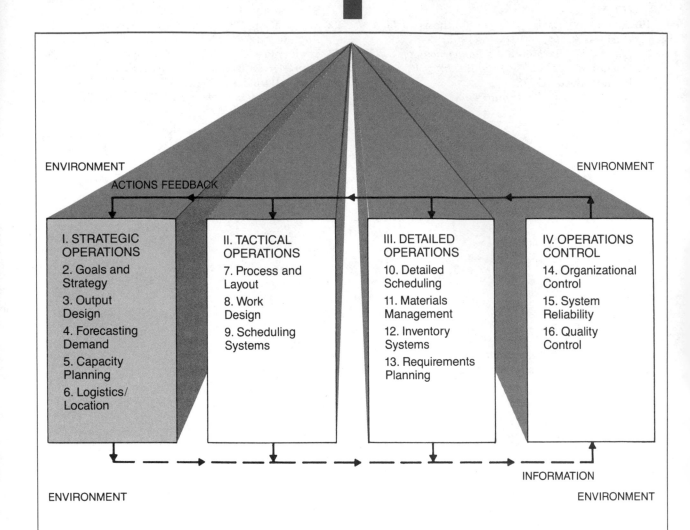

ENVIRONMENT

ACTIONS FEEDBACK

ENVIRONMENT

I. STRATEGIC OPERATIONS

2. Goals and Strategy

3. Output Design

4. Forecasting Demand

5. Capacity Planning

6. Logistics/Location

II. TACTICAL OPERATIONS

7. Process and Layout

8. Work Design

9. Scheduling Systems

III. DETAILED OPERATIONS

10. Detailed Scheduling

11. Materials Management

12. Inventory Systems

13. Requirements Planning

IV. OPERATIONS CONTROL

14. Organizational Control

15. System Reliability

16. Quality Control

INFORMATION

ENVIRONMENT

ENVIRONMENT

STRATEGIC OPERATIONS
GOALS, OUTPUTS, FACILITIES

"Would you tell me, please, which way I ought to go from here?"

"That depends a good deal on where you want to get to," said the Cat.

"I don't much care where—" said Alice.

"Then it doesn't matter which way you go," said the Cat.

"—so long as I get somewhere," Alice added as an explanation.

"Oh, you're sure to do that," said the Cat, "if you only walk long enough."

—Lewis Carroll, *ALICE'S ADVENTURES IN WONDERLAND**

Clearly, if you do not know where you are going, any path will get you there. Strategies are the paths that lead organizations to their goals. In establishing such strategies, a number of factors must be carefully considered by the organization:

The multiple goals of the organization.

The kinds of outputs that are feasible for the organization to produce and that can aid in achieving its goals.

The environmental demand for various outputs.

Ways of obtaining the capacity to produce the volume of output demanded in the marketplace.

The best location for its facilities, considering both production of the output and distribution to the market.

All of the above topics are "strategic" in nature and thus the concern of top managers. Because decisions about operations at this strategic level set both the form and the limits on the next, "tactical" sets of operations decisions, we must address them first.

In Chapter 2 we look in depth at the strategy formation process, its relationship to the organization's goals, and the critical role of an operations strength in the organization's strategic plan. Then in Chapter 3 we proceed to implement the strategy by selecting and developing the outputs the organization will offer in the marketplace. We examine the roles of (1) creativity and (2) Research and Development (R&D) in generating potential output candidates and methods by which the best outputs can be selected. Last, we describe the output design process and how it relates to the transformation process that will ultimately produce the output.

In Chapter 4 we look at the forecasting process and focus in particular on forecasting environmental demand for the outputs. The level of expected demand dictates how the output can most economically be produced, and thus forecasting is crucial to further development of the role of operations. Various forecasting methods are described and illustrated, and their utility for short-term or long-term forecasting is noted.

Using these forecasts to plan short-term and long-term capacity requirements is the subject of Chapter 5. Capacity alternatives in each of these cases are described and the unique requirements of pure service organizations are detailed. Last, because forecasts are never perfect, the role of risk in capacity planning is discussed and methods for addressing it are illustrated.

Finally, the process of "placing" the capacity through choice of a facility location is addressed. Two factors enter in this decision: (1) the effect on the production process and (2) the effect on the distribution of the output. The roles of transportation and logistics are discussed and the tradeoffs between location and transportation in the distribution of the output are noted. The single facility location problem is addressed in detail and a standard three-stage solution approach is illustrated. Last, the multifacility location problem is discussed and some solution approaches are described.

*Lewis Carroll, *Alice's Adventures in Wonderland*. New Junior Classics, Mabel Williams and Marcia Dalphin, eds. (New York: P. F. Collier and Son Corporation, 1949), V, p. 51.

ENVIRONMENT

ACTIONS FEEDBACK

ENVIRONMENT

I. STRATEGIC OPERATIONS

2. Goals and Strategy

3. Output Design

4. Forecasting Demand

5. Capacity Planning

6. Logistics/ Location

II. TACTICAL OPERATIONS

7. Process and Layout

8. Work Design

9. Scheduling Systems

III. DETAILED OPERATIONS

10. Detailed Scheduling

11. Materials Management

12. Inventory Systems

13. Requirements Planning

IV. OPERATIONS CONTROL

14. Organizational Control

15. System Reliability

16. Quality Control

ENVIRONMENT

INFORMATION

ENVIRONMENT

2
GOALS AND OPERATIONS STRATEGY

2

LEARNING OBJECTIVES

By the completion of this chapter the student should

- Be aware of the importance of operations in the development of the organization's strategic plan.
- Understand how an assessment aid can help evaluate the management of a firm's operations.
- Know the major categories of importance in assessing manufacturing operations and the possible problems they can involve.
- Be familiar with organizational goals and how management deals with multiple and often conflicting goals.
- Comprehend the process of developing both a strategic plan and a coordinated operations strategy.
- Appreciate the importance of an operations focus and the variety of operations strengths that can form such a focus.
- Be aware of the ways organizations lose their operations focus.

Top management's fault.

Synthesize.

It now appears that many operations problems in U.S. firms—low productivity, poor quality, and so on—are largely the fault of top management. This especially appears to be the case in top management's primary task: defining the strategy by which the firm will accomplish its goals. If the chief executive officer, or even worse, the entire executive committee lacks operations experience, the top managers of the firm cannot *synthesize* all the relevant functions of the firm to devise a coordinated strategy. What we find instead is a strategy coordinated in marketing, finance, and personnel that is dumped into the lap of operations to somehow implement. This approach typically fails because the strengths and limitations of operations were never considered in forming the firm's strategy.

In this chapter we will look in detail at the task of strategic planning, and especially the critical role of operations in strategy formation. First, we will describe an instrument to aid a manufacturing firm in evaluating the management of its operations and any particular strengths and weaknesses in the operations area. This will tell the firm what aspect of its operations strategy needs attention. Then in Section 2.2 we look at the relationship between the organization's goals and its strategic plan, concluding with the general process of formulating the strategic plan. In Section 2.3 we factor operations into the strategic plan and note the importance of an operations focus in the strategy. Finally, in Section 2.4 we conclude with the development of the operations strategy from the integrated strategic plan of the organization.

2.1 A MANUFACTURING OPERATIONS ASSESSMENT AID

Many firms do not know if they are doing a satisfactory job of including operations in their strategic planning. One way of determining this is to consider their current operations. If these are well managed, then they probably are including operations; if not, they probably are not. But how can a firm determine how well managed its current operations are? Who is to say that the operations function is well managed or not?

An assessment aid.

Plant tour.

Surrogates.

In Figure 2.1 is an **assessment aid**, adapted from Landel [7], for evaluating the management of a manufacturer's operations. (A similar aid is available for evaluating office operations.) This aid was devised for outsiders with minimal knowledge of the firm, or even the details of manufacturing, to be used during a "plant tour" of the manufacturer's facility. But it can also be used by the firm itself to assess the management of its own operations.

Note in the figure that most of the measures Landel employs are really **surrogates** for good management of the firm's operations. That is, they do not measure "good management" directly but rather "symptoms, signs, and characteristics" known to reflect good management procedures. Obvious examples here are "Inventory areas are well-lighted," "Restrooms are clean," and "Bulletin boards are up-to-date." Also note the categories of importance, as detailed by the manufacturing experts who participated with Landel in constructing the aid:

Categories of
importance.

- *Material control:* Representing attention to levels of investment, smooth operations, customer service.
- *Supervision and employee relations:* Showing concern for motivation, teamwork.
- *Productivity:* Illustrating the importance of cost, efficiency, and "throughput."
- *Maintenance:* Representing concern for technology, asset utilization, long-term attitudes.
- *Quality control:* Representing consideration for pride in achievement, value to the customer, morale.
- *Manufacturing/process engineering coordination:* Giving attention to product lead time, functional coordination, on-time delivery.

The number of questions in each category was selected to reflect the experts' estimate of the importance of each category to good overall management of the operations function. For example, "productivity" (14 questions) was deemed twice as important as "materials control" (7 questions).

In addition to an overall score, a score may be obtained for each category, to give an assessment of the strengths and weaknesses of the various operations functions. The score would be obtained by totaling the points in a category and dividing by the number of observations:

Final score.

4.0–5.0	Excellent
3.5–4.0	Good
2.5–3.5	Average
1.5–2.5	Poor
1.0–1.5	Unacceptable

Poor scores in individual categories may, for example, indicate the presence of some of the operations problems listed in Figure 2.2, thereby possibly warranting further, in-depth investigation.

A Beauty Products Firm

To illustrate the use of Figure 2.1, consider the following example, based on an evaluation of a leading consumer beauty products firm in Ohio. The production process of beauty products—soaps, creams, and liquids—is relatively simple but, with a large number of small products, materials control and order assembly are rather complex. Also, since the products are not ingested, quality is not an extremely high priority, just as long as the lotion or cream doesn't turn the customer's skin green. The assessment form results are given in Table 2.1.

The total score is 188, in the middle of the "good" category. Examining the operations area by area, we see that "materials control" and "supervision and employee relations" both score excellently (4.4 and 4.6). As stated, materials control in this type of firm is complex and requires considerable

Instructions: Score a "5" if your observations of actual conditions at the time of filling out this form are totally in agreement with, or surpass, the conditions stated in each question. Score a "4" if conditions seem very good though not perfect. Score a "3" if conditions seem "OK" but could be considerably better, though they could be much worse also. Score a "2" if conditions are actually poor. Score a "1" if no system seems to be in operation at all or conditions are actually bad.

Area 1: Materials Control

Score

_____ 1. Inventory areas are well-lighted and at the proper temperature and humidity.

_____ 2. Materials are clearly marked and segregated.

_____ 3. Aisles are clearly marked and not cluttered with material.

_____ 4. Waste or scrap on the floor is not allowed to accumulate.

_____ 5. Common parts are stored together.

_____ 6. Skids (pallets) are stocked carefully.

_____ 7. Access to stock is restricted.

Area 2: Supervision and Employee Relations

_____ 1. Supervisors are present on the shop floor.

_____ 2. Employees speak freely to supervisors.

_____ 3. Workers and supervisors speak knowledgeably and enthusiastically to visitors.

_____ 4. Machinery, work stations, and offices are painted, relatively clean, and uncluttered.

_____ 5. Safety/accident goals and performance records are posted throughout the facility.

_____ 6. Workers are moving at a normal (not hurried nor idle) pace.

_____ 7. Restrooms and eating areas are clean.

_____ 8. Supervisor's office is located near the shop floor.

_____ 9. Production schedules are clearly posted.

_____ 10. Bulletin boards are up-to-date.

Area 3: Productivity

_____ 1. Production process is orderly.

_____ 2. Workers are not idle waiting for tools, supplies, maintenance, inspection.

_____ 3. Few workers are in idle discussion groups away from work stations.

_____ 4. Machines are running (90% of *all* machines = 5, 80% = 4, 70% = 3, 60% = 2, 50% = 1).

_____ 5. Production goals and performance are posted and up-to-date.

_____ 6. Once set up, machines do not require continual operator adjustments.

Figure 2.1   Modified Landel plant tour assessment aid.

_____ 7. No bottlenecks (large amounts of work waiting on one machine or process) seem evident.

_____ 8. No handling or fork lift damage is evident.

_____ 9. Good environmental working conditions (noise, temperature, fumes, humidity, light, etc.).

_____ 10. Aisles are clear.

_____ 11. Tools and fixtures seem well organized and readily available.

_____ 12. Progress in automating manual operations is evident.

_____ 13. Progress in automating quality control activities is evident.

_____ 14. Paperwork is evident, kept with materials, or readily accessible.

Area 4: Maintenance

_____ 1. Facilities and equipment seem in good repair.

_____ 2. Equipment is tagged with a record of maintenance activity.

_____ 3. Maintenance shop is close to related operations.

_____ 4. Maintenance workers use tool carts to quickly reach breakdowns.

_____ 5. Safety devices are in place and warning signs posted.

_____ 6. Maintenance area is orderly.

Area 5: Quality Control

_____ 1. Quality inspection stations are adjacent to production stations.

_____ 2. An inspection station is located at material reception area.

_____ 3. Inspection stations are clearly marked.

_____ 4. Quality control specifications and details are clearly stated on shop orders.

_____ 5. Rejects are separated in their own area.

_____ 6. Rejects are tagged as to source, time, and condition.

_____ 7. Quality charts are up-to-date.

_____ 8. There is evidence of a recalibration system for inspection devices.

Area 6: Manufacturing/Process Engineering Coordination

_____ 1. Manufacturing engineers are well received by supervisors.

_____ 2. Manufacturing engineers are well received by workers.

_____ 3. Equipment is clean and running.

_____ 4. New equipment installations are evident.

_____ 5. Operator instructions are posted and current.

TOTAL SCORE
_____ (200–250: Excellent; 175–200: Good; 125–175: Average; 75–125: Very poor; 50–125: Unacceptable)

Figure 2.1 *(continued)*

Low Score Area	Possible Problems
Materials control	Long lead times, missed delivery promises, high inventory financing charges
Supervision and employee relations	High product costs, missed delivery promises, high defect rates
Productivity	Poor return on capital assets, high product costs, inability to meet demand
Maintenance	Higher equipment downtime, high defect rates, inability to meet demand, missed delivery promises
Quality control	High defect rates, many complaints and returns, decreased sales, lower than competitive product costs
Manufacturing/process engineering coordination	High defect rates, missed delivery promises, high product costs

Figure 2.2 Potential problem areas by category.

attention, which management is apparently giving it. Also, most of the hourly workers in the plant work in assembly, where close supervision is required. Again, this area demands, and apparently receives, close attention from management. It might be noted that attention to employees is very basic to the high margin, but highly competitive beauty products industry. In such industries, a large portion of the success of the firm hangs on the ability and motivation of its sales personnel.

Productivity in this firm also seems to be good (3.7), possibly another reflection of good employee relations. But attention to the production process seems weaker, with "maintenance" scoring at the high average level (3.5) and "manufacturing/process engineering coordination" barely above poor (2.6). From Figure 2.2 this latter score may indicate higher than necessary product costs. Last, quality control doesn't seem terribly critical, scoring only at average (3.1).

In sum, it appears that this firm is doing what's important in this particular industry and doing it well. Undoubtedly, that is why it is one of the leading firms in the industry.

2.2 GOALS AND THE STRATEGIC PLAN

The business plan.

Let us now look in more detail at organizations and their goals. Following this we will describe the construction of the organization's overall strategy, known in the private sector as **the business (or strategic) plan,** and how it relates to the organization's goals.

Table 2.1 Assessment Results of Beauty Products Firm

	Area						
Item Number	1 Materials Control	2 Supervision & Employee Relations	3 Productivity	4 Maintenance	5 Quality Control	6 Mfg./Process Engr. Coord.	
1	5	5	5	3	5	2	
2	5	4	4	2	1	2	
3	3	5	5	3	2	4	
4	5	4	3	4	4	2	
5	5	5	3	5	5	3	
6	4	4	3	4	2		
7	4	5	4		4		
8		5	3		2		
9		4	3				
10		5	4				
11			4				
12			4				
13			2				
14			5				
Total score	31	46	52	21	25	13	$\Sigma = 188$
Average	4.4	4.6	3.7	3.5	3.1	2.6	

Organizational Goals

> We the people of the United States, in order to form a more perfect union, establish justice, insure domestic tranquility, provide for the common defense, promote the general welfare, and secure the blessings of liberty to ourselves and our posterity, do ordain and establish this Constitution for the United States of America.
>
> —*Preamble to the Constitution of the United States*

The uses for goals. The **goals** of the U.S. government were clearly laid out in the Preamble to the Constitution. Goals are the intended destinations that indicate the direction for planning. They are guides to decision making and action, the basis for control of operations, and the logic for criteria for evaluating results. The organization selects plans and operating programs on the basis of their contribution to the achievement of its goals. The translation of the organization's goals into an operations strategy, then, sets the tasks for the operations managers.

Multiple Goals

Multiple goals. As the Preamble indicates, an organization typically has more than one goal. Even at the strategic level, multiple goals are common. In addition, organizations are made up of and represent many individuals and interests, each of whom has different motivations and goals. Employees want meaningful jobs with adequate and secure incomes. Stockholders desire a fair return on

Environmentally
imposed goals.

Business goals.

Public goals.

the money they have invested in the firm. And the managers themselves have their own personal goals and ambitions such as wealth, power, or prestige.

Beyond this, the environment also has some goals which it desires of organizations. Society, through the government and special interest groups, wants business firms to employ workers, pay taxes, and provide products and services but not pollute the environment, endanger the public health or safety, or prey on consumers. In addition, suppliers, competitors, customers, and others in the environment have an effect on the setting of an organization's goals.

Two major studies of top U.S. executives support the view that business firms subscribe to a large number of diverse organizational goals (see References 3 and 10). Table 2.2 lists those areas frequently mentioned as organizational goals. While profits were mentioned frequently in both studies, it is clear that profits are not the sole target of private enterprise.

Even more obviously than business firms, not-for-profit organizations (foundations, social clubs, charities) exhibit multiple goals. This is especially true for the largest category of the not-for-profit organizations, the federal, state, and local government. In general, governments attempt to satisfy a multitude of public needs through various programs. This naturally results in government units, at the various levels, maintaining multiple, and often even conflicting goals.

Conflicting Goals

Conflict among
goals.

The mere existence of multiple goals complicates the organization's activity planning. This is not only because resources must now be carefully allocated toward various objectives, a difficult enough problem in itself, but also because some of the goals will probably be in conflict: for example, paying top scale wages and minimizing labor costs, reducing taxes and providing increased veteran's benefits, and so forth. In addition to conflicting strategic goals, there clearly may be conflicts between organizational and personal goals (such as every manager wanting to be president).

Table 2.2   Selected Goals of Top Corporate Managers

To grow
To contribute to the community
To provide a quality product
To progress technologically
To pay dividends to stockholders
To provide for the welfare of employees
To gain prestige
To produce a profit
To develop the organization
To produce efficiently and effectively
To meet consumer needs

THE BORN LOSER   **by Art Sansom**

Born Loser: © 1978 NEA, Inc.

Resource restrictions on goal achievement.

Every organization must recognize and then meld these diverse interests and aspirations into a broader set of organization-wide goals. Whether goals conflict or not, an allocation of the available resources is necessary. Because resources are limited, it is seldom true that all organizational goals can be achieved simultaneously. The activities and operations required to achieve one goal consume the resources that could be used to move the organization closer to some of its other goals. Such limitations on resources have been clearly documented over the past few years with such examples as the energy crisis and the capital crunch.

Priorities

Setting priorities of the goals.

Even though they are faced with the problem of multiple goals and limited resources, organizations must still decide what new programs to initiate and which existing programs to increase or decrease. In order to make these decisions, organizations must establish **priorities** for each of the goals. Priorities are statements of the relative importance of the goals. That is, they indicate the *order* of importance to the organization (e.g., first priority) or the *weight* assigned to each goal. For example, President Kennedy placed a high priority on a moon landing before the end of the 1960s and thus the NASA budget was significantly increased. Likewise, President Johnson placed a great emphasis on social reform, and hence a high priority was assigned to his "Great Society" programs. It should be noted that, like goals, priorities also vary over time and between different individuals.

Tradeoffs

Establishing goal tradeoffs.

When resources are limited so that we cannot achieve all of our goals simultaneously, we are forced to make **tradeoffs.** A tradeoff is the substitution of achievement of one goal for another. We can, for example, trade the achievement of all of one goal for all or part of another. Or similarly, we can trade the achievement of one goal now for that of another goal later. The priorities are used to make the decisions regarding amounts of each goal to be traded or substituted for others. In our own personal selection of clothing, food, appliances, and automobiles, we must make tradeoffs between the goals of low price, high quality, and quantity. Also, we must trade purchases today for, perhaps, more important purchases later.

Together, the process of establishing priorities and trading off accomplishment of one goal for accomplishment of other goals allows the organization to reach a consensus of opinion regarding the most appropriate strategy to employ.

Reaching a goal consensus.

The Strategic Plan

With the goal consensus, priorities, and tradeoffs available to the organization, the next step is the formulation of the strategic plan. Given the number of books devoted to this subject (e.g., References 1, 5, and 8), we will not pursue this topic in depth here. Suffice it to say that all the approaches essentially follow these steps:

Step 1. Establish the organization's goals.

Step 2. Analyze the problems and opportunities in the competitive environment.

Step 3. Appraise the organization's present resources, strengths, and weaknesses.

The basic steps. **Step 4.** Match the organization's unique situation to a niche in the environment. Consider the goals, priorities, and tradeoffs available to the organization.

Step 5. Develop a strategy to exploit the environmental opportunity. Devise action plans and systems to monitor and evaluate the organization's progress.

Step 6. Put the strategy into action. Monitor the results and exert control to ensure that results conform to plan.

Of special interest to us is operations' input to Step 3 and the portion of the strategic plan incorporating the operations strategy. This latter subject is the topic of the next section.

2.3   OPERATIONS STRATEGY: THE ORGANIZATION'S COMPETITIVE ADVANTAGE

McKinsey's "successful companies" study.

In Steps 4 and 5 above we chose a key strength of the firm and exploited it to successfully enter a market. McKinsey & Company, a top management consulting firm, studied 27 outstanding successful firms to find their common attributes. Two of the major common attributes reported [9] were the following:

1. Stressing One Key Business Value. At Hewlett-Packard it is new product development, at Procter & Gamble it is product quality, at Dana

Corporation it is productivity improvement, at IBM it is customer service.

2. **Sticking to What They Know Best.** All the outstanding firms defined their strengths and then built on them. They resisted the temptation to move into new areas or diversify.

Two common attributes.

Hall's study [6] of 64 firms in major domestic markets characterized as "mature" and highly competitive found much the same thing.

The leading companies have demonstrated a continuous, single-minded determination to achieve one or both of the following competitive positions within their respective industries:

Lowest cost.

1. Have the lowest cost compared to the competition. If the output has an acceptable quality level then the firm can adopt a very competitive pricing policy that will gain profitable volume and market share growth.

A differentiated position.

2. Have an outstanding strength (short lead time, advanced technology, high quality, and so on) that differentiates them from the competition. Then, if they have an acceptable cost structure, the firm can adopt a pricing policy to gain large margins and fund reinvestment in their differentiated strength.

Focus.

Skinner [11] refers to this primary competitive strength of a firm as its **focus.** It is the task of top management to identify, or if necessary create, this unique focus and build on it. Most often the strength lies in the operations area—low cost, high quality, new technology; but on occasion it may lie elsewhere—the distribution chain or customer service. However, even if the strength lies in another function, the operations area must still be highly competitive on cost, quality, and the other competitive characteristics of the output. If the strength lies in the operations area, as it usually does, this is known as the operations focus or **competitive advantage.**

Competitive advantage.

Clearly, existing organizations once had some competitive advantage or they never would have survived. How do organizations lose this focus and get into trouble? This topic will occupy us for the remainder of this section.

Loss of Focus

The operations task.

The primary reason a company loses its operations focus is because the operations "task," or what the firm must do especially well to compete in the environment, has changed. It may, for example, in the initial stages of a product's life cycle have been *new technology*, then *variety* as the product caught on, and then *cost* as the product matured and became common. Or perhaps the marketing *environment* has changed so that lead time, or quality, becomes the competitive factor. Or again, the company itself may change the target market in which it wishes to compete, for example, in an attempt to increase its growth.

Regardless of the reason, top management may not realize that a new competitive task faces operations and the organization slowly will lose its previous competitive advantage. Experience indicates that this occurs in one

Three ways to lose focus.

of three primary fashions: (1) the task changes but the organization's focus does not, (2) new subtasks are added to operations, or (3) new outputs or attributes are added. Let us consider each of these separately.

Task Changes, Focus Does Not

This is typical of a change in the life cycle of the product or the competitive market. A new task is now required of operations but top management does not recognize it. For example, as new products become more popular, competitors enter the market and compete on quality, features, and so on. And as a market matures there is almost always heavy price competition. Either the firm must alter its competitive strength or abandon the market. There are many firms that do each. Most seem to stick with a product and meet competition, but many firms that see themselves as innovators sell out after an output is established and move on to other innovations.

New Subtasks

Quite often top management itself will add new tasks to operations such as reducing costs, raising quality, or improving product safety. These may be added because of new laws or regulations, union contract agreements, a desire to broaden a line, the need to meet new competitors' offerings, or

An unfocusing.

many other reasons. Yet, the result is often the "unfocusing" of the competitive weapon the firm has labored so hard to construct in the first place. Of course, this does not happen all at once. Instead, one small subtask at a time is added and eventually the incremental unfocusing takes its toll.

We often see this in food establishments that are small but successful because they make or do one thing well: fast service, home cooked food, or something similar. But in trying to broaden their appeal and grow (or just meet competition) they will defocus their strength by adding to their menu, using frozen foods, and so on.

New Outputs/Attributes

Probably one of the primary reasons a firm loses its focus is because top management keeps adding outputs that require a *different* operations task. The same effect results from adding attributes to the existing output that also require a different operations task. The usual justification for taking such actions is the larger volume of sales and supposed "savings" that will

Economies of scale.

be realized in overhead or resource utilization through combined operations.

When such decisions are made, top management is usually considering the additional units, volume, or time that is being added to operations and, percentagewise, it is usually small. This is a tremendous error! They should be looking instead at the operations "task" increases they are adding.

For example, adding a small amount of a second product that must be produced quickly at low cost to a facility that is focused on producing high-quality goods but more slowly increases the operations "tasks" by 100 per-

Volume or task increases?

cent. And if a small amount of a third product that requires high customization and frequent changes is also added, then the tasks have increased 200 percent and, for all practical purposes, the firm has now lost its competitive strength in quality production. What's more, it will *not* have gained a focus in quick, low-cost production or customized, fast-change production either.

A white elephant.

The result is that the product facility quickly becomes a big, complex do-everything, general purpose white elephant that is competitive at nothing. The firm begins to realize it is in trouble as sales and margins slip away and then tries various popular "fixes": MRP, CAD/CAM, robots, or many others. These do not work, of course, because the problem is in the unfocusing of what Skinner [11] calls the firm's **infrastructure**—the operations systems of the firm such as scheduling, supervising, quality, materials, purchasing, communication, and decision making. In spite of the expense and complexity of new technological equipment these days, technological change is *relatively* easy. Much more difficult to change is the organization's infrastructure where its real competitive strength lies.

Problems in the infrastructure.

2.4 STRATEGIC PLANNING FOR OPERATIONS

Let us now get more specific and examine some of the areas of operations focus that organizations may adopt, that is, their competitive edge. A partial listing is given in Table 2.3; other possible strengths are limited only by the creativity of the organization. As previously mentioned, if a firm maintains a focus in more than one area it is that much further ahead of its competition, particulary if one of the areas is "low delivery cost."

To reconsider our earlier beauty products example, which of the areas listed in Table 2.3 might be an appropriate operations focus for a firm in this industry? Low cost is inappropriate since the products do not compete on a price basis. Reliability is largely meaningless in this industry and, as mentioned, real quality seems irrelevant. But some of the remaining items on the list, when coupled with a strong sales force, could well give a firm a highly differentiated strength and set it apart from the competition. For example, dependable and rapid deliveries could be an important competitive strength. Similarly, marketplace responsiveness in terms of customization and flexibility would be a valuable asset. Thus, we see that a firm's focus must be appropriate to its industry, its customers, its output, and its competitors, as well as meet the goals, strengths, and weaknesses of the firm.

Table 2.3 Areas of Potential Operations Focus

Areas of operations focus.

Low delivery cost—price competitive
High quality—better overall craftsmanship
Superior reliability—consistent operation every time
Delivery dependability—delivery promises met
Short lead time—product can be obtained quickly
Good design—includes valuable features
Customization—modification to suit customers' needs
High capacity—high volumes produced
Flexibility—switch to producing variants or even different outputs easily

Determining the Organization's Focus

We shall now consider how an organization develops an operations focus for its outputs. First, we will look at the process of how to assess top management's attitudes toward the most appropriate focus for each of its product lines through an actual example.

Wheelwright [13] reports on a firm that attempted to assess the beliefs of its vice-presidents concerning the priorities of four potential areas of operations focus to support the firm's overall strategy. However, the priorities were also to be judged by individual product lines, both as they currently existed and as they "should" be, in the vice-presidents' opinions. The four areas of potential focus were low cost, quality, dependability, and flexibility. The VPs were to allocate 100 total points among these areas according to their estimate of each area's priority. As might be expected, the VPs' beliefs varied considerably, but through discussion a consensus finally emerged. The results are given in Table 2.4.

As the table shows, for Product 1 the VPs allocated 42 of the 100 points concerning the *current* ("as is") focus in that product to low cost, 17 points to high quality, 25 to high dependability, and 16 to high flexibility. However, the VPs apparently did not feel that the current focus distribution was ap-

Table 2.4 Current and Required Priorities as Assessed by Vice-Presidents (VP) and Manufacturing Managers (MM)

	Cost +		Quality +		Depend-ability +		Flexibility =		Total	
	VP	MM	VP	MM	VP	MM	VP	MM	VP	MM
Product 1										
As is	42	44	17	15	25	26	16	15	100	100
Should be	28	46	24	16	31	26	17	12	100	100
Needs more (less)	(14)	2	7	1	6	0	1	(3)		
Product 2										
As is	26	20	37	43	24	22	13	15	100	100
Should be	26	30	36	38	26	20	12	12	100	100
Needs more (less)	0	10	(1)	(5)	2	(2)	(1)	(3)		
Product 3										
As is	34	36	27	28	23	19	16	17	100	100
Should be	34	38	29	24	24	20	13	18	100	100
Needs more (less)	0	2	2	(4)	1	1	(3)	1		
Product 4										
As is	24	34	30	22	19	17	27	27	100	100
Should be	39	44	20	25	23	15	18	16	100	100
Needs more (less)	15	10	(10)	3	4	(2)	(9)	(11)		
Product 5 (Parts)										
As is	45	37	21	14	18	31	16	18	100	100
Should be	22	31	24	13	35	35	19	21	100	100
Needs more (less)	(23)	(6)	3	(1)	17	4	3	3		

propriate because they only allocated 28 of the 100 points concerning the "should be" focus from Product 1 to low cost and *raised* the points for quality and dependability.

But when the VPs considered Product 2, as shown in the table, there was very little disagreement about the current focus compared to what it should be. In sum, their overall conclusions for the five product lines were as follows:

Conclusions.

- Product 1 should have modest increases in quality and dependability at the expense of low cost.

- Products 2 and 3 should not be changed.

- Product 4 should have a significant improvement in its cost at the expense, if necessary, of quality and flexibility.

- Product 5 (parts) should have a significant increase in dependability at the expense of low cost.

VPs vs. MMs.

Out of interest, the same questions were then put to the firm's manufacturing managers (MM). Interestingly, these lower level managers did not perceive the focus priorities at all as the VPs. For example, the MMs thought Product 1 should have even a *stronger* focus on low cost, at the expense of flexibility. And they felt that the quality of Product 4 should be increased and its dependability *decreased* whereas the VPs felt just the opposite. The conclusion of the firm in this case was that the manufacturing managers are too cost oriented and need to receive better information regarding top management's priorities.

This study looked at priority deviations around an existing operations focus and illustrated a method for assessing top management's beliefs about competitive strengths. Next, we will look at the process of developing a *detailed* operations strategy once the organization's overall strategic plan, including operations' role, has been determined.

Developing the Operations Strategy

To illustrate the development of the operations strategy, we will adapt a manufacturing example from Skinner [11]. Here we are given the following statement of the organization's overall strategy:

> Our corporate objective is directed toward increasing market share during the next five years via a strategy of rapid product modification and customization at a modest price increment.

From this statement we must develop the details of the operations strategy and the tasks that will be faced. This involves 10 separate elements.

1. Write the operations strategy and tasks in sentence form, not outline, and state how this will be a competitive weapon for the firm.

2. Explicitly state the demands and constraints on operations derived from the organizational strategy, marketing and financial policies,

the product life cycle, and the technology and economics of the industry and firm.

3. Determine the implications of these demands and constraints for
   - Investment levels.
   - Fixed and variable costs and breakeven points.
   - Service levels.
   - Lead times.
   - Response times.
   - Risks (e.g., of assurance of supply, of excess capacity).
   - Quality.
   - Workforce management.
   - Organizational control.
   - Production scheduling and inventory management.
   - Competitive ability.
   - Opportunities.
   - Profitability.
   - Ability to ride economic cycles.
   - Flexibility (e.g., for product changes, for volume changes).
   - Delivery dependability.

4. Estimate how often the operations task should be reevaluated. What changes will make the task obsolete, when will this happen, and how will the task change?

5. State what operations must do especially well to support the organizational strategy and how this many have changed from the past.

6. Define the cost, quality, and other standards by which operations' performance will be judged.

7. Identify what will probably be operations' most difficult task and why. Consider human, competitive, and technological impediments.

8. Rank the activities in item 6 in order of priority and identify what may have to suffer to achieve the task.

9. Identify the impact of the requirements on the elements of the operations infrastructure.

10. Identify the combination of elements in the system that would be most likely to fail.

The following is a very condensed example of this process.

Our manufacturing task for the next three years will be to introduce specialized, custom-tailored new products into production, with lead times substantially less than our competitors'. Since the technology in our industry is changing rapidly, and since product reliability can be extremely serious for customers, our most difficult problems will be to control the new-product introduction process so as to solve technical problems promptly and to maintain reliability amid rapid changes in the product itself. Performance will be measured primarily in terms of flexibility for product redesign, then reliability, and then lead time. The standards for these measures will be three months to first production model and one year to defect-free performance. To achieve this result, efficiency, ROI, and costs will have to suffer. Since the technology in the industry is changing so rapidly we suggest reviewing this task within one year, screening for possible items which might represent a breakthrough in product technology and could be mass manufactured in another plant at a considerable profit. These requirements will necessitate a complete reorganization of our manufacturing engineering and quality control departments. New forms, procedures, and wage systems may be required as well. The most likely way that we might fail in this refocusing of our task is by putting out a product with poor reliability, so that we quickly gain a bad reputation and are shunned by the customers we most desire to serve. Thus, we must take extreme caution in the quality of our engineering designs and our quality control inspections, even to the extent of 100% inspection, something we have never done before.

2.5 SUMMARY AND KEY LEARNING POINTS

This chapter has reviewed the organization's goal-setting process, the development of the organization's strategic plan, and particularly the role of an operations focus in that plan. Considerable attention was given to assessing the management of existing operations and determining top management's belief in what the proper operations focus for the organization should be. Last, the process of developing the details of an operations strategy was described. The key learning points were as follows:

- It is imperative that operations be factored into the development of the organization's strategic plan early in the process; otherwise there is very little chance of it working.

- Assessment aids check surrogate measures for the telltale signs and symptoms of good management.

- Experts consider the major categories of operations to be materials control, supervision/employee relations, productivity, maintenance, quality control, and manufacturing/process engineering coordination.

- Organizations typically hold multiple, and even conflicting, goals but set priorities and make tradeoffs to attain them.

- This chapter described a typical 6-step process used in the formulation of strategic plans and a 10-element procedure for developing an operations strategy from the organization's strategic plan.

- Success in the marketplace seems to hinge on a firm's developing at least one unique strength, called its "focus," which is highly relevant to a particular market. Such strengths may be in quality, lead time, cost, or some other area.

- Organizations can easily lose their focus by not changing it when the product or market requires it, by adding new tasks to operations, or by adding new outputs that require a different operations focus.

2.6 KEY TERMS

assessment aid (p. 34)

surrogate (p. 34)

strategic (or business)
    plan (p. 38)

tradeoffs (p. 41)

priorities (p. 41)

key business value (p. 42)

goals (p. 39)

focus (p. 43)

competitive advantage (p. 43)

infrastructure (p. 45)

2.7 REVIEW AND DISCUSSION QUESTIONS

1. Which questions in Landel's Plant Tour Assessment Aid do you think would be most difficult to score? Why?

2. Do Landel's six categories seem appropriate? Where would good product design fit? Smooth scheduling?

3. Landel is also working on an assessment aid for clerical offices. How do you think the questions will differ?

4. What might the multiple strategic and tactical goals be for
   a. A "lonely hearts" club (nonprofit).
   b. A computer dating service.
   c. A religious foundation.
   d. A private charity.
   e. A public sanitation department.
   f. A drug manufacturer.
   What priorities would you assign to the goals above? What tradeoffs would you as a manager entertain?

5. What members of an organization should be consulted when goals are determined?

6. If you do not know where you are going, any path will get you there. Discuss the importance of knowing where you are before deciding on a path to take.

7. Discuss the necessity of tradeoffs if resources are not constrained.

8. What problems do you feel that a governmental manager faces in determining tradeoffs?

9. The text identifies customer service and the distribution chain as two *nonoperations* areas which a firm may exhibit as its focus. Can you think of others?

10. Contrast the philosophy of the conglomerate with that of the "focused firm." How can two such contradictory views each have successful proponents?

11. How might the approach developed in Table 2.4 be used to aid top managers in setting a firm's goals?

12. What difficulties would you anticipate in trying to use Landel's assessment aid to evaluate a firm's operations *strategy?* In implementing a strategy?

13. Why is the use of surrogate performance measures risky? Why might the risk not be too high?

14. Try out Landel's assessment aid on a manufacturing firm. Was it easy to use? What questions were hard to answer?

15. Are you familiar with any firms that lost their focus? Consider Braniff, Singer, and International Harvester.

2.8 REFERENCES AND BIBLIOGRAPHY

1. Andrews, K. R., *The Concept of Corporate Strategy*, rev. ed., Homewood, IL: Irwin, 1980.

2. Crosby, P. B., *Quality Is Free: The Art of Making Quality*, New York: McGraw-Hill, 1979.

3. Dent, James K., "Organizational Correlates of the Goals of Business Management," *Personnel Psychology*, 12:365–393 (1959).

4. Fleming, John E., "Study of a Business Decision," *California Management Review*, 8:51–56 (Winter 1966).

5. Glueck, W. F., *Strategic Management and Business Policy*, New York: McGraw-Hill, 1980.

6. Hall, W. K., "Survival Strategies in a Hostile Environment," *Harvard Business Review*, 58:75–85 (Sept.–Oct. 1980).

7. Landel, R. D., "Taking the Pulse of a Business: A Plant-Tour Guide for Assessing Management Effectiveness," *Operations Management Review*, 1:3–7, 44–48 (Fall, 1982).

8. McCarthy, D. J. et al., *Business Policy and Strategy*, Homewood, IL: Irwin, 1979.

9. "Putting Excellence into Management," *Business Week*, 21 July 1980, pp. 196–205.

10. Raia, A., *Management of Objectives*, Glenview, IL: Scott-Foresman, 1976.

11. Skinner, W., *Manufacturing in the Corporate Strategy*, New York: Wiley, 1978.

12. Utterback, J. M., and Abernathy, W. J., "A Dynamic Model of Process and Product Innovation by Firms," *Omega*, 3:639–656 (1975).

13. Wheelwright, S. C., "Reflecting Corporate Strategy in Manufacturing Decisions," *Business Horizons*, Feb. 1978, pp. 57–66.

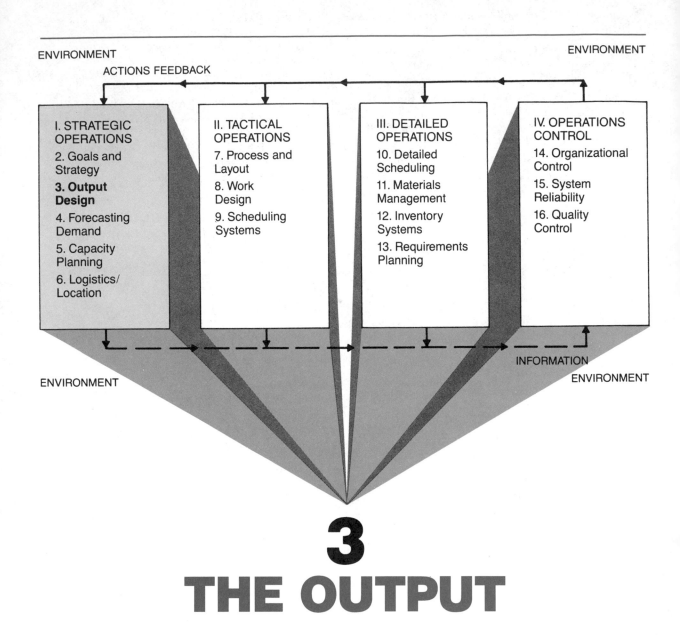

ENVIRONMENT   ENVIRONMENT

ACTIONS FEEDBACK

I. STRATEGIC OPERATIONS

2. Goals and Strategy

3. Output Design

4. Forecasting Demand

5. Capacity Planning

6. Logistics/ Location

II. TACTICAL OPERATIONS

7. Process and Layout

8. Work Design

9. Scheduling Systems

III. DETAILED OPERATIONS

10. Detailed Scheduling

11. Materials Management

12. Inventory Systems

13. Requirements Planning

IV. OPERATIONS CONTROL

14. Organizational Control

15. System Reliability

16. Quality Control

ENVIRONMENT   ENVIRONMENT

INFORMATION

3
THE OUTPUT

3

LEARNING OBJECTIVES

By the completion of this chapter the student should

- Be aware of the lengthy series of steps required to bring an output to market.
- Appreciate the implications of the mortality curve for new outputs.
- Understand the distinction between pure research, applied research, product research, process research, and development.
- Be familiar with the more common methods of idea generation.
- Have developed a sense of the risks of research and recent research trends.
- Know the major elements involved in the selection of new outputs.
- Comprehend the past history of output design, its characteristics and stages, and the difficulty of designing services.
- Appreciate the variety of design characteristics that must be considered and traded off.
- Be aware of the effect of product design on process design.

In the previous chapter we studied how organizations formulate goals and strategies and what tradeoffs and compromises are necessary in this process. In this chapter we trace the output decision from its conception as the organization's primary means of satisfying organizational goals through its final design to satisfy demand in the environment. Then, in the next chapter we will investigate the importance of forecasting this demand and develop some models that are frequently used for this purpose.

This chapter focuses on the organization's output: conceptualizing it, researching it, selecting it, developing it, and designing it. If there is one major strength of the United States it is probably in the area of creativity and innovation. We do everything our own way and *demand* the freedom to do so, even if we go bankrupt in the process. And it is exactly this independence that generates the great scientific and technological leaps of human endeavor: the electric light, the airplane, the atomic bomb, television, the computer, and so on. This crucial subject is the topic we will be exploring.

Spirit of independence.

First, we will look at the generic process of creating outputs, from imagination or pure research through design. Then in Section 3.2 we delve into idea generation: creativity, the innovation process, and technological forecasting. From there we move in Section 3.3 to the area of research, considering *process* research as well as product research, and look at the significant and sometimes negative effect that total reliance on marketing may have had on the ability of the United States to compete in world markets.

Next we consider the process of selecting outputs from the array of potential candidates to be designed and marketed by the organization. Then we describe the role of development and how it varies through the output's life cycle. Last, we consider the output design process and how the design of the output intimately relates to the transformation process that will be required to produce it.

3.1 THE OUTPUT PROCESS

All outputs are services.

Remember, all outputs can be viewed as services. A product, such as a wooden chair, is just the sum of a number of very specialized services. Some organization(s) located and purchased the wood, transported it, cut it, shaped and formed it, sanded it, painted it, stored it, sent it in the right quantity at the right time to a location where a customer could find it, informed the customer of its availability, kept its total cost low enough so that it could be purchased, and possibly even helped finance it, get it home, and repair it when it broke. It is clear then that we use the word *product* simply to indicate a very special set of services and that we do not have to fragment our thinking about the output of operations into product outputs and service outputs unless it is helpful to do so. This "services" perspective should draw attention to the fact that it is the *recipient* who defines what services are in demand, not the *organization*.

Many organizations in the past that lost sight of this point found themselves in trouble; for example, many railroads saw themselves as being merely in the business of running trains instead of the business of providing efficient transportation. Today we see attempts to break out of such restrictive thinking in an effort to orient to what the customer wishes to buy rather than what the producer wishes to produce; for example, "Sell the sizzle, not the steak," and Revlon's "In the factory we make cosmetics; in the store we sell hope." Today, we even find the gigantic oil companies quietly conducting research in solar and other forms of energy—they apparently see themselves as being in the "energy" business rather than just the petroleum business.

Selling hope and sizzle.

Figure 3.1 illustrates the process of creating, selecting, and designing the organization's outputs, and the general pattern of discussion we will follow in this chapter. As we see, output possibilities come from a number of sources: from customers through market research (customer surveys, opinion polls, consumer panels, and so on), from research labs themselves, and from deliberate, formalized attempts (we will look at some methods in Section 3.2) to generate ideas for outputs.

These ideas are then screened for viability in the market and fit with the organization, a process that eliminates about half of them. Next, a thorough economic analysis is conducted to determine the probable profitability of the output, a procedure that cuts another third from the original list. Development of the output, and the process to produce the output, is the next stage, followed by detailed design and testing. The remaining stages preceding a successful output are discussed below.

Throughout the entire output decision process, the interrelationships between the marketing, **R&D** (research and development), and operations de-

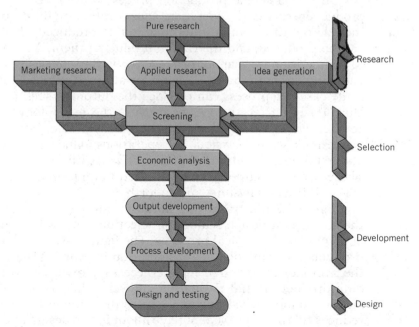

Figure 3.1 The stages of bringing a new output to market.

Role of marketing.

partments are crucial to the success of the output. Marketing plays a key role in judging environmental demand for various outputs, determining which outputs will be successful, and then following through by matching what the organization produces with the actual demand in the environment. These activities include suggesting new organizational product and service outputs (as well as new customers, new regions, and new technologies), market development and testing, and "commercialization" (getting the output to the right market and ensuring its success).

R&D defined.

R&D is responsible for creating and developing (but not producing) the organizational outputs. On occasion, R&D also creates new processes by which outputs, either new or old, may be produced. *Research* itself is typically divided into two types: pure and applied. Pure research is simply working with basic technology to develop new knowledge. Applied research is attempting to develop new knowledge along particular lines—for example, a cure for the common cold. *Development* is the attempt to utilize the findings of research and expand the possible applications, typically along the line of interest of the sponsor (e.g., the development of new drugs). We'll discuss R&D in more detail in Section 3.3.

The output selection process.

The selection and design of the product or service to be provided by the organization is a continually ongoing process. Various possible outputs are considered and general designs are developed to determine their approximate costs, efficient production possibilities, and performance characteristics. Of these, some are eliminated and others selected for further consideration through prototypes or redesign. This process contines until one or several outputs are finally selected for introduction.

The process along with the output.

On occasion, the production process must be designed *along with* the product or service. The operations considerations in the output decision process include the *variety* of outputs that can be produced, the *rate* at which they can be produced, and the *cost* of producing them. A firm leaves itself open to competition if it cannot produce the variations desired by the customers, enough volume to satisfy demand, or at a price the customer can afford. In some cases *no* process can produce the outputs—such as the wrist radio of Dick Tracy during the 1930s—because the technology is not available. Of course, wrist radios did finally become available, but by then Dick Tracy was using a wrist *television*. The operations manager must also be concerned about producing outputs that are *undesired* by society such as pollution. These negative outputs can also generate undesired returns for the organization—ill-will, lawsuits, and so forth.

New idea mortality curve.

Figure 3.2 illustrates the **mortality curve** (fallout rate) associated with the concurrent design/evaluation/selection process for a hypothetical group of 50 potential chemical products. The figure assumes that the 50 candidate products are available for consideration in year 3. (The first three years, on the average, are required for the necessary research preceding each candidate product.) Initial evaluation and screening reduces the 50 to about 22 and economic analysis further reduces the number to about 9. Development reduces this number even more, to about 5, and design and testing to perhaps

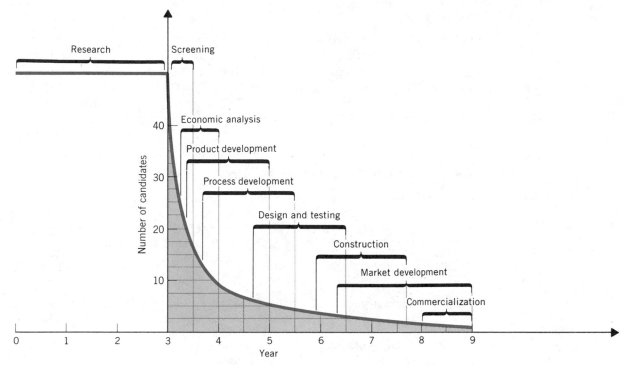

Figure 3.2 Mortality curve of chemical-product ideas from research to commercialization. (*Source:* Adapted from *This is DuPont 30*, Wilmington, Del., by permission of E. I. DuPont de Nemours and Co., 1966.)

3. By the time the construction for production, market development, and a year's commercialization are completed, there is only one successful product left. (Sometimes there are none!) And in a recent study [5], Crawford found that, beyond this, only 64 percent of the new products brought to market were successful, or about two out of three.

3.2 IDEA GENERATION

Idea sources.

There are a number of sources for ideas from which the organization can obtain a set of potential outputs for consideration. In business firms these new output possibilities come from the marketing department, company research laboratories, competitors, customers, and employees, as well as other sources. Some of these are the result of recognizing a new or potential improvement through contact with customers who use existing products or services. Many are the direct result of, and response to, new introductions of competitors. Also, customers themselves will often directly request a special improvement that may eventually be made standard for the product or service.

Creativity

Einstein has been credited with having said "Imagination is more important than knowledge." Both, though, are key ingredients to creativity—an essential element in the generation of new product and service ideas. Although creativity has been studied extensively [4, 6, 7, 10, 11, 12, 16], it is still not well understood. For example, Figure 3.3 contradicts the commonly held assumption that technological breakthroughs are becoming more and more

---

TIMETABLE OF TECHNOLOGICAL BREAKTHROUGHS

Is the pace of technological innovation really accelerating? Major breakthroughs in the last quarter century were fewer than in the previous 25 years—and fewer than in the two preceding quarter centuries. And many of the breakthroughs that have had visible impact on our daily lives came more than a half century ago.

	Years Ago		Years Ago
Use of antiseptic in surgery	100	Rocket engine	50
Storage battery		Commercial fertilizers	40
Dynamite		Hybrid seed	
Use of petroleum for heating, cooking, lighting		Air conditioning	
		Xerography	
Telephone		Electron microscope	35
Steam turbine		Radar	
Use of steel in construction		Antibiotics	30
Internal combustion engine		Artificial insemination	
Synthetic chemicals		Atomic bomb	
Electric generator	90	Television	
Elevator		Ballistic missile	
Recording and reproduction of sound		Electronic computer	
		Electronic transistor	
Electric light	75	Gas turbines	25
Electric motor		Jet engines	
Machine gun		Stimulated emission of radiation (Maser)	
Steel ships			
Aluminum		Nuclear power	
Submarine		Practical use of space satellites	10
Automobile		Holography	5
Synthetic drugs	65	Brain scanner	2
Synthetic fibers and plastics			
Radio			
Airplane	60		

Figure 3.3   One hundred years of technical creativity. (*Source:* IW and J. F. Kincaid. *Journal of the Association for the Advancement of Invention and Innovation,* July–Aug. 1976. Reprinted by permission of the Association for the Advancement of Invention and Innovation.)

frequent in our "future shock" society. Creativity does, however, appear to require the following basic elements.

The elements of creativity.

- *Intelligence:* To store and recall information and to understand and correctly conceptualize the manner in which things work.
- *Imagination:* To form unique and unusual combinations of elements and processes.
- *Motivation:* To be willing to concentrate on a problem for extended periods of time without becoming discouraged or fatigued.

Individual Creativity

Apparently, creativity can be fostered, or stimulated, in individuals by education and training in creativity techniques and processes. A number of the procedures used by "creative" persons have been studied and reported on [4, 6, 7, 12]. The general approaches such people use in being creative are summarized below.

Ways to increase creativity.

- *Ongoing practice:* Stay informed and stimulated, develop an "idea library" or reserve, be alert to unusual events and thoughts, vary your routine, watch for problems, carry a pad and pencil, drill your mind regularly in idea generation.
- *Preparation:* Relax your mind ahead of time ("sleep on it"); identify your most creative time of day; be enthusiastic, alert, and confident; organize your approach; use a place where you will not be distracted.
- *Getting started:* State the "problem" carefully, do not evaluate as you go or worry about poor ideas, be ready for inspiration, do not limit yourself to the short-term—look ahead, be specific with ideas rather than vague or general.
- *The session:* Build on previous ideas, use a checklist, divide the problem into pieces, try other senses than sight, skip over a temporary unsolvable aspect, change the words in the problem statement, state the old in new terms and the new in old terms, list the characteristics of the problem, work backward from the *ideal* solution.
- *Concluding:* Set a quota for new ideas, do not be satisfied with things as they are, do not worry about others' opinions, spot earlier mistakes, talk it over with someone else.

Group Methods

Brainstorming.

To facilitate the "imagination" phase of creativity, a number of special group procedures have been utilized, the best known of which is **brainstorming** [1, 3, 6, 10, 11, 16]. A brainstorming session encourages group members to present unusual ideas and to build on others' ideas, without evaluating the idea itself. A brainstorming session eliminates the "That's crazy!" or "It'll never work" responses that often result during group problem-solving sessions. This stage of the process is designed to allow the subconscious mind to "free associate" without being inhibited by the conscious (evaluating) mind. The review and evaluation stage, which is an analytic rather than a creative process, can be conducted at a later time.

Technological Forecasting

Technological forecasting (TF) is a significantly different approach to generating ideas for outputs. Here the purpose is to predict what technology will hold in store for future outputs. More specifically, TF is defined as a quantitative prediction, made through an explicit logic, of the timing and degree of change not only in technology itself but also in technological *capabilities*.

What, not how.   Note that TF is only meant to predict *what* will be achieved, not *how*. Also, it is not directed toward items of luxury or convenience but rather items based on new technology. Last, TF forecasts capabilities, not needs or wants (and thus, not demand or profit). One of the better known methods of TF is "Delphi." This very formalized group approach combines expert opinion to result in a consensus forecast. The details of the approach are presented in the next chapter.

3.3 RESEARCH

Product/Service Research

Many organizations, both public and private, sponsor both pure (undirected) and applied (problem-oriented) research in order to generate new ideas, processes, services, and "products." Table 3.1 lists the 1976 expenditures by government and industry for research and the general areas of application. Since that time, however, the government level of sponsorship has been

Decreasing investment in research. declining about 3 percent a year, and, initially, industry increased its contribution somewhat less than 2 percent a year, for a net decline in the amount of research being funded.

SX-70 research.   Unfortunately, the returns from such research are frequently meager whereas the costs are great. For example, Polaroid spent over $350 million on its new SX-70 camera in the early 1970s, anticipating large profits from the sale of *film* for the camera. Unfortunately, initial sales were much less than expected [13], and on 2 July 1975 Polaroid stock fell 11⅜ points, a drop

Table 3.1 Expenditures for Research

Source	Amount, in Billions of Dollars	Application	Amount, in Billions of Dollars
		Basic research	4.3
Government	20	Applied research	9.7
Industry	16	Development	22.0
Total	36		36

of 32 percent (representing $360 million), apparently due to the announcement that SX-70 sales were only one-third of company projections. (Sales improved later after SX-70 price cuts.)

Two frequent alternatives to research used by organizations are *imitation* of a proven new idea (e.g., electronic games) or outright *purchase* of someone else's invention. Although the former approach does not put the organization first on the market with the new product or service, it does give them the opportunity to study any possible defects in the original product or service and rapidly develop a better design, frequently at a better price. The latter approach, that is, purchasing an invention or the inventing company itself, eliminates the risks inherent in research, but still requires that the company develop and market the product or service before it knows whether or not it will be successful. Either route spares the organization the risk and tremendous cost of conducting the actual research leading up to a new invention or improvement.

Riskless innovation.

Important new R&D breakthroughs are usually *patented* in the U.S. Patent Office. This gives the patent holder the exclusive right to produce the new product or process, or license others to produce it, for 17 years. To obtain a patent, which now often takes over 3 years, the applicant must fully describe the invention and show that it is new, useful, tangible (i.e., not just an idea), and marketable. In a similar fashion, written, musical, and artistic creations can be *copyrighted* by sending two copies and an application fee to the U.S. Copyright Office in Washington, D.C. Last, trademarks can be *registered* at the U.S. Patent Office also (but, of course, have nothing to do with patenting or invention). The registering of a trademark, or brand name, prohibits others from using it without permission.

Patenting new ideas.

Because of the lack of patent protection, the difficulty of the task, and the impossibility of predicting marketplace response and profitability, there has been very little research on pure services, most of the effort being directed instead at the "facilitating good." Research on needs, availabilities, capacities, and other such aspects of pure services has been conducted, but the results are typically subject to controversy and interpretation.

Minimal service research.

Process Research

In addition to *"product" research* (as it is generally known) there is also *"process" research*. This involves the generation of new knowledge concerning *how to produce* outputs. Currently the production of so many familiar products out of plastic (toys, pipe, furniture, etc.) is an outstanding example of successful process research. Although not typically involved in the research side of such process innovation (a laboratory engineering function), the operations manager is intimately involved in *applying* these developments in the day-to-day production of the organization's outputs. The possible tradeoffs in such applications are many and complex. The new process may be more expensive but produce a higher quality output (and thus the repeat volume may be higher or the price can be increased). Or the new process may be more expensive and produce a *lower* quality output but be

Applying process research.

simpler and easier to maintain, resulting in a lower total cost and, ultimately, higher profits.

It is clear that many considerations involving labor, maintenance, quality, materials, capital investment, and so on, are involved in the successful application of research to operations. We will return to the subject of the production process in Section 3.6.

3.4 SELECTING THE OUTPUTS

Selection of the best ideas.

Once the organization has enumerated a number of potential new product or service ideas, the task still remains to evaluate and select the "best" ones. In some situations the selection of the appropriate product or service is relatively straightforward once the goals of the organization have been established. For example, a municipal fire department that has established "minimization of life and property losses due to fire" as its primary organizational goal will obviously select fire fighting and other fire prevention activities as a service. A restaurant on the other hand, which has established the primary goal of "earning a 15 percent profit on sales," has a broad range of service possibilities open to it. Decisions must still be made regarding the theme, the hours, the serving of alcohol, and many other such matters.

In general, the selection of a service is usually easier (but more subjective) than the selection of a product because of the following factors.

- The service organization's goal is usually directed to a generalized need on the part of the recipient or ability on the part of the organization (e.g., a recruiting firm, a podiatrist).

Services selection.

- Fewer elements such as plant, equipment, supplies, materials, and storage facilities, are usually involved in the production of a service. (Exceptions exist where large amounts of equipment are concerned, however: airlines, laundromats, laboratories.)

- If a change in the service is later found to be necessary, it can typically be accomplished with less difficulty and expense because services are typically labor, rather than equipment, intensive.

Lead time.

- Less lead time is involved in the development of a service since the product development and design stages, and much of the research stage, can be significantly shortened. The process design and production stages, however, are still required.

Whether the output is a product or a service, a number of guidelines exist for selecting among the candidate outputs. In general, these guidelines divide into the "screening" and "economic analysis" stages of Figure 3.1.

Screening and the Organizational Fit

Screening.

In the *screening* stage each candidate output is subjected to several tests to determine which outputs are most likely to succeed. Testing is based on the *fit* of the output to the organization. Any new output should capitalize on an organization's strengths and competitive advantage, complement the organization's existing outputs, and fit into the organization's structure, goals, and plans for the future.

The general areas of strength (or weakness) are

1. Experience with the particular output.
2. Experience with the production process required for the output.
3. Experience in providing an output to the same target recipients.
4. Experience with the distribution system for the output.

Evaluate weaknesses as well as strengths.

An organization must assess all its strengths and weaknesses, keeping in mind the goals of the organization, before a decision can be made to introduce a new output. A particular strength cannot necessarily be used as a justification for a new output if other major weaknesses exist. For example, an electronics company with the best professional staff and facilities for production of computer equipment may not find it advisable to enter the industrial computer market if past sales have been exclusively military. The bidding and contract experience gained through government procurement will provide no help in marketing computers to the industrial market. The company would have to develop a complete distribution system for the industrial level. This one major organizational weakness could be sufficient to convince management that entry into the industrial market is inadvisable, even though the technical capability exists.

Public competition too.

Organizational strengths and weaknesses cannot be considered in a vacuum. In the private sector there typically exist other firms that produce similar products or services. Even if the output is a new one, the firm can expect competitors to enter the market quickly if its own introduction is successful. Even a public sector organization is not exempt from an analysis of the marketplace and the existing and potential "competitors." While we generally do not think of a state park being in competition with a county park, or a city hospital in competition with a private hospital, these organizations do compete for demand in the community.

Competitive advantage.

The organization must consider the capabilities it possesses *relative* to the capabilities of other organizations in the marketplace and determine in which markets it might hold a competitive advantage due to such strengths as a particularly skilled labor force, a flexible set of facilities, an expensive and scarce piece of equipment, and so forth. In the great majority of organizations this competitive advantage must be reflected in the operations area, as illustrated above—it is the rare organization that can compete successfully with only a marketing, or financial, competitive advantage.

Effect on existing outputs.

Another aspect that the organization must address is the effect a new output will have on both the demand and the production methods used for existing outputs, a consideration of major importance to the operations manager. For example, introduction of color television sets reduced the demand for standard black and white TVs. Clearly, a new output may very well change the "best" production methods to be used for existing outputs in

Area of Fit	Poor	Fair	Good	Excellent
I. General				
1. Fits long-term organizational goals	———	———	———	———
2. Capitalizes on organizational strengths	———	———	———	———
3. Appealing to management	———	———	———	———
4. Utilizes organizational experience	———	———	———	———
II. Market				
1. Adequate demand	———	———	———	———
2. Existing or potential competition	———	———	———	———
3. In line with market trend	———	———	———	———
4. Enhances existing line	———	———	———	———
III. Economics				
1. Cost	———	———	———	———
2. Price	———	———	———	———
IV. Production				
1. Capacity availability	———	———	———	———
2. Material supply and price	———	———	———	———
3. Engineering know-how	———	———	———	———

Figure 3.4 Typical organizational fit checklist.

terms of labor skills, type of equipment, and possibly even the operations focus of the organization. It will certainly change the scheduling, routing, and other production planning aspects of the operations area.

Sometimes, of course, a new output totally changes the organization and its goals instead. On occasion, organizations do this on purpose to move into a new product or service area, especially if the old output is near the end of its life cycle.

The fit test.   One simple method for checking the organizational fit of the candidate outputs is to use a checklist, such as that shown for *products* in Figure 3.4. Although such a list is not a substitute for analysis, it does provide a starting point for analysis. We can begin by concentrating attention on the "Poor" fit areas and analyzing the impact of these and the tradeoffs available between areas checked as "Poor" and those checked as "Excellent."

Economic Analysis

The fit, in terms of economic costs and returns to the organization, must also be considered in this initial screening. Will the product or service result in an overall increase or decrease in returns to the organization? What will happen to demand for existing outputs? Will total costs stay the same? Generally speaking, the returns should exceed the costs—if not the monetary returns, then at least the other returns should provide a valuable benefit, such as acquiring experience in a new output area. Because new outputs

"You rang, Sir?"

(*Source: Wall Street Journal*, 30 Dec. 1976.
Reprinted by permission of Cartoon Features Syndicate.)

The time value of money.

usually involve heavy advance investments with returns coming in over a long future horizon, the economic analysis should include the element of time since time affects the value of both cost and returns. Time is usually incorporated into economic analysis through the concepts of *present value* and *internal rate of return,* topics that will be discussed in the appendix to Chapter 15 where equipment acquisition is treated.

Assuming that a preliminary output or outputs have been selected, we next focus on the development and design of the output and the critical role of operations in this process.

3.5 DEVELOPMENT

"Bugs" out!

The **development** end of R&D is more toward the applications side and often consists of modifications or extensions to existing outputs. Figure 3.5 illustrates the range of applicability of development as the output becomes more clearly defined. In the early years of a new output, development is oriented toward getting "bugs" out of the output, increasing its performance and quality, and so on. In the middle years, options and variants of the output

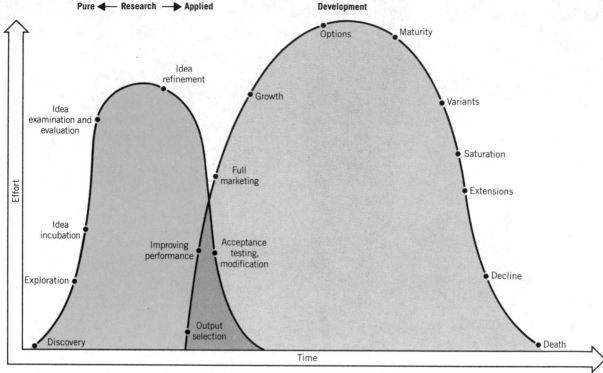

Figure 3.5 The development effort.

are developed. In the later years, development is oriented toward extensions of the output that will prolong its life.

Compared with 20 or 30 years ago, the development effort in R&D is currently much, much larger than the research effort. Some scholars of R&D [2] attribute the shift away from research and toward the simple extension of existing outputs to the impact of marketing's extensive influence on organizations. They postulate that the marketing approach of "give the customers what they want" is basically *wrong* because neither the customer nor the marketer has the vision to see what new technology can offer. By then draining off funds from research and spending them on ever-greater development of existing outputs, and the advertising of those outputs, the organization leaves itself open to those competitors willing to invest in research to develop entire new generations of outputs.

Misuse of marketing.

3.6 OUTPUT DESIGN

The History of Output Design

Once the outputs and production methods have been selected and developed, the task of *design* can begin. Design is the determination of the particular specifications (size, rating, capacity, etc.) of an output so that an organization can produce it economically. Many years ago the primary purpose of output design was only to facilitate the production process. Since demand for goods was plentiful as long as the price was low, companies desired to minimize the unit cost of items. One method of reducing unit cost was increasing capacity through *mass production* or assembly line manufacture. Thus, companies moved toward **standardization** and **interchangeability** of outputs and parts to minimize both costs and assembly difficulty. Standardization had the following cost-related advantages.

Standardization to increase capacity.

1. It minimized the number of different parts to stock.
2. It minimized the number of production equipment changes necessary to produce the outputs.

Some advantages.

3. It simplified operations procedures and thus reduced the need for many controls.
4. It allowed larger purchases with quantity discounts.
5. It minimized repair and servicing problems.

On the other hand, standardization had several drawbacks. For example, using standard parts rather than specially made parts sometimes meant lower quality products. But the major disadvantage of standardization was the inflexibility of production; little variety was possible. The classic comment exemplifying this fact was that of Henry Ford, who is reputed to have declared that his customers could have any color Model T they desired, as long as it was black!

The Marketing Phase

This standardization set the stage for the marketing phase of output design—designing for output characteristics other than cost, such as variety, quality, and appearance. Of course, cost could not be totally ignored. These other output characteristics had to be obtained while minimizing the increase in output cost. One method used to obtain variety, or at least the semblance of variety, and still hold down cost was **modularization.** This meant producing the output in "modules" or subassemblies that were interchangeable, thus giving the customer some choice in outputs. For instance, the purchaser of a new car can specify the engine size, type of transmission, upholstery, color, and numerous other aspects of the product. Such variety is *not* achieved by producing some number of every possible model but rather by producing modules (e.g., engines, transmission, bodies with varying colors, upholstery, tires and wheels, etc.) and then joining the appropriate modules together in final assembly according to the customer's order.

Modularization allows variety.

As an example of modularization, an automobile with three possible engines, two possible transmissions, five different exterior colors and three different interiors available to the customer requires only 13 modules for the operations manager to keep track of. But these 13 modules can be combined to form $3 \times 2 \times 5 \times 3 = 90$ different versions of the same model automobile, a blessing for the marketing staff.

Demand and Resource Shortages—The Impact of Operations

A recent addition to the output design problem has been recurring shortages of demand as well as the factors of production and the resulting direct decreases in capacity. Recently we have seen, and are likely to continue to live with, decreased consumer demand, the "capital crunch," and the "energy crisis," all of which tend to restrict output capacity. There have been a number of responses to this dilemma. The following are some of the major responses:

Recent shortages and some responses.

- *Reduction of product lines:* Marginal products have been dropped and a general retrenchment has taken place. Some new lines have been postponed and existing lines combined.

- **Simplification** *programs:* Simplifying products means fewer parts (thereby saving materials and labor), easier service, and greater reliability. Simplification can also be applied to the production process with equally important benefits.

- **Value analysis:** Value analysis (or value engineering) examines the *function* of an output and attempts to achieve it with less cost (for example, replacing metal parts with plastic parts). It considers cheaper methods, materials, processes, designs, and so forth.

Regulation

Another set of restrictions concerning output design, with some of the same responses as above, has been federal laws and regulations concerning pollution, occupational safety and health (OSHA), consumer protection, and other, similar problems. Some of these regulations are directed toward the product or service itself such as labeling of ingredients, health warnings, statements of true interest rates, mandated automobile gasoline mileages, emission restrictions, drug and chemical prohibitions (red dye #2, Freon, phosphates), and so on. These regulations directly affect the organization's output and hence the operations area that has the responsibility of producing the output.

Regulation affects capacity.

Other regulations, such as those regarding OSHA and pollution, concern the production process directly. Restrictions on the disposal of nuclear waste severely hamper electric generating capacity, for example. Similarly, safety restrictions in the workplace and the diversion of capital for pollution control tend to reduce productivity.

The Design of Services

Most of our design discussion up to this point has concerned the "facilitating good" more than the accompanying services. Let us now turn to the latter. As mentioned in Chapter 1, services are usually considered to be labor intensive rather than capital (equipment, facilities) intensive, and hence their design often centers on the skills of the person performing the service (e.g., physician, auto mechanic). As Levitt [9] points out, this may be a fatal perspective!

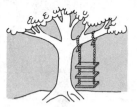
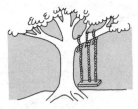

1. What Marketing suggested   2. What Management approved   3. As designed by Engineering

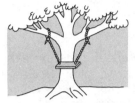
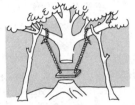
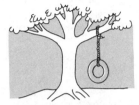

4. What was manufactured   5. As Maintenance installed it   6. What the customer desired

We have spent so many years in the mass production stage of output design that we now tend to erroneously focus on the output instead of the recipient, as illustrated below.

Focus on the recipient, not the output.

1. The design of services is labor intensive and typically includes personal attendance to the needs of the recipient. Improving the design of the service has been misdirected toward the *server* rather than the recipient.

2. The design of products is capital intensive. Improvements here have been misdirected toward improving the product itself or the capital equipment and facilities used to produce the product.

As mentioned earlier, this perspective is important to operations managers because many organizations still see the provision of customer service, financing, instruction, installation, promotion, and so forth as a necessary evil in the process of producing their product. Some managers tend to consider it in the same category as giving trading stamps with every purchase— a wasteful cost allocated to overhead that the entire industry would rather dispose with but cannot because it is used as a competitive tool.

Product services— something for nothing?

This attitude totally misses the truth. The demand is not only for the facilitating good but for the services as well. (In some instances the primary demand is not for the good *at all* but for the services.) In these instances redesign of the output would focus on the needs of the recipient. The provision of more services would probably be greatly increased and promoted as well.

Product and service design the same.

In pure service organizations output design should also refocus on the recipient rather than on the server. By considering what services the recipient is searching for, organizations can often design high-efficiency ap-

"Obviously, it'll have to inflate quicker than that."

(Reprinted with permission from *Changing Times*, © 1973, Kiplinger Washington Editors, Inc., Nov. 1973.)

proaches that minimize, or completely eliminate, the slow, highly variable result typically obtained through human labor. Levitt [9] gives as examples vending machines, packaged promotional displays, and modular servicing, all with the characteristics of complexity and attention to detail in their *concept and design* but simplicity in their *operation*. But these are the same characteristics as products!

Complex concept, simple operation.

Design Characteristics

Operations plays a major role in setting the final characteristics of the output. Some typical design characteristics of outputs that organizations should consider in relation to demand and capacity are

- *Function:* The new design must properly perform the function (meet recipient's need) for which it is required.
- *Cost:* The total cost (materials, labor, processing, etc.) cannot be excessive for the market under consideration.
- *Size and shape:* These must be compatible with the function and not distasteful or unacceptable to the market.
- *Appearance:* For some applications the appearance of the product or service is irrelevant; in other instances (e.g., art) the appearance is equivalent to the function.
- *Quality:* The quality should be compatible with the purpose. Excessive quality may increase cost unnecessarily; insufficient quality leads to complaints and decreased demand.
- *Reliability:* The output should function normally when used and last the expected duration. Outputs with complex combinations of elements, all of which must work, will tend to have lower reliabilities unless this is allowed for in the design.
- *Environmental impact:* The output should not degrade the environment or pose a hazard to the recipient.

- *Producibility:* The output should be producible with ease and speed.
- *Timing:* The output should be available when desired. This characteristic is especially relevant to service outputs.
- *Accessibility:* The recipient should be able to obtain the output without difficulty.
- *Recipient input requirements:* The amount and type of input required of the recipient should be considered in the design. "Do-it-yourself" projects are an example of this for product outputs and "self-service" for service outputs.

Tradeoffs are the key in design.

The design task is to "trade off" (as was described for goals in Chapter 2) the above characteristics in order to best meet the demands of the marketplace. For example, when Ford Motor Company introduced the Pinto, much of the initial advertising touted the "ease" of owner maintenance of the vehicle. Even the owner's manual contained specific instructions for undertaking the basic maintenance of the car. This improvement in maintainability was brought about by trading some aspects of size, function, and, to some minds, beauty. Another attribute of the new product that was greatly improved was cost, both initial purchase cost and operating cost. Recognition of a special need or desire in the marketplace is the first step, and a major one, in the design of a new product.

The rise of self-service.

In the service area, gasoline stations and fast food restaurants have become "self-service" to reduce the cost, as well as the service time, to the recipient. In return for the improvements in these two characteristics of the services, customers have had to give up such conveniences as battery, oil, and tire pressure checks, waiters and waitresses, full line menus, and individual attention. For those people who still desire these features, standard "full service" gas stations are available as are numerous dining alternatives.

Market "segmentation."

In both product and service design, many alternatives usually exist that will meet the basic function of the output. The key to good design is a recognition of the major characteristics of the demand and a detailed analysis of the tradeoffs available between and among the various attributes. Often, several different versions of the same output can be produced so that different market segments will find the output appealing. For example, Procter & Gamble offers a dazzling array of detergents, many of which undoubtedly even compete with each other to some extent. In the fast food business, the major companies experimented with expanding their menus (at the risk of loss of focus) to broaden the appeal to new markets (e.g., McDonald's experimented with offering chili, sundaes, and eggs and pancakes at many locations).

The Impact of Product Design on Process Design

Utterback and Abernathy [15] have noted the relationship of a product's life cycle to its production process life cycle, illustrated in Figure 3.6. The chart actually begins at the right-hand side of Figure 3.5, shown earlier, where

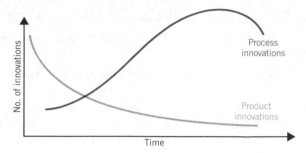

Figure 3.6 Product-process innovation history

product innovations such as variants and extensions are relatively frequent. At this point, the production process is relatively uncoordinated and very general since the product design is still changing. Toward the middle of Figure 3.6 the product design has stabilized and cost competition is forcing

Process innovation.   innovation in the production process, particularly the substitution of machinery for labor. At the right of Figure 3.6 this process has also died down and process innovations are the result of competitors' actions, government regulations, and other primarily external factors.

In Chapter 7, Transformation Process Design and Layout, we will continue this theme and get into considerably more detail concerning the nature of these process innovations.

3.7 SUMMARY AND KEY LEARNING POINTS

In this chapter we have briefly overviewed the subject of bringing outputs to market and the role of operations in that process. We have considered the subjects of idea generation, research, output selection and organizational fit, output and process development, and, finally, the design of the output. The key learning points have been

- The steps in bringing an output to market are idea generation and research, screening for organizational fit, economic analysis, output development, process development, design and testing, construction, market development, and commercialization.

- Throughout the above process, from the results of research onward, the success rate is only 1 to 2 percent.

- Pure research is undirected whereas applied research is problem oriented. Product research is oriented toward the output whereas process research is oriented toward the production process. Development occurs anywhere in the output life cycle following research and is oriented toward improving the output, modifying it, or extending it.

- Ideas can be generated individually, in group sessions (the best known method being brainstorming), or through technological forecasting, which tries to predict *what* will or can happen technologically rather than *how*.

- Research is very expensive and risky; much safer is common imitation. Much more development is now being funded than research, a partial outgrowth of firms' beliefs in marketing.
- Organizations select new outputs based on their goals and strengths, their experience in the market, their operations ability, the economics of the output, and the probable effect on their other outputs.
- The past history of output design was heavily product oriented, stressing standardization, interchangeability, and modularization. Current trends concern decreased demand and supplies, regulation, and, particularly, the design of services.
- Typical design characteristics include function, cost, quality, appearance, producibility, timing, and environmental impact.
- The stage in an output's life cycle determines how output design and innovation impact on the design and innovations concerning the production process for the output. In early dynamic years when the product is still changing form, process innovations are minimal. But once the form has stabilized and competition enters the market, an efficient production process is needed.

3.8 KEY TERMS

R&D (p. 55)
product research (p. 60)
process research (p. 61)
development (p. 65)
mortality curve (p. 56)

brainstorming (p. 59)
technological forecasting (p. 60)
standardization (p. 67)

interchangeability (p. 67)
modularization (p. 67)
simplification (p. 68)
value analysis (p. 68)

3.9 REVIEW AND DISCUSSION QUESTIONS

1. What kinds of organizations would have low new idea mortality rates? High rates?

2. Can creativity be learned?

3. What considerations are probably most important in the "fit" of an output to an organization?

4. Give examples of successful, and unsuccessful, attempts at tradeoffs in new products. In new services.

5. Is basic or applied research more profitable to society?

6. Was Kodak's Instamatic camera the outgrowth of research or development?

7. Name some instances in which the economic return to an organization did not justify the costs but the organization proceeded anyway. Why did it?

8. Has standardization hurt the service industry's image in any way?

9. How should an organization go about balancing the design characteristics of a contemplated output?

10. Do you agree or disagree that the recent emphasis on development at the expense of research is ultimately harmful to firms? Give an example to illustrate your case.

'1978 Target Car Results

	Points Possible	Olds Delta 88 Diesel	VW Dasher	Volvo 244DL	Mercedes 300D	SAAB 99 GLE	Chev Malibu 305	Datsun 810	Olds Cutlass 2608	Toyota Cressida	Audi 5000	Ford 2006 Fairmont	Peugeot** 504 Diesel*	Pontiac Le Mans 305	BMW 733i	Dodge** OMNI	Mercury Monarch 302	Plymouth Volare (318)	Lincoln Versailles 302	Mazda RX4*	Chrysler 318 LeBaron	Subaru DL 4 DR Sedan	Buick Electra 403	Cadillac 350 Seville	Jaguar** X6L
Fuel economy city	12	12	12	12	12	12	6	11	11	12	9	12	12	6	3	12	8	6	8	12	6	12	5	3	3
Fuel economy hwy	12	12	12	9	12	10	6	6	9	8	6	7	12	6	2	12	7	6	6	8	6	12	4	4	2
Interior front	5	5	4	4	5	4	5	4	5	4	4	4	5	4	4	2	4	5	4	5	5	4	5	5	5
Interior rear	12	11	6	10	6	8	10	9	6	5	5	8	9	8	9	2	8	10	5	4	10	2	9	10	9
Passing ability 40–60	5	4	5	5	0	5	5	5	4	5	5	4	0	5	5	5	5	5	5	5	5	2	5	5	5
Acceleration, 0–50	5	5	4	4	0	4	5	5	4	5	5	5	0	5	5	3	5	5	5	4	5	3	5	5	5
Crash worthiness potential	9	5	1	3	3	1	5	4	4	3	2	3	2	4	3	1	4	3	4	3	4	2	4	4	4
Noise @ 30 MPH	3	3	3	3	3	2	3	1	3	3	2	2	3	3	3	3	3	3	3	0	2	2	3	3	3
Noise @ 55 MPH	3	3	3	1	3	3	3	1	3	3	2	2	3	3	3	2	3	3	3	1	2	2	3	3	3
Noise @ 60 MPH WOT	3	3	3	2	3	1	3	3	3	3	3	3	2	3	2	2	3	3	3	2	3	2	3	3	3
Luggage/ Parcel capacity	6	6	5	4	5	3	5	3	5	2	6	5	4	5	6	2	4	4	4	4	4	2	6	3	5
Entry and exit	6	4	4	5	6	5	4	5	4	4	5	3	5	5	6	4	5	5	5	2	5	3	6	5	5
Slalom handling	6	5	6	6	6	5	5	6	3	6	6	5	4	6	6	6	1	3	4	6	3	6	0	4	4
Small exterior	5	1	5	3	3	5	4	4	3	3	3	3	4	2	3	5	2	2	2	5	2	5	0	2	2
Ride quality	5	4	3	4	5	4	4	4	4	4	5	4	3	4	5	4	4	4	5	3	4	3	4	4	5
Small turn circle	3	1	3	3	3	3	2	3	2	3	3	1	3	2	3	3	2	1	1	3	0	3	2	1	1
TARGET CAR TOTAL	100	84	79	78	75	75	74	74	73	73	71	71	71	71	68	68	68	68	67	67	66	65	64	64	64

Source: Auto Club of Southern California, © 1978 by the Automobile Club of Southern California.

3.10 READINGS

THE "TARGET CAR"

U.S. car manufacturers are looking good these days, following some "catch up" years during which foreign cars did better than domestics in meeting current needs such as fuel conservation while still maintaining other desirable characteristics.

For the first time, a U.S.-built car topped the list in the Auto Club's Target Car program. This results from a new U.S. trend of zeroing in on smaller size and greater fuel economy.

The new champ is the recently introduced Oldsmobile Delta 88 Diesel (reviewed in the February *Auto Club News Pictorial*). It scored a record 84 points in the Club's 1978 Target Car Program . . . five more points than any other production vehicle has achieved in the four-year history of the program. Oldsmobile achieved this record by combining a high fuel economy diesel with a body that has a spacious interior. The Oldsmobile diesel gives good acceleration, has an acceptable noise level and should last as long as the gasoline engine.

Also in the first group, following in the wake of the Oldsmobile Diesel, are the Volkswagen Dasher with 79 points and the Volvo 244DL with 78 points (see table for a complete listing of the cars tested).

After this, the cars begin to bunch up. The second group consists of 10 cars that scored between 71 and 75 points. The last group of 11 cars scored between 64 and 68 points—still a significant improvement over previous years.

The American manufacturers are getting more and more competitive with the imports. Last year only one American car made it to the top group of seven cars that scored 71 or more points. This year *13* cars scored at least 71 points, and 5 are of American origin.

In 1978, because of the efforts of domestic manufacturers in down-sizing automobiles to meet current and future federal fuel economy regulations and because of the foreign manufacturers bringing out new models to be competitive, the number of cars from which selections were made was much larger than before. Out of 24 cars that made our list this year, 8 are entirely new models.

These include the top scorer—the Oldsmobile Delta 88 Diesel, and three new foreign cars that respond to the American demand for bigger cars—the Toyota Cressida, Audi 5000 and the BMW 733i. Other new American entries are the Dodge Omni, Lincoln Versailles, the Chrysler Le Baron and the Ford Fairmont.

Now, more about the nature of the program.

As stated in previous articles, the Target Car is an "ideal," or optimum, design which exists only on paper.

The 11 characteristics measured are listed in the table and represent, for the most part, the independent variables challenging modern auto manufacturers. In simpler language, that means most of the characteristics measured ride a see-saw with one or more of the others. Consider fuel economy, for example. Miles-per-gallon may easily go up while acceleration goes down. Or desirable small exterior dimensions can be bought at the price of some passenger discomfort, and, perhaps, less adequate protection in a collision. A prime activity of the Target Car program is to urge a reasonable balance among all these variables, together with technological advances, which will permit us to push forward in all areas at once.

Several ingredients go into developing Target Car values:

1. The results of scientifically conducted surveys about automobile characteristics using the opinions of the Club's Membership Advisory Group (MAG).

2. The subsequent identification of key tradeoff characteristics.

3. The weighting of the 11 characteristics in terms of importance—see "points possible" in the table.

4. The use of test procedures, recognized in industry, or, as in some cases, established as a result of careful research and development. These procedures are designed to produce scores or ratings for each automobile characteristic.

Again, we caution readers concerning interpretation of results obtained in the Target Car program. First, let's consider limitations in connection with the testing performed. Where possible, generally recognized test procedures were used. In some cases, however, actual testing could not be performed. For example, crash testing was precluded because of cost. So a crashworthiness potential rating was substituted, using dimension data. Also, two characteristics, ease of entry/exit and ride quality, were evaluated subjectively.

The Target Car program was not designed to be a consumer guide to the purchase of a new car. However, the program can be used as one source of information for prospective buyers. To assist them, the cost of operating and owning various models can be compared to the Target Car score. Thus, the cost per Target Car point can be derived for various cars.

This and more detailed information about the 1978 Target Car program is contained in a full report which can be obtained by writing to the Automotive Engineering Department, Automobile Club of Southern California, 2601 South Figueroa Street, Los Angeles, Calif., 90007. Members interested in the test data and methodology are encouraged to ask for and review the full report. And, as always, all member comments are appreciated; they inform us of your concerns and are helpful in guiding the program.

3.11 REFERENCES AND BIBLIOGRAPHY

1. Bennett, Keith W., "Tomorrow's New Products, Today, by the Hunch Bunch," *Iron Age*, 209:49 (13 May 1972).
2. Bennett, R. C., and Cooper, R. G., "The Misuse of Marketing: An American Tragedy," *Business Horizons*, Nov.–Dec. 1981.
3. Bouchard, T. J., "Whatever Happened to Brainstorming," *Industry Week*, 170:26–27 (2 August 1971).
4. Covington, C. et al., *The Productive Thinking Program: A Course in Learning to Think*, Columbus, OH: Merrill, 1974.
5. Crawford, C. M., "New Product Failure Rates—Facts and Fallacies," *Research Management*, 22:9–13 (Sept. 1979).
6. Crosby, A., *Creativity and Performance in Industrial Organization*, London: Travistock Publication, 1968.
7. deBoro, E., *Lateral Thinking: Creativity Step by Step*, New York: Harper & Row, 1970.
8. Hayes, R. H., and Abernathy, W. J., "Managing Our Way to Economic Decline," *Harvard Business Review*, 58:67–77 (July–Aug. 1980).
9. Levitt, Theodore, "Production Line Approach to Service," *Harvard Business Review*, 50:41–52 (Sept.–Oct. 1972).
10. Oates, D., "The Boom in Creative Thinking," *International Management*, 27:18 (Dec. 1972).
11. Osborn, A. F., *Applied Imagination*, New York: Scribner's, 1963.
12. Summers, I., and White, D.E., "Creativity Techniques: Toward Improvement of the Decision Process," *Academy of Management Review*, 1:99–107 (1976).
13. "The SX-70 Camera Deglamorizes Polaroid," *Business Week*, 30 Nov. 1974, p. 90.
14. Uman, D., *New Product Programs: Their Planning and Control*, New York: American Management Association, 1969.
15. Utterback, J., and Abernathy, W. J. "A Dynamic Model of Process and Product Innovation," *Omega*, 3:639–656 (1975).
16. Whiting, C. S., *Creative Thinking*, New York: Reinhold, 1958.

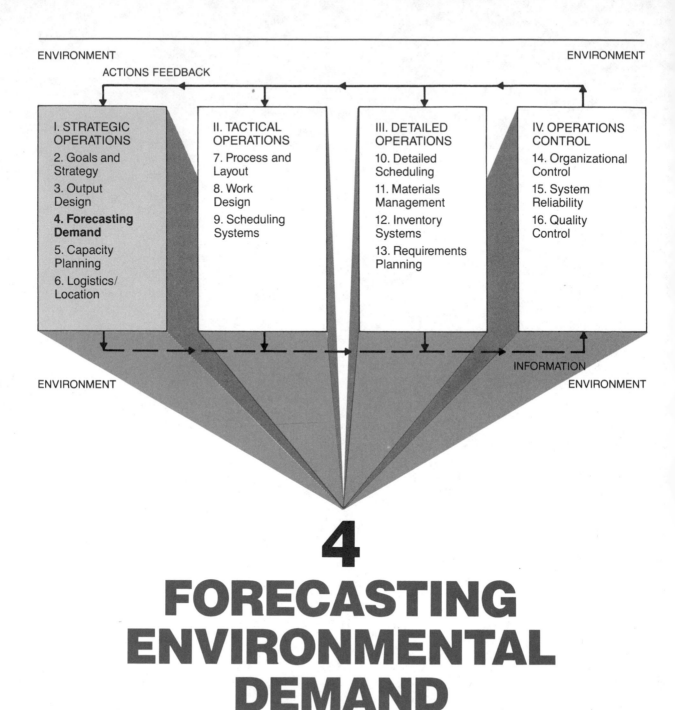

ENVIRONMENT   ENVIRONMENT

ACTIONS FEEDBACK

I. STRATEGIC OPERATIONS	II. TACTICAL OPERATIONS	III. DETAILED OPERATIONS	IV. OPERATIONS CONTROL
2. Goals and Strategy	7. Process and Layout	10. Detailed Scheduling	14. Organizational Control
3. Output Design	8. Work Design	11. Materials Management	15. System Reliability
4. Forecasting Demand	9. Scheduling Systems	12. Inventory Systems	16. Quality Control
5. Capacity Planning		13. Requirements Planning	
6. Logistics/ Location			

ENVIRONMENT   ENVIRONMENT

INFORMATION

4
FORECASTING ENVIRONMENTAL DEMAND

4

LEARNING OBJECTIVES

By the completion of this chapter the student should

- Be familiar with the types of returns that organizations receive.
- Appreciate the uses of forecasts in organizations.
- Have developed a sense for the general categories of forecasting methods.
- Be aware of the factors that influence the choice of a forecasting method.
- Comprehend the types of qualitative forecasting methods.
- Understand the four assumed components of time series.
- Know how to calculate a moving average and an exponential forecast.
- Be able to calculate the MAD and bias of a set of forecasts.
- Know how to calculate the linear regression equation and seasonal factors for a set of demand data.
- Be familiar with causal forecasting methods and their uses.

Forecasting demand for outputs.

In the previous chapters we discussed the goals of the organization and the potential outputs it can produce. Now we consider the prediction of environmental demand for the outputs. If insufficient demand exists for the output, it may not be a viable choice to produce the returns that the organization desires. Beyond that, at some demand levels the required transformation process may be beyond the skill level of the organization. Or the organization may not have the equipment or materials necessary to produce the output at that demand level. Thus we see that an accurate estimate of demand for the output is crucial to the efficient operation of the transformation process, and hence, to the operations manager.

Need for accurate forecasts.

For example, a hospital administrator who is contemplating the addition of a new emergency room must have a reasonable estimate of demand in order to determine the number of treatment rooms, the size of the waiting area, and so forth, to specify in the plans. Once the facility is constructed, a more specific forecast will be needed of demand each day of the week on each shift. Only with this forecast will the administrator be able to schedule staff for efficient utilization and high productivity. The same is true for capacity and scheduling/staffing decisions in a product organization. The size and capacity decisions regarding operations and the production/scheduling/staffing/materials decisions all require forecasting, whether it be a formal procedure or not.

Forecasting internal factors.

But it is not only demand for output that can be forecast. The tools of forecasting can also be used to predict the development of new technology, national and international economic conditions, and even many factors internal to the organization such as lead time changes, scrap rates, cost trends, personnel growth, and departmental productivity rates.

In this chapter we look at forecasting and demand for the organization's output. In Section 4.1 we focus on the returns organizations seek and then in Section 4.2 on means of developing forecasts to anticipate environmental demand that will generate those returns. We consider three primary types of forecasting methods: qualitative (Section 4.3), time series analysis (Section 4.4), and causal (Section 4.7). To develop and illustrate the concepts, we employ examples from public and municipal services: health care (Section 4.5) and mass transit (Section 4.6).

4.1 RETURNS TO THE ORGANIZATION

Before proceeding to the available forecasting methods, let us dwell first on some of the returns frequently desired by organizations: money, recognition, and sometimes just information.

Money

Money is an amazing invention. It is the *symbolic* equivalent of hard work, yet in a *physical* form that can be given by (and stolen from) one person to another in only seconds. It is no wonder that money is thus the most common

Money represents
hard work.

form of return to most organizations—it simply represents the hard work of people who value the organization's outputs. It can therefore be considered a measure of how well an organization is meeting the needs of its environment. Even nonprofit organizations can partially measure their success by the amount of monetary dues and donations they receive, as well as the budgets allocated to them by other organizations (e.g., the budget of a city parks department allocated by the elected city council).

Recognition

Recognition
important to
both profit and
not-for-profit
organizations.

Recognition is a highly-sought-after return desired by most organizations. Even profit-oriented organizations desire recognition, in part to convey a positive image, such as high quality or design, to their products. But especially for nonprofit organizations, recognition is usually a reflection of continuing success in meeting the needs of recipients. Such recognition is especially important to organizations that receive their monetary support through donations. Examples of high recognition organizations are the Red Cross, the Mayo Clinic, the NAACP, and the National Geographic Society.

Information

Desire for
feedback.

Even high recognition organizations usually desire and strive for another environmental return as well—knowledge, obtained through information feedback, that their activities have been of service to the recipients. For example, anonymous donors to charities may wish *not* to be "recognized" because of the publicity but still desire to know that their donation has been put to good use. Information regarding the results of organizational activities may be obtained indirectly through hearsay and news accounts, or may be directly solicited by the organization itself, as in surveys.

Undesired returns.

In addition to the returns an organization desires from the environment, there will frequently be undesired, or at least unexpected, returns. Examples of such returns are complaints and lawsuits as well as the literal return of merchandise found by the recipient to be unacceptable. Experienced organizations anticipate and prepare for such undesired returns in order to further foster the achievement of their goals. Thus, one of the reasons that Sears has become such a successful retailer is its deliberately liberal policy regarding the return of unsatisfactory merchandise.

4.2 FORECASTING ENVIRONMENTAL DEMAND

Forecasting for
efficiency.

To provide the organization with the returns it needs to satisfy its goals, the organization must usually interact with its environment. The organization provides outputs needed in the environment and receives certain returns in exchange. In order to most efficiently conduct this process the organization needs to know not only *what* to produce but also *when, how much,* and at *what price.* To a certain extent these last two items are interrelated—generally, the lower the price the more that can be exchanged with the environment. It is therefore useful to have a *forecast* of environmental demand for the output.

Sales or demand?

Before proceeding, it is important to note the difference between forecasting demand and forecasting sales. Given a particular output and price, the demand in the marketplace can be forecast, let us assume. Actual sales may differ substantially from this, however, even if the forecast was perfectly correct. Why? For many reasons. Perhaps the recipients did not know about the availability of the service, or maybe the service ran out and capacity could not meet the demand. The point is, actual sales are influenced to a great extent by management's own actions regarding advertising, stocking policies, and so on. If one attempts to forecast sales instead of demand, the result is an attempt to predict management's actions based, in part, on the prediction itself. Thus, the forecast would actually be altering the results, a situation we wish to avoid.

Use of Forecasts

Forecasts are used in organizations for three primary purposes.

Forecasting for new output introductions.

1. To decide whether environmental demand is sufficient to generate the returns desired by the organization. If demand exists but at too low a "price" to cover the "costs" the organization will incur in producing the output, then the organization should reject the opportunity.

Long-term forecasting for capacity needs.

2. To determine long-term capacity needs ("long-term forecasting") for facility design. An accurate projection of demand for a number of years in the future can save the organization great expense in expanding, or contracting, capacity to accommodate future environmental demands. Due to competitive forces in the environment, even in the not-for-profit sector, an organization that produces inefficiently, because of excess idle capacity, or insufficiently to meet demand is courting disaster.

Short-term forecasting for production planning.

3. To ascertain short-term (1 week to 3 months) fluctuation in demand ("short-term forecasting") for production planning, workforce scheduling, materials planning, and so forth. These forecasts are of special importance to operations management and crucially affect operational productivity (the "productivity crisis" currently of national interest), bottlenecks, master scheduling, meeting promised delivery dates, and other such issues of concern to top management and the organization as a whole. This area will be discussed in more depth in Chapter 10.

Forecasting Methods

Forecasting methods can be grouped in several ways. One classification scheme, illustrated in Figure 4.1, distinguishes between formally recognized forecasting techniques ("formal") and "informal" approaches such as intuition,

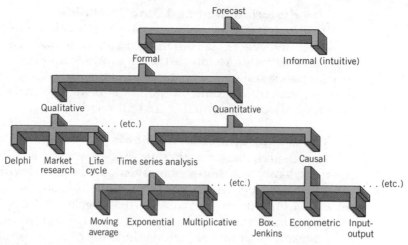

Figure 4.1 A classification of forecasting methods.

spur-of-the-moment guesses, and seat-of-the-pants predictions. Our attention in this chapter will obviously be directed to the formal methods.

Qualitative for long range.

In general, **qualitative** forecasting methods are often used for long-range forecasts, especially where external factors (e.g., the 1974 OPEC oil crisis) may play a significant role. They also see much use where historical data are very limited or nonexistent, such as in new product/service introductions. In Section 4.3 we will describe the variety of approaches available here.

The quantitative methods are commonly divided between those methods that simply project the past into the future **(time series analysis)** and those that also include external data **(causal).** Time series analysis is the simpler of the two and ranges from using a simple average of the past data to using regression analysis corrected for data cycles. Simple projection techniques such as this are obviously limited to, and primarily used for, very short-term forecasting. Such approaches often work fine in a stable environment but cannot react to changing industry factors or trends in the national economy. These approaches are described in Sections 4.4 through 4.6.

Time series for short range.

Causal for midrange.

Causal methods, which are usually quite complex, include histories of external factors, and employ sophisticated statistical techniques. These approaches, most appropriate for midterm (between short- and long-term) forecasting, are overviewed in Section 4.7, but for more specific information the reader should consult the Bibliography. There are many "canned" computerized forecasting packages available for the quantitative techniques, both time series analysis and causal, from computer manufacturers, software houses, consultants, and others. Again, consult the Bibliography for specific references.

Factors Influencing the Choice of Forecasting Method

The method chosen to prepare a demand forecast depends on a number of factors.

The Historical Demand Data Available

If such data are available one of the statistical forecasting methods described later can be used. Otherwise nonquantitative techniques are required. Attempting to forecast without a demand history is almost as hard as using a crystal ball. The demand history need not be long, complete, or even for exactly the same output as is being forecast. But some historical data base should be available if at all possible.

A crystal ball.

The Money and Time Available

The greater the limitation on time or money available for forecasting, the more likely it is that an unsophisticated method will have to be used. In general, management desires to use that forecasting method which minimizes not only the cost of making the forecast but also the cost of an *inaccurate* forecast; that is, management's goal is to minimize *total* costs. Costs of forecasting inaccuracy include the costs of over- or understocking or producing an item, the costs of under- or overstaffing, and the intangible and opportunity costs associated with loss of customer/client goodwill because a demanded item was not available. This tradeoff situation is depicted in Figure 4.2. The best forecasting method is the one for which the combined costs are minimized but, since some of these costs are difficult if not impossible to measure, a "best" method is seldom absolutely determined.

The costs of an inaccurate forecast.

With the advent of computers and preprogrammed, off-the-shelf forecasting routines, the cost and time of statistical forecasts based on historical data have been reduced significantly. It has therefore become more cost-effective for organizations to conduct more sophisticated forecasts causing the optimum forecasting method to shift to the right in Figure 4.2.

Requirements for methods of forecasting.

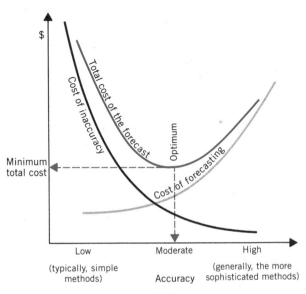

Figure 4.2   The costs of forecasting accuracy.

The Accuracy Required

If, for whatever reasons, the forecast must be very accurate, highly sophisticated methods are usually called for. Typically, long-range (3 to 10 years) forecasts require the least accuracy and are only for general (or "aggregate") planning purposes, while short-range (1 week to several months) forecasts require great accuracy since detailed workforce and machine scheduling as well as materials planning are based on these short-range projections.

4.3 QUALITATIVE FORECASTING METHODS

Uses of qualitative forecasts.

Some of the most significant decisions made by organizations, frequently strategic decisions, are made on the basis of qualitative forecasts. These often concern either new product or service introductions or long-range changes in the nature of the organization's outputs. In both cases, relevant historical demand data are typically not available. Qualitative demand forecasts for new output introductions will help operations managers decide the most efficient method of producing the output and whether the organization will gain or lose value ("profit") in the transaction.

Forecasts of long-range output changes will allow the operations manager to plan strategically for orderly replacement of facilities and modifications of the output production process. For example, a forecast of rapidly increasing demand for coal was used by many coal companies to justify changes in the technology used in coal mining. The process used to mine coal when 30 coal cars are being filled per day is neither economical nor feasible at 300 cars per day. Such forecasts also allow the operations manager to determine the cost of new production processes to meet these changes so top management can steer a wise course in maximizing the return to the organization.

Forecasting by historical analogy.

Qualitative forecasts are made using information such as expert opinion, surveys of consumer attitudes and intentions about the output, or analyses of demand information for similar products or services which were previously introduced and for which historical data are available. An example of the latter method, known as *historical analogy*, was the use of demand data for black-and-white television sets to predict the slope of the demand curve for color TV sets. Two qualitative forecasting methods are particularly common: the market survey and expert opinion.

The Market Survey

New products and services are often subjected to extensive *market research* before a final decision is made regarding their introduction. Such devices as the telephone survey, the mail questionnaire, consumer panels, and test markets are used to ascertain estimates of demand. For example, both the Nielson TV ratings and the Gallup public opinion poll are based on surveys of public attitude and behavior.

Telephone and personal interview surveys as well as mail questionnaires can provide information about current attitudes and behavior, about past actions, and about intentions for the future. *Consumer panels* which are made up of paid or volunteer participants, are provided with new and sometimes competing products and, after their use, requested to provide specific information to the market researchers. Also, consumer panels are often used to provide information about shopping and buying habits. Management can make use of a consumer panel over a long period of time to track changes in shopping and buying trends (called "longitudinal data").

Test marketing can also provide longitudinal data about a new product or service. A test market is usually some specific geographical region that is selected because it represents some segment of the organization's overall market for the new output. The test market requires that the product or service actually be introduced into the limited test area; thus, the output must be in its final stage of development and production capacity must exist to supply the test market demand.

Test marketing provides management with information about actual consumer behavior rather than simply consumer attitudes, opinions, or intentions; and, there are often great differences between a customer's attitudes and actions. This last point is particularly important and raises some of the drawbacks of this type of forecasting. Attitude and opinion surveys can be
very misleading. Subjects often try not to "disappoint" pollsters and thus tell them what they think the pollsters want to hear, rather than what the subject really thinks. Also, a subject may honestly believe that a new soap, or deodorant, really is needed on the market and would be a very good product. However, as it turns out, they do not personally happen to *need* that product. And even when subjects say that they *would* purchase a product, when the actual event presents itself they have often changed their minds.

In addition to these risks, market surveys are expensive because of packaging, mailing, analysis, and so forth. Current surveys sometimes even enclose $0.25 for the subject to fill out the questionnaire. Test marketing is also expensive in the sense that almost all development of the output must be completed. Since the in-depth study of market research is beyond the scope of this text, the student is referred to Reference 10 at the end of this chapter.

Expert Opinion

Consider, as an example, a company that over the years has introduced several dozen different consumer goods. It is conceivable that the experience of key managers, particularly those associated with the marketing of the
products, could provide better forecasts of demand for another new product than any survey of the potential market. In fact, this is often the case and methods have been developed to probe this expert knowledge. As "two heads are better than one," most expert judgment methods rely on the formation of a panel of experts who reach a consensus or compromise forecast based on their individual experiences and judgment.

The problems with committees.

But panel or committee solutions to the forecast problem are sometimes biased in favor of the opinion of one dominant member. Either that member is a better salesperson of ideas, is more "expert" than fellow committee members (perhaps others on the panel simply believe this whether it is a fact or not), or is simply more verbal than others on the panel. This bias may result in forecasts that are not good or as well thought out as predictions based on *all* of the information available from the committee members.

Delphi

Using Delphi to improve expert forecasts.

Rounds of questions are employed.

One method for combining individual experts' forecast opinions is called **Delphi.** The Delphi method was developed by the RAND Corporation as a technique for group forecasting that would eliminate the undesirable effects of interaction between members of the group. The method generally begins by having each expert provide individual forecasts along with any supporting arguments and assumptions. These forecasts are submitted to the Delphi researcher who edits, clarifies, and summarizes the data. These data are provided as feedback to the experts along with a *second round* of questions. Questions and feedback continue for several rounds, becoming increasingly more specific, until consensus among the panel members is reached. This method allows the benefits of multiple opinions and communication between group members of diverse opinions and assumptions, but avoids the negative effects of dominant behavior and stubbornness to change one's mind, which are often associated with committee solutions. For more details see Reference 8.

Life Cycle Analysis

Forecasting by life cycle analysis.

One device often used to aid in expert opinion forecasting is called **life cycle analysis.** Studies of successful new product introductions indicate that the *stretched S* growth curve provides a good pattern for the growth of demand for a new output. A typical growth curve is presented in Figure 4.3. The curve can be divided into three segments: introduction and early adoption, acceptance and growth of the market, and market saturation. After market saturation, demand may remain high or decline. Or the product or service may be improved and possibly start off on a new growth curve.

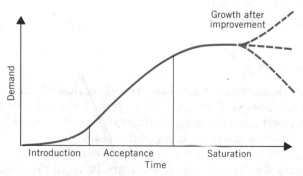

Figure 4.3   The life cycle curve.

Experienced managers who have introduced several new products, are often able to estimate the length of time that a product will remain in each of the stages of its life cycle. This forecast of the life cycle, coupled with other market information, can produce reasonably accurate estimates of demand in the intermediate to long range. This is useful to the organization in laying out long-range output plans. For operations management it indicates where periods of excess capacity might exist (and, thus, leasing out existing facilities or subcontracting might be required) or extra capacity might be required.

Operations management's use of life cycle forecasting.

4.4 TIME SERIES ANALYSIS

A time series is [3, p. 439] "an ordered group of values of a variable measured at successive points in time or for successive intervals of time." We measure the number of items in inventory at specific points in time and we measure the number of units sold over specific intervals of time. If, for example, we recorded the number of automobiles sold each month of 1983 by the Schroeder Oldsmobile Co. and kept those data points in the order in which they were recorded, the 12 numbers would constitute a *12 period time series*. We undertake *time series analysis* in operations planning because we believe that knowledge of *past behavior* of the time series might help our understanding of (and therefore our ability to predict) the behavior of the series in the future. In some instances, such as the stock market, this assumption may be unjustified, but in operations planning we assume that (to some extent, at least) history will repeat itself and past tendencies will continue. Time series analysis efforts conclude with the development of a *time series forecasting model* that can be used to predict future demand. To begin our discussion of time series analysis, let us consider the component parts of any time series.

Forecasting by time series analysis.

Time series analysis assumes that the historical demand data are composed of four component parts.

1. The *trend, T*.

2. A *seasonal* variation, *S*.

3. A *cyclical* variation, *C*.

4. *Random* variation, *R*.

Components of time series.

The Trend

The **trend** component is the long-run direction of the series, including any constant amount of demand in the data. Figure 4.4 illustrates three fairly common trend lines showing changes in the demand; a horizontal trend line would indicate a constant level of demand.

A straight-line or "**linear**" trend (showing a constant amount of *change* as in Figure 4.4a) could be an accurate fit to the historical data over some limited range of time even though it might provide a rather poor fit over an

Straight-line trend.

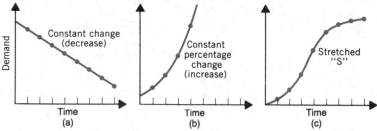

Figure 4.4   Three common trends.

entire time series. For example, the curve in Figure 4.4c could be approximated by three separate straight trend lines, as shown in Figure 4.5. Over each of these shorter ranges, a straight line provides a good approximation to the actual curve.

"Nonlinear" trends.

Figure 4.4b illustrates the situation of a constant *percentage* change. Here, change in demand depends on the current size of demand rather than being constant each period as in Figure 4.4a. Figure 4.4c indicates the trend line referred to earlier as the "stretched S" growth curve. Many new products follow this kind of growth pattern, which is characterized by a relatively slow start-up, a period of rapid product acceptance, and then a slowdown in the rate of adoption as the market becomes saturated.

The Seasonal

The bases for seasonal variation.

Seasonal fluctuations result primarily from nature but are also brought about by human behavior. Snow tires and antifreeze enjoy brisk demand during the winter months whereas sales of golf balls and bikinis peak in the spring and summer months. Of course, seasonal demand often *leads* or *lags* the actual season. For example, the production season to meet retailers' demand for Christmas goods is August through September. Sales of heart-shaped boxes of candy and Christmas trees are brought about by events that are controlled by humans. The **seasonal** variation in events need not be related to the seasons of the year, however. For example, fire alarms in New York

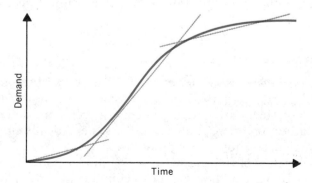

Figure 4.5   Straight trend approximation of stretched S growth curve.

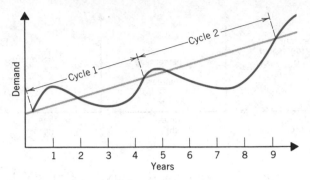

Figure 4.6 Typical cycles.

City reach a "seasonal" peak at 7 P.M. and a seasonal low at 7 A.M. every day. And restaurants reach three seasonal peaks every day at 7:30 A.M., 12:30 P.M., and 8 P.M.

The Cycle

Long-term cycles.

The **cycle** or **cyclic** component is only obvious in time series that span several periods. A cycle can be defined as a *long-term oscillation* or swing of the data points about the trend line over a period of at least three complete seasonals. National economic cycles of boom times and depressions and periods of war and peace are examples of such cycles. Figure 4.6 presents two complete cycles and the underlying straight-line trend of a time series where no yearly seasonal is assumed to exist. Note that the oscillations around the trend line are *not* symmetrical, as they seldom are in actual time series.

Cycles, particularly business cycles, are often difficult to explain and economists have spent considerable effort in research and speculation about their causes. Identification of a cyclic pattern in a time series requires the analysis of a long period of data. For example, only two cycles were completed in 9 years for the time series shown in Figure 4.6. For most operations, forecasting the cyclic component is not considered since data are typically unavailable to determine the cycle. Also, cycles are not likely to repeat in similar amplitude and duration; hence the assumption of repeating history does not hold.

Random Variation

Random variation is unpredictable.

Random variations are, as the name implies, without specific assignable cause and without pattern. Random fluctuations can sometimes be explained after the fact, such as the increase in energy consumption due to abnormally harsh weather conditions, but cannot be systematically predicted and, hence, are not included in forecasting models.

The objective of time series analysis models is to determine the magnitude of one or more of the time series components and to use that knowledge for the purpose of forecasting. Time series forecasts are more often found directly useful to the operations manager than are qualitative forecasts. For example, time series analysis is useful in planning annual production and inventory schedules based on previous demand patterns.

In the next two sections we will consider three time series analysis models.

Three models.

- Moving averages (trend component of the time series).
- Exponential smoothing (trend component of the time series).
- Linear trend multiplicative model (all three components).

Each of these models will be presented within the context of a sample situation.

4.5 DEMAND FORECASTING FOR THE INNER CITY HEALTH CENTER

The Inner City situation.

Inner City Health Center is a federally funded health clinic that serves the needs of the inner city poor. The center is currently in its fourth year of operation and is presently preparing its staffing plan for the upcoming quarter. The federal government requires that the center prepare a budget request each quarter for the coming quarter. The request is based largely on the forecast of demand for specific services during the next quarter.

Attempts at forecasting.

Demand data are available for each of the four quarters of the preceding three years and for the first two quarters of the current year. The data presented in Table 4.1 and plotted in Figure 4.7 are for emergency services at the center. The health center administrator has in the past tried using the last period's demand and has also tried using the average of all past demand to predict the next period's demand for the center. Neither of these two techniques has proven satisfactory. The use of the last period's demand as a predictor of the next period's demand produced erratic forecasts. For ex-

Table 4.1 Emergency Service Demand for the Inner City Health Center

Year	Quarter	Period Number	Number of Patient Visits
1971	1	1	3,500
	2	2	8,000
	3	3	5,500
	4	4	10,000
1972	1	5	4,500
	2	6	6,000
	3	7	3,000
	4	8	5,500
1973	1	9	5,000
	2	10	9,500
	3	11	7,500
	4	12	15,000
1974	1	13	13,500
	2	14	17,500

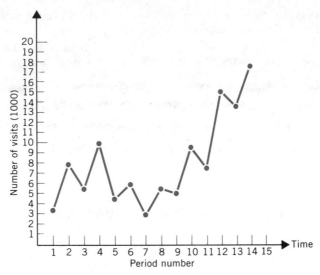

Figure 4.7 Plot of quarterly demand for emergency services—Inner City Health Center.

ample, using this method the administrator predicted (and staffed, scheduled, and purchased for) a demand of 3500 visits for the second quarter of 1971 when 8000 visits actually resulted (overtime and rush orders reached a peak during this quarter) and then predicted 8000 visits for the third quarter when only 5500 visits materialized. Clearly, this method could not sort out the fluctuations in the demand data and was therefore deemed unsatisfactory.

The administrator then turned to using the average of all demand data to predict the next period's demand. For the fourth quarter of 1971 the administrator predicted a demand of 5667 [i.e., (3500 + 8000 + 5500)/3] when 10,000 actually occurred and for the tenth period he forcast a demand of 5666 (i.e., the sum of the first nine periods' demand divided by 9) and 9500 occurred. The administrator recognized that this averaging method

Smoothing the produced forecasts that *smoothed* out the fluctuations, but did not ade-
fluctuations. quately respond to any growth or reduction in the demand trend. As a matter of fact, the averaging method performed progressively worse as the amount of data increased. This was because each new piece of demand data had to be averaged with *all* of the old data from period one to the present, and therefore each new element of data had less overall impact on the average. In fact, if the administrator were to use the averaging method to forecast the third-quarter demand for 1974 the forecast would be 8143, clearly a poor forecast when compared with demand in the past few periods.

After evaluating these two simple methods the administrator decided to consider the three time series forecasting methods mentioned earlier, each of which is capable of producing the needed forecasts. The remainder of this section will be devoted to an analysis of these three methods.

Moving Averages

To overcome the problem of using a simple average, the **moving average** technique generates the next period's forecast by averaging the actual demand for only the last n (n is often in the range of 4 to 7) time periods. Any data older than n are thus ignored. The choice of the value for n is usually based on the expected seasonality in the data, such as four quarters, or 12 months, in a year. If n must be chosen arbitrarily, then it should be based on experimentation; that is, the value selected for n should be the one that works best for the available historical data.

Using only the last few periods to average.

Mathematically, the moving average is computed as

$$F_{t+1} = \frac{1}{n} \sum_{i=(t-n+1)}^{t} D_i \qquad (4.1)$$

where t = period number for the *current* period

F_{t+1} = forecast of demand for the next period

$\sum$ = mathematical notation meaning "sum up"*

D_i = actual demand in period i

n = number of periods of demand to be included
(known as the "order" of the moving average)

For example, to forecast demand for the next quarter of this year (i.e., quarter 3 of 1974, or period 15, in Table 4.1) using a moving average of order four (that is, $n = 4$), the Inner City Health Center administrator would compute

$$F_{14+1} = \frac{1}{4} \sum_{i=14-4+1}^{14} D_i$$

or

$$F_{15} = \frac{1}{4} \sum_{i=11}^{14} D_i$$

$$F_{15} = (D_{11} + D_{12} + D_{13} + D_{14})/4$$

$$F_{15} = (7,500 + 15,000 + 13,500 + 17,500)/4$$

$$F_{15} = 13,375$$

The forecast for the next quarter using a moving average forecast of order four would therefore be 13,375 emergency services.

The moving average as a compromise.

The moving average is a *compromise* between the last period's demand forecast and the simple average, both of which the administrator has rejected as being unsatisfactory. The number of periods to be averaged in the moving average is dependent on the specific situation. If too few periods are included in the average, the forecast will be similar to the forecast obtained when

---

*The notation $\sum_{i=t-n+1}^{t}$ indicates a summation from $i = t - n + 1$ to $i = t$.

only the last period's demand had been used as the forecast. Using too many periods in the moving average will result in a forecast similar to the forecast obtained when the simple average was used.

Forecasting Difficulties

Time series analysis involves two inherent difficulties, and a compromise solution that addresses both must be sought. The first problem is producing as good a forecast as is possible with the available data. Usually, this can be interpreted as using the most current data because those data are more representative of the present behavior of the time series. In this sense, we are looking for an approach that is "responsive" to recent changes in the data.

Responsive or stable?

The second problem is to "smooth" the random behavior of the data. That is, we do not want a forecasting system that forecasts increases in demand simply because the last period's demand suddenly increased, nor do we want a system that indicates a "downturn" just because demand in the last period decreased. All time series data contain a certain amount of this erratic or random movement. It is impossible for a manager to predict this random movement of a time series, and it is folly to attempt it. The only reasonable conclusion is to avoid overreaction to a fluctuation that is simply random. The general interpretation of this objective is that several periods of data should be included in the forecast so as to "smooth" the random fluctuations that typically exist. Thus, we are also looking for an approach that is "stable," even with erratic data.

Measuring the accuracy of a forecast with the MAD.

Clearly, methods to attain both responsiveness and stability will be somewhat contradictory. Using the most recent data so as to be responsive results in only a few periods being included in the forecast, but a desire for stability results in large numbers of periods being included. The only approach to the problem of deciding on the number of periods to include is to experiment with several different numbers of periods and evaluate each on the basis of its ability to produce good forecasts and to smooth out random fluctuations. The *mean absolute deviation* (**MAD**) is one measure often used to evaluate a forecasting model. The MAD, which will be discussed in the upcoming section, is always the *lowest* for the best model.

Exponential Smoothing

Achieving the two objectives by exponential smoothing.

As noted above, we generally want to use the most current data and, at the same time, use enough observations of the time series to smooth out random fluctuations. One technique perfectly adapted to meeting these two objectives is **exponential smoothing.**

Exponential smoothing has an advantage over moving averages in that the computations required are much simpler and the data storage requirements are less, particularly in situations that require the use of data from a large number of past time periods.

The computation of a demand forecast using exponential smoothing is carried out with the following equation.

new demand forecast = (α)current demand
$$+ (1 - \alpha)\text{previous demand forecast}$$

or

$$F_{t+1} = \alpha D_t + (1 - \alpha)F_t \tag{4.2}$$

where α is a **smoothing constant** that must be greater than or equal to zero but less than or equal to 1 and the other symbols are illustrated in the following diagram.

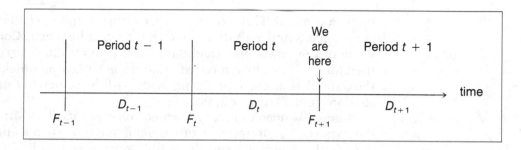

The smoothing constant as a weighting factor.

The smoothing constant α can be interpreted as the *weight* assigned to the last (i.e., the current) data point. The higher the weight assigned to this current demand, the greater the influence this point has on the forecast. For example, if α is equal to 1, the demand forecast for the next period will be equal to the value of the current demand, the approach used earlier by Inner City Health Center's administrator. The closer the value of α is to 0, the closer the forecast will be to the previous period's *forecast* for the current period. (Check these results by using Equation 4.2.)

Equal weights in a moving average.

In contrast, in a moving average all data are assigned equal weight in the determination of the next period's forecast. For example, in a four-period moving average, each of the four observations has a 25 percent weight in determining the forecast. In exponential smoothing, α determines the importance assigned to the most current data point and automatically weights the historical data simply by using Equation 4.2 above.

Selecting the Appropriate Value of α

Our objective in exponential forecasting is to choose the value of α that results in the best forecasts. Forecasts that tend to always predict too high or too low are said to be **biased**, positively if too high and negatively if too low. If forecasts are in error, then operations costs will be unnecessarily high due to idle capacity for the high forecasts (positive bias) and insufficient capacity (overtime, etc.) for low forecasts (negative bias). The value of α is critical in producing good forecasts, and if a large value of α is selected, the forecast will be very sensitive to the current demand value. With a large α, exponential smoothing will produce forecasts that react quickly to fluctua-

Bias.

Large values of α weight current demand the most.

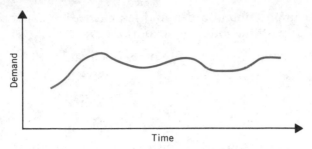

Figure 4.8   Data exhibiting low variability (use high α).

tions in demand. This, however, is irritating to those who have to constantly change plans and activities based on the latest forecasts. Conversely, a small value of α weights historical data more heavily than current demand and therefore will produce forecasts that do not react as quickly to changes in the data; that is, the forecasting model will be somewhat *insensitive* to fluctuations in the current data.

Use large values of α if the data is smooth.   Generally speaking, larger values of α are used in situations in which the data can be plotted as a rather smooth curve, such as in Figure 4.8. The data in this figure are said to exhibit *low variability*. If, on the other hand, the data look more like Figure 4.9, a lower value of α should be used. These data are subject to a high degree of variability. Using a high value of α in a situation like the one depicted in Figure 4.9 would result in a forecast that constantly overreacted to changes in the most current demand.

Values of α usually between 0.01 and 0.30.   The appropriate value of α is, like *n*, usually determined through a trial-and-error process; values typically lie in the range of 0.01 to 0.30. One method of selecting the best α value is to try several values of α with the existing historical data (or a portion of it) and choose the value of α that minimizes the average forecast errors. A simple computer program can greatly speed the evaluation of potential smoothing constants and the determination of the best value of α.

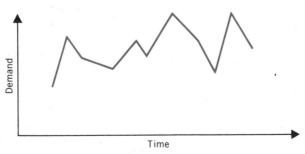

Figure 4.9   Data exhibiting high variability (use low α).

Forecasting Errors

Up to this point we have indirectly mentioned two methods of measuring forecast error: the mean absolute deviation (MAD) and the bias. Although there are others (such as the standard deviation and the running sum of errors), these two are commonly, and easily, calculated. Algebraically

$$\text{MAD} = \frac{1}{n} \sum_{i=1}^{n} |F_i - D_i| \tag{4.3}$$

$$\text{BIAS} = \frac{1}{n} \sum_{i=1}^{n} (F_i - D_i) \tag{4.4}$$

where F_i = forecast of demand in period i

D_i = actual demand in period i

n = number of periods of data

Very different effects.

MAD tells error.

Though very similar in appearance, these two variables measure extremely different forecasting effects. Since the MAD only sums **absolute values** of errors, both positive and negative errors add to the sum and the average size of the *error* is determined. This gives the manager a sense of the *accuracy* of the forecasting model. A manager might use this knowledge by saying, "Our forecasts are typically only accurate within 10 percent; we had better maintain a buffer stock of 10 percent or so to hedge against this potential error."

Bias tells if high or low.

The bias, on the other hand, tells whether the forecast is typically too low or too high and by how much. A manager knowing this might say, "We are almost always forecasting 10 percent too low; we had better make an extra 10 percent to hedge against this potential error." That is, MAD tells only the average size of the error while bias tells the average total error and the direction.

As mentioned earlier, the best forecast methods will exhibit the least error measurements. Suppose two methods of forecasting are tested against demand data for a 4-month period. Method A gave forecasts for January through April of 102, 107, 106, and 113 respectively; Method B gave 104, 105, 107, 110; and the actual demands were 103, 106, 106, and 111. The MAD for Method A would be $(|102 - 103| + |107 - 106| + |106 - 106| + |113 - 111|)/4 = 1$ and the bias would be $[(102 - 103) + \ldots]/4 = 0.5$. For Method B the MAD is also 1 but the bias is 0 (check the data). Thus, Method B is the better of the two. It may well happen that one method has a smaller MAD but a larger bias, or vice-versa. In such cases, the circumstances of the situation must be considered to determine whether MAD or bias is the more important measure.

A tracking signal.

The MAD is also sometimes used as a **"tracking signal"** in certain **adaptive forecasting** models (see References 12 and 14). Briefly, adaptive forecasting models *self-adjust* by increasing or decreasing the smoothing constant α when the tracking signal becomes too large. As long as the signal

Table 4.2 Actual and Exponentially Forecast Values of Quarterly Demand for the Inner City Health Center (Data in Thousands)

Year	Quarter	D Actual	F Forecast ($\alpha = 0.1$)	F Forecast ($\alpha = 0.3$)
1971	1	3.5		
	2	8.0	3.50	3.50
	3	5.5	3.95	4.85
	4	10.0	4.11	5.05
1972	1	4.5	4.69	6.53
	2	6.0	4.68	5.92
	3	3.0	4.81	5.95
	4	5.5	4.63	5.06
1973	1	5.0	4.71	5.19
	2	9.5	4.74	5.14
	3	7.5	5.22	6.44
	4	15.0	5.45	6.76
1974	1	13.5	6.40	9.23
	2	17.5	7.11	10.51
	3	?	8.15	12.61

remains within reasonable bounds, the model is presumed to be doing well. But if it increases beyond a set limit, the forecasting model increases α to catch up to whatever type of change has taken place.

Let us now use exponential smoothing to forecast demand for the Inner City Health Center example. We will use two different smoothing factors and calculate the MAD and bias in the forecasts to determine which is best. Table 4.2 presents the actual historical data for emergency services provided by the Inner City Health Center and the exponentially smoothed forecasts for the corresponding periods using α values of 0.1 and 0.3. Since there were no data on which to base a forecast for period one, F_1 (the forecast that would have been made in period zero), some value must be selected. We let F_1 be equal to D_1, the actual value of the series in period 1. Then F_2 is computed (using $\alpha = 0.1$).

$$F_2 = \alpha D_1 + (1 - \alpha)F_1 \tag{4.5}$$
$$= 0.1 \times 3.5 + (1 - 0.1) \times 3.5$$
$$= 0.35 + 0.9 \, (3.5)$$
$$= 3.5$$

In the same manner, we compute F_3 as

$$F_3 = 0.1(8) + 0.9(3.5)$$
$$= 3.95$$

The computations for the exponentially smoothed forecasts continue for each period using the previous forecast and the value of the current observation.

Table 4.3 Calculation of the Forecast Errors

Year	Quarter	Algebraic Difference (Forecast − Actual)		Absolute Difference |Forecast − Actual|	
		$\alpha = 0.1$	$\alpha = 0.3$	$\alpha = 0.1$	$\alpha = 0.3$
1971	1				
	2	−4.50	−4.50	4.50	4.50
	3	−1.55	−0.65	1.55	0.65
	4	−5.89	−4.95	5.89	4.95
1972	1	+0.19	+2.03	0.19	2.03
	2	−1.32	−0.08	1.32	0.08
	3	+1.81	+2.95	1.81	2.95
	4	−0.87	−0.44	0.87	0.44
1973	1	−0.29	+0.19	0.29	0.19
	2	−4.76	−4.36	4.76	4.36
	3	−2.28	−1.06	2.28	1.06
	4	−9.55	−8.24	9.55	8.24
1974	1	−7.10	−4.27	7.10	4.27
	2	−10.39	−6.99	10.39	6.99
	Sum	−46.50	−30.37	50.50	40.71
	Mean	Bias = −3.57	Bias = −2.33	MAD = 3.88	MAD = 3.13

The current data are weighted by α and the historical data (all of which are embodied in the previous period's forecast) by $(1 - \alpha)$. As can be seen from Table 4.2, F_{15}, the forecasts for the next quarter using each of the two α values, are 8150 and 12,610 emergency services, a considerable difference.

Table 4.3 presents quarterly errors needed for the computation of the final MAD and bias for the two forecasts.

Lagging.

Comparing values of α.

As indicated by the MAD calculations, the error is quite high with either value of α, though 0.3 seems the better of the two. The large negative value of the bias indicates that most of the error is due to negative bias in the model, in this case consistently forecasting too low or "lagging" the demand (a characteristic of the more simple exponential forecasting models such as this one). This result is also seen in Figure 4.10, which shows the actual demand data and the forecast values using $\alpha = 0.1$ and $\alpha = 0.3$. Notice, for example, that the downturn after quarter 4 and the upturn after quarter 9 are detected more quickly by the $\alpha = 0.3$ model, as we have indicated should be the case. You may notice that both models lag behind the upward trend after quarter 9. In general, if values of alpha greater than 0.3 seem to give the best results, exponential forecasting should probably not be used. A smoothing model like the one presented in Equation 4.2 is best used in situations where demand fluctuates around an overall level trend. If the trend is increasing or decreasing, other models are usually more appropriate. In the next section we consider a time series model more appropriate for data with an upward or downward trend than the models presented so far.

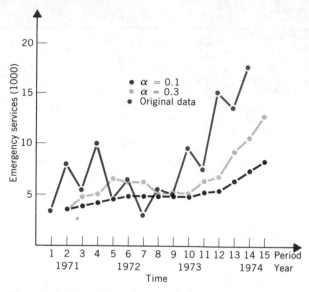

Figure 4.10 Plot of actual data and exponential forecasts.

4.6 LINEAR TREND, MULTIPLICATIVE MODEL

The linear trend model for trend and seasonals.

In Figure 4.11 and Table 4.4 the quarterly ridership volume (in thousands) for the new Inner City Mass Transit is presented. Demand is seen to be generally increasing. To forecast future ridership, the city manager has decided to try the linear trend time series model, which is based on a belief that demand follows both a fairly constant trend from quarter to quarter and a quarterly seasonal pattern. Just from observing the time series plot of the ridership demand data it is clear that demand is above average during the second and fourth quarters and below average during the first and third quarters, probably due to weather.

Versions of the linear trend model.

There are several versions of the linear trend time series model (for example, there are additive and multiplicative versions) and also many different approaches to the determination of the components of these forecasting models. We will present one method for determining the two demand components of a simple multiplicative model. Conceptually, the model is presented as

$$\text{forecast} = \text{trend component (or } T) \times \text{seasonal component (or } S) \quad (4.6)$$

In order to develop this model we must first analyze the available historical data and attempt to break down the original data into their trend and seasonal components.

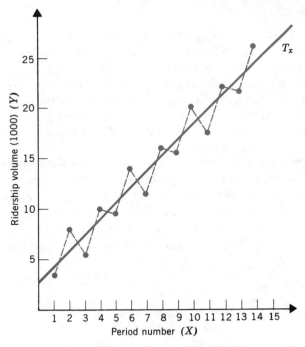

Figure 4.11 Quarterly ridership volume and trend line for the mass transit.

Table 4.4 Quarterly Ridership Volume and Least Squares Data for the Mass Transit

Quarter Number X	Ridership Volume (1000) Y	X^2	XY
1	3.5	1	3.5
2	8	4	16
3	5.5	9	16.5
4	10	16	40
5	9.5	25	47.5
6	14	36	84
7	11.5	49	80.5
8	16	64	128
9	15.5	81	139.5
10	20	100	200
11	17.5	121	192.5
12	22	144	264
13	21.5	169	279.5
14	26	196	364
$\Sigma X = 105$	$\Sigma Y = 200.5$	$\Sigma X^2 = 1015$	$\Sigma XY = 1855.5$

The Trend

As indicated earlier, the trend is the long-run direction of the series of data. In our example the trend in demand appears to follow a straight line; that is, to be a trend with respect to time. In order to project this linear trend into the future, we must first estimate the parameters of the trend line. The parameters of the straight line that must be estimated are the Y axis intercept and the slope of the line. The *Y axis intercept* is the value of Y where the trend line crosses the Y axis (at $X = 0$). The *slope* is the amount of change in Y for a one-period change in X.

The intercept and slope of the trend line equation.

There are several procedures for estimating the slope and intercept of a straight line from the observed value of X and Y, but a method known as **least squares regression** is the most widely used.* We will not attempt to derive the equations used in estimating the slope and the intercept, but will simply state and explain their use. The equation that we will use to forecast the trend into the future is known as the *regression equation* and is shown as

Least squares regression most commonly used for trend determination.

$$T_x = a + bX \tag{4.7}$$

where T_x = the trend forecast value of ridership volume Y
            for period number X
      a = the estimate of the Y axis intercept
      b = the estimate of the slope of the demand line
      X = the period number

The two equations used to determine a and b are

$$b = \frac{\Sigma XY - n\overline{X}\,\overline{Y}}{\Sigma X^2 - n\overline{X}^2} \tag{4.8}$$

$$a = \overline{Y} - b\overline{X} \tag{4.9}$$

where ΣXY = X times Y for each period, summed over all of the periods
      ΣX^2 = X squared for each period, summed over all of the periods
      $\overline{X}$ = the average of the X values
      $\overline{Y}$ = the average of the Y values
      n = the number of periods of data used in the regression

Using Least Squares Regression for the Inner City Mass Transit

Using the data for the Inner City Mass Transit, we can estimate the slope and the intercept of the trend forecasting equation for the transit's quarterly ridership volume. To simplify the computations we will arrange the data into four columns, as shown in Table 4.4. The numbers in column 3 are simply column 1 numbers squared, and the numbers in column 4 are com-

---

*The method derives its name from the way in which the parameters of the line are estimated. That is, the method minimizes the sum of the squares of the vertical deviations between the trend line and the original data points.

puted by multiplying the numbers in column 1 by the corresponding number from column 2. To compute the slope of the regression line (b) we need the average of column 1, which is

$$\bar{X} = \frac{\Sigma X}{n} = \frac{105}{14} = 7.5$$

and the average of column 2, which is

$$\bar{Y} = \frac{200.5}{14} = 14.32$$

In addition, we need the total of columns 3 and 4. In our algebraic notation, ΣX^2 is the sum of column 3 and ΣXY is the sum of column 4.

The slope can then be computed by using Equation 4.8.

$$b = \frac{1855.5 - 14(7.5)(14.32)}{1015 - 14(7.5)^2}$$

$$= \frac{351.9}{227.5}$$

$$= 1.55$$

which means that the ridership volume is, on the average, increasing by 1550 riders every quarter.

The Y axis intercept is computed from Equation 4.9.

$$a = 14.32 - 1.55(7.5)$$

$$= 2.69$$

which means that the initial ridership volume at $X = 0$ would have been 2690 riders.

The forecasting equation for the trend in ridership volume is therefore

$$T_x = 2.69 + 1.55X$$

Figure 4.11 shows the regression trend line and the original data.

It would be interesting to now apply the regression approach to the Inner City Health Center data of Table 4.1. By calculating its MAD and bias we could compare regression with the exponential forecasting approach to see which was best for this situation. This exercise is reserved for the problems section (Problem 14).

The Seasonal Component: Ratio-to-Trend Method

As noted earlier, and made even clearer in Figure 4.11, the data are above the trend line for all of the second and fourth quarters and below the trend line for all of the first and third quarters. Recognizing this distinct seasonal pattern in the data should allow us to estimate the amount of seasonal variation around the trend line (i.e., the seasonal component, S).

Calculating four seasonals.

The trend line is the long-run direction of the data and does not include any seasonal variation. We can compute, for each available quarter of data, a measure of the "seasonality" in that quarter by *dividing the actual ridership volume by the computed value of the trend* for that quarter. This method is known as the *ratio-to-trend* method. Using the notation developed thus far, we can write the seasonal component for any quarter X as

$$\frac{Y_x}{T_x}$$

Consider the second and third quarters of the first year. The computed trend value for each of these two quarters is

$$T_2 = 2.69 + 1.55(2)$$
$$= 5.79$$

and

$$T_3 = 2.69 + 1.55(3)$$
$$= 7.34$$

The actual ridership volumes (in thousands) in quarters 2 and 3 were

$$Y_2 = 8.0$$
$$Y_3 = 5.5$$

Dividing Y_2 by T_2 and Y_3 by T_3 gives us an indication of the seasonal pattern in each of these quarters.

$$\frac{Y_2}{T_2} = \frac{8}{5.79} = 1.38$$

$$\frac{Y_3}{T_3} = \frac{5.5}{7.34} = 0.75$$

In quarter 2 the actual volume was 138 percent of the expected volume (i.e., the ridership volume predicted on the basis of a linear trend) and in quarter 3 the volume was only 75 percent of that expected. Note that over the 14 periods of available data we have four observations of ridership volume for first and second quarters and three observations of volume for third and fourth quarters. We can compute the average of each of these sets of quarterly data and use the averages as the seasonal components for our time series forecasting model.

Averaging the Y/T ratios to get the seasonals.

Table 4.5 will simplify our computation of the seasonal values for each of the 14 quarters. Once Table 4.5 is complete, the seasonal factors for each of the four seasons or quarters are averaged as in Table 4.6. The seasonal components for each of the four quarters are found in the bottom row of Table 4.6.

Using both the trend and seasonal components, the city manager now can forecast the ridership volumes for any quarter in the future. First, the trend value for the forecast quarter is computed and is, in turn, multiplied

Table 4.5 Computations of Quarterly Seasonal Factors

X	Quarter	Y	T	Y/T
1	1	3.5	4.24	0.83
2	2	8.0	5.79	1.38
3	3	5.5	7.34	0.75
4	4	10.0	8.89	1.12
5	1	9.5	10.44	0.91
6	2	14.0	11.99	1.17
7	3	11.5	13.54	0.85
8	4	16.0	15.09	1.06
9	1	15.5	16.64	0.93
10	2	20.0	18.19	1.10
11	3	17.5	19.74	0.89
12	4	22.0	21.29	1.03
13	1	21.5	22.84	0.94
14	2	26.0	24.39	1.07

by the appropriate seasonal factor. For example, to forecast for the last quarter of the fourth year (quarter 16) and the first quarter of the fifth year (quarter 17) the city manager would first compute the trend values (in thousands).

$$T_{16} = 2.69 + 1.55(16) = 27.49$$

$$T_{17} = 2.69 + 1.55(17) = 29.04$$

Next, she computes the forecast by multiplying the trend value by the appropriate seasonal factor. For the fourth quarter S_4 is 1.07, so the forecast F, is

$$F_{16} = 27,490 \times 1.07 = 29,414$$

The seasonal factor for the first quarter is 0.90; therefore, the forecast for quarter 17 is

$$F_{17} = 29,040 \times 0.90 = 26,136$$

Table 4.6 Computations of Seasonal Component (S) for Quarters 1 through 4

	Quarter Number			
Year	1	2	3	4
1	0.83	1.38	0.75	1.12
2	0.91	1.17	0.85	1.06
3	0.93	1.10	0.89	1.03
4	0.94	1.07		
Total	3.61	4.72	2.49	3.21
Average (S)	$S_1 = 0.90$	$S_2 = 1.18$	$S_3 = 0.83$	$S_4 = 1.07$

These two forecasts correspond with the previous results for fourth and first quarters in that the fourth quarter forecast is above the trend and the first quarter forecast is below the trend.

This linear trend model can be useful to the operations planning and scheduling of Inner City Mass Transit. Procurement of new transit vehicles, scheduling maintenance and overhaul during slack seasons, and staff scheduling are all possible using this model. If data were available regarding ridership by route or area of the city, the operations staff could plan for new route additions or modifications and determine the number of buses to run on each route to produce acceptable wait times for riders.

Cautions

Inapplicability of linear models.

Although a simple linear trend model should be tried before more complex models, in many forecasting situations a linear trend model is simply not appropriate. The student is cautioned to recognize that a forecasting procedure produces useful results only if the input data conform to the assumptions of the model. Data that follow an obviously nonlinear pattern should not be subjected to a linear analysis. Also, models, for all their power in analyzing data, cannot think and reason intelligently about environmental changes that might affect demand, and external effects such as political events and recessions can clearly overwhelm a simple projection of past data.

External considerations may affect the forecast significantly.

For instance, in our earlier example of emergency services demand, there was a sudden upsurge after period 9, which the exponential forecasting models could only react to. But, suppose that the administrator knew that a local hospital was closing its evening clinic because it had not proved to be self-supporting. If the only medical services otherwise available in the community during the evening hours are those provided by the center's Emergency Services Division, the administrator could predict that demand would increase. This may, in fact, have been the cause for the noted increases.

To clarify the point of using a linear model to predict demand in an inherently nonlinear situation, consider again the demand data for emergency services (Figure 4.7). Demand first increases, then decreases, and then appears to be increasing at an accelerating rate. But, if the administrator were to use the least squares model on this data, the regression line would look like that shown superimposed on the plot of the original data in Figure 4.12. Note that a forecast for period 15 will be well under that which would be expected if demand continues to grow as it has over the past five quarters. Use of a nonlinear regression model would be appropriate in this case, whereas the use of a linear model is not. If a tracking signal were used in this situation, it would quickly indicate that the model needed to be altered.

4.7 CAUSAL FORECASTING METHODS

In the previous section we saw that demand for an organization's output could be related to time, that is, the demand changed as time changed. While

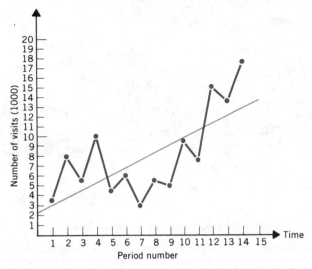

Figure 4.12 Plot of quarterly demand for emergency services—Inner City Health Center.

Considering the factors that cause demand.

Marriages as a predictor of housing demand.

High correlation.

a relationship existed, we could not say that time *caused* the demand. But there are factors other than time that are often related to demand and, in fact, these factors often cause, or at least precede, the demand.

For example, increases in single-family housing demand during a given quarter might be highly related to the number of new marriages during the previous quarter. While marriages do not directly *cause* new houses to be purchased, it is logical to argue that marriages (which cause new households to form) are a major precondition to new housing starts. Figure 4.13 illustrates the likely relationship between new marriages (the independent variable) and single-family housing starts, the dependent variable. This figure indicates a rather close relationship between the two variables. The variables are thus said to be highly **correlated.** The relationship between housing starts in one quarter and marriages in a previous quarter is an example of a *logical*

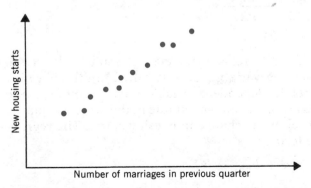

Figure 4.13 Plot of marriages versus housing starts, showing the close relationship.

"At last! A leading indicator I can understand!"

(Reprinted with permission from *Changing Times*, © 1975, the Kiplinger Washington Editors, Inc.)

relationship. Many causal models use such "leading indicators" to predict upcoming demand.

Predictor variables.

The least squares regression method used in the preceding section to determine the linear time series trend can also be used to estimate a *predicting equation* for new housing starts. The linear equation

$$Y'_x = a + bX \tag{4.10}$$

would be interpreted as

Y'_x = the predicted number of new housing starts
a = the Y axis intercept
b = the slope
X = the number of new marriages in the previous quarter

and the two parameters a and b are estimated in the same manner as before, that is

$$b = \frac{\Sigma XY - n\overline{X}\,\overline{Y}}{\Sigma X^2 - n\overline{X}^2}$$
$$a = \overline{Y} - b\overline{X}$$

Including many causative factors through multiple regression.

This linear regression methodology can be extended to situations in which more than one variable is used, called **multiple regression,** to explain the behavior of the dependent variable Y. For example, in addition to the number of marriages, the employment rate in the previous quarter might also explain a great deal of the change in housing starts. The regression equation would be of the form

$$Y'_{x_1 x_2} = a + b_1 X_1 + b_2 X_2 \tag{4.11}$$

where $Y'_{x_1 x_2}$ = the predicted number of housing starts based on new marriages *and* the employment rate

a = the Y axis intercept

b_1 and b_2 = the slopes (rates of change in Y') with respect to X_1 and X_2

X_1 and X_2 = the number of marriages and the employment rate, respectively, in the previous quarter

Generally, a computer is used to solve multiple regression models. As mentioned earlier, there are many "canned" routines available on time sharing, mainframe computers, and now even for microcomputers.

Econometric models.   A number of extensions of regression methodology are used in causal forecasting. One is the econometric model. In many cases the dependent and independent variables used in forecasting models are interdependent. That is, demand may be a function of personal income and personal income a function of demand. **Econometric models** take these interrelationships into consideration by formulating not one regression equation, but a series of simultaneous regression equations that relate the demand data to all of the interdependent factors, many of which are also predicted by the model.

Box-Jenkins.   Another extension is the *Box-Jenkins* approach (see Reference 4). This complex statistical method optimally fits time series models to the data and frequently results in quite accurate forecasts. However, it is also a costly and time-consuming process.

Input-output.   A different type of causal model is the *input-output* approach. Here interindustry demands are analyzed to determine the net effect on each industry of all the other industries combined. A forecast of total demands on each and all of the industries is then computed in one overall solution. The model is particularly useful for determining expected *changes* in demands due to changes in other industries.

The operations manager can use causal forecasting methods to help predict the impact on production costs of increases or decreases in volume and changes in the product mix. In addition, production time can be estimated on the basis of a number of independent factors. For example, the time required to design, program, and implement a new computer system has been estimated on the basis of such factors as the number of files required, the number of reports produced, the number of individual programs, and subjective factors relating to the level of complexity of various portions of the system.

Nevertheless, the complexity of causal models and the corresponding time and data required for their construction is an impediment to their use in operations. Most commonly a highly skilled statistician is required to design and validate these models, a person not commonly available in many organizations.

4.8 SUMMARY AND KEY LEARNING POINTS

This chapter continues the discussion in Chapter 3 on the organization's output in terms of determining the environmental demand for the output.

First, the returns the organization expects, and doesn't expect, from the environment were discussed. Then the need and uses of forecasts were described and the factors that influence the choice of the most appropriate forecasting approach were detailed. Last, the various forecasting approaches and techniques were described and illustrated. The key learning points have been

- Organizations usually expect money, recognition, or information as an environmental return for their output. Unexpected returns such as complaints and lawsuits also frequently occur.

- Forecasts are generally used for three purposes in organizations. One is to determine if demand is adequate for an anticipated output. Another is to determine long-run capacity needs based on long-term forecasts. And a third is to determine immediate scheduling and workforce plans based on short-term forecasts.

- One breakdown of forecasting approaches is formal versus informal (intuitive), where the formal can be further divided into qualitative and quantitative. Quantitative methods can, in turn, be categorized as either time series analysis methods or causal methods.

- The primary factors affecting the choice of a forecasting approach are the money and time available to make the forecast, the forecast accuracy required, and whether historical demand data are available.

- Two of the most common types of qualitative forecasting approaches are market surveys, which include market research, consumer panels, and test marketing; and expert opinion, which includes Delphi and life cycle analysis.

- Time series data are assumed to be composed of four parts: a trend, a seasonal, a cyclic, and random variation.

- A moving average is a simple average of the last n time periods. An exponential forecast is found by taking the weighted (by alpha) average of the most recent demand and the previous forecast of that demand.

- The mean absolute deviation (MAD) is simply the average error, ignoring whether the error is positive or negative, of a set of forecasts compared with the actual results. The bias is almost the same thing but includes the sign of the error, positive errors meaning that the forecast was too high. The forecasting method producing the smallest MAD and bias is best.

- The linear regression equation for a set of demand data is given as $T_x = a + bX$ where a and b are calculated from Equations 4.8 and 4.9, respectively. The seasonal factors are calculated as the simple average of all the ratios of actual demand for a season divided by the trend value for that season.

- Causal forecasting methods consist of multiple regression, econometric models, Box-Jenkins, and input-output. These complex models take much data and time for construction and are best made by skilled experts in this field.

4.9   KEY TERMS

qualitative forecasts (p. 83)

causal forecasts (p. 83)

trend (p. 88)

cycle, cyclic (p. 90)

seasonal (p. 89)

random (p. 90)

time series analysis (p. 83)

life cycle analysis (p. 87)

Delphi (p. 87)

least squares regression (p. 102)

linear (p. 88)

exponential smoothing (p. 94)

moving average (p. 93)

smoothing constant (p. 95)

MAD (p. 94)

bias (p. 95)

absolute value (p. 97)

adaptive forecasting (p. 97)

econometric models (p. 109)

multiple regression (p. 108)

correlation (p. 107)

tracking signal (p. 97)

4.10   REVIEW AND DISCUSSION QUESTIONS

1. Name some other types of undesired returns organizations may get.

2. Why do you think values of smoothing constants above 0.3 are rarely used?

3. If Delphi is so good why do we not see more of it?

4. Test marketing provides data regarding the monetary returns people really will provide as opposed to what they *say* they will. Why is there such a difference?

5. For many years it was believed that group forecasts were much more conservative than any individual's forecast in the group. Now it is known that just the opposite is true, a phenomenon known as the "risky shift." Why is this so?

6. In what situation might you have historical data but choose to use a qualitative forecasting method instead, ignoring the data?

7. What forecasting methods might be able to predict "turning points" in future demand (that is, effects that had not happened in the past history of demand)?

8. A linear trend *additive* forecasting model is of the form $Y = T + S$. How might forecasts with such a model differ from the multiplicative model?

9. What returns from the environment do regulatory agencies such as the Securities and Exchange Commission and the Federal Trade Commission desire?

10. Why do you think that technical analysts of securities, who as a group use time series analysis, have come to be called "mystics" by many investors?

11. How accurate do you think government forecasts need to be when business and labor often depend on such estimates as cost of living statistics and inflation indicators?

12. What techniques could you devise for forecasting what a competitor's price might be next year or what amount the competitor will bid on a project?

13. How can such events as strikes and disasters be integrated into a forecasting process to account for significant data shifts?

14. If MAD describes the average size of the error and bias the direction, what do you think the standard deviation and running sum of errors describe?

4.11   PROBLEMS

Practice Problems

1. How many periods n should be included in a moving average for each of the following sets of data?

   a. Hourly fire alarms.

  b. Daily output from a 40-hour-per-week manufacturer.

  c. Monthly sales.

  d. Quarterly earnings.

  e. Daily sales from a 24-hour convenience food store.

  f. Weekly bank deposits.

2. Plot the following data and then calculate and plot a moving average of order 3, order 4, and order 5.

Period	1	2	3	4	5	6	7	8	9	10
Data	6	5	5	4	5	3	2	4	3	3

3. Use the data from periods 6 to 10 in Problem 2 to make an exponential forecast for period 11. Try three values of smoothing constants, alpha, of 0.05, 0.30, and 0.90. Compare these with the moving average forecasts obtained from the answers to Problem 2.

4. Make an exponential forecast for period 5 with two values of alpha, 0.05 and 0.60, given the following data. Compare the results.

Period	1	2	3	4
Data	32	14	41	10

5. Calculate the MAD and bias based solely on periods 7 through 10 of the six forecasts in Problems 2 and 3 to determine the best forecast method.

6. Use the data in Problem 4 to calculate the MAD and bias for the two sets of forecasts based on periods 2 through 4. How do they compare?

7. Develop a linear regression equation to predict demand in the future from the following data.

Demand	23	24	31	28	29
Year	1979	1980	1981	1982	1983

8. Determine the linear regression trend equation and seasonals for the following.

Units	5	4	3	5	6	5	4	6
Quarter	1	2	3	4	5	6	7	8

9. Determine in Problem 7 if odd-numbered years are different from even-numbered years by calculating "seasonals" for each.

10. Predict quarter 10 in Problem 8 by linear regression and seasonals and calculate the current MAD and bias.

11. Develop a demand regression equation for the following data and predict demand at a price of $4 and $9.

Price, dollars	7	6	8	5
Demand	1050	1100	1020	1130

More Complex Problems

12. a. Demand for snow tires in Toronto depends on the snowfall with the history for the last 10 years given in the following table. Use the data to develop a linear regression equation for snow tire demand. Calculate the MAD and the bias and predict 1985 demand, if weather forecasters predict 22 inches of snowfall.

Year	Snowfall (inches)	Demand
1975	25.0	2050
1976	27.6	1944
1977	22.4	2250
1978	24.0	1700
1979	28.2	1842
1980	22.2	2404
1981	23.4	1756
1982	25.2	1780
1983	23.8	2144
1984	24.6	1862

b. A friend in the used auto business thinks you might get a better forecast by considering the possibility that demand *lags* snowfall by a year. That is, consider the possibility that demand is related to the snowfall in the *previous* year and develop a new regression equation, MAD, bias, and 1985 prediction. Is the result better or worse?

13. Consider the following data on Rube's Triangle, a toy for children from 5 to 85 years.

Month	J	F	M	A	M	J	J	A	S	O
Demand (in thousands)	0.2	0.5	1.0	2	4	8	25	45	59	66

a. Forecast November demand by a 3-month moving average.

b. Forecast November demand by exponential forecasting with an alpha of 0.3.

c. Forecast November demand by linear regression.

d. Plot the data and the linear trend line from *c*. What appears to be happening? Can you intuitively forecast November?

14. Calculate the linear regression trend line for the Inner City Health Center data in Table 4.1 and determine its MAD and bias. Also calculate the MAD and bias of the moving average of order 4. Compare these with the MAD and bias of exponential smoothing for an alpha of 0.3 found in Table 4.3. Which method appears to be best?

15. Economists have calculated that new home sales (*H*) are related to the number of new family formations (*F*), average annual income (*I*), average interest rate (R), and cost of construction (C) through the following equation:

$$H = 62{,}731 + 0.74F + 5.1I - 4126R - 0.9C$$

where I and C are in dollars and R is a percentage. If it is predicted that in 1988, F will be 100,000 new families, I will be $50,000, R will be 26 percent, and C will be $200,000, how many new homes will be sold? How sensitive are sales to a 1 percent increase in the interest rate; to a $1000 increase in the cost of construction; to a $1000 increase in average annual income? Do you think there may be any relationship between average annual income and new family formations? Or between average annual income and the cost of construction? If so, what effect might this have on our results?

16. To give the flexibility of emphasizing different portions of a time series, a *weighted* moving average is sometimes used, where each data point in the moving average has its own weight (between 0 and 1.0) and all the weights sum to 1.0. For example, a four-period moving average might weight the oldest data point only by 0.1, the next oldest by 0.2, the second most recent by 0.3, and the most recent by 0.4, thus acting much like exponential smoothing where the latest information receives the most weight and older data receive less. Use this method of weighting to calculate a weighted moving average of the Inner City Health Center data in Table 4.2 and plot the result in Figure 4.10 to compare to the two series of exponential forecasts. How does it compare?

17. Bobbie Sternham is trying to select a forecasting model to predict demand for new computer printers. She is using a multiple regression model with n variables and is trying to select n. She knows that the modeling cost (MC) as a function of the number of variables is approximately given by the following equation developed by the data processing group: $MC = \$2000 + \$1500n + 200n^2$. The cost of an inaccurate model is more difficult to assess, but she feels that it is probably $1000 for every 1 percent loss in accuracy. Last, Bobbie knows that simply adding more variables to a model doesn't increase its accuracy proportionally. She figures that doubling the number of variables will probably increase the accuracy, at most, 30 percent. As a base point Bobbie thinks that a simple, one-variable linear regression would be 75 percent accurate. Plot the results of your analysis in a fashion similar to Figure 4.2 and select the best value of n.

18. Recompute the exponential forecast for the Inner City Health Center using an alpha of 0.3, but use the MAD as a tracking signal. That is, whenever the MAD exceeds 3.0 switch to an alpha of 0.8. When the MAD drops to less than 3.0 return to an alpha of 0.3. Plot the result on Figure 4.10. Is this method of "adaptive smoothing" better than simple exponential smoothing for these data?

19. A conceptually simple method of adaptive smoothing is known as Chow's method. With this approach, after the actual demand is known for the forecast period, one recalculates the forecast two times using an alpha 0.05 larger and 0.05 smaller than what was previously used. Using the best result of the three, one then forecasts the next period using the value that performed best in the last period. Starting with an alpha of 0.3 try this approach on the Inner City Health Center data of Table 4.2 and plot the results on Figure 4.10. How does this method compare with the others?

4.12 CASE

BARDSTOWN BOX COMPANY

Bardstown Box Company is a small, closely held corporation located in Bardstown, Kentucky. The stock of the company is divided among three brothers with the principal shareholder being the founding brother, Bob Wilson. Bob formed the company 20 years ago when he resigned as a salesman for a large corrugated box manufacturer.

Bob attributes his success to the fact that he can better serve the five-state area which he considers "his territory" than can any of his large competitors. Bardstown Box supplies corrugated cartons to many regional distilleries and to several breweries. Also, standard size boxes are printed to order for many small manufacturing firms in the region. Bob feels that the large box manufacturers cannot economically provide this personal level of service to his accounts.

Bob recognizes the danger of becoming too dependent on any one client and has enforced the policy that no single customer can account for over 20 percent of sales. Two of the distilleries account for 20 percent of sales each, and hence are limited in their purchases. Bob has convinced the purchasing agents of these two companies to add other suppliers since this alternative supply protects them against problems Bardstown might have in shipping, paper shortages, or labor problems.

Bardstown currently has over 600 customers with orders ranging in size from a low of 100 boxes to blanket orders for 50,000 boxes per year. Boxes are produced in 16 standard sizes with special printing to customers' specifications. Bardstown's printing equipment limits their print to two colors. The standardization and limited printing allows Bardstown to be price competitive with the big producers but they also provide the service for small and "emergency" orders that large box manufacturers cannot provide.

Such personal service, however, requires tight inventory control and close production scheduling. So far, Bob Wilson has always forecasted demand and prepared production schedules through experience but because of the ever-growing number of accounts and changes in personnel in customers' purchasing departments, the accuracy of his forecasting has been rapidly declining. The number of backorders is on the increase, late orders are more common and inventory levels of finished boxes are on the increase. A second warehouse has recently been leased due to the overcrowded conditions in the main warehouse. Plans are to move some of the slower moving boxes to the leased space.

There has always been an increase in demand for boxes prior to the Christmas holiday season when customers begin stocking for holiday promotional demand. Such seasonality in demand has always substantially increased the difficulty of making a reliable forecast.

Bob Wilson feels that it is now important to develop an improved forecasting method. It should take both customer growth and seasonality into consideration. Bob believes that if such a method can be applied to forecasting total demand, it can also be used to forecast demand for the larger customers; the requirements of the smaller customers could then be integrated to smooth production and warehousing volume.

Bob has compiled the following demand data.

	Sales (in number of boxes)				
Month	1979	1980	1981	1982	1983
January	12,000	8,000	12,000	15,000	15,000
February	8,000	14,000	8,000	12,000	22,000
March	10,000	18,000	18,000	14,000	18,000
April	18,000	15,000	13,000	18,000	18,000
May	14,000	16,000	14,000	15,000	16,000
June	10,000	18,000	18,000	18,000	20,000
July	16,000	14,000	17,000	20,000	28,000
August	18,000	28,000	20,000	22,000	28,000
September	20,000	22,000	25,000	26,000	20,000
October	27,000	27,000	28,000	28,000	30,000
November	24,000	26,000	18,000	20,000	22,000
December	18,000	10,000	18,000	22,000	28,000
	195,000	216,000	209,000	230,000	265,000

Questions for Discussion

1. Develop a forecasting method for Bardstown and forecast total demand for 1984.
2. How might Bob improve the accuracy of the forecast?
3. Should Bob's experience with the market be factored into the forecast? How?

4.13 REFERENCES AND BIBLIOGRAPHY

1. Adam, E. E., Jr., "Individual Item Forecasting Model Evaluation," *Decision Sciences*, 4:458–470 (1973).
2. Berry, W. L. et al., "Forecasting Teller Window Demand with Exponential Smoothing," *Journal of the Academy of Management*, 22:129–139 (1979).
3. Boot, J. C. G., and Cox, E. B., *Statistical Analysis for Managerial Decisions*, 2nd ed., New York: McGraw-Hill, 1974.
4. Box, G. E. P., and Jenkins, G. M., *Time Series Analysis: Forecasting and Control*, San Francisco: Holden-Day, 1970.
5. Chambers, J. S. et al., "How to Choose the Right Forecasting Technique," *Harvard Business Review*, 49:55–64 (July–Aug. 1971).
6. Dancer, R., and Gray, C., "An Empirical Evaluation of Constant and Adaptive Computer Forecasting Models for Inventory Control," *Decision Sciences*, 8:228–238 (1977).
7. Hogarth, R. M. et al., "Forecasting and Planning: An Evaluation," *Management Science*, 27:115–138 (1981).
8. Linstone, H.A., and Turoff, M., *The Delphi Method: Techniques and Applications*, Reading, MA: Addison-Wesley, 1975.
9. Parker, G. C. et al., "How to Get a Better Forecast," *Harvard Business Review*, 49:99–109 (March–April 1971).
10. Ramond, Charles, *The Art of Using Science in Marketing*, New York: Harper & Row, 1974.
11. Rosen, G. R., "New Vogue in Forecasting," *Dun's Review*, Oct. 1979, pp. 94–100.
12. Thomopoulos, N. T., *Applied Forecasting Methods*, Englewood Cliffs, NJ: Prentice-Hall, 1980.
13. Wheelwright, S. C. et al., *Forecasting Methods for Management*, 2nd ed., New York: Wiley, 1977.
14. Whybark, D. C., "A Comparison of Adaptive Forecasting Techniques," *The Logistics and Transportation Review*, 8:13–26 (Jan. 1973).

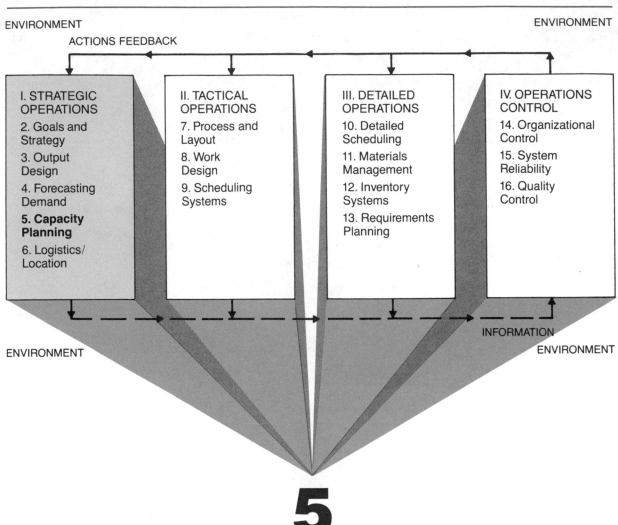

5

LEARNING OBJECTIVES

By the completion of this chapter the student should

- Understand the difference between capacity planning and scheduling.
- Be aware of the unique problems of capacity planning for pure services.
- Appreciate the range of alternatives for handling short-run capacity needs.
- Know the concepts underlying the learning curve and how to find the effect of learning on capacity.
- Be familiar with the role and importance of output life cycles on capacity utilization.
- Have developed a sense of the importance of breakeven concepts for capacity planning.
- Be able to calculate output rates and utilization efficiency as incremental changes are made to capacity.
- Have a feel for the use of linear programming to address the output mix problem and be able to formulate such a problem as a linear program.
- Know how to use a decision tree to evaluate uncertainty in managerial decision situations such as capacity planning.

Capacity defined.

In the last chapter we talked about determining the demand for the output that exists in the environment and the importance to the operations function of forecasting this demand. In this chapter we investigate the alternative methods available to obtain the *capacity* for economically supplying that demand. "Capacity" may be considered to mean the maximum available amount of output of the transformation process over some specified duration. For instance, airlines measure their capacity in "available seat miles" (ASMs) over a year. One ASM is one seat available for a passenger for 1 mile. Clearly, the number of planes an airline has, their size, how often they are flown, and the route structure of the airline all affect its ASMs, or capacity. An elementary measure of a hospital's capacity is often stated simply in terms of the number of beds in the hospital. Thus, a 50-bed hospital is "small" and a 1000-bed hospital is "large."

Capacity complicated by multiple outputs.

Notice that the above measures of capacity do not recognize the multiple types of outputs an organization may, in reality, be concerned with. ASMs say nothing about the freight capacity of an airline, but freight may be a major contributor to profits. Similarly, the number of beds says nothing about outpatient treatments, ambulance rescues, and other services provided by a hospital. Thus, capacity planning must often consider the capacity to produce multiple outputs. Unfortunately, this is frequently complicated by the fact that some of the outputs may be able to use the same organizational resources but require some specialized resources as well.

Service capacity a problem.

The provision of adequate capacity is clearly a generic problem, common to all types of organizations. Yet, in pure service organizations capacity is a special problem because the service output cannot normally be stored for later use. A utility, for example, must have capacity available to meet peak power demands, yet the *average* power demand may be much, much lower. Where the provision of the service is by human labor, low productivity is a danger when staffing is provided to meet the demand peaks.

We will look at all these situations. First, we address the short-term capacity issue and then use an example in "biofeedback" to illustrate the effect of learning on capacity. From there we move into long-term capacity, a significantly different problem with different solutions, and use an example in the manufacture of sports equipment to illustrate the breakeven concept, linear programming, and decision trees. In the appendix to the chapter we present the graphical approach to solving linear programs.

5.1 SHORT-TERM CAPACITY PLANNING

Capacity— acquiring resources.

The short-term capacity problem is to economically handle unexpected but imminent actual demand, either less than or more than expected. It is known, of course, that the forecast will not be perfect and, thus, the operations manager must plan what short-term capacity alternatives to use in either case. Such considerations are usually limited to, at most, the next 6 months, and usually much less, such as the next few hours. Thus, short-term capacity planning is very closely related to the scheduling function, a topic to be discussed in Chapters 9 and 10. The difference is that capacity is primarily oriented toward the *acquisition* of productive resources whereas scheduling concerns the *timing* of their use. However, it is often difficult to separate the two, especially where human resources are involved, such as in the use of overtime or the overlapping of shifts. In actual practice, scheduling and short-term capacity planning must often be conducted simultaneously. Why add expensive capacity if existing capacity is being inefficiently used?

As a simple example, suppose an organization has the two customers' jobs shown in Table 5.1 to complete within 2 weeks. The table shows the sequential processing operations still to be completed and the times required. (The operational resources may be of any form—a facility, piece of equipment, or specially skilled worker.) In total, 60 hours of resource A are needed, 45 hours of B, and 25 hours of C. It would appear that 2 weeks (80 hours) of capacity on each of these three resources would be sufficient and additional capacity would, therefore, be unnecessary.

Figure 5.1 is a sketch showing the resource requirements of the two jobs plotted along a time scale. Such a chart is called a **Gantt** chart (discussed further in Chapter 10) and can be used to show time schedules and capacities of facilities, workers, jobs, activities, machines, and so forth. In this case each job was scheduled on the required resource as soon as it finished on the previous resource, whether or not the new resource was occupied with the other job. This is called **infinite loading** because work is scheduled on the resource as if it had infinite capacity to handle any and all jobs. Note that in this way capacity conflicts and possible resolutions can be easily visualized.

The first resource conflict in Figure 5.1 occurs at 20 hours when job 1 finishes on resource C and next requires resource A, which is still working on job 2. The second conflict, again at A, occurs at 35 hours, and the third, on B, at 50 hours. It is quickly seen that deferring one job for the other has drastic consequences on resource conflicts later on as well as job completion times. Another consideration, not specified here, is whether an operation can be partially completed in stages or, once started, must be completely finished or else restarted from scratch.

Margin notes:
Scheduling— timing of their use.

Bottlenecks.

Gantt chart.

Infinite loading.

Short-term resource conflicts.

Table 5.1 Sequential Operations Required for Two Jobs

Job	Operational Resource Needed	Time Required (hr)
1	A	10
	C	10
	A	30
	B	20
	C	5
2	B	15
	A	10
	C	10
	A	10
	B	10

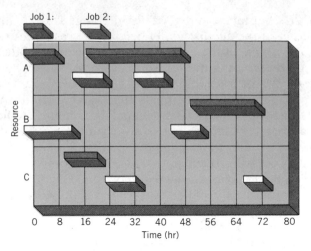

Figure 5.1   Gantt chart for capacity planning and scheduling.

Capacity Planning for Pure Services

Capacity planning for pure service operations is a much more difficult problem than for "products," and one with a clearer distinction between long- and short-run capacity planning. For services, the more difficult aspects of capacity provision occur in the short run, usually because services are subjected to daily peaks and valleys in their demands, and the output cannot be stored ahead of time to buffer this demand fluctuation. For example, doctors' offices see demand peaks at 9 A.M. and 1 P.M., and college classes at 10 A.M. Or there may be weekly peaks, monthly peaks, or yearly peaks such as Friday's demand on banks to deposit (or cash) payroll checks, and the first of the month demand on restaurants when social security checks arrive in the mail. Some services, such as fire departments, experience multiple types of peaks, as illustrated in Figure 5.2. In Figure 5.2*a* is depicted the regular *daily* cycle of fire alarms, with the peak from 3 to 7 P.M., and in 5.2*b* the *yearly* cycle of fire alarms, with the peak in April.

Service cannot be stored.

Multiple peaks.

To consider the alternative means of handling these capacity problems let us first focus on an example—the typical 1940s lunchroom during the noon rush hour (based on Reference 12):

As the customers started filling all the tables, a receptionist came on duty and attended to the parties queuing (waiting in line) for a table. More waitresses, bus boys, and an extra cook also showed up and started working. As customers got to a table and opened the menu they noticed the statement "No substitutions between 11 A.M. and 2 P.M." Waitresses were a long time in coming to take orders and service in general seemed slow. Hamburgers and other sandwiches were served plain with lettuce and tomato on the side, regardless of how they were ordered. Pre-prepared relish cups were included on every plate whether ordered or not. At the conclusion of the meal, signs on the table implored the customers to do their part to leave the table clean.

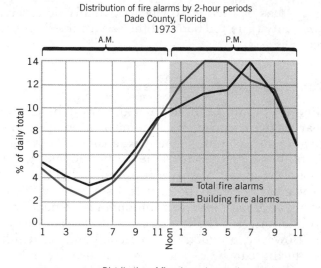

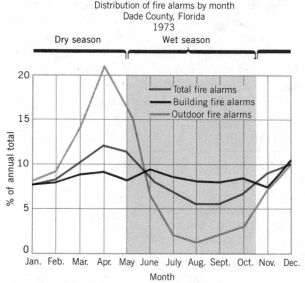

Figure 5.2 Fire alarm histories. (*a*) Hourly.
(*b*) Monthly.

We are more sophisticated in queuing for tables these days, of course. The receptionist takes our name and party size and tells us there will be a 20-minute wait (they must never tell a customer the wait will be longer than 20 minutes) and then motions us to a bar. This serves three purposes.

1. It gets us out of the receptionist's hair and into more comfortable surroundings where we are less likely to leave.

2. It makes money for the restaurant, whose greatest profits come from drinks, not food.

3. It deadens our senses so when we finally do receive our meal it does not really taste too bad and the service does not seem as terrible as it really is.

Short-Run Capacity Alternatives

From this lunchroom example, and the two-job scheduling example presented earlier, we can perceive a number of possible managerial short-run capacity alternatives to permanent expansion. These are listed in Table 5.2.

Problems with each alternative.

Most common alternative.

Each of the techniques in Table 5.2 has advantages and disadvantages. The use of overtime is expensive (time and a half) and productivity after 8 hours of work is typically poor. It is a simple and easily invoked process, however, that does not require additional investment and is one of the most common alternatives. The use of extra shifts requires hiring but no extra facilities. However, productivity on second and third shifts is usually poor. Part-time hiring can be expensive and is usually only feasible for low or unskilled work. Floating workers are flexible and very useful, but of course cost extra also. Leasing facilities and workers is often a good approach, but the extra cost reduces the profit, and these external resources may not be available during the high demand periods when they are usually needed. Subcontracting typically requires a long lead time, is considerable trouble to implement, and may leave little, if any, profit.

For daily demand peaks, shifts can be overlapped to provide extra ca-

Table 5.2 Techniques to Increase Short-Run Capacity

  I. Increase Resources
    1. Use overtime.
    2. Add shifts.
    3. Employ part-time workers.
    4. Use "floating" workers.
    5. Lease workers and facilities.
    6. Subcontract.
 II. Improve Resource Use
    7. Overlap or stagger shifts.
    8. Schedule appointments.
    9. Inventory output (if feasible) ahead of demand.
    10. Backlog or queue demand.
III. Modify the Output
    11. Standardize the output.
    12. Have the recipient do part of the work.
    13. Transform service operations into inventoriable product operations.
    14. Cut back on quality.
 IV. Modify the Demand
    15. Change the price.
    16. Change the promotion.
  V. Do Not Meet Demand
    17. Do not supply all the demand.

pacity at peak times, or staggered to adjust to changes in demand loads. Appointment systems can also help smooth out daily demand peaks, if feasible. If the output can be stocked ahead of time, as with a product, this is an excellent and very common approach to meeting capacity needs. If recipients are willing, the backlogging of demand to be met later during slack periods is an excellent strategy; a less accurate forecast is needed and finished goods investment is nil. However, this may be an open invitation to competition.

Storage is common.

Modifying the output is a creative approach. Doing less customization, allowing fewer variants, and encouraging recipients to do some assembly or finishing tasks themselves, perhaps with a small price incentive, are infrequently employed yet good alternatives. In service operations it is sometimes feasible to trade off service for products, as with the relish cups in the lunchroom example. The tradeoff here is, clearly, the reduced service for the increased capacity, a reduction which might be perceived as a decrease in the quality of the output, another available alternative.

Creative alternatives.

Attempting to alter or shift the demand to a different period is another creative approach. Running promotions or price differentials, or both, for slack periods is an excellent method for leveling out demand, especially in utilities, telephone, and similar services. Prices are not easily increased above normal in high demand periods, however. Last, the manager may simply decide not to meet the market demand, again, however, at the cost of inviting competition.

Inviting competition.

In actuality, many of these alternatives are not feasible except in certain types of organizations or in particular circumstances. For example, when demand is high, subcontractors are full, outside facilities and staff are already overbooked, second shift workers are employed elsewhere, and marketing promotions are already low-key. Thus, of the many possible alternatives, most firms tend to rely on only a couple, such as overtime and stocking up ahead of demand.

So far we have primarily discussed *increasing* capacity in the short run. But firms also have the need to decrease short-run capacity. This is more difficult, though, and most such capacity simply goes unused. If the output involves a product some inventory buildup may be allowed to make use of the available capacity, otherwise "system maintenance" activities are engaged in (cleaning, fixing, preprocessing, and so on).

The Learning Curve

Before we leave the topic of short-term capacity planning, an important issue needs to be addressed—the ability of humans to increase their productive capacity through "learning." This issue is particularly important in the short-term start-up of new and unfamiliar processes such as those involving new technologies like machinery and computerized word processing.

Capacity through learning.

The improvement in capacity, generally called the **learning curve** effect, is not necessarily due to learning alone, however. Better tools, improvements in work methods, upgraded output designs, and other such factors also help increase productivity, and hence such curves are also known as *improvement curves, production progress functions, performance curves*, and *experience curves*.

Japanese learning for long-term capacity.

The learning curve effect, when viewed in this fashion, also becomes a *long-term* capacity issue and is often factored into organizations' 5- and 10-year planning processes. The Japanese, in particular, count on the long-term capacity of a facility increasing through the workers' development of better work methods and tool improvements.

Based on airplane production.

The derivation of the learning curve is an outgrowth of the airframe manufacturing industry of the 1930s where it was found that the manhours needed to build each successive airplane decreased relatively smoothly. In particular, each time the output *doubled*, the manhours per plane decreased to a fixed percentage of their previous value—in this particular case, 80 percent. Thus, when the first plane of a series required 100,000 manhours (mh) to produce, the *second* took 80,000 mh, the *fourth* took 80,000 × 0.80 = 64,000, the *eighth* took 64,000 × 0.80 = 51,200 mh, and so on. This type of mathematical relationship is described by the *negative exponential function*

$$M = mN^{-r} \tag{5.1}$$

where M = the manhours for the Nth unit*
m = the manhours required to produce the very *first* unit
N = the number of units produced
r = the exponent of the curve corresponding
to the learning rate (= $\log_e$ [learning rate]$/-0.693$)

The plot of this function for the airplane example is shown in Figure 5.3.

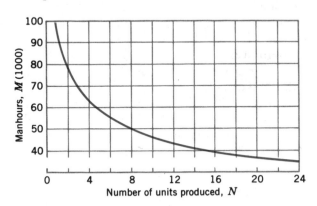

Figure 5.3   Eighty percent learning curve for airplane production.

*Two forms of the learning curve relationship are used in the literature. In one form M corresponds to the cumulative *average* manhours of all N units and in the other form M corresponds to the *actual* manhours to produce the Nth unit. The second interpretation is more useful for operations management and will be the interpretation used here. For example, then, a learning rate of 90 percent would mean that each time production doubled from, say, N_1 to N_2, unit N_2 will require 90 percent of the manhours that N_1 required.

To illustrate the equation let us find the time that the second airplane will take to build in the example mentioned.

$$M = (100,000)2^{-\log_e(0.8)/-0.693}$$
$$= (100,000)2^{-0.322}$$
$$= 80,000 \text{ mh}$$

Amount of human input is the key.

A number of factors affect the learning curve rate, but the most important is the percentage of human, compared to mechanical, input in the task and the complexity of the task. Greatest learning, sometimes with as much as a 60 percent rate, occurs for highly complex tasks consisting primarily of human inputs. A task that is highly machine automated clearly leaves little opportunity for learning to occur (only the human can learn, the machine generally cannot). In airframe manufacturing the proportion of human effort is about 75 percent and an 80 percent learning rate applies. For similar work of the same complexity and ratio of human-to-machine input, approximately the same rate will apply.

But learning curves are not limited to manufacturing, or even product-oriented organizations. These curves apply just as well to beauty shops, selling, finding a parking space, and preparing pizza. As indicated, they also apply to *groups* of individuals, and *systems* that include people and machines, as well as to individuals.

Applicable to groups and systems too.

The primary question, of course, is what learning rate to apply. If previous experience is available this may give some indication; if not, a close watch of the time it takes to produce the first few units should give a good indication. Let us illustrate the use of the learning curve, and some learning curve tables, with a simple example.

Biocontrol, Inc.

Biocontrol has just entered the growing brainwave feedback market with a contract from a semireligious organization to teach biocontrol techniques to the organization's 10 elders for alpha and gamma brainwave rhythm control (which it is hoped will enhance the elders' meditation abilities). The lessons for the last elder have just finished and the organization, considering the lessons highly successful, has engaged Biocontrol to give the same lessons to their congregation of 150 members. The lessons for the first elder were highly experimental, requiring 100 hours in all, but careful analysis and refinement of the techniques have gradually decreased this time to the point where the average time for *all* of the lessons was just under half that value, 49 hours each. To properly staff, schedule, plan, and cost out the work for the 150 lessons, Biocontrol needs to know how many hours of lessons will be required.

Learning Curve Tables

Biocontrol will use Tables 5.3 and 5.4 to solve their dilemma. These tables provide the fraction of time the Nth unit will require of what the first

Table 5.3 Unit Values of the Learning Curve
Example: Unit 1 took 10 hours. 80% learning rate. What will unit 5 require?
Solution: Unit 5 row, 80% column: value = 0.5956. Thus, unit 5 will take 10 (0.5956) = 5.956 hours.

Units	60%	65%	70%	75%	80%	85%	90%	95%
				Improvement Ratios				
1	1.0000	1.0000	1.0000	1.0000	1.0000	1.0000	1.0000	1.0000
2	0.6000	0.6500	0.7000	0.7500	0.8000	0.8500	0.9000	0.9500
3	0.4450	0.5052	0.5682	0.6338	0.7021	0.7729	0.8462	0.9219
4	0.3600	0.4225	0.4900	0.5625	0.6400	0.7225	0.8100	0.9025
5	0.3054	0.3678	0.4368	0.5127	0.5956	0.6857	0.7830	0.8877
6	0.2670	0.3284	0.3977	0.4754	0.5617	0.6570	0.7616	0.8758
7	0.2383	0.2984	0.3674	0.4459	0.5345	0.6337	0.7439	0.8659
8	0.2160	0.2746	0.3430	0.4219	0.5120	0.6141	0.7290	0.8574
9	0.1980	0.2552	0.3228	0.4017	0.4930	0.5974	0.7161	0.8499
10	0.1832	0.2391	0.3058	0.3846	0.4765	0.5828	0.7047	0.8433
12	0.1602	0.2135	0.2784	0.3565	0.4493	0.5584	0.6854	0.8320
14	0.1430	0.1940	0.2572	0.3344	0.4276	0.5386	0.6696	0.8226
16	0.1296	0.1785	0.2401	0.3164	0.4096	0.5220	0.6561	0.8145
18	0.1188	0.1659	0.2260	0.3013	0.3944	0.5078	0.6445	0.8074
20	0.1099	0.1554	0.2141	0.2884	0.3812	0.4954	0.6342	0.8012
22	0.1025	0.1465	0.2038	0.2772	0.3697	0.4844	0.6251	0.7955
24	0.0961	0.1387	0.1949	0.2674	0.3595	0.4747	0.6169	0.7904
25	0.0933	0.1353	0.1908	0.2629	0.3548	0.4701	0.6131	0.7880
30	0.0815	0.1208	0.1737	0.2437	0.3346	0.4505	0.5963	0.7775
35	0.0728	0.1097	0.1605	0.2286	0.3184	0.4345	0.5825	0.7687
40	0.0660	0.1010	0.1498	0.2163	0.3050	0.4211	0.5708	0.7611
45	0.0605	0.0939	0.1410	0.2060	0.2936	0.4096	0.5607	0.7545
50	0.0560	0.0879	0.1336	0.1972	0.2838	0.3996	0.5518	0.7486
60	0.0489	0.0785	0.1216	0.1828	0.2676	0.3829	0.5367	0.7386
70	0.0437	0.0713	0.1123	0.1715	0.2547	0.3693	0.5243	0.7302
80	0.0396	0.0657	0.1049	0.1622	0.2440	0.3579	0.5137	0.7231
90	0.0363	0.0610	0.0987	0.1545	0.2349	0.3482	0.5046	0.7168
100	0.0336	0.0572	0.0935	0.1479	0.2271	0.3397	0.4966	0.7112
120	0.0294	0.0510	0.0851	0.1371	0.2141	0.3255	0.4830	0.7017
140	0.0262	0.0464	0.0786	0.1287	0.2038	0.3139	0.4718	0.6937
160	0.0237	0.0427	0.0734	0.1217	0.1952	0.3042	0.4623	0.6869
180	0.0218	0.0397	0.0691	0.1159	0.1879	0.2959	0.4541	0.6809
200	0.0201	0.0371	0.0655	0.1109	0.1816	0.2887	0.4469	0.6757
250	0.0171	0.0323	0.0584	0.1011	0.1691	0.2740	0.4320	0.6646
300	0.0149	0.0289	0.0531	0.0937	0.1594	0.2625	0.4202	0.6557
350	0.0133	0.0262	0.0491	0.0879	0.1517	0.2532	0.4105	0.6482
400	0.0121	0.0241	0.0458	0.0832	0.1453	0.2454	0.4022	0.6419
450	0.0111	0.0224	0.0431	0.0792	0.1399	0.2387	0.3951	0.6363
500	0.0103	0.0210	0.0408	0.0758	0.1352	0.2329	0.3888	0.6314
600	0.0090	0.0188	0.0372	0.0703	0.1275	0.2232	0.3782	0.6229
700	0.0080	0.0171	0.0344	0.0659	0.1214	0.2152	0.3694	0.6158
800	0.0073	0.0157	0.0321	0.0624	0.1163	0.2086	0.3620	0.6098
900	0.0067	0.0146	0.0302	0.0594	0.1119	0.2029	0.3556	0.6045

Table 5.3 *(Continued)*

Units	Improvement Ratios							
	60%	65%	70%	75%	80%	85%	90%	95%
1000	0.0062	0.0137	0.0286	0.0569	0.1082	0.1980	0.3499	0.5998
1200	0.0054	0.0122	0.0260	0.0527	0.1020	0.1897	0.3404	0.5918
1400	0.0048	0.0111	0.0240	0.0495	0.0971	0.1830	0.3325	0.5850
1600	0.0044	0.0102	0.0225	0.0468	0.0930	0.1773	0.3258	0.5793
1800	0.0040	0.0095	0.0211	0.0446	0.0895	0.1725	0.3200	0.5743
2000	0.0037	0.0089	0.0200	0.0427	0.0866	0.1683	0.3149	0.5698
2500	0.0031	0.0077	0.0178	0.0389	0.0806	0.1597	0.3044	0.5605
3000	0.0027	0.0069	0.0162	0.0360	0.0760	0.1530	0.2961	0.5330

Source: Albert N. Schreiber, Richard A. Johnson, Robert C. Meier, William T. Newell, Henry C. Fischer, *Cases in Manufacturing Management* (New York: McGraw-Hill Book Company, © 1965), p. 464. Reprinted by permission of McGraw-Hill.

unit required or N^{-r} (Table 5.3) and the cumulative fraction of time that the first N units will take of what the first unit took or ΣN^{-r} (Table 5.4). Returning to our 80 percent learning curve airplane example for a moment, Table 5.3 shows that unit 2 (left-hand column) under the "80%" column will require 0.8 of what unit 1 required (100,000 mh), that unit 4 will require 0.64, unit 8 will take 0.512, and so forth. In addition, we also see that unit 3 will take 0.7021 and unit 6, for example, 0.5617 (i.e., 0.5617 × 100,000 or 56,170 mh). The *total* manhours to produce two, four, or eight planes can be found by adding the necessary values above together, or by looking at Table 5.4 where this has already been done. Again reading under the "80%" column for two, four, and eight units we get 1.8, 3.142, and 5.346 times 100,000, respectively, for 180,000, 314,200, and 534,600 mh, cumulative.

Solution to Biocontrol

To now consider Biocontrol's situation, the average of 49 hours each, times 10 elders, gives 490 hours, cumulative. This is 4.9 times what the first elder required (100 hours). Finding the value 4.9 in Table 5.4 for 10 units will then give the learning curve rate applying to these complex lessons. Reading across the 10 unit row we find 4.931 under the "70%" column (on occasion, interpolation between columns may be necessary).

Assuming the lessons are continuous and the teaching techniques are not forgotten (an important assumption), we can look further down the "70%" column of Table 5.4 to find the value corresponding to the *total* number of lessons to be given: 10 + 150 = 160. This value, 22.72, is then multiplied by the amount of time required for the first lesson (100 hours) to give a grand total of 2272 hours for the 160 lessons. Since the initial 10 elders required a total of 490 hours by themselves, the second group, consisting solely of the congregation, will require 2272 − 490 = 1782 hours. The time phasing of this 1782 hours is also available, if desired, from Table 5.3.

Table 5.4 Cumulative Values of the Learning Curve

Example: Unit 1 took 10 hours. 80% learning rate. What will be the total hours required to produce the first five units?

Solution: Unit 5 row, 80% column: value = 3.738. Thus, the first five units will require 10(3.738) = 37.38 hours.

				Improvement Ratios				
Units	*60%*	*65%*	*70%*	*75%*	*80%*	*85%*	*90%*	*95%*
1	1.000	1.000	1.000	1.000	1.000	1.000	1.000	1.000
2	1.600	1.650	1.700	1.750	1.800	1.850	1.900	1.950
3	2.045	2.155	2.268	2.384	2.502	2.623	2.746	2.872
4	2.405	2.578	2.758	2.946	3.142	3.345	3.556	3.774
5	2.710	2.946	3.195	3.459	3.738	4.031	4.339	4.662
6	2.977	3.274	3.593	3.934	4.299	4.688	5.101	5.538
7	3.216	3.572	3.960	4.380	4.834	5.322	5.845	6.404
8	3.432	3.847	4.303	4.802	5.346	5.936	6.574	7.261
9	3.630	4.102	4.626	5.204	5.839	6.533	7.290	8.111
10	3.813	4.341	4.931	5.589	6.315	7.116	7.994	8.955
12	4.144	4.780	5.501	6.315	7.227	8.244	9.374	10.62
14	4.438	5.177	6.026	6.994	8.092	9.331	10.72	12.27
16	4.704	5.541	6.514	7.635	8.920	10.38	12.04	13.91
18	4.946	5.879	6.972	8.245	9.716	11.41	13.33	15.52
20	5.171	6.195	7.407	8.828	10.48	12.40	14.61	17.13
22	5.379	6.492	7.819	9.388	11.23	13.38	15.86	18.72
24	5.574	6.773	8.213	9.928	11.95	14.33	17.10	20.31
25	5.668	6.909	8.404	10.19	12.31	14.80	17.71	21.10
30	6.097	7.540	9.305	11.45	14.02	17.09	20.73	25.00
35	6.478	8.109	10.13	12.72	15.64	19.29	23.67	28.86
40	6.821	8.631	10.90	13.72	17.19	21.43	26.54	32.68
45	7.134	9.114	11.62	14.77	18.68	23.50	29.37	36.47
50	7.422	9.565	12.31	15.78	20.12	25.51	32.14	40.22
60	7.941	10.39	13.57	17.67	22.87	29.41	37.57	47.65
70	8.401	11.13	14.74	19.43	25.47	33.17	42.87	54.99
80	8.814	11.82	15.82	21.09	27.96	36.80	48.05	62.25
90	9.191	12.45	16.83	22.67	30.35	40.32	53.14	69.45
100	9.539	13.03	17.79	24.18	32.65	43.75	58.14	76.59
120	10.16	14.11	19.57	27.02	37.05	50.39	67.93	90.71
140	10.72	15.08	21.20	29.67	41.22	56.78	77.46	104.7
160	11.21	15.97	22.72	32.17	45.20	62.95	86.80	118.5
180	11.67	16.79	24.14	34.54	49.03	68.95	95.96	132.1
200	12.09	17.55	25.48	36.80	52.72	74.79	105.0	145.7
250	13.01	19.28	28.56	42.08	61.47	88.83	126.9	179.2
300	13.81	20.81	31.34	46.94	69.66	102.2	148.2	212.2
350	14.51	22.18	33.89	51.48	77.43	115.1	169.0	244.8
400	15.14	23.44	36.26	55.75	84.85	127.6	189.3	277.0
450	15.72	24.60	38.48	59.80	91.97	139.7	209.2	309.0
500	16.26	25.68	40.58	63.68	98.85	151.5	228.8	340.6
600	17.21	27.67	44.47	70.97	112.0	174.2	267.1	403.3
700	18.06	29.45	48.04	77.77	124.4	196.1	304.5	465.3
800	18.82	31.09	51.36	84.18	136.3	217.3	341.0	526.5

Table 5.4   *(Continued)*

| | | | | Improvement Ratios | | | | |
Units	60%	65%	70%	75%	80%	85%	90%	95%
900	19.51	32.60	54.46	90.26	147.7	237.9	376.9	587.2
1000	20.15	34.01	57.40	96.07	158.7	257.9	412.2	647.4
1200	21.30	36.59	62.85	107.0	179.7	296.6	481.2	766.6
1400	22.32	38.92	67.85	117.2	199.6	333.9	548.4	884.2
1600	23.23	41.04	72.49	126.8	218.6	369.9	614.2	1001
1800	24.06	43.00	76.85	135.9	236.8	404.9	678.8	1116
2000	24.83	44.84	80.96	144.7	254.4	438.9	742.3	1230
2500	26.53	48.97	90.39	165.0	296.1	520.8	897.0	1513
3000	27.99	52.62	98.90	183.7	335.2	598.9	1047	1791

Source: Albert N. Schrieber, Richard A. Johnson, Robert C. Meier, William T. Newell, Henry C. Fischer, *Cases in Manufacturing Management* (New York: McGraw-Hill Book Company, © 1965), p. 465. Reprinted by permission of McGraw-Hill.

Plateaus, forgetting, relearning, and natural variability.

The learning curve is only a theoretical construct, of course, and it therefore only approximates actual learning. A more realistic learning pattern is illustrated in Figure 5.4. Initially, actual manhours per unit vary about the theoretical curve until a "learning plateau" is reached at, perhaps, the tenth unit. At this plateau no significant learning appears to occur, until a breakthrough materializes. Learning typically involves a number of such plateaus and breakthroughs. At about 30 units, production is halted for a period of time and "forgetting" occurs, rapidly at first but then tailing off. When production is later reinitiated, relearning occurs very quickly (as when relearning to ride a bicycle after 40 years) until the original efficiency is reached (at about 33 units). If the conditions are the same at this time as for the

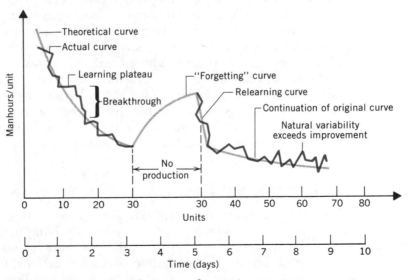

Figure 5.4 Typical learning-forgetting pattern.

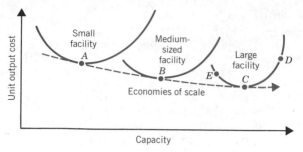

Figure 5.5 Decreasing output cost with facility size.

initial part of the curve, the original learning curve rate will then hold. After sufficient time passes, the improvement due to learning becomes trivial in comparison with natural variability in efficiency, and at that point we say that "learning has ceased."

5.2 LONG-TERM CAPACITY PLANNING

Strategic issue of long-term capacity.

Capacity planning issues over the long run relate primarily to the expansion and contraction of major facilities used in producing the organization's output. This is clearly a strategic operations issue rather than a tactical or detailed operations issue, as with short-term capacity planning. Figure 5.5 illustrates the facilities issue in terms of capacity and unit cost. Product cost curves are shown for three sizes of production facilities. Larger facilities, when operated at their optimal (lowest cost, here) production level (A, B, or C), will generally result in a lower unit cost of output. However, if nonoptimal production levels must be employed, the advantage of a larger sized facility may be lost. For example, point D is characterized by congestion and excessive overtime, and point E by idle labor and low equipment utilization.

There are many other considerations involved in the strategic decision of selecting long-run capacity and we will be looking in detail at the operations factors in this chapter. However, there are some financial considerations also, such as depreciation of the facility, leasing possibilities, and general tax considerations. These issues are addressed later in Chapter 15.

Demand and Life Cycles for Multiple Outputs

Capacity contraction.

Realistically, organizations are not always expanding their capacity. We usually focus on this issue because we are studying firms in the process of growth, but even successful organizations often reduce their capacity. Major ways of contracting capacity are to divest operations, lay off workers, and sell or lease equipment and facilities. Most organizations, however, only try to contract capacity that is inefficient or inappropriate for their circum-

Adding on outputs instead.

stances, due in part to a felt social responsibility to the community. If it appears that organizational resources are going to be excessively idle in the future, organizations often attempt to add new outputs to their current output mix rather than contracting capacity (the latter frequently being done at a loss). This entails an analysis of the candidate output's life and seasonal demand cycles.

Many organizations are oriented to a demand that is "seasonal" and hence find themselves in a frenzy at certain times and idly bored at other times. Figure 5.1 illustrated how this was true for fire departments.

Demand Seasonality

Adding an anticyclic output.

It is traditional in fire departments to use the slack months for building inspections, fire prevention programs, safety talks, and other such activities. The large investment in labor and equipment is thus more effectively utilized throughout the year by the organization's adoption of an *anticyclic* (counter to the fire cycle) output—fire prevention. For much the same reasons, many fire departments have been given the responsibility for the city or county's medical rescue service (although rescue alarms are not entirely anticyclic to fire alarms).

Furnaces and air conditioners.

Clearly, many organizations face this cyclic difficulty, such as the makers of Christmas ornaments, fur coats, swimming pool equipment, fireworks, and so forth. A classic case, however, is that of furnace dealers. For the last 100 years their business typically was all in the late autumn and winter months of the year, as illustrated in Figure 5.6. With the rapid acceptance of air conditioning in the 1950s and 1960s many furnace dealers eagerly added this product to their output mix. Not only was it conceptually along the same lines (environmental comfort) and often interconnected with the home furnace but, most important, it was almost completely anticyclic to the seasonal heating cycle. As shown in Figure 5.6 the addition of air conditioning considerably leveled dealers' sales throughout the year in comparison with furnace sales alone.

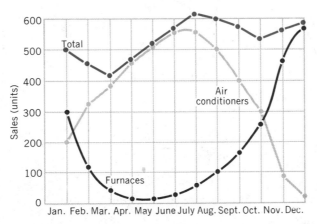

Figure 5.6 Anticyclic product sales.

Output Life Cycles

Multiple life cycles to even out capacity utilization.

In a similar manner, and for much the same reasons, organizations add outputs to their mix that are anticyclic to existing output *life cycles*. (Refer to the discussion on life cycle analysis in Section 4.3.) Figure 5.7 illustrates, in solid lines, the expected life cycles of an organization's current and projected outputs. Total required capacity is given by the heavy solid line, found by adding together the separate capacities of each of the required outputs. Note the projected dip in required capacity 5 years in the future, and, of course, beyond the 8-year R&D planning horizon.

The message of Figure 5.7 should be clear to the organization—an output with a 3-year life cycle (appearing similar to the dashed line) is needed between years 4 and 7 in order to maintain efficient utilization of the organization's available capacity. A priority output development program will have to be instituted immediately. At this point it is probably too late to develop something through R&D; a more effective strategy, especially in light of the relatively low volume and short life cycle, might be an extension of an existing output.

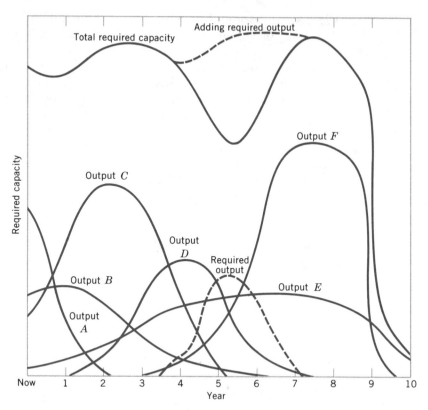

Figure 5.7 Forecast of required organizational capacity from multiple life cycles.

5.3 BREAKEVEN ANALYSIS

Breakeven analysis for new outputs.

The introduction of a new output into the organization's existing output mix should only be implemented if a complete economic analysis has been conducted beforehand. This analysis would consider the fixed cost of existing capacity, the variable costs of the output, the return from the output, and the effect of different volumes of demand. Such an evaluation is called a **breakeven** analysis (also known as "cost-volume-profit" analysis). It was originally developed as an accounting technique used in the preparation of a profit budget for the firm. The analysis is based on a simplified income or "profit and loss" statement, which can be written as

    revenue (price × units sold)
less   variable costs (variable cost per unit × units sold)
equals contribution margin
less   fixed costs
equals net profit

Simplifications of the breakeven concept.

Clearly, there are many simplifications in these quantities that will rarely hold in practice over a large range in output volume. For example, variable cost per unit may decrease, or increase, with larger output volumes. And small volumes of products are usually higher priced than if large volumes are sold. And in terms of our primary topic, capacity, fixed costs will certainly jump if additional facilities are necessary to increase output capacity.

Nevertheless, within small ranges of volumes the basic income statement relationship depicted above aids the operations manager in deciding whether or not a new product/service should be produced. Consider, for example, a sporting goods manufacturer who is faced with the decision of whether or not to produce a new fiberglass tennis racket.

Whataracket, Inc.

Sharon Rigg, operations manager for Whataracket, has determined a sales forecast for their new fiberglass tennis racket using one of the methods described in Chapter 4. The selling price assumed in preparing the forecast was $18. Sharon reasons that this price puts the racket somewhere in the medium price range for similar quality rackets. To determine total revenue she simply multiplies the selling price ($18) times the number of units (rackets) expected to be sold.

Revenue determination.

Variable costs from a number of sources.

Variable costs are the "per racket" costs of manufacturing and selling. The costs that would vary with the number of rackets sold are the fiberglass and bonding materials used in the racket, the nylon used to string the racket, the leather grip, and the labor and energy used to mold, string, assemble, and package the racket. Since the company has been in the sporting goods field for some time, and is familiar with the production methods required, a good estimate of variable costs can be made. Sharon estimates that the variable cost per racket will be $11.

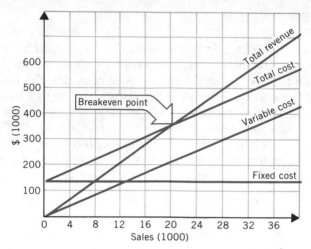

Figure 5.8 Breakeven graph for a tennis racket.

Elements of fixed costs.

Fixed costs are costs that do not vary with the volume of production or the number of rackets sold. In this case, the costs that would remain constant as production increased and decreased are building rent, insurance, property taxes, depreciation on equipment, administrative salaries, and interest on borrowed capital. Fixed costs are substantially determined through the selection of manufacturing equipment and the plant facility itself. The annual fixed costs associated with this new product have been determined to be $140,000. That is, the annual depreciation costs of the new molding equipment, the space rental, and other nonvariable costs total $140,000.

We can visually show each of the three factors bearing on net profit in the breakeven graph (Figure 5.8). Volume of sales is shown on the horizontal axis and dollars (of revenue or cost) are measured on the vertical axis. The point at which the total revenue (*TR*) line and the total cost (*TC*) line intersect (i.e., *TR* = *TC*) is called the *breakeven point*. It is given this name because the sales volume at this point is just enough to cover the fixed plus variable costs of operation without either earning a profit or suffering a loss. The firm just breaks even. For our sporting goods manufacturer we can see from the figure that the new tennis racket will break even if sales are about 20,000 units.

Breakeven point at the intersection of the revenue and cost lines.

For a more accurate analysis we should use algebra. The income statement can be written algebraically as follows.

revenue − variable costs − fixed costs = net profit

where

revenue = selling price × units sold

variable costs = variable cost/unit × units sold

If we let *SP* = selling price

$$U = \text{volume in units sold}$$
$$VC = \text{variable cost/unit}$$
$$FC = \text{fixed cost}$$
$$NP = \text{net profit}$$

then the income statement equation can be written as

$$(SP \times U) - (VC \times U) - FC = NP$$

and therefore the volume to meet a fixed net profit is

$$U = \frac{NP + FC}{SP - VC} \tag{5.2}$$

For example, to break even, and therefore earn a zero net profit, the number of units that must be manufactured and sold is

$$U = \frac{0 + 140,000}{18 - 11} = \frac{140,000}{7} = 20,000 \text{ units}$$

as surmised from the graph.

Another way to find the breakeven point is to set total revenue to total cost:

$$TR = TC$$

or

$$U(SP) = FC + U(VC)$$

so

$$U = \frac{FC}{SP - VC}$$
$$= 20,000 \text{ units}$$

as above. To earn a net profit of $10,000

$$U = \frac{10,000 + 140,000}{18 - 11} \approx 21,429 \text{ units}$$

If the best estimate for sales in units for the next period is less than 21,429 units, then the company will not earn the desired profit of $10,000 and should decide not to produce the product. If the sales forecast is for less than 20,000 units, then introduction of the new racket will result in a net loss for the firm.

One of the most useful aspects of the breakeven model for operations managers is its ability to clearly illustrate the overall effect of different managerial and environmental actions. For example, if inflation increases the variable costs by 10 percent, what will the new breakeven volume be? Or, what volume must be sold to maintain our current profit? Or, at current volumes what price increase will maintain current profits? For a discussion of the real importance of breakeven points to firms, see Figure 5.9.

Use of breakeven
for rules of thumb.

SLUMP FORCING FIRMS TO CUT COSTS
SO LOWER SALES STILL BRING A PROFIT

By Ralph E. Winter
Staff Reporter of The Wall Street Journal

After two recessions in two years, company executives are concentrating more on bringing down the break-even point, the sales level required to make a profit.

"A recession makes you analyze everything you do to see if it is worth continuing," says Robert H. Brethen, president of Philips Industries Inc., a Dayton, Ohio, maker of mobile-home parts and other products. "It's painful, but in a way it's healthy."

Such rigorous self-scrutiny is one of the few benefits business gets from a recession. (Collapse of competitors is another.) Besides keeping a company in the black when business is slow, a lower break-even point often permits a company to make extraordinarily good profits for a while after the economy improves.

Philips cut employment by about 700, or roughly 16%, during the past year, Mr. Brethen says. He notes that "hundreds of other nitty-gritty little savings," ranging from more-efficient manufacturing processes to cutting fuel consumption by the company's delivery trucks, have cut costs to the point that Philips could earn a profit if builders make only 200,000 mobile homes a year. That's down from a break-even point of about 230,000 two years ago. And if the industry turns out 280,000 homes, as Mr. Brethen hopes, profits could soar.

Unusually Severe Effort

This year, efforts to drive down the break-even point are unusually severe, even for a recession, because many company officials think the recovery may be weak and brief.

"Normal, as we have known it, just isn't going to return—ever," Carl R. Fiora, manager of Armco Inc.'s eastern steel division, told employees, explaining the need for a "comprehensive survival plan" to make the big Middletown, Ohio, works profitable when operating at less than 65% of capacity.

Prolonging the Slowdown

Concentrating on reducing the break-even point instead of on growth tends to pro-

long the slowdown, undermining the Reagan administration's hopes of a strong 1982–1983 recovery fueled by higher business investment. It also worsens unemployment.

Businessmen and economists add, however, that efforts to drive down the breakeven point help fight inflation, contributing to the recent decline in the basic inflation rate to 8% or less, from more than 12% two years ago. Moreover, a lower break-even point could help stave off bankruptcy if times get worse.

"There are two ways you can work at lowering the break-even point," says Leo W. Ladehoff, chairman and president of Dayton Malleable Inc., a foundry operator. "You can reduce costs through more-efficient methods and cutting overhead, or you can reduce capacity and the allied costs. . . . We've done both, and our break-even point is about 25% from what it was two years ago."

Another way to reduce the break-even point is to buy more parts from outside suppliers, cutting the number of plants a company must maintain in bad times. "Some manufacturers will own just the product design and engineering and then final assembly," says a manufacturing executive. "Everything else they will subcontract out, unless there's a critical component they don't trust anyone else to make. It's a very sensitive topic because it involves buying overseas and from nonunion shops parts that previously were made in union plants. But in a mature industry, you subcontract out a lot of cyclical risk."

Withdrawing from Markets

Still another approach is to withdraw from markets that generate profits only in good times. Retailers of all types are following that course these days. Restaurants are closing marginal units, and oil companies are pulling out of areas where they have only a few service stations. Marshall Field & Co. sold the Halle Bros. department store operation in Ohio, and the new owner is cutting it back to six stores from 16.

Companies usually pay a price for the lower break-even point. Severance pay, plant-closing costs and equipment write-offs frequently prevent any profit gain the first year. Polaroid Corp. last year established a $30.4 million reserve to cover the costs of getting

1,000 employees to retire early, and Jos. Schlitz Brewing Co. had a 1981 loss because of a $43.2 million charge for closing its old brewery in Milwaukee.

Furthermore, reducing the break-even point often requires cutting capacity, which could limit profits if an economic boom comes in 1983 or 1984. "I'm running my business like it's going to be painfully tough to get any growth in sales," says the owner of a privately held furniture-manufacturing concern. "People tell me, 'You won't be ready for the upturn when it comes,' " he says, "But I'll be happy to worry about that when it comes."

Figure 5.9 The importance of the breakeven point. (Reprinted by permission. *The Wall Street Journal*, 3 March 1982.)

Suppose, on the other hand, that, due to increased demand, management is planning on increasing capacity at a significant increase in fixed costs. Then what additional sales volume must occur to maintain current profits? Although the breakeven model is somewhat oversimplified, it is just this simplicity that makes it an ideal tool for operations managers. It allows quick, relatively accurate rules of thumb for small, day-to-day changes in production.

Simplicity as a virtue.

Comparing Capacity Alternatives

Comparing alternatives via breakeven.

Another important application of the breakeven concept for operations managers is the comparison of alternative methods of achieving capacity. For example, Figure 5.10 shows three different methods of producing a prod-

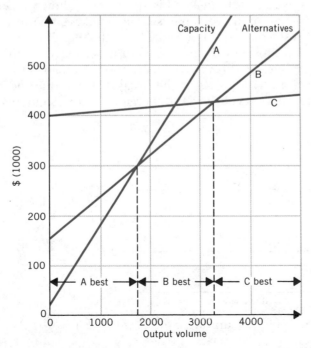

Figure 5.10 Capacity alternatives comparison.

uct. (Only the total cost functions are depicted.) Method A is an almost all-labor approach (VC = $160) with very little equipment (FC = $20,000) and hence is good for small volumes but very expensive for large volumes. On the other hand, Method C is a mass production automated factory with high fixed costs ($400,000) but low variable costs ($10) and hence is best for large output volumes. Method B (FC = $160,000; VC = $85) is a compromise between A and C.

Depending on the forecast of demand capacity required, now and in the not too distant future, either Method A, B, or C may be the wisest capacity choice. For example, for volumes in excess of 3200 units, Method C is best. This value can be determined by equating the costs of Methods B and C to find the intersection: $160,000 + 85U = 400,000 + 10U$ or $U = 3200$. But even though Method C can produce parts for much less than A or B, production must be quite high before C becomes the optimal alternative. Fixed costs add significantly to the total cost of operations, yet too often operations managers are attracted to investments solely on the basis of low *variable* costs. And then, after production has begun, they realize that their volume is not sufficient to reap these low variable cost rewards.

A managerial trap.

Application in the Public Sector

Because public sector organizations are not profit oriented, breakeven analysis is not directly applicable. But minor modification of the approach again makes the technique a useful aid for the public operations manager.

Public sector breakeven.

Although there are no "profits" involved in the operation of a public organization (e.g., a police department), there are revenues that are often fixed by the annual budget. This situation is shown in Figure 5.11. As with the traditional breakeven analysis, the breakeven point is the point at which the total cost line and the revenue line intersect. But, the interpretation here is somewhat different. To the right of the breakeven volume the organization exceeds its budgeted revenue—a situation analogous to a "loss" for a profit-oriented firm. To the left of the breakeven volume the organization is not "using up" all of its budget and therefore is not producing the level of service

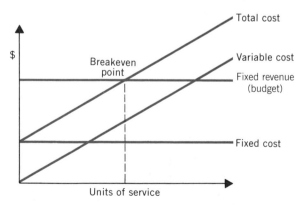

Figure 5.11 Fixed annual budget chart for public sector operations.

Ideal volume is the breakeven volume.

for which it was budgeted. The *ideal volume,* for the *public sector* organization, is the *breakeven volume.*

5.4 RESOURCE INVESTMENT TO GAIN CAPACITY

Capacity versus investment.

Up to this point we have considered the volume of productive capacity and the necessary resource investment to gain that capacity as proportional. In the case of one worker, or one machine, this is generally true but when many workers or machines or both are required to produce the output (as is usually the case) there is not a simple correspondence. That is, if rubber balls are molded in a machine run by one full-time worker at the rate of 100 per hour and a capacity of 1000 per hour is required, then the resource investment translates directly—10 workers and machines will be needed. For outputs involving more complex production operations the resource investment does not translate so directly with the required capacity, as illustrated in the example below.

Assume Whataracket produces a variety of rackets sequentially on four machines and the cycle time required for the fiberglass racket is as follows:

Machine 1: 4 minutes

Machine 2: 3 minutes

Machine 3: 10 minutes

Machine 4: 2 minutes

Cycle time based on the slowest machine.

To minimize the equipment cost, Sharon could use one of each machine and have a resulting output rate (based on the slowest machine cycle of 10 minutes) of six units per hour. In doing so, however, the first, second, and fourth machines would be idle 6, 7, and 8 minutes out of every 10-minute cycle for a utilization efficiency of only

$$\text{efficiency} = \frac{\text{output}}{\text{input}} = \frac{4 + 3 + 10 + 2}{4(10)} = 47.5\% \tag{5.3}$$

If Whataracket was willing to invest in a fifth machine of the same type as machine 3, Sharon could run machines 3 and 5 concurrently and put out *two* units every 10 minutes, obtaining an average cycle time of 5 minutes. The effect of this single investment would be to *double* her output rate to 12 units per hour and increase her efficiency to

$$\frac{4 + 3 + 5 + 2 + 5}{5(5)} = \frac{19}{25} = 76\%$$

Continuing in this manner results in the data shown in Table 5.5 and sketched in Figure 5.12.

Efficiency and output do not change at the same rate.

Note from the table and figure that efficiency of production does not always increase when machines are added, although the general trend is upward. This is because some systems are fairly well "balanced" to begin with (e.g., with 7 machines, the cycles are quite even, 2, 3, 3.33, 2; more so

Table 5.5   Return to Whataracket for Risking Use of More Machines

Number of Machines	Type Number of Next Machine	Machine Times (min)				Total Cycle Time	Hourly Output	Utilization Efficiency (%)
		No. 1	No. 2	No. 3	No. 4			
4	—	4	3	10	2	10	6	47.5
5	3	4	3	5	2	5	12	76.0
6	3	4	3	3.33	2	4	15	79.2
7	1	2	3	3.33	2	3.33	18	81.4
8	3	2	3	2.5	2	3	20	79.2
9	2	2	1.5	2.5	2	2.5	24	84.4
10	3	2	1.5	2	2	2	30	95.0
11	4	2	1.5	2	1	2	30	86.0
12	1	1.33	1.5	2	1	2	30	79.2
13	3	1.33	1.5	1.67	1	1.67	36	87.5
14	3	1.33	1.5	1.43	1	1.5	40	90.5

Natural operating points.

at 10 machines; and the addition of only one extra machine at such points does not pay for itself). If points of high efficiency are reached "early" (as machines are added), these points will tend to be natural operating solutions for Sharon's problem. For example, a tremendous gain in efficiency (and in output percentage) is reaped by adding a fifth machine to the system. Further additions do not gain much. The next largest gain is when the tenth machine is added to the system.

Although this analysis describes the general tradeoffs of the system, no mention has been made of demand. Suppose demand was 15 units per hour. Then, to minimize risk but still keep an efficient system, Sharon might use five machines and either work overtime, undersupply the market, or use a number of other strategies, as will be discussed later. Similarly, for a demand of 25 to 35 per hour, the use of 10 machines would be appropriate.

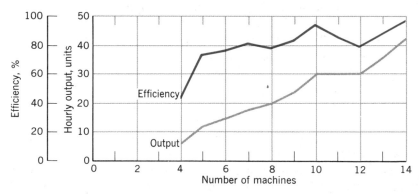

Figure 5.12   Efficiency and output increases from adding machines.

5.5 THE MULTIPLE OUTPUTS PROBLEM AND LINEAR PROGRAMMING

The best output mix.

Throughout our discussion of capacity planning we have referred to the complications that multiple outputs place on both capacity planning and scheduling. The objective, of course, is to maximize the returns to the organization by selecting the best mix of outputs which do not exceed the organization's resource capacity limitations. This problem is known as the **output mix problem.** To determine this best mix of outputs requires simultaneously considering three factors:

Three factors.

1. The forecast demand for each output.
2. The resource requirements for each output.
3. The relative return of each output.

The expected demand for each output provides an upper limit on the number of each that will be provided. There is no reason that an organization would want to produce more of a product or service than can be expected to be consumed. The organizational resource requirements for each output determine the maximum number of each type of output that can be produced. For example, if a social worker can make only five visits per day and the municipal social services department employs seven social workers, then we cannot expect to "produce" more than 35 visits per day.

The return to the organization from the production of each type of output does not limit or constrain the organization in the amounts that can be produced or sold but rather guides management in maximizing the returns to the organization. The contribution of each of the different outputs toward the objective of maximizing the total return to the organization is measured by the *contribution margin,* as it is called, which tells management the increase in return for providing one more unit of a given output.

Contribution margin.

Some products and services have higher marginal returns than others. For example, in a restaurant, the marginal profit on wines and liquors is higher than the return on the same dollar amount of food. And auto dealers earn a higher contribution for each dollar in sales from accessory items than they do from basic automobiles.

Limited resources.

Linear programming.

If demand and resources were both unlimited, then the obvious conclusion regarding optimal output mix would be to make and sell *"everything,"* that is, everything that has a positive contribution margin. But demand is *seldom* unlimited, even though it may appear to be for short time periods, and resources are *never* unlimited. The question then becomes: How do we simultaneously consider all three sets of factors to arrive at the best combination of outputs? One answer to this question is provided by **linear programming,** a mathematical tool demonstrated in the following example.

Addemup, Inc.

Addemup, Inc., is a relatively small firm in the fast-growing pocket calculator market. Addemup entered the business with the production of an inexpensive

Table 5.6 Variable Costs
of Calculator Production

	A-1000	A-2000
Labor	$ 3.00	$ 5.00
Material	6.00	12.00
Factory overhead	2.00	2.00
Total	$11.00	$19.00

four-function hand-held calculator, the A-1000, which sells for $15. It has recently added a more powerful version of the A-1000 (it has square, square root, and percent functions) named the A-2000. The A-2000 sells for $25.

The variable costs of producing an A-1000 and an A-2000 are given in Table 5.6.

Addemup produces its own integrated circuits (the internal logic of the calculator) and purchases all other materials from other firms. Manufacturing of integrated circuits is a complex operation, which requires precision equipment. Addemup has the capacity to produce, at most, 61,000 four-function circuit boards per month. One of these circuits boards is used in each A-1000 calculator produced. It takes three times as long on this precision equipment to manufacture the seven-function circuit board for the A-2000 calculator (i.e., add, subtract, multiply, divide, square, square root, percent) as it does for the A-1000. Therefore, if they made no four-function circuits at all, they could produce no more than 20,333 (i.e., 61,000/3) of the A-2000 boards. Addemup can manufacture any combination of A-1000 and A-2000 circuit boards, as long as the combined production time does not exceed the available capacity.

Assembly time on the two calculators is

A-1000: 0.2 hr
A-2000: 0.25 hr

If the company maintains its current two-shift operation it has available 8000 hours of assembly time per month.

The marketing manager has undertaken a detailed study of the calculator market and foresees a monthly demand of 40,000 units for the A-1000 calculator and 18,000 units for the A-2000.

If we assume that Addemup is interested in maximizing its monthly profit, we can begin to structure this problem in a way that will lead to a relatively simple solution procedure. Total monthly profit for next year will be equal to the marginal profit of each calculator times the number of each produced and sold.

If we let

$A1$ = number of A-1000s produced and sold
$A2$ = number of A-2000s produced and sold

then we can write an equation for the monthly profit as follows:

$$\text{profit} = (15 - 11)A1 + (25 - 19)A2$$
$$= 4A1 + 6A2$$

If the capacity were available and if the marketing manager's demand forecasts are correct, the company could expect to earn

$$\text{monthly profit} = 4(40,000) + 6(18,000)$$
$$= \$268,000$$

But there is only limited circuit manufacturing capacity so even though they may be able to *sell* 40,000 A-1000s and 18,000 A-2000s, the capacity is not available to produce these quantities. The capacity to produce circuit boards thus limits the number of calculators that can be manufactured and sold. Using the same notation as before, we can algebraically express this capacity limitation as

$$1(A1) + 3(A2) \leq 61,000$$

This inequality states that Addemup can produce either 61,000 A-1000s and no A-2000s, or 20,333 A-2000s and no A-1000s, or any combination of A-1000s and A-2000s that does not exceed the 61,000 equivalent circuit capacity.

But circuit manufacturing is not the only limited resource. Assembly time is limited to 8000 hours per month. This capacity restriction can be written as

$$0.2(A1) + 0.25(A2) \leq 8000$$

This inequality states that the hours used to assemble A-1000s (0.2 hours/unit × number of units) plus the hours to assemble A-2000s (0.25 hours/unit × number of units) must not exceed the available assembly time (8000 hours).

Finally, the restrictions on demand for the two models must be considered. The marketing manager expects to be able to sell 40,000 A-1000s and 18,000 A-2000s. Since we do not want to produce any more than we can sell, the following two **constraints** must also be included.

$$A1 \leq 40,000$$
$$A2 \leq 18,000$$

The first constraint states that the number of A-1000s produced cannot exceed 40,000 units and the second constraint states that the number of A-2000s cannot exceed 18,000.

Bringing together all of the previous equations and inequalities we have the following mathematical formulation of the problem.

maximize: profit $= 4A1 + 6A2$ (objective)
subject to the following limitations:

$$
\begin{aligned}
A1 + 3A2 &\leq 61,000 \quad \text{(circuit manufacturing capacity)} \\
0.2A1 + 0.25A2 &\leq 8,000 \quad \text{(assembly time capacity)} \\
A1 &\leq 40,000 \quad \text{(maximum demand for A-1000s)} \\
A2 &\leq 18,000 \quad \text{(maximum demand for A-2000s)}
\end{aligned}
$$

146 Part I STRATEGIC OPERATIONS

Again, our objective is to find the combination of A-1000s and A-2000s that can be produced and sold, within the limitations of capacity and demand, to maximize profit.

This output mix problem is in a form that can be solved by *linear programming*. Linear programming is a mathematical technique that can solve management problems characterized by

1. A single **objective** (e.g., maximize profit) that can be stated algebraically as a linear equation.
2. A set of **constraints** (e.g., capacities) that can be stated algebraically as linear equalities or inequalities.
3. One or more management decision variables (e.g., how much to produce of each output) that can assume only nonnegative values.

In this highly simplified example only two products and a few limited organizational resources were considered, but linear programming can and has been used to solve much larger, more realistic product mix problems. In the lumber and petroleum refining industries it is not uncommon to see computer solutions to linear programs with hundreds of constraints and thousands of variables. "Canned" (preprogrammed) computer packages are available from a number of computer manufacturers, research organizations, and universities [3] to solve linear programming problems.

Computer packages.

Although it is beyond the scope of this text to teach linear programming solution techniques, in the appendix to this chapter we present a simple graphical solution procedure for linear programming problems and demonstrate it with the Addemup example. (For other linear programming solution methods and further discussion see References 1 and 11.)

The solution to Addemup's output mix problem is to produce 25,000 A-1000s and 12,000 A-2000s for a total profit of $172,000. This solution uses all the assembly time capacity

$$0.2(25,000) + 0.25(12,000) = 8000 \text{ hr}$$

and all the circuit manufacturing capacity

$$1(25,000) + 3(12,000) = 61,000 \text{ equivalent boards}$$

Slack, surplus, and dual variables.

One of the advantages of using a computerized linear programming routine is the additional information it provides. For example, standard outputs will also include the values of "slack," "surplus," and "dual" variables for the four constraints. For our problem, there are no surplus variables, but the slacks on the constraints would be, in order, 0, 0, 15,000, and 6000. These values indicate the residual amount of each resource or the amount that was *not* used. We saw in the solution that *all* the circuit manufacturing and assembly time capacities were used, so there was no slack for these resources. However, we did not reach the maximum demand for either A-1000 or A-2000 model calculators, so slack existed here.

The dual variables for each constraint represent the incremental value to us of *one* more unit of that resource. Since there was slack in meeting the demand for A-1000 and A-2000 models, their dual variables are zero. That is, another unit of *demand* for either of these two models would not help our profit because we are at the limit of our resources already—we cannot even supply the existing demand! However, more circuit manufacturing capacity or assembly time capacity would have value to us. The dual variable is $0.60 for the former and $18 for the latter. This means that another hour of circuit manufacturing capacity would increase our profit by $0.60, but another hour of assembly time capacity would be worth 30 times as much.

5.6 CAPACITY AND RISK: THE DECISION TREE

Considering uncertainty in the capacity decision.

In previous examples we assumed that the operations manager, in trying to estimate future capacity needs, could reliably estimate the values of the factors that affect the profitability of a new output. Those factors were the selling price, the variable cost, the fixed cost, and the demand for which capacity would have to be available. If any one of these factors is uncertain (and generally all will be), the analysis becomes more complicated. Consider, for example, the following situation.

Whataracket is considering the introduction of one of two low-priced rackets: a standard wooden racket that would sell for the going rate, about $20, and a fiberglass racket that could sell either at the low end of the fiberglass range for $18 or in the middle of the range for $25. (It is not a "high quality" racket.) Sales for the wooden racket can be reliably predicted to be about 25,000 units. However, sales of the fiberglass racket are more difficult to predict. Sharon estimates that at the lower price there is a 50-50 chance that sales will either be slightly below expectations, averaging 30,000 units, or slightly above, averaging 40,000 units. At the higher price of $25 she feels there is a wider possible range of demand. She estimates there is a 20 percent chance sales will be as high as 25,000 units, a 50 percent chance they will be about 20,000 units, and a 30 percent chance they will be as low as 10,000 units.

The wooden racket requires only a minimal amount of additional production equipment since the manufacturer has some excess capacity for wood forming in the current plant. The annual fixed cost of this additional capacity will be $30,000. The variable cost per wooden racket is known to be $15. The annual fixed costs to add the capacity to produce the fiberglass racket are much higher, $140,000, but the variable cost is only $11. If no action is taken there is no cost (though in other situations there could be penalty or ill will costs).

All of the above data are summarized in Table 5.7. Understandably, given this mass of information, Sharon wonders how to determine which racket to select and, if she selects the fiberglass racket, at what price it should be sold. A modeling procedure developed primarily for sequential decisions, called a **decision tree,** will help Sharon analyze these data.

The decision tree construction.

The decision tree is formed, sequentially, from the left to the right, as **decision points** and **chance points,** both known as **nodes,** are encountered in

Table 5.7   Whataracket, Inc., Racket Data

Factors	Alternatives			
	$20 Wooden	*$18 Fiberglass*	*$25 Fiberglass*	*Nothing*
$ new fixed cost	30,000	140,000	140,000	0
$ variable cost	15	11	11	0
$ margin	5	7	14	0
Demand/probability	25,000/1.0	30,000/.5	25,000/.20	0
		40,000/.5	20,000/.50	
			10,000/.30	

time. Decision nodes are indicated by squares and chance nodes by circles. Connecting the nodes are **branches.**

Branches from decision nodes— choose one.

- Branches emanating to the right of decision nodes indicate all the possible management decision alternatives available at that point. If a cost or return accompanies any of the decisions, that fact is indicated in parentheses along the decision branch. At every decision node one branch must be selected by the decision maker.

Branches from chance nodes— calculate average.

- Branches emanating to the right of chance points indicate all the possible results that may occur. The decision maker has no alternative here but to observe what course nature takes. Each branch is labeled with its probability of occurrence, and if a cost or return is involved, it is so indicated in parentheses. At every chance node the expected value of the possible outcomes is calculated.

At the ends of the branches all costs and rewards are totaled to give the outcome of that path. The analysis then starts from this point on the right and works backward.

The decision tree for the sporting goods manufacturer is illustrated in Figure 5.13. At the left, the decision node indicates three possible decision alternatives: wooden (with an investment of $30,000), fiberglass ($140,000 investment), or neither (investment of 0). If the wooden alternative is chosen, only one result is expected: sales of 25,000 units. If neither racket is developed there will be no sales (but no loss either). If the fiberglass alternative is chosen (refer to figure), then another decision must be made: to price the racket at $18 for a contribution margin of $7 ($18–$11 variable cost) or to price it at $25 with a contribution margin of $14. Following the $18 branch, two results may occur, each with a 50 percent chance: sales of 30,000 units and sales of 40,000 units. Along the $25 branch, three outcomes are possible: sales of 10,000, 20,000, or 25,000 units with probabilities of .3, .5, and .2, respectively.

At this point the problem is formulated in the decision tree format. Next it must be solved. To solve the tree we start at the far *right* and work backward to the beginning of the problem at the left, the first decision node. To evaluate the branches of the tree we employ the expected value concept, as illustrated in Figure 5.13.

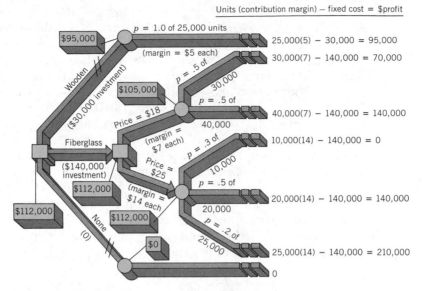

Units (contribution margin) − fixed cost = \$profit

$p = 1.0$ of 25,000 units

$95,000

(margin = \$5 each)

$p = .5$ of 30,000

$105,000

Wooden (\$30,000 investment)

Price = \$18

$p = .5$ of 40,000

Fiberglass

(margin = \$7 each)

$p = .3$ of 10,000

(\$140,000 investment)

Price = \$25

$112,000

(margin = \$14 each)

$p = .5$ of 20,000

$112,000

$112,000

None (0)

$p = .2$ of 25,000

$0

25,000(5) − 30,000 = 95,000

30,000(7) − 140,000 = 70,000

40,000(7) − 140,000 = 140,000

10,000(14) − 140,000 = 0

20,000(14) − 140,000 = 140,000

25,000(14) − 140,000 = 210,000

0

Figure 5.13 Whataracket, Inc., decision tree.

If the *wooden* racket is introduced, the net profit will be [25,000 units × (\$20 price − \$15 variable cost)] − \$30,000 fixed cost = \$95,000. This value is indicated in the rectangle attached to the result node at the top of the diagram. Similarly, "\$0" is indicated for the *"none"* alternative and is shown in the rectangle attached to its result node. The "price = \$18" decision branch of the fiberglass alternative is evaluated as

$$\begin{aligned} \text{expected net profit} = {} & .5[30{,}000 \text{ units} \times (\$18 \text{ price} - \$11 \\ & \text{variable cost}) - \$140{,}000 \text{ fixed cost}] \\ & + .5[40{,}000 \text{ units} \times (\$18 \text{ price} - \$11 \\ & \text{variable cost}) - \$140{,}000 \text{ fixed cost}] \\ = {} & \$105{,}000 \end{aligned}$$

which is shown in the rectangle attached to the "\$18 price" result node. Similarly, the "price = \$25" decision branch is evaluated as

$$\begin{aligned} \text{expected net profit} &= .3(\$0) + .5(\$140{,}000) + .2(\$210{,}000) \\ &= \$112{,}000 \end{aligned}$$

which is shown attached to the "price = \$25" result node.

At this point the manufacturer must decide between the \$18 racket and the \$25 racket. With the former the net profit is expected to be \$105,000 and with the latter, \$112,000. Since the expected net profit from the introduction of the \$25 racket is greater than the expected profit for the \$18 racket, the \$25 price should be chosen. An arrow is drawn on the "price = \$25" branch to indicate the decision and, correspondingly, hash marks on the nonchosen branches. The value \$112,000 is then indicated in a rectangle attached to the price decision node.

Last, we must decide whether to choose the wooden or fiberglass racket or to introduce no new rackets at all. Just as we did previously in deciding between the two prices for the fiberglass racket, we select the alternative with the *largest expected net profit*. The fiberglass racket with an expected net profit of $112,000 is the best alternative; it has the highest **expected value.**

Other decision criteria may also exist.

Note that in this analysis, the criterion of choice was the *expected value.* This may not, however, always be the best criterion. For example, the fiberglass, $25 price decision has a 30 percent chance of selling only 10,000 rackets, resulting in a net profit of $0. Thirty percent is a rather high chance of just breaking even. By choosing the wooden racket alternative the manufacturer would be "guaranteed" (assuming that the sales estimate is accurate and reliable) a $95,000 profit. Thus, the question the manufacturer must answer is: Is an additional $17,000 of *expected* profit worth the 30 percent risk of making nothing? This is a subjective decision, based on personal values, which only the manufacturer can make; the role of the decision tree is to *pose* these types of questions.

5.7 APPENDIX: GRAPHICAL SOLUTION TO A LINEAR PROGRAM

If a linear program has only two decision variables, as does the Addemup example, a simple solution procedure is the graphical method. The method begins by developing a graph that can be used to display the possible solutions (values of $A1$ and $A2$). We will show the solution to our linear program to be the most profitable number of A-1000s and A-2000s.

Plotting the Constraints

By using a graph to plot the constraints and objective we can begin to limit the set of solution points to only those that satisfy the constraints in the problem. But remember that only nonnegative values of $A1$ and $A2$ are possible. Consider, first, the constraint on circuit manufacturing capacity, which was of the form

$$A1 + 3A2 \leq 61,000$$

We want to locate all of the solution points that satisfy this relationship, and therefore we start by plotting the line corresponding to the equation

$$A1 + 3A2 = 61,000$$

Plotting the constraints.

To plot this line we need only find two points on the line and then draw a straight line through the points. The simplest way of finding two points on the line is to first set $A1$ equal to zero and solve for $A2$, and then set $A2$ equal to zero and solve for $A1$.

If $A1 = 0$, then $3A2 = 61,000$ or $A2 = 20,333$

Therefore, (0;20,333) is on the line.

If $A2 = 0$, then $A1 = 61,000$

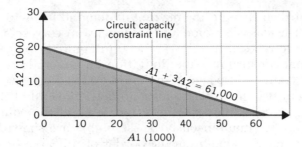

Figure 5.14 Circuit capacity constraint.

Therefore, (61,000;0) is on the line. With these two points we can plot the equation

$$A1 + 3A2 = 61,000$$

which is called the circuit capacity constraint. The line is shown in Figure 5.14. We know that for any ≤ constraints the solution points that satisfy the constraint are

1. All points on the constraint line itself.

2. All points below the constraint line.

All points that satisfy the circuit capacity constraint are shown by the shaded area in Figure 5.14.

Next, we can identify all points satisfying the assembly time capacity constraint

$$0.2A1 + 0.25A2 \leq 8000$$

Again, we draw the line corresponding to the equation

$$0.2A1 + 0.25A2 = 8000$$

as shown in Figure 5.15.

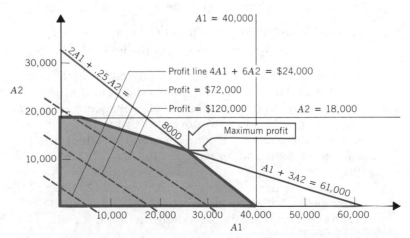

Figure 5.15 Feasible region with isoprofit lines.

Our third constraint, the maximum demand for A-1000s, is given by $A1 \leq 40,000$. The feasible region for this constraint corresponds to all points to the left of the vertical line $A1 = 40,000$ in Figure 5.15.

The final constraint is the limitation on demand for A-2000s, which is $A2 \leq 18,000$ and is also shown in Figure 5.15.

Finding the feasible region.

Since our original intention was to determine all of the points that satisfied the four constraints, we must locate all of the points that satisfy the four constraints simultaneously. These points are shown in Figure 5.15 by the shaded area. Any point on the border of this area or within the area is a *feasible solution* to the linear program. The whole set of points is called the *feasible region.* Any one of these points is a potential solution point, but only *one* of them (in this case) will be the *optimal solution point.*

Finding the Maximum Profit Solution Point

Because there are such a great number of feasible solution points, it is virtually impossible to determine the solution point that maximizes profit by trial and error. A less time-consuming method than this is to continue with our graphical analysis of the problem. The objective that we want to maximize is given by the equation

$$\text{profit} = 4A1 + 6A2$$

Plotting the profit line.

If we arbitrarily select some value of profit, we can then plot a profit line just as we plotted the constraint lines. For example, the set of points that yield a profit of $24,000 is given by

$$4A1 + 6A2 = 24,000$$

This profit line is superimposed on the feasible region in Figure 5.15.

Clearly, there are an infinite number of points that will yield a profit of $24,000; that is, all of the points on the "profit = $24,000" line that are in the feasible region. Since our objective is to maximize profit, we select larger and larger values for profit and plot the lines as shown in Figure 5.15.

What you should recognize by now is that

1. The profit lines are parallel to one another.

2. The further the line moves to the right, the higher the profit.

Moving the profit line to maximize profits.

Realizing this, a logical solution procedure is to simply move the profit line *parallel* to the lines already determined and to the *upper right.* As we do this, we are moving in the direction of higher and higher profits, but eventually we will not be able to move the profit line any farther without moving outside the feasible region. The point at which the profit line is farthest to the upper right and just touches the feasible region is the point of maximum profit.

Reading from the graph this point is (25,000; 12,000). That is, to maximize profit Addemup should produce and sell 25,000 A-1000 calculators and 12,000 A-2000 calculators, resulting in a net profit of $172,000 [4(25,000) + 6(12,000)].

5.8 SUMMARY AND KEY LEARNING POINTS

In this chapter we have looked at the task of translating forecasts of demand into capacity plans, both short- and long-term, and the capacity alternatives available to the manager. We studied the learning process and determined its effect on capacity needs. We examined output life cycles and saw the importance of balancing different life cycles to minimize changes in capacity requirements.

Breakeven analysis concepts were examined and their applicability for evaluating capacity alternatives, as well as "profitability" in both profit and nonprofit organizations, was demonstrated. Following this, measures of output capacity and utilization efficiency were calculated for incremental increases in capital resource investments. Linear programming was then employed to determine the best mix of outputs for a fixed level of production capacity. A graphical solution approach was then illustrated in the chapter appendix. Last, decision trees were presented as one way to handle uncertainty in demand, cost, and other such factors when capacity plans are being made.

The key learning points have been

- Capacity planning concerns the *acquisition* of productive resources whereas scheduling concerns the *timing* of their use. Poor scheduling can lead to "bottlenecks," which effectively limit the capacity of the production process.

- Capacity planning for pure services is more difficult in the short run because no facilitating good can be produced during idle periods and inventoried for later demand.

- Short-run alternatives fall largely into five categories: increasing resource levels, improving resource use, modifying the output, modifying the demand, and not meeting the demand.

- The effect of learning is to improve capacity levels, especially in the short term with new or unfamiliar tasks. Each time the output doubles, the required manhours per unit decreases to a fixed percentage of the previous value, this percentage being known as the "learning rate."

- The careful matching of output life cycles can minimize changes in the capacity needs of an organization and contribute to utilization efficiency.

- Breakeven analysis is a valuable tool for profitability and capacity planning in both profit and nonprofit organizations. For example, the costs of capacity alternatives can be compared as a function of output volume to make the best choice and minimize risk.

- Output rates in a productive system with sequential processing will always be limited to the slowest task in the system. Efficiency of the system is calculated as the value of the output divided by the value of the input.

- Linear programming can be used to find the best mix of outputs. The objective function is to either maximize profits or minimize cost. The constraints include capacity and demand limitations, as well as other unique considerations of the situation.

● A decision tree is constructed from the left to the right in chronological order but solved from the right to the left. Expected values are calculated for chance points and alternatives are selected at decision nodes until the tree is completely solved. Decision alternatives may be selected on the basis of maximum expected value, minimum risk, or some other criterion.

5.9 KEY TERMS

Gantt chart (p. 121)	**constraints** (p. 146)	**branches** (p. 148)
infinite loading (p. 121)	**objective function** (p. 146)	**decision points** (p. 148)
breakeven (p. 135)	**output mix problem** (p. 142)	**chance points** (p. 148)
learning curve (p. 125)	**decision tree** (p. 148)	**expected value** (p. 150)
linear programming (p. 143)	**nodes** (p. 148)	

5.10 REVIEW AND DISCUSSION QUESTIONS

1. Suppose per unit variable costs decrease as volume increases. Draw the breakeven chart. What happens to per unit profit above and below the breakeven point?

2. Frequently, simple models such as breakeven are much more appealing to management than more sophisticated ones (such as linear programming). Why might this be so?

3. What are the dangers for a not-for-profit organization in operating *below* the breakeven point? *Above* the breakeven point?

4. The decision tree example in the chapter alluded to the fact that a manager may decide *not* to follow the solution of the tree. For what conditions might such a strategy be appropriate?

5. How does the existence of multiple outputs complicate capacity planning?

6. Does the learning curve continue downward forever?

7. What marketing approaches are useful in capacity planning?

8. How do operations managers estimate what capacity will be needed with multiple, complex outputs?

9. Explain how the addition of equipment in Section 5.4 *lowered* efficiency. What does this say about replacing labor with machines to increase productivity?

10. Why is short-run capacity planning for services more difficult than for products? Are there more or fewer alternatives available?

11. Texas Instruments, like the Japanese, counts on long-term capacity increases through learning. Is this generally applicable to American industry?

12. Exactly what are the unit cost decreases that occur with larger facilities due to economies of scale? Might any costs *increase* with facility size?

5.11 PROBLEMS

Practice Problems

1. Solve this problem without using Tables 5.3 or 5.4. If a second unit requires 60 mh to produce and the fourth unit requires 42 mh, how many manhours will the eighth unit require?

2. If unit 1 requires 6 mh and unit 5 requires 1.8, what is the learning rate? What will unit 6 require? What have the first 5 units required in total?

3. If unit 1 required 200 hours to produce and the labor records for a contract of 50 units indicate an *average* labor content of 63.1 hours per unit, what was the learning rate? What total *additional* number of manhours would be required for another contract of 50 units? What would be the average labor content of this second contract? Of both contracts combined? If labor costs the vendor $10 per hour on this Air Force contract and the price to the Air Force is a fixed $550 each, what can you say about the profitability of the first and second contracts, and hence the bidding process in general?

4. All of the reports you wrote for one class had three sections: Introduction, Analysis, Conclusions. The times required to complete these sections (including typing, etc.) are shown below in hours.

Report	Introduction	Analysis	Conclusion
1	1.5	6	2
2	—	(lost data)	—
3	1	3	0.8

The class requires 5 reports in all. You are now starting report 4 and, though you are now working faster, you can only afford to spend 1 hour a day on these reports. Report 5 is due in one week (7 days). Will you be done in time?

5. Given a fixed cost of $2000, unit variable cost of $180, price of $200, and current sales volume of 120, how should $200 be invested? It can be used either to decrease variable cost by 10 percent or to increase sales volume by 15 percent. Find the net profitability of each alternative.

6. River City operates a Senior Services Department providing specialized services to senior citizens. One program, the Meals on Wheels program, is partially funded by the federal government and partially funded by collections from recipients who can afford to pay. The fixed cost of operating the program is $60,000 per year and the variable cost is $0.80 per meal. The federal contribution to the program is $140,000. If, on the average, $0.35 of the cost of each meal is covered by recipient contributions, how many meals can be served annually?

7. The breakeven volume had to be revised for a particular project which involved the manufacture of a component whose price was $3 per unit and unit variable cost was $1.50. Due to unforeseen material cost escalation, there was a 10 percent increase in unit variable cost, and thus the breakeven volume had to be revised. By what percentage does the breakeven increase or decrease?

8. Given the following four capacity alternatives, find the best production method for every production volume.

Method	Fixed Cost, dollars	Variable Cost, dollars/unit
A	200	5
B	100	10
C	150	4
D	250	2

9. Tom's Tom-Toms produces toy drums sequentially on three machines A, B, and C with cycle times of 3, 4, and 6 minutes, respectively. Determine the optimum utilization efficiency and output rates for adding 1, 2, . . . , 6 more machines.

10. Shootemup, Inc., makes fireworks for the holiday season. They have two skyrocket lines available to fill an order of 2000 skyrockets. Line "Wan," as it is called, can produce skyrockets at four per hour and is available for 600 hours at a cost of $10 per hour. Line "Tuo" is newer and can produce a skyrocket every 12 minutes but is only available for 340 hours at a cost of $8 per hour. Formulate a linear program to find the best production plan. What seems like a logical solution? Compare it with your formulation.

11. In another department Shootemup makes both firecrackers and Roman candles (RCs) on one automated line followed by hand assemblers. The line can handle either 1000 RCs or 2000 firecrackers (or any linear combination) per day. The assemblers can produce either 1500 RCs or 1700 firecrackers (or any combination) per day. The company has contracted to produce at least 800 firecrackers and 400 RCs a day. If the profit of firecrackers is $0.02 each and RCs is $0.03 each, formulate a linear program to determine the best production plan.

12. Solve the following decision tree.

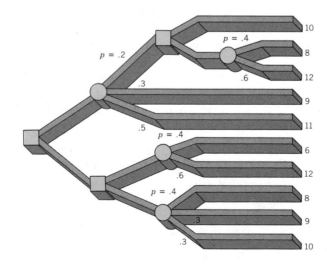

13. Solve the following tree where the rewards and costs are given along the branches instead of at the ends.

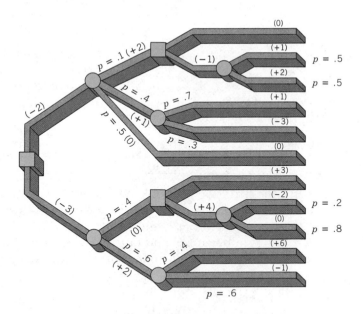

More Complex Problems

14. If, in Figure 5.1, Job 1 sequentially requires 10 hours on A, 10 hours on C, 29 hours on A, 20 hours on B, and 7 hours on C and Job 2 requires 15 hours on B, 10 hours on A, 8 hours on C, 11 hours on A, and 10 hours on B, how soon can both jobs realistically be completed? Does it help if operations can be split, that is, to take a job off a resource for a few hours to let the other job pass through?

15. A defense contractor is bidding on a military contract for 100 radar units. The contractor employs 30 machine operators who work 165 hours a month each. The first radar unit required 1145 machine operator hours, and the learning curve for this type of work is known to be 75 percent. It takes a month to order and receive raw material components, which cost $500 per radar unit. The material is then paid for in the month it is received. Fixed costs include a month to tool up, which costs $10,000, and then $5000 per month for every month of production. Direct labor and variable overhead is $8 per hour. The contractor can only deliver completed units and is paid the following month. Profit is set at 10 percent of the bid price. Find the bid price, derive the production schedule, and calculate the cash flow schedule.

16. The controller of ABC Co. arrived at the following cost structure relating to the introduction of a new product. Calculate the breakeven volume, assuming a price of $7.75 per unit.

	Production Volume	
	10,000 units	*20,000 units*
Capital costs	60,000	60,000
Material at 1.50 per unit	15,000	30,000
Labor at 0.75 per unit	7,500	15,000
Overhead:		
Fixed	10,000	10,000
Variable at 0.25 per unit	2,500	5,000
Selling and administrative expense:		
Fixed	5,000	5,000
Variable	7,500	10,000
Total costs	107,500	135,000

17. Assume the situation in Problem 9 but with two identical lines operating, each with machines A, B, and C. If new machines can be shared between the lines, how should 1, 2, and then 3 new machines be added? What are the resulting efficiencies and outputs of the two lines? Is it always best to *equally* share extra machines between the two lines?

18. Sherwood Acres, a central Kentucky farm, grows tobacco and soybeans on its 350 acres of land. An acre of soybeans brings a $150 profit and an acre of tobacco brings a $500 profit. Because of state agricultural regulations, no more than 150 acres can be planted in tobacco. Each acre of tobacco requires 100 mh of labor over the growing season and each acre of soybeans requires 20 mh. There are 16,000 mh of labor available during the growing season. How many acres should be planted in tobacco and how many in soybeans to maximize profit? Use the graphical method.

19. Robin, Inc., produces two different concrete products with the following price and input data.

	Selling Price ($)	Input Requirements		
		Material (lb)	Power Consumed (kWh)	Labor (hr)
Construction blocks	0.75	4	0.1	0.04
Decorative blocks	1.75	3	0.2	0.10

Labor cost is $5 per hour, materials cost $0.05 per pound and power costs $1.00 per kWh. If the company is limited to

100,000 lb of material
9000 kWh of power
1200 hr of labor

and if demand for decorative blocks is at most 3500 units, what quantity of each block should be produced to maximize profit? Use the graphical method to solve.

20. A company is trying to evaluate whether a second repair worker is needed to oversee two complex machines with daily failure probabilities of .05 and .08, respectively. With one machine down the company loses $1000 per hour; with both down it loses $3000 per hour. The time for a repair worker to repair one machine is 2 hours. With two repair workers the time is 80 minutes. The daily cost of a second repair worker, including the tools, is $200. Determine if the company should hire the second person. If so, how should the workers operate when both machines fail at the same time?

21. PDQ Co. is attempting to select between Method B and Method C in Problem 8. A history of their demand data indicates that they face an essentially normal distribution with a mean of 9 units and standard deviation of 6 units. Which method minimizes total costs for PDQ?

5.12 CASE

EXIT MANUFACTURING COMPANY

The planning committee of Exit Manufacturing Company (made up of the vice-presidents of marketing, finance, and production) was discussing the plans for a new factory to be located outside of Atlanta, Georgia. The factory would produce prehung metal-over-Styrofoam insulated exterior doors. The doors would be made in a standard format with 15 different insert panels which could be added after manufacture by a retail organization. The standardization of construction is expected to create numerous production efficiencies over competing factories that produce multidimensional doors. Atlanta was felt to be an ideal site because of its location in the heart of the sun belt with its growing construction history. By locating close to these growing states, distribution costs would be minimized also.

The capital cost for the factory was expected to be $14 million. Annual maintenance expenses were projected to total 5 percent of capital. Fuel and utility costs were expected to be $500,000 per year. An analysis of the area's labor market indicated that a wage rate of $7.50 per hour could be expected. The new facility was estimated to require 1.5 mh of operating labor per door. Fringe benefits paid to the operating labor were expected to equal 15 percent

of direct labor costs. Supervisory, clerical, technical, and managerial salaries were forecast to total $350,000 per year. Taxes and insurance would cost $200,000 per year. Other miscellaneous expenses were expected to total $250,000 per year. Depreciation was based on a 30-year life with use of the straight-line method and a $4,000,000 salvage value. Sheet metal, Styrofoam, adhesive for the doors, and frames were projected to cost $8.00 per door. Paint, hinges, door knobs and accessories were estimated to total $4.80 per door. The crating and shipping supplies were expected to cost $1.50 per door. Production labor has been estimated to be 1.5 hours per door produced.

Exit's marketing manager prepared the following price-demand chart for the distribution area of the new plant. Through analysis of these data the committee felt they could verify their belief of an increase from 15 to 25 percent in the current market share due to the cost advantage of standardization.

Average Sales Price ($/door)	Area Sales (in units)
$ 80	40,000
93	38,000
105	31,000
125	22,000

Questions for Discussion

Develop a breakeven capacity analysis for Exit's new door and determine

1. The best price, production rate, and profit.

2. The breakeven production rate and cost with the price in 1.

3. The breakeven price with the production rate in 1.

4. The sensitivity of profit to variable cost, price, and production rate.

What are the risks of operating so close the Break-even pt.

5.13 REFERENCES AND BIBLIOGRAPHY

1. Anderson, D. R., Sweeney, D., and Williams, T. A., *Linear Programming for Decision Making*, St. Paul, MN: West Publishing, 1974.

2. Hamel, Henry C., *Leasing in Industry*, New York: National Industrial Conference Board, 1968.

3. Harris, R. D., and Maggard, M. J., *Computer Models in Operations Management: A Computer Augmented System*, 2nd ed., San Francisco: Harper & Row, 1977.

4. Hinomoto, H., "Capacity Expansion with Facilities Under Technological Improvement," *Management Science*, 11:581–592 (1965).

5. Levitt, Theodore, "Production Line Approach to Service," *Harvard Business Review*, 50:41–52 (Sept.–Oct. 1972).

6. Magee, J. F., "Decision Trees for Decision Making," *Harvard Business Review*, 42:126 (1964).

7. Monroe, A. S., ed., *Investments for Capacity Expansion*, Cambridge, MA: M.I.T. Press, 1967.

8. Schmenner, R., "Before You Build a *Big* Factory," *Harvard Business Review*, 54:100–104 (July–Aug. 1976).

9. Schultz, R. S., "Profits, Prices, and Excess Capacity," *Harvard Business Review*, 41:68–81 (July–Aug. 1963).

10. Skinner, W., *Manufacturing in the Corporate Strategy*, New York: Wiley, 1978.

11. Turban, E., and Meredith, J. R., *Fundamentals of Management Science*, 2nd ed., Dallas: Business Publications, 1981.

12. Whyte, William F., *Human Relations in the Restaurant Industry*, New York: McGraw-Hill, 1948.

13. Yelle, L. E. "The Learning Curve: Historical Review and Comprehensive Survey," *Decision Sciences*, 10:302–328 (April 1979).

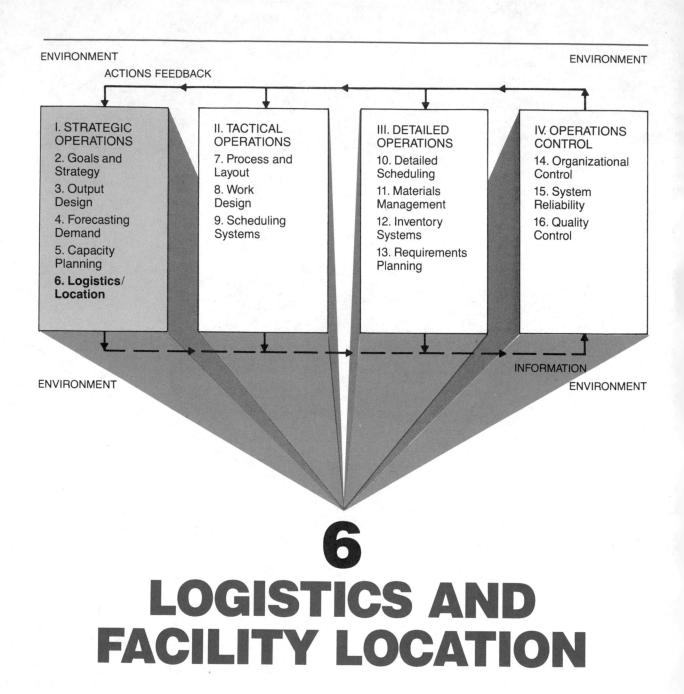

ENVIRONMENT

ENVIRONMENT

ACTIONS FEEDBACK

I. STRATEGIC OPERATIONS
2. Goals and Strategy
3. Output Design
4. Forecasting Demand
5. Capacity Planning
6. Logistics/ Location

II. TACTICAL OPERATIONS
7. Process and Layout
8. Work Design
9. Scheduling Systems

III. DETAILED OPERATIONS
10. Detailed Scheduling
11. Materials Management
12. Inventory Systems
13. Requirements Planning

IV. OPERATIONS CONTROL
14. Organizational Control
15. System Reliability
16. Quality Control

ENVIRONMENT

INFORMATION

ENVIRONMENT

6
LOGISTICS AND FACILITY LOCATION

6

LEARNING OBJECTIVES

By the completion of this chapter the student should

- Be aware of the tradeoffs between transportation and location in supply/distribution logistics.

- Be familiar with the categories of organizations whose unique characteristics dictate how they will locate their facility.

- Know the five basic modes of physical transportation and the meaning of the "routing problem."

- Be aware of the four major factors influencing the selection of a regional location for a facility.

- Understand the concepts employed in models to aid in the regional selection decision.

- Have a feel for the considerations of importance in the community selection decision and the use of the breakeven model for comparing them.

- Appreciate the elements of importance in selecting the actual site for the facility and how a scoring model can be used to compare these elements, particularly qualitative elements.

- Comprehend the nature and complexity of the multifacility location problem and the partial applicability of the transportation method in addressing the problem.

Up to this point in the design of the operations function we have selected the output, forecast the demand in the environment, and sized our production facility for sufficient capacity to economically meet the demand. The next step is to decide how best to get the output to the recipients. This decision must be made at this point because it will determine where we *place* the production facility and how much *transportation* of the output will be necessary. This function involves what is known as **logistics.**

The breadth of logistics management.

The term *logistics management* as currently used in organizations often includes the supply, storage, and movement of materials, personnel, equipment, and finished goods within the organization and between it and its environment. Such an all-encompassing interpretation would thus include the functions of purchasing, materials management, distribution, maintenance, and a number of others. In this chapter, however, we will primarily consider only the supply and distribution aspects of logistics. The other functions will be addressed later in separate chapters.

Impact on the operations manager.

The manner in which the output is distributed to the recipients is of special concern to the operations manager. First, the location of the production facility will affect the supply of labor, the shipment cost of materials, the timeliness of repair services, and numerous other aspects of the production process. Second, the transportation of the output will place certain additional constraints on the production process regarding weight, throughput time, sturdiness, and so forth. In addition, intermediate distribution points will impact on the functions of inventory control, materials handling, warehousing, routing, and so on.

In this chapter we will first address the generic subject of supply/distribution and then focus, in turn, on transportation and location. In the transportation section we describe the primary modes of traffic—water, rail, truck, air, and pipeline—and discuss the advantages and disadvantages of each. To discuss facility location, we divide the process into three stages: regional, community, and site. In each stage we describe the parameters of importance and some models of use for that stage. We employ examples from the pharmaceuticals industry, construction, and public health. Last, we look at the multifacility location situation and illustrate the interfacility allocation problem with an example from the food processing industry. We then solve the problem in the appendix with the transportation model of linear programming.

6.1 THE SUPPLY/DISTRIBUTION SYSTEM

The supply/ distribution system.

A major element of logistics is the *supply/distribution system*. The manner in which the organization's inputs are obtained and outputs are distributed is important because of its impact on the total cost of the output, the number of recipients that can be reached, and even the location of the organization itself. For example, the cost of *physical distribution*, that is, getting the product or service to the consumer, ranges from about 10 percent of sales in the mechanical equipment industry to 30 percent in the food industries.

Distribution improvements.

A good supply/distribution system will generally reduce supply/distribution costs and provide better service (faster deliveries, fewer stockouts, and greater variety) at the same time. For example, the move by many companies such as the Borden Company and Whirlpool Corporation in the early 1960s from multiple warehouses to only a few general-purpose distribution centers reduced the costs of order preparation, warehousing, materials handling, inventory control, and record keeping while simultaneously providing faster customer service, fewer stockouts, and greater variety of selection. This was accomplished primarily by utilizing the new technologies of *automatic data processing* for credit checking, record-keeping and inventory control, and *unit load* principles (this concept, which includes "containerization" and "palletization" is discussed later in Chapter 11: Materials Management) in materials handling.

Transporting-versus-locating tradeoffs.

Transporting services.

The determination of the best distribution system depends on the type of output being considered and the relative costs in dollars, time, and trouble of *transporting to* versus *locating near*. That is, the best choice depends on the costs of moving the output to the recipients from a centralized location as compared to *locating* the transformation activities in close proximity to the recipients. Since service outputs without a "facilitating good" are generally difficult, expensive, or even impossible to transport, service organizations have typically distributed their output by means of locating in the vicinity of their recipients. Examples of this approach are medical clinics, churches, parks and playgrounds, dry cleaners, and beauty shops. Of course, there are exceptions to this general practice when the recipients transport themselves to the service location. These situations usually occur where the service is of exceptional quality, scarce, or famous, such as the Mayo Clinic, to which people come from all over the world, or Yosemite National Park, which delights thousands of visitors every year.

Some pure service organizations, however, do attempt to transport their services, although frequently with a great deal of trouble. These instances occur when the nature of the service makes it impractical to remain in one fixed location for an extended duration (traveling carnivals, home shows), or, more commonly, when the service is deemed to be very important to the public but may otherwise be inaccessible (mobile x ray, blood donor vehicles, bookmobiles).

Locational categories of product organizations.

"Product" organizations, on the other hand, can generally trade transportation costs for location costs with more ease and, therefore, usually locate in an economically advantageous spot. Product organizations often fall into one of three categories, described in the following subsections, which dictate their distribution patterns as well as their most economic location.

Natural Resources

Those organizations that process natural resources as raw materials to obtain their facilitating good will locate near their raw material source if one of the following conditions hold.

1. There is a large loss in size or weight during processing.

2. High **economies of scale** exist for the product. That is, the operating costs of one large plant with the same total capacity as two smaller plants is significantly less than the combined operating costs of the two small plants.

3. The raw material is perishable (fish processing, canning) and cannot be shipped long distances before being processed.

Examples of these types of industries are mining, canning, and lumber. In these cases the natural inputs (raw materials) are either voluminous or perishable and the final product is much reduced in size, thus greatly reducing the cost of transportation to the recipients (either final users or further processors).

Immobile Outputs

The outputs of some organizations may be relatively immobile, such as dams, roads, buildings, and bridges. In these cases (referred to as "projects") the organization locates itself at the construction site and transports all required inputs to that location. The "home office" is frequently little more than one room with a phone, secretary, files, and billing and record-keeping facilities.

All Factors Relevant

The majority of product organizations do not have one single overriding transportation cost factor with which to contend. They must consider the costs of land, labor, capital, equipment, and transportation as well as other nonquantitative factors such as local zoning regulations or the supply of labor in choosing their pattern of distribution. These organizations have particular difficulty in selecting the best pattern of distribution since no one factor predominates.

6.2 SUPPLY/DISTRIBUTION BY TRANSPORTATION

In this section we will describe the main characteristics of the transportation approach to supply and distribution. Our treatment is very brief here because this topic constitutes an entire field in its own. Consult the Bibliography for further references.

We will focus here on two elements of the transportation area. First, we will describe the different modes of transportation and the advantages and disadvantages of each. Then we will briefly discuss the problem of how to actually transport goods between points, independent of the mode used. That is, what vehicle should take what goods to where? It should be noted that there are many topics in this field that we are *not* discussing, such as regulated carriers, traffic law, distribution channels (wholesalers, retailers, etc.), and others.

Transportation Modes

There are five basic modes of physical transportation.

- Water
- Pipeline
- Rail
- Truck
- Air

Table 6.1 lists the traffic shares held by these modes (excepting pipeline) and their relative costs per ton-mile (a railroad box car moving 90 miles with a load of 40 tons generates 3600 ton-miles). As indicated by the values in the table, trucks (and then railroads) carry the great majority of tonnage whereas water and then rail have the majority of ton-miles. This implies that rail and water are the major transportation modes in the high-tonnage, *long-haul* (over 800 miles) market whereas trucks and rail are the major modes in the short-haul market.

Long haul versus short haul.

Water

The least expensive mode of transportation is water, but this mode also has major drawbacks. It is slow, very limited in accessibility, and generally is used for bulky, nonperishable items of low unit value such as petroleum, coal, scrap iron, salt, and mineral ores, which accounts for the concentration of bulk product industries on rivers and coastlines.

Water is cheap but slow.

Pipeline

Piplining, frequently used for petroleum products and natural gas, has recently been extended to other products such as coal and sawdust, which can be formed into water-based mixtures called **slurries** and pumped through the line without damage to the pumps or the basic product. The disadvantage of using pipelines is their limited accessibility, slow rate of travel (about 15 miles per hour), and the requirement that the product be in a liquid or gaseous form. Another disadvantage in some locations is the scarcity of water used to form the slurries.

Pipelines are cheap but specialized and inaccessible.

Table 6.1 Traffic Shares and Costs for Major Transportation Modes

Mode	Tons (%)	Ton-Miles (%)	Average Cost/Ton-Mile
Water	26.3	43.7	$0.006
Rail	32.9	36.8	0.01
Truck	40.5	19.0	0.04
Air	—	0.1	0.10
Miscellaneous	0.3	0.4	—

Traffic shares by mode.

Source: Adapted by permission from E. W. Smykay, *Physical Distribution Management*, 3rd ed., New York: Macmillan, 1973.

Rail

Railroads handle a vast range of products such as cereals, coal, nonferrous metals, lumber, and food products. Rail offers a number of advantages as a form of transportation. It can transport large items as well as small, has good accessibility, offers services for specialized products [refrigeration, dock-to-dock *piggyback* (see Figure 6.1), trilevel auto handling, petroleum tank cars, etc.], and is relatively inexpensive.

Rail is inexpensive and accessible.

Truck

Truck transport has grown considerably, at the expense of rail, because of the following factors that either reduced the cost of trucking or improved service to the recipients:

- Liberalized trucking regulations (speed, size).
- Improved national highway system.
- Better trucking equipment.
- New, improved materials handling equipment.
- Speed, flexibility of service.
- Dock-to-dock availability.

Trucking offers accessibility and service.

Like rail, trucking is used for a vast array of products: office machinery, livestock, petroleum products, automobiles, and nonferrous metals.

Air

Air transport is typically used for items that are small or fragile but have high value, such as optical instruments, electrical recording instruments, and solid-state electronic components, or are highly perishable, such as live Maine lobsters for a Chicago restaurant or tropical fish from a Key West aquarium fish company. Speed of delivery is the major characteristic of air transport and for small, high-valued, or perishable products the use of air freight can significantly reduce inventory and warehousing costs with a corresponding improvement in customer service.

Air is fast but expensive.

The Routing Problem

Independent of the specific mode of transport there are additional transportation problems involving such considerations as the *number* of transporting vehicles, their *capacities*, and the *routes* that each vehicle will take. In general, these interrelated problems are frequently included under the heading of the **routing problem.**

The routing difficulties of transport.

Solving the routing problem involves finding the best number of vehicles and their routes to deliver the organization's output to a group of geographically dispersed recipients. When only one vehicle is serving all the recipients, the problem is known as the *traveling salesman problem*. In this problem a number of possible routes exist between the organization and all of the

The traveling salesman problem.

Myth:
Truck traffic can move only on the highways.

Fact:
More than two million truckloads moved by railway last year.

Piggybacking—the movement of truck trailers or containers by rail—is the fastest-growing part of the railroad business. It set a new record in 1977 and it's now our second-largest source of traffic—next to coal.

The piggyback concept has come of age. Better yet, it has generated a wealth of innovations and improvements. Containerized cargo destined for foreign countries now moves across America by rail. New designs in flatcars are saving fuel and increasing loads. Truck trailers that actually ride either roads or rails with two separate sets of wheels are being tested.

This is good news for the railroads, but it's better news for the consumer and the nation. Many piggyback trains move their cargo with about half the fuel that would be required by trucks to move the same goods.

Usually there's a cost saving in piggyback shipments, too, with the advantage of fast, long-distance travel and expedited door-to-door delivery service.

Because these truckloads travel on the railroads, not the highways, the motoring public enjoys a greater degree of safety and less congestion, while damage to the highway system is reduced.

Not all trucks can move by train, but thousands more are doing so every year. And the ones that do aren't leaving potholes in your favorite road.

Association of American Railroads, American Railroads Building, Washington, D.C. 20036

Surprise:
We've been working on the railroad.

Figure 6.1 Piggybacking truck trailers by rail. (Reprinted by permission of the Association of American Railroads.)

recipients but only a few or perhaps just one of these routes minimizes the total cost of delivery to all the recipients.

Although there are certain procedures available to minimize either the distance traveled or the cost in the routing and traveling salesman problems, quite often there are other considerations such as balancing the workloads among the vehicles or minimizing the idle or delay time. For approaches to such routing problems see Reference 16.

6.3 SUPPLY/DISTRIBUTION BY LOCATION

Advantages of proximity.

Organizations that supply a product to a recipient may locate close to their "market," not necessarily to minimize transportation costs of distribution, but to improve customer service. Being in close proximity to the market makes it easier for the recipient to contact the organization and also allows the organization to respond to changes in demand (both in quantity and variety) from current and new recipients. As in war, the people on the front line are closest to the action and are able to respond to changing situations faster than those far away simply because information about changes is available on a more timely basis and is generally more accurate.

Intermediaries in services.

For organizations that supply a pure service to recipients, there is usually little choice—they generally locate near their market because services are not easily transported. Frequently, the service is received directly by the recipient (surgery, hair cuts, counseling), but not always. That is, some intermediary may exist in the provision of the service. For example, the counseling/entertainment service "Dear Abby" uses newspapers as a communication medium and therefore Abby can "counsel" from a central location. College extension courses use both educational television and the U.S. Postal Service as intermediaries; patient symptoms and test results can be sent over telephone lines to a centralized health computer service for diagnosis and interpretation; and in-home shopping and bill paying can be conducted by telephone.

In each of these cases, the primary service facility can be considerably removed from recipients but some form of intermediary must be in contact with them. This allows the organization to locate the primary facility according to other requirements. For instance, "Abby" can reside in an attractive, quiet area conducive to creative counseling; the college can locate in a big city or at a teaching and research hospital with large capacity computer equipment and top medical specialists.

Branch facilities.

On occasion, the distribution function is handled by multiple, branch facilities, which may or may not perform the actual processing themselves. The problem of determining the best locations for the multiple facilities is known as the *multifacility location problem*. Franchises are a specialized form of branch facilities, as are warehouses, branch banks, and adult evening classes offered at local high schools and colleges.

Innovation in service distribution.

Recently, several examples of innovation in service distribution have appeared. The "bookmobile," a mobile branch library, has been around for a number of years, of course, providing a service to local communities, schools, and churches, that were physically distant from central or branch libraries. The Meals on Wheels program, originally developed under an Office of Economic Opportunity grant program, is widely used to provide prepared food for the elderly and handicapped who otherwise would find it difficult to provide or prepare their own meals. Other offshoots of this kind of program are the home health care (visiting nurse) programs, which provide health services without the need to go to the doctor's office, and homemaker services, which provide assistance for the elderly and handicapped, thereby allowing them to maintain their own residences rather than move into nursing homes. And finally, a mobile automotive tune-up service is also now being offered. A fully equipped van with an inventory of tune-up parts and electronic testing devices offers tune-ups and minor repairs at the customer's home or office. The result is a low overhead operation that offers both convenience and price advantages to the client.

Three stages in the location decision.
In general, the location decision is divided into three stages: regional (including international), community, and site selection. Sources of information for these stages are chambers of commerce, realtors, utilities, banks, suppliers, transportation companies, savings and loan associations, government agencies, and management consultants who specialize in relocation decisions. For pure service operations only the last stage (site selection) is typically relevant, because services are usually already focused on a specific region and community.

We will next discuss each of these three stages in turn, and provide some useful models for each of the decision steps. The location of pure services will be discussed in the section on site selection. We initially will limit our analysis to the single facility location decision. Then we broaden our scope and address the multifacility location problem.

6.4 REGIONAL/INTERNATIONAL SELECTION

The four major considerations in the selection of a national or overseas region in which to locate are the following:

1. The proximity of the region to the organization's recipients and raw materials, if any are used.

Four factors in the selection of a region.
2. The type and quantity of labor available in the region.

3. The availability of other inputs such as land, supplies, transportation, and utilities.

4. The acceptability of the "environment" (climate, tax rates, regulations, political situation).

Proximity

To minimize transportation costs and provide acceptable service to customers it is desirable that the facility be located in a region of close proximity to the customers and suppliers. Although methods of finding the location with the minimum transportation cost will be presented later in the chapter, a common rule of thumb within the United States is that the facility should be within 200 miles of major industrial and commercial customers and suppliers. Beyond this range, transportation costs begin to rise quickly.

For example, a major appliance firm found that annual distribution costs were $100,000 more if their plant was located even 50 miles from the geographically optimal center of distribution to their customers. However, the same figure held for not locating at the geographically optimal center for incoming supplies. Since the two centers were not at the same spot, the firm was forced to trade off between these two points to obtain the best overall location.

Labor Supply

The region should have the proper supply of labor available and in the correct proportions of required skills. One important reason for the expansion, during the 1960s, of American firms abroad was the availability of labor at wage rates much lower than U.S. rates. Currently, this disparity has been reduced significantly because of increased wages abroad; however, the real consideration should not be wage rates but the productivity of domestic labor as compared to productivity abroad. This comparison would thus involve skill level, equipment use, wage rates, and even work ethics (which differ even between regions within the United States) to determine the most favorable labor region in terms of output per dollar of wages and capital investment.

In addition to regional wage rates, the organization of the labor pool should also be given consideration, that is, whether all the skills are unionized or an open shop situation exists. Some states have passed *right-to-work laws* (see Figure 6.2) that forbid any requirement that all employees join the union in order to work in an organization. Often, these laws result in significantly lower wage rates in these states.

Availability of Inputs

The region selected for location of the facility should have the necessary inputs available. For example, those supplies that are difficult, expensive, or time-consuming to ship and those that are necessary (i.e., no reasonable substitutes exist) to the organization should be readily available. The proper type (rail, water, highway, air) and supply of transportation; sufficient quantities of basic resources such as water, electricity, gas, coal, and oil; and appropriate communication facilities should also be available. Obviously, many American industries are located abroad to use the raw materials (oil, copper, etc.) available there.

Environment

The regional environment should be conducive to the nature of the organization. Not only should the regional weather patterns be appropriate but

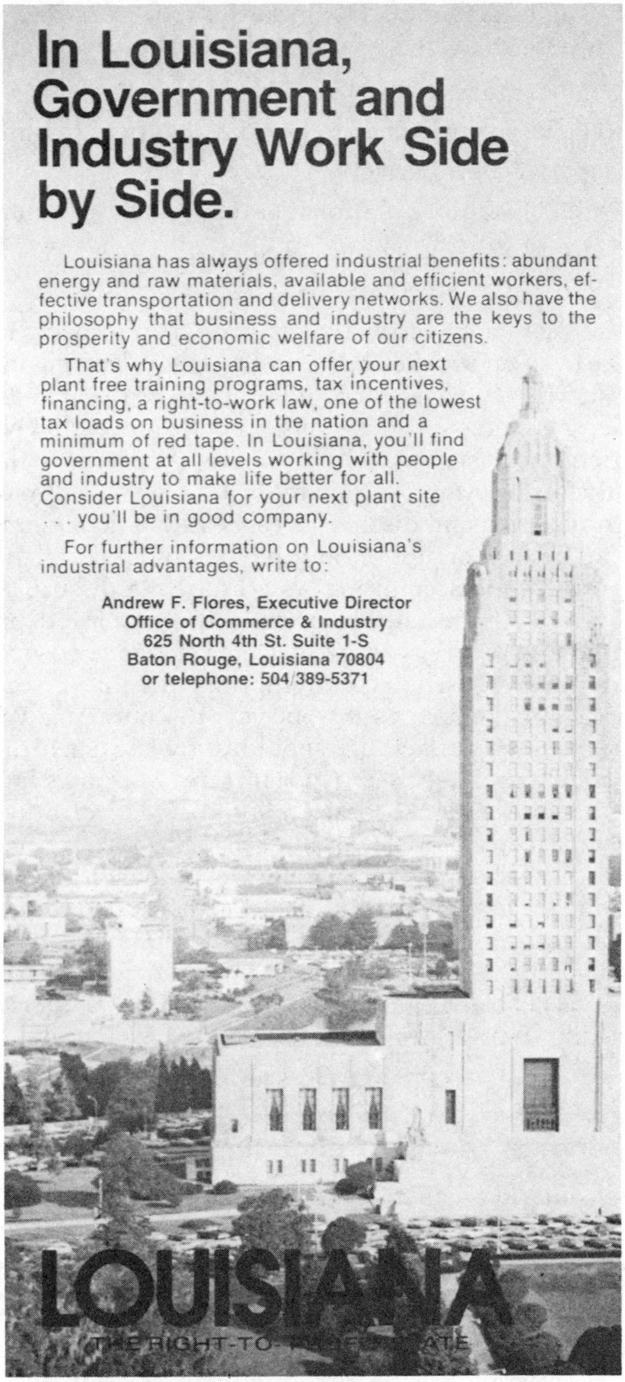

In Louisiana, Government and Industry Work Side by Side.

Louisiana has always offered industrial benefits: abundant energy and raw materials, available and efficient workers, effective transportation and delivery networks. We also have the philosophy that business and industry are the keys to the prosperity and economic welfare of our citizens.

That's why Louisiana can offer your next plant free training programs, tax incentives, financing, a right-to-work law, one of the lowest tax loads on business in the nation and a minimum of red tape. In Louisiana, you'll find government at all levels working with people and industry to make life better for all. Consider Louisiana for your next plant site . . . you'll be in good company.

For further information on Louisiana's industrial advantages, write to:

Andrew F. Flores, Executive Director
Office of Commerce & Industry
625 North 4th St. Suite 1-S
Baton Rouge, Louisiana 70804
or telephone: 504/389-5371

LOUISIANA
THE RIGHT-TO-... STATE

Figure 6.2 Location factors. (Reprinted by permission of the Louisiana Office of Commerce and Industry.)

the political, legal, and social climates should also be favorable. The following are several matters that should be considered:

1. Regional taxes.
2. Regional regulations on operating matters (pollution, hiring, etc.).
3. Import/export barriers.
4. Political stability (nationalization policies, kidnappings).
5. Cultural and economic peculiarities (e.g., restrictions on working women) of the region.

These factors are especially critical when locating in a foreign country, particularly an underdeveloped country. Firms locating in such regions should not be surprised to find large differences in the way things are done. For example, governmental decisions tend to move slowly with extreme centralization of decision-making authority. And very little planning seems to occur. Events appear to occur by "God's will" or by default. The pace of work is unhurried and discipline, especially among managers, seems totally absent at times. Corruption and payoffs often seem to be normal ways of doing business and accounting systems are highly suspect. Living conditions for the workers, especially in urbanized areas, are depressing. Transportation/communication systems (roads, ports, phone service) can be incomplete and notoriously unreliable. Attempting to achieve something under such conditions can, understandably, be very discouraging. When locating in such countries, a firm's timetable should allow for such difficulties and unexpected problems. In such an environment, Murphy's law thrives.

Not all international location situations involve firms locating outside the United States. Many location decisions are concerned with foreign firms locating in this country. In the new world marketplace it is becoming more common to see foreign firms locating in the United States to minimize transportation charges, import tariffs, and ill will. Japan, in particular, has placed many plants in the United States: Datsun at Smyrna, Tennessee, Kawasaki at Lincoln, Nebraska, and Sony at San Diego, California, are just three of many examples.

Center of Gravity and Incremental Analysis Models for Minimizing Transportation Costs

Importance of transportation costs. In many situations, such as the location of warehouses, the most important factor in locating the facility is the minimization of transportation costs. If the facility location is restricted to a given set of preselected sites, or even communities, then the evaluation is straightforward. All transportation costs into the facility and distribution costs out of the facility for each possible location are calculated and the least cost location is identified.

Minimum transportation cost. If the location is "open," however, another process is needed. In what follows we will only work with distribution expenses; in a real situation incoming transportation charges would be included as well, of course. We assume that the amounts and locations of demand by recipients are known

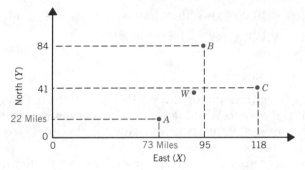

Figure 6.3 Location by center of gravity method.

and that the transportation cost to ship output to each demand location is known (or can easily be found) for any given facility location. We start by selecting a "promising" initial site for the facility. Such a location can be quickly determined by the **center of gravity** method of Coyle [5].

In essence, this method is simply a weighted mean of east-west transportation charges and a weighted mean of north-south transportation charges. No distinction is made between incoming (supplies and raw materials) goods and outgoing (finished) goods. For example, suppose a warehouse is to be located to receive goods from plants and to then supply customers. For simplicity, assume only three plants or customers are to be considered:

A, who supplies 10 tons at a cost of $5/ton/mile.

B, who desires 2 tons at a cost of $8/ton/mile.

C, who desires 8 tons at a cost of $4/ton/mile.

If A, B, and C are located as in Figure 6.3, where should the warehouse be built?

The weighted mean distance in any direction Z is

$$\bar{Z} = \sum_i T_i V_i Z_i \bigg/ \sum_i T_i V_i \qquad (6.1)$$

where $\sum_i$ is the sum over all points i

T_i is the transportation cost per unit volume

(or weight) per mile for each point i

V_i is the volume (or weight) to be transported

to or from each location i

Z_i is the distance in miles from any arbitrary

origin to each point i

Hence, in the easterly direction X

$$\bar{X} = (T_A V_A X_A + T_B V_B X_B + T_C V_C X_C)/(T_A V_A + T_B V_B + T_C V_C)$$

$$= [(5 \times 10 \times 73) + (8 \times 2 \times 95) + (4 \times 8 \times 118)]/$$
$$[(5 \times 10) + (8 \times 2) + (4 \times 8)]$$
$$= 8946/98$$
$$= 91.3 \text{ miles east}$$

Similar calculations for the northerly direction Y yield $\overline{Y} = 38.3$ miles. This point is shown as W in Figure 6.3. The center of gravity method typically determines an excellent starting point for the next procedure, or even an acceptable solution in itself.

For the incremental analysis model, we next calculate the total transportation cost to supply all the geographically dispersed demands. Then the facility is moved slightly north, east, south, and west of the initial site and the total transportation cost is calculated for each of these changes, in turn. *Incremental* This is a simple variant of a technique known as **incremental analysis.** If all *analysis.* four changes result in higher costs, then the initial site is best* and the problem is solved. However, if some movement results in a lower cost, the facility should be moved in that direction and the entire process repeated until a final location is found where none of the directional changes produces an improvement.

The method of calculating the total transportation cost is as follows. We use the following symbols.

T = the cost for the type of transportation needed, in dollars per unit volume (or weight) per unit distance [e.g., $/(lb \cdot mile)$]

V = the volume (or weight) being transported

D = the distance from the facility to the recipients' demand locations

C = the total cost

$1,2,3, \ldots, n$ = subscripts denoting the first, second, third, through the nth recipients

Then we compute

$$C = T_1V_1D_1 + T_2V_2D_2 + T_3V_3D_3 + \cdots + T_nV_nD_n = \sum_i T_iV_iD_i \qquad (6.2)$$

which is the total cost of shipping the desired quantities to all n recipients. This procedure is illustrated in the following example.

BRANDEX Medical Supplies

A new firm, BRANDEX, is entering the acetaminophen (aspirin substitute) market and plans to compete directly with Tylenol, the major acetaminophen supplier, by offering retailers a generic drug that could be sold as a "house brand" at a reduced price. BRANDEX has made contact with two

---

*At least among sites in that region. Although it does not happen frequently, there is occasionally a somewhat better site much farther away.

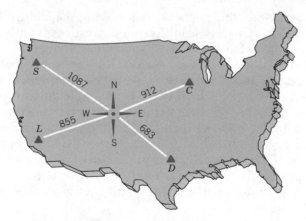

Figure 6.4   Nationwide distribution map.

large wholesalers in the Dallas (D) and Seattle (S) areas and has established two manufacturing representatives in Los Angeles (L) and Chicago (C) who would then further distribute the product on a house brand basis (Figure 6.4).

Denver, Colorado, has been suggested as a possible site at which to locate the production facilities. Trucking rates, T, for the product to the four demand cities and the mileages, D, from Denver (obtained from a truck routing map) are given in Table 6.2. (Note that rates among the four different trucking firms differ slightly.) Included in the table are the levels, V, of demand (in cartons) expected in the first year and the product of T times V, which (we assume here) is independent of the facility location.

At the bottom of Table 6.2 the total annual transportation cost is shown. The first figure, $13,064, represents the cost from Denver. The next figure $13,074, is the cost due to changing the distances involved simply by moving the facility 10 miles north. As can be seen in the table, the effect of this move, $D(N)$, is to *increase* the distance, and thus costs, to Los Angeles (L), an expensive, high-demand area, and Dallas (D) for a cost increase of 4133 − 4104 = 29 for L and 690 − 683 = 7 for D, thus totaling 36. But this move also *decreases* the cost for Seattle (S) and Chicago (C) for a decrease of 21 + 5 or 26. The net effect of this location shift is thus a total *increase* in cost of 36 − 26 or $10.

Table 6.2   Data and Calculations for Denver Location

Destination	T [($/carton mile)]	V (cartons)	TV ($/mile)	D (miles)	C = TVD ($)	D(N) (miles)	C(N) ($)	C(E) ($)	C(S) ($)	C(W) ($)
S	0.0015	2000	3	1087	3261	1080	3240	3282	3282	3240
L	0.0012	4000	4.8	855	4104	861	4133	4142	4075	4066
D	0.0010	1000	1	683	683	690	690	676	676	690]
C	0.0011	5000	5.5	912	5016	911	5011	4967	5022	5066
Total cost:					13,064		13,074	13,067	13,055	13,062

Comparing the total costs of next moving the facility 10 miles east, then south, and then west it is seen that the lowest cost results by moving south. Moving west also reduces the cost somewhat, though not nearly as much as moving south, so the next step is to look for an acceptable location somewhat south of Denver and perhaps a bit west and then repeat the entire process. A natural question, for which there is no single answer, is "How far should the facility be moved for the next test?" Clearly, we would not move farther south than Dallas because then the facility would be farther away from *all* the demand points. It is best to be conservative in this process and locate a city, or site, that is generally acceptable on other factors and is not very far from the previously tested location. In this case, Colorado Springs would be a logical next choice for BRANDEX and is only 75 miles away.

6.5 COMMUNITY SELECTION

Many of the considerations made at the regional level should be reconsidered here. For example, the availability of acceptable sites, local government attitudes, regulations, zoning, taxes, labor supply, market size and characteristics, and weather would again be considered. In addition, the pollution peculiar to the community, the availability of local financing, monetary inducements (such as tax incentives) for establishing operations in the community, and the community's attitude (Figure 6.2) toward the organization itself would be additional factors of interest to the organization. The tax and monetary differences may, by themselves, require that a comprehensive financial analysis, including a cash flow statement, be made.

Last, the preferences of the organization's staff should play a role in community selection. These would probably be influenced by the amenities available in the community such as homes, churches, shopping centers, schools and universities, medical care, fire and police protection, and entertainment as well as local tax rates and other costs. Upper level educational institutions may also be of interest to the organization in terms of opportunity for relevant research and development. For example, it is no coincidence that major IBM plants are located in Lexington, Kentucky; Denver, Colorado; and Austin, Texas, which are also sites of major state universities.

Breakeven Model for Fixed-Variable Cost Comparison

Uncertain variable costs.

However, although the relevant factors for comparison may be known, their values may be uncertain. This is particularly true of those factors that are a function of the output rate of the facility being located: utility costs, labor charges, materials usage, and so on. The community selection stage of the local decision is the time to consider this uncertainty. In the previous regional stage these factors still varied significantly *within* the regions. But in the next stage, site selection (Section 6.6), the factors typically do not vary between sites.

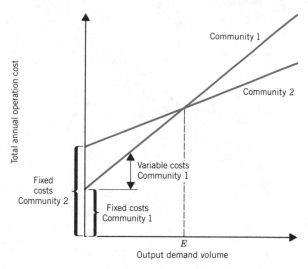

Figure 6.5 Breakeven location model.

Breakeven model
for uncertainty.

A useful technique for handling this uncertainty is the "breakeven" technique for cost comparison of different alternatives (presented in Chapter 5). Various location/distribution alternatives may be compared by graphing each alternative's total operating costs for the different demand levels, as in Figure 6.5.

This is accomplished by dividing the total operating cost into two components—fixed costs that do not vary with the demand for the output (e.g., land, buildings, equipment, property taxes, insurance) and variable costs such as labor, materials, and transportation—and plotting them on the axes of a graph. At the demand point E (the intersection of the two lines) the costs for the two alternatives are the same; for demand levels in excess of E, community 2 is best, and for levels less than E, community 1 is best. Thus, if the range of uncertainty concerning the output volume is entirely *above* point E the manager need not be concerned about which community to choose—community 2 is best. Similar reasoning holds for any uncertainty existing entirely *below* point E—community 1 is best. If the uncertainty encompasses point E, then two additional situations must be considered.

1. If the range of uncertainty is closely restricted to point E, then either community may be selected because the costs will be approximately the same in either case.

2. If the range of uncertainty is broad and varies considerably from point E in both directions, then the breakeven chart will indicate to the manager the extra costs that will be incurred by choosing the wrong community. The manager should probably try to gather more information to reduce the range of uncertainty in demand before selecting either community.

We will demonstrate with the following example.

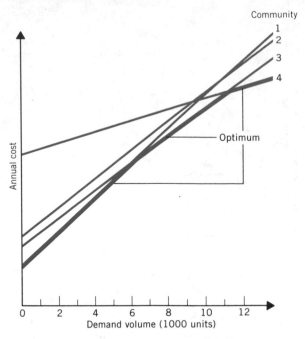

Figure 6.6   Cost comparison for four potential communities.

Upp and Adam Elevators, Ltd.

Figure 6.6 depicts the annual costs, calculated in Table 6.3, for four candidate locations for the Upp and Adam organization. Note from the figure that communities 1, 2, and 3 all have approximately the same fixed costs and the same variable costs compared with community 4, which has a very high fixed cost but low variable cost—beyond a demand volume of 11 (thousand units) community 4 is clearly the best. Also note from the figure that community 2 should never be considered because community 3 is *always* better than community 2; its fixed costs and its variable cost are *both* lower. Community 3 appears to be optimal between volumes (in thousands) of 6.5 and 11; below 6.5 community 1 is best and above 11 community 4 is best.

Suppose uncertainty in demand volume for Upp and Adam is relatively high because the product is a new one and may catch on quickly or, just as likely, languish for years at fairly low sales before any significant growth. Ms. Down N. Out, the operations manager, believes, under these circumstances, that the demand could range anywhere from 4000 to 12,000 units.

For such a situation, can the breakeven chart be helpful? Most certainly! For the majority of this range, community 3 is best. At demand volumes of 4000, although community 1 is best, community 3 is only slightly worse whereas community 4 is very poor. And at volumes of 12,000, although community 4 is best, community 3 is not much worse. Thus, community 3, as-

Table 6.3 Annual Costs for Four
Community Locations

Annual Costs	Community			
(in thousands of dollars)	1	2	3	4
Fixed:				
Interest	4	8	7	19
Rent	30	45	40	100
Insurance	6	10	9	15
Taxes	7	8	8	16
G & A	5	9	5	16
Marketing	5	8	7	17
Other	3	2	4	17
Total	60	90	80	200
Variable:				
Material	6	6	5	2
Transportation	3	3	3	1
Labor	7	6	6	3
Sales	5	4	4	2
Utilities	3	2	2	1
Other	1	1	1	1
Total	25	22	21	10

suming other factors are acceptable, appears to be a safe bet. Of course, for considerably higher volumes only community 4 would be economically acceptable; but, according to Ms. Out's estimate, such volumes are not expected to occur.

6.6 SITE SELECTION

Last, the *site*, the actual location of the facility, should be appropriate to the nature of the operation. Such matters as size; adjoining land; zoning; community attitudes; drainage; soil; the availability of water, sewers, and utilities; waste disposal; transportation accessibility; local market size; and development costs are typically considered in the site selection process. The development of industrial parks in some communities has alleviated many of the site selection difficulties of organizations since most of these matters are automatically taken care of by the developer.

Locating Pure Service Organizations

Now a service
focus.

In analyzing the location decision for pure services we must distinguish between two cases: where the recipient comes to the facility and where the service is taken to the recipient.

"We can be proud, gentlemen. Before we came, this was just desert!"

Cartoon by Chris Jensen. (Reprinted with permission from *Changing Times*, © 1973, Kiplinger Washington Editors, Inc., Aug. 1973.)

Recipient to Facility

First consider the case of a retail (nonpure) or professional (pure) service in which the facility is drawing from a local region in competition with other facilities of a like nature. Huff [10] found that the drawing power of a retail facility under these circumstances was primarily related to its size, S, and the typical customer's average travel time, T, to the facility. His results were expressed in the probability, P, of a customer patronizing a store or, equivalently, the fraction P of the customers in the region who would patronize a store.

Drawing power.

$$P = cS/T^n \tag{6.3}$$

where n = an exponent ranging, generally, between 2 and 3

   c = the factor of proportionality that makes all the stores' P values sum to 1.0

"Gravity equation."

This type of formula is known as a "gravity equation" because it operates in a fashion similar to gravity itself (where P is the power of attraction). Huff does not presume that size and travel time are the only important factors in drawing power, but given equivalence on the other factors, such as price and service, Equation 6.3 explains the effect of size and travel time quite well.

How to measure?

Next consider the situation of public services such as health care clinics, libraries, and colleges. Apart from the difficulty of framing a location model is the probably more significant problem of choosing a measure, or measures, of service: number of recipients served (a "surrogate" measure), change in the recipient's condition (a direct benefit measure), quantity of services offered (another surrogate), and so on.

Abernathy and Hershey [1] investigated a number of such measures in a study of the best locations for health service clinics in a community. Some of their recommended measures, which can be used for trial-and-error location procedures, were as follows:

1. *Facility utilization:* Maximize the number of visits to the facilities.
2. *Travel distance per citizen:* Minimize the average distance per person in the region to the nearest clinic.
3. *Travel distance per visit:* Minimize the average distance per visit to the nearest clinic.

No one location measure has been found to work best for these cases.

Facility to Recipient

These situations are common to the urban alarm services: fire, police, and ambulance. Again, how to properly measure service is a dilemma that involves such factors as number of recipients served, average wait time to service, value of property saved, and number of service facilities. Two general situations are encountered in this location problem, whether discussing the single or multiple facility problem:

Two different situations.

1. High-density demand for services where multiple vehicles are located in the same facility and vehicles are often dispatched from one alarm directly to another.
2. Widely distributed demand for services where extreme travel distances require additional facilities.

Typical of situation 1 above are the descriptions by Rider [18] of fire companies in New York City and Fitzsimmons [6] of ambulances in Los Angeles. Meredith and Shershin's work [15] in Miami illustrates the second situation. Queuing (waiting line) theory results are highly applicable in these situations (see Chapter 10).

Common findings.

Results in these cases have been basically the same. There is a significant dropoff in the returns to scale as more units are added to the system. Typically, the first three or four will improve all measures by up to 80 percent of the maximum improvement. Each additional unit gains less and less. A second common finding is that optimally located facilities only yield about a 15 percent improvement over existing or evenly dispersed facilities. Last, incremental approaches to selecting additional locations provide slightly poorer service than a total relocation analysis of all the facilities.

A Weighted Score Model for Site Selection

Multiple criteria.

The location decision, whether for products or services, is typically complicated by the existence of multiple location criteria such as executive preferences, maximization of facility use, and customer attitudes. These and other criteria may be very difficult to quantify, or even measure qualitatively; if they are important to the decision, however, they must be included in the location analysis.

The weighted score model for multiple factors.

There are a number of ways of handling the comparison of location criteria. The most common is probably just managerial intuition: which location is best on the important criteria? A simple formalization of this intuitive process that is useful as a rough screening tool for the problem of locating a single facility is the **weighted score** model. In this model a "weight" is assigned to each factor (*criterion*) depending on its importance to the manager. The most important factors receive proportionately higher weights. Then a "score" is assigned to each of the location alternatives on each factor, again with higher scores representing better results. The product of the factor weights and the location scores then gives a set of "weighted scores," which are added up for each location alternative. The location with the largest weighted score is considered best. This process is illustrated in the following example.

Venereal Disease Center

A county health department is investigating three possible locations for a specialized control clinic that will monitor both AIDS and the highly communicable viral venereal disease (VD), Herpes Simplex Type 2. The county director of public health is particularly concerned with four location factors.

1. The most important consideration in the treatment of VD is ease of access for infectives. Since they are generally disinclined to recognize and seek treatment for their health problem, it is foolish to locate a clinic where it is not easily accessible to as many patients as possible. This aspect of location is probably as much as 50 percent more important than the lease cost of the building.

2. The annual cost of the lease is not a minor consideration. The health department, unfortunately, is limited to a very tight budget and any extra cost for the lease will result in less equipment and staff being available to the clinic.

3. For some infectives it is of the utmost importance that confidentiality be maintained. Thus, although the clinic must be easily accessible, it must also be relatively inconspicuous. This factor is probably just as important as the cost of the lease.

4. Also, the director wants to consider the locational convenience of the clinic for its staff since many of the physicians will be donating their time to the clinic. This consideration is the least important of all, perhaps only half as important as the cost of the lease.

The three locations being considered are a relatively accessible building on Adam's Avenue, an inconspicuous office complex near the downtown bus terminal, and a group of public offices in the Civic Center, which would be almost rent-free.

The director has decided to evaluate (score) each of these alternative locations on each of the previous four factors. He has decided to use a four-point scale on which 1 represents "poor" and 4 represents "excellent." His

Table 6.4 Potential Clinic Sites

W: Importance Weight	F: Factor[a]	A: Adam's Ave.	B: Bus Terminal Complex	C: Civic Center
			Potential Locations	
2	1. Annual lease cost	1	3	4
3	2. Accessibility for infectives	3	3	2
2	3. Inconspicuousness	2	4	2
1	4. Accessibility for health personnel	4	1	2

[a]Factor scoring scale: 1, poor; 2, acceptable; 3, good; 4, excellent.

scores and the factor importance weights (derived from the relative importance of the four factors) are shown in Table 6.4. The problem now is to somehow use this information to determine the best location for the clinic.

To determine the weighted score for each location requires the multiplication of each location score by the importance weight for that factor and then the summation over all factors for each location, as illustrated in Table 6.5. Since larger scores indicate better ratings, the location with the largest score, B, the office near the bus terminal, is best, followed by C, the Civic Center.

6.7 THE MULTIFACILITY PROBLEM

Up to this point in our discussion of the transportation-location problem we have restricted our analysis to the single-facility situation in which, for example, one facility services a set of geographically dispersed recipients (Figure 6.7). The next level of complexity is the *multifacility* problem. The problem becomes complex because the best distribution pattern for each facility depends on the distribution patterns of *all* the other facilities. Hence, the problem cannot be solved by locating each facility one at a time. Rather, they must all be located "at once" since changing the distribution pattern of any one facility will change the distribution patterns of some or all of the other facilities as well. In addition to these complications is the fact that

Complication of multiple facilities.

Table 6.5 Factor Comparison by the "Weighted Score" Method

Factor	Weight	Sites:	A	B	C
1	2		2 × 1 = 2	2 × 3 = 6	2 × 4 = 8
2	3		3 × 3 = 9	3 × 3 = 9	3 × 2 = 6
3	2		2 × 2 = 4	2 × 4 = 8	2 × 2 = 4
4	1		1 × 4 = 4	1 × 1 = 1	1 × 2 = 2
Total			19	24	20

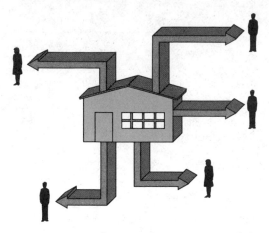

Figure 6.7 The single-source, multi-recipient location problem.

Multiple outputs.

most organizations produce more than one output, and thus the distribution problem must be solved with many products or services in mind. In addition, the potential locations may or may not be given. Furthermore, the *number* of facilities may not even be specified. However, even when the number of facilities is specified *and* their sites are given, the transportation cost is not immediately obtainable because it is still necessary to decide *which* facility, or more commonly facili*ties*, will supply *which* recipient. This is known as an *allocation* problem. This problem of allocating output from specific facilities to specific demand locations is a special type of linear programming problem and has been given a special name, the "transportation problem"; it is illustrated in the following example.

Solving allocation problems with the transportation model.

The Green Tomato Company

Tom, Green Tomato's operations manager, was having trouble trying to decide which processing plants should supply Green Tomato's new warehouse in Los Angeles. Green Tomato had opened their new warehouse in Los Angeles to serve the growing population in that region. But now management wondered which of their processing plants should supply the new warehouse, and to what extent, to minimize shipping costs.

Green Tomato has two processing plants for their Mexican tomatoes, one in Tijuana, Mexico (A), with a supply capacity of 100 tons per day, and one in Mexicali, Mexico (B), with a supply capacity of 110 tons a day. Green Tomato also has three warehouses: R in Calexico, California; S in Yuma, Arizona; and the newly added T in Los Angeles. The warehouses could use, if available, 80, 120, and 60 tons of tomatoes each week, respectively, to meet demands.

The shipping costs from each plant to each warehouse are given in Table 6.6.

Table 6.6 Green Tomato's Shipping Costs

From	To	Cost per Ton
A (Tijuana)	R (Calexico)	1
A (Tijuana)	S (Yuma)	2
A (Tijuana)	T (Los Angeles)	3
B (Mexicali)	R (Calexico)	4
B (Mexicali)	S (Yuma)	1
B (Mexicali)	T (Los Angeles)	5

Characteristics and Assumptions of the Transportation Problem

Green Tomato's distribution problem exhibits some typical characteristics.

1. A limited supply of a commodity is available at specific locations.

2. There is a specific demand for the commodity at other locations.

3. The *cost* of transporting the commodity from each supply point to each demand location is constant.

4. The *problem* is to minimize the total shipping cost by finding how many units each supply point should ship to each demand location.

Transportation problems often have a very large number of solutions. Although regular *linear programming* can solve such allocation problems, an especially simple variant of linear programming called "the transportation method" was developed specifically to solve this type of problem. The concept behind the transportation method, like linear programming and other such iterative methods, is to keep improving on *any* beginning, feasible solution. To determine whether a solution can be improved, one unit is shipped between every supply and demand route, one at a time, that does not have a flow in the current solution. This unit is allocated by "borrowing" units back and forth between other current shipping routes until all supplies and demands are again in balance. If any of these one-unit shipping possibilities *decreases* the cost of distribution, then as many units as possible are diverted to that route.

The details of this procedure are presented in the next section of this chapter (see also References 2 and 24) and illustrated using the Green Tomato Company problem. The optimal solution of Tom's problem is

$$
\begin{array}{lll}
80 \text{ units from A to R} & \text{cost of} & 80 \times 1 = 80 \\
10 \text{ units from A to S} & & 10 \times 2 = 20 \\
10 \text{ units from A to T} & & 10 \times 3 = 30 \\
110 \text{ units from B to S} & & 110 \times 1 = \underline{110} \\
& & 240
\end{array}
$$

Note that the demand at T, the most expensive shipping point, is not completely filled because of limited supply.

Locating the Multiple Facilities

With a solution to the allocation problem in hand, we can address the issue of locating the facilities. If the potential sites are given, a number of approaches may be used, most of them based on applying the transportation model of linear programming for each alternative site. Linear programming approaches have been used [8,12,21] to locate plants and warehouses and simulation (described in the appendix to Chapter 12) to locate warehouse distribution centers [14].

Linear programming and simulation solutions.

When the sites are not even specified, a more complex incremental analysis model, similar to that presented in Section 6.4, is called for. Initial trial locations that appear promising are selected for a number of facilities and then one of the facilities is optimally relocated with respect to the remaining set. Next, another of the facilities is chosen and optimally relocated, and so on until repeated trials with the same facility, after the others have been relocated, do not move it significantly. If desired, this process can be repeated for a different number of facilities until all reasonable sets have been examined. The primary difficulty with this approach is the extreme amount of computer time required to solve the problem. Hence, most multifacility location problems are, in practice, restricted to some set of acceptable or promising sites to begin with.

Iterative incremental analysis.

6.8 APPENDIX: THE TRANSPORTATION METHOD*

The transportation method is a search and evaluation process involving five steps, as shown in Figure 6.8.

Step 1 Arrange the Problem in Tabular Form. Transportation problems are presented in tabular form because it is a convenient form for applying special solution procedures. Table 6.7 shows Green Tomato's distribution problem. This table is explained in the following.

Left side: The sources of supply (plants) are listed on the left. Each source is represented by a row.

Top: The destination points (warehouses) are listed at the top. Each destination is represented by a column.

Right side: This column designates the capacity (supply) at the sources.

Bottom: The requirements (demand) of each destination are listed here.

Center: The center of the table is composed of "cells." In this case there are six. Each is designated by the letter of its row and column; for example, cell AR is in row A and column R. The corresponding shipping costs (per ton) are in the upper right-hand corner of each cell. For example, the

*Section 6.8 is adapted by permission from Efraim Turban and Jack R. Meredith, *Fundamentals of Management Science,* 2nd ed., (Dallas: Business Publications, 1981), pp. 228–244. © 1981 by Business Publications, Inc.

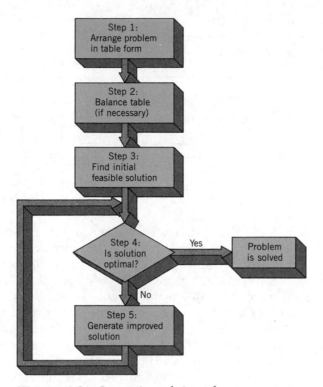

Figure 6.8 Steps in solving the transportation problem.

Table 6.7 Matrix Presentation of Green Tomato's Problem

From Plant \ To Warehouse	R	S	T	Supply
A	1	2	3	100
B	4	1	5	110
Demand	80	120	60	210
			260	

shipping cost from plant A to warehouse S is 2. For each cell there is to be determined the quantity to be shipped from the plant in that row to the warehouse in that column.

Step 2   Balance the Table.   The use of the transportation solution technique requires that the problem be balanced; that is, the total supply must equal

Table 6.8 Unbalanced Matrix (Excess Supply)

Source \ Destination	R	S	T	Supply
A	1	2	3	200
B	4	1	5	100
Demand	80	120	60	260 / 300

the total demand. If the matrix is not balanced, this must be done first. Two causes of imbalance are excess supply and excess demand. As an example, consider excess supply. Table 6.8 shows an example of an unbalanced matrix in which the modified total supply of 300 exceeds the total demand of 260. In this case there will be 40 unshipped units.

This matrix is balanced by adding a column for excess supply (sometimes labeled a "dummy" destination). The amount in this column equals the excess supply, as shown in Table 6.9. The "shipment" to this fictitious destination will, of course, not really occur. The cost of "shipments" to the dummy is usually set at zero: this ensures that all excess capacity will be absorbed by the dummy. For excess demands a dummy source is added in the same manner, as demonstrated further in the following step.

Step 3 The Initial Feasible Solution. An initial solution can be found by any of several available procedures. One of these is demonstrated next: initial assignment by the northwest corner rule.

a. Starting with the northwest corner (left, uppermost in the table), allocate the smaller amount of either the row supply or the column demand.

Table 6.9 Balanced Matrix

Source \ Destination	R	S	T	D (dummy)	Supply
A	1	2	3	0	200
B	4	1	5	0	100
Demand	80	120	60	40 (excess supply)	300 / 300

Table 6.10   Initial Solution by the Northwest Corner Rule

Source \ Destination	R	S	T	Supply	Remaining Supply
A	[1] 80	[2] 20	[3]	100	0
B	[4]	[1] 100	[5] 10	110	0
D (dummy)	[0]	[0]	[0] 50	50	0
Demand	80	120	60	260	
Remaining Demand	0	0	0		

   b. Subtract from the row supply and from the column demand the amount allocated.
   c. If the column demand is now zero, move to the cell next on the right; if the row demand is zero, move down to the cell in the next row.
   d. Once a cell is identified as per Step c, allocate to it an amount as per Step a.
   e. Repeat Steps a–d until all supply and demand are zero.

The advantage of this rule is that it is a simple mechanical process. The problem presented in Table 6.7 is balanced in Table 6.10 and serves as an example to illustrate an assignment by the northwest corner rule.

Initially, an amount of 80 tons is allocated to cell AR, out of the 100 available in source A, meeting all the demand of destination R. The remaining supply of 20 tons at source A is then allocated to cell AS, since that is the closest in the A row to AR. The capacity of row A has now been exhausted, but the demand of S has not yet been fully satisfied. Therefore, 100 tons of the 110-ton supply of source B is allocated to cell BS in order to meet the entire demand of destination S. Then, moving to the right in row B, the remaining supply of B (10 tons) is allocated to cell BT. This exhausts the supply in row B, but the destination T still needs 50 units. Moving down column T, the remainder (50 tons) is allocated to cell DT. In this fashion, the entire supply has been used and the entire demand has been satisfied. Cells that receive allocations are called "occupied" to distinguish them from the remaining empty or unoccupied ones.

The initial solution shown in Table 6.10 calls for shipments of

$$
\begin{aligned}
80 \text{ tons from A to R at a cost of } 80 \times 1 &= \$\ 80 \\
20 \text{ tons from A to S at a cost of } 20 \times 2 &= 40 \\
100 \text{ tons from B to S at a cost of } 100 \times 1 &= 100 \\
10 \text{ tons from B to T at a cost of } 10 \times 5 &= 50 \\
50 \text{ tons from D to T at no cost } &= 0 \\
\text{Total} \quad &\$270
\end{aligned}
$$

Note that warehouse T supposedly obtains 50 tons from D (dummy); that is, there is a shortage (unsatisfied demand) of 50 tons at warehouse T.

Once an initial solution is achieved, a test for optimality can be conducted.

Step 4 Testing for Optimality. The purpose of the optimality test is to check whether the proposed solution, just generated, is optimal or not. For each empty cell, the effect of changing it to an occupied cell is examined. If any of these changes are favorable, the solution is not optimal and a new solution must be designed. A general method for calculating the effect of such a change is called "the stepping stone method."

Note: The solution to be checked for optimality must be "nondegenerate"; that is, the number of occupied cells must be $m + n - 1$ (where m = number of sources and n = number of destinations). A method to handle degeneracy is given in Reference 24.

The Stepping Stone Method. The stepping stone method executes the final two steps of the transportation algorithm combined.

Step 4: Testing for optimality. This is done by calculating the "cell evaluators" for all the empty cells.

Step 5: Improving a nonoptimal solution. This is done by the following:
1. Identify the incoming cell.
2. Design an improved solution.

Details of Step 4: Start with Building a Closed Loop. A "cell evaluator" for an empty cell is a number designating the cost change that results from occupying that cell rather than one of the currently occupied cells. In order to fill an empty cell, a transfer has to be made from a currently occupied cell. Such a transfer, subject to the supply and demand constraints, will affect a total of four or more cells. The evaluator is calculated by determining the overall effect on the total cost of shifting one unit to that empty cell. The signs of the cell evaluators enable us to test for optimality.

In Table 6.11 a demonstration is given of how to calculate the cell evaluator for the empty cell AT (based on the Northwest Corner initial solution, Table 6.10). One unit is moved from the occupied cell AS to AT (following the top double arrow). Cell AT is called the *gaining cell* and a "plus" sign is placed there; cell AS is labeled the *losing cell* and a "minus" sign is placed there. However, since one unit is moved to cell AT, column T will now have $1 + 10 + 50 = 61$, which is more than the 60 required. Therefore, in order to maintain the demand requirement, one unit is moved from the occupied cell, BT, to occupied cell BS (follow bottom double arrow). The new number of units in each cell is now circled.

As a result of this transaction, the row supply requirements are maintained.

Table 6.11 Evaluation of Cell AT

Source \ Destination	R	S	T	Supply
A	1 80	2 (19) ~~20~~ ⟶ +	3 (1)	100
B	4 (101) ~~100~~ + ⟵	1	5 (9) ~~10~~	110
D (dummy)	0	0	0 50	50
Demand	80	120	60	260

For row A: 80 + 19 + 1 = 100
For row B: 101 + 9 = 110

So are the column demands.

For column S: 19 + 101 = 120
For column T: 1 + 9 + 50 = 60

The entire movement process is indicated by a *closed loop* of arrows. Such a closed loop will involve at least four, and sometimes more, cells.

Rule for Drawing Each Closed Loop. When tracing a closed loop, start with the empty cell to be evaluated and draw an arrow from it to an occupied cell in the same row (or column). Only occupied cells are used; otherwise it would not be clear which unoccupied cell the evaluator corresponded to. Next, move vertically or horizontally, but never diagonally, to another occupied cell. Follow the same procedure to other occupied cells until returning to the original empty cell. At each turn of the loop (the loop may cross over itself at times), plus and minus signs are alternately placed in the cells, starting with a + in the empty cell. One further important restriction is that there must be exactly one positive cell and exactly one negative cell in any row or column through which the loop happens to turn. This restriction is imposed to ensure that the requirements of supply and demand will not be violated when the units are shifted. Note that an even number of at least four cells must participate in a loop and the occupied cells can be visited once and only once.

Evaluation of Cell AT. Let us calculate the cost effect of the changes arising from the decision to ship one unit to the empty cell AT. In cells AT and BS, one unit is added so the additional cost is (3 + 1) = 4. In cells BT and AS, one unit is deleted and the cost is reduced by (5 + 2) = 7. Thus, by executing this exchange we simultaneously *increase* the total cost by 4 and *reduce* the total cost by 7, that is, alter the total cost by 4 − 7 = −3.

This value of -3 is then the *cell evaluator* of cell AT. The minus sign indicates a cost reduction; that is, the transaction in this case is favorable.

> *Definition.* The cell evaluator is the sum of the costs of all cells that gained one unit minus the sum of the costs of all cells that lost one unit.

This evaluation process must now be extended to *all* unoccupied cells.

Cost Analysis. By drawing these closed loops, *all* the empty cells of Table 6.10 can be evaluated. The results are as follows:

Empty Cell	Cell Evaluator
AT	-3
BR	$+4$
DR	$+5$
DS	$+4$

Test of Optimality. Once the cell evaluators for *all* the empty cells have been computed, their signs are examined.

Test for a Minimization (Cost) Problem. If one or more of the cell evaluators is negative,* the existing solution is not optimal.

The logic for this test is that an empty cell (not presently part of the solution) with a negative sign will reduce the total cost if it becomes occupied. The proposed solution is thus *improvable* and therefore not optimal.

In the example just presented, cell AT has a negative evaluator. Thus, the initial solution of Table 6.10 is not optimal.

Step 5. Improving a Nonoptimal Solution. Having discovered that a solution is not optimal, the next step in the transportation algorithm is to find a better solution. The operations in this step are

1. *Identify the "incoming" cell (empty cell to be occupied):* In a minimization case the incoming cell is located by identifying the *most negative* cell evaluator.† In the example, the incoming cell is AT (since only one cell is negative).

2. *Design an improved solution:* Once the incoming cell has been identified, an improvement is made by shifting *as many units as possible* along the "closed loop" into that empty cell. The quantity limit to this shifting process is reached when one of the two "losing" cells becomes empty.‡ In our case, of the two losing cells in Table 6.11, AS and BT,

---

*A cell evaluator of 0 indicates the existence of another solution just as good as the current solution. Thus, in the final solution, if cell evaluators of 0 exist, this indicates the existence of multiple optimal solutions.

†If two or more cells have the same value, the cell that can accept the most units is chosen.

‡If two or more of the losing cells contain the same number of units, both will become empty simultaneously and a "degenerate" solution will result (see Reference 24 for solution approaches).

Table 6.12 Improved Solution

Source \ Destination	R	S	T	Supply
A	1 80	2 10	3 10	100
B	4	1 110	5	110
D (dummy)	0	0	0 50	50
Demand	80	120	60	260

cell BT becomes empty first, when 10 units are shifted around the closed loop (10 from BT to BS, 10 from AS to AT). The improved solution is shown in Table 6.12. Once an improved solution is generated, the optimality test (Step 4) is repeated.

Optimality Test. The evaluators of all the empty cells are computed. The results are as follows:

Empty Cell	Cell Evaluator
BR	+4
BT	+3
DR	+2
DS	+1

Since *all* the empty cells have nonnegative cell evaluators, an optimal solution has been obtained. This optimal solution calls for a shipment of

80 units from A to R at a cost of $1/ton, total	$ 80
10 units from A to S at a cost of $2/ton, total	20
10 units from A to T at a cost of $3/ton, total	30
110 units from B to S at a cost of $1/ton, total	110
50 units from dummy to T at no cost	0
Total cost	$240

This, compared with the original Northwest Corner solution, represents a reduction in cost of $30. Notice that the demand requirements of destination T have, in reality, not been completely satisfied since 50 units are shipped out of the dummy source D.

6.9 SUMMARY AND KEY LEARNING POINTS

From the determination of the facility's capacity in Chapter 5, this chapter took us the next step—deciding the best place to locate the facility, including a consideration of the supply/distribution logistics. A brief overview of some aspects of transportation logistics was given, including the major traffic modes and the routing problem.

The location decision for a single facility was addressed in three consecutive stages. Regional location considerations, including international, were discussed first and some potentially helpful models were illustrated. Then, the factors entering the community selection decision were discussed and a breakeven-type model was suggested to compare some of these factors. Last, the considerations entering the site selection decision were noted, with special attention paid to the location decision for pure service organizations, and a "scoring" model was illustrated to help compare the quantitative and qualitative factors.

Finally, the multifacility problem was briefly addressed and an example was developed which used the "transportation method" of linear programming for its solution. The details of this method were explained in the chapter appendix.

The key learning points of this chapter have been

- Though many other considerations enter the facility location decision, the supply/distribution logistics are a primary factor. Because of the importance of logistics, there exist many tradeoffs between transportation of the output (primarily the facilitating good but, on occasion, pure services also) and location of the facility.

- Organizations that process natural resources will typically locate near their source. Organizations that produce an immobile output will locate where the output must finally exist. Pure service organizations will tend to locate near the center of their drawing, or service, area.

- Among the five traffic modes—water, pipeline, rail, truck, and air—water is the cheapest, air is the fastest for long distances, and trucks are the most flexible. The routing problem, addressed *after* a mode of transportation has been selected, concerns what vehicles will take what outputs to what recipients by what routes.

- The four major factors to consider in the regional selection decision are proximity to both raw materials and recipients, the nature of regional labor, the availability of other operations inputs, and the acceptability of the regional environment.

- Regional selection models such as center of gravity and incremental analysis are based on the concept of using the total cost of transportation (including rate, distance, volume, and weight factors) as the primary measure of good locations.

- At the community selection decision level, most of the regional factors would again be considered but additional factors would be added such as community attitudes toward the organization, staff preferences, and monetary (financing, tax) aspects. By plotting fixed and variable costs versus output volume, a breakeven-type analysis can be conducted to illustrate the cost differences of the alternative communities.

- Site selection factors include land variables such as size, zoning, and drainage, utility availability, development costs, and transportation accessibility. For organizations in which the recipient comes to the facility, centrality and accessibility are also critical. Scoring models in which weights are given to factors and the qualitative factor scores are then quantified can be helpful in comparing the site factors.

- The multifacility location problem is often complicated by the fact that a set of acceptable locations for the facilities may not be prespecified and the best location for each facility may depend on the locations of all the other facilities, which are yet to be determined. Last, even the *number* of facilities to be located may be unknown and to be determined.

  The transportation model can help address the multifacility problem by determining, once a set of facilities is tentatively located, the lowest cost to supply all needs from the multiple facilities. Then, other facility locations can be tested to see if their cost is still lower.

6.10 KEY TERMS

logistics (p. 164)

economies of scale (p. 166)

mode of transport (p. 167)

pipelining (p. 167)

slurry (p. 167)

routing problem (p. 168)

center of gravity (p. 175)

incremental analysis (p. 176)

weighted score (p. 184)

transportation method (p. 188)

6.11 REVIEW AND DISCUSSION QUESTIONS

1. When would an organization *not* use the three-stage location decision approach discussed in the chapter?

2. Describe other methods for handling multiple criteria. For handling uncertainty or risk.

3. What factors would be considered in locating an airport in a metropolitan area?

4. How much financial inducement should governments be allowed to offer companies to locate in their area?

5. For what service organizations is transportation a viable method of distribution?

6. How have the "piggyback," and now "fishy-back," concepts improved the transportation of goods?

7. Contrast the terms logistics, materials management, procurement, purchasing, distribution, and materiel.

8. Are there any other special categories of organizations than the two given in Section 6.1 whose characteristics might determine where they locate?

9. Interpret the meaning of the data in Table 6.1; in particular, trucking has 40.5 percent of the tonnage but water 43.7 percent of the ton-miles.

10. What other products might be suitable for slurrying for pipelines?

11. What transport modes does the U.S. Post Office use?

12. Interpret the routing problem for garbage trucks. For U-Haul trucks. For prescription deliveries out of a drugstore.

13. Which measures used to locate pure service organizations are direct benefit measures and which are surrogate measures of benefit? Can you think of better direct measures? Why aren't they used?

14. The text pointed out a number of risks when locating in a foreign country. What might be some offsetting advantages?

6.12 PROBLEMS

Practice Problems

1. Find the best point to locate an inspection/repair station to service five valves on a straight pipeline. The valves' locations and their weekly number of required inspections are as follows:

Valve No.	Miles East of Town	No. of Inspections/Week
1	5	3
2	3	6
3	1	2
4	10	2
5	8	4

2. A large waterproof container is used to store supplies for four underwater laboratories as follows. Find the best location for the container.

Lab No.	Location (ft) Depth	East	North	Supply Weight (lb)	Resupply Cost (cents/lb/ft)
1	240	560	320	40	1
2	130	425	270	120	3
3	405	190	485	60	2
4	340	85	170	80	1

3. A politician has suggested locating the inspection/repair station in Problem 1 at valve No. 2 since that valve has the most inspections required per week. Show by incremental analysis whether this is the best location and, if not, in which direction the station should be located.

4. A supply depot is located at $x = 3$, $y = 4$ to supply the following stores as indicated. Use incremental analysis to determine a better location and then test it to verify that it is indeed better.

Store No.	x	y	Trips
1	5	4	7
2	3	5	4
3	3	3	3

5. The head of the Campus Computing Center is faced with locating a new centralized computer center at one of three possible locations on the campus. The decision is to be based on the number of users in each department and the distance of the various departments from each possible location. Which location should be chosen?

Dept.	No. of Users	Distance by Location		
		1	2	3
1	25	0	3	5
2	30	5	4	3
3	10	2	0	1
4	5	3	2	0
5	14	6	2	3

6. A new product venture involves the following costs associated with three possible locations. If demand is forecast to be 3900 units a year, which location should be selected?

	Location		
	A	B	C
Annual fixed cost	$10,000	40,000	25,000
Unit variable cost	$10.00	2.50	6.30

7. The location subcommittee's final report to the board has focused on three acceptable communities. Table 15b in the appendix to the report indicates the cost of locating in communities 1, 2, and 3 to be approximately $400,000, $500,000 and $600,000 per year mortgaged over 30 years. Paragraph 2 on page 39 of the report indicates the variable cost per unit of product will increase 15 percent in community 1 but decrease 15 percent in community 3 due to labor rate differences. As plant operations manager you know that variable costs to date have averaged about $3.05 per unit and sales for the next decade are expected to average 20 percent more than the last 10 years, which saw annual sales vary between 40,000 and 80,000 units. Which location would you recommend?

8. Use a weighted score model to choose between three locations (A, B, C) for setting up a factory. The relative weights for each criterion are shown in the following table. A score of 1 represents unfavorable, 2 satisfactory, and 3 favorable.

Category	Weight	Location		
		A	B	C
Labor costs	20	1	2	3
Labor productivity	20	2	3	1
Labor supply	10	2	1	3
Union relations	10	3	3	2
Material supply	10	2	1	1
Transport costs	25	1	2	3
Infrastructure	10	2	2	2

9. A firm owns facilities at five geographically remote locations. It has man-ufacturing plants at points A and B with daily production capacities of 60 and 40 units, respectively. At points C, D, and E it has warehouses with daily demands of 20, 30, and 50 units, respectively. Shipping costs per mile between these points are the same. Mileages are shown in the following diagram. Given that the firm wishes to minimize its total trans-portation costs, formulate as a transportation problem.

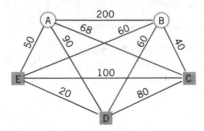

10. The Pollution Control Board of Alligator County has 100 employees: 20 live in city A, 35 in city B, and 45 in city C. The employees have inter-changeable skills and are to be assigned to various laboratories. The Water Laboratory requires 40 employees, the Air Lab requires 30 employees, the Solid Waste Lab requires 20 employees, and the Central Lab requires 10 employees. The distance between the cities and the labs is shown on the following map (in miles along the available streets).

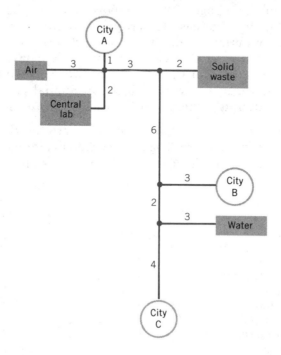

Workers travel by the shortest available route along the streets shown.

What worker-to-lab arrangement minimizes the total distances traveled by all the employees?

Formulate as a transportation problem.

More Complex Problems

11. Use a modified center of gravity method to locate *two* warehouses to service the following retail outlets.

Outlet	Miles North	Miles West
1	50	20
2	10	40
3	60	40
4	40	30
5	0	30
6	50	40
7	10	20

12. Use a map of the United States to optimally decide between Chicago and St. Louis to locate a single facility to serve the following cities. (a) Portland, Oregon—5 carloads per week. (b) Des Moines, Iowa—2 carloads per week. (c) New York, New York—1 carload per week. (d) St. Louis, Missouri—7 carloads per week. (e) Chicago, Illinois—10 carloads per week. (f) New Orleans, Louisiana—5 carloads per week. Assume the same transportation rate per carload to all destinations and a zero cost for same city delivery (e.g., Chicago to Chicago). Use straight-line distances measured by a ruler.

13. Consider Problem 12 again, assuming two small warehouses can be built and operated for 50 percent more than a single ($175,000/year) warehouse. What per-mile cost results in the same expense as the best answer in Problem 12 if the two warehouses are located in Chicago and St. Louis?

14. The Nuclear Energy Commission (NEC) is attempting to locate a nuclear waste dump in a region that is surrounded by three cities as described in the following table. Derive a method for locating the dump and find the best location.

City	Population (in thousands)	Miles East	Miles North
A	40	0	0
B	110	70	20
C	70	30	60

15. Reconsider Problem 6 if the demand forecast is revised as follows. Suggest two ways to solve the problem and then try them out. Might management have reason to select another alternative?

Forecast Demand	Probability
1000	.4
4000	.3
7000	.3

16. A manufacturing concern is considering three possible locations to construct its new factory. The choice depends not only on the operating costs at each location but also on the shipment costs of the product to its three major marketing regions. Given in the following table are the operating cost data and distribution costs. Which location would you recommend for a production volume of 80,000 units per year?

	Location A	Location B	Location C
Construction cost (amortize over 10 years)	$1,000,000	$1,800,000	$950,000
Material cost per unit	2.46	2.17	2.64
Labor cost per unit	0.65	0.62	0.67
Overhead: Fixed	100,000	150,000	125,000
Variable, per unit	0.15	0.18	0.12

Total Distribution Costs

	From Location		
To Region	A	B	C
1	$10,000	$20,000	$26,000
2	17,000	10,000	15,000
3	12,000	18,000	10,000

17. Nina Lewis is trying to decide in which of four shopping centers to locate her new boutique. Some cater to a higher class of clientele than others, some are in an indoor mall, some have a much greater volume than others, and, of course, rent varies considerably. Because of the nature of her store she has decided that the class of clientele is the most important consideration. Following this, however, she *must* pay attention to her expenses and rent is a major item, probably 90 percent as important as clientele. An indoor, temperature-controlled mall is a big help, however, for stores such as hers where 70 percent of sales are from passersby slowly strolling and window shopping. Thus, she rates this as about 95 percent as important as rent. Last, a higher volume of shoppers means more potential sales and she thus rates this factor as 80 percent as important as rent.

To aid her in visualizing her location alternatives she has constructed the following table. A "good" is scored as 3, "fair" as 2, and "poor" as 1. Use a weighted score model to help Nina come to a decision.

	Location			
	1	*2*	*3*	*4*
Class of clientele	Fair	Good	Poor	Good
Rent	Good	Fair	Poor	Good
Indoor mall	Good	Poor	Good	Poor
Volume	Good	Fair	Good	Poor

18. Solve Problem 9.

19. Solve Problem 10.

6.13 REFERENCES AND BIBLIOGRAPHY

1. Abernathy, W. J., and Hershey, J., "A Spatial Allocation Model for Regional Health Services Planning,"*Operations Research*, 20:629–642 (1972).
2. Anderson, D. R., Sweeney, D. J., and Williams, T. A., *Linear Programming for Decision Making: An Applications Approach*, St. Paul, MN: West Publishing, 1974.
3. Beckman, M., *Location Theory*, New York: Random House, 1968.
4. Brown, P. A., and Gibson, D. F., "A Quantified Model for Facility Site Selection—Application to a Multiplant Location Problem," *AIIE Transactions*, 4:1–10 (1972).
5. Coyle, J. J. et al., *The Management of Logistics*, 2nd ed., St. Paul, MN: West Publishing, 1980.
6. Fitzsimmons, J. A., "A Methodology for Emergency Ambulance Deployment," *Management Science*, 19:627–636 (1973).
7. Fulton, M., "New Factors in Plant Location," *Harvard Business Review*, 49:4–17 (May–June 1971).
8. Geoffrion, A. M., and Graves, G. W., "Multicommodity Distribution Systems Design by Benders Decomposition," *Management Science*, 20:822–844 (1974).
9. Hoover, E. M., "Some Programmed Models of Industry Location," *Land Economics*, 18:303–311 (1967).
10. Huff, D., "A Programmed Solution for Approximating an Optimal Retail Location," *Land Economics*, Aug. 1966, pp. 293–303.
11. Karasaka, G. J., and Browball, D. F., *Location Analysis for Manufacturing*, Cambridge, MA: MIT Press, 1969.
12. Khumawala, B. M., and Whybark, D. C., "A Comparison of Some Recent Warehouse Location Techniques," *The Logistics Review*, 7:63 (1971).
13. Magee, J. F., *Industrial Logistics*, New York: McGraw-Hill, 1968.
14. Markland, R. E., "Analyzing Geographically Discrete Warehouse Networks by Computer Simulation," *Decision Sciences*, 4:216–236 (1973).
15. Meredith, J. R., and Shershin, A., "Locating Emergency Medical Rescue Vehicles Under Conditions of Urgency," *Computers and Industrial Engineering*, 2:31–39 (1978).
16. O'Neil, B. F., and Whybark, D. C., "Vehicle Routing from Central Facilities," *The International Journal of Physical Distribution*, Feb. 1972.
17. ReVelle, C., Marks, P., and Liebman, J. D. C., "An Analysis of Private and Public Sector Location Models," *Management Science*, 16:692–707 (1970).
18. Rider, K. L., "A Parametric Model for the Allocation of Fire Companies in New York City," *Management Science*, 23:146–158 (1976).
19. Schmenner, R., "Before You Build a Big Factory," *Harvard Business Review*, 54:100–104 (Aug. 1976).
20. Smykay, E. W., *Physical Distribution Management*, 3rd ed., New York: Macmillan, 1973.
21. Sweeney, D. J. et al., "An Improved Long-Run Model for Multiple Warehouse Location," *Management Science*, 22:748–758 (1976).
22. Tertz, M. B., "Toward a Theory of Urban Public Facility Location," *Papers of the Regional Science Association*, 21:35–51 (1968).
23. Toregas, C. et al., "The Location of Emergency Service Facilities," *Operations Research*, 19:1363–1371 (1971).
24. Turban, E., and Meredith, J. R., *Fundamentals of Management Science*, 2nd ed., Dallas: Business Publications, 1981.

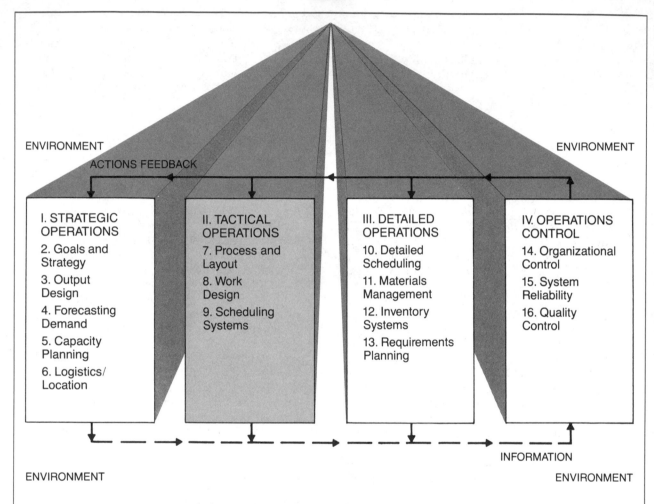

ENVIRONMENT

ACTIONS FEEDBACK

ENVIRONMENT

I. STRATEGIC OPERATIONS

2. Goals and Strategy

3. Output Design

4. Forecasting Demand

5. Capacity Planning

6. Logistics/ Location

II. TACTICAL OPERATIONS

7. Process and Layout

8. Work Design

9. Scheduling Systems

III. DETAILED OPERATIONS

10. Detailed Scheduling

11. Materials Management

12. Inventory Systems

13. Requirements Planning

IV. OPERATIONS CONTROL

14. Organizational Control

15. System Reliability

16. Quality Control

INFORMATION

ENVIRONMENT

ENVIRONMENT

TACTICAL OPERATIONS
DESIGNING THE TRANSFORMATION PROCESS

In this second part of the text we address the task of implementing the strategic operations plan designed in Part I. This procedure, designing the transformation operations, is known as "tactical operations." Here we select the transformation process, design and lay out the workplace activities, and plan the scheduling system that will bring all the inputs together to produce the desired output.

These activities are considered tactical because they are still concerned with designing and planning the organization's operations, but are not top level, strategic decisions such as those made in Part I. Rather, these activities directly follow from the previous strategic decisions concerning the output design, the capacity required, the facility location, and the distribution system. By completing this, the next stage of the design of the transformation system, we will be ready in Part II to plan the final, detailed level which is concerned with who does what on which job at which machine at what time.

In the first chapter of Part II, Chapter 7, we consider the task of selecting and designing the basic transformation process. There are four process alternatives: project, intermittent, continuous, and processing. In this chapter we also describe the procedure for laying out the transformation operations.

In Chapter 8 we look at the workplace activities and ways to design them so as to enhance their productivity. Placing the worker in the transformation process results in what is known as a sociotechnical system. We address the human element of productivity through consideration of the management system (Theory Z, quality circles, quality of worklife programs) and the physiological environment of the workplace (temperature, illumination, fatigue, safety, and so on). We also consider the human-technical elements combined, through the physical design and layout of the workplace as well as the workpace expected of the worker.

Last, in Chapter 9 we look at the first stage of the design of one of the more complex aspects of operations, the scheduling system. We first overview and describe the intricacies of the scheduling process, including the role of computers and the difficulty of scheduling pure services. We then address the "aggregate," or rough-cut, scheduling stage, illustrating its difficulty and describing some scheduling strategies that are appropriate.

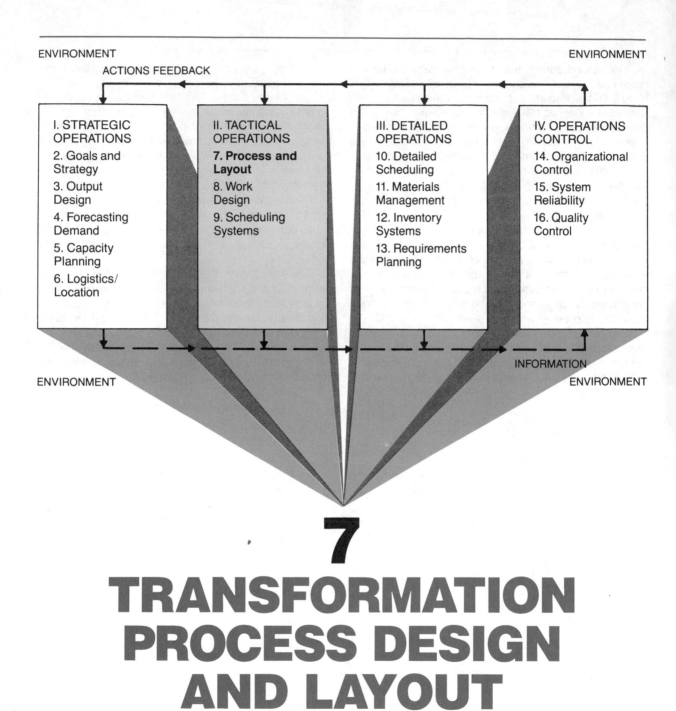

ENVIRONMENT

ENVIRONMENT

ACTIONS FEEDBACK

I. STRATEGIC OPERATIONS

2. Goals and Strategy

3. Output Design

4. Forecasting Demand

5. Capacity Planning

6. Logistics/ Location

II. TACTICAL OPERATIONS

7. Process and Layout

8. Work Design

9. Scheduling Systems

III. DETAILED OPERATIONS

10. Detailed Scheduling

11. Materials Management

12. Inventory Systems

13. Requirements Planning

IV. OPERATIONS CONTROL

14. Organizational Control

15. System Reliability

16. Quality Control

ENVIRONMENT

INFORMATION

ENVIRONMENT

7
TRANSFORMATION PROCESS DESIGN AND LAYOUT

7

LEARNING OBJECTIVES
By the completion of this chapter the student
should

- Have a feel for the general transformation
  process selection and design procedure.
- Know the four forms of transformation
  processes and their characteristics, tradeoffs,
  advantages, and disadvantages.
- Be familiar with the new technologies that are
  applicable to the transformation processes.
- Appreciate the concept of the process life
  cycle.
- Be aware of the types of charts and diagrams
  that aid in designing the transformation
  process.
- Understand the concepts underlying the
  models used to aid in laying out and balancing
  the transformation process.
- Be familiar with the computerized layout and
  line balancing programs.

Chapter 7 focuses directly on the central issue of operations management, designing the transformation process. This is where we decide whether to use mostly labor or mostly machines, whether to employ pushcarts or conveyor belts, whether to hire primarily physicians or nurses, and so on. Up to this point in our progress we have determined how much capacity we will need and how the output will be distributed to the recipients. Now, we will devote two chapters to the transformation design process. Chapter 7 deals with the form of the process and how the operations are laid out in the production facility. Then Chapter 8 looks at the design of the work itself in considerably more detail—the work environment, how individual workers do their job, the organization structure, and so forth.

This chapter concerns the design of the central element in the operations function: the transformation activities. The general procedure in designing the transformation process is to consider all available transformation alternatives in combination with all potential inputs to devise the best strategy for obtaining the desired outputs. The major considerations in this design, *efficiency*, *effectiveness*, *capacity*, *lead time*, *flexibility*, and so on, are so interdependent that changing the process to alter one will change the others as well.

The major considerations in process design.

Suppose, for example, that you decide to go into business for yourself to produce skateboards. There are many options open to you. In terms of the product, you could produce wooden skateboards, plastic boards, or even metal boards. The wheels, too, could be steel or high impact plastic, perhaps tinted or bright translucent red.

Wooden, plastic, or metal skateboards.

Now a wooden board would be simple to make—you could even work out of your own garage. On the other hand, each board would take quite a while to saw, plane, sand, and so on. Much faster would be injection molding a plastic board. You could produce them by the thousands, and at very low cost. But the molding dies will cost you about $30,000. (How much money did you say you had?) And you would have to subcontract the work because injection molding machines are way beyond your league.

So far we have been talking about efficiency, capacity, and flexibility. That is, garage produced wooden boards would be a low capacity, high flexibility operation efficient for low volumes at high prices. But is there a market for wooden boards at high prices? If not, such an operation will not be very *effective*—at least in terms of making a profit. Perhaps a more effective process would be to invest in some semiautomatic equipment to produce a higher volume at a lower unit price.

As you can see from this simple example, the design of the transformation process is a rather complex, but crucially important, procedure. Numerous tradeoffs are available between different materials, labor and equipment, quality and volume, efficiency and flexibility; and every tradeoff will affect the success of your business.

But the transformation design problem is one that never has a final answer; there are only answers given the present circumstances, and circumstances are always changing. Although successful organizations such as the Red Cross, IBM, and Sears, Roebuck and Co. may appear to be common,

Process design
is an
unending problem;
adaptation is the
key.

they in fact are exceptions in the world of organizations. Their key to continued success is that they have constantly redesigned their transformation process as the environment and demand changed; that is, they have *adapted*. Many organizations chose, or continued to use, a transformation process that was not viable for the environment or demand; in some cases *no* transformation process would have been viable because the market was insufficient, or the technology was unavailable.

Constant
environmental
change.

In an environment of constant change the transformation process may have to be constantly redesigned to cope with changing demands, new products and services, government regulations, and constant technological advances. Robots, decreased productivity, materials scarcities, minicomputers, and energy shortages are only a few examples of the changes in the past decade that have forced organizations to recognize the necessity of adaptation in their operations.

Generic focus.

Our discussion of these issues will again maintain a generic focus. In the first section we present the various forms of transformation processes, discuss their advantages and disadvantages, and then give examples from all kinds of product and service organizations. Section 7.2 addresses the issue of selecting one of these process forms, and the following section presents an example of designing the transformation process for the mass production of a ballpoint pen. Various charts and diagrams are described that can aid in the design of this process.

Sections 7.4 and 7.5 describe the procedure for laying out the workflow for intermittent and continuous flow operations, respectively. In the former, operations sequence analysis is used to lay out a university division's offices and a manufacturing plant. In the latter, the technique of line balancing is used to help lay out the workflow for a credit agency.

7.1 FORMS OF TRANSFORMATION PROCESSES

The general design
procedure.

A general schematic of the transformation process design is illustrated in Figure 7.1. Initially, the desired output is specified in terms of function (form, quality, etc.) and quantity for a given time horizon (e.g., 100 wooden skateboards a month for the first year). The output is then subdivided into a set of natural or logical components (wheels, boards, screws), each of which can be studied separately. This procedure may be repeated with subcomponents (ballbearings) and sub-subcomponents until some elemental component is reached. Each component is then analyzed to determine how it can be (1) obtained (make or buy) and (2) combined with other components (screws, glue). Consideration is given to equipment, staffing, leasing, subcontracting, workplace design, tooling, and so forth. Continuous specification and respecification of both the output (fiberglass boards?) and the process (100 percent hand made?) are required to remain competitive, simplify the process, make it more efficient, improve output quality, increase flexibility or output rate, eliminate bottlenecks, and so on.

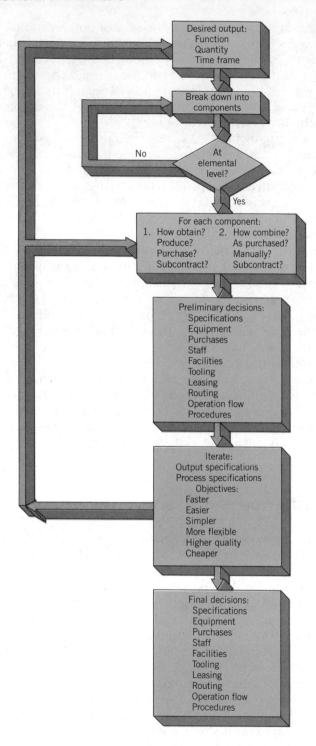

Figure 7.1 Designing the transformation process.

Volume/Variety Considerations

One of the most important factors in the design of the transformation process is establishing the volume and variety of outputs the organization will produce. High volumes tend to indicate that a highly automated, mass production process will be necessary. High variety, on the other hand, implies the use of skilled labor using general purpose tools and facilities.

Make-to-stock versus make-to-order.
A related consideration here is whether the output will be **make-to-stock** or **make-to-order.** A make-to-stock item is typically produced in some economical (for the firm) *batch size* and then stocked (in a warehouse, on shelves, etc.). As customers purchase them, the items are withdrawn from stock. A make-to-order item is usually produced in a batch size set by the customer (sometimes just *one*) and is delivered to the customer upon its completion. Generally, make-to-stock items are produced in large volumes with low variety whereas make-to-order items are produced in low volumes with high variety (quite often *every* item is different).

Clearly, services will not normally be of the type that can be stocked, even if every service is identical (e.g., a physical examination). Also, exceptions to the above cases are abundant. Automobiles, for example, are made-to-order, yet produced in high volume and with high variety. (However, autos are really *assembled* to order; the assembly components are produced to *stock*.) And general purpose machine shops often produce high volumes of low variety items for specific customers.

Assemble to order.

Figure 7.2*a* illustrates our previous comments as they relate to the various forms of transformation processes. The horizontal axis shows the volume, as measured by the batch size, and the left vertical axis shows the variety of outputs. Essentially, no organizations operate in the upper right and lower left segments of this grid. Those organizations that make a single unit of output that varies each time (such as dams, and custom-built machines) use the "project," or sometimes "intermittent" process form (described further below). Some services also fall into this region, as indicated by the upper left tip of the oval. Intermittent flow processes, however, are mainly used, as shown, when a considerable variety of outputs exists but in relatively small batch sizes. This is particularly descriptive of services.

The process forms.

When the batch size increases significantly, with a corresponding decrease in variety, then a "continuous" flow process form is appropriate. Some services also fall into this category. Last, when all the output is the same and the size of the batch is extremely large (essentially infinite in the ore, petrochemical, and food and drink industries), the "processing" form is appropriate (hence the term "the processing industries"). Very few services exist here. Again, these forms will be described further below.

Much overlap.

But before we leave Figure 7.2, note the overlap in the different forms. This means that, on occasion, some organizations will be using a continuous flow process for outputs with a smaller batch size or larger variety, or both, than the outputs of other organizations that are using an intermittent flow process, for example. There are many possible reasons for this including economical and historical factors. The organization may also simply be using

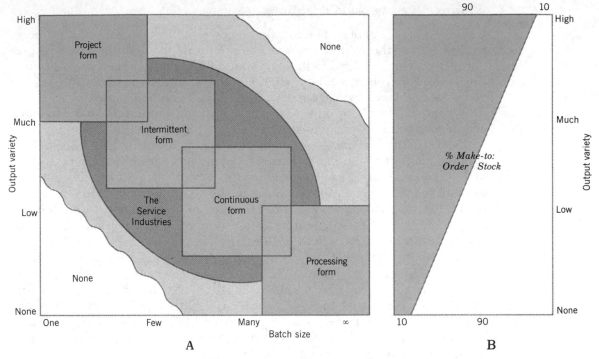

Figure 7.2 Effect of output characteristics on transformation process form. (Adapted from Reference 15.)

an inappropriate process. The point is that the categories are not rigid and many variations do occur. Many organizations also use hybrids or combinations of the processes, such as producing components to stock but assembling finished products to order, as in the auto industry.

Note in Figure 7.2b the general breakdown of make-to-order/make-to-stock with output variety and batch size. Project forms (high variety, unit batch size) are almost always make-to-order and processing forms (no variety, infinite batch size) are almost always make-to-stock, though exceptions occasionally occur. Let us now look further into these separate process forms, their attributes, and their advantages and disadvantages.

Project Processes

Project operations are typically of large scale and finite duration and are nonrepetitive, consisting of multiple, and often simultaneous, tasks that are highly interdependent. However, the primary characteristics of the tasks are limited duration and, if the output is a physical product, immobility during

Fixed position.   processing (referred to as **fixed position** assembly). Generally, staff, materials, and equipment are brought to the output and located in a nearby

Limited lives.   *staging area* until needed. Projects have particularly limited "lives." Resources are brought together for the duration of the project, some are consumed, and others, such as equipment and personnel, are deployed to other uses at the conclusion of the project.

Staging area. Frequently, the output is unique (dam, park) but need not be (airplanes, buildings). Furthermore, once at the staging area, the process may even appear to be more continuous in nature than intermittent. For example, housing reconstruction in Europe following World War II utilized mammoth equipment that would dig entire basements at once or pour complete foundations and then roll over to the next homesite and do the same thing. Following are examples of projects:

Constructing highways, bridges, tunnels, and dams.

Building ships, planes, rockets.

Typical projects. Erecting skyscrapers, steel mills, homes, and processing plants.

Locating and laying out amusement parks, camping grounds, and refuges.

Organizing conferences, banquets, conventions.

Managing R&D projects such as the Manhattan Project (atomic bomb).

Running political campaigns, war operations, advertising campaigns, or fire fighting operations.

Chairing ad hoc task forces, overseeing government agency planning, or conducting corporate audits.

As may be noticed in this list, the number of project operations is growing in our economy, probably at about the same rate as services (which many of them are). Some of the reasons for this growth in project operations are

1. *More Sophisticated Technology:* An outgrowth of our space age, and its technology, has been an increased public awareness of project operations (e.g., Project Apollo) and interest in using the project form to achieve society's goals (Operation Headstart).

2. *Better Educated Citizens:* People themselves are more aware of the world around them and techniques (such as project management) for achieving their objectives.

The growth of project processes.
3. *More Leisure Time:* People have the time available to follow, and even participate in, projects.

4. *Increased Accountability:* Society as a whole has increased its emphasis on the attainment of objectives (affirmative action, environmental protection, increased gasoline mileage) and the evaluation of activities leading toward those objectives.

5. *Higher Productivity:* People and organizations are involved in more activities, and more productive in those activities, than ever before.

Choosing the Project Form of Process Design

In designing a processing system there are a number of considerations that may indicate the appropriateness of the project design form. One of

Projects for high output diversity or differing technologies.

these is the diversity in the mix of outputs. If the technology for one output differs significantly from that of another (e.g., bridges, tunnels), then separate projects for the two outputs are appropriate. Another, similar consideration is the rate of change in the organization's outputs. If one department must keep current on a number of outputs (e.g., satellites, rockets, planes) that are rapidly changing, the organization will soon be falling behind its competition. The project form offers extremely short reaction times to environmental or internal changes; thus, separate project operations would again be called for. Last, if the tasks are for a limited duration only, the project form is indicated.

Not of value in advancing technology.

One of the advantages of the project form of process design is its ability to perform under crucial time and cost constraints. Therefore, if the performance time or cost are crucial factors for the output being considered, the project form is most appropriate. However, the project form, having a mixed personnel complement of different functional specialists (engineers, scientists, theoreticians, technicians, etc.) may be less capable of advancing high technology areas than process designs, in which operations are organized by specialty areas. In these latter designs, a number of specialists can be brought together to solve a problem. In addition, specialized resources (such as staff and equipment) often cannot be justified because of their low utilization; hence, generalized resources must be used instead.

Projects for coordinating multiple activities.

Last, the project design form is typically chosen when the output is of a very large scale with multiple, interdependent activities requiring close coordination. During the project, coordination is achieved through frequent meetings of the representatives of the various functional areas.

Project Process Design

The short life cycle of projects.

Since one of the main advantages of project processes is the ability to perform under time constraints, most projects are designed for a limited lifetime. The usual life cycle is characterized by an early buildup of resources and activities, a leveling off as work nears completion, and a cutting back as project termination approaches. This aspect of the design presents two problems.

Two personnel problems.

1. To quickly increase the staff, many of the personnel are borrowed from other ongoing areas in the organization. They therefore may have limited experience with the special duties of the project, short-lived interest, and limited loyalty.

2. Since everyone knows the project is of limited duration, as the end of the project draws near, the staff may begin spending more time getting prepared for the next job, leaving the project to drag out beyond its due date.

Managing professionals. The use of MBO.

However, the choice of the project form usually indicates the importance of the project objective to the organization. Thus, top-grade resources, including staff, are often made available for the project operations. The result is that project organizations typically become very "professionalized" and are often managed on that basis. That is, minimal supervision is exercised, administrative routine is minimized, and management by objectives (MBO) is the rule. In this MBO approach, the professional is given the problem and the performance (results, cost, time deadline) that is required. The individual is then given the privacy, comfort, and freedom to decide *how* to solve her or his portion of the problem.

A great many projects require varying emphases during their life cycle. For example, technical performance may be crucial at the beginning, cost overruns in the middle, and on-time completion at the end. The flexibility of making such spur-of-the-moment changes in emphasis by trading off one criterion for another is basic to the project design form. This ability results from the close contact of the project manager with the technical staff—there are few, if any, "middle managers."

Sudden changes requiring tradeoffs.

In physical project operations, such as bridge construction, most of the *production*, per se, is completed elsewhere and brought to the project area at the proper time. As a result, a great many project activities are *assembly* operations. The project design form concentrates resources on the achievement of specific objectives primarily through proper *scheduling* and *control* of activities, many of which are simultaneous. Some of the scheduling considerations in project management are knowing what activities must be completed and in what order, how long they will take, when to increase and decrease the labor force, and when to order materials so they will not arrive too early (thus requiring storage and being in the way) or too late (thus delaying the project). The control activities include anticipating what can, and might, go wrong, knowing what resources can be shifted among activities to keep the project on schedule, and so forth. In Chapter 10 we describe two techniques, critical path method (CPM) and program evaluation and review technique (PERT), that were designed specifically to address such issues. These techniques are also available as "canned" (preprogrammed) computer packages from computer manufacturers and consultants in the field.

Importance of scheduling and control.

CPM.
PERT.

Next, in Figure 7.2, let us consider the intermittent flow process form.

Intermittent Flow Processes

In this design each output is processed differently and therefore the flow of work through the facility tends to be of an **intermittent** nature. The general characteristics of this form are a *grouping* of staff and equipment according to function; a large *variety* of inputs; a considerable amount of *transport* of either staff, materials, or recipients; and large *variations* in system throughput times (the time it takes for a complete "job," a billable set of tasks, to be processed). In general, each output takes a different route through the organization, requires different operations, uses different inputs, and takes a different amount of time.

Intermittent design for one-of-a-kind outputs.

This type of process design is common when the outputs differ significantly in their form, structure, materials, or required processing. For example, an organization with a wide variety of outputs or one that does custom work (e.g., custom skateboards) would probably use an intermittent process form.

The job shop.   Product organizations of this type are often called **job shops.** Specific examples of both product and service organizations of this form are tailor shops, general offices, machine shops, public parks, physicians' offices, supermarkets, libraries, automobile repair shops, criminal justice systems, department stores, and wholesalers. By and large, the intermittent process is especially appropriate to service organizations because services are often customized and hence each service requires different operations. This is illustrated in the following example.

Little People's Day Care

Suppose you have decided to open up a local day-care service for neighborhood parents. As young couples tend to find out after a while, every child is different. This means that your care for such children will probably also have to be different. Some like to be read to, others like to be left alone, some like toys, others like television, still others like children like themselves to play with, and almost all like to eat (but different things). As you can imagine, this makes for quite a mess.

You will need "general purpose" equipment (television, play yards, bicycles, juice and crackers) that will appeal to general interests and varied ages. You cannot *afford* to buy equipment that only an 18-month old is interested in—you may not even *get* an 18-month old. Similarly, your staff should be broadly skilled—equally at home keeping records and forms, playing the piano, and making mud pies. Again, you cannot afford someone who can only keep books and hates mud.

The flexibility of intermittent processes.   What you have started is an organization designed along the *intermittent* transformation process form. An organization that desires to produce a wide variety of individualized outputs (reading, eating, playing) will probably utilize an intermittent production process to gain *flexibility*. To gain the flexibility required to produce the large variety of outputs, general purpose equipment and broadly skilled staff are necessary. Also, because of the variety of outputs there is usually a need for a variety of input materials.

Organizing around standard operations.   Since only small volumes of any one output are produced, it is not worthwhile to form "production lines" for the outputs. (In a production line each child, one at a time, would first eat, then play with toys, then go to the restroom, then to the playground, then listen to music, etc.) Instead of organizing around standard *outputs* the most efficient procedure for intermittent production is to organize around standard *operations functions*. In intermittent production, then, all similar types of operations are grouped together. For example, all the children have juice and crackers in one spot, sandbox play at another spot, and so on. Or in a hospital, all x-ray functions are grouped together, all pharmaceuticals together, and all obstetric patients together.

The result of such a process design is that each output, or small group of outputs, follows a different processing "route" through the facility, from one location to another. This type of process design, as a result, usually

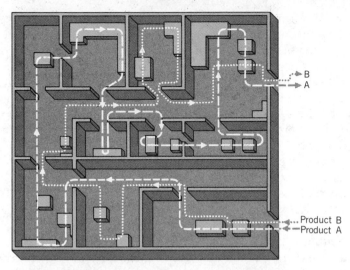

Figure 7.3 A generalized intermittent process design operation.

Characteristics of the intermittent process.

requires a considerable amount of transportation equipment: fork lifts, pallet trucks, little legs, dumbwaiters, wheelchairs, and so forth. It also typically results in large variations in throughput time. (Many children are ready to go home by 10 A.M.; others want to stay forever.) Each output may require different operations or sequences, thereby using different paths through the process. In some instances, all the outputs require one common operation (such as use of the restroom or, in manufacturing, inspection) and hence bottlenecks may occur.

The difficulty of management.

Clearly, the efficient management of an intermittent process is a difficult task since every output must be treated differently. Also, the resources available to process them are limited. Furthermore, not only is it management's task to ensure the performance of the proper functions of each output, where the outputs may have varying quality and deadline considerations, but management must also be sure that the available resources (staff, equipment, materials, supplies, capital) are being efficiently utilized. There is always a difficult tradeoff between efficiency and flexibility of operations. Intermittent transformation processes tend to emphasize flexibility over efficiency.

Figure 7.3 pictorially represents the flow through an intermittent process operation. This facility may be a library, an auto repair shop, or an office. Each particular "job" travels from one area to another, and so on, according to its unique routing, until it is fully processed. Temporary in-process storage may occur between various operations while jobs are waiting for subsequent processing (standing in line for the coffee machine). The widespread use of the job-shop process design form is due to its many advantages.

Advantages of the Intermittent Form

The intermittent design form is usually selected to provide the organization with the flexibility needed to respond to individual, small volume (or

Variety at low cost.

even custom) demands in the environment. The ability to produce a wide variety of outputs at reasonable cost is thus the primary advantage of this design form. Since general purpose rather than special purpose equipment is used, it is in greater demand and is usually available from more suppliers at a lower price than special purpose equipment. In addition, used equipment is more likely to be available, further reducing the necessary investment. There is a larger base of experience with general purpose equipment and therefore maintenance and setup problems are more predictable and replacement parts more widely available. Last, since general purpose equipment is easier to modify or use elsewhere and disposal is much easier, obsolescence expense is minimized.

Facility advantages.

Because of the functional arrangement of the intermittent process design form, other advantages accrue to the organization as well. Functions requiring special staff, materials, or facilities (e.g., painting or audiovisual equipment) may centralize the location of these resources at that function and save through high utilization rates. Distracting or dangerous equipment, supplies, or activities may also be segregated from other operations in facilities that are soundproof, airtight, explosion proof, and so forth.

Staff advantages.

An advantage to the staff of a functional arrangement is the increased responsibility, pride of workmanship, and reduced boredom that accompanies more highly skilled work involving constantly varying jobs. Other advantages to the staff are the concentrations of experience and expertise available and the increase in morale when similarly skilled staff work together in the centralized locations (all music teachers together). And because the pace of the work is not dictated by a moving "line," incentive pay arrangements may be set up to further benefit the staff. Last, because no line exists that must keep forever moving, the entire set of organizational operations does not halt whenever any one part of the operation stops working; other functional areas can continue operating, at least until in-process inventory is depleted. And commonly, other general purpose resources can substitute for the nonfunctioning resource: one machine for another, one staff member for another, one material for another.

Disadvantages of the Intermittent Form

Poor for high volumes.

The general purpose equipment of intermittent processes is usually slower than special purpose equipment, resulting in higher variable (per unit) costs. In addition, the cost of direct labor for the experienced staff necessary to operate general purpose equipment further increases unit costs of production above what semi- or unskilled staff would require. The result, in terms of costs for the outputs, is that the variable costs of production for the general purpose equipment, facilities, and staff are higher than for special purpose, but the initial cost of the equipment and facilities is significantly less. For small output volumes the intermittent-process design alternative results in a lower total cost. As output volumes increase, however, the high variable costs begin to outweigh the savings in initial investment. The result is that, for high production volumes, the intermittent process design form is not the most economic (although its use may still be dictated by other considerations such as when particular equipment threatens workers' health or safety).

Large in-process inventory.

Inventories are also frequently a disadvantage in the intermittent form of operations, especially in product organizations. Not only do many types of raw materials, parts, and supplies have to be kept for the wide variety of outputs anticipated, but *in-process inventories*, that is, jobs waiting for processing, typically become very large and thereby represent a sizable capital investment for the organization. Because there are so many inventory items that must travel between operations areas to be processed, the materials handling costs are also typically high. Since the job routings between operations are not identical, inexpensive fixed materials handling mechanisms like conveyor belts cannot be used. Instead, larger and more costly materials handling equipment is used, and therefore corridors and aisles must be large enough to accommodate them. This necessitates allocating even more facility space beyond the extra needed to store additional inventories.

Need for expeditors.

Finally, management control of the intermittent form is extremely difficult, as mentioned earlier. Because of the output variety in function, processing, quality, and timing, the management tasks of routing, scheduling, cost accounting, and such become nearly impossible when the output demand is high. "Expeditors" must track down lost jobs and reorder priorities. And, in addition to watching the progress of individual jobs, management must continually strive to achieve the proper balance of materials, staff, and equipment; otherwise, highly expensive resources will sit idle while bottlenecks occur elsewhere. (In Chapter 10 we discuss some of the available scheduling techniques to help manage such problems.)

New Technology for Intermittent Flow Operations

All related to computers.

Many new technologies of the last decade are making a significant impact on both intermittent and continuous flow operations. Acronyms such as ICAM, CAD, PICS, CAE, and others, almost all in some way related to computers, are sweeping through our trade, academic, and even public vocabularies and magazines. Those more appropriate to continuous flow operations will be discussed in the next section. Of those relevant to intermittent operations, the following are the most important.

PICS. These are computerized **p**roduction and **i**nventory **c**ontrol **s**ystems and include a host of proprietary software programs (e.g., COPICS, MAPICS, MACPAC, MANMAN) for manufacturing, transportation, distribution, retailing, and service industries. In general, the computer tracks inputs and outputs to the system, generates purchase orders, simulates schedules, and performs many other information functions. Of special relevance to operations are the scheduling and materials management functions; these are described in more detail in Chapters 9 and 13, respectively.

ICAM. These **i**ntegrated **c**omputer-**a**ided **m**anufacturing packages tie PICS-type systems into mechanical systems that control machinery (by **n**umerical **c**ontrol, or NC) and materials handling equipment. Thus, both planning and action are controlled together to increase productivity. The materials handling systems are described in more detail in Chapter 11.

MRP II. This term, "**m**anufacturing **r**esource **p**lanning," coined by Oliver Wight (a noted manufacturing consultant), relates to the concept of tying the PICS system into the firm's other planning and accounting systems. This would include the payroll, marketing, personnel, finance, and other systems to help plan cash flows, promotional needs, and so on. The advantages accruing to organizations that closely coordinate their activities are significant and improve the firm's ability to compete (on lead times, price, and quality) much more than normally expected.

Group Technology. This concept, translated primarily from first Russia and then Great Britain, relates to reorganizing an intermittent flow process into a set of multiple, continuous flow lines. The advantage gained is the reduction in lead time on jobs (e.g., from 5 months down to a week). The procedure begins by grouping parts into "families" that are all produced on basically the same set of machines and in the same sequence. Thus, all "rolled" parts are produced on one line, all "turned" parts on another, and so on. The disadvantage of this reorganization is the often necessary duplication of machinery and the task of "part-coding" into families in the first place. We will consider the general continuous flow process and its advantages and disadvantages next.

Families of parts.

Continuous Flow Processes

In this process form all of the outputs are basically treated the same and workflow is thus relatively **continuous.** Product organizations of this form are often called **flow shops** and are typically heavily automated with large, special-purpose equipment. The characteristics of this process design are relatively fixed inputs, operations throughput times, and outputs. Examples of the continuous form are pencil manufacturing, steel making, automobile production, the car wash, and life insurance processing.

Flow shops.

An organization that produces, or plans to produce, a high volume of a small variety of outputs will thus probably organize the operations on a continuous process basis. In doing so, the organization will take advantage of the simplicity and variable-cost savings that accrue from such a process. Since outputs and operations are standardized, specialized equipment can be used to perform the necessary operations at low per unit costs while the relatively large fixed costs of the equipment are distributed over a large volume of outputs.

Continuous operations for high volume, standardized outputs.

Continuous types of materials handling equipment, such as pipelines and conveyors, again operating at low per-unit costs, can be used because the operations are standardized and, typically, all outputs follow the same path from one operation to the next. Also, this standardization of treatment provides for a fixed, known throughput time, giving operations managers easier control of the process and marketing more reliable delivery dates. The continuous process is easier to manage for other reasons as well: routing, scheduling, and control are all facilitated by the fact that each output does not

Standard routes— standard operations.

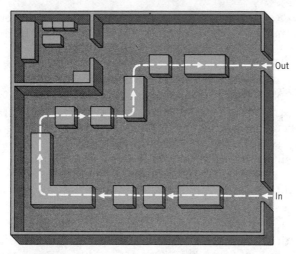

Figure 7.4 A generalized continuous process design operation.

have to be individually monitored and controlled. Standardization of operations means that lower worker skill levels can be used and each manager's span of control can increase.

The general form of the continuous process is illustrated in Figure 7.4. Shown here is a *production line*; if only assembly operations were being performed, as in many automotive plants, the line would be called an *assembly line*. This production line could represent new military inductees taking their physical exams, small appliances being assembled, or double-deck hamburgers being prepared.

The famous assembly line.

Advantages of the Continuous Form

Main advantage—low unit cost.

The primary advantage of continuous process operations is the low per unit cost that is attainable due to specialized, high-volume equipment, bulk purchasing, lower labor rates, efficient facility utilization, low in-process inventories, and simplified managerial problems. Because of the high rate of output, materials can often be bought in large quantities at significant savings. Also, because operations are standardized, processing times remain relatively constant so that large in-process inventories are not required to wait in queue for processing. This keeps in-process inventory investment and queue (buffer) space at minimal levels.

Low labor costs.

Because the machines are specialized, operator skills can be lower and, therefore, lower wages can be paid. Also, fewer foremen and supervisors are needed, further saving costs. Since the layout is continuous, with materials handling often built into the system itself, the operations can be designed to perform compactly and efficiently with narrow aisles, thereby making maximum use of facility space.

Simpler managerial control.

The simplification in managerial control of a well-designed continuous process operation should not be overlooked. Constant operations problems requiring unending managerial attention penalize the organization by distracting management from their normal planning and decision-making duties.

Disadvantages of the Continuous Form

Difficult to change the process or output.

In spite of the very important cost advantage of the continuous form of process design, there are some serious drawbacks. Not only is variety of output difficult to obtain; even changes in the *rate* of output are hard to make. Because of this, important product design changes are frequently not made, thereby weakening the marketing position of the organization.

Many worker problems.

A well-known problem in continuous manufacturing organizations is the boredom and absenteeism among the labor force. Since the equipment performs the skilled tasks there is no challenge for the workers. And, of course, the constant, unending pace of the manufacturing line dehumanizes the workers with its repetitiveness. (Current attempts to combat this effect are discussed in Chapter 8.) Since the work flow rate is generally set by the line speed (termed "paced"), incentive pay and other output-based motivation devices are not possible.

If the line ever stops. . . WIP.

The continuous production line form has another important drawback. If the line should stop for any reason, a breakdown of a machine or conveyor, a shortage of supplies, and so forth, production may come to an immediate halt unless work-in-process (WIP) is stored at key points in the line. Such occurrences are prohibitively expensive.

Other problems exist too.

Other requirements of continuous processes also add cost and problems. For example, parts must be standardized so they will easily and quickly fit together on the assembly line. And, since all machines and labor must work at the same repetitive pace in order to coordinate operations, the entire line is generally *balanced* (equalizing the work loads, described in Section 7.5) to the pace of the slowest element on the line. In so doing, work loads may be unequal and a sore point among workers. And to keep the line running smoothly, a large support staff is required, as well as large stocks and large **safety stocks,** of raw materials, all of which further add to the expense.

High initial cost for low unit costs.

Last, in the continuous process design form, simplicity in *ongoing operation* is achieved at the cost of complexity in the initial *setup*. Also, the planning, design, and installation of the typically complicated, special purpose, high-volume equipment is a mammoth task. The equipment is costly not only to set up originally but also to maintain and service. Furthermore, such special purpose equipment is very susceptible to obsolescence and is difficult to dispose of or modify for other purposes.

New Technology for Continuous Flow Operations

As with intermittent flow operations, new technology is having a significant impact on continuous operations as well. Daily we hear about robots, CAD/CAM, and the "factory of the future." We will briefly describe the more significant of these here. For more detail consult Reference 13. It should be noted that these technologies can also be used in intermittent processes but are more commonly seen in continuous processes.

CNC/DNC. These are **c**omputer **n**umerical **c**ontrol and **d**irect **n**umerical **c**ontrol, two methods for controlling machining operations by a small computer. Numerical control (NC) allows a machine to operate automatically through the use of coded numerical instructions. Until recently, these instructions were on punched paper tape, which directed the machine's operations in the same way that an operator would (e.g., a player piano). Numerical control of machines is considerably more flexible than automation since it can handle various operations, materials, speeds, and so forth.

Advantages of numerical control.

The advantages of NC are many: better utilization of the machine, fewer setups, fewer manual operations, fewer fixtures, less machining time, optimal machining speeds and feeds, automatic tool selection, potential for development of a *machining center* that has multiple tools, fewer rejects, less scrap, consistent quality, easy modification of processes, reduced inspection costs, and so on. Some disadvantages are the initial cost ($20,000 to $500,000), higher maintenance costs, expensive programming costs, and time.

Point-to-point versus continuous path programming. Open-loop versus closed-loop control.

NC programming is of two types. For machining to be done at one *point*, such as drilling, *point-to-point* programming is used. For machining over a *surface, continuous path* programming is used to keep the tool in constant contact with the workpiece. Two types of NC control can be used with either type of programming: *open loop* (without feedback) and *closed loop* (with feedback). The meat labeling machine discussed in Chapter 1 that kept "applying" labels even when there were no packages would be an example of the former and illustrates the dangers in such control mechanisms. An example of a closed-loop control system is given in Figure 7.5.

Robots.

Robotics. Robots (programmable materials-handling machines) as a tool for use in manufacturing have come of age. Initially used for fairly simple tasks such as welding and paint spraying, these machines have increased tremendously in ability in the last few years. They have much more sophisticated sensors and can perform very complex and difficult tasks, not

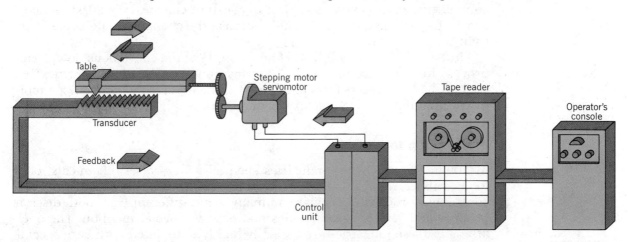

Figure 7.5 One-axis, closed-loop numerical control system. (*Source:* B. H. Amstead, P. F. Ostwald, and M. L. Begeman, *Manufacturing Processes*, 7th ed., New York: Wiley, 1977. Reprinted by permission.)

only in production but also in assembly. For its open house a few years ago, Cincinnati Milacron programmed one of its T^3-model robots to cook an entire meal, including a roast turkey, and set a table for eight.

Though there are a number of U.S. manufacturers of such robots, most of them are made, and used, in Japan. In a few factories there, the third shift is a "ghost" crew with robots performing all the work, the necessary materials having been loaded during the day by the first and second shifts. One worker oversees the entire plant operations during this ghost shift to make sure nothing goes wrong.

Ghost crew.

CAD/CAM/CAE. This trilogy of terms stands for **c**omputer **a**utomated **d**esign, **c**omputer **a**ided **m**anufacturing, and **c**omputer **a**ided **e**ngineering. The computer is used in design to store and rotate an image of the object being designed on a screen, such as a car, so the designer can view and analyze it from all angles. Light pens are used to draw right on the screen and add or delete lines, as the designer wishes. It appears that CAD can tremendously speed up the engineering design process.

CAM is the tying of NC machines into materials-handling equipment so the manufacturing operations are working together. (Compare to ICAM in the previous subsection and "automation" in Chapter 8.)

CAE is the use of the computer to aid in analyzing engineering problems, particularly structural analysis where the structure has been previously designed on the computer with CAD.

Factory of the Future. This is a vision of an almost totally automated factory in which all the computer systems are tied together: PICS, CAM, CAD, CAE, payroll, finance, accounting, and so on. The concept is the extension of Japan's ghost shift to all three shifts, much as a bottling plant operates today.

There are serious doubts about the viability of such a factory for discrete part manufacturing, however. In contrast to bottling, manufacturing in a competitive environment is subject to constant change. It is questionable if such a factory should even be built because the changes would come faster than the construction.

In Section 7.5 we will look at an example of the continuous flow design process for a service firm processing insurance applications. But next we look at the last process form of Figure 7.2, the processing industries, a more likely candidate for "the factory of the future."

Processing Industries

Although the processing industries such as water, gases, chemicals, ores, foods, rubber, flour, spirits, cements, petroleum, paints, milk, and drugs use continuous processing, they are, in many ways, different from both discrete product and service organizations and deserve special mention. The operations in these industries are typically highly automated with very specialized equipment and controls, often electronic and computerized. Such automation and expense is necessary because of the strict processing requirements for these products. The facility is typically a maze of pipes,

The automated processing industries.

conveyors, tanks, valves, vats, and bins. The layout follows the processing *stages* of the product and output rate is controlled through equipment capacity and flow and mixture rates. Labor requirements are typically low and are devoted primarily to monitoring and maintaining the equipment.

A single, fluid input.

The primary characteristic of processing industries is that there is usually one primary, "fluid"-type input material (gas, wood, wheat, milk, etc.). Commonly, this input is then converted to multiple outputs, although there may be only one (e.g., water). In (discrete) manufacturing, in contrast, *many* types of materials are commonly made or purchased and combined to form the output.

Analytic versus synthetic processes.

In a processing industry we typically visualize the process as having the singular input processed into many separate outputs. This is referred to as an *analytic process.* In *discrete* manufacturing, on the other hand, we typically visualize many materials coming together to form a singular discrete output, known as a *synthetic process.* (Synthetic fabrics require joining many inputs to make a single fiber, such as nylon.)

These concepts, as with job shops and flow shops, are not definitive but are merely aids in visualizing and understanding the differences between organizations. No organization probably uses a pure synthetic or analytic transformation process but rather many combinations of the two. And our definition of "fluid" inputs is itself rather fluid, including granulated plastics, crushed ores, powdered foods, and so forth.

The basic similarity of continuous processes.

Although more highly automated, the process design for processing organizations must follow the same steps laid out in this chapter for continuous flow processes. Specifications must include the order of adding various materials, the operations (including temperatures, times, etc.) to be conducted on the materials, where storage is to be held, what operations must be conducted simultaneously, and so on. And materials must come together in the proper amounts at the right time. Rates must be strictly regulated and operations carefully "balanced" to achieve perfect control over the process.

Very high initial costs to reduce unit costs.

Although human variation in processing firms does not usually make for the problems it does in unit manufacturing, the demands of processing are usually more critical. For example, chemical reactions must be accurately timed in their duration. The result is that initial setup of equipment and procedures is even more complex and critical than for continuous flow processing. Fixed costs are extremely high and the major variable cost is that of materials. Variable labor (excluding distribution) is usually insignificant.

7.2 SELECTION OF THE PROCESS

This section addresses the issue of selecting the appropriate process form, or mix of forms, for an organization to produce its output. In the following sections we will consider the actual design and layout of the transformation process. But the complete design of each of the transformation process forms is the purpose of the entire text and will be treated in the discussions of work design, scheduling, materials management, and operations control still to come.

From the discussion in the preceding section, it should be clear that the four processing forms are somewhat simplified extremes of what is likely to be observed in practice. Few organizations use one of the above four transformation processes in a pure sense; most combine two or more forms. For example, in manufacturing typewriters, some subassemblies are produced in *intermittent* form but then feed into a *continuous* final assembly line where a batch of one model is produced and then the line is modified to produce a batch of another model. Even in "custom" work, jobs are often done in groups of generally common items throughout most of their processing, leaving minor finishing details such as the fabric on a couch or the facade of a house to give the impression of customizing.

Most operations are combined forms.

Although services are typically of intermittent form, the emphasis has recently been on trying to "mass produce" (i.e., continuous form) them so as to increase the volume and reduce their unit cost [20]. Some examples are fast-food outlets, multiphasic medical screening, and group life insurance. Even with services we often find combined forms of process design: McDonald's prepares batches of Big Mac's but will accept individual custom orders. Burger King uses a conveyorized *assembly line* for its Whoppers but advertises its ability to customize its burgers to suit any taste.

Mass producing services.

Some examples of the process designs selected by various organizations are listed in Table 7.1. A few of these deserve special mention. The social and character-building goals of the Girl Scouts dictate a complex of activities such as trips and camp-outs (projects), training and counseling (intermittent), and cookie production (continuous). Similarly, the family has family *projects*, relatively *continuous* activities such as meal production and television viewing (assuming children are present), and *intermittent* activities such as baths, music lessons, and naps.

Family processes.

Table 7.1 Common Organizational Design Forms

	Process Design Form			
Organization	*Project*	*Intermittent*	*Continuous*	*Processing*
Utility				X
Hospital		X		
Railroad		X		
Farm	X		X	X
Supermarket		X		
University		X		
Family	X	X	X	
Construction	X			
Girl Scouts	X	X	X	
Church		X		
Charity	X			
Distributor		X		
Chemical processor			X	X

The problem for the operations manager is to decide what processing form is most appropriate for the organization, considering long-run efficiency, effectiveness, capacity, and flexibility. The selection task may be even more difficult due to the possibility, as mentioned previously, of combining processing forms to attain efficiency in some portions of the production process and flexibility or capacity in other portions. It is clear that the tradeoffs must be well understood by the manager and the expected benefits and costs well known.

Product/Process Life Cycles

A process life cycle.

In the previous chapters we described the life cycle of an output, how long it took to develop, bring to market, and catch on; how it quickly grew in popularity and different versions were developed for different market segments (refer back to Figure 3.5 in Chapter 3); and how the output reached market saturation and price competition emerged. Abernathy [1], Hayes and associates [14], and others have pointed out that a similar life cycle occurs in the production process for the output (refer to Figure 3.6), both output and process tending to follow the upper-left to bottom-right progress of process forms in Figure 7.2.

In the R&D stage many variations are investigated in the development project. When a feasible output is taken to market it is made in small volumes in a relatively inefficient, uncoordinated, intermittent flow manner and sold at a high price. As demand grows and competitors enter the market, price competition begins and high-volume, low-variable-cost continuous flow processes become preferred for selected operations. At the peak of the cycle the entire process is integrated into a high-volume, low-variable-cost continuous flow process.

Breakeven.

This progress is illustrated in Figure 7.6, a breakeven analysis of each of the three process forms (we assume here that the output is inappropriate for the processing industries). The heavy line illustrates the lowest cost process for each stage of the life cycle. At the development and initiation stage (R&D and initial production), fixed equipment cost is nil and labor is the predominant contributor to high variable costs. In the expansion stage, the intermittent form allows some tradeoff of equipment for labor with a corresponding reduction in variable unit costs, thus leading, at these volumes, to a reduction in overall unit costs. Finally, at the high volumes characterizing maturity, a virtually complete replacement of expensive labor for low-variable-cost equipment is possible.

Be advised, however, that not all outputs can or should follow this sequence. The point is that the process should evolve as the market and output evolve. But many organizations see their strength in particular segments of the process form, such as R&D, or low-cost production of large volumes. If their outputs evolve into another stage of the life cycle in which a different process form is preferable, they drop the output (or license it to someone else) and switch to another output more appropriate to their strengths.

Skinner [25] warns us that failing to maintain this focus in the organi-

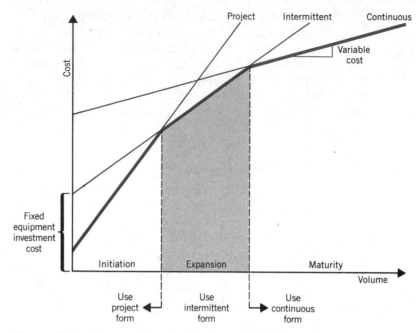

Figure 7.6 Process form selection with life cycle stage.

Focus or white elephant?

zation's production process can quickly result in a "white elephant" facility built to be efficient at one task but being inefficiently used for something else (refer to Chapter 2). This can also happen if the organization, in an attempt to please every customer, intermixes the production of outputs that require different process forms. Japanese plants are very carefully planned to maintain one strong focus in each plant. If an output requiring a different process form is to be produced, a *new* plant is acquired or built.

Next we will look at the task of designing a continuous flow process for manufacturing a high-volume, low-cost ballpoint pen.

7.3 TRANSFORMATION PROCESS DESIGN EXAMPLE

The importance of the explosion chart for proper assembly.

To illustrate the procedures involved in process design, consider the manufacture of the commonplace push-button ballpoint pen. The *explosion chart* of the pen, and a completed view, is shown in Figure 7.7 and the *assembly* and *operations process charts* in Figures 7.8 and 7.9. Note that we have only illustrated final assemblies—subassemblies such as SA-1 would typically be included in separate charts. The explosion diagram separates each of the parts as if they had been "blown apart" in exact order of their assembly. A centerline (— - —) is usually included to indicate how the parts fit together. In complicated explosions where it is impossible to fit all the parts in a straight line on the same piece of paper, the centerlines may be bent so as

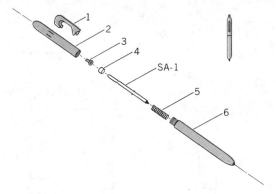

Figure 7.7 Ballpoint pen explosion chart.

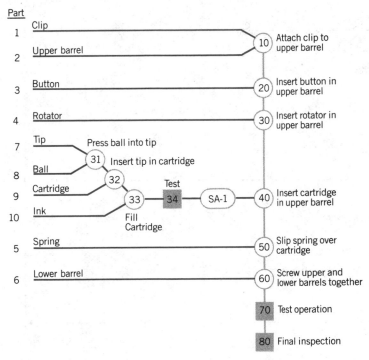

Figure 7.8 Assembly chart for ballpoint pen.

to draw the parts in an empty corner of the paper ($- \cdot -/\_ \cdot \_$). Such explosion charts are crucial to the proper assembly of even slightly complex parts.

Main and subassemblies on the assembly chart.

The assembly chart of Figure 7.8 gives more detailed assembly instructions than the explosion chart and includes subassemblies as well (such as SA-1 in the figure). Note, however, that the assembly chart does not tell what the raw materials are, or how to construct the parts—it is simply for assembly operations. The construction information is given in the operations process chart (Figure 7.9) and includes the standard time for each operation.

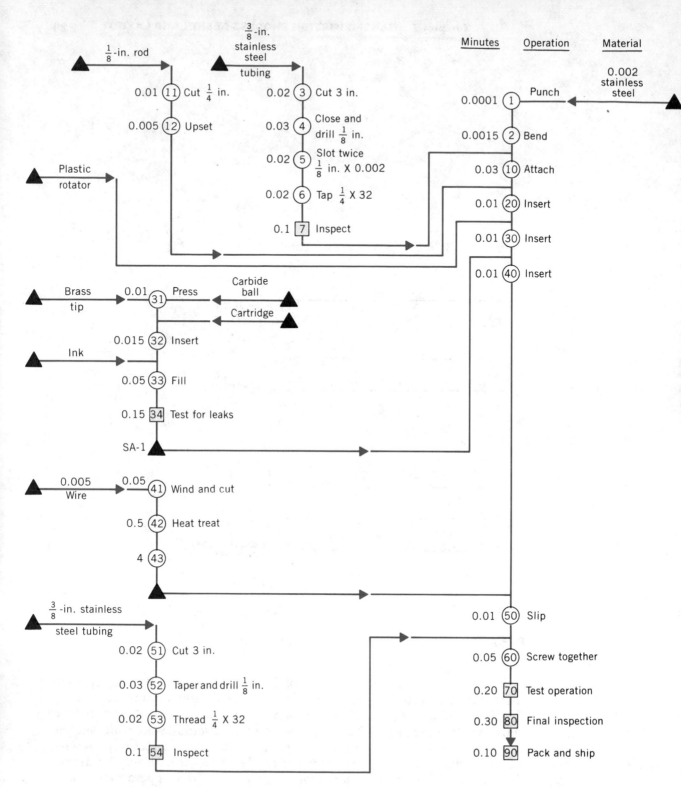

Figure 7.9 Ballpoint pen operations process chart.

230

Part name Cartridge subassembly		Date issued _____		Job _____		
No. SA-1		Date completed _____		Issued by _____		
Date	Oper. no.	Operation	Dept.	Setup (min)	Rate/min	Equipment
—	—	Tip and ball	Inventory	—	—	—
	31	Press ball into tip, 100 psi	Press	30	100	Sheridan press
	—	Cartridge	Inventory	—	—	—
	32	Insert tip into cartridge, 43 psi	Press	30	75	Low volume Cummings press
	33	Fill cartridge, 0.15 each	Paint	45	20	Simms high viscosity pump
	34	Test	Inspection	—	4	No. 1538 pressure tester, Fields Bros.
	—	Subassembly transport	Inventory	—	—	—

Figure 7.10   Route sheet for cartridge subassembly.

The symbols used in the assembly chart of Figure 7.8, the operations process chart of Figure 7.9, and the flow process chart of Figure 7.11 are as follows:

○: *Operation* being performed.

◊: *Transportation* of item takes place.

△: *Storage* of some item occurs.

D: *Delay* for further processing. Paperwork not required.

□: *Inspection* of an item occurs.

The *route sheet* for the cartridge *subassembly*, SA-1, is shown in Figure 7.10. Four departments (inventory, press, paint, and inspection) are involved in the production of this subassembly. As can be seen, the operations start at the inventory department where a batch of raw materials is requested. The operations finish at a later date, with the batch of subassemblies being stored back in inventory. The required equipment is also indicated, along with setup and run times.

If we wished to analyze this cartridge subassembly task for possible improvements, it would be helpful to have a chart listing each activity in detail, the time required, and the distance covered. This chart, the *flow process chart*, is illustrated in Figure 7.11. Items to consider in the possible improvement of the task are as follows:

Improvement questions.

- Can any operations be simplified? Eliminated? Combined?
- Are there any bottlenecks? Unnecessary storage points?
- Can the layout be improved in terms of ease of action? In terms of distance traveled?
- Can the working conditions be improved for productivity? Quality? Safety? Fulfillment?
- Can new tools, equipment, or facilities be economically employed?

Flow Process Chart							
Summary	No.	Min.	Operation: Cartridge subassembly				
◯ Operation	8	2.30	Dept.: _____ Part No. _____				
⇨ Transport	5	0.85	Sheet _1_ of _1_ Date: _____				
△ Store	1	0.10	Charted by: _____				
D Delay	1	0.30	Subject: _____				
☐ Inspect	1	0.45	Present method ☒				
Total	16	4.00	Proposed method ☐				
Feet of travel: 130							

No.	Dist. (ft)	Time (min)	Oper.	Transport	Store	Delay	Inspect	Description
1	30	0.20	◯	⇨	△	D	☐	Go to inventory
2		0.35	●	→	△	D	☐	Get tip, ball, cartridge
3	30	0.20	◯	⇨	△	D	☐	Return
4		0.40	●	→	△	D	☐	Install on Sheridan press
5		0.10	●	→	△	D	☐	Press ball
6		0.25	●	→	△	D	☐	Remove from press
7		0.50	●	→	△	D	☐	Install on Cummings press
8		0.20	●	→	△	D	☐	Insert tip
9		0.20	●	→	△	D	☐	Remove from press
10	10	0.05	◯	⇨	△	D	☐	Go to pump bench
11		0.30	●	→	△	D	☐	Fill cartridge
12		0.45	◯	→	△	D	■	Test pressure
13		0.30	◯	→	△	D	☐	Wait for pressure release
14	30	0.20	◯	⇨	△	D	☐	Take to inventory
15		0.10	◯	→	▲	D	☐	Store
16	30	0.20	◯	⇨	△	D	☐	Return

Figure 7.11 Flow process chart for SA-1.

> • Can the output be redesigned to improve the process? To reduce the cost? To increase the quality?

Activity charts for maximizing utilization.

Since one operator performs all of the press operations, we may analyze the operator's activities by a *man-machine chart* as in Figure 7.12. This kind of chart shows what the operator and each machine are doing at every point in time and thus facilitates obtaining the maximum use out of both the operator and the machines. As can be seen, once they are started, both machines are fully utilized but the operator is idle $2 + 0.5 + 1.5 + 1 = 5$ out of the first 12.5 minutes for a **utilization** rate of only

$$\frac{(12.5 - 5.0)}{12.5} = 60 \text{ percent}$$

Furthermore, there is no regularity in the activity. All of the idle times are of different durations and the machines "cycle" at different intervals. As seen in the chart, on the first cycle the operator loads the Sheridan and then immediately loads the Cummings. On the second cycle he must wait 0.5

| Part name | Cartridge subassembly | | Dept. <u>Press</u> | Operator _____ |
| No. | SA-1 | | Date _____ | |

Time (min)	Operator	1: Machine <u>Sheridan</u>	2: Machine <u>L.V. Cummings</u>
−0 − −1	Load and start Sheridan	Load	Idle
−2	Load and start Cummings		Load
−3 − −4	Idle	Run 300 units	Run 300 units
−5 −	Load and start Sheridan	Load	
−6	Idle		
−7	Load and start Cummings		Load
−8 −	Idle	Run 300 units	
−9 − −10	Load and start Sheridan	Load	Run 300 units
−11	Idle	Run 300 units	Load
−12	Load and start Cummings		

Figure 7.12 Press operator activity chart.

Differing cycles limit utilization.

minutes between loadings because the Cummings run is not completed when he finishes loading the Sheridan. On the third cycle he must wait 1.0 minute. Clearly, there will soon come a cycle when both machines complete their runs at the same time and then one machine must sit idle while the other is being loaded, as occurred in the first cycle. This is an inefficient use of equipment, as well as of labor (60 percent idle). Better "balancing" of the machine cycles by varying the run loads and perhaps adding other tasks to the operator's duties would significantly improve the utilization of all these resources.

Hand motion shown on the simo chart.

Figure 7.13 illustrates the right- and left-hand operations required to perform the cartridge subassembly leakage test by the inspector. Note that, as much as possible, use is made of both hands simultaneously, hence the

Left	Time (min)	Right
PartName <u>Cartridge subassembly</u> Dept. <u>Insp.</u> Operator_____ No. <u>SA-1</u> Date _____ Operation <u>Leakage test</u>		
Reach for cartridge	0.01	Reach for pressure probe
Pick up cartridge	0.02	Pick up probe
Carry to probe	0.03	Carry to cartridge
Position	0.04 / 0.05	Insert probe in cartridge
Hold probe-cartridge assembly	0.06 / 0.07	Reach for pressure switch
	0.08 / 0.09	Actuate switch
	0.10	Reach for probe
Hold cartridge	0.11	Replace probe
Check for leaks	0.12	Idle
Scribble	0.13	
Check for blotches	0.14	
Place into accept or reject bin	0.15 / 0.16	

Figure 7.13   Simo chart for leakage test.

name "simo chart." Principles such as this involving the efficient use of human labor will be discussed in more detail in Chapter 8.

Last, a preliminary *layout* can now be designed based on the previous analyses. For the ballpoint pen, this layout is depicted in Figure 7.14. In actual practice there are miniature two-dimensional cutouts and three-dimensional blocks representing machines, and so forth, available from firms specializing in layout to help visualize what a proposed layout would actually look like, its problems, and its advantages. The operation analysts (typically, industrial engineers) would then shift the pieces in this scale model around to check for safety problems, bottlenecks, materials flow, in-process storage, and other such complex, interrelated aspects of designing a continuous flow process. Alternative layouts would be considered and shown to operations managers and supervisors for their evaluation until, finally, a "best" layout would be selected for actual implementation.

Trial layouts with scale models.

7.4   PROCESS LAYOUT FOR INTERMITTENT OPERATIONS

Because of its relative permanency, the layout of the processing operations is probably one of the most crucial elements affecting the efficiency of an

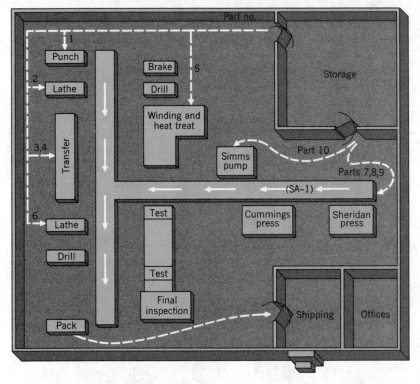

Figure 7.14   Preliminary operations layout diagram.

The layout
problem.

intermittent operation. In general, the problem of layout design for inter-mittent operations is quite complex. The difficulty stems from the variety of outputs and the constant change in outputs that are characteristic of orga-nizations with an intermittent process design. The optimal layout for the *existing* set of outputs may be relatively inefficient for the outputs to be produced *six months from now*. This is particularly true of job shops where there is no proprietary product and only outside customers are served. One week such a shop may produce 1000 ashtrays and the next week an 8000-gallon vat. Therefore, a process layout is typically based on the historically stable output pattern of the organization and expected changes in that pat-tern rather than on current operations or outputs.

In the layout of service operations, the emphasis may be directed much more toward the customer than toward technology or materials, as would be more typical of manufacturing. That is, parking lots, entry zones, receiv-ing procedures, waiting areas, and other such aspects of the layout are of top priority in nightclubs, exclusive restaurants, and savings and loans.

For example, Figure 7.15 presents the layout of a department store. No-tice that, even though an image of order and neatness prevails, the display racks, cabinets, and carousels are carefully arranged to break up any smooth flow of traffic. This is particularly the case in the entry/exitway where high margin items (jewelry and perfume) are conspicuously displayed. An enter-

Detour!

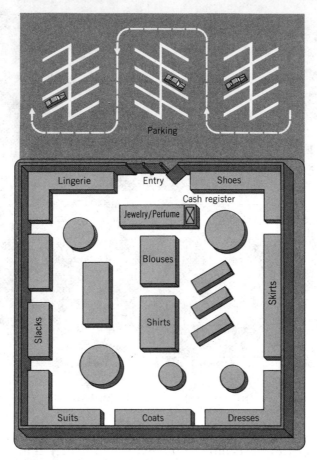

Figure 7.15   Department store layout.

ing customer who successfully outflanks the jewelry counter is then distracted by high visibility carousels and racks of merchandise, all seemingly aimed at him or her.

Purposes of relayout.   The main purpose of layout, or relayout, analysis is generally to maximize the profitability or efficiency of operations. But other purposes also frequently exist such as minimizing safety or health hazards, facilitating crucial staff interaction, freeing up bottleneck operations, and minimizing interference, noise, or distractions between different operational areas. Eilón [11] points out that most operations layouts are originally designed efficiently but as the organization grows and changes to accommodate a changing environment, the operations layout becomes less efficient, until eventually a relayout is necessary. The following are some operations problems that might indicate the need for relayout.

- Congestion.
- Poor utilization of space.
- Excessive amounts of materials in processing.

- Excessive workflow distances.
- Bottlenecks occurring in one location simultaneously with idleness in another.
- Skilled workers doing excessive unskilled work.
- Long operation cycles and delivery delays.
- Worker anxiety and strain.
- Difficulty in maintaining operational control of work or staff.

When such special reasons exist for a relayout analysis, then, of course, the layout criterion is based on the resolution of the particular difficulty. Two- and three-dimensional scale models of the operation, such as an interior decorator might use with model furniture, are often used to aid in resolving such problems. In general, however, the primary criterion for layout analyses is the "efficiency" of operations. Assuming every potential layout satisfies any *required* constraints (location of loading or shipping docks and restrooms, shape of certain departments, etc.), the efficiency criterion usually reduces to a concern for the *interrelations* between operations. Examples of such interrelations are the cost of materials handling when the main flows between operations are materials, staff time when the major flows are of people, or costs of lost or delayed information when the main flows are of paperwork.

The objective is then to minimize the costs of these interrelations between operations by locating those operations that interrelate close to one another. If we label one of the operations "i" and another operation "j" then the cost of i relating with j typically depends on the distance between i and j, D_{ij}, as measured by the route of the flow from i to j.

In addition, the cost will usually depend on the amount of relating from i to j, such as trips, cases, volume, weight, or some other such measure, which we will denote by V_{ij}. Then, if the cost of the flow from i to j per unit amount per unit distance is C_{ij}, the total cost of i relating with j is $C_{ij}V_{ij}D_{ij}$. Note that C, V, and D may have different values for different types of flows and that they need not have the same values from j to i as from i to j since the flow in this opposite direction may be of an entirely different nature. For example, information may be flowing from i to j, following a certain paperwork path (e.g., by pneumatic tube) but sheet steel may flow from j to i following a lift truck or conveyor belt path.

Adding the flows from i to every one of N possible operations, the total cost of interrelations with operation i is then

$$\sum_{j=1}^{N} C_{ij}V_{ij}D_{ij} \tag{7.1}$$

(It is normally assumed that $C_{ii}V_{ii}D_{ii} = 0$ since the distance from i to itself is zero.) Adding together the costs for all the other i operations relating to each of the j operations results in the total cost.

$$TC = \sum_{i=1}^{N} \sum_{j=1}^{N} C_{ij}V_{ij}D_{ij} \tag{7.2}$$

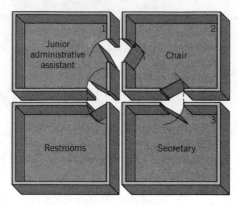

Figure 7.16 Office layout.

Our goal is to find the layout that minimizes this total cost. This may be done by evaluating the cost of promising layouts or, as in the following example, by evaluating *all possible* layouts.

The Department Chair's Office

The section of the business school containing the Operations Management Division's administrative offices is illustrated in Figure 7.16. Each office is approximately 10 by 10 feet so the walking distance (D) between adjacent offices is 10 feet whereas that between diagonal offices is 15 feet. The average number of interpersonal trips made each day is given in the travel or **load matrix** of Table 7.2.

The load matrix for travel.

Assuming the chair is paid approximately twice as much as the secretary and the junior administrative assistant, determine if the present arrangement is best (i.e., least costly) in terms of transit time and, if not, what arrangements would be better.

Analysis. For convenience in notation, the offices are numbered in the illustration. Before calculating total costs of all possible arrangements, some preliminary analysis is usually worthwhile. First, because of special utility connections, restrooms are usually not considered relocatable. In addition, the relocation of the restrooms in this example would not achieve any result that could not be achieved by moving the other offices instead.

Table 7.2 Load Matrix, V_{ij} (Trips)

		To		
	From	*1* *Assistant*	*2* *Chair*	*3* *Secretary*
1	Assistant	—	5	17
2	Chair	10	—	5
3	Secretary	13	25	—

Second, many arrangements are mirror images of other arrangements and thus need not be evaluated since their cost will be the same. For example, interchanging offices 1 and 3 will result in the same costs as the current layout. The essence of the problem then is to "determine which office should be located diagonally across from the restrooms." There are three alternatives: chair, assistant, or secretary.

Last, the number of trips times the relative earnings of each person constitute the effective cost per unit distance in this case (the distances must still be determined from the locations). Thus, *relative* cost-effectiveness will be a sufficient criterion here and *actual* costs need not be determined.

Letting V_{ij} represent "number of trips from i to j" and evaluating each alternative layout, that is, in terms of who is diagonally across from the restrooms, results in

$$\text{TOTAL COST} = C_{12}V_{12}D_{12} + C_{13}V_{13}D_{13} + C_{21}V_{21}D_{21} + C_{23}V_{23}D_{23}$$
$$+ C_{31}V_{31}D_{31} + C_{32}V_{32}D_{32}$$

Diagonal office

1. *Chair: TC* $= 1(5)10 + 1(17)15 + 2(10)10 + 2(5)10 + 1(13)15$
   $+ 1(25)10$
   $= 1050$

2. *Assistant: TC* $= 1(5)10 + 1(17)10 + 2(10)10 + 2(5)15 + 1(13)10$
   $+ 1(25)15$
   $= 1075$

3. *Secretary: TC* $= 1(5)15 + 1(17)10 + 2(10)15 + 2(5)10 + 1(13)10$
   $+ 1(25)10$
   $= 1025$

The best arrangement is therefore to put the secretary in the office diagonal to the restrooms for a cost of 1025. Next, let us consider a more complex situation using operations sequence analysis [4].

Layout by Operations Sequence Analysis

Table 7.3 shows the three products made by Topstar Co., the departmental processing sequence each requires, the transport cost per unit per foot moved, and the annual number of units of each product produced. Table 7.4 gives the required size of each of the nine departments.

Table 7.3 Topstar Product Operations Sequence

Product	Annual Production	Transport Cost	Department Processing Sequence
Tops	1000	$0.20	1-2-5-6
Deluxe tops	2000	0.25	1-3-6
Star tops	500	0.40	1-2-4-5-6

Table 7.4　Department Size

Department	Size (ft^2)
1	100
2	200
3	200
4	200
5	400
6	100

To begin the layout analysis we can calculate the costs per foot of moving products between departments and enter them on a grid, as in Table 7.5. For example, tops and star tops both move from department 1 to 2. The annual cost per foot of separation between these departments is the annual production rate times the transport cost

$$\begin{aligned} \text{Tops: } 1000 \text{ units} &\times \$0.20/\text{unit/ft} = \$200/\text{ft} \\ \text{Star tops: } 500 \text{ units} &\times \$0.40/\text{unit/ft} = \underline{\$200/\text{ft}} \\ &\text{Total} = \$400/\text{ft} \end{aligned}$$

Thus, the annual cost of materials handling will be $400 *for every foot* separating departments 1 and 2. Similar calculations result in the remaining values given in Table 7.5.* Note from the values that it is not important to have some departments close together, such as 3 and 5. On the other hand, it is extremely important that department 3 be near 1 and 6.

Returning now to our original example, how do we use Table 7.5 to lay out the departments? First we make an arbitrary diagram of the six departments, as in Figure 7.17, and label the total annual costs of flow per foot separating them. Next we analyze the diagram to ascertain if the depart-

Table 7.5　Annual Cost per Foot of Separation Between Departments

	Department					
Department	*1*	*2*	*3*	*4*	*5*	*6*
1		400	500	x	x	x
2			x	200	200	x
3				x	x	500
4					200	x
5						200
6						

*Suppose that transport cost depended on the departments between which products were moved rather than on the product. How would this be handled? This is shown in Table 7.6 where the interdepartmental transport cost (in dollars/unit/foot) is given in Table 7.6*b*. Multiplying the production units in Table 7.6*a* by the rates in Table 7.6*b* results in the cost-per-foot-of-separation grid (Table 7.6*c*).

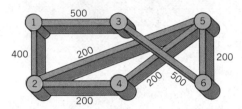

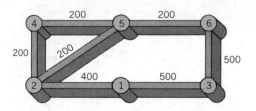

Figure 7.17 Initial department layout.

Figure 7.18 Final department layout.

ments can be better arranged to shorten the distances, particularly the high cost values. The final result of such a process is shown in Figure 7.18.

Last, we must consider the departmental sizes in Table 7.4. To fit a typically rectangular building may require relocating the arrangement of Figure 7.18. The initial and final results are shown in Figure 7.19.

Computer Layout Programs

One difficulty with this method is that the number of calculations for larger problems quickly becomes unmanageable. In general, the number of calculations required to locate N facilities in N different areas is $N!$ ($3! = 3 \times 2 \times 1 = 6$ in our example). Thus, for an organization with just 10 different operational areas, the number of calculations would be $10! = 3,628,800$. It is, therefore, usually necessary to use a computer to analyze realistic layout problems. However, even with the speed and power of a computer many problems are still too large to be economically evaluated and **heuristic***

Heuristics. routines must be employed.

Typical of such computer approaches to the layout problem is CRAFT, *Computerized Relative Allocation of Facilities Technique* [5]. This program

Three inputs for assumes that the cost of interrelations between operations is the product of

CRAFT. a "rate" matrix (such as cost per unit volume per unit distance) and a "load"

Table 7.6 Cost of Separation with Interdepartmental Rates

Depart-	Department																	
ment	1	2	3	4	5	6	1	2	3	4	5	6	1	2	3	4	5	6
1		1500	2000	x	x	x		$0.20	.30	x	x	x		300	600	x	x	x
2			x	500	1000	x			x	.20	.20	x			x	100	200	x
3				x	x	2000				x	x	.40				x	x	800
4					500	x					.50	x					250	x
5						1500						.40						600
6																		
	(a) Units of flow						(b) Interdepartmental rate					(c) Cost of separation						

*Heuristics are logically or experimentally derived rules of thumb. See Reference 27 for details.

Figure 7.19 Allocating space to the layout. (*a*) Initial. (*b*) Adjusted final.

matrix (such as volume or trips), both of which are inputs to the CRAFT program. Interoperation distances are obtained from an initial floor plan layout (existing or preliminary) which is read into the program; the computer routine itself then calculates distances between operational areas from the floor plan.

Interchanging two areas at a time to reduce costs.

The program's relayout heuristic is to interchange two areas at a time (more recent versions of CRAFT use three), recompute the total costs, and save the identity of the best switch. After all possible interchanges are evaluated, the best switch is then substituted for the original layout (if less costly) and the entire process repeated. Common results with CRAFT are 20 percent savings over initial layout costs. To analyze a 20-operation area takes about half a minute of computer time although CRAFT can handle up to 40 separate departments.

Limitations of CRAFT.

Even though CRAFT does not guarantee a least-cost layout, the nature of the layout problem is such that usually only trivially better solutions may exist. Although limited to single-story buildings, CRAFT does have the flexibility of allowing certain areas to be specified as fixed. A minor drawback of CRAFT is that the solution found is not allowed to alter the shape of the building, which is appropriate when the building is already in existence but perhaps inappropriate if a new building is being designed. Last, the realities of a particular situation may violate the CRAFT assumptions. For example, straight-line distances between operations areas may be inaccurate when only limited access exists to some areas (such as by fork lift), CRAFT designed shapes may not be appropriate for areas needing specialized shapes (such as L or T patterns), and certain areas may require other specific areas to locate (or not locate) near to them (e.g., inspection near shipping; painting away from sanding). Nevertheless, these difficulties can usually be resolved with slight manual modifications to the final CRAFT solution, quick relayouts on CRAFT using higher costs between areas to bring them closer together (or lower costs to space them farther apart), or by relayouts with fixed locations for certain areas.

Other computerized layout routines.

Other computerized layout routines also exist such as **ALDEP** (*Automated Layout Design Program*) [24] and **CORELAP** (*Computerized Relationship Layout Planning*) [19]. In these programs, department closeness preferences are specified directly (e.g., very important to be close to department A) and used as the criterion variable, which may or may not be more appropriate than interoperation cost. Also, as opposed to CRAFT, buildings of more than one story may be analyzed.

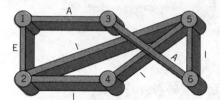

Figure 7.20 Initial layout.

Qualitative layout.　　An example of the specification of qualitative measures for interdepartmental separation is given in Table 7.7 and Figure 7.20, based on the Topstar Co. example. As can be seen by comparing Figure 7.20 with Figure 7.17, the procedure remains basically unchanged from this point on. Yet, this manner of specifying desired closeness between departments is more flexible and may be especially useful for some organizations, particularly service organizations in which materials flow may be much less relevant.

7.5　PROCESS LAYOUT FOR CONTINUOUS OPERATIONS

Dividing the workflow to smooth processing.

The crux of the problem of attaining the advantages of the continuous process form is whether the workflow can be subdivided sufficiently so that labor and equipment are utilized smoothly throughout the processing operations. If, for example, one operation takes longer than all the others, then this will become a bottleneck operation, delaying all of the operations following it and restricting output rate to *its* low value.

Bottleneck operations.

This is especially a problem where machines play a major production role as in the fabrication of parts. In these cases the utilization of machines waiting for a bottleneck operation to finish will be unprofitably low (refer back to Table 5.5 in Chapter 5) unless the machines are used for alternative purposes during slack times. But alternative uses will require special materials handling, storage space, and so forth, and will thus reduce the efficiency of both the alternative process and the original process.

Table 7.7　Qualitative Measures for Layout[a]

Department	Department					
	1	2	3	4	5	6
1		E	A	U	U	U
2			U	I	I	U
3				U	U	A
4					I	U
5						I
6						

[a]Note:
A = Absolutely necessary　　O = Ordinary closeness OK
E = Especially important　　U = Unimportant
I = Important　　　　　　　X = Undesirable

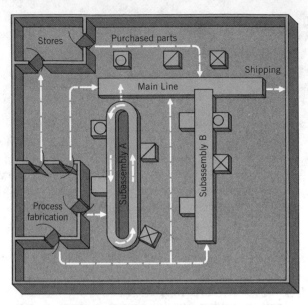

Figure 7.21   Typical configuration of off-line processing and subassembly.

The majority of production is off the main line.

The result in most organizations is that fabrication of basic parts and subassemblies occurs off the main production line either in intermittent process flow or on a subassembly line. When completed, these components are brought to the main assembly line, as in Figure 7.21. This procedure is also advantageous in that most subassembly lines can produce considerably more parts per period than the main assembly line. This is often required because multiples of some parts are used in each final output (e.g., every roller skate requires four wheels), and also because the organization must produce spares for its output or perhaps subcontract parts for sale to other companies. For example, a Chevrolet engine plant might produce engines for other cars (such as Oldsmobiles) or for other uses.

Conveyors for paced lines.

Final assembly operations usually have more labor input and less fixed equipment cycles and can, therefore, be subdivided easier for smooth flow. Either one of two types of lines can then be used. A **paced line** typically uses some sort of conveyor and moves the output along at a continuous rate while operators do their work as the output passes by them. For longer operations the worker may walk or ride alongside the conveyor and then have to walk back to the starting work station. Many disadvantages, such as boredom and monotony, are of course well known. An automobile assembly line is a common example of the paced line. Workers actually install doors, engines, hoods, and such as the conveyor moves past them.

Between-station storage in unpaced lines.

In unpaced lines, such as that used in IBM typewriter assembly plants, the workers build up queues between the work stations and can then vary their pace to meet the needs of the job or their personal desires; however, average daily output must remain the same. The advantage of an unpaced line is that a worker can spend longer on the more difficult outputs and balance this with the easier outputs. Similarly, workers can vary their work-pace to add variety to a boring task. For example, a worker may work fast to get ahead of the pace for a few seconds before returning to the task.

There are also some disadvantages to unpaced lines, though. For one thing, they cannot be used with large bulky products because of the excessive in-process storage space requirements. But more important, minimum output rates are difficult to maintain because short duration times in one operation usually do not dovetail with long durations in the next operation. And when long duration times coincide, operators downstream from these operations may run out of in-process inventory to work on and thus be forced to sit idle.

Choosing an output rate and balancing the line.

For operations that can be smoothed to obtain the benefits of a production line there are two main elements in designing the most efficient line. The first is deciding on the necessary output rate, and the second is subdividing and grouping job elements into balanced tasks. The approach to this task is discussed next.

Balancing a Continuous Process Production Line

In this subsection we will focus on the problem of "smoothing" the productive operations in a continuous process so that all operations work at approximately the same speed. If this were not done, the transformation process would be relatively inefficient with all operations delayed to the slowest rate of the most lengthy operation. For example, if a process consisted of three machines, A, B, and C, with individual output rates of 98, 50, and 100 units per day, respectively, then the resulting output of the entire system would be 50 units a day. The obvious solution is to use another machine B and increase the output to 98 units per day, assuming this volume is usable. The following example illustrates the general *line balancing* methodology of smoothing production operations.

Longform Credit, Inc., receives 1200 credit applications a day, on the average. Longform's advertising touts their efficiency in responding to all applications within a matter of hours. The daily application processing tasks, standard times, and required preceding tasks (those tasks that must be completed before other tasks) are listed in Table 7.8.

A precedence graph for order of assembly.

The *precedence graph* for these tasks is depicted in Figure 7.22 and is constructed directly from Table 7.8. This graph is simply a picture of the operations (a circle) with arrows indicating which tasks must precede each other task. The number or letter of the operation is shown inside the circle with the time directly above it.

Analysis

A common cycle time for all stations.

In *balancing* a line the intent is to find a **cycle time** in which each work station can complete its tasks. Conceptually, at the end of this time every work station passes its part on to the next station. Task elements are thus grouped for each work station so as to utilize as much of this cycle time as

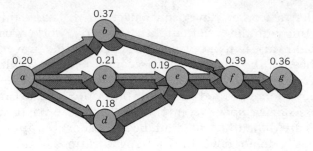

Figure 7.22 Credit application precedence graph.

possible but not to exceed it. Typically, each work station will have a slightly different *idle time* within the cycle time.

Cycle time is based on the output rate.

The cycle time is determined from the required output rate. In this case, the average daily output rate must equal the average daily input rate, 1200. If it is less than this figure, a backlog of applications will accumulate. If it is more than this, unnecessary idle time will result. Assuming an 8-hour day, 1200 applications per 8 hours means completing 150 every hour (2½ every minute) or *one* every *0.4 minutes*—this then is the cycle time.

$$\text{cycle time} = \text{available work time/demand} \qquad (7.3)$$

$$= \frac{(8 \text{ hr} \times 60 \text{ min})}{1200 \text{ applications}} = 0.4 \text{ min}$$

Adding up the task times in Table 7.8, it can be seen that the total is 1.9

Table 7.8 Credit Application Processing Tasks

Task	Average Time (min)	Immediately Preceding Tasks
a. Open and stack applications	0.20	none
b. Process enclosed letter; make note of and handle any special requirements	0.37	*a*
c. Check off form 1 for page 1 of application	0.21	*a*
d. Check off form 2 for page 2 of application; file original copy of application	0.18	*a*
e. Calculate credit limit from standardized tables according to forms 1 and 2.	0.19	*c, d*
f. Supervisor checks quotation in light of special processing of letter, notes type of form letter, address, and credit limit to return to applicant	0.39	*b, e*
g. Secretary types in details on form letter and mails	0.36	*f*
Total	1.90	

Finding the number of work stations.

minutes. Since every work station will do no more than 0.4 minute's worth of work during each cycle, it is clear that a minimum of 1.9/0.4 = 4.75 work stations are needed or, always rounding *up*, 5.

$$\text{number of work stations, } N = \Sigma \text{ task times/cycle time} \qquad (7.4)$$

$$= \frac{1.9}{0.4} = 4.75 \text{ (i.e., 5)}$$

Calculating the efficiency and balance delay of the line.

It may be, however, that the work cannot be divided and balanced in five stations and six, or even seven, may be needed. If this is the case, the production line will be less efficient. The *efficiency* of the line with N stations may be computed from

$$\text{efficiency} = \frac{\text{output}}{\text{input}} = \frac{\text{total task time}}{(N \text{ stations}) \times \text{cycle time}} \qquad (7.5)$$

$$= \frac{1.9}{5 \times 0.4} = 95\% \text{ if the line can be balanced}$$
$$\text{with 5 stations}$$

$$= \frac{1.9}{6 \times 0.4} = 79\% \text{ if 6 stations are required}$$

On occasion, the *inefficiency* of the line is calculated instead; this is called the **balance delay.**

$$\text{balance delay} = 1.0 - \text{efficiency} \qquad (7.6)$$
$$= 1.0 - 0.95 = 5\% \text{ with 5 stations}$$

The balancing process.

At this point we can attempt to balance the line by assigning tasks to stations. We begin by assuming that all workers can do any of the tasks and check back on this later. There are many heuristic rules for which task to select next. We will use the "LOT" rule; select that task with the *longest operation time* next.

The general procedure for line balancing is as follows.

The line balancing procedure.

Construct a list of the tasks whose predecessor tasks have already been completed. Consider each of these tasks, one at a time, in LOT order and place them within the station. As a task is tentatively placed in a station new follower tasks can now be added to the list. Consider adding to the station any tasks in this list whose time fits within the remaining time for that station. Continue in this manner until as little station idle time remains as possible.

We will now demonstrate this procedure. The first tasks to consider are those with no preceding tasks. Thus, task a, taking 0.2 of the 0.4 minute available, is put into station 1. This then makes tasks b (0.37 minute), c (0.21 minute), and d (0.18 minute) available for assignment. Trying the longest first, b, then c, and last d, we find that only d can be assigned to station 1 without exceeding the 0.4-minute cycle time; thus, station 1 will include

Table 7.9 Station Task Assignments

Station	Tasks Available	Tasks Assigned	Minutes	Idle Time
1	a; b, c, d	a, d	0.38	0.02
2	b, c	b	0.37	0.03
3	c; e	c, e	0.40	0
4	f	f	0.39	0.01
5	g	g	0.36	0.04

tasks a and d. Since only 0.02 minute remain unassigned in station 1 and no task in the job is that short, we enter the results in Table 7.9 and then consider assignments to station 2.

Only b and c are available for assignment (since e requires that c be completed first) and b (0.37 minute) will clearly require a station by itself; b is, therefore, assigned to station 2. Only c is now available for assignment since f requires that both e and b be completed and e is not yet completed. But by assigning c (0.21 minute) to station 3, task e (0.19 minute) becomes available and can also be just accommodated in station 3. Task f (0.39 minute) is the next available task and clearly requires its own station, 4, leaving g (0.36 minute) to station 5. These assignments are illustrated in Figure 7.23 and Table 7.9.

We now check the feasibility of these assignments. In many cases a number of aspects must be considered in this check (as discussed further later), but here our only concern is that the clerk or the secretary does not do task f and that the supervisor does not do task g (or, hopefully, very much of a–e). As it happens, task f is a station by itself so there is no problem.

Some realistic complications. This example is, of course, highly simplified. In realistic situations many other difficulties and considerations are present, which complicate the problem even more. Some of these complications are listed here.

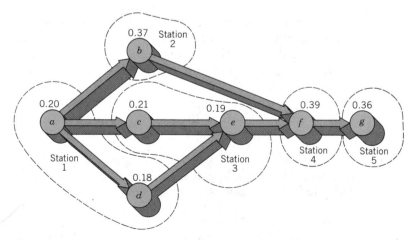

Figure 7.23 Station assignments.

- Many, many more tasks are involved with more interactions and precedence relationships. Considerable research has been done on this problem and numerous heuristic techniques (e.g., choose as the next task the one with the longest operation time) are available to aid in obtaining a solution (see References 6, 17, and 21 for details). Worthy of special mention are the computerized techniques COMSOAL [3] and MALB [6], which can handle hundreds of tasks in only a few minutes.

- Some sets of tasks require the same skills, tools, parts, equipment, worker positioning, or facilities and might be more efficiently grouped together than is indicated from the pure line balancing solution. Thus, it is always worthwhile to inspect the time-oriented solution for further possible efficiencies.

- In the spirit of job enrichment (discussed further in Chapter 8) it may be worthwhile to group some tasks together that normally would not be, simply to ward off boredom and allow some variety, or even pride of workmanship.

- Potential task interference should be considered. For example, noisy, dangerous, or polluting tasks should be grouped and confined in facilities designed for them.

- Frequently, some tasks exceed the cycle time by themselves. If the task cannot be further broken down, the best approach in this case is to assign such tasks to two (or more) stations, each completing their task *every other* cycle. An approach to the opposite situation where one uncombinable task has a *low* cycle time is to utilize two (or more) complete parallel lines with the one, short cycle task in common.

7.6 SUMMARY AND KEY LEARNING POINTS

From the strategic decision in Chapter 6 of where to best locate the facility, this chapter has covered the tactical decisions of how to choose, design, and lay out the transformation process. The general transformation design procedure and an introduction to the four forms—project, intermittent, continuous, and processing—was given first. Then the relationship of each form to volume, batch size, and output variety was noted and the tradeoffs described. Following this, each form was discussed in detail, its advantages and disadvantages were outlined, and relevant new technologies were described.

The next two sections discussed process selection and design and illustrated the procedure with a ballpoint pen example. Last, the layout procedure for intermittent and continuous process forms was described and some potentially helpful models and computer programs were noted and illustrated.

The key learning points were

- The transformation process selection procedure is made by comparing the volume and variety of outputs, high volume with low variety tending to indicate a processing, or continuous, transformation process and low volume with high variety indicating a project or perhaps intermittent transformation process. The general transformation design procedure, as illustrated in Figure 7.1, is to determine the output characteristics, break down the output into components, decide how to obtain and combine the components, and then iterate until a coherent process is formulated.

● The four forms of transformation processes are project, intermittent, continuous, and processing. Each form exhibits the characteristics and advantages listed in Section 7.1 that are unique to that mix of variety and volume/batch size it was designed to handle. Natural tradeoffs between the forms may indicate the superiority of one form over a more commonly adopted form due to a particular organization's unusual situation.

● New technologies, particularly computer-based ones, are significantly altering intermittent and continuous processes. These include PICS, ICAM, MRP II, group technology, CNC/DNC, robotics, CAD/CAM/CAE, and the concept of the factory of the future.

● The transformation process follows a life cycle that parallels the product's life cycle. As the product design becomes standardized and higher volumes at cheaper cost are required, the process moves from project to intermittent to continuous.

● Some aids in the transformation process design are explosion charts, assembly charts, operations process charts, route sheets, flow process charts, worker-machine (or activity) charts, simo charts, and layout diagrams.

● Most of the concepts used in layout models are based on the importance of locating departments close together or the cost of activity (such as transporting materials) between departments. Determining coordination requirements, space needs, transport costs, and product flows will usually generate the needed information.

   Line balancing models are based on breaking the work into small tasks that are then grouped into stations that follow the required precedence and complete the tasks within the required cycle time to meet the demand rate. The variation in models lies in the heuristic used to select tasks for inclusion in stations.

● Some of the more common computerized layout programs are CRAFT, ALDEP, and CORELAP. The common line balancing programs are COMSOAL and MALB.

7.7 KEY TERMS

7.8 REVIEW AND DISCUSSION QUESTIONS

1. Why is managing a high-volume continuous operation easier than, for example, a low-volume job shop?

2. Are there more or less inventories with a continuous process than with an intermittent process?

3. Why is the special purpose equipment for continuous processes especially susceptible to obsolescence?

4. How are explosion charts drawn for overlapping, interconnected, and hidden assemblies?

5. Why are irregular cycles in activity charts considered undesirable instead of desired for their change of pace and elimination of boredom?

6. What other considerations might an operations analyst have to consider in a layout other than those mentioned?

7. How would a task that takes longer than the cycle time be handled if it can be broken into smaller subtasks? If it cannot?

8. Can you think of any logical heuristics to aid in balancing a line?

9. Where might the term "balance delay" have come from?

10. In calculating the number of stations in line balancing, why must we always round up?

11. Could tasks be taken out of precedence if it were easy to route them back to earlier stations in order to achieve better balance?

12. Project processes such as building construction often focus upon scheduling techniques to aid in planning the project. How do such techniques help improve the production process?

13. Is a logging mill an analytic processing operation or a synthetic continuous operation?

14. The equipment of a job shop is less specialized than that of a flow shop. Is the labor also?

15. How would a relayout be conducted if the objective was to minimize congestion?

16. What might the advantages of CORELAP's criterion of closeness be compared to CRAFT's?

17. Contemporary approaches to the solution of skyrocketing labor costs have been aimed at increasing corporate operating leverage by utilizing automated machinery wherever feasible. What are the advantages and disadvantages of such a strategy?

18. Consider a typical grocery store operation. What type of process design would be best? How might this operation be analyzed for layout and facilities requirements?

19. What operations setup would be best suited for processing college registration changes under deadline conditions?

20. Review the "new technologies" of Section 7.1. Which are *not* related to the development of the computer? What advantages of computerization (e.g., speed, storage) do the others make use of?

21. As the process life cycle changes with the product life cycle, should a firm change along with it or move into new products more appropriate to its existing process? What factors must be considered in this decision?

22. In Figure 7.2 where the four process forms are illustrated, why don't firms operate in the regions marked "none"? Why don't the service industries extend all the way to the upper left corner?

7.9 PROBLEMS

Practice Problems

1. Five departments, located in two separate buildings as shown in the following figure, all use the same fork lift truck. The fork lift can be located in one of two locations as indicated by points A and B in the figure. The departments make use of the fork lift with the following approximate weekly frequencies.

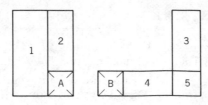

Dept.	Weekly Frequency
1	30
2	15
3	10
4	25
5	35

The time (in minutes) to travel to and from each of the departments to the two possible locations is given below.

	Location	
Dept.	A	B
1	10	15
2	5	12
3	15	10
4	12	5
5	20	10

Which location would result in the least total travel time?

2. In Problem 1, suppose travel time for an operator and the equipment is worth $0.50 per minute. What weekly rental cost for a second fork lift would be justified on the basis of travel time eliminated?

3. PVT Co. makes three products, as listed in the following table. They are moving into a 40- by 60-foot building and have five departments with space needs as indicated. Suggest a layout for the building.

Product	Annual Volume	Cost/Unit/Foot	Processing Sequence
Peas	300	$0.05	1-2-4-5
Vees	700	0.03	1-2-3-5
Teas	600	0.04	1-2-3-4-5

Department:	1	2	3	4	5
Size (ft²):	400	400	600	500	500

4. Resolve Problem 3 if the cost in cents to transport units between departments is as shown here for all products:

	To Dept.				
From Dept.	1	2	3	4	5
1	x	3	x	x	x
2		x	4	5	x
3			x	3	4
4				x	4
5					x

5. An office is laid out as in the following table. The office manager is considering switching departments 2 and 6 to reduce transport costs. Should she? (Use rectangular distances. Assume offices are 10 feet on a side.) What is the difference in annual cost assuming a 250 day work year?

Trip Matrix

	To					
From	1	2	3	4	5	6
1	x	40	x	x	x	40
2	30	x	20	30	60	0
3	x	70	x	x	x	20
4	x	0	x	x	x	30
5	x	10	x	x	x	0
6	40	50	20	0	10	x

1	2	3
4	5	6

Trip Cost (to any *department*) per Foot From					
1	2	3	4	5	6
$0.02	$0.03	$0.01	$0.03	$0.02	$0.02

6. **a.** Relayout PVT's new building in Problem 3 if the desired closeness ratings are as given below (based on definitions in Table 7.7). Compare with the solution in Problem 3.

Dept.	1	2	3	4	5
1		E	O	U	X
2			I	I	U
3				E	I
4					E
5					

b. Resolve the problem given the following ratings and compare with the previous solutions.

Dept.	1	2	3	4	5
1		U	O	I	A
2			X	U	I
3				U	U
4					X
5					

7. Relayout the office in Problem 5 given the following desired closeness ratings:

Dept.	1	2	3	4	5	6
1		I	A	X	O	U
2			X	E	I	O
3				O	X	I
4					I	E
5						A
6						

8. Demand for a certain subassembly in a toy manufacturing facility is 96 items per 8-hour shift. The following six tasks are required to produce one subassembly.

Task	Time Required (min)	Predecessor Tasks
a	4	—
b	5	a
c	3	a
d	2	b
e	1	b, c
f	5	d, e

What is the required cycle time? Theoretically, how many work stations will be required? Balance the line. What is the line's efficiency? What is the balance delay?

9. An assembly line has the following tasks (times shown in minutes).
   a. Six assemblies are required per hour. Balance the line.
   b. What is the efficiency of the line?

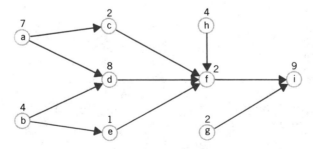

10. Balance the following line to a cycle time of 10 minutes and determine the balance delay. (Times are given in minutes.)

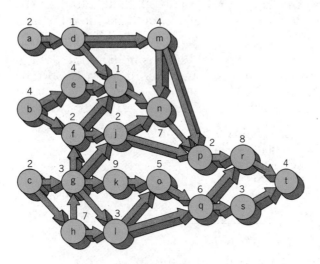

More Complex Problems

11. Ace Machinery is forecasting a major increase in demand for their product next year: 70,000 units total demand. They are currently producing 50,000 units a year on the equipment they have. By employing a third shift they could reach 75,000 units but the per unit variable cost would rise from $1.10 each currently to $1.50 each for the extra units. By adding capital equipment this cost could be cut to as low as $1 each.

Two alternatives are available: (1) buy $100,000 worth of new equipment (20,000 unit capacity) and attain a unit variable cost of $1.20 for the extra units or (2) buy $120,000 worth of new equipment and attain a unit cost of $1 for the extra units. In both cases the equipment would last 10 years and their capacities would be the same. Management is strongly leaning toward the second alternative as being worth the extra $20,000. Construct a breakeven-type chart and recommend a decision.

12. Design an operator activity ("man-machine") chart for one operator running the two machines M and N described in the following table. Compare the output rate and cost per unit when two operators (one on each machine) are used. An operator's hourly wage is $4.50 per hour. Can you think of a way to make use of the single operator's idle time?

	Machine M	Machine N
Unload time (min)	0.24	0.18
Load time (min)	0.08	0.06
Run time (min)	0.95	0.85
Cost ($/hr)	5.00	4.00

13. Use the given layout and trip costs in Problem 5 to perform *one iteration* (with department 1) of the CRAFT algorithm. Assume the trips marked "x" in the trip matrix are all 30. Calculate the existing layout cost and determine if department 1 should be interchanged with any other department.

14. Relayout PVT's new building using *both* the data in Problem 3 and the data in Problem 6b. Assume that the cost-importance correspondence is as follows:

Annual Transport Cost ($)	Importance
0–300	U
300–600	O
600–900	I
900–1200	E
1200–up	A

15. Resolve Problem 10 if:
    a. The cycle time is 20 minutes.
    b. The cycle time is 7 minutes.
    c. The task time for k is 19 minutes (10-minute cycle time).

16. Solve Problem 10 for a cycle time of 14 minutes using the following task selection heuristics:
    a. LOT.
    b. Shortest operation time (SOT).
    c. Most follower tasks (MFT).
    d. Longest (in minutes) follower tasks (LFT).

17. Use the data in Problem 10 for various cycle times from 9 to 40 and then plot the efficiencies of the line versus cycle time. Show solutions of constant numbers of work stations. Are there "natural" solutions of high efficiency? What are they?

7.10 REFERENCES AND BIBLIOGRAPHY

1. Abernathy, W. J., "Production Process Structure and Technological Change," *Decision Sciences*, 7:607–619 (1976).

2. Amstead, B. H., Ostwald, P. F., and Begeman, M. L., *Manufacturing Processes*, 7th ed., New York: Wiley, 1977.

3. Arcus, A. L., "Comsoal: A Computer Method of Sequencing Operations for Assembly Lines," in E. S. Buffa, ed., *Readings in Production and Operations Management*, New York: Wiley, 1966.

4. Buffa, E. S., "Sequence Analysis for Functional Layouts," *Journal of Industrial Engineering*, 6:12–25 (March–April 1955).

5. Buffa, E. S., Armour, G. C., and Vollman, T. E., "Allocating Facilities with CRAFT," *Harvard Business Review*, 42:136–150 (March–April 1964).

6. Buffa, E. S., and Miller, J., *Production-Inventory Systems: Planning and Control*, 3rd ed., Homewood, IL: Irwin, 1979.

7. Buxey, G. M., Slack, N. P., and Wild, R., "Pro-

duction Flow System Design—A Review," *AIIE Transactions*, 5:37–48 (March 1973).

8. Chase, R. B., "Survey of Paced Assembly Lines," *Industrial Engineering*, 6:14–18 (Feb. 1974).

9. Davis, E. W., ed., *Project Management: Techniques, Applications, and Managerial Issues*, Norcross, GA: American Institute of Industrial Engineers, 1976.

10. Decker, R., "Computer Aided Design and Manufacturing at GM," *Datamation*, May 1978, pp. 159–165.

11. Eilon, S., *Elements of Production Planning and Control*, New York: Macmillan, 1962.

12. Francis, R. L., and White, J. A., *Facility Layout and Location: An Analytic Approach*, Englewood Cliffs, NJ: Prentice-Hall, 1974.

13. Groover, M. P., *Automation, Production Systems, and Computer-Aided Manufacturing*, Englewood Cliffs, NJ: Prentice-Hall, 1980.

14. Hayes, R. H. et al., "Link Manufacturing Process and Product Life Cycles," *Harvard Business Review*, 83:133–140 (Jan.–Feb. 1979).

15. Hayes, R. H., and Wheelwright, S. G., "The Dynamics of Process Product Life Cycles," *Harvard Business Review*, 57:127–136 (March–April 1979).

16. Helgeson, W. G., and Birnie, D. P., "Assembly Line Balancing Using the Ranked Positional Weight Technique," *Journal of Industrial Engineering*, 12:394–398 (1961).

17. Ignall, E. J., "A Review of Assembly Line-Balancing," *Journal of Industrial Engineering*, 16:244–254 (1965).

18. Kilbridge, M. D., and Wester, L., "A Heuristic Model of Assembly Line Balancing," *Journal of Industrial Engineering*, 12:292–298 (1961).

19. Lee, R. S., and Moore, J. M., "CORELAP—Computerized Relationship Layout Planning," *Journal of Industrial Engineering*, 18:195–200 (1967).

20. Levitt, T., "Production Line Approach to Service," *Harvard Business Review*, 50:41–52 (Sept.–Oct. 1972).

21. Mastor, A. A., "An Experimental Investigation and Comparative Evaluation of Production Line Balancing Techniques," *Management Science*, 16:728–746 (1970).

22. Middleton, C. J., "How to Set Up a Project Organization," *Harvard Business Review*, 45:73–82 (March–April 1967).

23. Remick, C., "Robots: New Faces on the Production Line," *Management Review*, 68:27 (May 1979).

24. Seenot, J. J., and Evans, W. O., "Automated Layout Design Program," *Journal of Industrial Engineering*, 18:690–695 (1967).

25. Skinner, W., *Manufacturing in the Corporate Strategy*, New York: Wiley, 1979.

26. Tonge, F. M., "Assembly Line Balancing Using Probabilistic Combinations of Heuristics," *Management Science*, 11:727–735 (1965).

27. Turban, E., and Meredith, J. R. *Fundamentals of Management Science*, 2nd ed., Dallas: Business Publications, 1981.

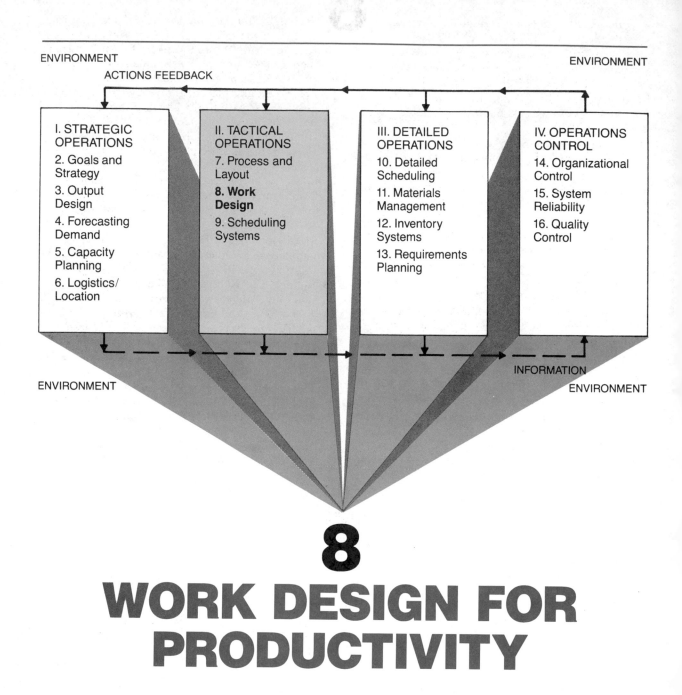

ENVIRONMENT   ENVIRONMENT

ACTIONS FEEDBACK

I. STRATEGIC OPERATIONS

2. Goals and Strategy

3. Output Design

4. Forecasting Demand

5. Capacity Planning

6. Logistics/ Location

II. TACTICAL OPERATIONS

7. Process and Layout

8. Work Design

9. Scheduling Systems

III. DETAILED OPERATIONS

10. Detailed Scheduling

11. Materials Management

12. Inventory Systems

13. Requirements Planning

IV. OPERATIONS CONTROL

14. Organizational Control

15. System Reliability

16. Quality Control

ENVIRONMENT   INFORMATION

ENVIRONMENT   ENVIRONMENT

8
WORK DESIGN FOR PRODUCTIVITY

8

LEARNING OBJECTIVES

By the end of this chapter the student should

- Have a better feel for the multiple meanings of productivity, its trends, and the factors that have apparently hampered it in the United States.

- Be familiar with the common approaches to increasing productivity.

- Be aware of the physiological elements of the workplace that influence workers' productivity.

- Understand the roles of motion study and work measurement in worker productivity.

- Know the terminology and procedures used in a time study.

- Comprehend how a work sampling study is conducted and how to determine the number of observations.

- Appreciate the use and application of predetermined data in setting standards.

We have reached the point in the transformation design part of this text where the design of the processing operations is largely complete. The only thing missing is the worker. But have we taken into account the fact that humans get bored with repetitive tasks? And that physically strenuous tasks require more rest than less strenuous tasks? And all the other multiple facets of people that affect their work performance?

Work design to maximize productivity.

This chapter now addresses the issue of integrating the *worker* into the transformation process. Our goal is to design the work environment so the long-run organizational competitive ability is maximized. An important element of this ability is the organization's *productivity*. As an example of what we are talking about, consider the fact that General Motors produces about 8 cars per worker each year while Toyota produces *40!* All in all, the average amount of labor put into Japanese cars runs about half of what U.S. manufacturers require, for a resulting cost savings of about $1500 per car, and we have not yet even broached the subject of quality.

Five times U.S. productivity.

In this chapter we focus on the important effect of the worker and the workplace on productivity, particularly the social and behavioral aspects, the physiological environment, and the physical elements. We begin our discussion in Section 8.1 by looking a little deeper into productivity and the elements that affect it. We specifically consider the issues of *quality circles,* the *quality of worklife,* and the relatively recent *Theory Z* approach to management based on Japanese methods of managing.

QC, QWL, and Z.

From this largely managerial perspective we narrow our focus in Section 8.2 to the physiological environment of the workplace, considering the worker-machine interface and the temperature, humidity, illumination, noise, and, particularly, health and safety conditions. We note especially the role of OSHA (Occupational Safety and Health Act) standards in the design of the workplace.

Role of OSHA.

Finally, we come in Section 8.3 to the physical aspects of work. Here we discuss motion study, time study, work measurement, and work simplification. The quantitative aspects of this section are illustrated with an example from the service sector, processing applications for insurance. An appendix to the chapter delves into some ancillary aspects of work design—human resource planning, compensation, and evaluation—and how they relate to the operations function.

8.1 PRODUCTIVITY

Productivity has, in recent years, become a major national issue. We have come to expect that our sociotechnical systems can become more and more advanced and that productivity can and should continue to grow in all areas of operations. In simple terms, productivity is defined as "output (units, gallons, visits, etc.) per worker hour." However, the interpretation of outputs, and worker hours, is not always uniform across industries. And at the national level the government computes U.S. productivity as the total national income divided by total paid employee hours. There are other common definitions of productivity also, such as labor productivity, capital productivity, total factor productivity, and so on, where the outputs and relevant inputs are measured in dollars rather than hours. Another problem in measuring productivity is that the output being counted is not always constant. It is easy enough to increase productivity by letting quality decrease. Rapidly changing technology has made output comparisons almost meaningless in many areas, such as electronics. And in the service sector the definitions are even more difficult: if arrests per police officer go down in one year compared to the year before, has police protection improved because of prevention or worsened because, perhaps, of a slackening in apprehension efforts?

The difficulty of measuring productivity.

Note that it is difficult to talk about productivity without also talking about quality, technology, output rates, and many other terms inherent in the language of operations management. Indeed, successful operations management, in large part, *is* the attainment of productivity. To help attract attention to the overwhelming importance of productivity, two national centers have recently been established, the National Center for Productivity and Quality of Working Life, in Washington, D.C., and the American Productivity Center, in Houston, Texas.

OM is productivity.

Productivity Trends and Reasons

Figure 8.1 illustrates the trend in productivity in the United States since 1890. Note that up to 1945, productivity gains increased at about 2 percent per year and then at about 3 percent per year thereafter. In the early 1960s annual productivity increases hit a peak of almost 4 percent a year but since that time the *rate* of productivity increases has been declining. Indeed, in the late seventies productivity *itself* started decreasing, thereby drawing significant attention to the problem, though this trend turned around in the 1980s.

Decreasing productivity!

For example, it was noted [7] that all the increases in productivity since 1947 evaporate when plotted as output *per dollar* of employee labor rather than per hour. In fact, it appears that throughout this entire period one dollar of labor consistently produced a dollar and a half worth of goods, and the late seventies were no exception. Yet, even on this measure the late seventies showed a higher drop than had ever occurred previously.

Many explanations were offered. These largely fell into four areas: capital investment, external factors, labor, and management.

Capital Investment

These reasons were based on industry's reduced investment in labor-saving, productive equipment. The causes were seen to be less cash available for investment due to the following factors:

1. Excessive wage demands by workers.
2. Excessive dividends to stockholders.

Some causes.

3. Forced investment by the government into unproductive pollution and safety equipment.

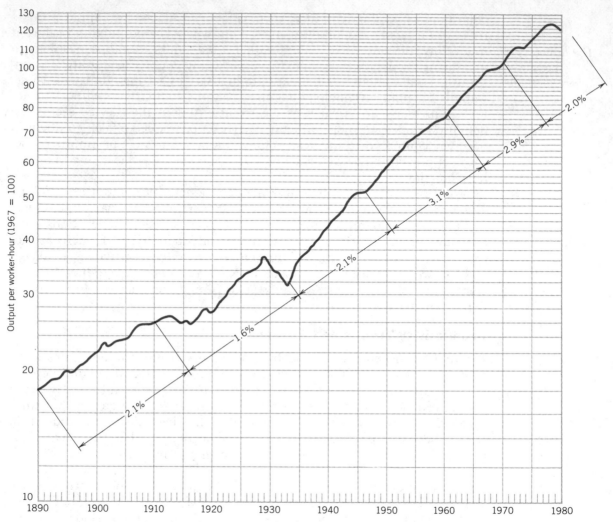

Figure 8.1 History of productivity in the United States. (Adapted from J. L. Riggs, *Production Systems Planning, Analysis and Control*, 2nd ed., New York: Wiley, 1976.)

4. Government-forced rollbacks in price increases. For example, President John Kennedy forced big steel to roll back their price increases in the early 1960s. The profits lost at that time could have gone to replace aging blast furnaces with basic oxygen furnaces to keep the U.S. steel industry competitive. Instead, steelmaking in the United States now appears to be largely uncompetitive with foreign-produced steel.

External Factors

Cost of energy.   Some explanations note the contribution of aggravating, if not causative, external factors such as the increases in the cost of energy (thereby forcing businesses to use less energy-intensive but also less productivity facilities).

Growth of services.   Another explanation in this category is the national growth in services, which are known to be much less efficient than manufacturing.

Labor

This category consists of explanations relating to the workers.

1. The increased militancy of workers and unions in their demands on business. Abetting this is the government's perceived support of the unions.

The worker's fault.

2. The governmentally enforced social programs businesses must adhere to regarding the aged, the poor, veterans, and so on.

3. A decrease in the work ethic due to youth's attitudes toward business and wealth, the decreasing marginal contribution of additional income, inflation, tax levels in the higher brackets, the increased availability of services, and a general reduced dedication to both employers and work itself, with more interest in enjoying one's free time.

Management

Many in-depth analyses [21] of the productivity problem have concluded

Really the fault of management.

that it is largely the fault of top management itself and is *not* due to the usual reasons of energy prices, inadequate capital investment, government meddling, or even the workers. It was found, for example, that workers are

GOOD NEWS • BAD NEWS

"Mr Bruckner would like a word with you in his office."

(Reprinted by permission of the Chicago Tribune–New York News Syndicate, Inc.)

45 percent idle time!

Causes of low productivity.

Ignorant of costs.

Goods available due to specialization.

only *working* 55 percent of the time. The managers in charge had been promoted on the basis of their technical, rather than supervisory, skills and often did not even know how long workers should take to do a job. Productivity losses have been found to largely derive from the following:

30 percent: poor planning and scheduling.

30 percent: poor coordination of resources.

25 percent: poor instructions to workers.

15 percent: inadequate ability to alter capacity to meet demand.

In part, the fault was also deemed to be due to the managerial fad in the United States of "hands-off" management taken to the extreme of not monitoring, helping, or even caring about lower level managers in their duties. To a great extent, U.S. managers do not know what the details of their costs are or even which customers' orders are profitable and which are not. Accounting reports often do not break out costs for managerial use but instead present "averages" for the use of bankers, security analysts, the IRS, the SEC, stockholders, and other such "externals."

Skinner [20] warns us, however, not to focus solely on productivity as the problem but rather on overall competitive ability. We will not regain industrial leadership by trying to work "harder" than the Japanese or the Germans. Any solution must include quality, lead time, innovation, and a host of other such factors as well.

But it is feared by some that the United States is not yet ready for such a solution. Managers are still looking for faster machines to solve their problems, having in too many cases bargained away every other response. When the answer comes this time, it must start from the very top of the managerial pyramid—factory floor fads will not be sufficient. There will be no quick solutions; patience will be required.

Approaches to Increasing Productivity

In the meantime, efforts to improve basic productivity in both product and service areas are proceeding along three fronts: through equipment, the workers, and the work methods employed. We will look at what is happening in each of these areas next.

Equipment

In Chapter 1 we described how the division of labor increased specialization, thereby increasing productivity and reducing costs. This enabled the public to obtain the products of the Industrial Revolution by both decreasing the *cost* of the products and, simultaneously, increasing the general public's ability to pay for the products through wages earned in the factories.

People supplied factories with physical labor and were often considered by managers to be relatively interchangeable commodities that could be bought or sold at will. Quite naturally, management was interested in producing the organization's output at minimal cost, and human labor was most cost-effective. They were generally not concerned with an employee's satisfaction with the job, except as it affected job performance. As human labor became more expensive, either directly in terms of wages, or indirectly in terms of requiring special consideration (such as managerial attention and fringe benefits), machines became relatively more cost-effective and began to substitute for human labor. Where this substitution was less feasible, such as in service operations, costs rose in relation to product costs because the same substitution advantages could not be used.

Machines replace labor.

The increasing technological sophistication since the Industrial Revolution has had major effects. The substitution of machines for labor, in addition to significantly improving productivity, has resulted in both increased *and* decreased skill levels being required of the humans working with these systems. For example, a high degree of skill is necessary to set up a large, numerically controlled machine center. But, on the other hand, the skill levels required in a large auto assembly plant have, on the whole, declined. Automation results in challenging jobs for some, those designing the sophisticated equipment, but tedious and boring jobs for others, those being paced by the equipment.

Automation changes the skill levels.

The overall result has been to substitute mechanical power for human physical labor (called *mechanization*) and, in the process, to create needs for both higher and lower levels of human skills. This trend is continuing even today where electronic equipment is replacing human sensing skills (called *automation*). It is not hard to imagine complex equipment doing much of the work occupying humans in their jobs today.

Mechanization led to automation.

"They told me I'd be a plant supervisor...."

(*Source: Industry Week,* Aug. 1, 1977. Reprinted, courtesy of *Industry Week.*)

Mechanization, automation, and computerization are commonplace and expected in our society's organizations. In fact, as consumers we get irritated and indignant on the few occasions when the computer mis-bills us for merchandise or loses our reservation, when the vending machine dispenses cold coffee, or when the traffic signal gets stuck on red. We forget the savings in cost, increase in speed, and enlarged service capacity this equipment has also provided.

Automation certainly appears promising for our productivity crisis. We have, however, noted in Chapter 1 the trend in our economy toward services, and many of these service occupations appear somewhat more difficult to replace mechanically or electronically: the teacher, the waiter, the masseur, the doctor. Nevertheless, someone will only too quickly point out the computerized teaching machine; the vending machine; the vibrating beds and recliners, roller massage chairs, and pulsating showers; and computerized diagnosis and multiphasic screening. There is even a computer game called "Psychiatrist" whose "patients," communicating through a terminal connected to the computer, swear there is a real person on the other end and have even felt significant psychological improvement following "sessions" with the computer.

Computerized psychiatry.

The question that often arises is: What can machines, like the computer, *not* do? Some researchers (e.g., McCormick [13]) have attempted to answer this question. To summarize their views, human abilities surpass machines in terms of

Are humans superior to computers?

- *Organizing* patterns and information, using *judgment*, reasoning *inductively.*
- Responding *flexibly* to situations, *selecting* appropriately.
- Being *innovative* and *creative, synthesizing* elements of a situation or problem.

In a way, all of these abilities seem to relate to each other; for example, an important element of creativity is the ability to organize information and respond flexibly. And one aspect of reasoning inductively is selecting and synthesizing. It might be noted also that humans have a considerable amount of *redundancy* in their makeup and this too might contribute to the abilities above as well as to increased reliability (as will be discussed in Chapter 15).

The human use of human beings.

Ideally, workers would only be used for their highest abilities, as previously mentioned: creativity, synthesis, organization, judgment, flexibility, and so forth. Although society is clearly advancing in this direction, the achievement of this goal is still a long way off. In the meantime, there is work to be done, much of it menial, and to the extent that this work can be made more palatable to the indispensable human worker, productivity will be improved.

The sociotechnical approach to high productivity.

In spite of the tremendous potential of machines to replace human endeavor in organizations, virtually all of today's productive systems are still combinations of facilities, equipment, materials, and *humans*. These organizations are frequently referred to as **sociotechnical systems** because they

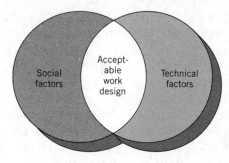

Figure 8.2 The sociotechnical approach to work design.

intimately combine people and technology in complex forms to produce outputs. To the extent that the worker is considered to be simply a cheaper substitute for a machine there will be managerial problems. The sociotechnical approach to work design is illustrated in Figure 8.2. Although there are clearly certain *technical* requirements for each job, there are also certain human (*social*) factors that must be considered (comfort, interest, etc.). Work designed to lie in the region of overlap of these factors, then, is expected to have continuing high productivity.

Workers

A considerable amount of attention has been focused on directly improving the worker's performance through good management as well as by such specialized techniques as four-day workweeks, profit-sharing, absentee programs, "sensitivity training," job "enrichment," and so on. Here we will look at three more recent, yet relatively encompassing, programs: quality of worklife, Theory Z, and quality circles.

Quality of Worklife (QWL). The **QWL** program incorporates many of the earlier worker programs and varies significantly in application. That is, it is not a singular approach but is conceived and applied in every company according to their situation and desires. It has, in some form, been applied at General Motors, Eaton Corp., Procter & Gamble, and a number of other firms.

The conceptual basis of the program is that an improved QWL will lead to long-term productivity payoffs through better communication of ideas on improvements, less absenteeism and waste, and better employee-employer relations. The aim is to change the complete *culture* of the workplace so both the worker and the firm benefit.

Change the culture.

There appear to be four specific areas of emphasis in the various QWL programs employed thus far: compensation, working conditions, the work itself, and opportunity.

- *Compensation:* Attention in this category has usually concerned adequate, fair, and secure compensation (especially unemployment compensation). Yet, most workers already fare well in this area and their concerns now lie with benefits, particularly health and pensions, and forms of profit-sharing such as bonus plans, stock ownership, and others.

Profit-sharing.

- *Working conditions:* Here the focus has historically been twofold: a safe, healthy working environment and the "rights" of workers. More recent concerns are the physiological work environment (supportive, low stress, low pressure, unforced overtime) and egalitarian treatment of all workers. This last aspect focuses on the historical perquisites of management: no time clocks; minimal rules; greater freedom of movement and access; and private lunchrooms, lockers, offices, and parking. A democratic workplace with participation of the workers in the setting of workplace policies is one step in this direction.

Equal treatment.

- *Work:* Much attention has been devoted to this aspect of worklife with job rotation, cross-training, enlargement, enrichment, and team programs. The goal here has been to make the work more fulfilling, allow greater responsibility, and give workers some pride in their work. Yet, our current predicament has, in part, derived from our historical narrowing of the job scope, through greater and greater specialization, to increase productivity in the first place.

A bit of pride.

- *Opportunity:* Finally, attention to the *growth* of the worker is a unique element of some QWL programs. This includes the opportunity for advancement, of course, and the ability to take pride in the firm and its image as well. But the focus is more on the overall development of the worker as a unique human resource available to the firm.

Worker growth.

Theory Z. This concept, articulated by Professor William Ouchi at UCLA [15], presents a third alternative to the two classic management approaches: Theory X, the "lazy worker" theory, which holds that people basically do not like to work and must be coerced into it, and Theory Y, also sometimes called the "contented cow" theory, that says people do like to work and, if happy in their job, will work even harder.

The lazy worker.

The contented cow.

Theory Z, in contrast, holds many of the tenets of QWL. The emphasis here is on mutual commitment and loyalty between worker and firm, the growth and development of the individual, and equality among employees, including participation in decision making. More specifically, the following practices directly support these tenets:

- Lifetime employment for up to 35 percent of the workforce.
- Equal sacrifice by all, such as in pay cuts, when problems occur.

Specific Z practices.

- Slow but steady promotion on the basis of total experience gained with the firm.
- Total within-company job rotation among *all* functions.
- Decision making by consensus and compromise in a bottom-up fashion.

Won't work here?

Critics of Theory Z state that such an approach cannot work in the culture of the United States. But indeed, it already has, and with American workers, at Sony Corp. in San Diego, at Kawasaki in Nebraska, and in many other places. What's more, many American firms follow these same tenets already, in large part: Hewlett-Packard, IBM, Procter & Gamble, Intel, and others.

Quality Circles (QC). The **quality circle** movement started in Japan around 1961, although attention to quality had become a national obsession much before then. This obsession was largely due to the work of two eminent statisticians, Doctors W. Edward Deming and J. M. Juran, both of the United States.

A U.S. invention.

A QC is a group of employees from the same work area who voluntarily meet together on a regular basis to address job-related issues and problems. The characteristics of most of these circles are as follows:

- Top management support.
- Voluntary participation.
- Groups of 10 to 12 maximum.

QC characteristics.

- Wide range of representation.
- Regular (usually weekly) meetings.
- Meetings held outside regular hours but time paid for by the company.
- Self-selected problems for analysis.
- Emphasis on instruction in problem-solving techniques.

The worker needs help.

The belief behind a QC is in stark contrast to traditional American attitudes and again reflects the tenets of QWL and Theory Z: Quality problems are *not* due to a lack of motivation on the part of the worker. Rather, the worker does not know the cause of the problems, nor even which ones are the main problems. To determine this, the worker needs to learn to use statistical tools and analysis: data collection, histograms, Pareto techniques (discussed in Chapter 12), brainstorming, cause-effect diagrams, and so on. These techniques are used by the group to identify primary problems, design experiments, determine ways to measure effects, develop alternatives, and evaluate solutions. This is the purpose of the QC.

Not just quality.

In fact, circles are not limited to considering only quality problems; they investigate all ways of improving the firm, from work methods to cafeteria menus. Yet, the purpose of the circles remains problem solving: teaching techniques, measuring, evaluating, analyzing, and solving problems.

Lockheed Industries introduced quality circles to the United States in late 1973 but many, many firms, both service and product oriented, have quickly adopted the idea: GE, 3M, Ford, Bank of America, American Airlines, and many others.

Up to 8:1 ROIs.

Not all solutions proposed by the circles are implemented but typically about 80 percent are, with a return on investment ranging from 4:1 to 8:1, though not all solutions are successful, either. A point requiring an early decision by the firm is whether the workers, or circle, will participate in the savings accruing from their solutions. In Japan they do not, but in the United States mutual commitment, trust, and loyalty are not as great and an added incentive may be necessary. Last, quality circles work best in a firm that already has a good relationship with its workers and a democratic style of management.

Methods

A number of changes in work methods often help in improving productivity, such as

- Suggestion plans.
- Parts interchangeability (Chapter 3).
- Unitization and containerization (Chapter 11).
- Standardization (Chapter 3).
- Better work design (Chapter 8).
- Cost reduction programs (Chapter 8).
- Improved workplace organization (Chapter 8).
- Waste reduction programs (Chapter 16).
- Zero-defects programs (Chapter 16).
- Value analysis programs (Chapter 3).
- Managerial aids such as control charts (Chapter 14), computer models, and so on.

We will next consider some of these methods' approaches to improving productivity in Sections 8.2 and 8.3.

8.2 PHYSIOLOGICAL ENVIRONMENT OF THE WORKPLACE

Considering the complete workplace environment.

In this section we focus on the workers' *environment* as it relates to work design and productivity. We consider the workplace arrangement itself of course, such as proper seat height, as well as temperature, noise, illumination, and so forth. We we also consider *neurological* factors, such as the design of hand controls, and other such concerns that may affect the workers' safety or health. We will divide our discussion of workplace design among *anthropometric* factors (body measurements), neurological factors, muscular factors, temperature and humidity, illumination, noise, and safety and health.

Anthropometric Factors

The necessity of body measurements.

In designing the workplace, information concerning the proper desk height, handrail size, tool length, and so on must all be available. Without knowing standard body measurements, and variations in those sizes, it would be impossible to design the cab for a truck, or the faucets for a sink. Much of the data available concerning the body measurements of people were originally gathered for special purposes such as cockpit sizes for pilots in World War II. Nevertheless, such data have been put to extensive use in many other organizations and situations.

Note that simple average values will not suffice. An average value for the height of a chair is acceptable but not for the size of a door, or the weight of a fire extinguisher. For these items it is desired that some very large fraction of the population be able to use them, so it is necessary to know the variation in "widths" of people, and their lifting strengths. Then a doorway large enough to accept 99.9 percent of all people, or an extinguisher that can be lifted by 99.98 percent of all people, can be designed. Standard figures and tables of average body dimensions and fifth and ninety-fifth percentiles for both males and females are available in References 5, 13, and 24.

Neurological Factors

Designing knobs and dials.

Many of the tasks that workers perform relate to sensory perception, speed of reaction, and ability to perform simultaneous tasks. All these tasks are concerned with *neurological* responses and the design of the workplace can improve or hinder such responses considerably. For example, Figure 8.3 illustrates two ways to set dials, one the wrong way and the other the right way. The *natural* way they would be installed is shown in the left "Off" half of Figure 8.3*a*. The meters are, of course, not connected when they are installed, so all the pointers point upward to zero, which also probably agrees with the labels and writing on the meters. However, when the meters are connected and operating they point in all different directions, as illustrated in the right "On" half of Figure 8.3*a*. We have shaded, as an example, the range of dial readings that corresponds to "normal" indications and for which no managerial intervention is required. Note that two dials do *not*

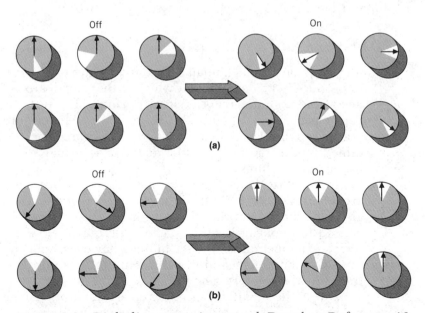

Figure 8.3 Dial alignments in a panel. Based on Reference 13. (*a*) Zero values aligned. (*b*) Shaded ("normal") ranges aligned.

indicate a normal reading and thus require attention. But every meter must be carefully examined to determine if any are in need of such attention.

In contrast, in Figure 8.3b all the meters are installed (the left "Off" half) with their *normal* ranges pointing *up*. By so doing, when the meters are operating, all the pointers point *up* (the right half of Figure 8.3b) except those requiring managerial attention, which now are quite obvious.

Controls should operate as expected.

There are many similar such considerations (see References 13 and 24) but, in general, workplace controls should be designed to operate in the manner a worker would expect: turning a handle clockwise to *shut off* a flow, pushing a lever to *increase* a mechanism, and so forth. Many airplane crashes in test flights have been linked to the anti-intuitive workings of controls; for example, rudder controls that turn the plane to the right by pushing *down* on the right pedal.

Muscular Factors

Although less common than in earlier days, workers' muscular abilities are sometimes important. Similar to anthropometry tables, there are also tables of muscular strengths available (see Reference 13).

Fatigue considered through allowances.

Of more probable importance than strength in a workplace design is the consideration of fatigue. Unfortunately, very little progress has been made in this area although many studies have been conducted. One of the main problems is that fatigue is not totally a muscular reaction—boredom, anxiety, and stress play important roles as well. To date the most common approach has simply been the use of an "allowance," a percentage increase in time allowed, for particularly fatiguing work.

Temperature and Humidity

Although the normal human body temperature is 98.6°F, workers attempting to produce in an environment which is that warm are extremely ineffective. According to studies reported in McCormick [13] the limit of efficient human performance is at about 92°F; beyond this temperature, performance degrades rapidly. The reason is that our 98.6-degree body temperature is maintained by the "burning" of fuel (food) in a normal external environment of lower temperatures.

Limit of efficient human performance is 92°F. Heating and cooling the workplace.

In the past, it has been common for organizations to heat their work areas during cold periods of the year. In recent years many organizations also air condition during the hot (or smoggy) period of the year. Even advanced technological equipment often requires close environmental monitoring of temperatures. For the human, however, temperature is not the only important environmental variable. Humidity is important as well, as illustrated by the **comfort zone** in Figure 8.4.

Due to the simultaneous occurrence of a natural gas shortage and several severe winters, many organizations have found it necessary to lower average temperatures in offices and factories. In fact, many factories have had gas allotments cut by 80 percent and more. The effect of working in significantly

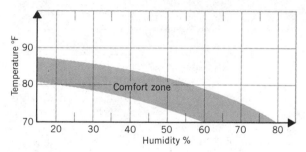

Figure 8.4 Temperature-humidity comfort zone.

lower than "normal" temperatures is not yet known, but it is bound to have some impact on worker productivity.

Illumination

The proper lighting of the workplace, in intensity, contrast, and color, is an important element of work design. Few things are as irritating as not being able to see what you are doing. Table 8.1 lists the accepted illumination levels for various situations and tasks based on American Illumination Engineering Society standards.

Natural versus artificial lighting.
Workers generally prefer natural to artificial light, perhaps as much for claustrophobic reasons as anything else. But natural light varies considerably in intensity, from 800 footcandles on a bright summer day to 50 footcandles during rainy ones. And windows are expensive to clean, repair, and insulate.

Minimizing glare.
Glare and color are two other aspects of illumination that are important in workplace design. Glare should be minimized by moving or diffusing the source or raising visors or shields to block it. The use of color in the work-

Table 8.1 General Illumination Levels

Illumination (footcandles)	Task
1800	Operating room surgery
1000	Welding (at work point)
500	Detailed inspection of fine work
300	Fine assembly work
200	General machining, drafting
100	Sewing
80	Polishing, typing, benchwork, art
50	Filing papers, general reading and writing, assembly
20	Rough machining, dining
10	Shipping and receiving, general lighting
5	Soft lighting, back lighting
0.5	Moonlit night
0.1	Movie theater

Table 8.2 OSHA Color Standards

White	Red	Orange	Yellow
Traffic lines	Fire equipment	Dangerous machinery	Caution lights
Refuse locations	Flammable liquids	Energized equipment	Guard rails
Room corners	Barricade lights	Enclosed mechanisms	Construction
Food and drink	Emergency	Start buttons	equipment
dispensing	switches		Suspended fixtures
	Alarm boxes		Pillars, posts
			Combustible scrap
			containers

Green	Black	Blue	Purple
Safety	Traffic lines	Equipment under	Radiation hazards
First aid	Direction signs	repair	Radiation storage
Go lights		Inoperative controls	Radiation disposal
		Faulty valves	Radiation
			equipment

place is often helpful as well as psychologically beneficial. Table 8.2 lists the OSHA (Occupational Safety and Health Act) color standards for marking facilities, pipes, and equipment as an example of the utility of color.

The uses of color. The psychological use of color in hospitals, banks, and modern offices is a recent trend also. Brightly colored furniture is often used to promote a sense of sureness or progressiveness. Frequently the cool colors, blues and greens, will be used for quiet and rest areas while the warm colors, yellows, oranges, and reds are used for active areas. In addition, light colors reflect illumination well and give a sense of spaciousness to rooms.

Noise

There are two serious negative effects of noise: potential hearing loss and workplace inefficiency. Noise is typically measured in *decibels (dB)* where *A logarithmic* each increase of 10 decibels means a *tenfold* increase in intensity. Some *decibel scale.* common noise levels are given in Figure 8.5. We see that a vacuum cleaner at 70 decibels is 10 times as loud as a noisy office (60 decibels), that heavy traffic is 100 times as loud, an exhaust fan 1000 times, a circular saw 100,000 times, and a siren 100,000,000 times as loud. Included in the figure is the OSHA limit for continuous noise.

Table 8.3 lists the permissible noise levels for shorter durations also. For example, a circular saw (110 decibels) is permissible for ½ hour, or a passing subway train (100 decibels) for 2 hours (a very long train). But intensity of noise is not the only distraction; high pitched or irregular noises are also distracting. The following are some methods of dealing with noise.

● *Controlling* the noise by reduction of vibration, and so forth.

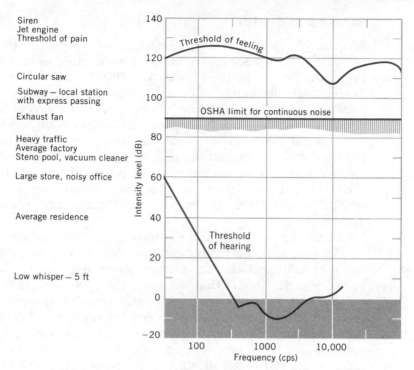

Figure 8.5   Decibel levels of some common noises. (Adapted by permission from W. E. Woodson and D. W. Conover, *Human Engineering Guide for Equipment Designers*, 2nd ed., Berkeley: University of California Press, 1966.)

(Reprinted by permission of the Chicago Tribune–New York News Syndicate, Inc.)

- *Isolating* the noise.
- *Protecting* the worker through ear plugs, helmets, or even carpets and drapes.
- *Piping* in music to provide a pleasant background for working.

Table 8.3   OSHA Permissible Noise Levels

OSHA permissible
noise levels.

Duration per day (hr)	Sound Level (dB)
8	90
6	92
4	95
3	97
2	100
1½	102
1	105
½	110
¼ or less	115

Safety and Health

OSHA began
in 1971.

Frequently in the preceding discussion we referred to the *OSHA standards* for various workplace design factors such as color or noise. In 1971, the U.S. Occupational Safety and Health Act (**OSHA**) took effect. This act provides for much tighter safety and health regulations of organizations than ever before. The National Institute for Occupational Safety and Health (NIOSH), which administers OSHA, has the authority to inspect workplaces, issue citations for violations of standards, and even obtain court orders closing down operations until unsafe practices are corrected. OSHA initially earned a negative reputation because of some poor judgments in its early regulatory activities, but most of this has now been cleared up. In addition to safety responsibilities, OSHA is also responsible for unsafe noise and chemical regulations.

The expense of
accidents.

Designing for safety in the workplace is of special importance—not only accident-related safety but health as well. Management knows that health and accident expenses can be tremendous, not only to the worker but also to the organization. It thus behooves the operations manager to try to anticipate and prevent both accidents and health hazards. Since we are becoming more and more aware of work environments that can produce health problems (mining of various minerals, asbestos production and use, spray painting, arc welding) it is reasonable to expect more regulations and precautions against materials and occupations that result in long-term health problems.

Accidents as two
unsafe acts.

Most accidents seem to be combinations of multiple unsafe events: an unsafe act in the presence of unsafe conditions, or two unsafe acts occurring simultaneously. This is why accidents do not occur more often than they do. In some sense, it also explains why people are lulled into thinking accidents only happen to someone else—they have often done unsafe acts themselves and never had an accident. Since it is usually *two* unsafe events that produce accidents, there is an early opportunity to prevent accidents by watching for the *first* unsafe event. In addition to observation, another way to identify unsafe events is by reviewing all previous accidents. It has generally been found that, for every major injury, there were over 300 noninjury accidents. If the location and nature of these noninjury accidents can be identified, it might be possible to prevent a major injury.

300 noninjuries per
injury.

8.3 PHYSICAL WORK DESIGN AND MEASUREMENT

Designing the
workplace.

The first aspect of physical work design should perhaps concern the design of the workplace within which the work will be conducted. This is a continuation of the layout analyses of Chapter 7 but now in relation to the human worker's place in the system. The objectives of the work to be done should, in large measure, dictate the basic workplace design. If customer service is the task, then a work arrangement that optimizes customer contact should be used. Entry and exit should be easy, waiting should be minimal, and so on. If committee work is the task, then the workplace should allow for the

easy, interpersonal communication that is necessary. The ⌐
quiet, comfortable, and segregated from distractions such as ⌐
comings and goings of others.

But in considering the various aspects of work design, th⌐
to backtrack without end. *Is this the best way to serve a cusⱡⱺⱨⱨⱨ.*
tool be employed? Can a machine do the work instead? Could this task be more
efficiently combined with an earlier or later one? Is this task necessary? Could
redesigning the output eliminate the task? These are all fruitful questions for
simplifying work, and cutting costs as well, and should precede the purely
physical aspects of work design. Some useful questions to aid in simplifying
work are

Work
simplification
questions.

1. Is this task necessary?
2. Can the task be shortened?
3. Can the task be more efficiently combined with an earlier or later one?
4. Is there a better way to do the task?
5. Can a machine be used more effectively?
6. Would tools or equipment help in this task?
7. Can handling be minimized?
8. Are the working conditions best for this task?
9. Is necessary idle time more usefully employed elsewhere?
10. Is fatigue minimized?
11. Are worker skill levels appropriate to the task?

One classic area of physical workplace design has been known as "time
and motion study," popularized in the media of the 1950s by the concept of
the "efficiency expert." The reason that time and motion study is important
to the operations manager is that these studies set the *capacity* of the productive process and thus help determine the output rate of the operation.
Without a "standard" output rate no planning can be done, nor for that
matter can anyone tell if work is taking longer or shorter than it should.

Time study versus
motion study.

Actually, these are two separate areas of study—**motion study** is oriented
toward *improving* productivity and **time study** toward *measuring* productivity. We will consider each of them separately. Motion study should always
precede time study so the most efficient work process is timed rather than
a less efficient one.

Motion Study

As with the previous task analysis process, the purpose of motion study is
to increase the worker's efficiency of movement and decrease fatigue. There
are also a number of accepted "principles" of economy of motion, primarily
based on Barnes [2]. These principles can be divided into worker and workplace guidelines, as indicated in the following partial list of Barnes' principles.

Worker

1. Minimize all movements (including eye movements) by eliminating unnecessary ones, combining movements, and shortening them.

2. Make all movements smooth, continuous, curved, and rhythmic instead of zig-zagged, angular, stop and go, and so forth.

3. Balance motions by using both hands with symmetry, simultaneity, and equality of effort.

4. Do work with the smallest muscle group necessary; use gravity if possible.

5. Provide variety with foot controls, intermittent muscle use for tension relief, perceptual variety (shape, color) for control.

Principles of economy of motion.

Workplace

6. Use holding fixtures, guideways, and stops to minimize the muscular forces required.

7. Optimally locate tools and equipment to suit the task.

8. Use equipment that can be easily operated in the proper manner.

9. Workplace conditions such as lighting, temperature, and seat height should be appropriate to the task and the worker.

Therblig Analysis

Therblig analysis for basic elemental motions.

One of the techniques for describing task motions has come to be called *therblig analysis.* Frank and Lillian Gilbreth, who developed the technique, needed a term to describe the most basic elemental motions of which all tasks are composed. Since any name was sufficient, they simply chose a reverse spelling of their own, with the t and h transposed. (If the authors had invented the technique we probably would have called the motions "Sbbigs" or "Thiderems," clearly much better terms.)

The analytic technique consists of breaking any task down to its elemental component movements, therbligs, and analyzing these to eliminate wasted motion and improve the overall task. Typical therbligs, represented in the analysis by letters, are reach (R), move (M), and grasp (G). These motions, and others, will be discussed again in the next subsection. Such studies are relatively rare these days because they are expensive and are only useful when a task is repeated many, many times. Today, many such tasks are typically automated instead.

Micromotion Study

Micromotions through a high speed camera.

The determination of the exact sequence of therbligs is rather difficult since they are all "micromotions" (very small motions) and occur quickly. To aid the analysis, a high-speed videotape or motion picture camera is often used in what is called a *micromotion study.* The task is filmed at high speed and then replayed in the laboratory over and over, both forward and backward, and in slow motion, until a full analysis can be made to obtain the time durations for each motion. Either a high-speed clock, *chronometer,* is included in the background of the film or speed of the camera itself is used to time the worker's mov

Memomotion Study

Slow speed memomotion.

A similar type of study, but for very *long* duration tasks, is *memomotion study* in which a *slow speed* camera is used in a fashion similar to "time lapse" photography. The film is then run at a higher rate of speed to visualize the continuous motions.

In all of these cases, the same procedure is employed of analyzing basic movements in an attempt to improve the efficiency of the task. In the process, many of the worker and workplace principles of motion economy stated earlier are drawn upon.

Work Measurement

The need to measure work.

When human labor is used as part of the productive operations, it is necessary to know the productivity of that labor for capacity planning, process design, and scheduling considerations. Thus, there is a need for work measurement to establish standards for output rates. A study by Rice [18] indicates that two-thirds of all "standards" are set by time study, either at the time of need or by referring to earlier time studies of similar jobs. Another, similar approach we will describe is called work sampling, but this is only used to set standards very infrequently. Of the remaining times that standards are set, half the time historical accounting records are simply used, calculating average output rates and work times. The other half of the time, a method we will discuss later called "predetermined standards" is employed. However, all of these methods only relate to physically observable work done by humans. Machine-paced work and mental activity, for example, would not fall into these categories.

Time Study

Continuous versus snapback timing.

The basic tool used in time study is a stopwatch, typically one that measures in hundredths of a minute. Two timing methods are common. One is to start the watch at the beginning of the study and let it run *continuously,* observing and recording the times at the end of each task element in sequential fashion. The other method, called **snapback timing,** is to read the time at the end of each task element and then reset the time to zero by depressing the crown for the next task element. (This procedure has occasionally been criticized as being less accurate.)

Time study is a sensitive subject.

In preparing a time study, considerable care must be taken. Time study, and motion study as well, has had especially bad press, and workers often view the process with at least suspicion, if not irritation; in some unionized organizations time study is not even allowed.

Changing pace under observation.

Beyond this basic consideration, the operations analyst will want to make sure the worker has been properly trained for the job and is aware of what the analyst is doing. Frequently, workers will change their pattern of work

TLEY'S CREW

(Reprinted by permission of the Chicago Tribune–New York News Syndicate, Inc.)

while being observed, sometimes to try to increase the allowed time for the task or in an attempt to perform well (fast) under a test situation. The well-trained analyst can detect and compensate for these changes, however, by methods we will discuss later.

Time the job elements. The analyst should be thoroughly familiar with the job being timed. This is necessary in order to divide the job into meaningful, timeable elements. It is desirable to time elements of a job rather than complete job *cycles* for a number of reasons.

- Performance speeds may vary among elements.
- Standards for *similar* jobs involving the same elements can later be set without repeating the study.
- The job is better described in terms of its elements. Some elements may be of relatively consistent duration whereas other elements may vary widely. This can then give considerable insight into ways to improve the productivity of operations.
- Timing errors or performance aberrations (dropping a tiny screw in a hole) can more easily be spotted when timing by elements.
- Different multiples of elements (e.g., assembling wheels onto carts) may exist in one cycle of the job.

Number of cycles to time. Last, the analyst should know about how many cycles must be timed to give a reliable time standard. To be 95 percent confident that the observed times will be within 5 percent of the actual required times, refer to Table 8.4.

To illustrate the various aspects of time study, let us consider the following simple office paperwork example.

The Insurance Form

In a mail order insurance company, applicants apply for insurance by filling out a multiple copy form. The daily mail of forms is delivered to Ms.

Table 8.4 Number of Cycles for Time Study

Cycle Time (min)	If Annual Number of Cycles Is	
	<10,000	*>10,000*
0.25	40	80
0.50	30	60
1	20	40
5	10	20
10	7	13
20	5	9
50	3	6
100	2	4
400	1	2
1000	1	2

Note: 95 percent confidence of being within ±5 percent of actual time.

"Trip" L'Cutt who handles them according to a special procedure. She cuts open each envelope, lays any enclosed letters in one stack, locates the *second* page of the application and pulls out the snap-apart original and carbon copy, separates them on her desk, snaps out the original and carbon copy of the first page, lays them on top of the second page, staples the originals together and sets them in a stack, and staples the copies together and sets them in a separate stack.

The time study form for 40 cycles is shown (abbreviated here for simplicity) in Figure 8.6 filled in with continuous time readings in hundredths of minutes. Note the stapler problem indicated on the form by an asterisk; such "aberrations," or "outliers," are ignored in determining standard times. Alongside the continuous times are listed the *elemental times*, Δt, obtained by subtraction of the continuous time from the preceding continuous time. The average of all these element times is then listed at the far right.

A performance rating for normalization.

The next column lists a **performance rating,** R, a subjective estimate based on the experience of the operations analyst of how fast Ms. L'Cutt is working on each element compared to an "average" worker doing this task day in and day out. A rating such as 0.90 means that she is only 90 percent as fast as expected of an average worker, perhaps due to a lack of manual dexterity or such. The next column to the right lists the frequency of each task element in one job cycle. In this example every task is done every cycle, so f is one for all tasks, but in other situations, such as opening and unpacking a box of 12 cans, it may be done one-twelfth of the time, or perhaps every other time. The task **normal times** are obtained by multiplying these last three columns. This is the time it would take a normal worker to do the task elements. Again, using the 0.90 rating, the effect would be to *decrease* the amount of time a normal worker would take for this element, which is indeed the proper correction. (This multiplying, instead of dividing, should

Worker __Ms. L'Cutt__   Date _____   Times Allowance __15%__

Task __Insurance Form__   Analyst __R.P.G.__   __Feb. 20, 1979__   Cont. 0.01 min

Element	1	Δt	2	Δt	3 Δt	......	40 Δt	Average Δt	Performance Rating, R		Frequency, f		Normal Times
Open envelope	05	5	47	3	......	......	......	4	× 0.90	×	1	=	3.6
Papers out, envelope trash	07	2	49	2	......	......	......	2	× 1.10	×	1	=	2.2
Letters stacked	09	2	51	2	......	......	......	2	× 1.00	×	1	=	2.0
Locate page 2	10	1	54	3	......	......	......	2	× 0.90	×	1	=	1.8
Snapout, separate page 2	13	3	55	1	......	......	......	2	× 1.20	×	1	=	2.4
Snapout, separate page 1	15	2	57	2	......	......	......	2	× 1.20	×	1	=	2.4
Staple, stack original	16	1	58	1	......	......	......	1	× 1.10	×	1	=	1.1
Staple, stack copy	44*	X	60	2	......	......	......	2	× 1.00	×	1	=	2.0
											Total	=	17.5

Comments: *Stapler jammed

Normal time: 17.5
Allowance: + 2.6
Standard time: 20.1

Figure 8.6 Time study of insurance form.

have confused you for a second. If it did not, reread the last par
you are sure you understand what is happening.)

Adding up the elemental normal times then results in the
time, NT, for this job, 17.5 hundredths of a minute.

$$NT = \sum_i \Delta t_i R_i f_i = 17.5 \tag{8.1}$$

Allowance for
fatigue, and
so forth.

On top of this, an **allowance** is given for such unavoidable delays as a
jammed stapler, conferring with a supervisor, visits to the restroom, fatigue,
and so forth. Typically, about 5 percent is allowed for personal needs; fatigue
allowances depend on the strenuousness of the task but usually only apply
to those task elements that *are* strenuous, not the entire task. For highly
strenuous task elements (ditch digging, tapping molten steel from a furnace),
allowances of up to 30 percent are sometimes used. Appropriate allowances
can often be developed by work sampling, a technique discussed later, but
in many cases allowances are determined as part of a labor-management
bargaining agreement.

Standard time
from normal time.

In Figure 8.6 and quite commonly, 15 percent is used as an average
allowance. Adding the 15 percent of normal time for unavoidable delay to
the 17.5 then results in the **standard time**, ST, of 20.1 hundredths of a minute
(12 seconds).

$$ST = NT (1 + \text{allowance}) \tag{8.2}$$
$$= 17.5 (1 + .15)$$
$$= 17.5 + 2.6$$
$$= 20.1$$

This is now the time that can be used to verify the number of cycles
needed for the study (about 40 from Table 8.4) and to design the insurance
form processing operation for the organization. For example, the hourly rate
for this job, called a standard hour, SH, would be

$$SH = 60/ST \tag{8.3}$$
$$= (60 \text{ min/hr})/(0.201 \text{ min/job})$$
$$= 300 \text{ jobs/hr}$$

At a pay scale of $4.50 per hour, this results in a *piece rate*, PR, of

$$PR = \text{wage rate}/SH \tag{8.4}$$
$$= (\$4.50/\text{hr})/(300 \text{ jobs/hr})$$
$$= \$0.015/\text{job}$$

One of the reasons that time study has come under fire is the necessity
of making a *subjective* performance rating of the worker being timed. Considerable effort has been expended by organizations to ensure that time
study analysts have been properly trained by using training films, certified
by time study organizations, and so forth.

One way of avoiding the interpersonal problems associated with time study is through **work sampling** in which case the worker is not directly timed and often is not even aware of being studied.

Work Sampling

Another way of acquiring information similar to that obtained in work measurement is through *work sampling*. In work sampling a large number of random observations are made of a worker, and in each case, a note is jotted down regarding what the worker is doing. A number of advantages accrue to this procedure: it is simple, no stopwatch is needed, less training is required, the worker is often not even aware of being observed, and true work performance is more likely to be observed.

On the negative side, work sampling may involve a considerable number of observations in order to obtain 95 percent confidence. The required number of observations N, is given by the formula

$$N = \frac{4p(1 - p)}{e^2} \tag{8.5}$$

where p is the percentage of time the worker spends on the activity being observed and e is the allowable error in percentage points, expressed as a decimal. That is, the observed percentage should be within ± 0.01 if 1 percent accuracy is desired. This formula is also, indirectly, the basis for the values given in Table 8.4. To demonstrate the use of the formula, suppose an activity is to be timed that is expected to represent 20 percent of the working day and an accuracy of ± 3 percent with 95 percent confidence is deemed sufficient (that is, from 17 to 23 percent or, if the initial estimate was wrong, from, say, 22 to 28 percent, of the working day). The required number of observations is then

$$N = \frac{4(0.2)(1 - 0.2)}{(0.03)^2} = \frac{0.64}{0.0009} = 711$$

A common and valuable use of work sampling is the establishment of allowances. If a worker is observed a sufficient number of times and in 5 percent of the observations is idle for personal reasons and 7 percent for unavoidable reasons, then a total allowance of 12 percent may be used for this task.

The full use of work sampling is to establish standards for a job as a whole or even subelements of a job. To illustrate, reconsider the insurance form example and assume we are interested in setting a standard for the overall job. Since the standard allowance is 15 percent we will assume p, the proportion of time spent on the mail, is 0.85. If the allowable error is four percentage points, then the number of observations required is

$$N = \frac{4(0.85)(0.15)}{(0.04)^2} = 319$$

If these 319 random observations are collected over a week's duration this will require an observation about every 8 minutes, on the average.

Suppose the results of the week's study were that 80 percent of the time Ms. L'Cutt was working (with an average rating of 110 percent), 3 percent she was avoidably idle, and 17 percent of the time she was unavoidably idle for both personal and work-related reasons. During the week of observation (40 hr × 60 min/hr = 2400 min) she processed 12,000 applications.

The standard time would be determined as follows.

$$\text{normal time} = \frac{\text{actual work time} \times \text{performance rating}}{\text{number of applications processed}} \tag{8.6}$$

$$= \frac{(2400 \text{ min} \times 80\%) \times 1.10}{12,000}$$

$$= 0.176 \text{ min}$$

$$\text{standard time} = \text{normal time} + \text{allowance} \tag{8.7}$$

$$= 0.176 + (0.176)\,0.15$$

$$= 0.202 \text{ min}$$

Note in this example that the 15 percent allowance is not in agreement with Ms. L'Cutt's 20 percent idle time. However, when she was working Ms. L'Cutt worked 10 percent faster than normal to produce *more* than the standard number of applications per week.

$$\frac{2400 \text{ min/week}}{0.202 \text{ min/application}} = 11{,}881 \text{ applications/week}$$

Predetermined Standards

Another way to determine output rates is to use **predetermined** data (e.g., from a previous time study) concerning the movements involved in a task. A knowledge of the movements then allows the synthesis (adding together) of known normal times to arrive at a total normal time for the task.

The MTM system for constructing a synthetic time study.

One of the most popular sets of such standard time elements is that used in the *methods-time-measurement* (**MTM**) system, a sample of which is shown in Figure 8.7. This system uses predetermined times measured in units called *time measurement units* (**TMUs**) to measure various elementary micro-motions (discussed in the previous subsection) such as reach, grasp, and turn. These times (each TMU) are stated in 0.00001 hour. The time it takes to reach, for example, is listed as a function of the distance and the "clarity" of the object being reached for (if it is moving, very small, covered, etc.).

The MTM procedure is thus to break each job down into the required elemental motions for both left and right hands. A chart similar to a *simo chart* (refer back to Figure 7.13) is then constructed and TMUs are assigned to the elemental motions in order to obtain a final normal time for the job. The obvious advantage of MTM is avoiding the need for a time or work sampling study. Nevertheless, a time study may still be easier to do than the rather complex MTM.

METHODS-TIME MEASUREMENT
MTM-I APPLICATION DATA

1 TMU	=	.00001	hour	1 hour	= 100,000.0 TMU
	=	.0006	minute	1 minute	= 1,666.7 TMU
	=	.036	seconds	1 second	= 27.8 TMU

Do not attempt to use this chart or apply Methods-Time Measurement in any way unless you understand the proper application of the data. This statement is included as a word of caution to prevent difficulties resulting from mis-application of the data.

**MTM ASSOCIATION
FOR STANDARDS
AND RESEARCH**
16-01 Broadway
Fair Lawn, N.J. 07410

TABLE I – REACH – R

Distance Moved Inches	Time TMU				Hand In Motion		CASE AND DESCRIPTION
	A	B	C or D	E	A	B	
3/4 or less	2.0	2.0	2.0	2.0	1.6	1.6	A Reach to object in fixed location, or to object in other hand or on which other hand rests
1	2.5	2.5	3.6	2.4	2.3	2.3	
2	4.0	4.0	5.9	3.8	3.5	2.7	
3	5.3	5.3	7.3	5.3	4.5	3.6	B Reach to single object in location which may vary slightly from cycle to cycle
4	6.1	6.4	8.4	6.8	4.9	4.3	
5	6.5	7.8	9.4	7.4	5.3	5.0	
6	7.0	8.6	10.1	8.0	5.7	5.7	
7	7.4	9.3	10.8	8.7	6.1	6.5	C Reach to object jumbled with other objects in a group so that search and select occur.
8	7.9	10.1	11.5	9.3	6.5	7.2	
9	8.3	10.8	12.2	9.9	6.9	7.9	
10	8.7	11.5	12.9	10.5	7.3	8.6	
12	9.6	12.9	14.2	11.8	8.1	10.1	
14	10.5	14.4	15.6	13.0	8.9	11.5	D Reach to a very small object or where accurate grasp is required
16	11.4	15.8	17.0	14.2	9.7	12.9	
18	12.3	17.2	18.4	15.5	10.5	14.4	
20	13.1	18.6	19.8	16.7	11.3	15.8	
22	14.0	20.1	21.2	18.0	12.1	17.3	E Reach to indefinite location to get hand in position for body balance or next motion or out of way.
24	14.9	21.5	22.5	19.2	12.9	18.8	
26	15.8	22.9	23.9	20.4	13.7	20.2	
28	16.7	24.4	25.3	21.7	14.5	21.7	
30	17.5	25.8	26.7	22.9	15.3	23.2	
Additional	0.4	0.7	0.7	0.6			TMU per inch over 30 inches

TABLE II – MOVE – M

Distance Moved Inches	Time TMU			Hand In Motion B	Wt. Allowance			CASE AND DESCRIPTION
	A	B	C		Wt. (lb.) Up to	Dynamic Factor	Static Constant TMU	
3/4 or less	2.0	2.0	2.0	1.7				
1	2.5	2.9	3.4	2.3	2.5	1.00	0	A Move object to other hand or against stop.
2	3.6	4.6	5.2	2.9				
3	4.9	5.7	6.7	3.6	7.5	1.06	2.2	
4	6.1	6.9	8.0	4.3				
5	7.3	8.0	9.2	5.0	12.5	1.11	3.9	
6	8.1	8.9	10.3	5.7				
7	8.9	9.7	11.1	6.5	17.5	1.17	5.6	
8	9.7	10.6	11.8	7.2				B Move object to approximate or indefinite location.
9	10.5	11.5	12.7	7.9	22.5	1.22	7.4	
10	11.3	12.2	13.5	8.6				
12	12.9	13.4	15.2	10.0	27.5	1.28	9.1	
14	14.4	14.6	16.9	11.4				
16	16.0	15.8	18.7	12.8	32.5	1.33	10.8	
18	17.6	17.0	20.4	14.2				
20	19.2	18.2	22.1	15.6	37.5	1.39	12.5	
22	20.8	19.4	23.8	17.0				
24	22.4	20.6	25.5	18.4	42.5	1.44	14.3	C Move object to exact location.
26	24.0	21.8	27.3	19.8				
28	25.5	23.1	29.0	21.2	47.5	1.50	16.0	
30	27.1	24.3	30.7	22.7				
Additional	0.8	0.6	0.86				TMU per inch over 30 inches	

TABLE IV – GRASP – G

TYPE OF GRASP	Case	Time TMU	DESCRIPTION	
PICK-UP	1A	2.0	Any size object by itself, easily grasped	
	1B	3.5	Object very small or lying close against a flat surface	
	1C1	7.3	Diameter larger than 1/2"	Interference with Grasp
	1C2	8.7	Diameter 1/4" to 1/2"	on bottom and one side of
	1C3	10.8	Diameter less than 1/4"	nearly cylindrical object.
REGRASP	2	5.6	Change grasp without relinquishing control	
TRANSFER	3	5.6	Control transferred from one hand to the other.	
SELECT	4A	7.3	Larger than 1" x 1" x 1"	Object jumbled with other
	4B	9.1	1/4" x 1/4" x 1/8" to 1" x 1" x 1"	objects so that search
	4C	12.9	Smaller than 1/4" x 1/4" x 1/8"	and select occur.
CONTACT	5	0	Contact, Sliding, or Hook Grasp.	

TABLE III A – TURN – T

Weight	Time TMU for Degrees Turned										
	30°	45°	60°	75°	90°	105°	120°	135°	150°	165°	180°
Small 0 to 2 Pounds	2.8	3.5	4.1	4.8	5.4	6.1	6.8	7.4	8.1	8.7	9.4
Medium - 2.1 to 10 Pounds	4.4	5.5	6.5	7.5	8.5	9.6	10.6	11.6	12.7	13.7	14.8
Large - 10.1 to 35 Pounds	8.4	10.5	12.3	14.4	16.2	18.3	20.4	22.2	24.3	26.1	28.2

TABLE III B – APPLY PRESSURE – AP

FULL CYCLE			COMPONENTS		
SYMBOL	TMU	DESCRIPTION	SYMBOL	TMU	DESCRIPTION
APA	10.6	AF + DM + RLF	AF	3.4	Apply Force
APB	16.2	APA + G2	DM	4.2	Dwell, Minimum
			RLF	3.0	Release Force

Figure 8.7 Motion study by MTM analysis. (Reprinted by permission of the MTM Association for Standards and Research. No reprint permission without written consent from the MTM Association, 16-01 Broadway, Fair Lawn, NJ 07410.)

8.4 APPENDIX: HUMAN RESOURCE PLANNING, COMPENSATION, AND EVALUATION

Human Resource Planning

Human resource planning objectives.

Simply put, the objective of *human resource planning* is to ensure that the organization has the correct *number* of people, with the appropriate *skills*, at the right *time*, and in the proper *location*. Five steps are required in good human resource planning.

1. Analyze short- and long-range organizational plans.
2. Determine current human resources.
3. Determine probable losses.
4. Develop a short- and long-range human resource forecast.
5. Develop action plans to meet the forecast.

Plans

Human resource plans tied to organizational goals.

All plans are based on organizational goals and specific organizational objectives. The short- and long-range production plans are based on these underlying directions and, therefore, the human resource plan is "tied to" organizational goals through these plans. Human resource requirements are determined by the actions the organization expects to take in the future (e.g., new output mix, higher volume, better quality), and, if not achieved, can severely limit the organization's ability to act on higher level plans.

Importance of timing in training.

Meeting skill and timing requirements are critical and often elusive objectives of human resource planning. For example, a large regional fast-food chain is growing rapidly. Financing for expansion and profits are both good. A plan to open 50 new stores each year for the next 3 years must be severely altered because of poor human resource planning. Cooks and counter help are available, but store managers, who require 6 months training, and district and regional managers, requiring 1 to 2 years training, will not be available. The necessary backscheduling of human resources was not done and opening without adequate managerial skill is a sure route to failure. As seen, the production plan and the human resource plan are interdependent. The production plan must recognize the current human resource status for short-range actions and the human resource planning system must react to new production plans or changes in them.

Current Resources

Human resource audit.

To paraphrase the Cheshire Cat, as mentioned earlier, "If you don't know where you are going, any path will get you there." Equally important in "getting there" is knowing where you are. Before beginning any human resource plan, a complete human resource inventory should be available. This inventory should include at least the following information about all present personnel.

Name

Age

Sex

Department or organizational unit

Education

Job category

Experience on current job

Other experience

Performance rating

Promotability to other positions

Predicting changes.
This basic information about current employees enables human resource planners to anticipate possible promotions and to plan training and additional experience to upgrade existing employees into expected future positions. It also provides the baseline data from which needed personnel additions can be determined. Human resource inventory information also pinpoints job categories that will experience declines and for which layoffs or job transfers will be required.

Losses

Human resource losses usually result from deaths, disabilities, retirements, employee terminations (voluntary or otherwise), and intracompany transfers. Deaths, disabilities, and retirements can be predicted with reasonable accuracy based on past organizational history and current trends. Quitting rates are generally higher for employees in the first 2 or 3 years of employment and for younger employees. The expected rate of termination due to unacceptable performance is dependent on availability of good employees in the community and on the system of employee selection used. A poor selection system will result in a higher rate of termination. Transfer losses are not net losses to the organization, but are clearly redistributions of human resource needs. This problem is particularly burdensome in governmental organizations for which the Civil Service system allows high employee mobility between government departments and agencies. While a transfer from HUD to the DOD is not a loss for the federal government, the HUD planning unit has lost an employee.

Forecast

Anticipates requirements.
The human resource forecast is based on the production plans and the current human resource inventory, adjusted for expected losses. The human resource forecast begins with the estimate of operational activity requiring labor. For example, a fast-food restaurant may operate two shifts of four employees and a store manager for each shift. One district manager has a span of control of eight stores and each regional manager controls six district managers. Therefore, to open 50 new stores next year will require

$$50 \times 4 \times 2 = 400 \text{ cooks and counter helpers}$$
$$50 \times 2 = 100 \text{ store managers (50 day, 50 night)}$$

$$50 \div 8 = 7^* \text{ district managers}$$
$$8 \div 6 = 2^* \text{ regional managers}$$

As for timing, the regional and district managers need to be employed and involved in most of the planning for the new stores. The store managers will be hired 6 months prior to the opening of a new store so that they can be adequately trained, and cooks and clerks will begin 2 weeks to 1 month prior to opening.

Actions

Personnel activities to meet plans.

Finally, once the human resource forecast exists, the personnel manager must develop plans to meet the forecasted needs. Parts of this plan might include such activities as college campus recruiting, newspaper advertising, and employee training and development programs. An obvious necessity in developing these plans is a consideration of equal employment opportunity laws and affirmative action programs to upgrade the skills and employment levels of women and minorities.

As you can well imagine, this human resource planning process requires a significant amount of information and also necessitates the integration of numerous objectives, assumptions, and quantitative factors into an overall planning system. Once the human resource requirements for an organization have been estimated, it still remains to implement a plan of action to meet these requirements. An early element in this plan of action is job evaluation to determine the rates of pay of the various jobs.

Compensation

Compensation plans are invariably of two types, either time-based or output-based (sometimes the latter is called "incentive wages"). When members of organizations are paid for their services, they are often considered to be either salaried or hourly. All salaried and most hourly workers are compen-

Time-based systems.

sated on a *time-based system*, typically weekly, biweekly, or monthly. The advantages of a time-based system are that compensation is easy to calculate, precise output standards do not have to be calculated, record keeping is minimal, workers are generally considered to be self-motivated by standards of professionalism or fairness, labor relations are smoother (since output-based incentive wages do not exist), and quality need not suffer in attempts to increase quantity.

The primary disadvantage of time-based systems is that no direct incentive exists for working harder than "average." Only far-removed merit increases and possible promotion provide direct incentives for working harder, but they also provide incentives for "playing politics," "favoritism," and a host of other dysfunctional organizational behaviors. Of course, in many types of work, the nature of the work itself, the working conditions, and other such factors provide natural motivation to the workers.

---

*Assumes a new manager is required after each preceding manager reaches specified span of control. Thus, $50 \div 8 = 6.25$, or 7 district managers.

Output-based
systems.

Although the main advantage of *output-based compensation systems* is that a direct incentive is applied to increase output, there are also many disadvantages.

- The determination of "standard" output is difficult.
- The system itself requires a considerable amount of time and cost to develop and implement.
- Loopholes frequently exist in such systems and are quickly exploited by workers.
- Quality and service may decrease in an attempt to increase the output rate.
- Workers resent the manipulative aspect of such plans.
- Record keeping becomes a monstrous task.
- The calculation of compensation becomes extremely complicated.
- The plan is often the subject of grievances and union contract negotiations.
- Not all jobs can be put on incentive systems and charges of unfairness often result.
- Social problems and peer pressure may be encouraged.
- An incentive is created for the worker to devise improved work methods and equipment but keep both secret from management so the standard will not be raised.

In addition to these disadvantages, management must be careful that the increased output can be profitably used. For example, if automobile production is 60 per hour there is little value in putting transmission workers on an incentive system that increases transmission output to 100 per hour.

Individual
incentive plans.

The simplest *incentive plan* is the straight *piece-rate system* whereby the worker, such as a harvester, is paid for the amount of output produced (bushels picked). Modifications to this basic system also exist. A *base-rate system* (also called *100 percent premium plans*) guarantees the worker a minimum wage based on standard output with a *piece-rate* bonus beyond the standard. In some cases, instead of a piece-rate bonus beyond the standard, a *sharing plan* (e.g., Halsey plan, Rowan plan) is used in which the organization shares the increased value of the output at some rate, such as 50:50, with the worker.

Group incentive
plans.

In addition to individual incentive plans, there are also *group plans* wherein a particular group can earn a bonus, as in the *Scanlon plan*, where all the organization's workers gain, as in profit sharing. To illustrate, the basis of the Scanlon plan is the formation of committees who seek out ways in which the organization can cut labor costs. The group is then rewarded on the basis of the value of their suggestions. Some controversy has arisen with this plan when worker committees make suggestions regarding unproductive *managerial* policies and inefficiencies. Nevertheless, top management has usually encouraged such constructive criticism.

Some useful guidelines to aid in setting up incentive plans are the following:

1. The bonus should follow the action as soon as possible.
2. The plan should be simple and the bonus easy to calculate.
3. The plan should be fully communicated to all the workers.
4. Precise standards should be stated and guaranteed to remain unchanged for some period of time.
5. The manner and time points of re-evaluating standards should be specified.
6. Clear policies should be given regarding bonuses under conditions beyond the control of the worker, such as when a machine breaks down.
7. No upper limit should exist on bonuses.
8. Standards should be monitored for fairness in case of changes in products, production methods, quality requirements, or equipment.

Evaluation

Importance of evaluation. Members of an organization are typically evaluated regarding their performance on a regular basis, usually annually. The purpose of these evaluations is to give the worker some formal feedback on his or her performance and

Employee Performance Evaluation Sheet

Performance	Exceeds Job Requirements	Meets Job Requirements	Needs Some Improvement	Does Not Meet Minimum Requirements
Quality	Leaps tall building with a single bound	Requires running start to leap tall buildings	Can leap short buildings only	Can only leap candlesticks
Timeliness	Is faster than greased lightning	Is faster than a greased pig	Is faster than a pig in molasses	Is slower than molasses
Drive	Works in overdrive	Works in high gear	Works in low gear	Works in reverse gear
Adaptability	Walks on water consistently	Walks on water in emergencies	Swims in water	Requires flotation device
Communication	Talks with God	Talks with the angels	Talks to animals	Talks to self

also provide an opportunity for the worker to identify, for management, any problems that are impairing the employee's ability to perform. These sessions are usually held in connection with changes in pay and promotion. Union guidelines concerning the conduct and frequency of these sessions are often spelled out since promotions, raises, tenure, terminations, and other such personnel actions may be bargaining issues.

In some organizations the evaluation interviews are held with a superior *two* grades higher so that the worker can air any complaints regarding an immediate superior, and correspondingly, any criticism of the worker's performance will have more authority and seem less like personal criticism. Both good and bad performance are normally identified and the best method for growth on the part of the worker is spelled out—skill requirements, further education, and so forth.

8.5 SUMMARY AND KEY LEARNING POINTS

Continuing with the design of the transformation process in Chapter 7, this chapter has addressed the issue of designing the process so the human worker can be productive within it. We first addressed productivity, its trends, some possible explanations for the trends, and approaches for increasing productivity. We then looked at the design of the workplace itself and considered the impact of workplace layout, illumination, environment, and other such aspects on the human worker.

Next we considered physical work design and measurement in terms of motion study, work simplification, and time study. We particularly considered the many different ways of setting time standards: direct time study, work sampling, and the use of predetermined standards. In the appendix to the chapter we looked at the ancillary issues of workforce planning, compensation, and evaluation.

The key learning points have been

- Productivity is basically measured as output per working hour, but other measures are also employed such as output per dollar of labor or capital. In the 1950s and 1960s the annual rate of U.S. productivity increases had reached about 3 percent a year but since the 1970s the rate has slipped back to 2 percent a year; in the late 1970s productivity actually started to decrease, though this has turned around in the early 1980s. The major factors hampering productivity are postulated to be low capital investment, external effects such as government regulations and the high cost of energy, poor labor attitudes toward work, and, perhaps most important, poor management.

- Common approaches to increasing productivity are through new equipment, the workers, and work methods. The former is simply the substitution of mechanization and automation for labor. Typical of worker-centered approaches are the employment of quality-of-worklife programs, Theory Z management, and quality circles. Work method approaches include cost reduction, zero-defects, suggestion plans, and so on.

- The following are the major physiological aspects of the workplace that affect the productivity of workers:
  - Anthropometric factors such as table heights.
  - Neurological factors such as dial designs.
  - Muscular and fatigue aspects.
  - Temperature.
  - Humidity.
  - Illumination.
  - Noise.
  - Health and safety considerations.

- All the forms of motion study—work simplification, principles of motion economy, therblig analysis, micromotion, and memomotion study—are oriented toward improving the efficiency of the worker doing a task. Work measurement is used to set "standards" for normal productivity so that capacities can be estimated and schedules set.

- Time study uses either continuous or snapback timing of task elements to set time standards for jobs. A predetermined number of cycles are timed, performance ratings on the task elements are judged, and the frequency of each task element in the job is noted. Multiplying these three values and summing over all task elements gives the normal time for the job. Adding the appropriate allowance results in the standard time.

- In a work sampling study a large number of short observations, determined from Equation 8.5, are made of the worker and it is noted what task the worker is performing at the time. The normal time is then given by the total work time times the percentage of observations represented by the task or job of interest times the performance rating divided by the output during the observation time.

- Standards are frequently set by using predetermined motion data measured in TMUs. One of the most popular sets of such data is the MTM system.

8.6 KEY TERMS

productivity (p. 260)

sociotechnical systems (p. 266)

quality of worklife (p. 267)

Theory Z (p. 268)

quality circle (p. 269)

anthropometric (p. 270)

OSHA (p. 276)

motion study (p. 277)

time study (p. 277)

work measurement (p. 279)

snapback timing (p. 279)

performance rating (p. 281)

normal time (p. 281)

comfort zone (p. 272)

allowance (p. 283)

standard time (p. 283)

work sampling (p. 284)

predetermined standards (p. 285)

MTM (p. 285)

TMUs (p. 285)

8.7 REVIEW AND DISCUSSION QUESTIONS

1. How can a company justify to its stockholders the installation of air conditioning in its machine shop?

2. How valid do you think the listed explanations for the productivity drop are?

3. Do you think the United States is willing to take the difficult measures necessary to increase productivity?

4. Federal guidelines now call for wheelchair facilities in newly constructed machine plants. Do you feel this is appropriate for all industrial plants?

5. How might the productivity of resources other than labor be defined such as a pump, $1000, a warehouse, a kilowatt-hour, a market survey?

6. Workers frequently regard new approaches such as Theory Z and quality circles as management fads to get them to work harder. Are they right?

7. The sociotechnical approach to work design deals with the overlap of two areas. Might you add more factors to consider in this overlap?

8. Why is the performance time *multiplied* by the rating instead of divided? Does this not seem backward?

9. Since work sampling seems so much easier and less irritating to the workers, why is it not always used instead of work measurement?

10. How do those workplace measurements requiring *average* dimensions differ from those requiring extreme percentiles?

11. How does *adding* background noises reduce noise distraction?

12. Why is human resource procurement so much more difficult than materials procurement?

13. Should companies require new employees to contract to work a specified number of years after the training program?

14. What might the drawbacks be in group incentive plans such as Scanlon's?

8.8 PROBLEMS

Practice Problems

1. Mr. I. R. Service is employed by the H & R Blop income tax service. I. R. prepares 1040s, all day, every day, from January 1 to April 15 each year. Work sampling was done for one week and the following results were recorded:

Number of 1040s completed	82
Available work time	2400 min
Performance rating	95%
Actual work percentage	80%

H & R Blop uses a 10 percent allowance. Based on this information, what should the standard time be for preparation of a 1040 tax return?

2. John Pressman has performed the following time study for a bending operation on a metal press. The times are recorded using the continuous reading method.

	Cycle 1	2	3
Get sheet from stack	0.10	0.49	0.92
Place against back and side guides	0.25	0.66	1.12
Depress safety activator switches with both hands	0.30	0.70	1.19
Remove and stack part in crate	0.40	0.81	1.31

The performance ratings for the four activities are 0.90, 0.85, 1.05, and 0.95, respectively. Assuming a 15 percent allowance, what should be the standard time for a complete cycle?

3. Jake Idletime has been observed 1000 times over the last 300 hours during which time he produced 27,000 parts. Jake was busy at work 600 times, but idle 400 times. Jake is rated at 80 percent of normal performance and normal allowance is 10 percent. What is the standard output per hour? What is the piece rate if Jake makes $5 per hour? Jake's sister, Jane, works at the same job, but Jane has a 110 percent performance rating. How many parts can Jane be expected to produce in an hour?

4. The following time study results were obtained using the snapback method.

	Cycle 1	Cycle 2	Cycle 3
Get carton	0.02	0.03	0.03
Pick up six cans	0.08	0.10	0.10
Place cans in carton	0.13	0.12	0.15
Seal carton	0.06	0.07	0.06

If the performance rates are 1.0, 0.9, 1.1, and 1.0, respectively, and a 20 percent allowance is used, what is the standard time for one cycle?

5. How large a work sample will be required to estimate within ±2 percent the proportion of the working day a worker spends in travel to and from the tool crib if he is expected to use about 30 percent of his day in travel and a 95 percent confidence level is required?

6. Calculate the standard time using a 15% allowance.

Observation period	1200 min
Performance rating	110%
Work percentage	90%
Number of parts made	1000

What percent is the worker over- or underproducing?

7. Calculate a standard time to rotate five tires on a car using a 20% allowance.

	Cycle 1	Cycle 2	Cycle 3	Cycle 4	Cycle 5 (spare)
Get car	2.1	—	—	—	—
Remove tire	1.5	1.4	1.6	1.5	1.4
Rotate tire	1.0	0.9	0.9	1.0	1.1
Mount tire	1.4	1.5	1.4	1.3	1.5
Return car	—	—	—	—	2.0

8. A work sampling study is to be conducted to determine an allowance for a job where the workers are commonly idle 15% of the time for personal reasons and 10% for unavoidable reasons. If an accuracy of $\pm 2\%$ is desired with 95% confidence, how large a sample should be taken?

More Complex Problems

9. How many times louder is heavy traffic than an average residence?

10. Construct a time standard using the predetermined data in Figure 8.7 for reaching across an 18-inch desk, grasping a golf ball out of a box of golf balls, transferring it to the other hand, and rotating it 180 degrees for visual inspection.

11. Some approaches to setting performance standards recommend the formula

$$ST = \frac{NT}{1 - \text{allowance}}$$

   a. What is the difference between this formula and Equation 8.2?
   b. Which gives the larger standard time?
   c. Which formula would labor unions support?
   d. Which formula is "right"?

12. Management wishes to conduct a work sampling study on a 4-hour job where the time is believed to be distributed as shown in the following data. They wish to be 95 percent confident that the individual task element times are accurate within ± 1 minute and nonworking times are accurate within ± 2 minutes. How many observations should be taken? How close together, on average, and over what time period would you recommend they be taken?

Fasten on jig	7 min
Mount tools	15 min
Cut face	35 min
Reposition	10 min
Cut side	20 min
Read drawings (total)	55 min
Cut back	40 min
Finish cuts	30 min

Idle (total)	8 min
Personal time (total)	20 min

13. In a work sampling study consisting of 1000 observations over 6 hours, a worker was observed to be working 700 times. The standard output per hour was computed to be 79 units with an allowance of 15 percent. The actual output of the worker during the sampling happened to be 420 units. What was the performance rating applied? Was the number of observations adequate for 95 percent confidence and a 3 percent error level?

14. The IE Department of a company is trying to determine a standard for the following job that involves 20-pound castings.

    Select 2 castings
    Carry them 25 feet to lathe
    Mount one on lathe
    Turn down 0.1 inches
    Remove from lathe and place in bin

    They have the following data available from previous time studies. What standard time would you recommend for this job?

Select and lift two 25-pound motors	30	sec
Carry 35 pounds 20 feet	12	sec
Walk 15 feet carrying 35 pounds	9	sec
Carry 50 pounds a distance of 16 feet	12	sec
Mount a 22-pound casting on a lathe	1.5	min
Turn down a medium-size casting	17	min/inch of depth
Remove a 25-pound casting from lathe and set down	0.45	min

15. Accounting is in the process of redetermining piece rates for jobs based on the new union contract that raised pay rates 10 percent and allowances from 15 percent previously to 20 percent now for all jobs. One job in particular had a piece rate of \$0.50 each based on a \$7 per hour wage. What should the new piece rate be?

16. Compute a standard time for one average cycle of the following job. Use a 15 percent allowance.

	Cycle							
Task	*1*	*R*	*2*	*R*	*3*	*R*	*4*	*R*
Get case of 4 cans	0.19	0.90	—	—	—	—	—	—
Lift out a can	0.05	1.10	0.07	0.85	0.04	1.20	0.06	1.00
Open can	0.11	0.85	0.09	1.20	0.10	1.00	0.11	0.85
Pour contents	0.07	0.95	0.06	1.00	0.06	0.95	0.06	1.00
Dispose of can	0.02	1.10	0.03	0.95	0.02	1.10	0.03	0.95
Dispose of case	—	—	—	—	—	—	0.05	1.10

8.9 CASE

BALDWIN MOTOR WORKS INC.

Baldwin Motor Works Inc. is a manufacturer of small electric motors for model trains and cars. Their first plant was opened in Cincinnati, Ohio, in 1970. Demand for Baldwin's products became so great (there are several major toy manufacturers located in the Cincinnati vicinity) that production had to be carried on around the clock. The company began making a profit after its second year of operation and has been profitable every year since.

Although employee relations have been acceptable, the workers who solder the motor lead wires to their bases have consistently been complaining. Each worker is seated in front of a large revolving table which receives motors from three assembly lines. A worker must pick up the next motor in line, place it on a solder jig, solder the two leads to the base, and place the motor on a conveyer belt, which moves on to inspection. The workers argue that, while they were able to keep up with the three production lines when the plant opened, this is no longer true due to improvements in production further up the line from them. They contend that if they are to keep from becoming a "bottleneck," they must work feverishly without time to take care of personal needs.

The plant superintendent sets production rates for all three shifts. The production rate for each shift is set at an identical level so that there are no complaints about one shift carrying the load of another shift. All three shifts complain about the solder job.

Bob Dennler, the industrial engineer for Baldwin Motor Works, has convinced management to conduct a work sampling study on the soldering job. He has decided that a sample of 2000 observations would be required to establish the degree of confidence necessary for the sample. Work samples were taken for each of the three shifts over a 20-day period (four work-weeks). To remove the effect of any sampling bias, the hours of the day within each shift and the workers sampled were both randomized by using a table of random numbers. There are four soldering workers operating on each shift. The following table shows the results of the work sampling at the end of each of the four weeks.

	Total No. of Observations	No. of Observations During Which Productive Work Was Being Performed
End of week 1	510	460
End of week 2	480	430
End of week 3	520	440
End of week 4	490	430

Questions for Discussion

1. Assuming that the industry's standard for idle time ranges between 8 and 10 percent, evaluate the results of this work sampling study.

2. From your limited knowledge of the situation, what suggestions might you have to resolve or alleviate part of the problem?

8.10 REFERENCES AND BIBLIOGRAPHY

1. Adam, E. E., Jr., et al., *Productivity and Quality: Measurement as a Basis for Improvement*, Englewood Cliffs, NJ: Prentice-Hall, 1981.

2. Barnes, R. M., *Motion and Time Study: Design and Measurement of Work*, 6th ed., New York: Wiley, 1968.

3. Chase Manhattan Bank, "Behind the Productivity Slowdown," *Business in Brief*, Sept.–Oct. 1979.

4. Davis, L.E. et al., *Quality of Working Life: Problems, Prospects, and State of the Art*, Glencoe, IL: Free Press, 1975.

5. Dreyfuss, H., *The Measure of Man: Human Factors in Design*, New York: Whitney Library of Design, 1967.

6. Goodfellow, M., "Quality Circles—Supervisory Training Is the Key to Success," *Production Engineering*, June 1981.

7. Henrici, S. B., "How Not To Measure Productivity," *New York Times*, 7 March 1982.

8. Herzberg, F. H., *Work and the Nature of Man*, New York: Harcourt Brace & World, 1966.

9. Herzberg, F. H., "One More Time: How Do You Motivate Employees?" *Harvard Business Review*, 46:53–62 (Jan.–Feb. 1968).

10. "How the Japanese Manage in the United States," *Fortune*, 15 June 1981.

11. Kellogg, M. S., *What to Do About Performance Appraisal*, New York: American Management Association, 1965.

12. Konz, S., "Quality Circles: Japanese Success Story," *Industrial Engineering*, 11:24–27 (Oct. 1979).

13. McCormick, E. J., *Human Factors Engineering*, 3rd ed., New York: McGraw-Hill, 1970.

14. Moore, B. E. et al., *The Scanlon Way to Improved Productivity*, New York: Wiley, 1978.

15. Ouchi, W., *Theory Z*, Reading, MA: Addison-Wesley, 1981.

16. Peterson, J. E., *Industrial Health*, Englewood Cliffs, NJ: Prentice-Hall, 1977.

17. Rendell, E., "Quality Circles—A Third Wave Intervention," *Training and Development Journal*, March 1981.

18. Rice, R. S., "Survey of Work Measurement and Wage Incentives," *Industrial Engineering*, 9:18–31 (July 1977).

19. Rosow, J., "Quality of Work Life Issues for the 1980's," *Training and Development Journal*, March 1981.

20. Skinner, W., *Manufacturing in the Corporate Strategy*, New York: Wiley, 1978.

21. "Study Says Management to Blame for U.S. Productivity Decline," *Industrial Engineering*, Nov. 1980, p. 14.

22. Taylor, J. C., "Experiments in Work Systems Design: Economic and Human Results," Parts I and II, *Personnel Review*, Summer and Autumn 1977.

23. Walton, R. E., "Improving the Quality of Work Life," *Harvard Business Review*, 78:52–62 (May–June 1974).

24. Woodson, W. E., and Conover, D. W., *Human Engineering Guide for Equipment Designers*, 2nd ed., Berkeley: University of California Press, 1966.

25. Yoder, Dale, *Personnel Management and Industrial Relations*, 6th ed., Englewood Cliffs, NJ: Prentice-Hall, 1970.

26. Zell, S. P., "Productivity in the U.S. Economy: Trends and Implications," *Economic Review* (Federal Reserve Bank of Kansas City), Nov. 1979.

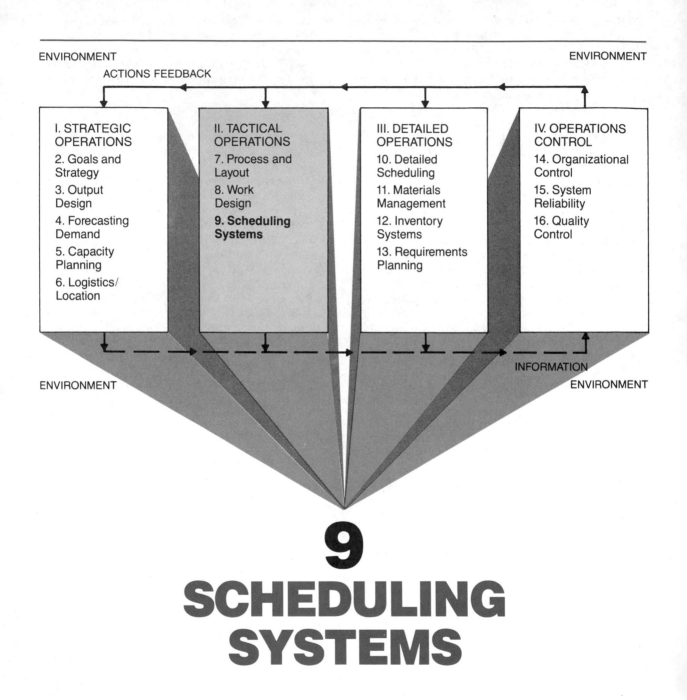

ENVIRONMENT   ENVIRONMENT

ACTIONS FEEDBACK

I. STRATEGIC OPERATIONS	II. TACTICAL OPERATIONS	III. DETAILED OPERATIONS	IV. OPERATIONS CONTROL
2. Goals and Strategy	7. Process and Layout	10. Detailed Scheduling	14. Organizational Control
3. Output Design	8. Work Design	11. Materials Management	15. System Reliability
4. Forecasting Demand	**9. Scheduling Systems**	12. Inventory Systems	16. Quality Control
5. Capacity Planning		13. Requirements Planning	
6. Logistics/ Location			

ENVIRONMENT   INFORMATION
                                                       ENVIRONMENT

9
SCHEDULING SYSTEMS

9

LEARNING OBJECTIVES

By the completion of this chapter the student should

- Know the sequence of activities involved in the scheduling function.
- Comprehend the difference between forward and backward scheduling.
- Be familiar with the role of computers in scheduling.
- Be aware of the difficulties of implementing computer-based scheduling systems.
- Appreciate the complexities and strategies involved in aggregate scheduling.
- Have a feel for the difficulty of scheduling pure services, their unique scheduling requirements, and some common approaches to the problem.

The previous chapters have dealt with the design of the operations to produce the organization's output. But this has been a static snapshot of the operations system, with workers, machines, and materials all frozen in space and time. The next function adds the dimension of *time* to this static picture, transforming it into a running, operating set of activities that are producing products or services for live, demanding people and organizations. Ensuring that the *right* tasks are conducted at the *right* time on the *right* items to produce the output is, in a sense, a matter of "orchestration," more generally known as *scheduling*.

The need for scheduling.

Our productivity problems in the United States are, in large part, attributable to problems in the scheduling function: *not* having the right items when they are needed, *not* having equipment available when it is needed, and so on. The scheduling function addresses the issues that the operations manager must face on a daily basis: where each input (material, machine, worker) must be, when it must be there, what form it must be in, how many must be available, and other such details.

However, the scheduling function for continuous flow and processing organizations is not anywhere near the problem that it is for batch and intermittent flow producers. This is because the scheduling process is largely *built into* the transformation process when the facility is designed and therefore need not, in fact *cannot*, be constantly changed. To reschedule these facilities, beyond just increasing or decreasing the rate of input, requires a rebalancing of the entire flow process, as was illustrated in Chapter 7 under the topic of "line balancing."

Scheduling built into flow operations.

On the other side, the scheduling of project operations is probably the most important single planning function in the successful management of projects. Because of the extent of this topic we will defer its treatment to the next chapter, Detailed Scheduling.

Major task of project management.

In this chapter we will primarily treat scheduling in intermittent process flow organizations, for services as well as products. We begin, however, by looking at the generic sequence of scheduling activities in product firms, since these functions in product firms are better developed and more common than those in service organizations. We also note the increasing role played by computers in these scheduling systems and, in a brief aside, explore the functions of the computer and the difficulties of implementing computer-based scheduling systems. In passing, we might note that the Japanese "just-in-time" scheduling system is, in actuality, more of a materials management system and is hence discussed in Chapter 12: Inventory Management Systems.

Major role of computers.

Just-in-time.

Following this general view of intermittent process scheduling we look at the first major function in the sequence of activities: aggregate scheduling. Using a manufacturing example, we illustrate the aggregate scheduling concept and its application. Solution approaches are described in Appendix II.

After this treatment of the scheduling problem in primarily product organizations, we turn our attention to the scheduling of service operations and specifically consider hospitals, urban alarm services, and educational institutions.

Scheduling services.

The more detailed scheduling functions, such as loading and sequencing, are deferred to the following chapter which initiates Part III of our text, Detailed Operations.

9.1 THE SEQUENCE OF SCHEDULING ACTIVITIES

The Production Planning and Control Department.

In most organizations there is a department (or individual) specifically responsible for scheduling the organization's operations. In product organizations it is frequently called *Production Planning and Control* or some similar name. The breadth of this department's responsibility varies considerably and may consist only of planning gross output levels, for example, or may include all of the scheduling activities illustrated in Figure 9.1.

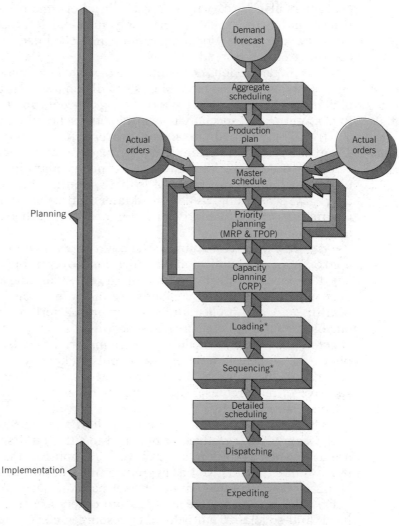

Figure 9.1 Scheduling activity relationships. (*Described in greater detail in Chapter 10.)

This figure does not describe a *standardized* scheduling system, such as might exist in an available computer package, but rather the complex of activities and terms that are often grouped under the phrase "scheduling." Many of these have only become major activities since the advent of computerized scheduling. Prior to that, the activities were simply judgmental ones (as some of the activities still are). Let us look at each of the scheduling activities on the chart and their interrelationships; in the remaining sections of the chapter we will then look more intensively at some of the major activities and describe some approaches in dealing with them.

Demand Forecast. The foundation that supports the entire scheduling process is, in most cases, the forecast of demand for the upcoming planning horizon. In some organizations, such as the machine tool industry, customers place orders up to a year ahead of time because of the long lead times and order backlogs. Thus only minimal forecasting, if any, is conducted and organizational operations are scheduled on the basis of actual customer orders instead.

Demand forecast as the basis for scheduling.

Most organizations do not operate in such a fortunate environment, however, and their success often hinges heavily on the accuracy of their forecasts of demand. In these cases the forecasting concepts and techniques illustrated in Chapter 4 are especially relevant for the scheduling functions.

Different uses of forecasts.

It might be noted that forecasts over different periods are used for different purposes. For example, long-range forecasts (i.e., 2 to 20 years) are typically used more for facility and capacity planning than for any scheduling function. In the range of 9 to 18 months the forecasts are used for aggregate scheduling, as described later, and detailed forecasts for the next few months are particularly crucial in near-term scheduling such as loading and sequencing.

Aggregate scheduling a first rough-cut.

Aggregate Scheduling. The **aggregate schedule** is a "rough-cut," or approximate, schedule of an organization's overall operations that will satisfy the demand forecast at minimum cost. Planning horizons, the period over which changes and demands are taken into consideration, are often 1 year or more and broken into monthly or quarterly periods. This is because one of the purposes in aggregate scheduling is to minimize the short-sighted effects of day-to-day scheduling where material may be ordered from a supplier and workers laid off one week, only to have to reorder more material and rehire the workers the following week. By taking a longer term perspective of resource use, short-term changes in requirements can be minimized with a considerable cost savings.

The basic approach in minimizing short-term variations is to work only with "aggregate" (grouped or bunched together) units. Aggregate resources are used, such as total number of workers, hours of machine time, and tons of raw materials, as well as aggregate units of output—gallons of product, hours of service delivered, number of patients seen, and so on—totally ignoring the fact that some are blue and others are red, some soft and some hard, and so forth. That is, neither resources nor outputs are broken down into more specific categories; that occurs at a later stage.

On occasion, the units of aggregation are somewhat difficult to determine, especially if the variation in output is extreme (such as when a manufacturer produces dishwashers, clothes washers, and dryers). In such cases, *equivalent units* are usually determined based on value, cost, worker hours input, or some similar basic measure. For the appliance manufacturer above, the aggregate schedule might be: January—5000 "appliances," February—4000 "appliances," and so forth.

Aggregate scheduling to minimize total costs.

The resulting aggregate scheduling problem is to minimize the long-run costs of meeting forecasted demand. The relevant costs are typically those of hiring and laying off workers, storing finished goods if a product is involved, wages and overtime charges, shortage and *backordering* costs, subcontracting costs, and so on. As it turns out, the use of inventory to buffer production against variations in demand is an extremely important managerial option. In service organizations this option is usually not available since services, such as plane trips, typically cannot be inventoried. The result is increased cost to produce the service with a resulting increase in the price of the service.

The topic of aggregate scheduling will be discussed in considerably more detail in Section 9.3.

The output of aggregate scheduling is the production plan.

The Production Plan. The result of the aggregate scheduling task is the organization's **production plan** for the planning horizon used by the organization (e.g., 1 year). Sometimes this plan is broken down (i.e., *disaggregated*) one level into major output groups (still aggregated); for example, by models but not by colors. In either case, the production plan shows the resource requirements and output changes over the future: hiring requirements, capacity limitations, the relative increases and decreases in materials inventories, the output rate of goods or services.

The Master Schedule. The driving force behind the scheduling process is the **master schedule.** There are two reasons for this.

1. It is at this point that *actual* orders are incorporated into the scheduling system.

2. This is also the stage where aggregate scheduled outputs are broken down into individual scheduled output groups (called **"level zero items"**) by model, size, color, and so forth, specifically checked against lead time (time to produce or ship the items) and operations capacity (if there is enough equipment, labor, etc.) for feasibility.

The actual scheduling itself is usually an iterative process, with a preliminary schedule being drawn up, checked for problems, and then revised. Initial schedules are usually obtained by either **forward scheduling,** in which jobs are scheduled in the order they come in, or by **backward scheduling,** in which due dates are used to determine the *latest* possible time a job can be started. The situation in which this master scheduling problem arises is as follows: Marketing usually makes promised delivery dates to customers based on some fixed lead time specified by operations. As new jobs come in, operations then attempts to slot the new jobs' processing requirements between that of existing jobs already scheduled on the equipment. Backward scheduling is usually used in this situation because starting at the latest acceptable time for each task will indicate where the bottlenecks exist.

Forward scheduling is usually conducted when a delivery date is to be *directly* set for the job by operations rather than by marketing based on fixed lead times. The job is then simply scheduled into each facility as the facilities are expected to become available, and the resulting expected completion date is transmitted to the customer. After either scheduling method is applied the following problems are checked:

1. Does the schedule meet the aggregate plan?
2. Does the schedule meet the end item demand forecasts?
3. Are there priority or capacity conflicts in the schedule (see next two scheduling activities)?

Typical scheduling problems.

4. Does the schedule violate any other constraints regarding equipment, lead times, supplies, facilities, and so forth?
5. Does the schedule conform to organizational policy?
6. Does the schedule violate any legal regulations or organization-union rules?
7. Does the schedule provide for flexibility and backups?

The difference between the scheduling process using forward and backward scheduling is illustrated in the following example. Table 9.1 describes three jobs in terms of when they are due and their processing requirements. The requirements are shown as the first processing facility required and, in parentheses, the hours required on that facility, the second facility and hours, and, for Jobs A and B, the third facility and hours required. Job A, for example, requires that facility 3 be used first for 1 hour, then facility 2 for 3 hours, and last, facility 1 for 2 hours. We assume in this situation that job tasks can be split. That is, a job can be started on a facility, taken off for a higher priority job to be worked on that facility, and then put back on to continue its processing. To simplify the illustration we will also assume there are no existing jobs on the facilities.

Figure 9.2*a* illustrates the forward scheduling process for the three jobs. Job A comes in first and thus is scheduled first. Its first processing task is on facility 3 for 1 hour only, so it is scheduled there for hour 1 as shown circled in Figure 9.2*a*. Following this, Job A requires 3 hours on facility 2, so it is scheduled there for hours 2, 3, and 4, also shown circled. Last, it spends 2 hours on facility 1, so hours 5 and 6 are scheduled there.

Next, Job B is scheduled when it comes in sometime later. It first requires

Table 9.1 Jobs to be Scheduled

Job	Hour Due	Facility, Hours Required (in Order of Processing)
A	8	3 (1), 2 (3), 1 (2)
B	6	2 (2), 3 (1), 1 (1)
C	4	1 (2), 3 (1)

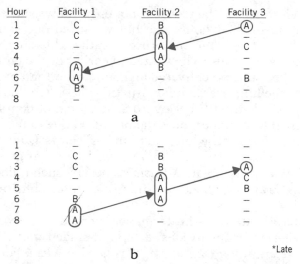

Hour	Facility 1	Facility 2	Facility 3
1	C	B	A
2	C	A	–
3	–	A	C
4	–	A	–
5	A	B	–
6	A	–	B
7	B*	–	–
8	–	–	–

a

	Facility 1	Facility 2	Facility 3
1	–	–	–
2	C	B	–
3	C	B	A
4	–	A	C
5	–	A	B
6	B	A	–
7	A	–	–
8	A	–	–

b

*Late

Figure 9.2 Forward versus backward scheduling. (*a*) Forward scheduling. (*b*) Backward scheduling.

2 hours on facility 2, so it is started there in hour 1, but because Job A has previously been scheduled on facility 2 for hours 2, 3, and 4, Job B must be removed to let Job A "pass through," and B is finished up on facility 2 in hour 5. (If Job B could *not* be split we would have to delay its processing on facility 2 until hour 5 when it could be scheduled for hours 5 and 6.) Next it spends 1 hour, hour 6, on facility 3 and last, hour 7 on facility 1. But it was due at the end of hour 6 and hence is an hour late. Last, Job C is scheduled with no difficulty.

The backward scheduling procedure for the same three jobs is illustrated in Figure 9.2*b*. Again, Job A is scheduled first but since it is due in hour 8 it is scheduled for its last hour of processing on the last facility, 1, at hour 8. Since 2 hours of processing are required on facility 1 in the final stage, Job A is also scheduled there for hour 7. Then 3 hours are required on facility 2, hours 6, 5, and 4. Last, 1 hour is required on facility 3, hour 3. This process is also illustrated in Figure 9.2*b*.

Job B is then backward scheduled from hour 6 on its last processing facility, 1. Since only 1 hour is required there, it is next scheduled on facility 3 for hour 5 (no conflict appears), and, last, on facility 2 for 2 hours. But it cannot be scheduled there for hour 4 because Job A is there. The next available backward hour is 3, so it is scheduled there for hours 3 and 2. (Note that another job might have totally occupied facility 2 and Job B could not have been successfully scheduled to be completed by hour 6 *at all*. Backward scheduling *may not* result in a successful schedule but *if it is possible*, one will usually be found. Forward scheduling, on the other hand, never results in such a conflict but it may not meet desired due dates either.) Last, Job C is scheduled on its final facility, 3, for its due hour, hour 4, and then on facility 1 for 2 hours, hours 3 and 2.

Of interest here is the fact that not only did we successfully schedule all the jobs to meet their hours due but we saved one complete hour on the three facilities (hour 1) in the process. Either this hour could now be used for later oncoming jobs to be slotted in earlier or the entire set of Jobs A, B, and C could be run and delivered an hour earlier than promised. This is why backward scheduling is used for situations in which due dates are set externally. The problem with backward scheduling, of course, is that the shop sometimes simply cannot meet the promised due date.

The major role of the master schedule.

It is the master schedule, then, that specifies *what end items* are to be produced *in what periods* to *minimize costs* and that gives some measure of assurance that such a plan *is feasible*. Clearly, such a document is of major importance to any organization—it is, in a sense, a blueprint for future operations.

Priority planning for materials.

Priority Planning.   This term, popularized by Oliver Wight [32], relates not to giving priorities to jobs (a topic included under "sequencing"), but rather to determining *what material* is needed *when*. For a master schedule of production to be feasible, the proper raw materials, purchased materials, and manufactured or purchased subassemblies must be available when needed, top priority going to immediate needs. The key to production planning is the "needed" date. Previous scheduling attempts concentrated on *order launching*; that is, when to *place* the order. Priority planning concentrates on when the order is actually needed and schedules *backward* from that date. For example, if an item is needed July 18 and requires a 2-week lead time then the order is released July 4 and not before. Why store inventory needlessly?

TPOP system for independent demand.

The systems that have been devised for accomplishing this task are inventory control systems based on lead times and expected demands. The classic inventory systems are most appropriate for organizations *producing to stock* (e.g., continuous flow organizations). These are called "order point" systems because new orders for materials are sent out when the inventory on hand reaches a certain low point. Although delivery lead time is *generally* known, as well as a distribution of demand, the *specific* demand for materials cannot be easily anticipated. Materials must therefore be stocked in quantity to meet this random or "independent" demand. For example, demand for spare parts is typically independent of current orders. Manual systems based on *economic order quantities* (to be discussed in Chapter 12) have followed this approach for years; recent trends have been to computerize this mass of order quantities and reorder points for the thousands of items organizations normally use. These systems are now called *time-phased order point* (**TPOP**) systems.

MRP systems for dependent demand.

For organizations that *produce to order* (e.g., many job shops) materials requirements are known with almost certainty because they are tied to specified outputs (thus known as *dependent demand*). For example, every car requires four wheel covers—the number of wheel covers *depends* only on the number of cars. For these situations the computer unlocked an undreamed of world to the production scheduler. Computerized *materials requirements planning* (**MRP**) systems were specifically developed to anticipate materials needs, consider lead times, release purchase orders, and schedule production in accord with the master schedule, a capability almost unimaginable twenty years ago. MRP is also useful in producing "to stock" when demands are again dependent. That is, the critical issue in choosing between an MRP system and a TPOP system is not *how* the item got ordered but whether the demand is *dependent* or *independent*.

If insufficient lead time exists to produce or obtain the necessary materials, under either TPOP or MRP systems, or other problems arise, the master schedule must be revised or other arrangements made. These inventory systems are discussed in much greater detail in Chapters 12 and 13.

Capacity Planning. The inventory control system and master schedule drive the *capacity requirements planning* (**CRP**) system. This system projects the job orders and demands for materials into equipment, workforce, and facility requirements and finds the total required capacity of each over the planning horizon. That is, during a given week how many nurses will be required, how many hours of kidney machine operation, how many syringes, and so forth?

Checking the master schedule against the CRP.

This may or may not exceed *available* capacity. If it is within capacity limits, then the master schedule is finalized, *time-phased work orders*, also known as *route sheets*, are released according to schedule, materials orders are released by the priority planning system, and *load reports* are sent to work centers listing the work facing that area based on the CRP system. Note that external lead times (usually longer than internal lead times) from suppliers have already been checked in the priority planning stage, so the master schedule can indeed now be finalized.

Human intervention if capacity limits are exceeded.

However, if the capacity limits are exceeded, something must be changed. Either some jobs must be delayed, a less demanding schedule devised, or extra capacity obtained elsewhere (e.g., by hiring more workers or using overtime). It is the role of Production Planning and Control to solve this problem.

Allocating jobs to work centers.

Loading. **Loading** means deciding which jobs to assign to which work centers. Although the capacity planning system determined that sufficient gross capacity existed to meet the master schedule, no *actual assignment* of jobs to work centers was made. Some equipment will generally be superior for certain jobs and some equipment will be less heavily loaded than other equipment. Thus, there is often a "best" (fastest, or least costly) assignment of jobs to work centers. We will consider the loading problem in more detail in Chapter 10.

Properly ordering the execution of the jobs through priority rules.

Sequencing. Even after jobs have been assigned to work centers, the *order* in which to perform the jobs must still be decided. Unfortunately, even this seemingly small final step can have major repercussions on the organization's workload capacity and the timeliness of job completions. A number of **priority rules** have been researched in this regard and some interesting results are available which will be discussed in Chapter 10.

A final schedule, at last.

Detailed (Short-Term) Scheduling. Once all the foregoing has been specified, detailed schedules itemizing specific jobs, times, materials, and workers can be drawn up. This is usually only done for a few days in advance,

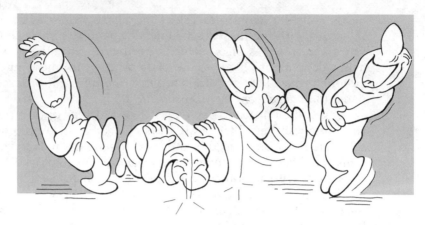

You want it when?!

however, since changes are always occurring and detailed schedules become outdated quickly. It is Production Planning and Control's responsibility to ensure that when the job is ready to be worked on, all the items, equipment, facilities, and information (blueprints, operations sheets, etc.) are available as scheduled.

Dispatching. All of the previous activities constitute schedule *planning*; no production, per se, has taken place yet. **Dispatching** is the physical *release* of a work order from the production planning and control department to operations. The release may be manual, from the *dead load file* as it is called, or through the computerized master scheduling system.

Expediting. Once Production Planning and Control has released a job to operations (or the *shop floor*, as it is sometimes called) they usually have no more responsibility for it and it is the operations manager's task to get the job done on time. As jobs fall behind schedule, managers have historically tended to use *expediters* to help push these "hot" jobs through the operations.

Before computerized scheduling techniques, the extensive use of expediters was common (and still is in many organizations). The problem was the impossibility of the scheduling task facing production planning and control. Not only could they not determine a good production schedule; they often could not even tell when insufficient capacity existed. Operations managers thus relied heavily on expediters to gather all the necessary materials together (often cannibalizing parts from other jobs) in order to get important jobs completed. Of course this further delayed the remaining jobs so that more and more jobs tended to become "hot."

Instances are common of the use of yellow tags on jobs to label the "hot" ones until, pretty soon, all the jobs had yellow tags. To identify the "especially hot" jobs, then, red tags were used. After a while the operations' area resembled a rainbow whereupon no new orders were accepted, the backlog was worked off, and the cycle started from scratch.

It may be presumed that a clear indication of the failure of a scheduling

Releasing the work orders.

Checking on delays.

The overuse of expediters.

Hot jobs.

The need to de-expedite.

system is the existence of a great many expediters. One of the problems of the informal scheduling system, of course, was the lack of a *de-expediting* (delaying jobs that have dropped in priority) system to reflect changes in required due dates and, thus, in the priorities and schedules for jobs. This process has been built into the computerized scheduling systems.

9.2 THE ROLE OF COMPUTERS IN SCHEDULING

The critical importance of the computer.

Requirements-based scheduling systems, because of their relatively large-scale and complex nature, necessitate the use of a computer system for implementation. The role of the computer here is extremely important. The concept of requirements-based scheduling is not novel; it simply was previously too cumbersome to pursue in a clerically oriented system. Construction management has for years recognized the need for detailed requirements planning and scheduling. If material, labor, or equipment was at the job site in the wrong sequence or at the wrong time, not only would bottlenecks be unending but wasted time and material losses from weather damage and theft would raise the cost of construction to unreasonable levels. The computer has simply allowed all of these clerical data processing activities and file handling tasks to be accomplished more efficiently; hence, what once was conceptually feasible but technically infeasible is now both technically and conceptually possible.

The PICS scheduling system.

An example of a computerized scheduling system is the Production Information and Control System (**PICS**)* designed by IBM [15]. PICS accepts a sales forecast and basic engineering data for each product and, using an MRP subsystem, develops the "time phased materials requirements." Once this information is available, the purchasing, capacity planning, and operations scheduling components of PICS take over to produce purchase order requirements, route the product through the operations, generate capacity requirements by individual operations, and load and schedule operations for production.

We might ask how the system handles the inevitable last minute changes such as breakdowns or rush orders. When these changes are input to the computer, the program works *backward* to see what new resources are needed, or what old resources are now not needed, and *time phases* (schedules) the requirements. When an order is scheduled earlier, this is called "expediting"; when an order is intentionally delayed it is referred to as "de-expediting." One of the Production Planning and Control (PP&C) Department's more important tasks when a computerized system is used is to determine the need for reasons for expediting and de-expediting. That is, an equipment failure input to the system may indicate the need to delay (de-expedite) a particular job. However, PP&C should not simply let the system delay the job but should attempt to find alternative ways to maintain the original schedule, if possible.

*Compare to PICS in Section 7.1.

Net change versus
regenerative
systems.

If changes, such as the above, are input to the MRP system on an immediate basis, this is called a *net change* system and is virtually always up-to-date (at the cost of computing time and program complexity). If such changes are stored until, for example, a weekend, and then the entire MRP program rerun, this is called *regeneration*. Clearly, this latter system will always be somewhat out of date, except on Monday morning.

The importance of
data base integrity.

Generally speaking, the integrity of the *data base* is the most critical element in computerized scheduling systems. If incorrect data are fed to the system, the confidence of the workers in the validity of the schedule will be lost and they will turn once again to an expediter to identify the hot jobs. The use of the computer to handle and store the massive amounts of data concerning the hundreds of jobs and thousands of items is a revolution in the information base available to operations managers.

Let us briefly examine computer systems and their use and implementation in scheduling systems.

Types of Computerized Systems

Batch versus real
time systems.

Electronic data processing systems in organizations are either *batch* or *real time* systems. In both cases, organizational data processing is typified by high volumes of input and output, with relatively simple and repetitive computations and logic. Typical business data processing applications include payroll processing, billing and collection, inventory management, and accounts payable processing.

File maintenance.

Many data processing applications consist of maintaining up-to-date data files. That is, files are updated with new information as organizational transactions take place. It is common for input documents, which contain the information from each transaction, to be accumulated in batches that, at specified intervals, are used to update the necessary files. Batch processing applications are those that do not require a constantly up-to-date file. For example, a general ledger system that is used to produce a monthly income statement and balance sheet for a company does not have to be constantly made up-to-date. Journal entries to this system can be batched until the end of the month whereupon they are keypunched and processed at one time.

On the other hand, many operations data processing systems must be real time systems. That is, data files (such as inventory or job status) must always be up-to-date because of inquiries regarding that data. Rather than batching transactions for subsequent processing, real time systems process transaction data and update files as the transactions take place. Data files

On-line systems.

must be maintained *on line* to the computer at all times in order to allow constant interaction between the file and those desiring to update or inquire into the status of a particular record.

Real-time systems
for reservations.

The most widely recognized of the real time systems are the airlines and hotel reservations systems. These systems constantly maintain the status of, for example, all flights and passengers so that a reservationist at any location can inquire into the availability of a seat and can update the file to indicate the sale of a seat. Typically, real time processing systems are most often

"Good news, Miss Morgan . . . your keypunch will be here tomorrow."

justified in terms of providing better service to customers or for day-to-day organizational decisions that require a high degree of timeliness in the information used.

Minis and Micros

The general-purpose minicomputer.

The 1980s have already seen an exciting trend toward even smaller computers (see Figure 9.3). A *minicomputer* is simply a lower cost, physically small, general purpose computer. While there is no standard price, commercial minicomputers range in price from $10,000 to $70,000. They are physically smaller and more adaptable than their larger counterparts. Minicomputers typically require no special environmental conditions such as raised floors, temperature/humidity control, and so forth. But, the minicomputer has its limitations. A minicomputer's primary memory is usually smaller, accessing and processing times are slower, and the CPU can usually process one or only a few programs at a time.

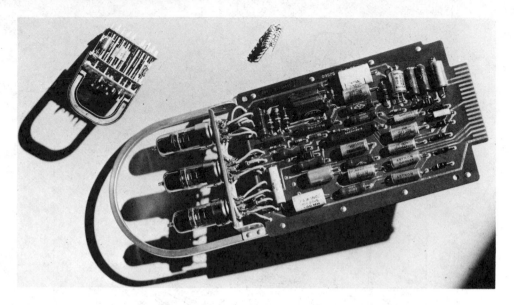

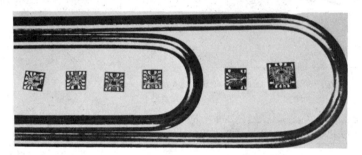

Figure 9.3   Four generations of computer circuitry (courtesy of Burroughs Corporation.)

The special
purpose
microcomputer.

A *microcomputer* is composed of one or more microprocessors, virtually "computers on a chip." The silicon chip, which is an integrated circuit produced in microminiature size, was first used in the early 1970s. Originally intended as the brain of modern "pocket" calculators, the silicon chip has allowed computerization of numerous pieces of equipment. Among the most widely recognized uses are manufacturing process control, numerical control of machine tools, automotive ignition and fuel injection timing, and energy control. The microprocessor, when used by itself, is typically developed for a specific function. The mini and microcomputers, on the other hand, are intended to be general-purpose data processing systems. The exciting aspects of microcomputers, whether IBM, Apple, or whichever, are their relatively low price, from $100 to $10,000, and their amazing capability.

The continuing
growth of small
computers.

From an operations standpoint, both minis and micros have and will continue to revolutionize the operations environment. Further applications in production process control and materials management will be found for microcomputers. The minicomputer will continue to bring more and more data processing power to even lower levels in the organization. As computer costs drop, availability will increase. Such methods of inventory/production control as MRP are simply impossible to apply without the aid of the high-speed computers. Minis are bringing these methods to smaller organizations and are giving departments of larger organizations access to the computer which was previously unavailable. In many cases small microcomputers such as Apples and TRS-80s are being installed in offices and connected to the organization's mainframe computer for updating, a technique called "distributed data processing" (discussed in Chapter 14).

The Implementation Problem

Difficulty of implementation.

The productivity gains promised by computerized scheduling systems are, unfortunately, more difficult to achieve than might be thought. Recent studies [22] point out some of the pitfalls. There are three separate sets of factors that constitute the significant impediments to implementation.

Technical Factors

These factors constitute a set of minimum necessary criteria for implementation and relate primarily to the *mechanics* of the process. That is, although these are not, by themselves, sufficient, no system will probably work without them. The factors here include the following:

- Valid data.
- Simple, transparent system (understandable to all).
- Adaptable system (as the organization changes).
- Low-cost system (to install and run, both).
- Complete user training.
- Representative project team (of all users).
- Implementation as a major goal.

The last point brings up a subsidiary issue, the difference between "installation" of a computerized system and "implementation," or full and continuing use of the system. Many computerized systems are installed, and even running, but no one is using them. Also, implementation must be a continuing process. Many "successful implementations" later failed when the project team went on to another project.

Process Factors

These factors are concerned with supporting the initiation and use of the system and are more complex and less well understood than the technical factors. Included here are the following:

- *Top management support:* This support must be broad based and *knowledgeable.* Managers would rather keep a problem they understand than employ a solution they don't. An MRP system, for example, commonly requires an investment of $240,000, 10 hours a month of a vice-president's time, and takes 16 months to successfully implement. Managers must be prepared for this amount of time, money, and effort, or more.

● *User support:* The users (those who are intended to eventually use the system in their jobs) should help design and implement the system. In fact, they should fund and *own* the system.

Inner-Environmental Factors

These two factors may well provide the foundation for all the preceding factors:

● *A crucial situation:* If the problem or opportunity is not of crucial, *and current,* importance to the organization, with significant resources already committed or about to be, the cost and difficulty of a computerized system will strongly mitigate against successful implementation.

● *Willingness to change:* Management must be willing to change the way they operate the firm. These systems *demand* it! If the VP still plans to have old Joe run the "hot" jobs through the shop for him, the computerized system is doomed to failure because *two* systems cannot ever both be in use. One will always be the "real" system and the other will be a phony. Management must be willing to make changes and give up some power to the system. More than that, they must *use* this new system and *stop using* (and thereby *rewarding*) the old system.

Eighty percent failure rate. With all these potential traps in the implementation process it may come as no surprise that fully 80 percent of all attempts to implement computer-based scheduling systems fail to come near their potential. Yet, this is an improvement—10 years ago 95 percent of them failed!

9.3   AGGREGATE SCHEDULING

The aggregate scheduling problem. The aggregate scheduling problem arises in the following context. The manager of operations has a month-to-month forecast of total demand for all outputs combined for the next year or so. She is expected to capitalize on this demand by supplying that portion of it that will maximize long-run profitability. That is, not all of the demand need be satisfied if attempting to fill it will result in lower overall profits. But a loss of market share might thereby result, which, in turn, may reduce long-run profitability.

The manager has a set of productive facilities and workers with some maximum capacity to supply demand. There may also be some finished output available in inventory to help meet the demand but there may, as well, be a backorder of unsatisfied demand. The manager must decide how to employ the resources at her disposal to best meet the demand. If excess capacity is available the manager may lease it out, sell it, or lay off workers. If insufficient capacity is available, but only for a short time in the future, she may employ overtime or part-time workers, subcontract work, or simply not meet the demand.

As discussed in Chapter 5, there are a number of ways of changing the capacity available to the manager to meet demand at minimum cost such as

Managerial variables.

1. Overtime.
2. Additional or fewer shifts.
3. Hiring or laying off workers (including part time).
4. Subcontracting.
5. Building up inventories during slack periods.
6. Leasing facilities or workers, or both.
7. Backlogging demand.
8. Changing demand through marketing promotions or price changes.
9. Undersupplying the market.

The need for a long-range view.

Each of these strategies has advantages and disadvantages associated with it and perhaps certain restrictions on its use (such as legal or union regulations). The manager must plan her strategy carefully because a short-sighted strategy, such as laying off workers when they will later be needed again, can be very expensive to rectify. However, an excessively long-range perspective may also be incorrect, such as keeping an idle worker for a year when it would be much cheaper to lay off and then rehire the worker.

Pure Strategies

There are two *baseline* aggregate scheduling strategies, known as *pure strategies*, which, although rarely used in practice, can give the manager a feel for some upper limits on cost. They are as follows:

Two baseline strategies.

I. **Chase demand:** In this strategy, production is identical to the expected demand for the period in question. This is typically obtained either through overtime or hiring and laying off. The advantage of this policy is that there is no finished goods inventory cost (except perhaps for *buffer*, or *safety*, *stock* as discussed in Chapter 12) or shortage cost.

II. **Level production:** Here finished goods inventories (or backlogged demand) are used to meet variations in demand, at the cost of inventory investment and shortage or stockout expense. The advantage is steady employment with no workforce or overtime expenses. Since service outputs cannot generally be inventoried, this strategy results in a constant, but poorly utilized, workforce of a size large enough to meet peak demand (e.g., repair crews, firefighters).

The vast majority of realistic aggregate scheduling strategies achieve much lower costs than the baseline costs of these pure strategies by trading off investment in finished goods inventories for capacity level changes or vice versa. Let us demonstrate with an example.

Aggregate Scheduling Example

Demand forecasts for each of the quarters of the year for your product are 40, 60, 30, 10, with this pattern repeating in the future as far as can be foreseen. The current workforce is three and each worker can produce 10 units per quarter. Inventory costs are $10 per unit per quarter whereas shortage costs for expediting backorders are $13 per unit per quarter. Hiring and layoff costs have been estimated as $100 per worker but idle workers effectively cost $150 per quarter. The cost to produce units on an overtime basis is an additional $15 each. Find the best production plan if all demand *must* be met, either immediately or through backorders. Assume no initial inventory exists and only consider the incremental costs noted here.

Analysis

Figure 9.4 displays the expected demand over a 2-year (eight-quarter) period, and the two extreme production strategies.

 I. Production equal to demand.
 II. Level production (dashed line) at a rate equal to the average demand of (40 + 60 + 30 + 10)/4 = 35 units per quarter. (Producing in excess of this would continue to build up unnecessary inventory; producing less than this would build up a continuing backlog. See the example in Figure 9.6a.)

The shadings in Figure 9.4 illustrate periods of inventory use (or backlog) and then buildup (unshaded) under a 35 unit level production strategy.

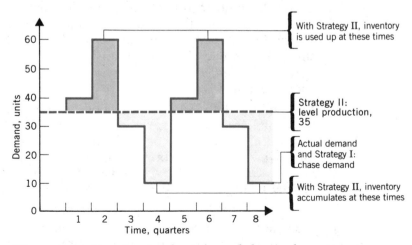

Figure 9.4   Quarter production and demand.

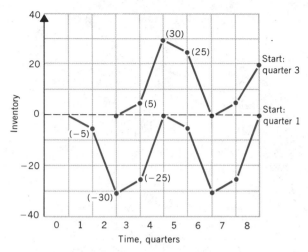

Figure 9.5 Inventory accumulation for two level-production strategies.

Figure 9.5 illustrates the resultant inventory level for the given demands under Strategy II as either positive or negative (or alternately both), depending on the quarter during which you begin to market your product. If production and sales *began* in quarter 3, for example (i.e., you entered the market in quarter 3), then inventory level under the constant 35-unit production would always be at or above zero. But if production and sales began in quarter 1, then the inventory level would be permanently at or below zero using the same production level. That is, there would always be backorders simply because sales exceed production in both of the first two quarters and production is level at 35 units thereafter.

When you enter is important.

Note that the shapes of the inventory curves are identical. *When* you start production simply shifts the curve up or down in proportion to the amount of inventory initially on hand. As another example, suppose you entered the market in quarter 2. Then by the end of that quarter your inventory level would be − 25 (a backlog). The message here is that strategy can be changed from, for example, one of backlog to inventory buildup by "reentering" the market at a different point. This may be done by temporarily dropping out of the market (at the risk of losing market share), working overtime to "catch up" on the market, subcontracting, or any number of other *mixed* strategies, which we will consider in the following section.

Mixed Strategies

Using a cumulative chart for mixed strategies. Inventories and shortages.

A way to combine Figures 9.4 and 9.5 in order to obtain a working graph for better analysis is the "cumulative" chart shown in Figure 9.6. Here, both demand and production are accumulated so positive inventories are shown (shaded in color) *below* any production (heavy) line and shortages (shaded in gray) *above* it. Figure 9.6a illustrates two level-production strategies, which are always straight lines, and a chase-demand strategy. The upper level-

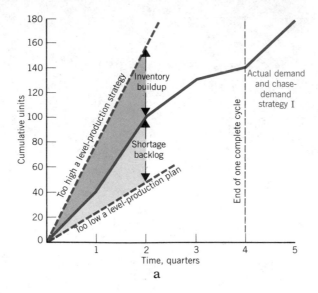

a

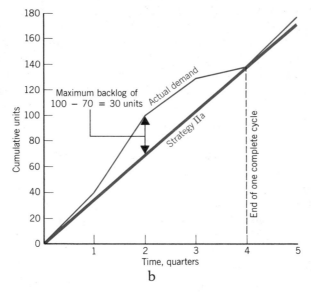

b

Figure 9.6 Cumulative demand and production strategies. (*a*) Actual demand, chose-demand Strategy I, and two examples of level-production strategies. (*b*) Strategy IIa: Produce 35 units per quarter level production. (*c*) Strategy IIb: Produce 50 first 2 quarters, 35 thereafter. (*d*) Strategy III: Produce 40, 40, 40, 20 and Strategy IV: Produce 50, 50, 20, 20.

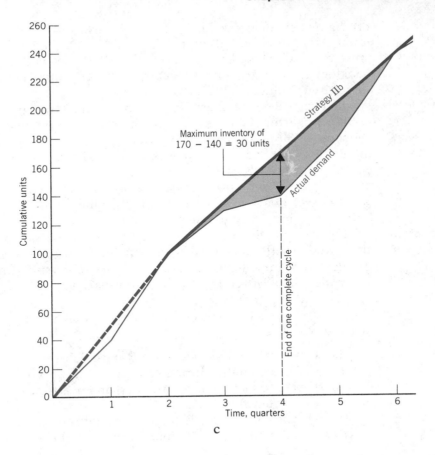

c

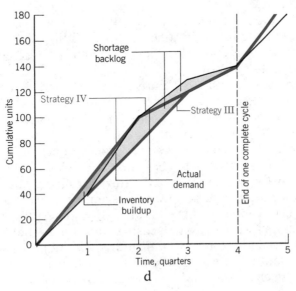

d

production strategy produces at an excessive level and continues to accumulate inventory over the actual demand while the lower level-production strategy produces at an insufficient level and continues to build a shortage backlog. The chase-demand strategy (I) exactly matches, and thus falls on top of, the actual demand curve.

Two level production strategies.

In Figure 9.6*b*, Strategy IIa is plotted. This strategy produces at a rate of 35 per quarter. As is seen, it immediately stocks out and runs a maximum shortage of 30 units. This is essentially the lower curve of Figure 9.5. The upper curve of Figure 9.5, always building up inventory, is attained by Strategy IIb, shown in Figure 9.6*c*. Here the production rate is set at 50 units a quarter for the first two quarters so as to start at the zero point at the *beginning* of quarter 3. Then 35 units a quarter are produced thereafter, building up inventory to a maximum of 30 units.

Two mixed strategies.

Figure 9.6*d* illustrates two mixed strategies. Strategy III is the lower curve and exactly matches demand the first quarter but runs shortages for the next three quarters. Strategy IV more evenly splits the demand curve and runs a small inventory the first two quarters and then a small shortage the last two quarters.

The total costs for some of the strategies shown in Figure 9.6 are derived in Table 9.2.

Ia. Chase demand using overtime and idle time: $900 total cost.
Ib. Chase demand by hiring and laying off: $1000.
IIb. Level production (three workers) and overtime (start regular cycle in quarter 3): $900.
III. Produce 40, 40, 40, 20 (four workers): $690.
IV. Produce 50, 50, 20, 20 (four workers) and overtime: $1130.

In cases III and IV the cost of *permanently* hiring the fourth worker increased the cost by $100 for 1 year only. This increase was *amortized over an infinite horizon* and thus effectively added nothing to the total *annual* costs. Hiring and laying off is only expensive when used as a *continuing* strategy to balance production and demand.

As seen in Table 9.2, the pure chase demand Strategy Ia only incurs overtime and idle cost. To produce 40 units with three workers requires 10 units from overtime at $15 for a cost of $150. In quarter 4, two workers were idle (20 units of production) for an "effective" cost of $2 \times \$150 = \$300$. Idle time is charged as a cost since no revenues are considered here.

Strategy Ib is also a pure chase demand strategy but accomplished in a different way (with a different cost) through hiring and laying off workers. The cost calculations are skipped in quarter 1 because the previous quarter's workforce is unknown at this point; it will be determined later from quarter 4. We therefore start calculating costs in quarter 2 when we have to hire two workers beyond the four (from 40 units production divided by 10 units/worker) we had in quarter 1 at a cost of $100 per worker. The total cost of achieving the chase demand strategy in this manner is seen to be $100 per year more expensive than with Strategy Ia.

Table 9.2 Relevant Costs for Various Strategies

Case	Quarter	Demand	Production	Inventory Cost	Overtime Cost	Idle Cost	Shortage Cost	Hire-Layoff Cost	Total
Ia	1	40	40	0	10 × $15 = 150	0	0	0	$150
	2	60	60	0	450	0	0	0	450
	3	30	30	0	0	0	0	0	0
	4	10	10	0	0	2 × $150 = 300	0	0	300
									$900
Ib	1	40	40	0	0	0	0	(Calculate in quarter 5)	$200
	2	60	60	0	0	0	0	2 × $100 = 200 (hire 2)	300
	3	30	30	0	0	0	0	300 (layoff 3)	200
	4	10	10	0	0	0	0	200 (layoff 2)	300
	5	40	40	0	0	0	0	300 (hire 3)	
									$1000
IIb	3	30	35	5 × 10 = 50	5 × $15 = 75	0	0	0	$125
	4	10	35	(5 + 25) × $10 = 300	75	0	0	0	375
	5	40	35	(30 − 5) × $10 = 250	75	0	0	0	325
	6	60	35	(25 − 25) × $10 = 0	75	0	0	0	75
									$900
III	1	40	40	0	0	0	0	0	$ 0
	2	60	40	0	0	0	20 × $13 = 260	0	260
	3	30	40	0	0	0	130	0	130
	4	10	20	0	0	2 × $150 = 300	0	0	300
									$690
IV	1	40	50	10 × $10 = 100	10 × $15 = 150	0	0	0	$250
	2	60	50	0	150	0	0	0	150
	3	30	20	0	0	2 × $150 = 300	10 × $13 = 130	0	430
	4	10	20	0	0	2 × $150 = 300	0	0	300
									$1130

Strategy IIb uses extra workers (or overtime) to reach quarter 3 where regular operations (and our calculations) then begin with three workers and overtime. Five units are always produced on overtime for a constant cost of $5 \times 15 = \$75$ every quarter. Inventory builds up 5 units in quarter 3 plus another 25 units in quarter 4 and then is drawn down in quarters 5 and 6.

Strategies III and IV employ four workers with combinations of either shortage and idle time cost or inventory with overtime and idle time costs. In spite of the fact that Strategy IV more equally split the demand curve, Strategy III is the least costly, but there are undoubtedly even better policies. Note the difficulty of even such a simple problem: constant (from year to year) demands, clear-cut costs, limited strategies, and all for only a *single* "aggregate" product.

The next step in computerized manufacturing information is the tying together of financial and operations systems (called "Manufacturing Resource Planning" or "MRP II"). The greatest benefits will come when all such systems are integrated on the computer.

Trial-and-error solutions.

In Appendix II at the end of this chapter we present four approaches that have been developed for analyzing the aggregate scheduling problem. Yet, such analytical approaches are rarely used in industry. More use is made of the trial-and-error capabilities of computerized manufacturing information systems such as COPICS by IBM and MAC-PAC by Arthur Anderson. These systems allow various aggregate schedules to be test run on the computer to see what loads they generate on the facilities before a final schedule is chosen. Although *detailed* schedules are not derived at this time, at least *gross* capacity is known to be sufficient to handle the load.

9.4 SCHEDULING SERVICES

In this section we consider the scheduling of pure services. Much of what was said previously applies to the scheduling of services, as well as products, but here we consider some scheduling issues of particular relevance to services.

Resource scheduling when the jobs cannot be scheduled.

Up to now we have dealt primarily with situations where the jobs (or recipients) were the items to be loaded, sequenced, or scheduled. There are, however, many operations for which scheduling of the jobs themselves is either inappropriate or impossible, and it is necessary to concentrate instead on scheduling one or more of the input resources. Therefore, the staff, the materials, or the facilities are scheduled to correspond, as closely as possible, with the expected arrival of the jobs. Such situations are common in service systems such as libraries, supermarkets, hospitals, urban alarm services, colleges, restaurants, and airlines.

The complications of scheduling staff.

In the scheduling of jobs we were primarily interested in minimizing the number of late jobs, minimizing the rejects, maximizing the throughput, and maximizing the utilization of available resources. In the scheduling of resources, however, there may be considerably more criteria of interest, especially when one of the resources being scheduled is staff. Staff desires in terms of shifts, holidays, and work schedules become critically important when work schedules are variable and not all employees are on the same schedule. In these situations there usually exist schedules that will displease everyone and schedules that will satisfy most of the staff's more important priorities—it is crucial that one of the latter be chosen rather than one of the former.

Approaches in Resource Scheduling

Match the resources to demand.

The primary approach to the scheduling of resources is to match resource availability to demand on the resources (e.g., 7 P.M.–12 A.M. is the high fire alarm period). In so doing we are thus not required to provide a continuing high level of resources that are poorly utilized the great majority of the time. However, this requires that a good forecast of demand be available for the proper scheduling of resources. If demand cannot be accurately predicted, the resulting service with variable resources might be worse than using a constant level of resources.

Methods to increase resources.

Methods used to increase resources for peak demand include using overtime and part-time help and leasing equipment and facilities. Also, if multiple areas within the organization tend to experience varying demand, use of *floating workers*, or combining departments to minimize variability, is often helpful. On occasion, the employment of new technology can aid the organization such as 24-hour computerized tellers and bill paying by telephone.

Changing demand through promotion.

And, as mentioned previously, the use of promotion and advertising to shift *demand* for resources is highly practical in many situations. Thus, we see *off-peak pricing* in the utilities and communication industries, summer snowblower sales in retailing, and cut rates for transportation and tours in both the off-peak seasons (fall, winter) and off-peak times (weekends, nights). Let us now consider how some specific service organizations approach their scheduling problems.

Hospitals

There are multiple scheduling needs in hospitals. Although patient arrivals (the jobs) are in part uncontrollable (e.g., emergencies) they are, to an extent, controllable through selective admissions for hernia operations, some

Selective admissions to control demand.

maternity cases, in-hospital observation, and so on. By selective admissions the hospital administrator can smooth the demand faced by the hospital and thereby improve service and increase the utilization of the hospital's limited resources.

Scheduling equipment.

Very specialized, expensive equipment such as a kidney machine is also carefully scheduled to allow other hospitals access to it, thus maximizing its utilization. Two-stage scheduling may thus exist in some cases: equipment availability may be scheduled for a hospital only during certain periods of various days of the week (such as 7–11 A.M. Mondays; 9 P.M.–4 A.M. Thursday–Fridays; and 2–6 P.M. Sundays), and the job (patient) scheduling for those periods of availability may be conducted by the hospitals (Mr. R. from 2 to 2:30 Sunday the sixth; Miss S. from 2:30 to 5).

By sharing such expensive equipment among a number of hospitals, more hospitals have access to modern technology for their patients at a reasonable level of investment.

Scheduling the nursing staff.

Of all the scheduling needs in hospitals the most crucial is probably the scheduling of the nursing resources. This is because (1) it is mandatory, given the nature of hospitals, that nurses always be available, (2) nursing resources are a large expense for the hospital, and (3) there are a number of constraints on the scheduling of nurses such as the number of days per week, hours per day, weeks per year, hours during the day, and so on.

Approaches to nurse scheduling.

Abernathy et al. [1] review the difficulty of the nurse scheduling problem, point out the deficiencies in present practices, and conclude that an integrated scheduling system is what is required to solve the problem. Warner and Prawda [31] approach the nurse scheduling problem in terms of a programming model that determines the number of nursing personnel of each skill level to allocate among wards and shifts. In a pilot test of their model they reduced nursing costs by two-thirds (primarily in the night shift) and increased service by a factor of three.

Urban Alarm Services

Scheduling police, fire, and rescue services.

In those urban services that respond to alarms, such as police, fire, and rescue, the jobs (alarms) appear randomly and must be quickly serviced with sufficient resources or extreme loss of life or property may result. In many ways this problem is similar to the hospital problem in that the staffing cost of personnel is a major expense but floating fire companies and police S.W.A.T units may be utilized where needed and some services (such as fire inspection) can be scheduled to help *smooth* demand.

Scheduling duty tours.

However, there is sometimes a major difference that vastly complicates some of these services (particularly fire) and that is the use of *duty tours* of extended duration, as opposed to regular shifts, which run over multiple days. These tours typically vary from 24 to 48 hours in teams of two to four personnel each. Common schedules for such services are "two (days) on and three off" and "one on and two off" with every fifth tour or so off as well (for a running time off, every 3 weeks, of perhaps 3 + 2 + 3 = 8 days). Because living and sleeping-in are considered part of the job requirements, the standard workweek is in excess of 40 hours with common values being 50 and 54 hours. Clearly, the scheduling of such duty tours is a complex problem, not only because of the unusual duration of the tours but also because of the implications concerning overtime, temptations of "moonlighting," and other such issues. For further discussion of such problems consult References 13, 18, and 23.

Educational Services

The scheduling requirements of schools.

Colleges and universities have scheduling requirements for all of the various types of transformation processes: intermittent (such as counseling), continuous (English 1), batch (committee meetings), and project (regional conferences). In some of these situations the jobs (students) are scheduled, in some the staff (faculty, administrators) are scheduled, and in some the facilities (classrooms, convention centers) are scheduled.

The difficulty of scheduling classes.

The primary scheduling problem, however, involves the scheduling of classes, assignment of students, and allocation of facility and faculty resources to these classes. Three difficult elements must be coordinated in this process to obtain a manageable schedule.

1. An accurate forecast of student class demand.
2. The limitation on available classroom space.
3. The multiple needs and desires of the faculty such as
   - Number of "preparations."
   - Number of classes.
   - Timing of classes.
   - Level of classes.
   - Leave requirements (sabbatical, without pay, etc.).
   - Release requirements (research, projects, administration).

The need for a multicriteria approach.

Because of the number of objectives in such scheduling problems, a variety of multicriteria approaches have been employed to aid in finding acceptable schedules including simulation [16], goal programming [12], and interactive modeling [7].

In summary, the scheduling approach to services is usually to attempt to match resources to the forecasted demand for service. Since the demand cannot be controlled, inventory buildup ahead of time is impossible, and backordering is usually infeasible. Careful scheduling of staff, facilities, and materials is employed instead with (limited) flexibility achieved through floating, part-time, and overtime labor and off-peak rates to encourage leveling of demand.

Scheduling techniques for services similar to scheduling jobs.

Scheduling techniques for resources are similar to those used for scheduling jobs: the use of indexes, weights, priorities, programming, simulation, and so forth. Simulation appears to be an especially relevant approach since it can handle multiple criteria in highly varied situations [9,16,25]. The main advantage of simulation is that the reality of operational conditions—equipment breakdowns, emergencies, and so forth—can be easily included to determine their effect. Various schedules can be tested and their impact on resource utilization and level of service under varying distributions of demand can be found with ease. The best schedule is often not the one that optimizes the use of resources or minimizes lateness for the expected demand but rather the one that gives acceptable results under all likely operating conditions.

Simulation as an important aid.

The tendency of queues to form.

An important element in the scheduling of operations to produce either products or services concerns the waiting lines, or *queues*, that tend to build up in front of the operations. With an unpaced production line, for example, buffer inventory between operations builds up at some times and disappears at other times due to the natural variability in the difficulty of the operations.

In the production of services this variability is even greater because of both the amount of highly variable human *input* and the variable service *requirements*. What is more, the "items" in queue are often people, who tend to complain and make trouble if kept waiting too long. Thus it behooves the

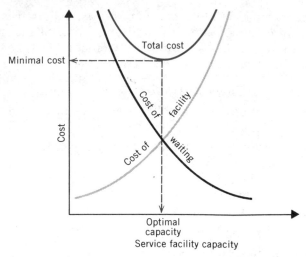

Figure 9.7 The relevant queuing costs.

operations manager to provide adequate service to keep long queues from forming. This, however, costs more money for service facilities and staff. But long queues cost money also, in the form of in-process inventory, unfinished orders, lost sales, and ill will. Figure 9.7 conceptually illustrates, as a function of the capacity of the service facility, the tradeoffs in these two costs:

1. *The cost of waiting:* In-process inventory investment, ill will, lost sales, which decreases with service capacity.
2. *The cost of service facilities:* Equipment, supplies, staff, which increases with service capacity.

The tradeoff between ill will and cost of service. At some point the total of the two costs is minimized and it is at this point that managers typically wish to operate. The field of *queuing theory*, presented in the appendix to Chapter 10, has developed to address exactly these kinds of situations.

9.5 APPENDIX I: MASTER OPERATIONS SCHEDULING GAME*

Marketing Considerations

Your company manufactures a consumer product which is purchased for resale by numerous wholesale and retail establishments. The market for your product is highly competitive and subject to both cyclical and seasonal fluctuations. The timing and extent of seasonal peaks are influenced by weather conditions and thus can be forecast with only moderate accuracy. Although the annual sales forecast made each November has been, on the average, within ±10 percent of total actual sales, there had been years in which the

*Adapted by permission from the "Simuload Game" of General Electric Co.

forecast total varied from the actual results by as much as ±20 percent. Moreover, the forecast of sales for any of the four 13-week "operating periods" into which the year is divided is sometimes in error by as much as ±33 percent of the results actually obtained.

These forecasting inaccuracies are tempered somewhat by the fact that certain customers usually negotiate purchase contracts for at least a portion of their requirements 60 to 120 days in advance of the shipping date. As a result, in most years anywhere from 10 to 30 percent of the shipping requirements for a given operations period are "booked" sometime during the second operating period ahead of the period in which delivery has to be made. An additional 20 to 60 percent are booked one period ahead. In total, therefore, "Advanced Commitment Sales" already on the books at the start of a period rarely represent less than 30 percent—and sometimes amount to as much as 90 percent—of the shipments that the factory will be called to make out of current production or finished goods inventory during the period.

The remaining delivery commitments, known as "Single Period Sales"— that is, sales that are booked and shipped during the same operating period— sometimes involve as little as 3 weeks' lead time. Since such sales frequently represent supplemental orders placed by important customers, your company makes every effort to meet even the tightest delivery deadline, as do its major competitors.

Customers rarely cancel an order once it has been booked. On the other hand, since the product is bulky and therefore costly to handle and store, customers are unwilling to accept delivery much in advance of the date requested. Therefore, if factory production runs ahead of the actual shipping requirements during a given operating period, your company has to carry the excess units as finished goods inventory.

Advertising: Basic Programs and Special Supplementary Campaigns

Within your company and the industry there is agreement that industrywide sales for any operating period are more decisively influenced by weather conditions than any other single factor. Moreover, research studies have indicated that "brand loyalty" is significant to only about half of the customers who regularly purchased this product. Therefore, even though weather plays a major role in determining when and in what quantities retail customers buy such items, the choice between competing brands can be considerably influenced by advertising.

In common with all major companies in the industry, prior to the start of each calendar year your company commits itself to a carefully planned basic advertising program for the ensuing year. This entails the commitment of a specific amount of money. The exact amount usually is a predetermined percentage of the sales revenues forecast for the coming year. Experience has convinced your organization's top management that under certain circumstances it is profitable to augment this basic program with supplemental advertising (SA) during all, or part, of particular operating periods. To assess the advisability of launching such campaigns, the following "rules of thumb" have proven useful:

Type of Supplemental Advertising Campaign	Extra Costs per Period Incurred from Supplemental Campaign	Approximate Percentage Increase in Sales for the Period that Can Probably Be Achieved Over the Sales that Would Result from the Basic Program Alone
Type X (Modest stepup in efforts)	$10,000	10%
Type Y (Major stepup in efforts)	$20,000	20%
Type Z (Maximum stepup in efforts)	$50,000	30%

For any of these supplemental campaigns to yield results during a given operating period it is essential that commitments be made no later than the start of the period. Nor is it possible, except at prohibitive cost, to abandon a campaign once it has been undertaken. Furthermore, experience indicates that even if the extra expenditures are increased substantially beyond $50,000, sales are not likely to exceed 130 percent of the level they will reach with only the basic program.

In commenting on this phase of operations, one of your senior executives has stated, "It is imperative that a decision regarding an SA campaign be based on a painstaking analysis of the total situation. I am referring not only to the status quo then surrounding the company, but also the probable future course of events, the plans being launched by the other sectors of the business, and so on. This can be tricky. It is a nightmare to find yourselves committed to a 'maximum effort' Type Z campaign during a period in which actual sales are so favorable that the factory is unable to meet even the demand that would have been generated by the basic program. On the other hand, not to have launched an SA campaign during a period in which sales fall seriously short of the factory output appears, by hindsight, to be inexcusably poor management. But by digging and analyzing, it is possible to assess if a supplemental campaign is likely to be helpful."

Factory Output Capabilities and Direct Labor Costs

As noted previously, your company divides the calendar year into four consecutive operating periods of 13 weeks each. The range of factory output capabilities per period, and the average direct labor cost per unit under each of the three factory operating conditions that management believes to be feasible, are as follows:

Factory Operating Conditions	Output Capabilities per Operating Period[a]	Average Direct Labor Cost per Unit
Single shift without overtime	60,000 units or less	$5.00
Single shift with overtime	61,000 to 80,000 units	$5.00 for first 60,000 units, $7.50 per unit thereafter
Two shifts	61,000 to 110,000 units	$5.00 for first 60,000 units, $5.50 per unit thereafter

[a]For planning and scheduling purposes, factory output is always expressed in multiples of thousands of units.

Scheduling and Planning Factory Activity

Until recently, your company's policy has been to increase or to decrease the rate of factory output frequently. This has been accomplished by hiring or laying off workers, increasing or decreasing overtime, changing the number of shifts, and so on, whenever sales fluctuations seemed to warrant it. After careful study, however, your board of directors has become convinced that the costs and inefficiencies associated with such frequent changes are excessive and that with careful planning a more stable, and hence more profitable, pattern of operations could be achieved. Instructions have been given, therefore, to your operating management that until further notice it is to adhere to a policy decision that the level of factory operations can be changed no more than four times per calendar year and that such changes can only occur at the start of an operating period. Once the level of factory activity has been determined for a given period, it cannot be changed until the start of the next period.

In commenting on this new policy, your board chairman has stated, "Granting that forecasting is difficult in our industry, we feel that it still is not unreasonable to expect our operating management to do a sufficiently sound job of planning to be able to live with their decisions for at least a 3-month period."

Extra Costs Arising from Scheduling or Forecasting Problems

Simultaneously with announcing the new policy regarding the number and frequency of changes in factory output rate, your company's directors announced their intention to employ the results of a recently completed cost analysis. This study had been undertaken by representatives of the Sales, Production, Finance, and Accounting Departments to provide information on the extra costs incurred whenever problems of scheduling or forecasting caused your company to adopt any of the following three types of action:

1. *Making Changes in the Rate of Factory Operations:* That is, the extra costs incurred from having to recruit, hire, and train additional employees—or from having to lay off present employees; from having to place rush orders for additional materials; from increases in state unemployment taxes arising from an irregular employment record; and so on.

2. *Carrying Finished Goods Inventories:* That is, the extra costs incurred from the physical movement and storage of finished products; the cost of insurance, the risk of theft, damage, deterioration, or obsolescence, or all of these; the cost of the capital tied up in such inventories; and so on.

3. *Defaulting on a Delivery Promise Made to a Customer:* That is, extra costs arising from the use of air freight to expedite delivery on a delayed order; losses arising from a customer's refusal to accept late delivery; estimates, based on past experience, of the risk that such nondeliveries will result in legal action or in the loss of future sales from the customer in question or from other customers who learn of the situation; and so on.

The results of the study were as follows:

Extra costs incurred from changes in the rate of factory output: $2.00 per unit of change, regardless of whether the change is upward or downward.

Extra costs, in addition to those cited above, from changes in the number of shifts employed in the factory:

1. Going from one shift to two shifts: $7000.

2. Going from two shifts to one shift: $3000.

Extra costs from overtime or second-shift premiums:

1. *Overtime:* $2.50 per unit for each unit of factory output in excess of 60,000 units per period.

2. *Second shift:* $0.50 per unit for each unit of factory output in excess of 60,000 units per period, plus $20,000 per period of second-shift operation.

(Note: Single shift plus overtime can be used only up to a maximum factory output rate of 80,000 units per period. To obtain an output rate in excess of 80,000 units requires the use of a second shift. To obtain an output rate between 61,000 and 80,000 units, operating management can choose either single-shift-plus-overtime, or two-shift operations.)

Extra costs of missed delivery promises: $6.00 per unit per period. Extra costs of carrying finished goods inventory: $4.00 per unit per period (to be applied to the average size of the inventory, that is, one-half of the sum of the beginning inventory plus the closing inventory for the period).

Special Internal Controls

One of top management's objectives in obtaining such cost information was to establish a special system of internal controls which would help the directors make a continuing assessment of the performance of operating management. Therefore, in addition to the conventional profit and loss statement, the directors also now require that at the close of each operating period operating management complete and submit the form shown in Exhibit 1.

Exhibit 1   Computation Sheet

Company: _____   Period N: __*1*__

I.   *ACTIVITIES DURING THIS PERIOD*
   (a) Factory Operations (circle one): Single Shift without Overtime; (Single Shift with Overtime;)
       Two Shifts.

   (b) Factory Rate this period **62,000** units; Rate prior Period __**71,000**__ units;
       Change in Rate therefore equals __**9,000**__ units.

   (c) Supplementary Advertising Campaign (circle one):
       None   Type X ($10,000)   (Type Y ($20,000))   Type Z ($50,000)

II. *SHIPPING REQUIREMENTS THIS PERIOD* (units)	III. *SHIPPING CAPABILITIES THIS PERIOD* (units)
Delivery Deficits from prior Periods and Advance Commitment Sales booked for delivery this Period **44,000**	Starting Finished Goods Inventory **10,000**
+ Single Period Sales this Period **32,000**	+ Factory Output Rate this Period **62,000**
equals TOTAL SHIPPING REQUIREMENTS **76,000**	equals TOTAL SHIPPING CAPABILITIES **72,000**

IV.   *SHIPMENTS MADE DURING THIS PERIOD* (i.e., the total shown in either item II or item III
      above, whichever is the *lower*)   **72,000** units

V.   If item II above is greater than item III, the difference equals a *DELIVERY
     DEFICIT* of   **4,000** units

VI.   If item II above is less than item III, the difference equals an *ENDING FINISHED GOODS
      INVENTORY OF*   **0** units

VII.   *POTENTIAL OPERATING CONTRIBUTION FOR THIS PERIOD*
       Shipments made this period (item IV above, **72,000** units) × $3 $ **216,000**

VIII.   *EXTRA COSTS AND EXPENSES INCURRED THIS PERIOD*

   (a) Supplementary Advertising (see item I-c above) $ **10,000**

   (b) Change in Factory Rate (item I-b above × $2)   **9,000** $ **18,000**

   (c) Change in # of Factory Shifts (changing from 1 to 2 costs $7,000; from 2 to 1
       costs $3,000) $ **0**

   (d) Overtime or 2nd Shift Premiums (Overtime costs $2.50 per unit for all units
       in excess of 60,000; 2nd shift costs $20,000 + $.50 per unit over 60,000
       units) $ **5,000**

   (e) Inventory Carrying costs (i.e., Starting Inventory + Ending Inventory) × ½
       × $4 $ **20,000**
                                              4,000
   (f) Missed Delivery Promises (item V above × $6) $ **24,000**

                TOTAL EXTRA COSTS & EXPENSES INCURRED $ **77,000**

IX.   *NET OPERATING CONTRIBUTION FOR PERIOD* (item VII minus item VIII) $ **139,000**

   − Auditing Fee ($10,000 per error) $ **0**

   + Cumulative Operating Contribution from prior Periods $ **0**

   equals NEW CUMULATIVE NET OPERATING CONTRIBUTION $ **139,000**

* * * * * * * * * * *

YOUR COMPANY'S DECISIONS REGARDING *NEXT* OPERATING PERIOD (fill in blanks)

Factory Operations: Factory Rate _____ units; SA Type _____ ; Shifts _____
Period N + 3 Forecast (SA of None) **58,000** Total Bookings to Date:
   Period N + 1 **68,000** Period N + 2 **28,000**

These internal controls are based on the conviction that, on the average, each unit shipped from the factory generates a potential contribution of $3.00. That is to say, if operations are at maximum efficiency, your company can meet all variable costs arising from the production of the unit in question and still have $3.00 of the selling price available as a contribution toward its fixed costs, taxes, and profits. This potential contribution is reduced, however, by any extra costs incurred during the period.

Use of this concept requires that the following computations be made for each operating period:

1. Number of units actually shipped × $3.00 = potential contribution for the period.

2. Extra costs incurred during period = cost of any supplementary advertising or sales promotion campaign plus any extra costs arising from scheduling or forecasting problems.

3. Net operating contribution for period = potential contribution minus extra costs incurred.

An Example of the System at Work: The First Operating Period of the Current Year

During the final week of the year just concluded, your factory was operating at an output rate of 71,000 units per period, that is, the rate that had been set at the start of the period. This had been accomplished through use of single shift plus overtime. All orders calling for shipments during the fourth period have now been received, and it has been determined that after meeting these your company will end the current year with a finished goods inventory of 10,000 units.

The sales forecast for the coming year, prepared by the Sales Department in November, is as follows:

Period No.	Delivery Requirements Forecast
1	70,000 units
2	82,000 units
3	125,000 units
4	59,000 units
Total	336,000 units

By late December, your company's operating management also knew that 44,000 units of advance sales commitments calling for delivery during period 1 of the coming year were already on the books. Of this total, 18,000 units had been booked in the third quarter of the year just concluding, and 26,000 units during the fourth quarter. An additional 29,000 units of advance commitments had been booked in this last period for delivery during period 2 of the coming year.

After studying these facts, your company's operating management decided that during period 1 of the new year, the factory would be operated on a single-shift-plus-overtime basis at an output rate of 62,000 units; that is to say, a reduction of 9000 units would be made in the rate maintained during the fourth period of the year then concluding. In addition, it was decided that a "Type X" supplementary advertising campaign would be launched during period 1 in an effort to stimulate sales by about 10 percent.

During the actual operations in period 1, the following sales results were achieved:

Period in Which Shipment Called For	Amount of Orders Booked
1 (This Period N sales)	32,000 units
2 (Period $N + 1$)	40,000 units
3 (Period $N + 2$)	28,000 units

As a result of these developments, total delivery requirements for period 1 turned out to be 76,000 units: the 44,000 units of advanced commitment sales booked prior to the start of period 1, plus the 32,000 units of single-period sales booked during period 1. However, your company was able to ship* only 72,000 units of this total: the 62,000 units that were produced by the factory during period 1, plus the 10,000 units that were available in the form of finished goods inventory at the start of the period.

Therefore, your company will enter period 2 with a shipping deficit of 4000 units in overdue orders which will have to be met at the earliest possible date out of period 2 factory output.

Under your company's internal control system, period 1 operations resulted in a net operating contribution of $139,000, computed as shown in Exhibit 1.

Now, operating management must make various decisions regarding operations during period 2. It knows positively that as early as possible in period 2 your company must ship the 4000 units of delayed deliveries, that is, the shipping deficit incurred in period 1. It knows also that during period 2 the factory will have to ship an additional 69,000 units to satisfy advanced sales commitments booked for period 2: the 29,000 units booked during the last period of the previous year, plus the 40,000 units booked during period 1 of the current year. Before deciding on the rate at which to operate the factory during period 2, your management will also have to reach a conclusion regarding the additional shipping requirements that are likely to arise from single-period sales that will be booked during period 2. Attention will

---

*In most instances, orders shipped from the factory during the last few days of a period are not received by the customer until early in the following period. This brief lag is not considered important within the industry, however, and all shipments leaving the factory during a particular period are assumed to be applicable to the shipment requirements of the period.

have to be given to the possibility that the factory should begin building up its inventory position in anticipation of shipping requirements in period 3. Decisions on these points will be based, of course, on a careful analysis of the sales forecasts and the sales trends that seem to be developing, as reflected in sales to date for the year.

An Unexpected Development

Several hours prior to the time they were to reach final decisions regarding period 2 operations, the entire operating management of your company was "pirated en masse" by a desperate competitor who tripled their salaries and offered them lavish stock options.

In light of this crisis, you have accepted an assignment to join a newly formed management group which will assume full responsibility for the company's operating decisions. You and your new associates have agreed to meet as soon as possible to decide on the organizational techniques and procedures you will employ in meeting your new responsibilities. In recognition of the difficulty of your situation the directors have given you and your associates complete latitude regarding who, among you, will assume what executive positions.

While congratulating you on your new responsibilities one of the directors offers you a few words of advice:

> Look, the secret of success in our company—like any other—is organizing an effective management team. In a technical sense, there are only three things that *have* to be done: (1) before the start of each period you have to decide on the rate at which the factory is going to be run during the ensuing 13 weeks; (2) you have to decide whether or not to employ a supplemental advertising campaign during the forthcoming period and, if so, which one; and (3) you have to compute the net operating contribution for the period just ended, and submit this figure to the directors. Note that our external auditors charge us a fee of $10,000 every time they have to correct any error we made in our calculations on the computation sheet. Clearly it's imperative that you assign specific responsibility to each of these steps.
>
> But these formal requirements represent only part of the story. Sound decisions regarding the factory rate and the desirability of a supplemental advertising campaign can only grow out of careful analysis of various known facts and a resourceful prediction regarding certain unknowns. There are data, and trends, and other evidence that helpfully can be brought to bear on both of these matters. The trick is to organize for the analytical job that is required. The task is too complex—and the time pressure too great—for any one person to do alone. And the situation is undergoing too rapid a rate of change to permit operating management to rely merely on intuition, or on the hope that the disorganized efforts of able individuals will somehow yield wise results. Instead, each manager must assume some portion of the total job, and all of these individual efforts must then be blended into an effective whole.
>
> I urge you and your colleagues to start by making a careful analysis of our company, the market it serves, the relationship between the various costs it encounters, and so on. Then reach agreement regarding the precise information

and data that you need to compile to sharpen your judgment regarding the various decisions you know you will have to make. For example, might there be some way to highlight the constantly changing relationship between sales forecasts and actual sales results? Might there be some way to ensure that before committing the factory to a given output rate for the next period, you examine the costs under several different output rates? Is there some device that will ensure that the plans of the factory, and of the Sales Department, are carefully coordinated? And so on.

Once you decide the analytical approaches you want to employ, pin down responsibility for executing them. And decide in advance just how you plan to go about making final decisions. Is the president alone going to have the "final say," with all of the other managers acting as staff advisers to him? Or are decisions to be divided up functionally, with a Sales Manager deciding matters relating to sales, a Production Manager deciding factory matters, and so on? Or should the management group act as a committee, reaching decisions via majority vote? Or would some still different organizational approach be better suited to management's needs?

Well, best of luck. We're up against some tough competition. But the other directors and I expect you to run circles around them.

9.6 APPENDIX II: ANALYTICAL APPROACHES FOR THE AGGREGATE SCHEDULING PROBLEM

A number of interesting approaches for the aggregate scheduling problem have been developed, especially with the increased power of the computer, and we will investigate some of these in detail.

Linear Programming

The use of *linear programming* to meet aggregate production demands was first developed by Bowman [3] in 1956. The objective is assumed to be to minimize the costs of monthly production plus storage, subject to the constraints of meeting monthly sales demands, capacity limitations, and desired initial and ending inventory levels. The model is quite flexible in that productive resources may include regular time production, overtime production, outside subcontracting, extra shifts, inventory stockpiling between periods, and backordering. Constraints on productive capacity in each period may also be included. And infeasible allocations, for any reason, may simply be dropped and not considered.

The transportation model for aggregate scheduling.

Bowman recognized that the format of this problem matched that of the *transportation model* (Chapter 6) of linear programming and thus presented it in that form. An example illustrating the capabilities of such a format is depicted in Figure 9.8 for the 3-month period June, July, and August. Across the top of the matrix the months are listed, with the monthly demands shown at the bottom of the matrix. Demand in the final month, September, represents the required August ending inventory. A dummy column for unused (idle) capacity picks up any slack in the productive abilities of the three sources, shown in the far right column as "available."

		June	July	August	(September)	Unused	Available
	Begin. Invent.	0	2	4	6	0	200
June	Regular time	50	52	54	56	0	500
	Overtime	60	62	64	66	0	100
	Subcontract	65	67	69	70	0	300
July	Regular time	55	50	52	54	0	500
	Overtime	65	60	62	64	0	100
	Subcontract	70	65	67	69	0	300
August	Regular time*	60	55	50	52	0	250
	Overtime*	70	65	60	62	0	50
	Subcontract	75	70	65	67	0	300
	Demand	1000	700	500	150	250	2600

*Two week vacation in August.

Figure 9.8 The linear programming approach to aggregate planning.

Backordering and subcontracting available.

Along the left side of the matrix are the three productive sources of supply for each month: regular time, overtime, and subcontracting. In the upper right corner of each cell is listed the cost of using that supply source for each month's sales requirements. Note that backordering is possible (e.g., July production for June), but at a cost of $5 extra per unit per month. Subcontracting is also possible for future months but with an inventory carrying charge of $2 per unit per month, as with regular production.

An advantage of this approach to aggregate planning is that multiple outputs may be included in the model if their demands can be transformed to aggregate units (such as hours of work). There are also some limitations to the model, however; the most important of these is that workforce hiring and firing costs are not included when production changes are significant (as demand is between June and July). If production is fairly steady, then this limitation does not become a problem.

Other limitations enter through the lack of shortage costs when demand is lost and the linearity of the cost functions with output level (which undoubtedly are not strictly proportional); however, the approximations may be sufficiently close for the situation at hand. Extensions of Bowman's approach include workforce hiring and firing costs and shortage costs through a general linear programming model.

The Linear Decision Rule

In the early 1950s a group of researchers at the Carnegie Institute of Technology developed a set of managerial "decision rules" to aid managers in determining two aspects of aggregate scheduling: the lowest cost monthly production and workforce levels for their organizations [14]. These rules were simple linear equations involving

1. The size of the workforce the preceding month.
2. The ending inventory in the preceding month, less any units on backorder.
3. Demand forecasts for the next 12 months.

The rules were derived from a process that minimized the total monthly cost of four separate elements.

Four costs.

- *Regular payroll:* The cost of direct labor (Figure 9.9*a*).
- *Hiring and layoffs:* Need not be symmetrical. Approximated by a curve (Figure 9.9*b*).
- *Overtime:* Includes time and a half and double time (Figure 9.9*c*).
- *Carrying inventory:* Includes stocking out and setup costs (Figure 9.9*d*).

Approximating costs with quadratic equations.

These costs were approximated by a series of curves, as shown in Figure 9.9. Note that some of the relationships are straight (linear) whereas others are *parabolic* (*quadratic* or of *second degree*). Due to the simple form of these four curves, there exists a minimum point on the monthly *total* cost curve (i.e., the sum of the four curves for each month), which can be located through calculus to give the least cost values of monthly production and workforce levels.

The simplicity of LDR in use.

Although perhaps difficult to generate the initial cost curves, the linear decision rule is a simply applied approach to aggregate production planning. To use the rules, the manager or production scheduler solves two simple equations at the beginning of every month. For the actual company considered by the researchers, the use of the rules would have lowered production costs significantly. The criticism of the approach, beyond the difficulty of collecting the cost data, is that it does not consider many constraints such as overtime restrictions, capital limitations, and so forth.

For the company data used by the researchers, the resulting decision rules looked like

$$P_t = (aF_t + bF_{t+1} + \cdots + 1F_{t+11}) + mW_{t-1} + nI_{t-1} + p$$
$$W_t = (qF_t + \cdots + wF_{t+11}) + xW_{t-1} + yI_{t-1} + z.$$

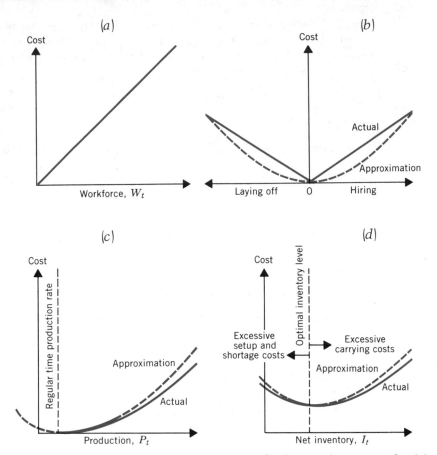

Figure 9.9 Cost approximations in the linear decision rule. (*a*) Payroll cost approximation. (*b*) Work force cost approximation. (*c*) Overtime cost approximation, (*d*) Inventory cost approximation.

where $a, b, \ldots, z$ = constants
P_t = the production rate for the upcoming month t
W_{t-1} = the workforce in the preceding month
I_{t-1} = the ending inventory level of the preceding month less any outstanding backorders
F_t = the forecast demand for month t

Although these equations look overwhelming, they are not really difficult. The analysts studying the operations are responsible for deriving the constants $a, b. \ldots, z$. For simplicity, suppose all the constants are 0.2. And let us also suppose production last month was 30, the workforce was 20, and the ending inventory was 20. And last, suppose the forecast of demand for every month in the future is 9. Then the linear decision rules say that next month's production should be

PEANUTS®   **By Charles M. Schulz**

The use of rule-of-thumb heuristics. (Reprinted by permission of United Feature Syndicate.)

$$[0.2(9) + 0.2(9) + \cdots + 0.2(9)] + 0.2(20) + 0.2(20) + 0.2 = 29.8$$

and the workforce should be

$$[0.2(9) + 0.2(9) + \cdots + 0.2(9)] + 0.2(20) + 0.2(20) + 0.2 = 29.8$$

or, use 30 workers (hiring is required) to produce 30 units. In the next month the forecasts, workforce, and inventory would be updated to produce new production and workforce values.

Management Coefficients Heuristics

A heuristic is a procedure used in facing a problem situation: how to find an item in an unfamiliar store, how to remember when the next committee meeting is, how to decide the amount to produce next month. Although similar to "rules-of-thumb," heuristics are usually more scientifically based; for example, they may be based on simulation, experimentation, rigorous analytical analysis, or logical reasoning combined with experience. In the world of organizational operations most decisions are probably based on heuristics and rules-of-thumb.

Using managers' own decision rules to improve the decisions.

It might be expected that the managers faced with operational decisions would themselves know best what the critical variables were in those decisions. Thus, there should somehow be a way of synthesizing their experience to capitalize on this knowledge.

Multiple regression to find the heuristic rules.

A number of interesting studies have been conducted that analyzed the performance of managers with the aim of trying to uncover their heuristic decisions rules (e.g., see References 24, 29 and 33). The research process used in these studies is usually the same. The researcher talks with a number of managers involved in the decision situation and generates a list of all the possible variables that the managers feel might bear on the decision. Historical data relating to the occurrence of the decision in the past and all of the identified variables are then collected for analysis. A *multiple regression analysis* (Chapter 4), or some other analytical method, is then used to uncover the significant variables and how, on the average, they affect the decision. This model is thus an approximation to the manager's decision heuristic. The last step is to try this heuristic on historical data and new decision data to see how well it imitates the manager's actual decisions.

When these heuristic rules were *reapplied* to the same historical data the managers had worked with, performance was usually improved *significantly*. The major reason for such a result was the erratic, though normal, behavior on the part of the manager. That is, interruptions, headaches, lack of time, and other such facts of managerial life were more typically the cause of bad decisions than lack of managerial skill. On the other hand, models employing the skills distilled from the manager are not subject to the same pressures and problems.

Bowman conducted a study of this sort relating to aggregate production planning [4]. He adopted the variables used in the linear decision rule but, instead of using the calculus derived coefficients, he derived them by multiple regression, as described previously. His general results were excellent.

Search Methods

Computer search.

Another way to approach the aggregate production planning problem is to formulate the exact costs as accurately as possible, program them on a computer, and then attempt various production plans to see which one has the least cost. The problem, of course, is that in this trial-and-error method there are an unending number of plans that might be tried (cf. Table 9.2). The basis of "search" methods is thus to develop efficient procedures for picking trial alternatives from the infinite number of possible aggregate production plans and identifying the best one.

Hill-climbing and gradient heuristics.

There are a number of heuristic procedures for searching a set of decision variables to identify extreme (e.g., least cost) points. Some of these, known as *hill-climbing* or *gradient* methods, start at one spot and check the effect of changing one variable at a time *just a little* to see the effect on cost. The most promising variable (the one that reduces cost most quickly) is thereby identified and is changed first (sometimes combinations of favorable variables are used).

Search techniques to locate an optimum.

The next question concerns *how much* to change the variable. Again, this is answered by testing. The selected variable is changed a bit more than it was the previous time. This information tells the computer routine *how fast* the selected variable is lowering the cost and thus lets it approximate how much to change the variable. For example, suppose the first change was to add one worker and the effect was to reduce the total cost by 3 percent (more than any other change). And suppose the second change, adding another worker, reduced the total cost another 2 percent. The computer would then conclude that the next best aggregate plan to examine would be to add three workers (expecting to thereby reduce the total cost 6 percent). In the chemical industry, one such method is known as "evolutionary operation." Production variables are changed on the basis of earlier successes and failures and the process "evolves" in a rational manner, improving at almost every step.

Evolutionary operation in the chemical industry.

Sometimes this elementary logic does not work. In those cases the search routines use varied strategies. The rule may be to backtrack to the previous best (least cost) point (adding two workers) and reinitialize the search or, alternatively, to go half the distance instead and examine that point.

One problem with search methods is that they do not guarantee that the *best* solution has been located. There may be another point with quite different values of the variables that has a lesser cost.

Taubert used this type of search methodology, called the *search decision rule* (SDR) to test its performance on the company data used for the linear decision rule [30]. The results were gratifying in that the search rule converged to essentially the same results as the linear decision rule.

Of these methods considered for solving the aggregate scheduling problem, the SDR has the greatest potential. It is not limited in its assumptions as the other rules are and the full power and cost effectiveness of the computer can be brought to bear on the problem. Lee and Khumawala [19] tested the methods against actual company decisions in a capital goods job shop and found all of them superior to actual results, with the search decision rule improving profits the most (14 percent increase).

The superiority
of the SDR.

9.7   SUMMARY AND KEY LEARNING POINTS

Following work design as the last aspect of tactical operations, this chapter has addressed the issue of scheduling: incorporating the input "time" into operations so as to properly mesh all of the previous inputs and produce the desired output. We looked in detail at how this process is accomplished starting with the demand forecast and ending with the inputs to detailed scheduling. We also looked at the increasing role of computers in the scheduling task and the difficulty of successfully implementing computerized scheduling systems.

From this conceptual overview we discussed the details of aggregate scheduling and described the variety of strategies available through the use of an extended example. Last, we looked at some of the scheduling approaches and systems used for scheduling pure services and the unique difficulties encountered here.

Appendix I presented a scheduling game to give the reader some experience in the difficulties and techniques of scheduling. Appendix II then presented some well-known analytical solution approaches for the aggregate scheduling problem.

The key learning points of this chapter have been

- The sequence of activities involved in scheduling is as follows: the *forecast*, which is then used in *aggregate scheduling* to derive a *production plan*, which, with the help of *firm orders*, is further disaggregated into a *master schedule.* From this schedule, material availabilities are checked in *priority planning* and capacity limits are checked in *capacity planning.* When these two checks are satisfied, *loading* of the facilities and *sequencing* of the jobs at each facility can be conducted, leading to the final planning step of *detailed scheduling.*

- Forward scheduling is done by loading jobs on facilities when the job is ready for that facility. The job then starts at the next opening on the facility. This process is used when operations sets the dates for delivery.

   Backward scheduling is used to meet a desired customer due date or marketing promise date based on fixed lead times. In backward scheduling, the due date is used to help schedule the job for the latest possible times it can be loaded on each facility.

- There are many commercial computerized scheduling systems available. Some are batch and others are real time systems. Some are designed for large mainframe computers while others can run on minicomputers. Microcomputers are making extensive inroads into scheduling for individual data analysis and input to larger computers through distributed data processing.

- Successful implementation of computerized systems is still relatively uncommon because of three major sets of factors: (1) technical factors, which constitute minimal requirements for the system to perform the mechanics of the process, (2) process factors, which include top management and user support, and (3) inner-environmental factors, which provide the foundation of a critical, current situation and a managerial willingness to change.

- Two "baseline" aggregate scheduling strategies are to chase demand or level production. The manager can employ different methods to achieve either strategy such as using overtime, hiring and firing, building up inventories, and backordering.

- The major problem of scheduling in pure service organizations is finding an economic way to meet variable, peak demands when the output cannot be inventoried. Common approaches are to use floating workers, overtime, overlapping shifts, part-time employees, duty tours, and off-peak pricing.

9.8   KEY TERMS

aggregate schedule (p. 304)	MRP (p. 308)	sequencing (p. 309)
production plan (p. 305)	CRP (p. 309)	detailed scheduling (p. 309)
master schedule (p. 305)	loading (p. 309)	expediting (p. 310)
forward scheduling (p. 305)	priority rules (p. 309)	chase demand (p. 317)
backward scheduling (p. 305)	dispatching (p. 310)	level production (p. 317)
TPOP (p. 308)	PICS (p. 311)	level zero items (p. 305)

9.9   REVIEW AND DISCUSSION QUESTIONS

1. How could top management overcome lower level resentment of the installation of a computerized scheduling system?

2. Why are special-purpose digital electronic devices not considered computers?

3. What is the primary motivating force behind the explosive adoption of new technology (such as microcomputers)?

4. Which of the three sets of implementation impediments is probably the most important? The most common?

5. Given the immensity of the computerized scheduling task, how did it ever get accomplished previously?

6. What are the implications of the use of multiple expediters for the value of inventory and utilization reports to management?

7. Why is de-expediting important?

8. What are the advantages of "net change" versus "regeneration" scheduling systems?

9. In what sense is "chase demand" a "pure" aggregate scheduling strategy?

10. To what other areas might management coefficients heuristics be applied?

11. Why do loading and sequencing not apply as well to continuous processes?

12. What are some practical ways of matching staff availability to expected demand?

13. How do overtime and moonlighting become issues when duty tour scheduling is used?

14. Under what other conditions can queues form besides when the service cannot be stored ahead of time?

9.10 READINGS

SCHEDULING IS NOT THE PROBLEM

Kenneth L. Campbell
Honeywell Information Systems, Inc.
Cleveland, Ohio

Abstract

It has often been said that scheduling is no problem, but rescheduling can kill you. In this article, the author supports this theme and points out the causes and penalties of rescheduling. He also makes pertinent suggestions as to how to avoid the causes and reduce the penalties.

At a conference on shop scheduling, the principal speaker was extolling the virtues of a particularly complex scheduling system when one of the attendees spoke up and said, "Scheduling is no problem, it's the rescheduling that kills me."

While that remark may have sounded facetious to the speaker, it is a concise statement of fact. When one stops to analyze the situation, it becomes quite clear how well that comment expresses a truly profound observation.

What Is a Schedule?

When we isolate the act of scheduling from its related activities, such as loading, dispatching and rescheduling, it becomes clear that scheduling is, in fact, no problem.

First, it is an abstract. It cannot be specifically related to a real life situation. The schedule, as prepared for a manufacturing organization, is based on a given capacity, the availability of specific materials or a given job content. In most cases, due to the lapse of time between the conception and the execution of a schedule, one or more of these factors has changed.

The typical schedule in itself is not dynamic, and is, therefore, a poor instrument to associate with the usual manufacturing shop which, as we all know, is a dynamic beast, continually out of control and continually going off in an unpredictable direction.

Schedules come in a large number of varieties. They can be grouped into three major families: forward, backward and (for the lack of a better word) non-directional. In the first family, we begin with where we are and find out when we will arrive. In the second, we decide when we wish to arrive and determine when we should get started.

With the third family, the non-directional, we may start now to get there by then without any regard to the route, the terrain, or the other travelers who may be encountered along the way. (Sound silly? Check the systems where the Sales Department dates the customers' orders!)

Scheduling techniques are often described as being related to finite or infinite capacity. Some aren't (or can't be) described at all in terms of capacity.

Some schedules are based on very sophisticated rules and formulas, some on very simple ones, and, of course, some are based on no rules at all.

There are, in the first category, scheduling systems that take into consideration such factors as the order quantity, resource capacity, material availability, setup and process time, in-house transportation delays and even order values.

In the second category, one would group those having only one or two factors to consider: perhaps the product complexity, the current shop loading, or the time of the year. Into the third group, we could toss the schedules based strictly on external factors: customers' requested date, a sales forecast, and Joe's best guess.

What Are the Problems of Rescheduling?

The majority of the problems caused by the need to reschedule can be divided into three groups: (1) cost, (2) capacity, (3) confusion.

Naturally, cost, in terms of reduced dollar profits, is the major concern of every red-blooded manufacturing man. And rescheduling can be a real drain on the profits. In most shops, a rescheduling can involve untold manhours of both direct and indirect labor. If there is any doubt about this, count the number of "expediters" found on our payrolls. "Expediters prevent rescheduling," you say? Well, perhaps that viewpoint does have some merit, but, at the same time, it supports our premise that rescheduling does cost profit dollars—otherwise we would not be willing to spend so much money on the salaries of the expediters.

Rescheduling also costs labor dollars when it involves the premature breakdown of a setup, the paying of overtime, or the use of a less efficient resource.

When capacity utilization is adversely affected by rescheduling, it is lost forever. If a resource is in short supply, its scheduling is critical and extreme care must be taken to be sure that rescheduling will not waste any of the resource.

Confusion, for most people, is a detractor and has a detrimental effect on their morale, their production and their respect for those who are responsible for its creation or permit its prolonged existence. If it could be quantitatively expressed, confusion would undoubtedly increase exponentially with the amount of rescheduling.

Now that we have considered the problems associated with rescheduling, what should we do about them?

Rescheduling Is Here to Stay

At first thought, it would seem as though the best solution to the rescheduling dilemma would be to eliminate the practice of remaking our schedule and stick to it come what may. Unfortunately, this solution could soon put most manufacturers out of business. This is primarily due to the source of some of the causes of the failure of our scheduling systems. A list of some of the causes of schedule failures would include such things as:

1. *Materials not available:* The vendors have failed to meet deliveries or the previous operation has not been completed.

2. *Tools are not available:* They haven't been received or they have not been repaired.

3. *Machines have broken down:* An alternate is not available or is less efficient.

4. *Customers requirements have changed:* Order quantities have changed or new delivery dates are required.

5. *Overloaded capacity:* Unrealistic master schedules or promise dates have been prepared without regard to available capacity.

6. *Loose discipline in job selection:* A good schedule is ignored for such reasons as make-out, personal preferences or simply unawareness of the need for first-things-first.

Obviously, some of the listed causes are external and, as such, *are not fully* under control of the organization. Others, such as overloaded capacity, are internal and can be controlled by management once they are recognized and the problem given some attention.

In either case, it is only practical to acknowledge the fact that things do happen to upset even the best, well prepared, schedule and, as a consequence, rescheduling will be necessary.

Reduce the Problems of Rescheduling

There are a few basic things that can be done in any shop and using any system that will reduce the penalties caused by the act of rescheduling. Included among these are:

1. Release Fewer Jobs

In many shops the manufacturing information is prepared, typed, duplicated and distributed to the shop floor as rapidly as it can be done, without regard to *start dates, due dates* or *capacity*. This creates a large portion of the problem when rescheduling is necessary.

Someone must scurry about the shop locating the paperwork, collecting, correcting or replacing it with updated information. Naturally, the more jobs in the queue, the more likely changes will be required and, therefore, the more involved the task. Likewise, the more jobs in the queue, the more likely a rescheduling will be *required*. This may mean rescheduling shop orders which have been previously rescheduled.

When the situation gets too far out of control, it is natural that we throw in the towel and no longer attempt to keep the dates (start and/or finish) corrected. Instead, a Hot List is published and we hire more expediters to get the jobs on the list pushed to the front of the queue.

Where the system is computerized, it is logical to delay the preparation of all the manufacturing information until the last practical moment. The storage of the basic facts within the computer will permit it to be factored into the scheduling system (or rescheduled) as often as required, with or without changes.

Some scheduling systems distinguish between "PLANNED" orders and "RELEASED" orders. In those systems a planned order is one which has been entered into the computer but not yet "exposed" to the shop through the preparation of shop papers. Planned orders may be altered (date or quantity) or cancelled for any reason. Released orders are those for which the shop papers have been prepared and distributed to the shop. On these orders, it takes a virtual act of Congress to change them and they will be cancelled only by feeding back the information that they were "completed" with an increased quantity or "closed out short."

It pays then, to release orders only far enough in advance to permit the tools, materials and resources to be "staged" soon enough to prevent lost time between jobs. Where the processing cycle is longer than the staging time, the opti-

mum would be to release only the next job ahead of each machine, production line or employee. When the processing time is shorter, it would be best to have several released orders ahead.

2. Demand Shop Floor Discipline

Assuming that it is not practical at this time in your shop to release only the next job, it is then necessary to enforce a system of job selection. The lack of such discipline generally makes effective scheduling difficult. Perhaps, in such cases, each job entering a particular queue should be given a sequence number and a firm rule be established that jobs be started in order of their sequence numbers.

Good scheduling systems should be directly associated with a corresponding monitoring system in which job completions are fed back in a timely manner. Systems permitting time or labor banks will suffer unless, of course, the payroll input is divorced from the scheduling feedback. Naturally, that would be a duplication of effort and is not recommended.

Overruns should be controlled since they will generally be an unnecessary drain on available resources. Overruns are often again the result of releasing too many shop orders to a given machine, particularly when the orders have identical raw materials and the material is not clearly "bundled" by order.

3. Use Realistic Dating Procedures

If your shop orders from a master schedule, the persons preparing that schedule should be aware of the time required to process the quantities on that schedule. They must also be aware of the capacities available on the various resources involved.

A two-way exchange between the master scheduling function and the shop scheduling system is desirable. Using a computer, it is quite easy to "explode" the master schedule into its requirements and to those requirements against available capacity. Where conflicts exist the master schedule can be adjusted to avoid them.

If, on the other hand, your shop load is basically the direct result of customer orders, it is prudent to withhold the promise date until a similar test has been made of the required resources.

These systems need not be complicated. They can be very effective even when available capacity and capacity requirements are only roughly known.

One company, using a small computer, has developed a loading system which permits the computer to automatically apply promise dates to customer orders up to a predetermined amount (say 85%) of capacity. Unless a "special" date is requested, the computer assigns the date of the next available time period. The sales department has the option of assigning the remainder of the available capacity (in this example 15%) to rush orders, etc.

When it comes time to schedule the orders for the next week's production, a tentative schedule for that week is produced along with a list of the orders loaded into the next time period. The total accumulated required machine time is printed. If less than 100% of capacity is scheduled for the coming period, the scheduler has the authority to select orders from the following period to make up a full schedule of 100% of capacity. If, for some reason, the tentative schedule shows more than 100% of capacity, the scheduler can make the necessary adjustments (overtime or rescheduling) to get a workable schedule.

The benefits of such systems include realistic schedules, fewer overdue shipments, less panic and more profits. The system is relatively uncomplicated and easily administered by those responsible for getting the job done.

Summary

Since rescheduling is really the problem, scheduling systems *should* be so designed to recognize the need for and make it as convenient as possible to reschedule. In designing such a system, every factor should be considered. However, only those factors of major importance may need to be used in the scheduling rules. To attempt to use all factors may make the logic too complex, and therefore, impossible to administer.

Source: Production and Inventory Management, 3rd quarter, 1971. American Production and Inventory Control Society, © 1971. Reprinted by permission.

9.11 PROBLEMS

Practice Problems

1. Use both forward and backward scheduling to add another job, D, to the schedules in Figure 9.2*a* and *b* that is due in hour 8 and has the following facility processing requirements: 3(2), 1(1), 2(2).

2. Same as in Problem 1, above, but the requirements are 1(2), 2(2), 3(1). What can you conclude from Exercises 1 and 2?

For Problems 3 to 6 use the following information. Quarterly demand for the next four quarters is 140, 215, 80, 20. Inventory holding cost is $10 per unit per quarter, and backordering cost is $12 per unit per quarter. All demand must be met by the end of the fourth quarter.

3. Devise a level-production strategy, a beginning inventory level, and an ending inventory level that minimize costs over the four quarters.

4. Devise a level-production strategy and a beginning inventory level to minimize total costs if the ending inventory level must be zero.

5. Devise a level-production strategy and an ending inventory level to minimize total costs if the beginning inventory level is zero.

6. Devise a two-level production strategy (i.e., nonlevel) that begins and ends the four quarters with no inventory. The level of production can change at any quarter.

7. Find a better aggregate schedule than those shown in Table 9.2 for the example problem.

More Complex Problems

8. Schedule the following jobs on two shifts to best meet their due hours.

Job	Hour Due	Facility, Hours Required (in order)
A	10	3(2), 1(2), 2(2), 1(1)
B	3	2(1), 3(2)
C	7	1(3), 2(2), 3(1)
D	12	2(1), 3(2), 2(2), 1(2), 3(1)
E	15	3(1), 2(3), 1(3), 3(3), 2(1)

9. Accept as many of the following jobs as possible on the loaded (with jobs W, Y, and Z) facilities below and set promised delivery hours, as early as possible, for them. All the jobs must be completed, if accepted, within the 8-hour period.

Job	Facility, Hours (in order)	Hour	Facility 1	Facility 2
A	2(1), 1(2), 2(1)	1	W	Y
B	1(2), 2(1), 1(1)	2	W	—
C	1(1), 2(1), 1(2), 2(1)	3	—	W
D	2(1), 1(1)	4	Z	—
		5	—	Z
		6	—	—
		7	—	—
		8	—	—

10. Demand forecasts for each of the quarters of the year for your product are 120, 140, 110, 90 with this pattern repeating in the future as far as can be told. Current workforce is 11 and each worker can produce 10 units in a quarter. Inventory costs are $10 per unit per quarter while shortage costs with backordering are $13 per unit per quarter. Hire and fire costs are each $100 per worker but idle workers cost $150 a quarter. Cost to produce units on overtime is an additional $15 each. Find the best long-term production plan if all demand must be met.

9.12 REFERENCES AND BIBLIOGRAPHY

1. Abernathy, W. J., Baloff, N., and Hershey, J. C., "The Nurse Staffing Problem: Issues and Prospects," *Sloan Management Review*, 13:87–109 (Fall 1971).

2. Berry, W. L. et al., *Master Scheduling*, Washington, DC: American Production and Inventory Control Society, 1979.

3. Bowman, E. H., "Production Planning by the Transportation Method of Linear Programming," *Journal of the Operations Research Society*, Feb. 1956.

4. Bowman, E. H., "Consistency and Optimality in Managerial Decision Making," *Management Science*, 9:310–321 (1963).

5. Buffa, E. S., "Aggregate Planning for Production," *Business Horizons*, 10:87–97 (Fall 1967).

6. Buffa, E. S., et al., "An Integrated Work Shift Scheduling System," *Decision Sciences*, 7:620–630 (Oct. 1976).

7. Dyer, J. S., "A Time-Sharing Computer Program for the Solution of the Multiple Criteria Problem," *Management Science*, 19:1379–1383 (1973).

8. Eilon, S., "Five Approaches to Aggregate Production Planning," *AIIE Transactions*, 7:118–131 (1975).

9. Fetter, R. B., and Thompson, J. D., "The Simulation of Hospital Systems," *Operations Research*, 13:689–711 (1965).

10. Fisk, J. C., "Integration of Aggregate Planning with Resource Requirements Planning," *Production and Inventory Management*, third quarter 1978, p. 87.

11. Fuller, J. A., "A Linear Programming Approach to Aggregate Scheduling," *Academy of Management Journal*, 18:129–137 (1975).

12. Harwood, G. B., and Lawless, R. W., "Optimizing Organizational Goals in Assigning Faculty Teaching Schedules," *Decision Sciences*, 6:513–524 (1975).

13. Heller, N. R., McEwan, J. T., and Stengel, W. W., *Computerized Scheduling of Police Manpower*, Vols. I and II, St. Louis: N. R. Heller and Associates, March 1973.

14. Holt, C. C., Modigliani, F., Muth, J. F., and Simon, H. A., *Planning Production, Inventories, and Work Force*, Englewood Cliffs, NJ: Prentice-Hall, 1960.

15. IBM, *The Production Information and Control System*, GE20-0280-2.

16. Judy, R. W., and Levine, J. B., *A New Tool for Educational Administrators*, Toronto: University of Toronto Press, 1965.

17. Krajewski, L. J. et al., "Disaggregation in Manufacturing and Service Organizations: Survey of Problems and Research," *Decision Sciences*, 8:1–18 (Jan. 1977).

18. Larson, R. C., *Urban Police Patrol Analysis*, Cambridge, MA: MIT Press, 1972.

19. Lee, W. B., and Khumawala, B. M., "Simulation Testing of Aggregate Production Planning Models in an Implementation Methodology," *Management Science*, 20:903–911 (1974).

20. Mabert, V. A., and Raedels, A. R., "Detail Scheduling of a Part-Time Work Force," *Decision Sciences*, 8:109–120 (Jan. 1977).

21. Mellichamp, J. M., and Love, R. M., "Production Switching Heuristics for the Aggregate Planning Problem," *Management Science*, 24:1242–1251 (1978).

22. Meredith, J. R., "The Implementation of Computer Based Systems," *Journal of Operations Management*, 2:11–22 (Oct. 1981).

23. Meredith, J., and Shershin, A. C., *EMS and Fire Activities in the South Florida Region*, Working paper 75-4, School of Business, Florida International University, Nov. 1975.

24. Miller, M. H., and Orr, D., "An Application of Control-Limit Models to the Management of Cash Balances," in A. A. Robicheck, ed., *Financial Research and Management Decisions*, New York: Wiley, 1967.

25. Reitman, J., *Computer Simulation Applications*, New York: Wiley, 1971.

26. Sasser, W. E., "Match Supply and Demand in Service Industries," *Harvard Business Review*, 80:133–140 (Nov.–Dec. 1976).

27. Schwarz, L. B. et al., "An Appraisal of the Empirical Performance of the Linear Decision Rule for Aggregate Planning," *Management Science*, 24:844–849 (1978).

28. Shapiro, S., "An Automated Court Scheduling System," Twelfth American Meeting of TIMS, Detroit, Sept. 1971.

29. Simon, H. A., and Newell, A., "Heuristic Problem Solving: The Next Advance," *Operations Research*, 6:1–10 (1968).

30. Taubert, W. H., "Search Decision Rule for the

Aggregate Scheduling Problem," *Management Science*, 14:343–359 (1958).

31. Warner, D. M., and Prawda, J., "A Mathematical Programming Model for Scheduling Nurses," *Management Science*, 19:411–422 (1972).

32. Wight, O. W., *Production and Inventory Management in the Computer Age*, Boston: Cahners, 1974.

33. Willoughby, T., Paterson, W., and Drummond, G., "Computer Aided Architectural Planning," *Operational Research Quarterly*, 21:91–99 (1970).

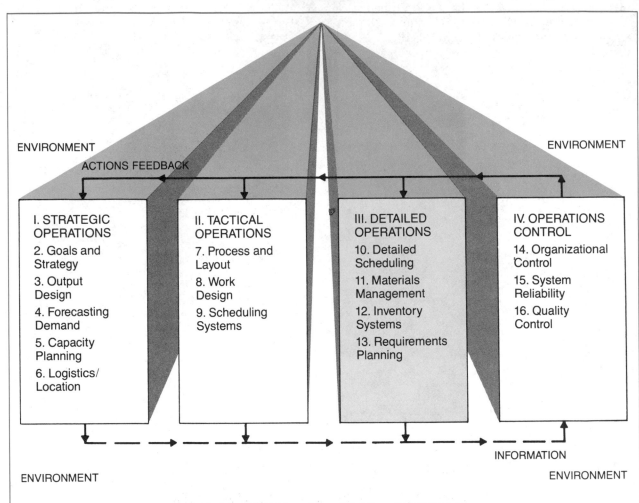

ENVIRONMENT

ACTIONS FEEDBACK

I. STRATEGIC OPERATIONS

2. Goals and Strategy

3. Output Design

4. Forecasting Demand

5. Capacity Planning

6. Logistics/ Location

II. TACTICAL OPERATIONS

7. Process and Layout

8. Work Design

9. Scheduling Systems

III. DETAILED OPERATIONS

10. Detailed Scheduling

11. Materials Management

12. Inventory Systems

13. Requirements Planning

IV. OPERATIONS CONTROL

14. Organizational Control

15. System Reliability

16. Quality Control

ENVIRONMENT

ENVIRONMENT

INFORMATION

ENVIRONMENT

DETAILED OPERATIONS
PROCESSING THE INPUTS

At this point of the text we have completed both the strategic and tactical design of the organization's operations. At the strategic level we have set goals and strategies, chosen and designed the outputs, forecast demand, determined the necessary operations capacity, and selected a facility location and distribution system. At the tactical level we have chosen a transformation process type and roughed out its general outlines. This includes the layout of the facility, the design of the workplaces and jobs, and the plan for the operation of the scheduling system.

We are now ready to get into the details of the operating system. There are only two major systems that require further intensive examination, and they both concern the coordination of inputs to focus on bringing the intended output into final form. The first of these is the scheduling system and it is critical not only to product firms but particularly to pure service organizations. The second is the materials management system, which is clearly oriented toward the facilitating good, though the concepts also apply, and are used, when services are directly applied to the recipient.

In Chapter 10 we look extensively at the subject of detailed, or "minute-by-minute," scheduling. We start with the subject of loading, or assigning jobs to work centers and equipment. We then move into the subject of sequencing jobs that are waiting at the work centers to be processed. We also cover in this section the sequencing problem for continuous flow operations where many products must be run on the same facility. We then move into the scheduling problem for project organizations, a totally different type of problem, and describe and illustrate the use of project scheduling techniques such as PERT and CPM. Last, the appendix to the chapter addresses the subject of queuing theory, particularly relevant to pure service organizations that directly treat the recipient, and present and illustrate formulas and graphs to aid in analyzing the service process.

Chapter 11 introduces the second major system in the subject of detailed operations, materials management. Here the entire materials flow process is described and tied back into the logistics system discussed in Chapter 6. Now we get into the details and start with the purchasing or procurement function and move into the materials handling and warehousing functions, noting particularly the tremendous technological leaps created by automation and computers. Last, we introduce inventory management, the subject of the next two chapters.

The inventory systems of Chapters 12 and 13 also are intimately concerned with the subject of scheduling, as they must, and in fact cover the topics that fall between aggregate scheduling in Chapter 9 and loading in Chapter 10. In Chapter 12 we discuss inventory systems to manage items whose demand is independent of other items made by the same organization. That is, we are primarily speaking of finished goods though other items, such as spare parts and some supplies, also fall into this category. We describe the variety of inventory systems available and some models to help decide when and how much to order to resupply these systems for both intermittent and continuous processes. Last, we discuss the concept of using safety stocks to improve service levels and illustrate the use of marginal analysis, decision trees, and simulation to aid in the selection of an appropriate safety stock level.

Chapter 13 completes our discussion of detailed operations by covering the case of managing materials that experience *dependent* demand, that is, subassemblies, components, parts, and supplies that are needed to produce a finished good whose demand is already known. We first describe how inventory systems for these items must be different from those in Chapter 12 and then discuss the critical importance of computers for these material requirements planning (MRP) systems. We discuss the computerized information inputs the MRP systems require and the common outputs they deliver and then detail the mechanics of such systems. The subject of lot sizing in MRP, how much and when to order, is also covered and some techniques are illustrated. Finally, an extensive MRP example concludes the chapter.

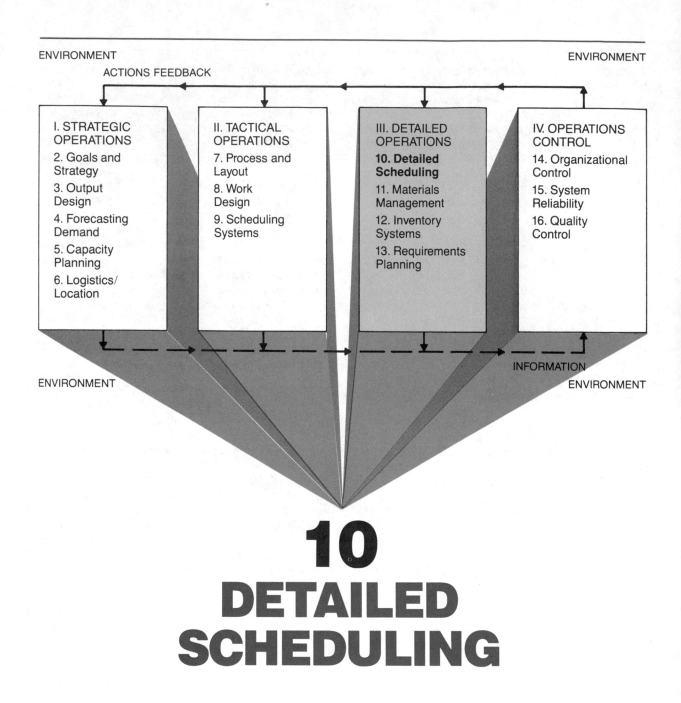

ENVIRONMENT

ACTIONS FEEDBACK

ENVIRONMENT

I. STRATEGIC OPERATIONS

2. Goals and Strategy

3. Output Design

4. Forecasting Demand

5. Capacity Planning

6. Logistics/ Location

II. TACTICAL OPERATIONS

7. Process and Layout

8. Work Design

9. Scheduling Systems

III. DETAILED OPERATIONS

10. Detailed Scheduling

11. Materials Management

12. Inventory Systems

13. Requirements Planning

IV. OPERATIONS CONTROL

14. Organizational Control

15. System Reliability

16. Quality Control

ENVIRONMENT

INFORMATION

ENVIRONMENT

10
DETAILED SCHEDULING

10

LEARNING OBJECTIVES

By the completion of this chapter the student should

- Have developed a feel for the loading problem and know the typical solution approaches used.
- Know how to solve an assignment problem.
- Be able to employ the index method.
- Better appreciate the nature of the sequencing problem and be familiar with the common aids and heuristics used.
- Understand how to read and construct a Gantt chart.
- Be aware of the common priority rules for sequencing and their strengths and limitations.
- Be able to use Johnson's rule in the proper situations.
- Know how and when to use the runout and critical ratio heuristics.
- Realize the importance of scheduling for project processes.
- Know the terminology employed in PERT and how to use PERT to plan project schedules.
- Understand CPM terminology and its procedure for expediting project tasks.
- Be familiar with some of the extensions of the PERT/CPM procedures.

In the previous chapter we looked at the various types of scheduling systems used in manufacturing and service industries and the crucial new role of computers in those systems. In keeping with the "tactical" level of that part of the book we focused on *aggregate* scheduling and production planning.

In this part of the text we move into "detailed" operations and hence will examine the generic task of operations scheduling at a much finer level. It is at this level in particular that plans so often go awry and productivity is lost—a machine unexpectedly breaks down, a skilled employee gets sick, or other such problems arise to ruin the carefully worked out plans. Yet, even without emergencies, productivity can be poor. In intermittent processes, for example, it is common for parts to spend 95 percent of their time waiting to get on facilities. Thus, a job that normally takes only a week to complete will require a five-month lead time to finally get it into the customer's hands.

We first look at the loading problem and illustrate its nature and some limited solution procedures with two examples. We then move into the sequencing/priority planning problem and discuss some useful tools and heuristics for these situations, illustrating one of the heuristics with a medical example involving sickle cell screening. Last, we consider the problem of scheduling the tasks in *project* operations and examine in detail the primary tools used here: PERT (program evaluation and review technique) and CPM (critical path method). We illustrate these tools with examples from public service organizations. An appendix to the chapter details the application of waiting line, or "queuing," theory to scheduling situations.

10.1 LOADING

For continuous process systems such as assembly line operations and chemical processors, loading is a moot problem because all output goes through essentially the same processes. And the load on each facility is fairly constant. But in electrical power generation an interesting loading problem arises in which an organization places a "load" on the utility at various times and in various amounts throughout the day. Linear programming-type models are currently being used in conjunction with mini- and microcomputers to optimally allocate the load so as to minimize energy cost. One IBM publication [15] indicates that a supermarket with $3000 per month electrical bills (for lighting, cooling food cases and freezers, etc.) can reduce costs up to 20 percent and more through proper scheduling of compressor use to produce an optimal load on the utility.

Allocating intermittent and batch jobs to facilities. But for many intermittent transformation systems there is considerable choice in determining which facilities should handle which jobs. Some choices are much better than others, however, because particular processes are more efficient for some jobs than for other jobs. It is desirable to process the operations as quickly as possible to minimize both job lateness and facility use time.

Table 10.1   Costs of Assigning Jobs to Various Work Centers

Work Centers	Jobs	1	2	3	4	5
R		$ 30	$ 50	$40	$ 80	$20
S		90	40	30	50	70
T		110	60	80	100	90
D		60	100	40	120	50
F		30	50	60	40	90

The Assignment Model

Allocation by the assignment model.

When the problem consists of deciding which of a number of jobs to allocate among a number of facilities on a one-to-one basis, the *assignment model* is a useful aid. For example, suppose the costs of producing five jobs at each of five different work centers is as shown in Table 10.1. Use of the assignment method will indicate which job should be allocated to which work center in order to minimize costs.

Solution Procedure

Although the problem appears simple enough, the solution is not always easy to obtain. For example, in Table 10.1 it appears by inspection that job 3 should go to center S. It costs less to assign job 3 to center S than any of the other jobs, *and* assigning job 3 to center S is cheaper than assigning it to any other center. Nevertheless, this would be a poor assignment, as we will soon see. Overall, it is less expensive to assign job 4 to center S, even though it costs $20 more initially. A better procedure than simple inspection is derived from the following logic.

Inspection is insufficient.

Since the assignments are on a one-to-one basis, then adding (or subtracting) a *constant* to every cost in the same row, or the same column, will not alter the relative costs of the assignments. For example, adding $10 to all the costs in column 1 of Table 10.1 still leaves the cost of assigning job 1 to center S $20 cheaper than assigning it to center T. Therefore, the least cost solution (which job to which center) will be unchanged by this process even though the *values* will be different.

Using *relative* costs.

One way, then, to identify good assignments is to subtract amounts from the rows and the columns so as to generate zeros in some of the cells, being careful not to generate negative numbers in the process. Then, if a feasible assignment can be made to only zero-valued cells this will result in the lowest possible cost assignment. The assignment method uses the essence of this approach in a five-step procedure. We will illustrate it with the example.

Step 1.   Subtract the lowest cost in each row from all the other costs in that row (Table 10.2).

Table 10.2   Row Reduction

	1	2	3	4	5
R	$30 - 20 = 10$	$50 - 20 = 30$	$40 - 20 = 20$	$80 - 20 = 60$	$20 - 20 = 0$
S	$90 - 30 = 60$	$40 - 30 = 10$	$30 - 30 = 0$	$50 - 30 = 20$	$70 - 30 = 40$
T	$110 - 60 = 50$	$60 - 60 = 0$	$80 - 60 = 20$	$100 - 60 = 40$	$90 - 60 = 30$
D	$60 - 40 = 20$	$100 - 40 = 60$	$40 - 40 = 0$	$120 - 40 = 80$	$50 - 40 = 10$
F	$30 - 30 = 0$	$50 - 30 = 20$	$60 - 30 = 30$	$40 - 30 = 10$	$90 - 30 = 60$

Step 2.   Next, subtract the lowest remaining cost in each column from all the other costs in that column. (Steps 1 and 2 may be reversed.) See Table 10.3.

Table 10.3   Column Reduction

	1	2	3	4	5
R	10	30	20	$60 - 10 = 50$	0
S	60	10	0	$20 - 10 = 10$	40
T	50	0	20	$40 - 10 = 30$	30
D	20	60	0	$80 - 10 = 70$	10
F	0	20	30	$10 - 10 = 0$	60

Step 3.   Since all costs at this point are nonnegative, the minimum possible assignment cost using these "new" cost elements would be zero. *If* a one-to-one assignment can be made to only cells with zero costs, this would be an optimal assignment. Rather than attempting to make an optimal assignment by trial and error we follow a special procedure: cover all the zeros in the matrix with the *fewest* possible number of straight horizontal and vertical lines. If the number of lines is equal to the number of rows (or columns) an assignment can be made. (The *minimum* number of lines never exceeds the number of rows or columns.) If not, then it is possible to improve the solution. (In Table 10.4 all the zeros can be covered with only four lines; hence, it is possible to improve the solution.)

Table 10.4   Optimality Test

10	30	2̶0̶	50	0̶
60	10	0̶	10	4̶0̶
~~50~~	~~0~~	~~2̶0̶~~	~~30~~	~~3̶0̶~~
20	60	0̶	70	1̶0̶
~~0̶~~	~~20~~	~~3̶0̶~~	~~0~~	~~6̶0̶~~

Step 4.   If an assignment can be made, go to Step 5. Otherwise, inspect the values *not* covered by lines and select the lowest one (10 in Table 10.4). *Subtract* this value from all the *uncovered* values and *add* it to the values at the *intersections* of the lines. Return to Step 3. (See Tables 10.5 and 10.6. We

find that, following the first improvement, it requires five lines to completely cover all the zeros in Table 10.6. An optimal assignment can therefore be made.)

Table 10.5 First Improvement

10 − 10 = 0	30 − 10 = 20	20	50 − 10 = 40	0
60 − 10 = 50	10 − 10 = 0	0	10 − 10 = 0	40
50	0	20 + 10 = 30	30	30 + 10 = 40
20 − 10 = 10	60 − 10 = 50	0	70 − 10 = 60	10
0	20	30 + 10 = 40	0	60 + 10 = 70

Table 10.6 Second Optimality Test

0	20	20	40	0
50	0	0	0	40
50	0	30	30	40
10	50	0	60	10
0	20	40	0	70

Step 5. To identify the optimal assignment, make the first assignment, if possible, to a row or column with only one zero in it. Delete that row and column and then continue the procedure. If more than one optimal solution exists, this process will quickly indicate that fact. (Table 10.7 illustrates the procedure. Assignments R-5, T-2, or D-3 are identified first. In this case there is only one solution: R-5, S-4, T-2, D-3, F-1, with minimum cost, from Table 10.1, of 20 + 50 + 60 + 40 + 30 = $200.

Table 10.7 Optimal Solution

	1	2	3	4	5
R	0	20	20	40	[0]
S	50	0	0	[0]	40
T	50	[0]	30	30	40
D	10	50	[0]	60	10
F	[0]	20	40	0	70

The most economical assignment of jobs to centers will therefore cost $200. The assignment method is quite flexible in handling special assignment conditions. Prohibited assignments, for example, can simply be marked out with an X without disrupting the solution process. The *maximization* problem can be treated simply by converting it to a minimization problem. This is accomplished by subtracting every entry in the original table from the largest entry. Once the optimal assignment is found, the original values (to be maximized) are used to determine the value (profit) of the solution.

Table 10.8 Stereo Repair Times in Hours

	John	Mary	Bo
Total Hours Available	20	15	5
Stereo			
Lloyds	4	3	3
Panasonic	2	3	2
Sound Design	5	(?)	3
Juliette	1	1	1
Heathkit	3	4	5
Realistic	2	3	1

The Index Method

Allocation through use of an efficiency index.

A simple variant of the assignment model can be used where more than one job is assigned to each work center. The approach, called the *index method*, is to calculate an "efficiency" index for each job on each work center and then to load the centers with those jobs that have the best indices for that center. Simply put, this method assigns jobs to the centers best able to do them. Let us demonstrate with a simple example.

Stereo Re-Pairs, Inc.

Bill, owner-manager of Stereo Re-Pairs, employs three part-time electrical engineering students, John, Mary, and Bo, to service the stereos customers bring to the shop. Bill knows that the three students have different experience on the various stereo brands and also knows on which stereo each of the students works best. Bill can usually estimate their repair times fairly accurately. On this particular Monday, six stereos, brought in on Saturday, are awaiting repair. Table 10.8 shows Bill's estimate of the repair times for each unit, depending on who services it, and the weekly hours each student works for him.

Assuming the students are all paid the same hourly rate, it is desirable to load the tasks on the students who are expected to be fastest on that repair. Letting the smallest repair time take an index value of 1.00 and giving other times an index equal to the ratio of repair time to the minimum repair time gives the results shown in Table 10.9.

We now attempt to load the tasks on those facilities where the index is 1.00. Notice, however, that if Bo is loaded first, the total hours will exceed the 5 hours available, so the procedure is initiated with John, who has the most hours available. John then gets the Panasonic, Juliette, and Heathkit, as indicated and circled, for a total of 6 hours, leaving $20 - 6 = 14$ hours available for the rest of the week. Mary next takes the Lloyds (3 hours), leaving the Sound Design and Realistic to Bo (4 hours total).

In case a facility with the lowest index becomes overloaded, jobs are simply shifted to the facility with the next lower index that is not already

Table 10.9 Index Loading Procedure

Stereo	John Hours	John Index	Mary Hours	Mary Index	Bo Hours	Bo Index
Lloyds	4 (4/3 =)	1.33	3	1.00	3	1.00
Panasonic	2	1.00	3	1.50	2	1.00
Sound Design	5	1.67	(?)	—	3	1.00
Juliette	1	1.00	1	1.00	1	1.00
Heathkit	3	1.00	4	1.33	5	1.67
Realistic	2	2.00	3	3.00	1	1.00
Hours remaining	14		12		1	

overloaded. In some situations the work may have to be split between facilities. For example, if Mary only had 1 hour available to spend on the Lloyds and then was to leave the rest of the job to John, he would *not* spend (Mary's remaining) 2 hours on it. Rather, he would have two-thirds of the job left to finish, which would take him ⅔ × 4 = 2.67 hours.

The model is simple enough that pay rates can also be easily included. This is done by deriving indices based on Bill's *labor* cost (rate × hours) rather than just the hours. The hours available would still constrain the allocations, however, not the labor cost per student.

10.2 SEQUENCING

The next scheduling topic we will consider is sequencing, which is most relevant for intermittent processes. Sequencing refers to ordering the jobs so as to achieve some operations goal such as maximizing job throughput, minimizing job lateness, and so forth. An illustration of the importance of the sequencing problem was given in Chapter 5 (Figure 5.1) where the effect of poor scheduling was shown to restrict capacity quite seriously by overloading facilities at critical times.

Approaches to efficient job ordering.

In this section we will consider first the historical use of Gantt charts to pictorially aid in the sequencing problem and then look at some priority rules that have been extensively tested to determine their value in maximizing facility utilization, getting jobs through the operations, and minimizing late deliveries. We will then expand our horizon and consider some sequencing heuristics such as Johnson's rule, critical ratio, and runout time.

Gantt Charts

The flexibility of Gantt charts.

Probably the oldest, most useful, and yet most easily understood graphical aid for conveying the sequence and status of operations is the *Gantt chart*, developed by Henry L. Gantt, a scientific management pioneer, around 1917. The Gantt chart usually shows planned *and* actual progress on a number of

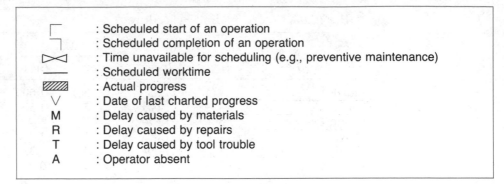

Figure 10.1 Gantt chart symbols.

items displayed against a horizontal time scale. The items may be jobs, machines, departments, parts, staff, and so forth. A variety of symbols may be added to the chart, depending on the activity being charted. Some common symbols are given in Figure 10.1 and their use is illustrated in Figure 10.2. This latter figure illustrates job loadings for three facilities. As of July 15, 5 P.M., job 481 was completed as planned, even with the shutdown of facility A-2 on July 9; and job 502, although completed, took half a day longer than expected. Job 563 was delayed one day due to lack of materials and still is incomplete and job 459, besides starting late, was delayed for repairs. Last, job 496 is half a day ahead of schedule.

Sequencing by Gantt chart.

The use of a Gantt chart for sequencing is illustrated in Figure 10.3. In this situation the jobs to be considered over the next two weeks with their facility and time requirements, in order, are as shown below the figure.

Figure 10.3 shows only one possible sequencing; a better one might have been to put job 703 on facility A-2 first at day 6½ and then job 717 on A-2 so facility A-5 would be better utilized over the two-week duration. What is "best" depends on a number of factors such as the importance and due dates of the jobs, the relative expense of the facilities, and so on. If the objective is to meet due dates, *backward scheduling*, as described in Chapter 9, is useful. This is also the basic approach of *priority planning* techniques, such as *materials requirements planning* (MRP), which we discuss in detail in Chapter 13.

Backward scheduling to meet due dates.

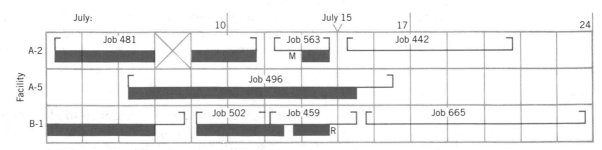

Figure 10.2 Typical Gantt status chart.

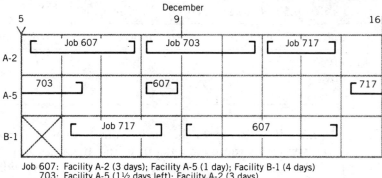

Job 607: Facility A-2 (3 days); Facility A-5 (1 day); Facility B-1 (4 days)
    703: Facility A-5 (1½ days left); Facility A-2 (3 days)
    717: Facility B-1 (2½ days); Facility A-2 (2 days); Facility A-5 (6 days)

Figure 10.3 Sequencing by Gantt chart.

A number of variations of the basic Gantt chart have been developed with the use of pegs, colored string, colored tape, and so forth. Nevertheless, the purpose remains the same: to clearly communicate the current status of operations, facilities, and jobs for purposes of expediting, sequencing, resource allocation between idle and bottleneck facilities, and so forth.

Although the Gantt chart performs the function of communicating job and facility status quite well, it is not a scheduling technique per se, and is thus not especially useful for determining the best sequence of activities, or for rescheduling activities. Other approaches, described in the following section, have been found more useful for these situations.

Priority Rules for Sequencing

An ideal sequencing rule would be one that resulted in all jobs being completed on time, with maximum facility utilization but minimal in-process inventory. Since no rule is perfect, the task is to identify that rule which minimizes the sum of these interrelated costs. In some organizations, the cost of lateness will far overshadow the other costs (e.g., ambulance services) while, in other organizations, equipment utilization (e.g., machine shops), or inventories (e.g., retailers), will result in the largest cost. It may also be that, at different times in an organization's life, different factors will be of first importance and so the best rule will change. Such rules are known more generally as "decision rules." When applied to the sequencing problem they are known as **priority rules.**

Best sequence depends on goals.

Let us look at some of these priority rules, how they are used, and what costs they tend to minimize. The situation is this: There is a work station with a number of jobs waiting to be run. Which job should be selected next? Table 10.10 illustrates such a situation in which three jobs are waiting for processing. The due date (assuming the current time is zero) and expected operation (processing) time for each job are given in the table, plus a calculation of the "dynamic slack" for each job: its due date less its expected operation time.

Table 10.10 Characteristics of Three Jobs

Job	Due Date	Operation Time	"Dynamic Slack"
ABC	4	1	3
PDQ	7	5	2
XYZ	2	2	0

Four priority rules.

FCFS.

Table 10.11 presents the performance results of invoking four different priority rules for these jobs. Let us follow the analysis conducted using Priority Rule 1: first come (to the work center), first served (FCFS). We assume the jobs arrived in the order listed in Table 10.10. First we repeat the operation times given in Table 10.10 and from this calculate the **flow time** for each job—the time it takes for the job to get through this process, that is, the job's operation time plus its **queue time** while waiting for other jobs to finish on the facilities. For example, PDQ's queue time waiting for ABC is 1 day. The derivation of these flow times is illustrated for Rule 1 in Figure 10.4.

Next is listed the due date, again from Table 10.10. The last column showing lateness is then simply the flow time less the due date. If the job is not late it has a 0 in this column, although we track the "algebraic differ-

Table 10.11 Priority Rule Results

Job Order	Operation Time	Flow Time	Due Date	Days Late
RULE 1: FCFS				
ABC	1	1	4	0 (−3)
PDQ	5	6	7	0 (−1)
XYZ	2	8	2	6
Average		5.0		2.0(0.7)
RULE 2: Due date				
XYZ	2	2	2	0 (0)
ABC	1	3	4	0 (−1)
PDQ	5	8	7	1
Average		4.3		0.3(0)
RULE 3: Minimum slack				
XYZ	2	2	2	0 (0)
PDQ	5	7	7	0 (0)
ABC	1	8	4	4
Average		5.7		1.3(1.3)
RULE 4: SOT				
ABC	1	1	4	0 (−3)
XYZ	2	3	2	1
PDQ	5	8	7	1
Average		4.0		0.7(−.3)

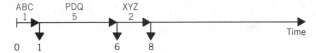

Figure 10.4 Rule 1 flow times.

ence" (days early) in parentheses also. Last, we calculate the average (per job) flow time and lateness for this rule.

Due date.   Rule 2 orders jobs by when they are due, thereby trying to minimize lateness but not being concerned with how long jobs take to get through operations (thus ignoring the cost of materials "in-process"). Yet we see that this rule lowered the flow time somewhat while significantly lowering the lateness.

Rule 3 applies the logic that those jobs that cannot "afford" to be delayed should be processed first. Thus those jobs that have more slack are all held back, and the slack used up, while more critical jobs are worked on. We see

Min slack.   from the average flow time for this rule that jobs are, on average, held longer with this rule than with either of the two preceding rules (for this particular situation). Yet the average lateness is worse than for the due date rule.

SOT.   Rule 4 orders those jobs with the smallest operation times (and probably the easiest) first. We see that the use of this rule minimizes the average flow time of the jobs, as would be expected. But, perhaps surprisingly, it also seems to give good results on lateness, running second only to the due date rule, and, "algebraically," (values in parentheses), is best. This is no accident; the SOT rule is indeed superior, as we will discuss somewhat later.

There are quite a few priority rules; for example, Conway investigated 92 of them [7]. Such rules can be categorized on a number of different bases, such as on the costs they most often minimize. Another basis is whether they are static (based on situations existing at the time the job came in, such as order of acceptance) or dynamic (taking current events into account such as delays and rush orders).

A number of researchers [1, 3, 10, 11, 16] have investigated the characteristics of many of the more common priority sequencing rules and have come to some interesting conclusions. The following rules are in most common use:

- FCFS   First come, first served. The first job to arrive at a work center (not into the organization) is processed first. This rule is based on "fairness" to all jobs waiting at the same work center and is probably the most common rule used in processing people for service.

- DUE DATE   A job entering the organization first will be given an earlier due date independent of job length. The rule is justified to recipients on the basis of "fairness": "His job came in first— then yours is next."

- SOT   Shortest operation time. Do the short, easy jobs first and get them out of the way.

- LOT   Longest operation time. The longer jobs are often the bigger, more important (and profitable) ones and should be done first.

- SS   Static slack. "Slack" here equals the due date minus the time of arrival at the work center. Jobs with the smallest slack are done first.

- SS/RO   Static slack per remaining operation. If two jobs have the same static slack but one has more operations remaining to be completed, it should have the higher priority because it will require more setups.

- DS/RO   Dynamic slack per remaining operation. The dynamic slack is defined as the remaining time until the due date *less* the remaining expected processing time.

- COVERT   Priority is given to the job with the *highest* ratio of cost of delay, c, over processing time, t (c over t). This rule attempts to operate like the SOT rule but to also consider the cost of delays, c.

- RAND   Random order.

The general superiority of the SOT rule.

In terms of maximizing work flow through the operations, maximizing facility utilization, and minimizing lateness, the SOT rule was often found to be the best. Not considering the COVERT rule for the moment (which was not included in most of the research), the SOT rule results in more jobs being finished early, shorter average flow times, shorter in-queue waiting times, and higher labor and equipment utilization. In addition, the SOT rule ranks second only to the DS/RO and Due Date rules in minimizing the percentage of jobs completed late. However, it is this one characteristic of the SOT rule that hampers its use—when short jobs are always taken before long jobs there will invariably be some *very* long jobs that just *never* seem to get done. Perhaps this is a legitimate justification for expediting.

Improving the SOT rule.

Researchers have attempted to devise SOT-type rules that would negate this one drawback of SOT. And that, of course, was the basis for devising the COVERT rule [3]. However, the determination of the "cost" of delay is a difficult matter and not easily identified with a particular job once it is in processing. Also, such modifications to the SOT rule destroy one of its most important characteristics—its simplicity of use. Any worker can usually tell which job among those available is going to be easiest, thereby eliminating the sequencing task and freeing the operations manager to handle bottlenecks, overdue jobs, and so forth.

In addition to the formal priority rules above, there are also informal priority systems. Examples are most important customer first, most profitable item first, and most crucial subassembly first. Although well justified, these priority rules are sometimes not used at all in organizations. Instead, "chaos" rules. That is, a worker may be told to start on one job, and 15 minutes after a customer's call, told to work on that customer's job instead.

The hat switching problem. This "hat switching" often consumes more of a day than actual productive work.

Johnson's Rule for Sequencing Jobs

The general sequencing problem usually involves getting jobs through the operations as quickly as possible. The dual objectives are to (1) maximize facility utilization by smoothly processing a large number of jobs, and (2) avoid excessively delaying any one job. As a simple motivating example, consider the situation of two jobs, J_1 and J_2, going through two facilities in the *same order*: F_1 and then F_2. Suppose one of the jobs (say J_1) requires 4 hours on F_1 and 5 hours on F_2 and the other job (J_2) requires 7 hours on F_1 and 4 hours on F_2. In what order should the jobs be run to minimize the total facility time?

Sequencing two jobs on two facilities.

This problem is simple enough that we may enumerate both of the possible solutions: start J_1 first or J_2 first. Figure 10.5 illustrates the Gantt charts for each solution. In the case of J_1 first, Figure 10.5a, we see that due to our scheduling there exists some delay on facility 2 before the second job can begin. Hopefully, scheduling job 2 first will eliminate this delay. And we see in Figure 10.5b that indeed it does; however, even with the delay eliminated, it takes *longer* to process both jobs: 16 hours with J_2 scheduled first compared with 15 hours with J_1 first.

Upon further examination we can see the reason why. No matter which job was scheduled first, the two jobs completed work on facility 1 in 11 hours. Therefore, if the job with the longest time on facility 2 is scheduled last, the overall duration for completion of both jobs would be greatest. The message then is clear: schedule the job with the *shortest* time on facility 2 *last*.

Scheduling the shortest jobs.

By the same token, it would be well to get jobs *started* on facility 2 as soon as possible. Hence, the *short* jobs on facility 1 should be scheduled as *early* as possible. These intuitive conclusions have been formalized by S. M. Johnson [16] in a form now referred to as **Johnson's rule,** which deals with the task of optimally sequencing N jobs through two facilities in the same order.

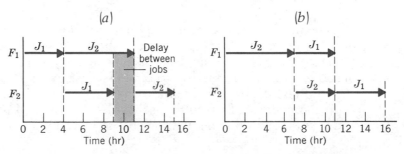

Figure 10.5 The result of two sequencing possibilities: (a) J_1 first; (b) J_2 first.

Johnson's rule.

> If the shortest time for a job is on the *first* facility, schedule the job as *early* as possible. If it is on the *second* facility, schedule it as *late* as possible. Delete that job and repeat the procedure.

Let us consider an example.

Sickle Cell Screening

Five patients who had positive tests on "sickledex" are to be scheduled for definitive testing by electrophoresis and then consultation with a physician for genetic education. A mobile laboratory is to be used, starting at 8 A.M. Naturally, it is desirable to conclude the screening and education tasks as quickly as possible, so that the mobile lab may be used elsewhere. Based on the sickledex results, the nurse estimates that the screening and education times (in minutes) listed in Table 10.12 will be required. In what order should the patients be scheduled and when may the work be expected to be completed?

Table 10.12 Sickle Cell Screening Time Estimates in Minutes

	Patient				
	1	2	3	4	5
Lab (electrophoresis)	120	30	20	40	60
Genetic education	10	60	120	30	60

Analysis. Applying Johnson's rule, the shortest time is 10 minutes in the second task with patient 1. Thus, this patient should be scheduled last. The problem now appears as

P_1	P_2	P_3	P_4	P_5					
120	30	20	40	60					P_1
10	60	120	30	60					

The next shortest time is for P_3 on task 1 (20 minutes), so it is scheduled first. Deleting this patient, the next shortest time is 30, but this appears twice. In general, ties may be broken arbitrarily; but here there really is no problem, since for P_2 the 30 is on the first task and for P_4 it is on the second. Hence, P_2 is scheduled right after P_3 (see below) and P_4 just before P_1, leaving P_5 in the middle. The resulting schedule is illustrated in Figure 10.6; it appears that the mobile lab will be able to leave by about 1 P.M.

P_3	P_2	P_5	P_4	P_1

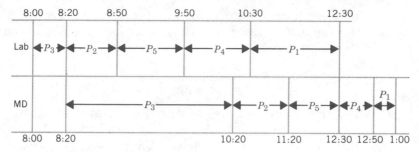

Figure 10.6 Mobile lab schedule.

The multiplicity of optimal schedules. Although Johnson's rule will find an optimal schedule, it is not necessarily the *only* optimal schedule—there may be others also, but none will finish *sooner*. It should also be noted that there are extensions to Johnson's rule concerning the case of two *jobs* and *N facilities*, and for certain *N* jobs—three facilities situations, but there is not a solution to the *general* sequencing problem, although Johnson's approach usually gives good results even in these cases. However, the general sequencing problem is not just limited to jobs undergoing the same sequence of operations.

The need for a policy. Under certain conditions the more general sequencing problem can be formulated and solved by linear programming, but, by and large, such decisions must be made on the spot and often by someone who is not a manager but "just works there." What is needed is a *policy*, rather than a solution model, which will give good results most of the time under real operating conditions. This is the purpose of the priority rules discussed earlier. It might be noted that some of these priority rules are based on the general approach embodied in Johnson's rule.

Runout and Critical Ratio Heuristics*

N-job, one-machine problem. The "runout" and "critical ratio" approaches to sequencing extend our analysis to entire processing lines but only one job can be using the facilities at a time. In a sense, this situation is the same as the *N*-job, one-machine problem which we looked at first in this section. The situation is actually quite different, however, in that priority rules are employed when there will be a number of following operations on the job before it is completed. In the case here, we consider a facility that will *complete* all the work on the job. Moreover, we are producing "to stock" rather than "to order" and there are usually some stores of the items that are still available for use. These stores will be depleted soon, though, and must be replenished.

In the **runout** method, we simply produce next the item that we will run out of first.

$$\text{runout time} = \frac{\text{inventory remaining}}{\text{demand rate}} \tag{10.1}$$

*Refer to the discussion on heuristics in Appendix II to Chapter 9.

In the **critical ratio** (CR) method, this logic is carried one step further and the remaining processing time is also factored in so that jobs with greater remaining processing times are viewed as more important. The equation is

$$\text{critical ratio} = \frac{\text{runout time}}{\text{processing time}} \tag{10.2}$$

For critical ratios above or near 1.0, we are not usually concerned because stock is being used up slower or at about the same rate as processing time. But for values near 0.8 or less, the stock is being used significantly faster than the remaining processing time and there is a good chance of a shortage. Clearly, the lower the critical ratio the greater the priority, and the greater the need for management intervention.

CR < 1?

Only the next job.

Table 10.13 illustrates these rules. As can be seen, the runout rule sequences the jobs in the order R3S, X17, and 27Y because this is the order in which they will be depleted. It should be noted, however, that the runout method is only used to select the *next* job. After R3S has completed processing, a new runout analysis should be conducted. There are two reasons for this: (1) conditions may have changed the urgency of the other jobs or (2) a recently completed job may now again be more urgent than one of the other jobs. For example, if X17 is run next, it may be that, following its completion, job R3S is again due to run out and job 27Y still has quite a while before it will run out. That is, not every job may need to be run in every "cycle" of processing, or to state it another way, some jobs may need to be run more often than all the others.

The calculation of the critical ratio in Table 10.13 totally reorders the sequencing of the jobs: X17, 27Y, and R3S. This rule operates similar to the minimum slack priority rule and says that even though job R3S is due to run out soon, a new batch can also be run very quickly so we should not worry about it. Though responsive to lateness considerations, the critical ratio rule often delays the processing of items until the need is more critical. This may, then, result in increasing the in-process inventory investment significantly and if the jobs are run in the new sequence derived, R3S will be *extremely* late. Again, the message is to use this approach only for the *next* job and reevaluate when that job is completed.

We will address the issue of producing multiple products on one set of facilities again in Chapter 12, but more from the perspective of minimizing

Table 10.13 Runout and Critical Ratio Sequencing Heuristics

Job	Units of Inventory Remaining	Daily Demand (units)	Runout Time (RT) (days)	Sequence by Runout	Batch Process Time (PT) (days)	CR = RT/PT	Sequence by CR
X17	12	4	3	2nd	4	0.75	1st
R3S	8	4	2	1st	2	1.00	3rd
27Y	20	2	10	3rd	12	0.83	2nd

production and inventory investment costs while maintaining feasible production schedules. We will find that the runout concept has application in that case also.

10.3 PLANNING AND SCHEDULING PROJECTS

In this section we will focus in some detail on the scheduling of projects. In the area of project management the scheduling function is probably the single most important element in the success of the project, and considerable research has been done on the topic.

Most important element.

It has been found, for example, that progress in a project is not at all uniform, but instead follows the life cycle curve shown in Figure 10.7. As the project is initiated, progress is slow as responsibilities are assigned and organization takes place. But the project gathers speed during the implementation stage and much progress is made. As the end of the project draws near, the more difficult tasks that were postponed earlier must now be completed, yet people are being drawn off the project and activity is "winding down" so the end keeps slipping out of reach.

Life cycle.

One of the major responsibilities of the project manager during the project initiation stage is to define all the project tasks in as much detail as possible so they can be scheduled and costed out, and responsibility can be assigned. This set of task descriptions is called the "work breakdown structure" and provides the basis for the project "master schedule."

WBS.

Such a schedule is illustrated in Figure 10.8 for an assembly-line robot installation project. Milestone, commitment, and completion points are illustrated and actual progress is graphed on the chart as well. We see from the last status update that the project is a month behind schedule.

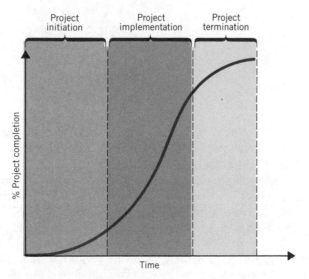

Figure 10.7 Life cycle of a project.

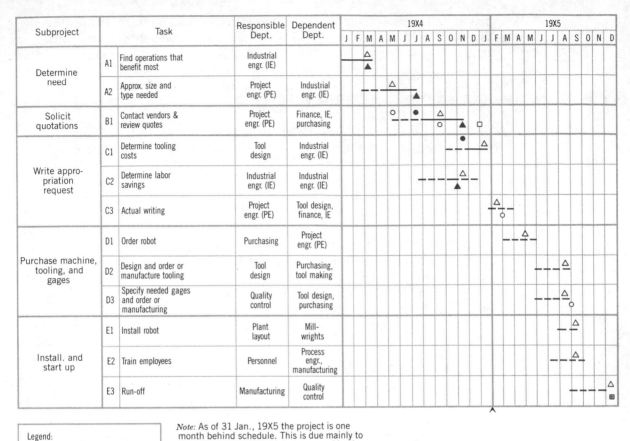

Subproject	Task		Responsible Dept.	Dependent Dept.	19X4 J F M A M J J A S O N D	19X5 J F M A M J J A S O N D
Determine need	A1	Find operations that benefit most	Industrial engr. (IE)		△ ▲	
	A2	Approx. size and type needed	Project engr. (PE)	Industrial engr. (IE)	△ ▲	
Solicit quotations	B1	Contact vendors & review quotes	Project engr. (PE)	Finance, IE, purchasing	o ● △ o ▲ □	
Write appropriation request	C1	Determine tooling costs	Tool design	Industrial engr. (IE)	● △	
	C2	Determine labor savings	Industrial engr. (IE)	Industrial engr. (IE)	△ ▲	
	C3	Actual writing	Project engr. (PE)	Tool design, finance, IE		△ o
Purchase machine, tooling, and gages	D1	Order robot	Purchasing	Project engr. (PE)		△
	D2	Design and order or manufacture tooling	Tool design	Purchasing, tool making		△
	D3	Specify needed gages and order or manufacturing	Quality control	Tool design, purchasing		△ o
Install. and start up	E1	Install robot	Plant layout	Mill-wrights		△
	E2	Train employees	Personnel	Process engr., manufacturing		△
	E3	Run-off	Manufacturing	Quality control		△ ⊞

Note: As of 31 Jan., 19X5 the project is one month behind schedule. This is due mainly to the delay in task C1, which was caused by the late completion of A2.

Legend:
+ Project completion
□ Contractual commitment
△ Planned completion
▲ Actual completion
⋏ Status date
o Milestone planned
● Milestone achieved
- - Planned progress
— Actual progress

Figure 10.8 Project master schedule.

How project scheduling differs from other processes.   The scheduling of project activities is highly complex because of (1) the number of activities required, (2) the precedence relationships among the activities, and (3) the limited-time nature of the project. Project scheduling is similar to that discussed earlier in some ways but still differs significantly. For example, the basic network approaches, **PERT*** (program evaluation and review technique) and **CPM*** (critical path method), are based on variations of the Gantt chart. Figure 10.8 is, in a sense, a type of Gantt chart

*PERT was developed by the U.S. Navy with Booz-Allen Hamilton and Lockheed Corporation in the late 1950s to manage the Polaris missile project. CPM was developed independently in the same time period by Du Pont, Inc.

but is inadequate for scheduling the multitude of subtasks that compose, for example, Task A1. That is, a project schedule has to handle an enormous number of different operations and materials that must be coordinated with each other in such a way that following activities can take place and the entire project (job) be completed by the due date. For example, the use of a shortest operation time (SOT) priority rule would be entirely inappropriate here. Rather, the *critical* operation, which must precede all the remaining operations, should be performed next.

SOT versus PERT.

The scheduling procedure for project operations must be able to not only identify and handle the variety of tasks that must be done but also handle their time sequencing. In addition, it must be able to integrate the performance and timing of all the tasks with the project as a whole so that control can be exercised, for example, by shifting resources from operations with *slack* (permissible slippage) to other operations whose delay might threaten the project's timely completion. The tasks involved in planning and scheduling project operations are

Slack.

Planning: The determination of *what* must be done and which tasks must *precede* others.

Scheduling: The determination of *when* the tasks must be completed; when they *can* and when they *must,* be started; which tasks are *critical* to the timely completion of the project; and which tasks have *slack* in their timing and how much.

Next we will investigate the use of PERT and CPM for these tasks.

PERT/CPM For Project Scheduling

Although PERT and CPM originally had some differences in the way their activities were determined and laid out, many current approaches to project scheduling minimize these differences and present an integrated view of an approach instead, as we shall see here. It will be helpful to define some terms first.

An integrated methodology is used.

- *Activity:* One of the project operations, or tasks, that requires resources and takes some amount of time to complete.
- *Event:* The completion of an activity, or series of activities, at a particular point in time.
- *Network:* The set of all project activities graphically interrelated through the precedence relationships. In this text we let the network lines (or *arcs*) represent the activities, the connections between the lines (called *nodes*) represent the events, and arrows on the arcs represent the precedence relations. (This is typical of the PERT approach; in CPM the nodes represent the activities.)
- *Path:* A series of connected activities between two events.
- *Critical:* Activities, events, or collections of activities and events, which, if delayed, will delay the entire project. The **critical paths** of a project

are those continuous paths from the start to the finish of a project that contain the critical activities and events.

We will use an example to illustrate the PERT/CPM technique.

Black Cross Plan "E"

The Black Cross is a volunteer organization recently formed in California to prepare for and respond to the long-overdue earthquake expected there in the last decade. They have developed a single, efficient, uniform response plan (termed "plan E") consisting of 10 major activities for all cities where the earthquake causes major damage. Clearly, completing the project activities as quickly as possible is crucial in saving lives and property and aiding victims in distress. The staff of Black Cross has determined not only the most *Three activity time* likely times for each activity but the fastest times in which they could prob-*estimates.* ably be done (termed *optimistic time*) as well as the slowest (termed *pessimistic time*) that might be encountered by a project team out in the field (when everything went wrong). The project operations and the optimistic, most likely, and pessimistic times, in hours, are listed in Table 10.14, along with the activities that must precede them.

Construction of the Network: Ordering the Activities

Following A project "network" illustrating the activities and their interdependence *precedence in* is constructed by first examining Table 10.14 for those activities that have *constructing the* no activities preceding them. These activities *a*, *b*, and *c*, are all drawn out *network.* of a starting node, which, for convenience in Figure 10.9, we have labeled **1**.

Next, the activity list is scanned for activities that require only that activities *a*, *b*, or *c* be completed. Thus, activities *d* through *h* can be drawn in the network next. Activity *d* can be drawn directly out of node **2**, and activity *h* can be drawn out of node **4**. But if node **3** indicates the completion *The use of dummy* of activity *b*, how can activities *e*, *f*, and *g* be drawn since they also depend *activities.* on the completion of activity *c*? This is accomplished by the use of a *dummy*

Table 10.14   Plan "E" Activity Times (Hours)

Project Activity	Optimistic Time, t_o	Most Likely Time, t_m	Pessimistic Time, t_p	Required Preceding Activities
a	5	11	11	none
b	10	10	10	none
c	2	5	8	none
d	1	7	13	*a*
e	4	4	10	*b, c*
f	4	7	10	*b, c*
g	2	2	2	*b, c*
h	0	6	6	*c*
i	2	8	14	*g, h*
j	1	4	7	*d, e*

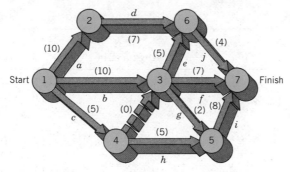

Figure 10.9 Plan "E" project operations network.

activity from event **4** to event **3**, which indicates that event **3** depends on activity *c* (event **4**) being accomplished as well as activity *b*. The dummy activity, shown as a dashed line in Figure 10.9, requires no time to accomplish, but the linkage is necessary, so that activities *e*, *f*, and *g* cannot start before *both* activities *b* and *c* are completed.

What if activity *e* did *not* require that activity *c* be completed whereas *f* and *g* did? If this was the case, the diagram would be drawn as shown in Figure 10.10. Care must be taken to ensure that the *proper* precedence relations are drawn in the diagram; otherwise, the project might be unnecessarily delayed.

The remainder of the diagram is drawn in the same manner. Activity *i*, which depends on activities *g* and *h*, comes out of node **5**, which represents the completion of *g* and *h*. A similar situation occurs with activity *j*. All of the remaining activities without completion nodes (*f*, *i*, and *j*) are then directed to the project completion node **7**.

Calculating Activity Durations

We have now completed a *graphic* network representation of the precedence information shown in Table 10.14. We next need to place expected activity times on the network so we can see which activities must be scheduled first and when they must be completed for the project not to be delayed.

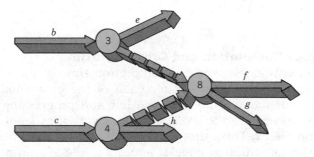

Figure 10.10 Proper use of dummy activities.

Table 10.15 Activity Expected, Variance, and Slack Times

Activity	Expected Time, t_e	Variance, σ^2	Slack
a	10	1	0*
b	10	0	$11 - 0 - 10 = 1$
c	5	1	$8 - 0 - 5 = 3$
d	7	4	0*
e	5	1	$17 - 10 - 5 = 2$
f	7	1	$21 - 10 - 7 = 4$
g	2	0	$13 - 10 - 2 = 1$
h	5	1	$13 - 5 - 5 = 3$
i	8	4	$21 - 12 - 8 = 1$
j	4	1	0*

*On critical path

The estimation of the three activity times in Table 10.14 is typically based on the assumption that the events that can go wrong when doing a task are not necessarily the same, nor do they even have the same effect, as the events that can go right. For example, a critical piece of equipment may be wearing out, which, if it is working well, can do a task in 2 hours that normally takes 3 hours. But if the equipment is performing poorly, the task may require 10 hours. Thus, we may see nonsymmetrical optimistic and pessimistic task times for project activities such as for activities *e* and *h* in Table 10.14. Note also in the table that for some activities, such as *b*, the durations are known with certainty.

Beta distribution. The general form of nonsymmetrical or skewed distribution used in approximating PERT activity times is called the *Beta* distribution and has a mean (the expected completion time, t_e) given by Equation 10.3 and a variance, or uncertainty in this time, σ^2, given by Equation 10.4. The results of these calculations are listed in Table 10.15 and indicated on the network of Figure 10.11 in parentheses.

$$t_e = \frac{t_o + 4t_m + t_p}{6} \tag{10.3}$$

$$\sigma^2 = \left(\frac{t_p - t_o}{6}\right)^2 \tag{10.4}$$

Project Completion and Critical Paths

Calculating early start time. To determine the expected completion time of the entire project, *early start times*, T_E, are calculated for each of the event nodes in the project, working from the *start* node on the left and progressing to the right. The early start times are the soonest that *all* activities leading into each node can be completed. These times are shown next to each of the nodes in Figure 10.11. Starting with 0 at node **1**, nodes **2** and **4** are simply the times of the activities preceding them. However, node **3** is the *latest* of activity *b* or *c*

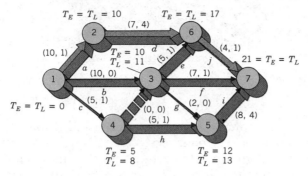

Figure 10.11 Early start times, latest allowable times, and critical path.

since *both* of these activities must be completed before activities following event **3** can begin.

Similarly, event **5** is the later of the two paths **3-5** or **4-5.** Thus, the time for event **5** is 12 (10 + 2 for **3-5** is greater than 5 + 5 for **4-5**). Completing the project nodes, it is found that node **7**, project completion, has a time of 21 (hours); this is then the soonest that the project can be completed. The activity path that resulted in this value (and sometimes there is more than one) is identified as the *critical path* of the project and is shown with a heavy arrow in Figure 10.11. This means that any delay in the activities along this path will delay the entire project. In addition to a project critical path, each node has its own critical path. For example, the critical path to node **5** is **1-3-5** since this is the path that defines the earliest that node **5** can be realized and the activities following it begun.

Slack Time

All activities on the critical path have zero "slack"—that is, there is no room for delay in any activity on the critical path without delaying the entire project. Activities off the critical path may delay up to a point where further delay would delay the entire project. This is called their *slack.* A number of ways exist to calculate this slack but one of the easiest involves calculating another set of times for each event node, its **latest allowable time,** T_L. This is the latest time that an event can be delayed without delaying the entire project. It is calculated similarly to the early start time but is initiated from the *end* of the project, node **7**. Any event on the critical path will, of course, not have *any* allowable delay, so its T_L value will equal its T_E value, such as for nodes **2** and **6**. The T_L for event **5**, for example, is simply 21 − 8 or 13.

A better example occurs with node **3.** Here there are three activities that exit the node, each of which will give a separate value of T_L. Similarly to the early start times, the correct value is the *smallest* of all the possible values (anything larger than this is "not allowable"). Then for node **3**

Activity *e*: $T_L = 17 - 5 = 12$
Activity *f*: $T_L = 21 - 7 = 14$

Finding the slack in activities. Calculate latest time.

Activity g: $T_L = 13$ (T_L for node **5**) $- 2 = 11 \leftarrow$ smallest

These values are also listed in Figure 10.11.

The activity slack values can now be simply found by Equation 10.5.

$$\text{activity slack} = T_L \text{ (at activity end)}$$
$$- T_E \text{ (at activity beginning)} - t_e \text{ (activity time)} \quad (10.5)$$

These values are calculated for each activity in Table 10.15. Knowing these slacks then allows the manager to transfer resources from noncritical to critical activities in order to keep the project on schedule. But in doing so, the manager must not delay a noncritical activity in excess of its slack.

Probabilities of Completion

Finding the probability of completing the project on time.

Knowing the variance in each activity (the variances in Table 10.15) we can compute the likelihood of completing the project in a given time period, assuming the activity durations are independent of each other. The distribution of project completion times will be approximately normally distributed if the critical path has a large number of activities on it, with a mean and variance found from the critical path. The mean time along the critical path was found to be 21 hours. The variance is found by summing the variances of each of the activities on the critical path. In our example, this would be

$$V = \sigma_a{}^2 + \sigma_d{}^2 + \sigma_j{}^2$$
$$= 1 + 4 + 1$$
$$= 6$$

The probability of completing the project in, say, 23 hours is then found through the table of the standard normal probability distribution in the appendix with a standard normal deviate of

$$Z = \frac{\text{desired completion time} - \text{mean completion time}}{\sqrt{V}} \quad (10.6)$$
$$= \frac{23 - 21}{\sqrt{6}}$$
$$= 0.818$$

which results in a probability (see Figure 10.12) of 79 percent.*

Expediting the Project with Cost-Time Tradeoffs

Earlier we spoke of transferring resources from activities with slack to critical activities to expedite the project. When this is not feasible there is often another way to expedite the project—by expediting *individual* activities, though

---

*The variances of "almost-critical" paths should also be investigated if they might affect the probability of completion in the desired time. For further details, refer to References 2, 14, or 18.

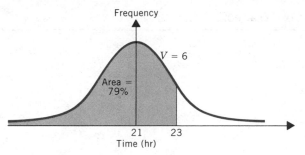

Figure 10.12 Probability distribution of project completion times.

usually at a significant cost. Although this can, of course, be planned before the project is even initiated, more often it is considered after some activity has been delayed in the project. This comparison of the planned completion of activities from the PERT chart and actual performance allows managers to adjust schedules through additional resource reallocations so as to keep the project on course when delays have been experienced. The speeding up *Crashing activities.* of critical activities is known as *crashing* and is derived from the original concepts employed in the critical path method, CPM. The technique is described as follows.

Cost of crashing.   Activities can be *expedited* (or *crashed*) up to a limit, at some increase in cost. The assumption is usually made that the activity duration-cost relationship is linear between the "normal" schedule and the "crash" schedule. For example, a normal 3-week activity may cost $2000 and a crash 2-week schedule may cost $3000. Then a 2.8-week duration is assumed to cost $2200. Each activity usually has its own minimum duration and expediting cost, some activities being more efficient than others.

As the more efficient *critical* activities are expedited (there is no point in crashing noncritical activities—they will not speed up the delayed project), more and more activities and paths become critical and must be simultaneously expedited to further reduce the project duration. Thus, the cost for expediting the project increases faster and faster until the point is reached where the project can be expedited no further: all activities on one (or more) critical path are at their crash point. An application of this concept is provided in the next section.

The Bonfire Boys

Local fathers and their sons in Brood 22 of the Bonfire Boys are planning a special Biannual Bonfire Blast beginning in three days. However, there are a number of expensive and time-consuming project activities remaining before the Blast can get underway, as shown in Table 10.16. Every day the Blast is delayed will be discouraging to the boys. But every extra $10 spent unnecessarily will be discouraging to the fathers. What is the minimum cost of expediting the remaining activities for various project durations?

Table 10.16   Network Time-Cost Tradeoffs

Activity	Precedence	Normal Duration (days)	Normal Cost ($)	Crash Duration (days)	Crash Cost ($)	Cost/Time "Slope" ($/days)
a	—	2	20	1	40	20
b	a	4	30	1	60	10
c	a	2	10	2	10	—
d	a	2	10	1	40	30
e	d	3	10	1	30	10
			Total = 80		Total = 180	

The network and critical path are shown in Figure 10.13; note the *dummy activity*. In the figure, activity *c* is shown for its actual two-day duration to the arrowhead and then the line thinly continued to node **5** to show project completion.

Inspecting the critical activities *a*, *d*, and *e* in Table 10.16 for the most efficient activity to crash in order to gain one day in completion time, activity *e* is best. The six-day schedule from expediting activity *e* by one day is shown in Figure 10.14. Note that there are now *two* critical paths—*a-d-e* and *a-b-dummy*.

To expedite completion by another day will require expediting *both* critical paths. This can be done in this case by expediting activities *common* to both paths (such as activity *a*, for $20) or separate activities on the two paths (*b* and *d*, for $10 + $30 = $40, or *b* and *e*, for $10 + $10 = $20). Either way, a reduction of one day (five days total) will cost at least $20 and then $20 again for another day (four days total). The final result of both $20 reductions is shown in Figure 10.15.

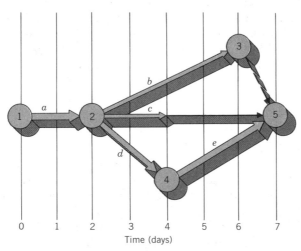

Figure 10.13   All normal, seven-day schedule.

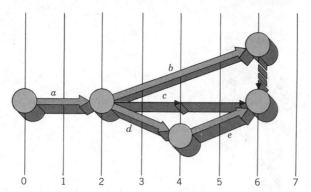

Figure 10.14   Two-critical path, six-day schedule.

One more day's reduction can only come about by expediting activities *b* and *d*; activities *a* and *e* are already fully crashed. The cost of this reduction, to three days' project duration, is $10 + $30 = $40. The result, shown in Figure 10.16, is the maximum reduction possible because all activities along critical path *a-d-e* have been crashed. In addition, path *a-c* is now also critical and cannot be further reduced. Figure 10.17 shows the cost increases as a function of the shortened project duration.

It should be noted that for use as a feedback control technique the crashing of activity *a* would probably not be applicable since it is the *first* activity that might be delayed. That is, by the time control was necessary, activity *a* would probably already be completed. Of more use for control purposes would be the reduction possible in activities *b* and *e* and the initial slack in activities *b* and *c*. Thus, for example, one day's delay in activity *d* could be negated by expediting activity *e*.

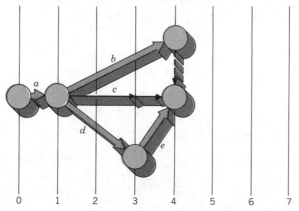

Figure 10.15   Second and third reduction, four-day schedule.

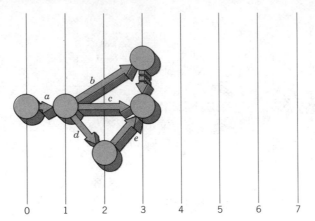

Figure 10.16 Final reduction, three-day schedule.

PERT/CPM Extensions

There have been an extremely large number of extensions to the basic ideas of PERT and CPM which are oriented toward handling some problem situations more flexibly, computerizing some of the aspects, specializing some of the concepts for particular environments, and tying various management approaches into the PERT concept. Here we will discuss two of these extensions: PERT/cost and GERT.

PERT/Cost

DOD idea.   A natural extension to the basic PERT idea is to add cost elements to the network. This extension was developed by the Department of Defense in the early 1960s and has also been used by General Electric and others in one form or another. The objective is to think about and plan for cost aspects of the project just like time aspects. Using a cost network will show what to monitor, where and when to intercede, and, in general, provide needed feedback to the project manager concerning costs.

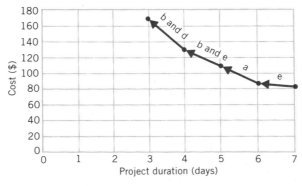

Figure 10.17 Project cost duration.

The approach taken is to develop costs for each work package and monitor actual costs by using accounts for individual packages. Either a single cost is estimated or three costs may be used: an optimistic, most likely, and pessimistic cost, just as with PERT. Rather than control costs by accounting periods, or even by volume (as in "flexible budgeting"), the costs are monitored by individual tasks and activity time.

"Earned value."

In some applications of PERT/cost an "earned value" curve is used rather than cost since it is felt that cost is not necessarily linear with progress. (It is frequently necessary to spend large amounts of money up front before progress can be made.) In these cases earned value is tracked through subjective estimates of the workers, either alone or in addition to cost. Cost and earned value charts are discussed in more detail in Chapter 14 on Organizational Control.

GERT

Complex networks.

Two parameters.

The graphical evaluation and review technique (GERT) is a network model that was developed to handle much more complex modeling situations than PERT. It combines probabilistic networks, PERT, and decision trees all into a single framework. Its components consist of nodes and directed arcs (or branches) with *two* parameters: the probability that the arc is taken (or "realized," as it is called), and the mathematical function describing the time the activity requires. Evaluation of a GERT network results in the probability of each node being realized and the elapsed time between each of the nodes. In Figure 10.18 is a comparison of GERT and PERT.

GERT	PERT
1. Branching from a node is probabilistic.	1. Branching from a node is deterministic.
2. Various possible probability distributions for time estimates exist.	2. Only the Beta distribution for time estimates exists.
3. Flexibility in node realization is present.	3. No flexibility in node realization is present.
4. Looping back to earlier events is acceptable.	4. Looping back is not allowed.
5. Difficult to use as a control tool.	5. Easy to use for control.
6. Arcs may represent time, cost, reliability, etc.	6. Arcs represent time only.

Figure 10.18   Comparison of GERT and PERT.

10.4   APPENDIX: QUEUING THEORY ANALYSIS AND SCHEDULING

It was stated earlier in the chapter that a large portion of the lead ("flow") time on jobs is the idle time they spend waiting (or "queuing") to be placed on machines. The analysis of this queuing phenomenon is highly relevant to the scheduling task because even a small reduction in queue time can significantly improve an organization's overall productivity. This is even more important in the case of service organizations because the waiting "job" for them is more than likely the customer, who makes unpleasant and disrupting noises if kept waiting too long.

Unhappy jobs.

In this appendix we therefore address the nature of the queuing situation and apply some elementary queuing theory results to a few scheduling examples for illustration. We begin by closely examining the queuing system, as commonly encountered in most organizations.

The pioneer analyst in queuing theory was a Danish telephone engineer named A. K. Erlang who developed the theory in the 1920s to predict telephone call service. Given an arriving population and a service facility (or facilities) with a certain speed of service, the theory will determine, given certain assumptions, the expected (average) length of the queue, number of people or items in the queue, idle time of the facility, and other such criteria of service facility performance.

What descriptive queuing theory will determine.

The structure of the queuing system to be considered here is illustrated in Figure 10.19. It is assumed that the arrivals wait in *one* queue (or take a number for service or add their names to a list) and, as they come to the front of the line, go to the next available service facility. (This system is called first come, first served, FCFS, and is commonly adopted for reasons of fairness.) The arrivals are assumed to come at random, with the average rate λ (arrivals per unit time). Service is also assumed to be random, with the average rate μ (services completed per unit time).

The structure of the queuing system.

If the service can be performed *before* the recipients arrive and then stored until their arrival, a queue will *not* form (unless the demand rate exceeds the service rate). For example, if punch is being served as a refreshment at a party where people arrive for refreshments, on the average, every 4 seconds and it takes 4 seconds to pour a drink there will never be a queue, over the long run (say, after at least 10 minutes). This is because even when people are not coming for a drink the server keeps on pouring drinks; then, when a batch of people all come at once, the drinks are ready.

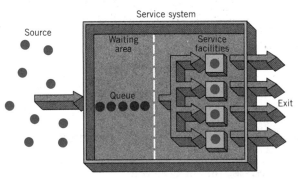

Figure 10.19   Queuing system structure.

Table 10.17   The Formation of a Queue

Time (sec)	Waiting	Time (sec)	Waiting
1	—	26	G, F
2	A	27	G, F
3	A	28	G
4	A	29	G
5	A	30	G
6	—	31	G
7	—	32	H
8	B	33	H
9	B	34	I, H
10	C, B	35	I, H
11	C, B	36	I
12	C	37	I
13	C	38	I
14	C	39	I
15	C	40	J
16	D	41	J
17	D	42	K, J
18	E, D	43	K, J
19	E, D	44	K
20	E	45	K
21	E	46	K
22	E	47	K
23	E	48	L
24	F	49	L
25	F	50	M, L

How a queue tends to form.   However, if mixed drinks are being served so that the mix cannot be poured *until the person gives an order,* a queue will tend to form under exactly the same conditions. To see this, let us assume that people arrive consecutively 2 and then 6 seconds apart (thereby averaging 4). The results are tabulated in Table 10.17.

As seen in the table, following the arrival of person B there is never a time that someone is not waiting for a drink. On many occasions there is a queue of one person waiting to be served (while another is being served). Starting from the arrival of B at 8 seconds there are 11 seconds (out of 50 − 7 = 43 seconds or 11/43 = 26 percent of the time) when a person is waiting to be served. The *expected queue length* in this case is thus said to be 0.26 × 1 = 0.26 persons.

Assumptions and Results of Queuing Theory

Queuing theory can determine the expected queue length, and many other such variables, for situations much more realistic than this—such as for variable service and arrival rates and for more than one server. There are, however, some basic assumptions that must be satisfied.

- *The system is in steady state.* Note in the preceding example that we ignored the 7-second *start-up transient* in Table 10.17. This time to reach "steady state" is usually a small fraction of an ongoing service system and may be ignored. (However, some systems, such as banks, may always be in transient states such as 9:00 A.M. start-up, 10:00 A.M. coffee break, 11:30 A.M.–1:30 P.M. noon rush, 2:00 P.M. break, 2:30 P.M. closing rush. In these cases queuing theory is inappropriate and simulation must be used.)

- *First come, first served priority discipline.* We assume people (items) are served in the order they join the queue and only one queue exists, even if there are multiple service facilities.

- *An unlimited source exists.* We assume we never run out of recipients from the source. Chapter 15 includes an approach for queuing situations where the source *is* limited (e.g., machines that are breaking down and must be repaired).

- *Unlimited queue space is available.* We assume there is sufficient space in the (single) queue to hold any recipient who desires service.

- *Standard queue behavior which prohibits:*
  Balking—refusing to join the queue.
  Reneging—leaving the queue before being served.
  Jockeying—switching between queues as their lengths vary.
  Cycling—returning to the queue following service.

- *Random arrivals and service.* As stated earlier, the *random arrivals* occur at the average rate λ and the services at the average rate μ.

Although some limited results have been obtained for situations that relax some of these restrictions, we will not consider them here. The interested reader is referred to References 12 and 18.

Poisson arrivals and services.

The assumption of random arrivals and services results in a *particular* distribution of arrival and service rates known as the *Poisson distribution.* With the assumptions given above, these distributions allow us to find a number of characteristics (discussed later) that describe the waiting line and the service process. Since these characteristics are usually related, only one of them need be found and the others will follow from it.

Here we choose as the major characteristic the expected (average) length of the queue, L_q, that is waiting for service (not including those being served). This characteristic is presented in Figure 10.20 as a function of three parameters of the queuing situation.

- λ—The average arrival rate to the service facility.

- μ—The average service rate at a facility, *when busy.* The average service *time* is $1/\mu$.

- K—The number of servers or service facilities, known as *channels* (four shown in Figure 10.19) in the service system.

- λ/μ—The *utilization* of the facility. If the arrival rate λ exceeds the service rate of a single server μ the queue will grow indefinitely unless

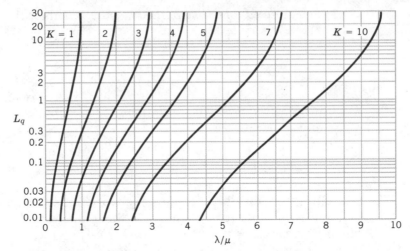

Figure 10.20 The multichannel queue. [Reprinted by permission from Efraim Turban and Jack R. Meredith, *Fundamentals of Management Science* (Dallas: Business Publications, 1977), p. 432. © 1977 by Business Publications, Inc.]

more than one server is available. Then the facility utilization is given by $\lambda/K\mu$.

Note in Figure 10.20 that as curves of constant K reach values of $\lambda/\mu = K$ (near the top of the chart), the length of the queue, L_q, gets greater and greater. This is because the arrivals tend to fully utilize the capacity of the system. For example, if the arrival rate is twice that of the service rate this will keep two servers busy full time.

Finding the
other queue
characteristics.

Once a value for L_q is found, many other interesting characteristics describing the process can be derived from it.

1. The *average number of items in the system*, both in the queue and in service combined, L_s. The number being served, on the average, is simply the utilization of the service facility, λ/μ. Thus

$$L_s = L_q + \frac{\lambda}{\mu} \tag{10.7}$$

2. The *expected waiting time in the queue*, W_q. This is *not*, as might be expected, simply the average length of the queue times the average service time because the average service time is calculated on the basis of *continuous service*, but in reality the facility is not always busy. Rather another relationship is used: the average *length* of the queue will equal the average *waiting time* multiplied by the average *arrival rate*: $L_q = W_q\lambda$. Rearranging terms

$$W_q = \frac{L_q}{\lambda} \tag{10.8}$$

3. The *expected total time in the system, W_s.* This will be the queuing time plus the service time, $1/\mu$.

$$W_s = W_q + \frac{1}{\mu} \tag{10.9}$$

4. For service systems composed of a *single server* (channel) we can determine the *probability of n items occupying the system* (both queuing and in service).

$$P_n = \left(\frac{\lambda}{\mu}\right)^n \left(1 - \frac{\lambda}{\mu}\right) \qquad \text{for } K = 1 \tag{10.10}$$

Equations exist for the multiple server case but are extremely involved (see Reference 18). Note that when $n = 0$ this reduces to the *probability that the system is empty.*

$$P_0 = 1 - \frac{\lambda}{\mu} \qquad \text{for } K = 1 \tag{10.11}$$

The *probability that the system is busy,* otherwise known as the *utilization* of the facility, is thus $1 - P_0$ or

$$P_{\text{busy}} = \frac{\lambda}{\mu} \qquad \text{for } K = 1 \tag{10.12}$$

Unexpected results.
One of the most confounding aspects of waiting line analysis is that it defies normal expectations. For example, if a service system with one server results in an average queue length of 12 recipients, then most people expect that adding a second server will cut the queue in half, to 6 recipients. But consider the following situation. A one-person service facility can serve on the average, 10 customers per hour and customers arrive, on the average, every 7.5 minutes. What will happen if a second server is added?

Analysis

$$\lambda = \frac{60}{7.5} = 8/\text{hr}, \qquad \mu = 10/\text{hr}, \qquad \frac{\lambda}{\mu} = 0.8, \qquad K = 1$$

From Figure 10.20, $L_q = 3$, approximately. If a second server is added then reading from Figure 10.20 at $K = 2$ and $\lambda/\mu = 0.8$ we find $L_q = 0.14$. That is, the expected line length reduces by

$$\frac{3.0 - 0.14}{3.0} = 0.95$$

Queue reduction much greater than expected.
or 95 percent. This is much greater than just one-half (50 percent). The reason is because of the randomness of the arrivals and the fact that services cannot be produced during idle periods and stored for use in busy periods. A second server is no help when the facility is idle or only one customer is being served but when *groups of people* arrive, the second server is a *great* help.

Let us consider an example now of using queuing theory to solve a scheduling problem.

Kee Pon Trucking, Ltd.

Mr. Kee Pon is trying to estimate the best number of work crews to employ in a local excavating job at Bandini, India. The crews can each load, on the average, four trucks per hour but cost $10 per hour in total wages. (Only one crew can work on a truck at a time.) On the other hand, the idle time of trucks is charged at $16 per hour. If the trucks arrive every 20 minutes, on the average, how many crews should Mr. Pon hire? (Assume loading and arrivals rates are random.)

Analysis

$$\lambda = 60/20 = 3/hr$$

$$\mu = 4/hr$$

$$\frac{\lambda}{\mu} = 0.75$$

One Crew. From Figure 10.20 at the intersection of $\lambda/\mu = 0.75$ and $K = 1$, we find $L_q = 2.3$. Hence, the total hourly waiting cost of the trucks is

$$2.3 \times \$16 \quad = \$37$$
$$\underline{+ \$10} \quad \text{(cost of one crew)}$$
$$\text{Total} \qquad \$47/hr$$

Two Crews. From Figure 10.20 $L_q = 0.12$

Waiting cost of trucks	$0.12 \times \$16 =$	$2
Cost of two crews		$20
Total		$22/hr

Three or More Crews. The most that can now be saved from the cost of waiting trucks is $2, so clearly it is not worthwhile to add another $10 crew. The best answer, therefore, is *two* crews.

Scheduled Services

When jobs can be scheduled by appointment.

There are some situations where the recipients do *not* arrive randomly but are *scheduled*, as in medicine and dentistry. If possible, appointments in such a case should be scheduled so that the first recipient has the most *definite* required service time and the last recipient the most *variable* service time. For similar types of recipient needs, the variability is often proportional to the expected length of service. That is, a 10-minute appointment may run 5 to 15 minutes but a 4-hour appointment may run 3½ to 4½ hours. Scheduling in this manner then minimizes the potential wait for all the *following* recipients.

10.5 SUMMARY AND KEY LEARNING POINTS

This chapter has continued the discussion of scheduling in Chapter 9 and taken it to its final level of detail. The loading and sequencing issues were discussed and some potentially helpful charts, models, and heuristics were illustrated. The subject of scheduling projects was then discussed in some detail and the well-known PERT and CPM models were explained and illustrated. Extensions of these models to handle cost and more complex situations were briefly described. Last, the subject of queuing, or waiting line, theory was discussed and solution methodologies and graphs were explained and illustrated.

The key learning points of the chapter were

- The loading problem concerns allocating tasks or entire jobs to facilities. The assignment model and index method are two common approaches used to address the loading problem.

- The assignment model is appropriate for solving a type of linear programming problem where one-to-one loadings of resources to tasks is required.

- The index method is used for loading problems when *more than* one job can be assigned to each facility.

- The sequencing problem is that of choosing an order for jobs waiting for processing on a facility. Gantt charts, priority rules, Johnson's rule, and the runout and critical ratio heuristics are common approaches used for sequencing.

- Gantt charts graphically depict jobs, facilities, or resources over time and aid in visualizing what is happening dynamically on multiple entities. A number of symbols are employed to indicate special events and problems.

- The most common priority sequencing rules are first come, first served (FCFS) which exhibits fairness; shortest operation time (SOT), which maximizes the job output rate and minimizes average lateness; due date, which get jobs out closest to their promised delivery time; and various slack rules, which attempt to meet delivery dates at lowest cost.

- Johnson's rule is an extension of SOT for the *n*-job, two-facility problem. It minimizes the total time the set of jobs takes on both facilities by scheduling short jobs on the first facility early and short jobs on the second facility late.

- The runout and critical ratio heuristics identify the next job to run on one common set of facilities. Runout schedules the next job as the one that will run out of inventory next whereas critical ratio also considers the amount of time it will take to produce the items, longer times receiving a higher priority.

- Scheduling is one of the most critical functions in project processes because of the size and singularity of the project (only one job).

- Project evaluation and review technique (PERT) uses optimistic, most likely, and pessimistic task times to determine expected task times. A network using the expected times, plus their variances, and required precedence then allows the identification of project completion times, their probabilities, critical tasks, and tasks with slack time available.

- The critical path method (CPM) uses normal and crash durations and costs for tasks to develop cost-time tradeoffs for the network. Crashing tasks along the critical path allows the project to be expedited at minimum additional cost and a project cost-versus-time function can thus be derived.

- Two basic extensions to the PERT/CPM procedures are PERT/cost, which attempts to schedule costs throughout the project, and the graphical evaluation and review technique (GERT), which is appropriate for more complex projects.

10.6 KEY TERMS

loading (p. 356)	**priority rules** (p. 363)	**runout** (p. 369)
assignment model (p. 357)	**flow time** (p. 364)	**critical ratio** (p. 370)
index method (p. 360)	**queue time** (p. 364)	**PERT** (p. 372)
sequencing (p. 361)	**SOT** (p. 365)	**CPM** (p. 372)
Gantt chart (p. 361)	**Johnson's rule** (p. 367)	**critical path** (p. 373)

10.7 REVIEW AND DISCUSSION QUESTIONS

1. Might some of the scheduling techniques be extended into other realms such as investment analysis and information systems planning?

2. How would the scheduling of bottleneck operations involving a single machine (printing press, computer) be accomplished?

3. Do the available priority rules differ in product and service organizations?

4. What problems arise when the SOT rule is used?

5. What are the critical ratio and runout methods actually minimizing to determine priorities? Which method is best?

6. Is flow time the same as customer wait time? If not, why not?

7. Why can the SOT rule not be used for projects?

8. What is the difference between PERT and CPM?

9. What might a "late start time" indicate? What could it be used for?

10. Could there ever be a negative slack?

11. Some texts define a term called "free slack" along a path. What might this be?

12. Can the variance of a "near-critical" path possibly invalidate a computed probability of completion based on the critical path? How?

13. Do you think people's estimates of the optimistic or pessimistic activity times are the most accurate?

14. What types of situations would GERT be best for but not PERT?

15. Why is balking disallowed in queuing theory?

16. Why is λ/μ called the "utilization" of the facility?

17. Why is the expected waiting time in the queue not simply L_q/μ?

18. Can you explain why adding a second server does not cut the queue length in half?

10.8 PROBLEMS

Practice Problems

1. Solve the following minimization assignment problem.

Job	A	B	C	D	E
1	3	9	11	6	3
2	5	4	6	10	5
3	4	3	8	4	6
4	8	6	10	12	4
5	2	7	9	5	9

2. John, Mary, and Henry have been asked to work this Saturday morning but the union contract calls for double-time pay on Saturday. Since the work must get out, the production supervisor has decided to load the three jobs so as to minimize the total cost of overtime. The jobs and the time required for each person are shown below. John earns $12 per hour, Mary $16 per hour, and Henry $20 per hour on overtime.

	John	Mary	Henry
Job 1	2	1.5	1.5
Job 2	1.5	1.5	1
Job 3	1	2	1

Who should do which job if one job is assigned to each worker?

3. Solve Problem 2 using the index method. Note that none of the employees is willing to work more than 4 hours on Saturday morning.

4. Interpret, by task, the Gantt chart in Figure 10.8.

5. a. Draw a Gantt chart to depict the schedule for four jobs on two machines, A and B. Today is Wednesday, August 5. The business is closed on Saturday and Sunday.

   Job
   1: Two days on A, one on B, one on A.
   2: One day on B, one day on A.
   3: One day on B, two on A.
   4: One day on A, two on B.

   Machine
   A: Preventive maintenance August 12.
   B: Operator called in with a toothache this morning; will be in at noon for a half day today.

Material
Job 2: Materials delayed for work on machine A, will arrive August 10.

b. Show the actual progress as of August 11, 8 A.M.

Aug. 6: Machine B is down all day for repairs.
Aug. 10: Materials for job 2 on A did not arrive. Job 3 finished (or is) a day ahead of schedule. Job 4 delayed a day on A due to defective materials.

6. More information is given below about the three jobs in Table 10.10. Continue Table 10.11 for rules LOT, SS, SS/RO, and DS/RO.

Job	Days Ago Arrived*	No. Remaining Operations
ABC	6	2
PDQ	2	6
XYZ	1	1

*Today is Date 0.

7. Sequence the following jobs by Johnson's rule.

					Job					
Machines	A	B	C	D	E	F	G	H	I	J
1	33	37	31	38	35	36	43	34	32	30
2	41	35	30	39	32	30	38	43	31	30

8. Chippo Bakery Co. has five cakes that must be produced today for pickup this evening. Each cake must go through the bakery department and then the decorating department. Each department can process only one cake at a time. If the following estimates are available for production in each department, in what order should the cakes be scheduled?

	Baking (min)	Decorating (min)
Cake 1	30	30
Cake 2	20	15
Cake 3	20	45
Cake 4	15	35
Cake 5	15	15

9. Calculate and diagram when each cake will be completed in Problem 8. What is the total idle time of the two departments while the cakes are being made?

10. Use the runout and critical ratio rules to derive a processing sequence for the following jobs.

Job	Inventory	Daily Demand	Processing Time (days)
1	30	5	4
2	110	7	10
3	70	3	12
4	50	10	3
5	20	2	1
6	90	8	8

11. The following PERT chart was prepared at the beginning of a small construction project.

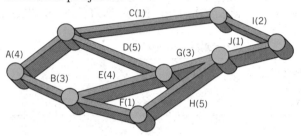

The duration, in days, follows the letter of each activity. What is the critical path? Which activities should be monitored most closely?

At the end of the first week of construction, it was noted that activity A was completed in 2.5 days, but activity B required 4.5 days. What impact does this have on the project? Are the same activities critical?

12. Consider Problem 11, again. Suppose the duration of both activities A and D can be reduced to one day, at a cost $15 per day of reduction. Also, activities E, G, and H can be reduced in duration by one day at a cost of $25 per day of reduction. What is the least cost approach to crash the project two days? What is the shortest "crashed" duration, the new critical path, and the cost of crashing?

13. Given the following project find the probability of completion by 17 weeks. By 24 weeks. By what date is management 90 percent sure completion will occur?

| | Times (weeks) | | |
Activity	Optimistic	Most Likely	Pessimistic
1–2	5	11	11
1–3	10	10	10
1–4	2	5	8
2–6	1	7	13
3–6	4	4	10
3–7	4	7	10
3–5	2	2	2
4–5	0	6	6
5–7	2	8	14
6–7	1	4	7

If the firm can complete the project within 18 weeks it will receive a bonus of $10,000. But if the project delays beyond 22 weeks it must pay a penalty of $5000. If the firm can choose whether or not to bid on this project, what should its decision be if the project is only a breakeven one normally?

14. The emergency room of a local hospital employs three doctors. Emergency patients arrive randomly at the average rate of 3.5 per hour. Service is good and averages about ½ hour per patient so the hospital is considering reducing the number of doctors to two. What effect would this have on patient waiting time?

15. Jim sells tickets at a counter where the customers randomly arrive, on the average, every 2 minutes. He finds that he can service no more than 10 customers per hour. For management to maintain an average queue length of no more than one customer, how many more ticket sellers must they provide to help Jim?

More Complex Problems

16. The following table shows the profits to a company from assigning salespersons to different regions. Find the best overall assignment if only one salesperson can be assigned to one region.

| | Salesperson | | |
Region	A	B	C
I	5	6	8
II	4	7	11
III	7	3	2

17. In the Sunset Nursing Home the director is attempting to assign nine practical nurses to nine patients. Six of the patients are difficult and three are easy. The nurses' experience with such patients varies also: three have only one year of experience, four have two years, and two have three years. Based on her experience the director expects the following number of complaints from each type of assignment. How should she assign the nurses to the patients?

| | Years of Experience | | |
Type Patient	1	2	3
Hard	24	28	20
Easy	10	9	12

18. The following table gives the hours to run each job if placed on each machine, machine costs per hour, and machine hours available. If jobs can be split, what jobs should go on which machines for how many hours?

| | Machine | | |
Job	A	B	C
1	50	40	75
2	25	40	50
3	27	30	54
4	40	100	80
5	20	100	50
Cost, $/hr	4	2	3
Hours available	75	75	75

19. a. Try to devise a better schedule than that shown in Figure 10.3. Do not split tasks.

   b. Devise a better schedule if tasks can be split.

20. Data Tronics produces custom engineered testing equipment. The following four orders are currently in the design department.

Order No.	Due Date	Date Order Received in Design Dept.	Operations Time (days)	No. Operations Remaining
1	12/1/79	10/15/79	30	1
2	1/15/80	11/15/79	40	3
3	2/10/80	11/5/79	20	5
4	1/30/80	11/1/79	35	2

In what sequence should these four orders be processed through the design department if the following priority rules are used?

1. FCFS

2. SOT

3. SS

4. Due date

5. SS/RO

21. Derive the flow times and lateness (as in Table 10.11) for the four jobs in Problem 20 according to each of the five priority rules listed. Today is 15 November 1979 and the firm works a full shift every day, even holidays.

22. Johnson's rule can be extended to three machines under certain circumstances. Using the following rule, solve the problem in the table and find the completion times for each job. If the minimum time on the first machine is greater than or equal to the maximum on the second machine, *or* if the minimum on the third machine is greater than or equal to the maximum on the second—add the time on the second to both the time on the first and the time on the third, and solve as a two-machine problem.

Machine	Job				
	J_1	J_2	J_3	J_4	J_5
M_1	2	3	0	1	3
M_2	1	2	2	1	2
M_3	3	2	3	3	4

23. Assume the process times in Table 10.13 are 2, 1, 6, respectively (instead of 4, 2, 12). Track the inventories of the three jobs under each of the two processing sequences given in Table 10.13. What happens? Resolve the problem by resequencing the orders as the facilities complete a job. Use both sequencing methods. What sequence do you now get with each method? Are there still problems?

24. The network shown in the following table has a fixed cost of $90 per day, but money can be saved by shortening the project duration. Find the least cost schedule.

Activity	Normal Time	Crash Time	Cost Increase ($) (1st, 2nd, 3rd day)
1-2	7	4	30, 50, 70
2-3	9	6	40, 45, 65
1-3	12	10	60, 60
2-4	11	9	35, 60
3-4	3	3	—

25. Sloe Bank is trying to determine how to staff its teller windows so the average number of customers waiting for service in the single line ("cattle stall") queue does not exceed eight. On average, one customer arrives every minute and one teller can service 20 customers an hour. On the average, how long will a customer have to wait in the cattle stall? Find the utilization of the facility. How many square feet of space will be required if every teller needs 50 square feet and every waiting customer requires 15 square feet?

10.9 CASE

MICROSERVICE INC.

In January 1978, Rollie Bolton, who had been a customer engineer for both Burrows Corporation and IB2 Corporation, opened the doors to his new microcomputer service company. Rollie had spent 14 years repairing computers and peripheral hardware for Burrows and IB2 and had spent a considerable amount of time learning the microcomputer business. He was the immediate past president of the Tri-City Computer Club, which was made up principally of computer hobbyists.

Within Rollie's "service area" there were eight microcomputer stores selling to small businesspersons and hobbyists. Only three of those stores provided service for the equipment they sold.

Rollie's business grew rapidly over the first 18 months, but at that point he began to falter. Rollie was receiving subtle hints from many of his friends in the computer club that service times were becoming longer than acceptable. Several of the computer stores were complaining that they were unable to sell hardware because of the rumored poor service.

Rollie recognized the problem and knew that lack of staff was not its source. His staff were often idle waiting for the testing and diagnostic equipment. Rollie currently had five microcomputers or components in his shop. He estimated the amount of time required for each of the operators to complete their respective tasks. These estimates are shown in the following table. Rollie wants to minimize the amount of waiting time and minimize the time required in total to get the five components shipped out the door. He is, however, uncertain as to the sequencing of these five components to accomplish his objective.

Equipment	Diagnostic Check (hr)	Repair/Part Replacement (hr)
TRS-80	9	8
IMSAI	12	6
Tektronics Printer	10	3
Adds Terminal	8	7
Ohio Scientific	14	2

Questions for Discussion

1. How should Rollie sequence the computer equipment through his shop to minimize the waiting time and the total time taken?

2. Provide Rollie with a scheduling method to use in place of his trial and error scheduling.

10.10 REFERENCES AND BIBLIOGRAPHY

1. Baker, K. R., *Introduction to Sequencing and Scheduling*, New York: Wiley, 1974.

2. Brennan, J., *Applications of Critical Path Techniques*, New York: American Elsevier, 1968.

3. Buffa, E. S., and Miller, J., *Production-Inventory Systems: Planning and Control*, 3rd ed., Homewood, IL: Irwin, 1979.

4. Campbell, H. G. et al., "A Heuristic Algorithm for the *n* Job *m* Machine Sequencing Problem," *Management Science*, 16:B630–B637 (June 1970).

5. Campbell, K. L., "Scheduling Is Not the Problem," *Production and Inventory Management*, 11:53–59 (No. 3, 1971).

6. Clayton, E. R., and Moore, L. J., "PERT vs. GERT," *Journal of Systems Management*, 23:11–19 (1972).

7. Conway, R. W., Maxwell, W. L., and Miller, L. W., *Theory of Scheduling*, Reading, MA: Addison-Wesley, 1967.

8. Davis, E. W., "Networks: Resource Allocation," *Industrial Engineering*, April 1974.

9. Davis, E. W., *Project Management*, Norcross, GA: American Institute of Industrial Engineers, PP&C Monograph No. 3, 1976.

10. Day, J. E., and Hottenstein, M. P., "Review of Sequencing Research," *Naval Research Logistic Quarterly*, 27:11–39 (March 1970).

11. Gavett, J. W., "Three Heuristic Rules for Sequencing Jobs to a Single Production Facility," *Management Science*, 11:B166–176 (1965).

12. Gross, D., and Harris, C. N., *Fundamentals of Queuing Theory*, New York: Wiley, 1974.

13. Hershauer, J. C. et al., "Search and Simulation Selection of a Job-Shop Sequencing Rule," *Management Science*, 21:833–843 (March 1975).

14. Horowitz, J., *Critical Path Scheduling: Management Control Through CPM and PERT*, New York: Ronald Press, 1967.

15. IBM, "Shopwell's One Million $ Promise," *Viewpoint*, 8:26–28 (July–Aug. 1978).

16. Johnson, S. M., "Optimal Two and Three Stage

Production Schedules with Set-up Time Included," *Naval Research Logistics Quarterly*, 1:61–68 (March 1954).

17. Nanot, Y. R., "An Experimental Investigation and Comparative Evaluation of Priority Disciplines in Job Shop-Like Queuing Networks," Ph.D. Dissertation, UCLA, 1963.

18. Turban, E., and Meredith, J. R., *Fundamentals of Management Science*, 2nd ed., Dallas: Business Publications, 1981.

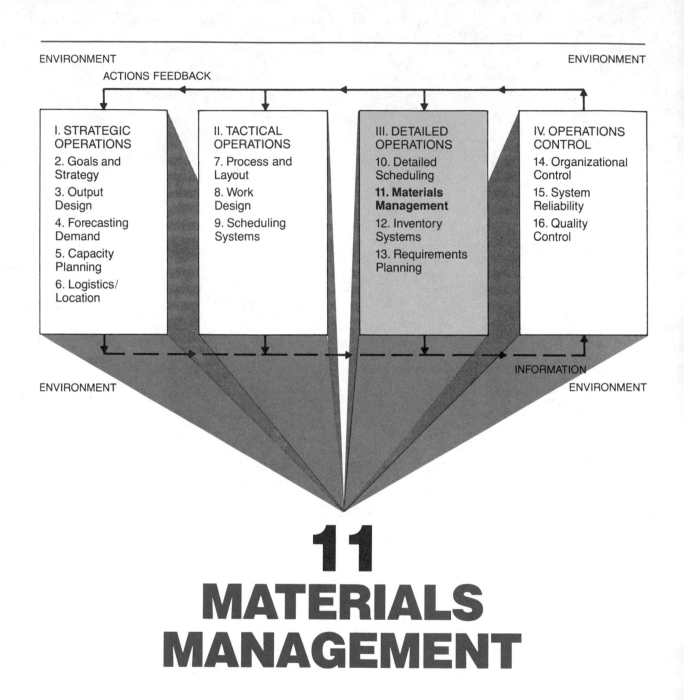

ENVIRONMENT   ENVIRONMENT

ACTIONS FEEDBACK

I. STRATEGIC OPERATIONS	II. TACTICAL OPERATIONS	III. DETAILED OPERATIONS	IV. OPERATIONS CONTROL
2. Goals and Strategy	7. Process and Layout	10. Detailed Scheduling	14. Organizational Control
3. Output Design	8. Work Design	**11. Materials Management**	15. System Reliability
4. Forecasting Demand	9. Scheduling Systems	12. Inventory Systems	16. Quality Control
5. Capacity Planning		13. Requirements Planning	
6. Logistics/ Location			

ENVIRONMENT   ENVIRONMENT

INFORMATION

11
MATERIALS MANAGEMENT

11

LEARNING OBJECTIVES

By the completion of this chapter the student should

- Have a better appreciation for the nature of purchasing/procurement and the tasks involved.
- Know the basic principles of materials handling.
- Be familiar with materials handling equipment and the new concepts and techniques.
- Realize the extent of the revolution occurring in warehousing.
- Comprehend the variety of types, classes, and uses of inventories.

Inventories as stocks of goods.

A major aspect of the detailed operations of most organizations concerns the management of their raw materials and supplies: obtaining them, inspecting them, storing them, moving them, using them, and, finally, shipping them. These raw materials and supplies, called inventories are, respectively, the stocks of materials that become part of the output or are used in the production of the organization's output. A retail store stocks dresses and slacks for sale to final consumers. An auto parts distributor stocks inventories of parts for sale to retail outlets. A furniture manufacturer stocks wood, glue, and fabrics, among other items, to be used in the production of lounge chairs. And, a government office stocks supplies of forms to be used in providing its particular services.

How a product organization manages its materials probably has more of an impact on its product costs than any other single factor. Trying to use defective or poor-quality raw materials, being out of a critical part, not having the materials at the right location when they are needed, having an insufficient supply of materials, not being able to locate the materials—all these and many other similar materials problems plague firms who do a poor job of either *planning* their materials flows or *controlling* them. Materials management consists primarily of these two major tasks, planning and control. Yet many organizations do not realize that they are very different functions. Materials "planning" consists of the design of the materials flow systems and the policies that govern them. Materials "control," on the other hand, is concerned with the proper execution and maintenance of these systems. Should the accuracy of inventory levels fall to 80 percent, for example (i.e., 20 percent of actual inventory parts do not agree with the records), this is probably a failure in *control* rather than in *planning*. If reorders of supplies are always initiated according to plan, yet stockouts are common, this would more likely indicate a failure in the setting of materials policy, such as reorder points, and thus a planning problem.

"P&IC."

It should be clear that the materials flow systems must fit hand-in-glove with the scheduling systems described in the preceding chapters. In fact, such systems are typically known as "production and inventory control" systems or "scheduling and materials control" systems. This close tie-in has accelerated with the development of computerized production planning and control systems since the management of tremendous quantities and varieties of materials is not the problem for computers that it was for manual systems. This has allowed the two systems to be joined, for both substantial savings in costs and significant improvement in the control of materials and operations, thereby resulting in higher productivities, the meeting of promised due dates, and other such benefits of better control.

Such close-knit systems seem to hold the most immediate promise for U.S. industry to compete with the better managed manual systems of Japan, such as "Kanban" (discussed later), and other foreign competitors. The elements of these systems, both U.S. and foreign, will be described in more detail in Chapter 12. Here we will briefly address the more general aspects of materials management such as purchasing, handling, and storing. We discussed the distribution and traffic elements, that is, *logistics*, earlier in

Chapter 6, and we will discuss the inspection function later, in Chapter 16.

Importance of purchasing.

Our first topic in this chapter is purchasing. The operations function depends heavily on the purchasing area to dependably obtain materials by the time they are needed in the production process. Purchasing must make some important tradeoffs in this process. Particularly in the current age of fierce price competition from abroad, the purchasing operations of matching varying prices, qualities, quantities, and lead time to meet the needs of production, inventory control, quality control, and the other operations functions are crucial.

"UPC."

"AS/RS."

Following this, we address the materials handling function, paying particular attention to new technologies for handling and control such as shrink-wrap, containerization, and UPC (bar code) labeling. The next section on warehousing closely relates to the materials handling section and stresses, once again, the new technologies in warehousing such as the use of stacker cranes and automatic storage and retrieval systems (AS/RS). We then close this short chapter with a general discussion of the need for inventories and their various classes and types.

Figure 11.1 illustrates how these topics relate to each other in the organization. The materials inputs from vendors (and scrap, on occasion, also) are initiated by purchase orders and scrap recycling requisitions from procurement. Receiving confirms the quality and amount of the shipments from vendors and sends the goods to storage, from which they are withdrawn, as

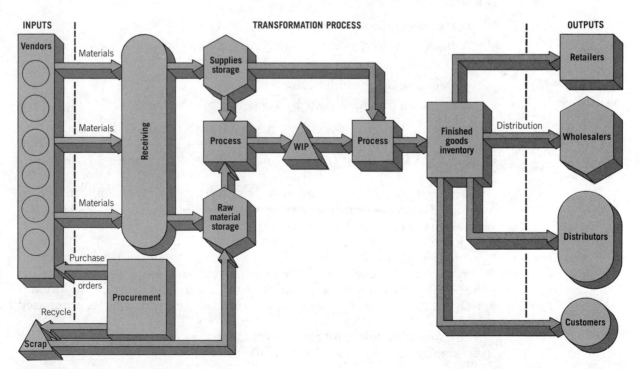

Figure 11.1   The materials management system.

needed, by operations. In the process of transformation, goods are temporarily stored as "work-in-process" (WIP) and as they become finished products, as finished goods inventory. From there they are distributed to various outlets such as directly to customers, manufacturing representatives, wholesalers, and so on.

11.1 PURCHASING/PROCUREMENT

Profit potential.

Many organizations, particularly wholesale, retail, and manufacturing firms, spend half their revenues for outside materials and services. Thus, the purchasing system also has a major potential for cost/profit improvement, perhaps the most powerful within the organization. Consider the following data concerning a simple manufacturing organization.

$$
\begin{aligned}
\text{total sales} &= \$10,000,000 \\
\text{purchased materials} &= 7,000,000 \\
\text{labor and salaries} &= 2,000,000 \\
\text{overhead} &= 500,000 \\
\text{profit} &= 500,000
\end{aligned}
$$

To double profits to $1,000,000, one or a combination of the following five actions could be taken.

1. Increase sales by 100 percent.

2. Increase selling price by 5 percent (same volume).

3. Decrease labor and salaries by 25 percent.

4. Decrease overhead by 100 percent.

5. Decrease purchase costs by 7.1 percent.

Although Action 2 looks best, it may well be impossible since raising prices almost always reduces the sales volume. In fact, raising prices often *decreases* the total profit (through lower volume). Alternative 5 is thus particularly appealing.

Decreasing the cost of purchased material provides significant profit leverage. For every 1 percent decrease in the cost of purchases, a 14 percent increase in profits results. This potential is often neglected in both business and public organizations.

Procurement defined.

Another common term for the purchasing function is **procurement.** Whereas "purchasing" implies a *monetary* transaction, "procurement" is simply the responsibility for acquiring the goods and services the organization needs and thus may include, for example, scrap, as well as purchased materials.

Organizational procurement is similar to the consumer purchasing of an individual except for the following differences.

1. The volume and dollar amounts are much larger.

Individual versus
organizational
purchasing.

2. The buyer may be larger than the supplier, whereas in consumer purchases the buyer is typically smaller than the supplier.

3. Very few suppliers exist for certain organizational goods whereas many typically exist for consumer goods.

4. Certain discounts are available for organizations (discussed later).

Purchasing Forms and Procedures

Purchasing forms and procedures in most organizations have become relatively standardized. *Purchase requisitions* are the forms sent to the purchasing department from another department within the organization authorizing it to obtain needed materials, supplies, or equipment. The standard purchase requisition usually includes the items indicated in Figure 11.2. On occasion, a *traveling requisition* is used when a standard item must constantly be resupplied. This form is simply a heavy duty card with the standard information listed on it which can just be pulled and sent to purchasing when new items are needed.

Purchase requisitions for departments.

In some computerized production systems, such as materials requirements planning (MRP) systems, vendor lead time, dependability, price, and so forth are stored internally and when an item is determined to be in need a computerized **purchase order** is automatically generated. In manual systems purchasing will draw up the purchase orders authorizing a vendor to ship items, directly from the requisitions (see Figure 11.3). The required information is similar to that for the purchase requisition and is also shown in Figure 11.2. However, a purchase order is considered a legally binding contract in the Uniform Commercial Code whereas a purchase requisition is not. For items that are in constant need, there is a *blanket purchase order* (corresponding to the traveling requisition) through which the originator in an organization can order without having to go through purchasing. This order system is usually negotiated by purchasing with individual suppliers for a year's duration at a time. Blanket purchase orders are also used for

Purchase orders for vendors.

Standard Purchase Requisition	Standard Purchase Order
*Identification number	*P.O. no.
*Date of request	*Date of issuance
*Originator	*Vendor name, address
*Billing account and authorization	*Item description and amount
*Item description and amount	*Delivery date
*Date needed	*Carrier
*Vendor information: Name	*Price, terms, conditions
P.O. no.	
Carrier	
Promised delivery	

Figure 11.2 Standard purchase forms information.

25275 - INSTRUCTIONS TO DEPARTMENT: COMPLETE FORM IN FULL. USE TYPEWRITER ONLY. THIS FORM CAN BE USED ONLY WHEN THE TOTAL AMOUNT OF GOODS OR SERVICES BEING REQUESTED IS $25.00 OR LESS. MULTIPLE ORDERS MUST NEVER BE USED AS A MEANS OF CIRCUMVENTING THE $25.00 LIMITATION. THIS FORM MUST

BE AUTHORIZED (SIGNED) BY THE DEPARTMENT HEAD BEFORE SEPARATING AND DISTRIBUTING ALL COPIES. MAIL ORIGINAL COPY TO VENDOR, SEND THIRD COPY TO PURCHASING DEPARTMENT, AND RETAIN SECOND AND FOURTH COPIES. IMMEDIATELY UPON RECEIPT OF INVOICE, DEPARTMENT MUST COMPLETE SECOND COPY (RECEIVING REPORT AND RECOMMENDATION FOR PAYMENT) AND FORWARD THIS COPY ALONG WITH THE INVOICE TO OFFICE OF CONTROLLER FOR PAYMENT. FOURTH COPY SHOULD BE RETAINED FOR DEPARTMENTAL FILES.

A-116 20M 7-75

UNIVERSITY OF CINCINNATI

DEPARTMENTAL PURCHASE ORDER

Cincinnati, Ohio 45221

No. D 38374

DATE ____________

TO: ____________ VENDOR NAME

DELIVER & INVOICE TO: ____________ NAME OF ORIGINATING DEPARTMENT

____________ ADDRESS

____________ ADDRESS

CITY STATE ZIP CODE

DEPARTMENTAL TELEPHONE NUMBER

QUANTITY	DESCRIPTION	PRICE	AMOUNT

1. **Invoice in duplicate to Department issuing order.** Do not invoice for partial shipments; send one invoice only upon completion of order.
2. The articles specified herein are to be used exclusively by the University of Cincinnati and are not subject to Ohio State Sales Tax or Federal Excise Tax.
3. This order is valid only if the total amount of purchase is twenty five dollars ($25.00) or less.
4. PLEASE READ DIRECTIONS on reverse side.

VENDOR CAUTION!

Do not accept this order 1) unless it has been signed, 2) unless you know its bearer, 3) unless you have been paid for all previous shipments made to the department shown above. Contact the originating department concerning any overdue payments or the validity of this order.

DO NOT WRITE IN THIS SPACE

Authorized By:

Department Head Signature
(Order Valid Only When Signed)

Figure 11.3 A typical purchase order.

small-valued purchases where the cost of ordering might even exceed the cost of the item.

Bidding. For high-cost and high-volume items, an intensive analysis is usually conducted before a decision is made as to which vendor will receive the purchase order. Bids are usually solicited from vendors and an analysis of all bidding suppliers conducted to aid in the supplier selection decision. The considerations in such an analysis will be discussed in the next section.

The Supplier Rating/Selection Decision

Dickson [4] has listed a number of evaluation criteria that are used in the supplier **vendor** rating/selection process. His list contains many of the qualifications of a good supplier. Some of these general characteristics are as follows:

Supplier qualifications.

1. Deliveries made on time, of the quality, and in the quantity specified. This maintains the consistent flow of processing operations for the purchasing organization.
2. Fairly priced.
3. Able to react to unforeseen changes such as an increase or decrease in demand, quality, specifications, or delivery schedules, all frequent occurrences in operations.
4. Continually improving products and services.

Suppliers with all of these characteristics are difficult to find. The purchasing function must recognize these selection criteria and not be swayed by cost/price considerations alone.

The vendor evaluation and selection process can be divided into two segments: evaluating existing suppliers and evaluating potential new suppliers.

Evaluating Existing Suppliers

Current suppliers can be evaluated monthly or quarterly on the basis of three elements of objective data and one subjective assessment. The objective variables are

- Price.
- Percentage of material rejected.
- Percentage of delivery dates met.

Evaluation factors for existing suppliers.

The subjective data can be gathered through periodic questionnaires to company engineers, purchasing agents, and others within the organization. This subjective information relates to the level and quality of technical and service help provided by the vendor. Vendors who fall below the acceptable standards should be notified and, if improvement is not forthcoming, dropped as suppliers.

Evaluating Potential Suppliers

Evaluating *potential* sources of supply is less objective but, according to the *Guide to Purchasing* of the National Association of Purchasing Management, Inc. [10], it can be divided into four major areas.

Evaluation factors for potential suppliers.

1. Technical and engineering capability.
2. Manufacturing strengths.
3. Financial strengths.
4. Management capability.

Capability.

Each of these four areas can be evaluated through generally available information and through meetings with the potential vendor. The vendor's technical and manufacturing capability can often be evaluated through meetings with engineering and manufacturing personnel, through bid evaluation, plant tours, and through the use of a trial order.

Financial strength.

Financial strength is an important consideration, for even though a company is technically competent, it may not be financially sound enough to meet deliveries. Recent examples of this problem include Rolls Royce's difficulty in delivering jet engines and Lockheed's difficulty delivering jet planes to buyers. An analysis of financial statements, including financial ratio analysis of ability to repay short- and long-term debt, profitability, and the general trend of the capitalization structure of the firm, should also be undertaken.

Management strength is paramount in long-term and high-dollar contracts. For example, management of construction contractors for buildings, bridges, and highways or airframe manufacturers for aircraft must be evaluated to determine their ability to successfully complete the project. The technical capability may well exist, but managerial talent and organization may not be available to guide the project. Even for short-term arrangements, the ability of the vendor's management to control its own operations will lead to better prices, delivery performance, and quality.

Vendor Rating/Selection Models

One method of combining the various decision factors for several vendors is to use a simple expected value model. Suppose the vendor selection decision is to be determined on the basis of three decision criteria.

1. Ability to meet price.
2. Ability to meet shipping date.
3. Ability to meet quality specifications.

A simple selection model.

Importance scores can be assigned to each of the three criteria and *probabilities* of meeting each criterion can be estimated for each vendor. The vendor with the greatest expected importance score should be selected.

Table 11.1 Supplier Selection

		Smith	Jones
	1	.8	.7
Criterion Number	2	.6	.85
	3	.9	.75

Smith Versus Jones

A simple example will illustrate the procedure. Two suppliers, Smith and Jones, are being evaluated. Their chances of meeting the three criteria are shown in Table 11.1, with the probability ranging from 0 to 1.0.

The importance scores for the three criteria are

1. Ability to meet price, 5.

2. Ability to meet shipping date, 10.

3. Ability to meet quality specifications, 8.

A score of 0 is given for failure on any of the three criteria. The expected score for Smith is computed as

$$.8(5) + .6(10) + .9(8) = 17.2$$

and for Jones

$$.7(5) + .85(10) + .75(8) = 18$$

On the basis of this simple analysis, the best supplier is Jones, with an expected importance score of 18.

This kind of decision model is important in selection decisions such as the vendor selection problem and for other purchasing problems such as specification selection. Because there are multiple criteria and most of them are subject to uncertainty, a decision analysis, or expected value, approach is often useful.

Other evaluation models.
Other models are the aviation industry's CASE program [8], General Motor's SPEAR program [5], and Ford Motor Company's Q-101 program [8]. These and other methods, such as those used by the Department of Defense, offer a significant addition to the precision of at least one component of the purchasing function.

Other Considerations

Using local vendors.
Other factors often considered by purchasing managers are the location of vendors and the use of multiple vendors for the same item. Local vendors are often preferred to nonlocals for two primary reasons. First, expediting orders is often less complicated if the purchasing agent can easily travel to the supplier's plant. Communications are less difficult, and a better rapport can be established between the representatives of the two organizations.

Second, for less tangible reasons, a local vendor is often desirable. The economic condition of the community affects the company and its employees. Buying local means that the local economy is stimulated, causing tax receipts to increase and thus improving the lot of employees through better schools, parks, and other public services. It also improves the general social conditions of the community, making it a more desirable place to locate and thus improving the organization's ability to attract good employees.

Using multiple vendors.

Multiple vendors are often desirable, assuming that more than one feasible source exists. The reasons for using more than one vendor include

1. Reduced risk compared with **sole source** buying.

2. Competition among vendors.

Risk of stockout.

Buying from one vendor increases the risk of missed deliveries due to a strike, natural catastrophe, or equipment failure. Diversification of purchasing reduces this risk since it is unlikely that all vendors would be affected at the same time. Also, knowledge on the part of the vendor that other suppliers are getting some of the business increases the vendor's sense of competition and keeps all of the suppliers aware of the need for good performance.

Competition.

Buying foreign.

A considerable amount of purchasing is conducted in the foreign markets. With competitive, and frequently even superior quality, and significantly lower prices, foreign firms are getting many purchase orders that used to go to U.S. firms. General Motors recently announced a policy of buying many more of its parts from foreign suppliers. After years of "buying American," GM can no longer afford to be so patriotic, not if it is to stay competitive. It appears that more and more of our standard parts and supplies will be imported from abroad and purchasing departments may have to learn more about "buying foreign."

The "80-20 rule."

Last, a word might be said about keeping good relations with suppliers. The **80-20 rule*** works in purchasing just like everywhere else: 80 percent of the materials will come from 20 percent of the suppliers. Thus, it behooves purchasing management to stay on good terms with their major suppliers.

Cost/Price Analysis

Price is an important element in any purchase. Whether the item being purchased is a new dress or a ton of coal, the purchasers are expected to search for the best value possible for themselves or their organization. In the process of establishing a price, the purchasing agent or buyer will expect the supplier's costs to come down in accordance with the learning curve concept, discussed earlier in Chapter 5. As the volume increases, the supplier can make the items with less expense and the buyers expect that savings to be passed on to their firms. Frequently there will be a good deal of argument

Role of price.

---

*This is also known as Pareto's rule and is the basis of the ABC concept (see Chapter 12): 20 percent of inventory represents 80 percent of the value; 20 percent of the customers make 80 percent of the complaints.

concerning the *rate* of learning (the supplier saying it is slow and the buyer trying to prove that it should be fast).

However, price is not the only consideration. A great price cut is meaningless if the material purchased is of insufficient quality to be used or is not delivered on time to meet operations schedules.

Discounts

There are typically four standard types of discounts that purchasing managers should take advantage of.

1. **Trade discounts:** These are discounts to the retailer from the distributor, or to the wholesaler from the manufacturer. Only the final customer ever buys at the "manufacturer's suggested price."

2. **Quantity discounts:** These discounts are available for buying in large quantity and thus should be especially important to purchasing. They will be analyzed in detail for inventory purposes in Chapter 12.

3. **Seasonal discounts:** These discounts are available to purchasers for buying in the "off" season and help the vendor or manufacturer to level out their production. If storage is available, excellent discounts can be obtained in this fashion.

4. **Cash discounts:** These are cash and "near cash" purchases (prompt payment). The most common is "2/10, net 30" which means a 2 percent discount if the bill is paid within 10 days; otherwise the entire amount is due in 30 days. Such discounts represent a significant cost savings to organizations and should rarely be passed up.

Discounts.

A purchasing manager is also concerned with determining the price that will ensure a reliable source of supply in the right quantities, quality, and timing. She or he must be able to enter negotiations with suppliers with a reasonable estimate of the price the organization is willing to pay and must be aware both of prices that are excessive and prices that cannot possibly earn the supplier a profit.

The right price.

While discussing materials pricing, mention should be made of the Robinson-Patman and other such federal acts affecting pricing in interstate commerce. While originally intended to curb discriminatory practices of large retailers, the Robinson-Patman Act has also become applicable to manufacturers. The effect of the act has been to make it illegal, in most circumstances, for sellers to offer different customers different prices for the identical material in the same quantities. In addition to the Robinson-Patman Act, there are many others (Miller-Tydings, Clayton, Sherman) of importance that the operations manager should be acquainted with. For further information, consult References 1, 2, and 6.

Federal pricing regulations.

Last, it is commonly said that buyers are underpaid, underappreciated, and under temptation. The ethical considerations in purchasing are a major problem, and companies' policies regarding what gifts and services employees may accept from suppliers, and potential suppliers, varies considerably.

Under temptation.

(Copyright © 1978 Universal Press Syndicate. Reprinted by permission.)

Since it is so difficult to draw the line, wise purchasing personnel refuse *all* gifts, services, and meals from outside sources. It is best to avoid all situations in which your judgment could even be *challenged* because of something you accepted from someone.

11.2 MATERIALS HANDLING

A generic problem.

As mentioned earlier, a major disadvantage of the intermittent process design is the amount of movement required between operations. In the case of product organizations this becomes a serious materials handling problem. But the problem is a generic one and applies to all types of organizations whether it is "people handling" in libraries, "paper handling" in home offices, "food handling" in restaurants, or "money handling" in banks.

For example, think back a couple of months ago to when you stood in line to register for your classes, or sent your registration material in through the U.S. Post Office, another intermittent process design. Or remember that time when you had classes on opposite sides of the campus and 10 minutes to make the trip? And the extra difficulty of the trip in the rain or snow?

The importance of materials handling.

Depending on the organization, these costs of "materials" handling can be as high as 75 percent of total expenses. In the manufacturing industry these costs run about 25 percent of factory payroll. Therefore, the subject of materials handling deserves special consideration in the design of the organization's operations.

Principles of materials handling.

Before discussing the types and costs of various materials handling systems it will be useful to examine some of the basic "principles" of materials handling. These principles are grouped under two general approaches to materials handling: (1) minimizing the amount of handling, and (2) improving the efficiency of the handling that must be done.

Minimize Handling

The principles here are as follows:

1. *If possible, do not handle the material at all:* Sometimes this is possible when the operations are arranged so that the output of one is the input to the next (as in continuous processes). Closer analysis of sequential operations, or perhaps output redesign, may allow the combining of separate operations and thus eliminate a handling step.

2. *Minimizing handling by shortening travel distances:* Layout (and relayout) analysis focusing on travel distances and costs of materials handling equipment can save a significant proportion of materials handling costs. And rearrangement of aisles, doorways, and impediments can often allow the use of nearly straight-line distances between locations.

3. *Use gravity to move materials whenever possible:* The creative use of chutes, roller conveyors, pipelines, ramps, and other such gravity-based equipment can save significant costs over equivalent power equipment. In addition, it is fast, reliable, and typically maintenance-free.

Improve Efficiency

There are five general principles used in improving the efficiency of materials handling.

1. *Clearly identify materials:* Incorrect, unknown, and misplaced materials critically hamper operations and add considerably to the costs of materials handling. Not only must the materials be located and/or identified, a costly process in itself, but the materials handling cycle must be repeated again for twice the cost.

2. *Avoid partial loads:* Using high capacity equipment on small loads is an expensive policy. Operations should be scheduled and coordinated so that full or nearly full loads can always be carried. In addition, full loads should be carried in *both* directions to maximize the utilization of expensive labor and equipment.

3. *Minimize pickup and delivery delays:* To increase the utilization of expensive equipment, its idle time while waiting to receive and deliver materials should be minimized. It is this concept that has been used

in rail transit for years where carloads of materials are dropped off on sidings for unloading at the recipient's convenience while the main train continues on its way. Also in rail transit, the piggyback railroad car is an example of the application of this principle. In trucking, the classic dump truck best illustrates the principle.

4. *Use unit loads when feasible:* The objective of **unitization** is to standardize the weight and form of materials in order to systematize not only their handling but their storage as well. There are three main types of unitization: *palletization, containerization,* and *general packaging.* We will briefly describe these before listing the last principle, 5.

Palletization. The use of *pallets*, or platforms (see Figure 11.4), upon which materials are stacked is the most common form of unitization. Typically, the pallets are constructed of wood, 4 by 4 feet, and are carried around by forklift trucks whose blades enter between the pallet boards to lift the entire load. The load is attached to the pallet either by straps, metal bands, chains, nets, or *shrink-wrap*, a plastic film that, when heated, shrinks around the load and pallet and seals it tight (Figure 11.5). This keeps the load from falling off the pallet during transport as well as protecting it from contamination, weather, and theft.

Containerization. Containerization is a unitization method that encloses the material being transported and thus offers environmental protection and security, as well as unit handling efficiency and economy. Containers vary from tote boxes, cushioned mailing bags (for books and small parts), bins, and drums, to large rectangular metal shipping containers (called "rigid containers"). These are designed to load conveniently on railroad flatcars (called *piggyback,* Figure 11.6), airplane cargo compartments (*birdyback*), and the holds of ships (*fishyback*) but require specialized handling equipment.

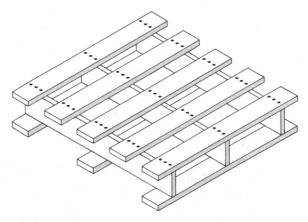

Figure 11.4 Typical wooden pallet.

Figure 11.5 A stretch/shrink-wrap machine wrapping a pallet. (Photo courtesy of Herbert S. Warmflash & Associates and MIMA, Inc.)

Figure 11.6 Piggyback containerization. (Santa Fe Railway photo.)

General Packaging. Used for both commercial and industrial purposes, general packaging serves the objectives of standard quantity dispensing (three different sized boxes of cereal), product identification and differentiation, protection, and, sometimes, advertising. Through the use of unitization, often by means of shrink-wrap, products can be made available which were not previously possible, such as packaged sets of nails in supermarkets. One important innovation in general packaging is the use of the *Universal Product Code* (**UPC,** see Figure 11.7) to permit more efficient handling of supermarket items. This set of bars of varying widths was selected as a standard code by industry after years of study. An optical scanning device can "read" the code, which identifies the company and product only, and can communicate the information to a computer which then can be used to ring up the product price, keep track of any reorders and the shelf inventory, and maintain cash sales information.

Universal Product Code (UPC)

The series of dark lines and white spaces set over numbers is the symbol for the Universal Product Code (UPC), an industry-developed way of identifying food producers and products.

Each participating manufacturer is permanently assigned the first five digits as its own number—this allows identification of about 100,000 companies. The firm uses the second set of five digits to designate each of its products.

For instance, Hunt's tomato paste in the 6-oz size is 27000 (the company number) 38815 (the product number); Kellogg's Special K cereal in the 15-oz box is 38000 01620, and a 2-lb can of Maxwell House regular grind coffee is 43000 70297.

The widths of the dark bars and the white spaces between them are different for each product. Each of the numbers and its version of the symbol is printed on the product's label.

What the grocery receipt might look like

1. You'll be told what you are buying either by brand name or product type. The receipt you now get usually uses cryptic abbreviations, such as "gro" for canned and packaged groceries, "pro" for fresh produce, "mt" for fresh meat.

2. "T" indicates taxable item.

3. Sweet peas were programmed at 22 cents a can or five cans for $1. The system allows the items to go through the checkout counter in a random order but still gives you a price break when you buy the appropriate number of items to get the savings.

4. The system weighs and correctly prices the produce after the proper code numbers have been manually keyed into the computer.

5. At the bottom of the receipt you are told the name of the checker, the number of the checkout lane, the store name or location, the date, and the time.

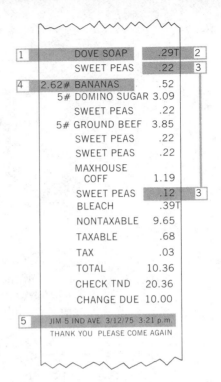

Figure 11.7 A UPC label. (Reprinted with permission from *Changing Times*, © 1975, Kiplinger Washington Editors, Inc., February 1975.)

5. *Mechanize handling tasks whenever cost-effective:* In these days of ever-higher labor rates and extensive development of mechanical methods of materials handling there are relatively few tasks for which manual handling is most economical. Mechanical materials handling equipment is generally classified as either variable-path or fixed-path equipment. We will therefore consider the various general equipment forms under these two categories next.

Variable-Path Equipment

This type of equipment is generally self- or labor-powered and quite flexible in its routing. It handles materials in separate batches, or lots, such as cartons, and therefore is especially suited to intermittent process operations. It generally consists of some form of truck.

Trucks. The two common types of materials handling trucks are the interterminal trucks, seen on the road, and intraplant trucks. The former type range from pickup trucks to garbage trucks, concrete trucks, and tank trucks. Of the intraplant trucks the *forklift* (Figure 11.8) is without doubt the most universal. It generally has two forks (or *tines*) in front but can be specially rigged to handle barrels, drums, bales, rolls, and so forth.

Tractors. The advantage of tractors is that terminal pickup and delivery time can be minimized by loading and unloading the trailers without the tractor, and remaining trailers, standing idle. We see this concept in

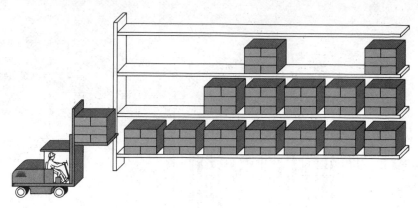

Figure 11.8   Forklift trucks.

"semi's" and tractor-trailers on the road and intraplant trailer trains such as is commonly used for baggage handling at airports.

Manual Vehicles.   Dozens of varieties fall into this inexpensive category, which includes supermarket carts, wagons, hand trucks, and dollies.

Fixed-Path Equipment

This equipment usually handles materials continuously without need for separate identification of the materials. In initial cost it is usually more expensive than variable-path equipment but for large volumes it is more cost-effective. It is usually driven by a central power unit between fixed locations and therefore is best for continuous process operations. A vast amount of this type of equipment is used in automobile assembly.

Conveyors.   The countless varieties of conveyors (roller, screw, overhead, work level, floor height) constitute the main type of fixed-path materials handling equipment. One example is illustrated in Figure 11.9. The advantages of conveyors are many: they operate independently of workers; they can position, transfer, and hold the work (as with *automatic transfer machines*); they can be used for temporary in-process storage; they can pace a production line; and they can buffer operations by, for example, allowing the proper time for cooling, drying, filling, heating, and so forth. A recent innovation in conveyerized systems is the use of bar codes, such as in Figure 11.5, that are machine read and direct, through computerization, items to their correct destination. This will be discussed in more detail in the next section on automated storage and retrieval.

Although typically used for continuous horizontal motion as in supermarket checkout counters and moving sidewalks at airports, they can also move up and down inclines or stop and go. Turntables constitute another specialized form of conveyor.

Elevators.   Closely related to conveyors are the various forms of vertical lifting equipment such as grain elevators, hydraulic lifts (e.g., truck tailgates), dumbwaiters, and man lifts (a vertical belt conveyor with regularly spaced platforms and handles).

Figure 11.9 A typical conveyor. (Reprinted by permission of American Chain and Cable Company, Inc., Acco.)

Cranes. There are typically three types of cranes. One is the large overhead indoor type that runs on tracks near the ceiling, controlled by an operator in a suspended cage, and uses hooks, buckets, or magnets to raise and lower materials. The outdoor equivalents of this are the mobile and fixed cranes used for building construction, loading and unloading of ships, and earth-moving. The third type is the small, self-powered crane, or hoist, with suspended controls used by workers on the floor to move heavy equipment and parts.

Pipelines. These types of equipment can be either powered or gravity-fed and include pipes, chutes, ducts, and tubes. The powered type are either hydraulic, air-pressure, or vacuum, and transport oils, slurries, water, effluents, gases, fumes, dust, and other common bulk materials. Pneumatic tubes and gravity-assisted chutes are used to move rigid materials.

General Considerations

The primary consideration in choosing a materials handling system is, of course, the nature of the material and the operations; for example, liquids cannot be moved by hand cart alone. Next in line are the comparative costs. The breakeven chart is of use here. As shown in Figure 11.10, each type of equipment will have its own fixed and variable (per unit) costs that also depend on the distance the materials must be moved. The number of possible

(Reprinted from *Changing Times*, © 1975, Kiplinger
Washington Editors, Inc., February 1975.)

alternatives can be limited by knowledge of the amount of volume that must
be moved. For high volumes more mechanized and specialized equipment
can be used than for low volumes.

Other considerations include equipment lifetime, salvage, resale value,
operating costs, maintenance, ease of use, safety, and reliability. Also, the
rate of technology development for the equipment should be considered since
new and better equipment may be available in the near future. Last, the rate
of change and growth in the organization itself should be considered since
the organization's operating needs may change significantly in a short time.

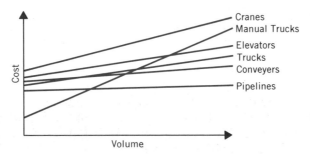

Figure 11.10 An illustration of typical cost
tradeoffs in materials handling.

11.3 WAREHOUSING

A quiet revolution has been occurring in the warehouse in the last decade and we will thus address this issue separately from materials handling, though it is clearly a part of it. A number of seemingly small improvements in various aspects of warehousing and materials handling have joined together to produce a true leap in productivity and performance in this area of materials management. What's more, the success is spreading back into the main operations of the organization.

The following are the independent elements that have joined together:

A quiet revolution.

- Computer hardware.
- Computer software.
- Scanning equipment.
- Sortation devices.
- Conveyance equipment.
- Unit load concepts.
- High-density automated storage and retrieval systems **(AS/RS).**
- Warehouse construction.
- Simulation modeling.
- Management interest.

The computer again.

The driving force behind many of these individual improvements, such as bar code labeling, simulation, and AS/RS is, of course, the development of the computer and associated software, particularly the powerful mini- and microcomputers. Probably even more significant than the impact of the computer on each of the warehousing elements, however, has been the *tying together* of all the elements, again through the computer. We will look at these elements in closer detail.

Automatic Storage and Retrieval Systems

There are four major components of AS/RS:

1. Storage/retrieval (S/R) equipment.
2. Storage structures.
3. Conveyance equipment.
4. Control systems.

Of the S/R equipment, there are two types, unit load systems and order-picking systems.

Unit Load

High-density storage.

These are the relatively older, better known systems such as high-rise stacker cranes for high-density palletized storage (Figures 11.11 and 11.12). Unit load warehousing systems now exceed 100-foot heights and have travel speeds of up to 500 feet per minute (fpm) horizontally and 150 fpm vertically.

Figure 11.11 High-rise unitload AS/RS saves up to 75 percent of conventional warehouse floor space. (Photo courtesy of Litton Unit Handling Systems, division of Litton Systems, Inc.)

Load capacities are in the neighborhood of 2 tons. Aisle sizes have shrunk to the width of the standardized load plus only a few inches. The storage and retrieval equipment is mounted on a rail in the aisle with guidance provided at the top.

New developments.   Very recent developments in unit load systems include "deep lane storage," which stores pallets two deep, thus eliminating half the aisles, and "rackless storage," which accesses the material through an overhead monorail and thereby uses no aisles at all.

Orderpicking

Orderpicking systems fill small, partial loads of multiple items such as a retail store might order. These "less than unit load" systems are of two

Figure 11.12 High-rise unitload AS/RS stores loads up to 4000 pounds at heights to 50 feet. (Photo courtesy of Litton Unit Handling Systems, division of Litton Systems, Inc.)

types: in-aisle and out-of-aisle. The in-aisle systems consist of the person going to the part location and picking the part; the out-of-aisle systems bring the parts, or a container holding the parts, to the person at the end of the aisle. The latest innovation in in-aisle systems consists of a microprocessor controller that horizontally and vertically drives a "man-aboard crane" (Figure 11.13) directly to the appropriate container from which the parts are picked.

Carousels.   Recent developments in out-of-aisle systems include microcomputer-controlled carousel loops (Figure 11.14) that rotate the containers on the carousel until the proper container is accessible at the end of the loop. A second major innovation in out-of-aisle systems is the microprocessor controlled miniload crane. These systems were originally devised for locating

Figure 11.13   Litton's Man-Rider™ stacker crane. (Photo courtesy of Litton Unit Handling Systems, division of Litton Systems, Inc.)

and retrieving manila folders in high-density information storage files but have been adapted very successfully to small parts retrieval.

In-aisle systems are less expensive to purchase and maintain and give the most flexibility. However, out-of-aisle systems make the best use of space and require fewer people. They also provide the best control.

Storage Structures

There is a tremendous interest in making better use of space, not just to reduce the cost of real estate and plant, but also to reduce the costs of utilities and maintenance. The resulting trend to high-density storage systems is referred to as "maximizing the cube," or in other words, using all the volume in the storage location, particularly the empty space so common *above* the

Max the cube.

Figure 11.14 Overhead track, large-bin carousel storage/orderpicking system. (Photo courtesy of Saratoga Conveyer Corp.)

storage bins. The S/R systems described in the previous section directly relate to this trend, particularly concepts such as rackless storage.

But even in the design of the structure there have been exciting innovations. The most recent is called a "rack supported" building, where the storage structure supports the walls and roof of the building. The result is a savings of over 20 percent in costs and much higher utilization of space. An especially favorable aspect of such structures is that for tax purposes they are treated as depreciable equipment rather than buildings.

Conveyance Equipment

Both fixed-path and variable-path conveyance equipment have seen numerous innovations. One of the major innovations in the latter is the automated guided vehicle system (AG/VS). These self-loading and unloading vehicles now follow an *electronic* guidepath in the floor, for significant reliability improvements over their nonelectronic predecessors.

"AG/VS."

A major development in fixed-path systems has been in the area of sortation devices, particularly bar coding and its associated scanning equipment. Sortation equipment of the diverter type can now handle up to 120 items per minute and 100 pounds. Tilt sorting machines have reached speeds of 300 items per minute and 200 pounds.

Control Systems

Role of the computer.

As mentioned previously, this area has probably provided the major breakthrough for all the systems. The computer can be used for receiving, inspection, inventory counting, stock allocation, orderpicking, backordering, billing, scheduling, and numerous other warehousing functions. Its benefits include better space utilization, reliable control of equipment, higher warehouse productivity, better customer service, lower error rates, and better working conditions with higher worker morale as a result. These benefits are all in addition to the major benefit of simply better managerial control.

300 percent increase.

Since 1975 there has been a 300 percent increase in the number of computer-controlled AS/RS systems. The primary direction has been to distributed systems with microcomputers tied to a plant computer, either by cable or, more frequently, by microwave radio. These microcomputers work independently but are directed and feed back to the host computer for information updates. They are dedicated in use, thereby performing independently and more reliably.

Warehousing in the Future

New designs

These developments will clearly continue in the future. For example, in the 1970s only 20 percent of the warehouses were rack supported but fully 50 percent will be in the 1980s. Separate storage locations will soon exceed 5000 and load capacities will exceed 4000 pounds. In the future, new factories will be designed *around* the materials handling systems.

More integrated systems.

Yet some aspects seem to have stabilized. Vertical heights for unit load AS/RS systems will tend to be between 65 to 85 feet and 20 to 30 feet for miniload systems. There will be a trend toward *smaller* AS/RS systems located nearer the storage items. There will be more *integration* of existing warehousing systems, and also of warehousing with plant floor operations. Computer uses will continue to expand; even the *design* of the warehouse will be by computer modeling and simulation.

Last, the interest shown by management in adopting these systems, perhaps the most important element of all, will continue to expand as the abilities of the computer are better recognized and productivity, quality, and foreign competition become more important.

11.4 GENERAL INVENTORY CONSIDERATIONS

Different attitudes toward inventories.

While inventory is inanimate, the topic of inventory and inventory control can arouse completely different sentiments in the minds of people in various departments within an organization. The sales people generally prefer large quantities of inventory to be on hand. In this way they can meet customer requests without having to wait. Customer service is their primary concern. The accounting and financial personnel see inventory in a different light. High inventories do not translate into high customer service in the accountant's language; rather, they translate into large amounts of tied-up capital which could otherwise be used to reduce debt or for other more economically advantageous purposes. From the viewpoint of the operations manager, inventories are seen as a tool that can be used to promote efficient operation of the production facilities. Neither high inventories nor low inventories, per se, are desirable—they are simply allowed to fluctuate so that production can be adjusted to its most efficient level. And top management's concern is with "the bottom line"—what advantages the inventories are providing versus their costs.

Types of Inventories

There are often many purposes for holding inventory but, in general, there are only five types of inventories that an organization can use to accomplish these purposes. The student should be aware that these various types of inventories will not be identified and segregated within the organization and that not all types will be represented in all organizations. The five types are

1. Transit (pipeline) inventories.
2. Buffer inventories.
3. Anticipation inventories.
4. Decoupling inventories.
5. Cycle inventories.

Transit Inventories

Inventories to fill the pipeline.

Transit inventories exist because materials must be moved from one location to another. (These are also known as **pipeline inventories.**) Five hundred tons of coal moving slowly on a coal train from the mines of southeastern Kentucky to an industrial northeastern city cannot provide customer service by powering furnaces or generators. This inventory results because of the transportation time required. If no time were necessary for transport (e.g., inventory could be "beamed" from factory to warehouse á la "Star Trek"), then transit inventories would be unnecessary. Transit inventories also exist between facilities of the same organization. For example, transmissions assembled in the Cincinnati Ford transmission plant are shipped to numerous assembly plants via truck and train.

Buffer Inventories

Inventory as a cushion.

Another one of the purposes of inventories is to protect against the uncertainties of supply and demand. **Buffer inventories** or, as they are sometimes called, **safety stocks** serve to cushion the effect of unpredictable events. The amount of inventory over and above the *average* demand requirement

Variation in
demand for items.

Inventory provides
safety against
stockouts.

Stockouts and
backorders.

Backordering not
always practical.

Inventory buildup
for surges in
demand.

is considered to be buffer stock held to meet any demand in excess of the average. A grocery store manager may know that average daily demand for rye bread is 58 loaves. Does that mean that the manager can stock 58 loaves of bread each morning and be assured of having enough for that day's customers? Obviously not. Even though *average* demand and *average* delivery time are known, actual demands and deliveries vary from these averages and therefore can never be predicted prefectly. These fluctuations in demand and lead time are normally protected against by carrying more inventory than is necessary just to meet "average" demand.

The higher the level of inventory, the better the customer service; that is, the fewer the **stockouts** and **backorders.** A stockout exists when a customer's order for an item cannot be filled because the inventory of that item has run out. Some systems allow backorders in such a case: an order for the demanded item that will be filled as soon as the next shipment of the item is received. In many cases, backordering is practical (such as in a clothing store or a furniture store) and results in a minimum loss of customer goodwill.

But there are many cases in which backorders are not practical, either because of the clerical expense involved in keeping track of what is on backorder or because of the customer's basic unwillingness or inability to wait. For example, gas stations cannot backorder gasoline because the customer can find many substitutes and would be unwilling and generally unable to wait. Better yet, what would you think of a McDonald's manager who has just run out of Big Mac's but wants to backorder one that you can pick up tomorrow?

Buffer inventories are unavoidable because we can never perfectly predict the level of demand or supply for a given period. In Chapter 12 we will consider methods for determining the optimum amount of buffer inventory to be maintained.

Anticipation Inventories

An anticipated future demand is the reason for holding anticipation inventories. Rather than operating with excessive overtime in one period and then allowing the productive system to be idle or shut down because of insufficient demand in another period, inventories can be allowed to build up before an event and consumed during or after the event. Examples of the use of *anticipation inventories* are numerous. Manufacturers, wholesalers, and retailers build anticipation inventories prior to occasions such as Christmas and Easter when demand for specialized products will be high. Anticipation inventories are built up when strikes are expected in a supplier's plant, when a supply price increase appears imminent, or when a large sales promotion is expected to significantly increase demand.

In addition, without anticipation inventory a manufacturing plant would have to produce goods to meet immediate demand, and only immediate demand. For services this is most generally true since the services themselves cannot be inventoried. A painting contractor cannot produce and store "painted walls" and then wait for a customer to demand them. A hospital surgical team cannot produce and store open heart surgeries in their spare time and then use them later when a patient requires one. But, a bathing suit manufacturer could produce bathing suits all year long or it could produce them only during the three-month bathing suit buying season. If corporate policy stated that no inventories of bathing suits were to be stocked, then the company would have to produce only to meet demand.

What this means to the utilization of equipment and workforce can be seen from Figure 11.15. In order to keep inventory level at zero all year long, as depicted in Figure 11.15*b*, the company must only produce during the buying months and must produce only the amount that will be demanded. Thus, the production level remains at zero for 9 of the 12 months of the year and increases to the level of demand for the 3 buying months. This would pose obvious problems. However, if inventory is allowed to fluctuate over the year, as in Figure 11.15*a*, production (and workforce levels) can be maintained at a year-round constant level. The *annual* amount of production will equal the amount of demand over the *three-months* buying period. Figure 11.15*a* also illustrates the effect on the inventory level. Inventory is depleted, due to sales, at the end of July and begins to increase at a constant rate from August through April. Then, beginning in May, demand outstrips production so that inventory falls and continues to decline until the end of July, at which time the cycle begins again. Production is going on at all times whether or not demand exists.

Inventories increase resource utilization.

What efficiencies are produced in this example by allowing a capital investment of inventory to accumulate? First, the productive capacity of the operations system can be one-fourth the size of the system required if no inventories are allowed. Second, the costs of hiring, training, and firing em-

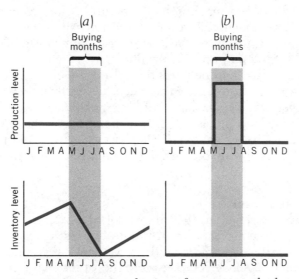

Figure 11.15 Producing for seasonal demand. (*a*) Year-round production. (*b*) Production to meet demand.

ployees are avoided (as well as union trouble) with year-round production. Third, production capacity is used continuously rather than being allowed to sit idle for nine months out of the year. There are indeed some costs associated with keeping inventory, but, as we shall see in this chapter, they must be balanced against other costs, such as the three just mentioned.

Decoupling Inventories

It would be a rare production process in which all equipment and personnel operated at exactly the same rate. Yet, if you were to take an inspection tour through a production facility you would notice that most of the equipment and people were producing. Products move smoothly even though one machine can process parts five times as fast as the one before or after it. An inventory of parts between machines, or fluid in a vat, known as *decoupling inventory,* acts to disengage the production process. That is, inventories act as shock absorbers, or cushions, increasing and decreasing in size as parts are added to and used up from the stock. Even if a preceding machine were to break down, the following machines could still produce (at least for a while) since an "in-process inventory" of parts would be waiting for production. The more inventories that management carries between stages in the manufacturing-distribution process, the less coordination is needed to keep the process running smoothly. Clearly, there is an optimum balance between inventory level and coordination in the operations system.

But without decoupling inventories, each operation in the plant would have to produce at an identical rate (a *paced line*) to keep the production flowing smoothly, and when one operation broke down, the entire plant would come to a standstill. Figure 11.16 illustrates two machines that produce at different rates and the inventory between them which is used to disengage these two machines. If machine A, for example, could produce twice as fast as machine B, then A could possibly be used to produce other parts for a third machine after running an appropriately large batch of inventory for B to work on. If A produced at a *slower* rate than B, then more type A machines would be needed or else B would sit idle. Thus, there is no place or capacity for maintaining decoupling inventory in a paced line; the system must always run smoothly, or not run at all. This is exactly the approach used in Japanese "just-in-time" production systems (discussed in Chapter 12) such as "Kanban." They take the time and trouble to maintain a system like this just so expensive decoupling inventory can be dispensed with.

Smoothing production through in-process inventories.

Paced lines without inventory.

Cycle Inventories

Cycle inventories or, as they are sometimes referred to, lot-size inventories exist for a different reason from the others just discussed. Each of the previous types of inventories typically serve one of the major purposes for holding inventory. Cycle inventories, on the other hand, result from management's attempt to minimize the total cost of carrying and ordering inventory. If the annual demand for a particular part is 12,000 units, management could decide to place one order for 12,000 units and maintain a rather large in-

Inventory lots to minimize total costs.

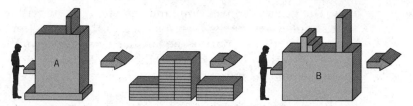

Figure 11.16 Inventory used to disengage and smooth production.

ventory throughout the year or place 12 orders of 1000 each and maintain a lower level of inventory. But the costs associated with ordering and receiving would increase. Cycle inventories are the inventories that result from ordering in batches or "lots" rather than on an "as needed" basis.

As you can see from this discussion, the inventory system and the operations system within an organization are strongly interrelated. Inventories affect customer service, facility and equipment utilization, capacity, and labor efficiency. Therefore the plans concerning the acquisition and storage of materials, or "inventories," are vital to the production process. This chapter initiates the discussion of these plans. A recurring point of focus in the discussion is: How *much* to order and *when*. All of the analyses and plans eventually boil down to addressing these two issues, as we shall see.

Inventory Classes

Inventories are also usually classified into four groups, some of which correspond directly with the previous inventory types but some of which do not.

1. Raw materials.
2. Spares, supplies, stores.
3. Work-in-process.
4. Finished goods.

Raw Materials

Raw materials are the objects, commodities, elements, and items that are received (usually purchased) from outside the organization to be used directly in the production of the final product. Typically, when we think of raw materials we think of such things as sheet metal, flour, paint, structural steel, chemicals, and other basic materials. But nuts and bolts, hydraulic cylinders, engines, frames, integrated circuits, and other assemblies purchased from outside the organization would also be considered part of the *raw materials inventory* of an organization.

Spares, Supplies, Stores

Spares are sometimes produced by the organization itself rather than being purchased. These are usually machine parts or supplies, crucial to production. The term "supplies" is often used synonymously with inventories. The general convention, and the one that we will adopt in this book, is that supplies are stocks of items used in the production of goods or services but not directly as a part of the finished product. Examples are carbon paper, staples, pencils, and packing material. "Stores" commonly includes both supplies and raw materials.

Work-in-Process

Work-in-Process (WIP) inventory consists of all of the materials, parts, and assemblies that are being worked on or are waiting to be processed within the operations system. Decoupling inventories are an example of work-in-process. That is, they are all of the items that have left the raw materials inventory but have not yet been converted or assembled into a final product.

Finished Goods

The finished goods inventory is the stock of completed products. Goods, once completed, are transferred out of work-in-process inventory and into the finished goods inventory. From here they can be sent to distribution centers, sold to wholesalers, or sold directly to retailers or final customers.

Another class of inventory that should also be considered is *components*. Components are subassemblies of a finished product, that is, some assembly of parts that enter as a unit into the final assembly of the product. Components can be found in each of the preceding classes of inventories. Some components are purchased directly from outside the organization and stocked in raw materials inventory. Other components are produced from raw materials by the organization and are stocked until needed in final production. Still other components are stocked as replacement parts in finished goods inventory. General Motors, for example, must produce engines, transmissions, doors, fenders, and other components of each style of automobile produced, to be sold as replacement and maintenance parts. These components are classified as finished goods, even though they are not automobiles, but parts of automobiles.

11.5 SUMMARY AND KEY LEARNING POINTS

In this second chapter of Part III on Detailed Operations, we moved from a focus on all inputs to examining just the materials flows. First, we studied the procurement/purchasing system and its procedures and forms. We then looked at the supplier rating and selection process and illustrated some useful models for this task. Last, we considered cost/price aspects and described the common types of discounts.

Then we moved into the plant and looked at materials handling and storage equipment. We noted some principles of materials handling, the common equipment and machines, and a number of new techniques and technologies such as unitization, bar code labeling, AS/RS, and rack-supported buildings. Last, we introduced some general inventory considerations, such as inventory classes and types, that will be elaborated further in Chapter 12.

Key learning points have been

- Procurement/purchasing is a critical, but often unappreciated, function responsible for the disposition of great sums of money. They must rate, evaluate, and select vendors/suppliers based on price, quality, accessibility, service, competence, risk, and other factors. They must be familiar with the terms and discounts in their trade and obtain favorable terms with vendors. Many forms and contracts are used in their daily work such as purchase orders and requisitions.

- The basic principles of materials handling fall into two categories: minimizing handling and improving efficiency. In the former category there are three principles: do not handle at all, shorten the distance, and use gravity. In the latter are five principles: clearly identify materials, avoid partial loads, minimize pickup/delivery delays, use unit loads, and mechanize handling.

- Materials handling equipment is generally one of two types: variable-path (trucks, manual vehicles, and so on) and fixed-path (cranes, conveyors, pipelines, elevators). The new concepts in materials handling relate mainly to the unit load principle: palletization, shrink-wrapping, and containerization. Another new concept is using bar code labeling such as UPC to identify loads.

- The computer has created a revolution in the warehousing storage and retrieval function. AS/RS equipment is computerized and can handle larger, heavier loads at a greater distance, much faster, and in significantly less space than previously. Orderpicking systems are also very advanced, exhibiting man-aboard cranes, automated carousels, and miniload systems for small parts and papers. Storage structures have also been revolutionized, to the point of totally rack-supported buildings being used for ultrahigh-density storage. And AG/VS conveyance and sortation systems have seen many innovations.

- There are five common purposes, or types, of inventories: transit or pipeline, buffer, anticipation, decoupling, and cycle. Four classes, or physically different forms, of inventories are raw materials, spares and supplies, WIP, and finished goods.

11.6 KEY TERMS

procurement (p. 404)	seasonal discount (p. 411)	buffer inventory (p. 427)
vendor (p. 407)	cash discount (p. 411)	safety stock (p. 427)
sole source (p. 410)	unitization (p. 414)	backorders (p. 428)
purchase order (p. 405)	UPC (p. 416)	stockouts (p. 428)
80-20 rule (p. 410)	AS/RS (p. 421)	work-in-process (WIP)
trade discount (p. 411)	transit inventory (p. 427)	(p. 432)
quantity discount (p. 411)	pipeline inventory (p. 427)	

11.7   REVIEW AND DISCUSSION QUESTIONS

1. In what ways might organizational purchasing differ from individual purchasing other than those named in the text?

2. On what basis would you evaluate a potential supply source?

3. When might an organization *not* wish to take advantage of each of the four types of discounts?

4. Should a company prohibit its purchasing agent from socializing with vendors?

5. Interpret the principles of materials handling for a library.

6. At grocery checkout counters with UPC scanning equipment, about one-third of all items still must be keyed in by hand. Why is this so? How could it be improved, or can it?

7. Many of the advances in automated warehousing have brought multiple benefits to users beyond what was expected. What would be the direct, expected benefits and what might be the derivative, unexpected benefits?

8. Under what conditions might automated warehousing *not* be desirable?

9. What inflexibilities are forced on service organizations as a result of their inability to inventory their output? Is it possible to inventory any of these outputs? Give examples.

10. What effect(s) on the types of inventories would "beaming" á la "Star Trek" produce?

11. Contrast the division of inventory "types" with "classes." Does every class exist for each type or are some classes more common for certain types?

12. Why does the UPC not include the price of the product?

11.8   CASE

CLASSIC AUTO PARTS COMPANY

Classic Auto Parts Company began eight years ago when Don Murphy, frustrated at his inability to find needed parts for his 1961 356B Porsche, purchased two rusted Porsches for parts. Don had always been a sports car enthusiast and the 356B was the third of his auto restoration attempts. Parts for the old Porsches were extremely scarce and prices for available components were at a premium.

Don was able to complete his restoration with the parts obtained from the two parts cars. He was also able to sell, with no advertising, all the usable parts of the two cars which he did not need. He wound up with a 2000 percent profit on the purchase of the two cars. He also received numerous phone calls about parts long after the two cars were both "parted out" and their remains shipped off to the junk yard.

Don began to search for old Porsches that were not in restorable condition and purchased as many as he could find. He called his company Classic Auto Parts and placed an ad in the yellow pages of several telephone books in the surrounding communities. After two years in business, Don quit his full-time job and devoted his entire attention to Classic Auto Parts.

Calls were coming in constantly for body components (fenders, rocker panels, lower pans, hoods, trunk lids, doors, etc.) which were typically rusted on the cars that Don had. Don approached a local sheet metal fabrication company with the idea of manufacturing stamped floor pans identical to those of the original Porsches. The dies for the press were manufactured at a cost of $8200 and Don had 100 floor pan sets produced. His cost in the floor pans (including the cost of the die) was $140 each. He sold all the sets within the first six months at a selling price of $175 each. With this initial experience, Don decided to become actively involved in the NOS (new-old stock) business. Since that time, Don has taken on several additional suppliers for sheet metal parts and has produced floor pans for all model Porsches including the newer 911s and 912s, and is producing fender panels, inner fender wells, trunk lids and deck lids, rocker panel assemblies, and a variety of chrome and rubber body parts. The business has grown from an initial part-time activity to a $13 million per year business.

Dick Sandmeyer, Don's vice-president in charge

of purchasing, has recently secured quotes on NOS battery hold-down brackets. Four suppliers have bid on the order for 1000 brackets and have quoted the following prices.

Supplier	Price	Terms	FOB	Tooling Cost
A	$8.62	2/10 net 30	shipping point	$ 750
B	7.50	1/10 net 30	Classic Auto Parts	550
C	9.01	net 30	Classic Auto Parts	1000
D	7.40	net 30	shipping point	500

Dick has only specified that the battery hold-down bracket be equivalent in construction and workmanship with the original Porsche hold-down bracket. The vendors have not been given prints or other engineering specifications from which to develop their bid. Classic has purchased previously from vendors A and C, and has not purchased from vendors B and D. Dick feels that a fair price for the part would be in the $8.50 to $9.00 range. He has some doubts about vendor D's ability to produce the part although they are doing NOS work for several companies specializing in NOS Chevrolet parts. The two vendors that Classic has used before have both called to talk with Dick and have indicated that their prices have gone up due to inflation in both labor and materials costs.

Vendor A is located 800 miles from Classic's plant. Vendor C is located in the same city as Classic. Vendor B is located 300 miles away and vendor D is located 75 miles away. The part weighs approximately 3 pounds.

Questions for Discussion

1. Which supplier should Classic choose? Make whatever assumptions and analysis that are necessary.

2. What special studies might be useful here?

3. What cautions would you give to Dick in making his decision to select one of the new vendors?

11.9 REFERENCES AND BIBLIOGRAPHY

1. Aljian, G. W., ed., *Purchasing Handbook*, 3rd ed., New York: McGraw-Hill, 1973.

2. Ammer, D. S., *Materials Management*, Homewood, IL: Irwin, 1974.

3. Apple, J. M., *Materials Handling Systems Design*, New York: Ronald Press, 1973.

4. Dickson, G. W., "An Analysis of Vendor Selection Systems and Decision," *Journal of Purchasing*, 2:5–17 (Feb. 1966).

5. Edwards, M. G., "Supplier Management Evaluation," *Journal of Purchasing*, 3:28–41 (Feb. 1967).

6. England, W. B., and Leenders, M. R., *Purchasing and Materials Management*, Homewood, IL: Irwin, 1975.

7. *Industrial Engineering*, special issues: *Materials Handling*, Sept. 1980, March 1982. *Warehousing*, June 1980, June 1981.

8. Lamberson, L. R., Dredenck, D., and Wuori, J., "Quantitative Vendor Evaluation," *Journal of Purchasing and Materials Management*, 12:19–28 (Spring 1976).

9. Love, S. F., *Inventory Control*, New York: McGraw-Hill, 1979.

10. National Association of Purchasing Agents, Inc., "Vendor Supplier Evaluation," *Guide to Purchasing*, New York, 1967.

11. *Production and Inventory Management*, issue on automated storage/retrieval systems, April 1982.

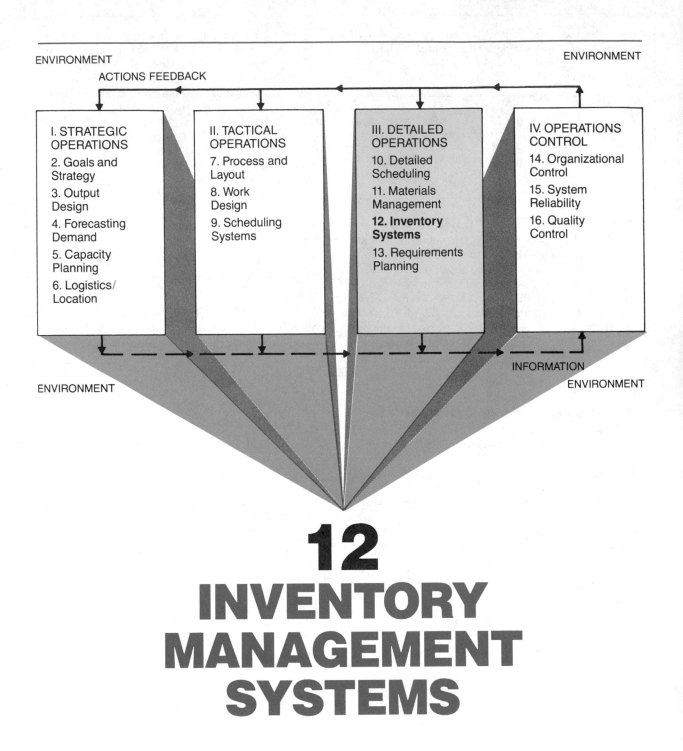

ENVIRONMENT ENVIRONMENT

ACTIONS FEEDBACK

I. STRATEGIC OPERATIONS

2. Goals and Strategy

3. Output Design

4. Forecasting Demand

5. Capacity Planning

6. Logistics/ Location

II. TACTICAL OPERATIONS

7. Process and Layout

8. Work Design

9. Scheduling Systems

III. DETAILED OPERATIONS

10. Detailed Scheduling

11. Materials Management

12. Inventory Systems

13. Requirements Planning

IV. OPERATIONS CONTROL

14. Organizational Control

15. System Reliability

16. Quality Control

ENVIRONMENT

INFORMATION

ENVIRONMENT

12
INVENTORY MANAGEMENT SYSTEMS

12

LEARNING OBJECTIVES

By the completion of this chapter the student should

- Be aware of the various costs involved in inventory systems.

- Know the two basic questions that inventory models must answer.

- Be familiar with the three major types of inventory management systems and their method of operation.

- Be able to use the ABC classification concept.

- Understand the assumptions, development, and use of the economic order quantity (EOQ) model.

- Know how to analyze an inventory ordering problem that includes discounts for quantity purchases.

- Comprehend the economic production lot size (ELS) situation and the development of the ELS model.

- Have developed a sense for the difficulties that arise when multiple products are produced on the same facilities and ways to circumvent this.

- Appreciate the complexity demand and lead time uncertainty poses for inventory management and the solution approaches employed for these difficulties.

- Know how to use decision tables, incremental analysis, probability trees, and Monte Carlo simulation to handle inventory problems involving uncertainty.

In the previous chapter we addressed the general problem of materials management from purchasing through handling to storage, and discussed the various types and classes of materials. In this chapter we now consider the issue of managing those materials stores, called "inventories."

Significant improvements through computerization of their inventory management system have allowed many organizations to both reduce their inventory management labor, thereby improving their productivity, and reduce their levels of inventory, thus freeing up capital for other investments. Yet, at the same time they have improved their customer service. In this and the following chapter we will analyze these various systems and their characteristics. We will also compare them to the famous Japanese "Kanban" system used at Toyota.

First we look at inventory costs and the variety of inventory systems in use. We derive the economic order quantity and demonstrate its use in a retailing situation. We move from this to some extensions such as optimal order quantities under discounting, finite production rates, and multiple products produced on the same facilities. Last, we discuss the concept of using safety stocks to improve service levels, illustrating, when suitable, the alternative use of decision trees and simulation (in the appendix). Our examples include a police department, a paint company, an oil company, a newsboy, a jewelry store, and a manufacturer.

12.1 DESIGN OF OPTIMAL INVENTORY SYSTEMS

The inventory system balances the costs of inventory with its advantages.

The ultimate objective of any inventory system is to produce decisions regarding the level of inventory that will result in an optimum balance between the purposes for holding inventories and the costs associated with them. Typically, we hear inventory management practitioners and researchers speaking of "total cost minimization" as the objective of an inventory system. If we were able to place dollar costs on interruptions in the smooth flow of goods through the operations system, on not meeting customer demands, or on failures to provide the other purposes for which inventories exist, then "total cost minimization" would be a reasonable objective. But, since we are unable to assign costs to many of these subjective factors, we must be satisfied with obtaining a good "balance" between inventory costs and inventory functions.

Costs Involved in Inventory Decisions

There are essentially five broad categories of cost associated with inventory system decisions:

Five inventory costs.

1. Ordering or setup costs.
2. Carrying or holding costs.
3. Stockout costs.
4. Capacity-associated costs
5. The cost of the goods themselves

Ordering or Setup Costs

Ordering costs are the costs associated with the outside procurement of material, and *setup costs* are the costs associated with the internal procurement (i.e., the internal manufacture) of parts of material. Ordering costs include the cost of writing the order, processing the order through the purchasing system, postage, invoice processing, accounts payable processing, and receiving department costs such as handling, testing and inspection, and transporting. Setup costs also include order writing and processing for the internal production system, the cost of the setup labor, the machine downtime due to a new setup (i.e., cost of an idle, nonproducing machine), the cost of parts damaged during setup (e.g., actual parts are often used for tests during setup), and costs associated with the employee learning curve (i.e., the cost of early production spoilage and low productivity immediately after a new production run is started). Learning curve costs are often referred to as "hat-switching" costs.

Inventory Carrying or Holding Costs

Inventory carrying or *holding costs* consist of the following major components:

Three components of carrying costs.

1. Capital costs

2. Storage costs.

3. Risk costs.

Capital costs include interest on money invested in inventory and in land, buildings, and equipment necessary to hold and maintain the inventory. These rates often exceed 20 percent these days. If these investments were not required, the organization could invest the capital in an alternative which would earn some return on investment.

Storage costs include rent, taxes, and insurance on buildings, depreciation of buildings, maintenance and repairs expense, heat, power, light, salaries of security personnel, taxes on the inventory, labor costs in handling inventory, clerical costs of inventory record keeping, taxes and insurance on equipment, equipment depreciation, equipment fuel and energy costs, the costs of repairs and maintenance, and so forth. Some of these costs are variable, some fixed, and some "semi-fixed."

Inventory risk costs include the costs of obsolete inventory, insurance on inventory, physical deterioration of the inventory, and losses from pilferage.

Carrying costs are frequently 35 percent of the value of the inventory.

While some of these costs are relatively small, the total costs of carrying items in inventory can be quite large. Studies have demonstrated that the cost for a typical manufacturing firm are frequently as large as 35 percent of the cost of the inventoried items. A large portion of this cost is typically the cost of the invested capital.

Stockout Costs

If inventory is unavailable when customers request it, or if inventory is unavailable when it is needed for production, a stockout occurs. There are

The cost of not having inventory when it is needed.

several costs associated with each type of stockout. A stockout of an item demanded by a customer or client can result in lost sales or demand, lost client goodwill (very difficult to estimate), and costs associated with back-order processing (such as extra paperwork, expediting, special handling, and higher shipping costs). A stockout of an item needed for production results in production rescheduling costs, costs of downtime and delay caused by the shortage, the cost of "rush" shipping of needed parts, and possibly the cost of substituting a more expensive part or materials.

Capacity-Associated Costs

Capacity-associated costs are those costs incurred because a change in productive capacity is necessary or because a temporary shortage or excess in capacity exists. Why would capacity be too great or too small? If, for example, a company tried to meet seasonal demand (or any fluctuations in demand) by changing production level rather than by allowing inventory level to increase or decrease, capacity would have to be increased during high demand periods and reduced during low demand periods.

Inventory-capacity tradeoffs.

Capacity-associated costs include the overtime required to increase capacity, the costs of hiring, training, and terminating employees, the cost of using less skilled workers during peak periods, and the cost of idle time if capacity is *not* reduced during periods when demand decreases. The trade-offs in these costs were considered earlier in Chapter 9 in terms of aggregate scheduling.

Cost of Goods

Last, the goods themselves must be paid for. Although they must be acquired sooner or later anyway, *when* they are acquired can influence their cost considerably, such as through quantity discounts.

Decisions in Inventory Management

As we have stated, the objective of an inventory management system is to make decisions regarding the appropriate (optimal) level of inventory and changes in the level of inventory. To maintain the appropriate level of inventory, "decision rules" are needed to answer two basic questions.

Two questions an inventory control system must answer.

1. When should an order be placed to replenish the inventory?

2. How many items should be ordered when inventory is reordered?

The role of the decision rules is to guide the inventory manager in evaluating the current state of the inventory and deciding if some action, such as replenishment, is required. Various types of inventory management systems incorporate different decision rules to answer the "when" and "how much" decisions. Some are time dependent and others are dependent on the level of inventory, but the essential decisions are the same. Even when complexities, such as uncertainty in demand and delivery times, are introduced into the inventory management problem, the "how many" and "when to order" decisions still remain the basis of sound inventory management.

Types of Inventory Management Systems

All inventory systems can be classified as one of three varieties, based on the approach taken to the "when to order" decision.

Three types of inventory control systems.

1. Reorder point systems.

2. Periodic review systems.

3. Material requirements planning (MRP) systems.

Before we describe these three systems, let us consider a simplified inventory management situation to provide a background for our subsequent discussion.

Consider the Hard Charger Corporation, a wholesaler that sells 1000 generators per month to auto parts retailers in the Southeast. Demand for generators is constant throughout the year. Suppose that Hard Charger has a policy of ordering 2000 generators per order and that they have just received a shipment of 2000, bringing their inventory level to 2000.

Hard Charger sells 1000 generators per month, and therefore the beginning inventory of 2000 units will be depleted by the end of the second month. In order to keep from "stocking out" an order must be placed and shipment received prior to the end of the second month. To keep the costs of carrying inventory as low as possible, it is desirable to schedule receipt of the order at the time that the previous inventory supply is exhausted. Assuming this perfect scheduling and "instantaneous replenishment" (the immediate resupply of the order quantity when the inventory level reaches zero), a graph of the inventory level as it changes over time would appear as in Figure 12.1.

Inventory is used at the rate of 1000 per month and orders are received so that the inventory level is replenished before a stockout can occur. No stockouts occur and the inventory level never exceeds the order quantity of 2000. As we progress through this chapter we will eliminate the unrealistic assumptions of constant demand and instantaneous replenishment and introduce other more "realistic" assumptions into our discussion. For now, let us turn to a discussion of the three types of inventory control systems.

Reorder Point Systems

In reorder point systems an inventory *level* is specified at which a replenishment order for a fixed quantity of the inventory item is to be placed.

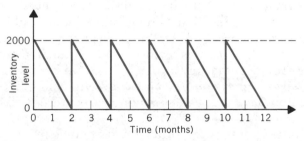

Figure 12.1 Inventory fluctuation.

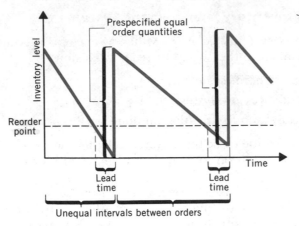

Figure 12.2   A reorder point system illustrated.

Reorder points and lead times.

Whenever the inventory on hand reaches the predetermined inventory level (or **reorder point**) an order is placed for a prespecified amount, as illustrated in Figure 12.2. The reorder point is established so that the inventory on hand at the time an order is placed is sufficient to meet demand during the **lead time** (i.e., the time between placement of an order and receipt of the shipment). The quantity of inventory to be ordered is typically based on the **economic order quantity** (EOQ) concept (one answer to the "how much to order" question), an approach illustrated in the next section. But, other "how much" decision rules such as ordering "six-weeks supply" are also used in reorder point systems.

The "two-bin" system.

A simplified and much used variation of the reorder point system is the **two-bin** system. In this system, parts are stored in two bins, one large and one small. The small bin usually holds sufficient parts to satisfy demand during the replenishment lead time. Parts are used from only the large bin until it is empty. At that time, a replenishment order is placed and parts are used from the small bin until the replenishment order is received.

Who should reorder?

Two-bin systems have been developed in many variations. In some systems it is simply the responsibility of the employee who removes the last item from the large bin to place a materials requisition with the purchasing department or with the supervisor. In others, a completed requisition is placed at the bottom of the larger bin and only needs to be picked up and submitted when the last item is removed. In others, an 80-column computer card is affixed to a wrapped quantity of items in the small bin. When these items are opened, the card is removed and sent to data processing to generate an order. The advantage of the two-bin system is that no detailed records of inventory use (a **perpetual inventory system**) must be kept and inventory level need not be continually recounted to determine whether or not a reorder should be placed.

The perpetual inventory system. Constantly checking the inventory level.

This latter point is important. A perpetual inventory system requires either a manual card system or a computerized system to keep track of daily usage and daily stock levels. Also, each day the cards or computer file must be "searched" to find all items whose balances have fallen below the reorder point. Note that these are clerical functions that remove the burden of assessing proper inventory levels from the people who use the inventory. Typically, perpetual systems run into problems because those who use the inventory fail to report the use. Management controls over the inventory system must be fairly rigid to ensure that perpetual records remain accurate and, in turn, result in proper orders being placed for inventory. This also requires a regular physical check of the inventory to be sure that the records are accurate. A reorder point system could not perform adequately without either a two-bin type system or a perpetual inventory control system. Without one of these, someone would have to record the inventory balances for all items each day in order to have accurate counts and, therefore, to know when to order. The recent development of "real time" inventory control systems that include computerized order entry and invoicing have greatly eased the perpetual system difficulties and reduced the need for two-bin types of systems.

"Real time" computer systems.

Periodic Review Systems

The periodic review system.

In **periodic review** systems the inventory level is reviewed at equal time intervals and at each review a reorder is placed to bring the inventory level up to a desired quantity. Such a system is especially appropriate for retailers when ordering families of goods. The amount of the reorder is based on a "maximum" level established for each inventory item. The quantity that should be reordered is the amount necessary to bring the *on-hand* inventory, plus the *on-order* quantity, less the expected demand over the lead time to the maximum level. That is

On-hand plus on-order.

$$\text{reorder quantity} = \text{maximum level} - \text{"on-hand" inventory}$$
$$- \text{"on-order" quantity} + \text{demand over lead time} \quad (12.1)$$

The on-hand inventory is the amount actually in stock. If the system allows back orders, then on-hand could be negative, at least in concept. If back orders are not used, then a stockout condition simply results in a zero on-hand quantity. The on-order amount is the quantity for which purchase orders have been issued, but delivery has not yet been made. We deduct the on-order quantity to ensure that an order is not placed for the same goods. Figure 12.3 illustrates such an occurrence. Suppose at review point A an order is simply placed for Q_A. At review point B, the first order has not arrived so an order for Q_B is placed. No attention was paid to the on-order quantity. Now, some time later, Q_A is received, and then Q_B. At review point C, inventory exceeds the desired maximum.

Is an order due in?

Fixed review period or fixed reorder amount?

In periodic review systems the *review period* (and therefore reorder period) *is fixed* and the *order quantity varies* (see Figure 12.4) according to the above rule. This system is more appropriate when it is difficult to keep track of inventory levels and the cost of stockouts or when safety stock is not excessive. In reorder point systems the *order quantity is fixed* and the *reorder period varies* (see Figure 12.2). This system is best where a continuing watch of inventory levels is feasible and stockouts or safety stock would be expen-

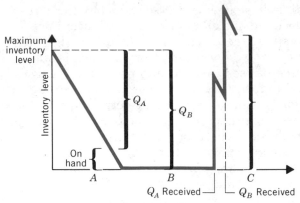

Figure 12.3 Periodic review systems without considering on-order quantity.

sive. If demand increases during the period, the reorder point system would simply place an order sooner than normal. The periodic review system would review and place an order at the regularly scheduled time but for a larger than normal quantity. However, in both systems there is a risk that a stockout will occur because the demand during the lead time may be greater than the amount on hand at the time the order is placed. As we shall see later in the chapter, there are ways to compensate for this risk.

Material Requirements Planning (MRP) Systems

The two previously discussed systems operate best for inventory items with fairly constant, and independent, demand. **Independent demand** simply means that demand for an item is not based on demand for some other item. Examples include clothing, furniture, automobiles or retail items, and supply type items (paper, pencils) in a manufacturing or office environment. The most likely applications for the two previous systems are for finished

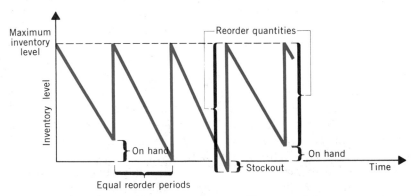

Figure 12.4 Periodic review system illustrated (assumes none on order at time of reorder).

goods inventories and for some continuously used raw materials. But, for a wide range of raw materials, component parts, and subassembles, the **MRP** system, a materials application of the requirements planning concept presented in Chapter 9, produces better results.

MRP for dependent demand.

For most component parts and assemblies used in production, demand tends to be intermittent rather than continuous because demand for those components is *dependent* on demand for higher level assemblies,* or finished products. For example, many manufactured products are entered into production in batches, the size of the batches and the scheduling of entry into production being dependent on anticipated orders for the product. Entering an order for a batch of 100 Model X-72 room air conditioners would result in a (dependent) demand for 100 "wood grained" front covers. There is little sense in stocking large quantities of these covers if they will only be demanded a few times throughout the year. A better inventory strategy would obviously be to order the 100 covers so that they will be received just prior to the time they are needed in production, that is, the last stage of assembly prior to packaging.

Order dependent demand items when they are needed.

MRP was primarily designed by Joe Orlicky of IBM in the early 1960s to take advantage of the capabilities of computers for storing and monitoring the millions upon millions of parts requirements of modern production. We will discuss the MRP approach in detail in Chapter 13.

Kanban.

Another version of MRP used by many Japanese firms is called "just-in-time." The famous "Kanban" system of Toyota is a **just-in-time (JIT)** system that uses large cardboard cards (the kanban) to withdraw stock as needed from continually replenished supplies. The JIT procedure did not derive from MRP but arose independently; yet it is very similar in its application.

Goal: to eliminate waste of space.

The impetus behind JIT is different, however: to eliminate waste, particularly in facility space which is scarce in Japan. Stores of unused materials (WIP) are perceived as using up precious space. The goal is to turn every production system into a continuously flowing system of materials where items pass through the system one by one and are never in storage; that is, to have no "decoupling" inventory.

Clearly, equipment setup times to vary product mixes must be extremely short or else items will start stacking up and occupying space. The reduction of setup times has been a major breakthrough for Japanese industry. Machines that five years ago required 4 hours to disassemble and set up again now take 10 minutes. Mold changes, for example, are done in minutes by using "lazy Susans" to swing the old molds out and new ones in.

"Lazy Susans" in the factory.

Many side benefits.

The JIT system has produced many unexpected side benefits for the Japanese as well, however. With no stores of material sitting idle there is little inventory investment cost (raw materials are delivered three and four times a day rather than weekly, or monthly). And with each worker passing a completed item to the next worker, defects are caught immediately (and the responsible reason corrected immediately). Scrap also becomes immediately

*Assemblies are subcomponents of products composed of multiple parts and were discussed in Chapter 7.

apparent and thus efforts are made to eliminate it. And without bins of material to store, locate, and move, the scheduling and management process is greatly simplified. The result, in a sense, is that an intermittent process is converted to a continuous process.

The JIT system has many advantages to recommend its use but requires a facility that is extremely well controlled, which is not typically a strength of U.S. manufacturers, as we shall see in Chapter 14 on Organizational Control.

12.2 PRIORITIES FOR INVENTORY MANAGEMENT: THE ABC CONCEPT

Varying importance of inventories. In practice, all inventories cannot be controlled with equal attention. Some inventories are simply too small or too unimportant to warrant intensive monitoring and control activity. Additionally, in implementing new inventory management systems a priority ranking must be developed to allow management to decide the order in which to include the inventoried items in the control system. One simple procedure of common use is the ABC classification system.

The **ABC classification system** is based on the annual dollar purchases of an inventoried item. As can be seen from Table 12.1, a relatively small proportion of the total items in an inventory account for a relatively large proportion of the total annual dollar volume, and a large proportion of the items account for a small proportion of the dollars. This phenomenon is often found in systems in which large numbers of different items are maintained, and is also in evidence in marketing where a small number of customers represent the bulk of the sales, in complaint departments where a large volume of complaints come from a relatively small group, and so forth.

The three classifications used in the ABC system are

A. *High value items:* The 15 to 20 percent or so* of the items that account for 75 to 80 percent of the total annual inventory value.

Table 12.1 Inventory Value by Item

Number of Items	Percentage of Total Items	Annual Dollar Purchases	Percentage of Total Purchases
521	4.8	$15,400,000	50.7
574	5.3	6,200,000	20.4
1,023	9.4	3,600,000	11.8
1,145	10.5	2,300,000	7.6
3,754	34.0	1,800,000	5.9
3,906	36.0	1,100,000	3.6
10,923	100.0	$30,400,000	100.0

*The percentages are somewhat arbitrary and vary to suit individual needs.

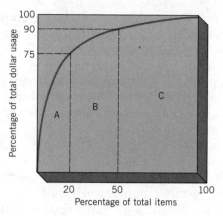

Figure 12.5   ABC inventory categories.

Three value classes.

B. *Medium value items:* The 30 to 40 percent of the items that account for approximately 15 percent of the total annual inventory value.

C. *Low value items:* The 40 to 50 percent of the items that account for 10 to 15 percent of the annual inventory value.

This classification is presented in the ABC chart of Figure 12.5, which presents the cumulative distribution of the dollar value of inventory items. In practice, the A items are first identified, then the C items, and what is left is usually considered to represent the B items.

A common misconception is that the ABC classification is based on the dollar value of the individual items. Relatively costly items can still be classified as C items if the annual usage is low enough. Table 12.2 presents a simple table of cost/volume combinations and the inventory class likely to result.

Annual usage important also.

ABC levels of control.

The ABC classification is management's guide to the necessary control priority of inventory items. A items should be subject to the tightest control with detailed inventory records being maintained and accurate, updated

Table 12.2   Classification of Inventory Items

Dollar Value/Unit	Volume/Year	Category
High	High	A
High	Medium	A
Medium	High	A
High	Low	B
Medium	Medium	B
Low	High	B
Medium	Low	C
Low	Medium	C
Low	Low	C

values of order quantities and reorder points being employed. B items are subject to normal control with order quantities being set by EOQ (as shown in the next section) but with less frequent updating of records and review of order quantities and reorder points. C items are subject to little control; orders are commonly placed for six month's to one year's supply so that relatively little control must be exercised and inventory records can be kept simple. Essentially, the control time and effort saved by *not* controlling C items is used to tighten control of A items.

Other uses of ABC.   The ABC concept is not only used for inventory control—it is also frequently used to determine priority levels for customer service and for deciding on safety stock levels, a subject we will address later in this chapter. The concept is also known by other names such as the "80-20 rule" and the "Pareto principle" (the economist who discovered the effect).

12.3 THE ECONOMIC ORDER QUANTITY

EOQ for batch rather than continuous delivery.   The *economic order quantity* (**EOQ**) concept applies to inventory items that are replenished in *batches* or *orders* and are not produced and delivered continuously. While we have identified a number of cost categories associated with inventory decisions, only two, the carrying cost and the ordering cost, are considered in the elementary EOQ model. The shortage and capacity-associated costs are not relevant because shortages and changes in capacity should not occur if demand is constant, as we assume in this elementary case. And the cost of the goods is considered to be fixed (for the moment) and, hence, does not alter the decisions as to *when* inventory should be reordered or *how much* should be ordered.

We assume the following in the EOQ model:

1. Rate of demand is constant (e.g., 50 units per day).
2. Shortages are not allowed.
3. Stock replenishment can be scheduled to arrive exactly when the inventory drops to zero.

Assumptions.

4. Ordering cost and per-unit holding cost are independent of the quantity ordered.
5. Items are ordered independently of each other. (We ignore families of items, common suppliers, and joint ordering.)

The Hard Charger Corporation

Let us again consider the Hard Charger Corporation, which sells 1000 generators per month (30 days) and purchases in quantities of 2000 per order. Lead time for the receipt of an order is six days. The cost accounting department has analyzed the inventory costs and has determined that the cost to place an order is $60 and that the annual cost of holding one generator

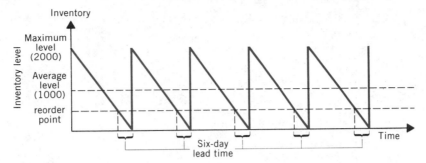

Figure 12.6   Hard Charger Corporation's inventory pattern.

in inventory is $10.* Under its present policy of ordering 2000 per order, what is Hard Charger's total annual inventory costs?

Hard Charger's inventory pattern is represented by the "sawtooth" curve of Figure 12.6. For simplicity of presentation, let us define the following notation.

Q = order quantity

U = annual usage

C_O = order cost per order

C_H = annual holding cost per unit

In order to determine the total annual incremental cost of Hard Charger's current inventory policy we must determine two separate annual costs, the total annual holding cost and the total annual ordering cost.

The *ordering cost* is determined by C_O, the cost to place one order ($60) and the number of orders placed per year. Since Hard Charger sells 12,000 generators per year and orders 2000 per order, they must place six (12,000/2000) orders per year for a total ordering cost of $360 (6 orders per year × $60 per order). Using our notation, the annual ordering cost is written as

$$\text{annual ordering cost} = \frac{U}{Q} \times C_O \qquad (12.2)$$

The annual holding cost is determined by C_H, the cost of holding one generator for one year ($10) and the number of generators "cycle stock" held. Notice that the inventory level is constantly changing and that no single generator ever remains in inventory for an entire year. On the average, though, there are 1000 generators in the inventory. Consider one cycle of Hard Charger's inventory graph as shown in Figure 12.7.

The inventory level begins at 2000 units and falls to 0 units before the next cycle begins. Since the rate of decline in inventory is constant (i.e., 1000

---

*Sometimes holding cost is given as a fixed value per year and other times as a percentage of the value of the inventory, especially when interest charges represent the major holding cost. Then $C_H = iC$ where C is the cost of the inventory item and i is the interest rate.

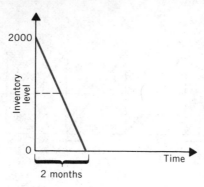

Figure 12.7 Hard Charger's inventory graph.

per month), the average level is 1000 units or simply the arithmetic average of the two levels: $(2000 + 0)/2 = 1000$.

If, on the average, there are 1000 generators in inventory over the entire year, then the annual inventory holding cost is $10,000 ($10 per unit $\times$ 1000 units). Or, in our general notation, the annual holding cost is

$$\text{annual holding cost} = \frac{Q}{2} \times C_H \qquad (12.3)$$

Adding the annual ordering cost and the annual holding cost gives the following equation for total annual cost (TAC)

$$\text{TAC} = \left(\frac{Q}{2}\right)C_H + \left(\frac{U}{Q}\right)C_O \qquad (12.4)$$

For Hard Charger, the TAC is $360 + $10,000 = $10,360.

Improving Hard Charger's Inventory Policy

Hard Charger's current inventory policy of ordering quantities of 2000 generators is costing $10,360 per year. Is this the best policy or can it be improved? Using a simple trial and error approach we can answer this question.

First, let us see what happens if we increase the order quantity to 5000 units.

$$
\begin{aligned}
\text{TAC} &= \left(\frac{5000}{2}\right)10 + \left(\frac{12,000}{5000}\right)60 \\
&= 2500 \times 10 + 2.4 \times 60 \\
&= 25,000 + 144 \\
&= \$25,144
\end{aligned}
$$

The annual holding cost increases and the ordering cost decreases, but the

Table 12.3   Costs of Various Order Quantities

Order Quantity	Annual Holding Cost	Annual Ordering Cost	Total Annual Cost
2000	$10,000	$ 360	$10,360
5000	25,000	144	25,144
1000	5,000	720	5,720
500	2,500	1440	3,940
100	500	7200	7,700

overall result is a significant increase in the total annual inventory cost. This is clearly an uneconomical choice. Let us try some other values. The resulting costs are given in Table 12.3.

We see from the table that 100 units is too small and the costs are beginning to increase again. But, we have bounded the range of solutions. The best order quantity is somewhere between 100 and 1000 items.

Finding an Optimal Policy

As you can imagine, the trial-and-error aproach used above could go on for quite some time before an optimal policy is determined. A more straight-forward approach to finding an optimal policy is to use the graphical approach or an algebraic solution.

We can graph the annual holding cost and annual ordering cost as a function of the order quantity as shown in Figure 12.8. Since the annual holding cost is $(Q/2)C_H$, which can be written $(C_H/2)Q$, we see that holding cost is linear and increasing with respect to Q. Annual order cost is $(U/Q)C_O$, which can be rewritten as $(UC_O)/Q$. We can see that ordering cost is nonlinear with respect to Q and decreases as Q increases.

Now, if we add together the two graphed quantities for all values of Q we have the TAC curve as shown in Figure 12.8. Note that the TAC first decreases as ordering cost decreases but then starts to increase quickly. The point at which the TAC is a minimum is the optimal order quantity; that is, it gives the quantity Q which provides the least total annual inventory cost. This point is called the *economic order quantity* or the EOQ and, for this inventory problem, happens to occur where the order cost curve intersects the holding cost curve. (The minimum point is not *always* where two curves intersect, it just happens to be so in the EOQ case.) From Figure 12.8 we can see that the EOQ is approximately 400 generators per order.

Finding the EOQ where the curves intersect.

We can compute an accurate value algebraically by noting that the value of Q at the point of intersection of the two cost lines is the EOQ. We can find an equation for the EOQ by setting the two costs equal to one another and solving for the value of Q that satisfies the equality. That is

$$\left(\frac{Q}{2}\right)C_H = \left(\frac{U}{Q}\right)C_O$$

Multiplying both sides by Q gives

$$\left(\frac{Q^2}{2}\right)C_H = UC_O$$

and dividing both sides by $C_H/2$ gives

$$Q^2 = \frac{2UC_O}{C_H}$$

Finally, taking the square root of both sides gives

$$Q = \sqrt{\frac{2UC_O}{C_H}}$$

The Q is the economic order quantity* and is most often written as

$$EOQ = \sqrt{\frac{2UC_O}{C_H}} \tag{12.5}$$

For the Hard Charger Corporation we can compute the EOQ as

$$EOQ = \sqrt{\frac{2(12,000)60}{10}} = \sqrt{144,000} = 379.5$$

Obviously, since we cannot order half a generator, the order quantity would be rounded to 380 units.

The total annual cost of this policy would be

$$TAC = \left(\frac{380}{2}\right)10 + \left(\frac{12,000}{380}\right)60$$
$$= 1900 + 1894.74$$
$$= \$3794.74$$

*For those students with an understanding of calculus, we could find the minimum of the TAC equation by taking the first derivative and setting it equal to zero as follows.

$$TAC = \left(\frac{Q}{2}\right)C_H + \left(\frac{U}{Q}\right)C_O$$
$$\frac{\partial TAC}{\partial Q} = \frac{C_H}{2} - \left(\frac{U}{Q^2}\right)C_O$$

Setting this equal to zero we have,

$$O = \frac{C_H}{2} - \left(\frac{U}{Q^2}\right)C_O$$

or:

$$\left(\frac{U}{Q^2}\right)C_O = \frac{C_H}{2}$$
$$UC_O = \frac{Q^2 C_H}{2}$$
$$\frac{2UC_O}{C_H} = Q^2$$
$$\sqrt{\frac{2UC_O}{C_H}} = Q$$

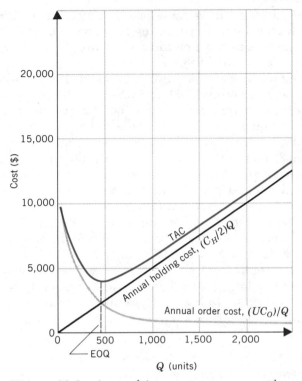

Figure 12.8 Annual inventory costs graph.

Note that this is an improvement in total annual cost of $6565.26 over the present policy of ordering 2000. But also note that the optimal policy of ordering 380 per order provides only a $145.26 savings over the "order 500" policy which we considered in our trial-and-error procedure. Actual inventory situations often exhibit this relative "insensitivity" to quantity changes in the vicinity of the EOQ. To the operations manager what this means is added flexibility in order quantity decisions. If, for example, shipping and handling was more convenient or economical in quantities of 500 (perhaps the items are wrapped in quantities of 250), the additional 120 units per order would only cost the organization an extra $145.26 per year.

Cost insensitivity in the EOQ region.

Cautions Regarding EOQ Computations

The GIGO rule.

The EOQ is a computed minimum cost order quantity. As with any model or formula, the GIGO rule (garbage in–garbage out) applies. If the variables used in computing the EOQ are inaccurate, then the EOQ will be inaccurate, though, as mentioned previously, a slight error will not increase costs significantly. EOQ determination relies heavily on two variables that are subject to considerable misinterpretation. These are the two cost elements, holding cost (C_H) and order cost (C_O). In the derivation of the EOQ we assumed that by ordering fewer units per order the cost of holding inventory would be reduced. Likewise, it was assumed that by reducing the number of orders placed each year the cost of ordering could be proportionately reduced. Both of these assumptions must be thoroughly questioned in looking at each cost element that is included in both C_H and C_O.

For example, if a single purchasing agent is employed by the firm, and orders are reduced from 3000 per year to 2000 per year, does it stand to reason the purchasing expense will be reduced by one-third? Unless the person is paid on a "piece-work" basis the answer is clearly NO. Likewise, suppose that we rent a warehouse that will hold 100,000 items and we currently keep it full. If the order sizes are reduced so that the warehouse is only 65 percent occupied can we convince the owners to charge us only 65 percent of the rental price? Again, the answer is NO. Clearly then, when costs are determined for computations, only real, out-of-pocket costs should be used. Those costs that are committed or "sunk," no matter what the inventory levels or number of orders are, should be excluded because they violate the assumptions of the EOQ model.

Use only out-of-pocket costs in the EOQ.

Also, very small EOQ values (e.g., 2) will not be valid because the cost functions will be in question for such small orders. Last, EOQ reorder sizes should not be blindly followed. There may not be enough cash just now to pay for an EOQ or storage space may be insufficient.

Using the EOQ in Reorder Point and Periodic Review Inventory Systems

As we mentioned in the previous section, both reorder point systems and periodic review systems rely on the EOQ concept for reorder level and review interval. Consider first the inventory level graph for the optimal "order 380" policy shown in Figure 12.9.

The reorder point is based on LT.

Hard Charger's maximum inventory level will be 380 units. Selling at the rate of 1000 per month, or 33.34 per day, the beginning supply of 380 will be sold in 11.4 days. An order must be placed six days (the *lead time,* LT) prior to the time the original supply will be exhausted so that an order will be received in time to avoid stockouts. In order to avoid stockouts,

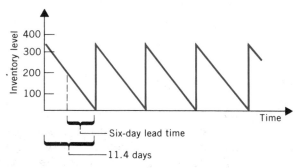

Figure 12.9 Optimal inventory pattern for Hard Charger Corporation.

therefore, Hard Charger must reorder when the inventory level falls to 200 units (6 days × 33.34 per day). We can also see this result from Figure 12.9. If the inventory is used uniformly (this is one of the assumptions we have made), then six days prior to the time the inventory level will fall to zero, the inventory level must be 200 units in order that 33.34 units can be sold (on the average) in each of those remaining days before an order is received.

For the periodic review system our concern is not with the optimal order quantity, but with the *time interval* for review and reordering. Using information provided by the EOQ model we can derive an effective period review policy. If Hard Charger orders 380 generators per order, then, on the average, they will place 31.6 orders per year. That is, since the number of orders is given by U/Q, Hard Charger will place 12,000/380 = 31.6 orders. The review period in a periodic review inventory system is constant; only the order quantity changes. Therefore, to space 31.6 orders equally throughout the year Hard Charger should order every 7.91 working days (practically, this would be rounded to 8 for convenience). That is, 250 working days per year/31.6 orders per year = 7.91.

Practical Aspects of Inventory Management

Inventory managers often pride themselves in the fact that they have been ordering quantities very near to the EOQ, even before an EOQ system was implemented. This should not come as a surprise since the natural forces within an organization tend to produce reasonable, if not optimal, inventory policies. That is, the sales people desire large quantities of inventory, accounting and financial personnel desire low quantities of inventory, and the operations manager desires fluctuating inventories so that production can operate most efficiently. The combination of these forces tends to produce an inventory policy that is a compromise of all the individual departmental (and, thus, organizational) objectives. But, if one of the department managers is significantly more influential than the others (and this is often the case) an imbalance, and possibly a poor inventory policy, will come about.

Setting inventory levels by compromise.

12.4 EOQ WITH QUANTITY DISCOUNTS

As was briefly noted earlier, our total annual cost equations for the EOQ model have not included a term for the cost of the item itself. The reason for this omission is that we have assumed a constant unit cost for all of the items ordered or produced and therefore this unit cost does not change with changes in the order quantity.

Quantity discounts affect optimal order sizes.

In practice, though, this assumption is often not true. *Quantity discounts* are common practice in many businesses and are used by selling companies as incentives for purchasing companies to buy in larger quantities. With quantity discounts the total annual cost of the items purchased *does* change with changes in order quantity and therefore unit cost must be considered in the EOQ model.

The Pinchpenny Co.

Consider the Pinchpenny Company, which uses a small alloy casting in the production of one of its machines. Currently, annual usage of this item is 5000 parts. The cost accountant has estimated that the cost to place an order is $49 and the inventory carrying cost is $1 per casting per year. Pinchpenny's supplier of castings, Buymorfromus, Inc., has just released the following discount schedule (Table 12.4) to the purchasing agent of Pinchpenny. The current policy employed by Pinchpenny is to order in EOQs. Pinchpenny's purchasing agent must answer two questions regarding his purchasing policy now that discounts have been offered. Should they change this policy on the basis of the new discounts offered? If so, what should the new order quantity be?

The total annual cost equation for Pinchpenny, including the cost of the casting, is

$$\text{TAC} = \left(\frac{Q}{2}\right)C_H + \left(\frac{U}{Q}\right)C_O + UC \tag{12.6}$$

where C is the unit cost of the castings and the other notation is as defined earlier.

A rather simple two-step procedure is used to determine the answers to the above two questions. First, we compute Pinchpenny's current EOQ. If the EOQ is large enough to receive the greatest discount, there is no problem to solve; the current EOQ will be maintained *and* the best discount will also be received. But, if the EOQ is less than the minimum order size to qualify for the largest discount (in our example, 2500) then the second step is entered. The current EOQ for the alloy casting is

$$\text{EOQ} = \sqrt{\frac{2(5000)49}{1}} = 700$$

which falls in the lowest class and, therefore, qualifies for no discount.

In the second step, we establish trial order quantities equal to the minimum order quantities qualifying for each discount level. For Pinchpenny's casting the two trial order quantities are $Q_1 = 1000$ and $Q_2 = 2500$, corresponding to the minimum order quantities that qualify for the $4.85 and 4.75 prices from Buymorfromus. Then, we evaluate the total annual cost of the current EOQ and these two trial order quantities.

Table 12.4   Discount Schedule From Buymorfromus

Order Quantity	Unit Cost of Casting, C
0– 999	$5.00
1000–2499	$4.85
2500–over	$4.75

If we order the EOQ, the annual cost is

$$\text{TAC} = \left(\frac{700}{2}\right)1 + \left(\frac{5000}{700}\right)49 + 5000(\$5)$$

$$= 350 \qquad + 350 \qquad + 25{,}000$$

$$= \$25{,}700$$

If we order 1000, the total annual cost is

$$\text{TAC} = \left(\frac{1000}{2}\right)1 + \left(\frac{5000}{1000}\right)49 + 5000(4.85)$$

$$= 500 \qquad + 245 \qquad + 24{,}250$$

$$= \$24{,}995$$

If we order 2500, the total annual cost is

$$\text{TAC} = \left(\frac{2500}{2}\right)1 + \left(\frac{5000}{2500}\right)49 + 5000(4.75)$$

$$= 1250 \qquad + 98 \qquad + 23{,}750$$

$$= \$25{,}098$$

The costs for each of the three policies are summarized in Table 12.5.

Table 12.5 shows the results of changing the order quantity from 700 to 1000 and 2500, respectively. In both cases the ordering cost decreases and the holding cost increases. The decrease in holding cost is more than offset by the increase in ordering cost for both trial order costs, resulting in net increases in cost. But the annual cost of purchasing the castings decreases enough for the order-1000 policy to more than offset the net increase in the other inventory costs. Such is *not* the case in moving from 1000 to 2500 per order. The order quantity of 1000 has the minimum total annual cost of the three and therefore the Pinchpenny policy should be changed to "order 1000."

But, how do we know that some other quantity, such as 1500, or 3000, would not result in an even lower cost? In the Pinchpenny case the EOQ for all three prices breaks was, we assumed, at the same quantity: 700. Therefore, for quantities greater than 700, at the same unit cost, the TAC would be increasing. Figure 12.10 illustrates this point.

Sketching the TAC curves is a useful device for determining the best order quantity in more complex situations. More than two price breaks are

Table 12.5   TAC for Three Ordering Policies

Order Quantity	Annual Holding Cost	Annual Ordering Cost	Annual Purchase Cost	TAC
700	350	350	25,000	25,700
1000	500	245	24,250	24,995
2500	1250	98	23,750	25,098

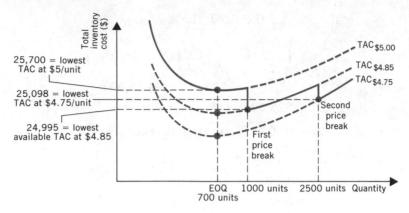

Figure 12.10 Illustration of Pinchpenny quantity discount problem.

common, which adds to the computation involved. Also, it is often true that the inventory carrying charge is related to the cost of the items being carried. If this is so, then the EOQ must be recomputed for each price rather than simply for the base price.

The "rule" for evaluating quantity discount situations is thus:

Rule for discounts.

Calculate the EOQ for the best discount rate. If this EOQ value lies in the range where the discount applies, then this is the best order quantity. If not, do the same with the second best discount rate and compare the total cost with the total cost at the order rate to achieve the best discount. Continue in this manner until the lowest total cost at an EOQ is found.

To illustrate, consider this simplified price break situation.

Quantity	Unit Cost
1–99	$2.00
100 and over	1.00

The inventory carrying cost, to illustrate the other method of calculation mentioned earlier, is computed as *20 percent of the value of the item*, 250 items are used per year, and order cost is $5. Computing the two EOQs, we have

$$\text{EOQ}_{\$2.00} = \sqrt{\frac{2(250)5}{0.2(2)}} = 79$$

$$\text{EOQ}_{\$1.00} = \sqrt{\frac{2(250)5}{0.2(1)}} = 112$$

Note that the optimal order quantity for the $1.00 price is 112 units and not 100, the minimum quantity that qualifies for the lower price. Figure 12.11

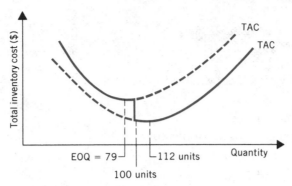

Figure 12.11 Quantity discounts and EOQs when holding cost is computed as a percentage of the unit cost.

illustrates the TAC graph for this situation in which the EOQ changes as the unit cost changes (i.e., where the holding or carrying charge is computed as a percentage of the unit cost).

12.5 THE ECONOMIC PRODUCTION LOT SIZE (ELS)

ELS for continuous production and use.

If an internally used part or assembly is also manufactured internally, rather than being procured from an outside vendor, it is often possible to use individual items *as they are produced* rather than waiting for an *entire lot*, such as a caseload, to be produced. The economic lot size model is used to determine the optimal inventory policy under these conditions. The following example will clarify the ELS problem.

Brush and Ladder Paint

Consider the Brush and Ladder Paint Manufacturing Company, which manufactures and sells latex interior wall paint. B&L is a small local company selling through three retail outlets in the same city as the manufacturing plant. Because B&L's best selling paint (80 percent of all sales) is eggshell white, management wishes to establish an inventory policy for this one product. Demand for eggshell white has averaged 300 gallons per day. The setup cost for production of a new paint color is $250 including downtime of the machines, cleanup, and setup labor. The annual holding cost of a gallon of paint is $1.50. B&L's production management wants to know how many gallons of eggshell white should be produced in each lot in order to minimize the combined total annual cost of holding inventory and setting up for production.

Let us use the following notation.

Q = production lot size

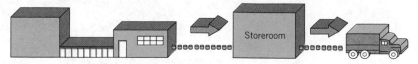

Figure 12.12   B&L production system.

$$U = \text{annual demand rate}^*$$
$$P = \text{annual production rate}^*$$
$$C_O = \text{setup cost per lot}$$
$$C_H = \text{annual holding cost}$$

When a new order for paint production is given to the factory the previous lot of paint is terminated, all machines are disassembled for complete cleaning, all adjustments are made and the machines set up for the new production run. Once the setup is complete, production will begin and filled cans will exit the filling line at the rate of 800 one-gallon cans per day. These cans are moved by conveyor belt to the finished goods storeroom, from which sales and shipments to the three retail outlets are made. The system is graphically represented in Figure 12.12. Note that cans are available for use as they leave the filling line. The storeroom does not have to wait for a completed batch before using the paint.

Inventory level in the finished goods storeroom will simultaneously increase at the rate of 800 gallons per day and decrease at the rate of 300 gallons per day (the average daily sales), for a net increase of 500 gallons per day while the eggshell white is being produced. At the end of the production run, the inventory level will continue to decrease at the rate of 300 gallons per day until production of eggshell white resumes. In our notation, inventory will increase at the rate of $P - U$ while the lot is being produced and will decrease at the rate of U when eggshell white is not being produced.

One final question remains to be answered before we can draw the inventory level graph for B&L's eggshell white paint. We must know the duration of a production run in order to compute the maximum inventory level. If the production lot size is Q gallons and the facility can process and fill P gallons per year, then it will take the fraction Q/P years to complete the production run. The inventory level will grow to a maximum, computed as

$$\text{maximum inventory level} = (P - U) \times \frac{Q}{P} \tag{12.7}$$

which can be rewritten as

$$\left(1 - \frac{U}{P}\right)Q$$

That is, the maximum inventory level is achieved at the point where eggshell

*Annual rates need not be used. It is only important that the demand and production rates be the *same duration*, such as "per day."

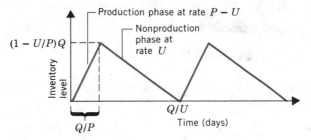

Figure 12.13   Inventory level graph for B&L.

white production terminates, the fraction Q/P years after it starts. Since the rate of increase in finished goods inventory is $(P - U)$, the maximum level is given by the rate of increase times the duration or $(P - U)$, times Q/P. We can now present the inventory level graph (Figure 12.13) for eggshell white paint.

For this inventory pattern the holding cost and setup (ordering) costs are computed similarly to the computation of these costs in the outside procurement (EOQ) model. Annual holding cost is computed as the average inventory level times the annual holding cost per unit in inventory. Using our notation

$$\text{average inventory level} = \frac{1}{2}\left(1 - \frac{U}{P}\right)Q$$

$$\text{annual holding cost} = \frac{1}{2}\left(1 - \frac{U}{P}\right)QC_H$$

Annual setup cost is computed as the number of annual setups times the individual setup cost.

$$\text{number of setups} = \frac{U}{Q}$$

$$\text{annual setup cost} = \left(\frac{U}{Q}\right)C_O$$

The total annual cost (TAC) is therefore given by

$$\text{TAC} = \frac{1}{2}\left(1 - \frac{U}{P}\right)QC_H + \left(\frac{U}{Q}\right)C_O \tag{12.8}$$

The optimal lot size is determined, in a fashion similar to that used for the EOQ model, to be*

*The first derivative of the TAC equation is

$$\frac{\partial\text{TAC}}{\partial Q} = \frac{1}{2}\left(1 - \frac{U}{P}\right)C_H - \left(\frac{U}{Q^2}\right)C_O$$

Setting this expression equal to zero and solving for Q gives

$$Q = \sqrt{\frac{2UC_O}{(1 - U/P)C_H}}$$

$$ELS = Q = \sqrt{\frac{2UC_O}{\left(1 - \frac{U}{P}\right)C_H}} \tag{12.9}$$

For B&L, the economic production lot size for eggshell white paint is (assuming 250 working days per year)*

$$
\begin{aligned}
ELS &= \sqrt{\frac{2(75,000)250}{\left(1 - \frac{300}{800}\right)1.50}} \\
&= \sqrt{\frac{37,500,000}{0.9375}} \\
&= \sqrt{40,000,000} = 6325 \text{ gal}
\end{aligned}
$$

Using this lot size the maximum inventory level will be

$$\left(1 - \frac{300}{800}\right)6325 = 3953 \text{ gal}$$

The length of a production run will be

$$\frac{6325}{800} = 7.91 \text{ days}$$

and the total annual inventory cost will be

$$
\begin{aligned}
TAC &= \frac{1}{2}\left(1 - \frac{300}{800}\right)6325 \times 1.50 + \left(\frac{75,000}{6325}\right)250 \\
&= 2964.84 + 2964.43 \\
&= \$5929.27
\end{aligned}
$$

It is useful to note that the ELS formula (Equation 12.9) reduces to the EOQ formula (12.5) when P tends to infinity. That is, as the production rate, or resupply time, becomes instantaneous (the EOQ assumption) the ELS simply becomes the EOQ. Hence, the EOQ is just one particular version of the ELS. Also, as P reduces to the level of U, the ELS tends to become infinite, or in other words, production is constant.

EOQ a version of the ELS.

Neither the ELS nor the EOQ are very useful when a number of items must all be produced, sequentially, on the same facilities. In these cases, the facilities are usually not available when another lot needs to be produced and more complex lot sizing methods are required. This situation will be considered next.

---

*Note in this equation we are using the daily rather than annual demand and production rates. Clearly, both numerator and denominator can be multiplied by 250 without affecting the results.

12.6 LOT SIZING FOR MULTIPLE RECURRING BATCHES

The problems of scheduling batches.

The two basic problems of multiple batch production are (1) what size batches should be produced? and (2) how should the batches be sequenced and scheduled? These two problems are highly interrelated, however—specifying the batch size to a large extent fixes the schedule, and vice-versa.

Lot sizes for multiple batches.

For multiple batches, more than one output is competing for the *same* facilities. Inventories of the various outputs are used up (demanded) at different rates, can be produced at other rates, and undoubtedly have different "economic lot sizes." Given that the production capacity is limited, what are the "best" batch sizes for each of the products?

Consider the following very simple situation. A manufacturer has limited equipment available to produce two products, A and B, which have the demand rates, production rates, and economic lot sizes shown in Table 12.6. Note that the manufacturer can produce all the monthly demand for A in half a month (demand rate/production rate = 100/200 = 0.5) and all the demand for B in 2/5 (or 0.4) months. In total, production of both A and B only requires 0.9 months and, therefore, productive capacity seems quite adequate. The economic lot size for A is only 20 units, which takes 20/200 = 0.1 months to produce and will last for 0.2 months. The economic lot size for B is 180 units, so this requires 180/500 = 0.36 months to produce. Presuming A is scheduled on the equipment first, A finishes at 0.1 months and product B finishes at 0.46 months (0.1 for A + 0.36). In the meantime, however, product A will suffer a stockout (at 0.3 months). This situation is illustrated in Figure 12.14 for greater clarity.

Inferiority of ELS for multiple batches.

The conclusion is that "economic lot sizes" computed for products on a single item basis are not at all "economic" when other products compete for the same production equipment. One way to avoid this problem is by producing in lots other than the economic lot size—for example, in lots for each product that last an equal length of time. This approach is called "the equalization of runout time" (see Section 10.2).

In the previous two-product case, this would mean producing A for some fraction of a month and then B for the remainder of the month so that the units of A and B produced would each last X months. The amount to be produced within the month would thus be

$100X$ units of product A + $200X$ units of product B

Table 12.6 Demand and Production Rates for Two Products

	Product A	Product B
Monthly demand, units	100	200
Production rate, units/month	200	500
Economic lot size, units	20	180

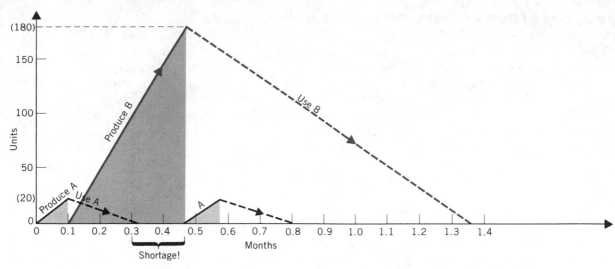

Figure 12.14   Two-product scheduling by economic lot size.

The amount of time to produce the A product would be $100X/200$ months and for the B product would be $200X/500$ months. Considering a one month production plan

$$\frac{100X}{200} + \frac{200X}{500} = 1$$

or

$$0.5X + 0.4X = 1$$

and therefore

$$X = \frac{1}{0.9} = 1.11 \text{ months}$$

$100X = 111$ units of A taking $111/200 = 0.555$ months to produce

$200X = 222$ units of B taking $222/500 = 0.444$ months to produce

This schedule is shown in Figure 12.15. As seen, due to the extra capacity of the equipment it can be shut down (for maintenance, etc.) for 0.11 month every cycle. Although shown in Figure 12.13 as following the production of B, this shutdown could be divided between the two runs or allocated in any other manner. And although Figure 12.15 represents a *feasible* schedule it is not very efficient (although the ease of scheduling may outweigh any loss in cost efficiency). More complex techniques do exist for determining economic lot sizes for multiple-product batch operations, however (see Reference 1).

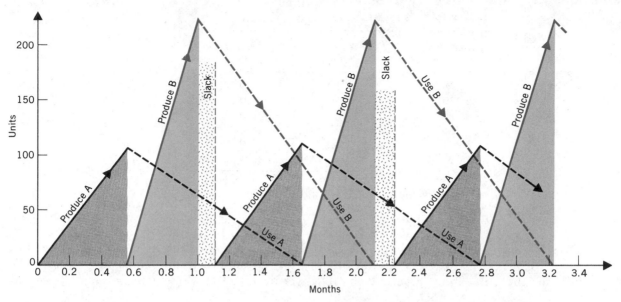

Figure 12.15 Two-product scheduling for equal usage periods.

12.7 MANAGING INVENTORIES IN AN UNCERTAIN ENVIRONMENT: THE SINGLE-PERIOD, "NEWSBOY" PROBLEM

Introducing uncertainty into the inventory situation.

In the previous sections we discussed the fundamental concepts and terminology of inventory management. The systems we described presumed an absolute knowledge of the parameters that determined optimal order quantities. We also discussed the notion of an order point based on a known demand and a known lead time. Now it is appropriate to relax these assumptions so as to consider more realistic inventory situations. That is, we will introduce uncertainty into the inventory environment.

Demand uncertainty for a perishable commodity.

First, we will consider a problem that has been traditionally referred to as the "newsboy" problem, but which is applicable in numerous situations in which a *perishable* commodity is purchased in some order size (before demand is known) and is then either sold or scrapped, depending on the demand level. The following example will clarify the problem.

Clark Kent has, for three years, sold newspapers each morning at the corner of Upper and Downer Streets. Clark purchases the morning edition of the *Daily Planet* at 6:00 A.M. and stands on the corner from 6:30 to 8:30 each morning before walking two blocks to school. Clark buys the newspapers for $0.10 each and sells them for $0.15. Even though Clark is making a good profit on each newspaper sold and has developed quite a sizable bank account for a lad his age, he knows that he can do better.

It seems that he is always running out of papers before 8:30 A.M. and therefore missing potential sales, *or* having several papers left over that cannot be sold or returned to the newspaper publisher. He reasons that there

Table 12.7 Clark's Newspaper Demand

Demand (newspapers)	Frequency (days)	Relative Frequency
28	10	0.10
29	20	0.20
30	35	0.35
31	25	0.25
32	10	0.10
	100	1.00

Overstocking versus understocking.

must be some "best" order quantity to stock each day which will produce the largest average profit over the long run. Clark knows that he cannot perfectly predict daily demand and that he is bound to run out on some days and to overstock on others. But, he is sure that a consistent policy will maximize his expected profit over the long run. How many newspapers should Clark stock each day?

To answer this question we must first consider the demand for newspapers on Clark's corner. Suppose that Clark has kept a record of the number of papers demanded each day for 100 days. That is, even when he ran out of papers, Clark remained on the corner until 8:30 A.M. to count the number of people who asked for a paper, even though he had to tell them he had none left. His summary of the 100 days' demand is presented in Table 12.7.

Clark's lowest demand was for 28 newspapers and his highest demand was for 32. Therefore, he at least knows that he should never order more than 32 or less than 28.* But, Clark could order any of the five quantities in between on any given day. Which number will maximize profits? Table 12.8, which is called a **payoff table** presents the daily profit for each "order/demand" combination.

Table 12.8 Payoff Table for the Newsboy Problem

Order Quantity	Demand				
	28	29	30	31	32
28	$1.40	$1.40	$1.40	$1.40	$1.40
29	1.30	1.45	1.45	1.45	1.45
30	1.20	1.35	1.50	1.50	1.50
31	1.10	1.25	1.40	1.55	1.55
32	1.00	1.15	1.30	1.45	1.60

*We are making the assumption here that 100 days' history is enough to predict the future. Obviously, demand can change; Clark must simply be aware of the possibility and monitor for it.

Decision Table Analysis

The rows of Table 12.8 are labeled with the five potential order quantities and the columns are labeled with the five potential demands. Each combination of order quantity and demand will result in a different payoff, as seen in the body of the table.

Each entry in the payoff table is computed as follows. If Clark orders enough to equal or exceed demand, then

$$\text{profit} = \text{no. demanded} \times \$0.15 - \text{no. order} \times \$0.10 \qquad (12.10)$$

For example, if he orders 30 and 28 were demanded

$$\begin{aligned} \text{profit} &= 28 \times \$0.15 - 30 \times \$0.10 \\ &= 4.20 - 3.00 \\ &= \$1.20 \end{aligned}$$

If Clark orders less than is demanded on a given day, then he can only sell what he has in stock and therefore

$$\text{profit} = \$0.05 \times \text{no. ordered} \qquad (12.11)$$

If 32 were demanded and he had ordered only 30

$$\begin{aligned} \text{profit} &= 0.05 \times 30 \\ &= \$1.50 \end{aligned}$$

With the information provided in the payoff table, Clark now knows the profit that will be earned for each of the potential order quantities and each of the possible daily demands. He can now determine the best order quantity by determining the expected profit to be earned using each order quantity.

Clark knows the relative frequency of occurrence of each level of demand. On the average, 28 newspapers are demanded 10 percent of the time, 29 newspapers are demanded 20 percent of the time, 30 newspapers are demanded 35 percent of the time, and so on. If Clark plays it safe and orders 28 newspapers each day, then the expected daily profit will be

$$\begin{aligned} E(P_{28}) &= 0.1(1.40) + 0.2(1.40) + 0.35(1.40) + 0.25(1.40) + 0.1(1.40) \\ &= \$1.40 \end{aligned}$$

That is, his expected daily profit is *$1.40* if he orders 28 newspapers each day and the relative frequency of the demand levels remains as it was for the 100-day data collection period. This result is obvious since he is sure of selling at least 28 papers at a nickel profit each.

If Clark orders 30 newspapers each day his expected daily profit is

$$\begin{aligned} E(P_{30}) &= 0.1(1.20) + 0.2(1.35) + 0.35(1.50) + 0.25(1.50) + 0.1(1.50) \\ &= \$1.44 \end{aligned}$$

Therefore, even though he will not sell all of the 30 newspapers each day (in fact, he will not sell all of them 30 percent of the time) his expected long-run daily profit is greater than the more conservative approach.

Table 12.9 Clark's Expected Profits

Order Quantity	Expected Daily Profit
28	$1.400
29	$1.435
30	$1.440 (best)
31	$1.392
32	$1.307

Table 12.9 contains the expected profits for each of the five possible order quantity decisions. Since the expected profit for the "order *30*" decision is the greatest, the optimal policy is to order 30 newspapers each day.

Does this mean that Clark will never run out of newspapers, or that Clark will never have bought more than he can sell? The obvious answer is NO! In fact, Clark can expect to *run out* 35 percent of the time; that is, the times that demand is 31 or 32, and to stock *more* than he needs 30 percent of the time, the times that demand is 28 or 29. This policy, though, is one that produces the greatest long-run profit.

Marginal (Incremental) Analysis

Consider ordering
one more unit.

There is another, more flexible, method for solving Clark's problem called **incremental (or marginal) analysis.** The idea here is to start with a very small order for items and compare the advantages of ordering *one more item* to the disadvantages. The advantage, of course, is the potential profit (or cost reduction, in some cases) the unit might bring. The disadvantage is that the item may not be sold (or needed) and then a loss might be sustained. Of course, for very small initial order sizes the probability of one more unit being sold is quite high, so it probably makes sense to order at least one more. For example, in Clark's case if he is at an initial order size of 27 or less, it certainly makes sense to order at least one more paper because the probability of selling it is 100 percent.

The next step is to consider adding still another unit to the order: Is the expected gain greater than (or equal to) the expected loss? This process is continued until ordering one additional unit cannot be justified based on the expected return for that unit.

Let us frame this process mathematically. We will use the following symbols:

p = the probability of selling (or using) *at least* one more unit

$1 - p$ = probability of *not* selling or using the unit

MCO = marginal cost of *overordering*

MPU = marginal profit (or marginal cost of *underordering*)

Then the expected gain from ordering one more unit is the probability of selling the unit times either the profit to be gained or the cost that would be incurred if the unit was not available. (The latter more general and inclusive definition includes the lost opportunity cost of the potential profit but also any costs from not having the unit available such as goodwill costs, expediting costs, penalties, etc.). Mathematically

expected gain $= p(\text{MPU})$

Similarly, the expected loss from ordering the unit is the probability it does not sell (or is not needed) times the loss incurred (its price, or price less salvage value)

expected loss $= (1 - p)\text{MCO}$

Now, it is logical to keep increasing the order size as long as the expected marginal profit (or marginal cost of underordering) exceeds the marginal cost of overordering. Stating this conclusion mathematically will allow us to identify that value of p *below which* it is not worthwhile ordering another unit.

$$p(\text{MPU}) \geq (1 - p)\text{MCO}$$

or

Critical value of p.

$$p \geq \frac{\text{MCO}}{\text{MCO} + \text{MPU}} \tag{12.12}$$

In Clark's problem MCO $= \$0.10$ (the cost of the papers; there is no salvage value) and MPU $= \$0.05$ (the profit; there are no goodwill losses or penalties). Thus

$$p \geq \frac{0.10}{0.10 + 0.05} = 0.67$$

Now we need a table showing the probability of selling N or more units as a function of order size, N. This is shown in Table 12.10.

Notice that our value for $p = 0.67$ falls between $N = 30$ and 31. That is, if our current order size was 29, then at $N = 30$ the probability 0.70 of selling 30, 31, or 32 units is *greater* than the critical probability of 0.67, so 30 is acceptable. But at $N = 31$ the value of 0.35 is *less* than 0.67, so 31 cannot be justified.

The "newsboy" problem" in other situations.

This problem is a common one. Retailers purchase seasonal clothing, perishable foods, and other items such as Christmas trees, Valentine candy

Table 12.10 Probability Table for Newsboy Problem

Order Size, N	Probability of N	Cumulative Probability of Selling N or More
28	0.10	1.00
29	0.20	0.90
30	0.35	0.70
31	0.25	0.35
32	0.10	0.10

and cards, and fruit and vegetables in anticipation of demand. If too little demand is realized, then the remaining goods are scrapped if not salable or "reduced for clearance," either at a loss or at a reduced profit.

12.8 SAFETY STOCK FOR UNCERTAINTY IN DEMAND: STERLING'S JEWELERS

In the newsboy problem, the concern was with ordering quantities of a perishable commodity for a *single* period. The reorder point model, on the other hand, is concerned with *multiple* periods. Now we will consider *demand* uncertainty with multiple periods. The case of *lead time* uncertainty is treated in the following section.

Sterling's Jewelers sells a relatively inexpensive man's watch, which it orders directly from a New York distributor. Tom O'Malley, the store's owner, recently attended a conference on inventory control, learned about EOQs, and immediately decided to put this concept to work in his store. Tom collected the demand data shown in Table 12.11 for 20 weeks and computed an average weekly demand of 13 watches. Order cost was determined to be $30 and holding cost was calculated to be $2 per watch per year. The EOQ (for a 50-week year) was calculated to be 140 watches. Lead time was known

Table 12.11 Watch Demand for Sterling's Jewelers

Week	Weekly Demand
1	10
2	13
3	12
4	16
5	11
6	13
7	16
8	13
9	14
10	12
11	15
12	10
13	16
14	14
15	15
16	13
17	11
18	12
19	13
20	11
	260

Average weekly demand = 13 units

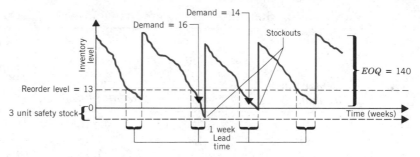

Figure 12.16 Graph of inventory level for Sterling's Jewelers.

to be one week, so Tom instituted the EOQ system with a reorder point of 13.

Soon after implementing this new policy Tom started receiving complaints from his clerks and customers that this particular watch was often out of stock. Sterling's has constantly advertised a policy of always meeting customer demand, so this problem especially concerned Tom. After two months he realized that he was losing numerous sales and that something must be wrong with his new inventory policy.

Uncertain demand over lead time.

Figure 12.16 presents a graph of the actual inventory level of the watches that Tom has recently placed on the 13 watch reorder point policy. As you can see, the inventory level is not constantly decreasing, as in the inventory graphs of the previous sections, but decreases randomly. Tom's inventory policy was based on a constant demand (and therefore a constant rate of decrease in inventory level) since this is one of the EOQ assumptions. The numerous stockouts were the result of insufficient inventory available to meet the demand *between* the time the order was placed and the time the shipment was received. This demand is known as the "demand over the lead time" and is abbreviated as **DOLT.** As you can see from Table 12.11, weekly demand ranges from 10 to 16 watches. If an order is placed at the reorder point of 13 watches and either 14, 15, or 16 watches are demanded, there will be a stockout.

Safety stock to protect against demand uncertainty.

In order to avoid stockouts, Sterling's must maintain a *safety stock* of watches. That is, a certain number of watches must be kept on hand solely to act as a buffer against the uncertainty in demand. For example, since Sterling's demand ranges up to 16 watches per week, a 3 watch safety stock [calculated as maximum demand over lead time (16) − reorder point (13) = 3] would result in zero stockouts. This is shown in Figure 12.16 as the dotted horizontal time axis. Adding safety stock, in effect, lifts the inventory graph by the amount of safety stock, in this manner providing protection against stockouts. The appropriate level of safety stock depends on the number of stockouts management is willing to allow each year. No stockouts is the ideal but, because of the increased holding cost resulting from the safety stock, can also be an expensive policy.

How many stockouts a year are acceptable?

Sterling's lead time from the New York distributor is one week. Since demand has been recorded on a weekly basis we can use the data in Table

Table 12.12 Sterling's Frequency Distribution for Demand

Demand over Lead Time, DOLT	Frequency	Relative Frequency	Cumulative Frequency (i.e., Probability That Demand Will Be Less Than or Equal to DOLT)
10	2	0.10	0.10
11	3	0.15	0.25
12	3	0.15	0.40
13	5	0.25	0.65
14	2	0.10	0.75
15	2	0.10	0.85
16	3	0.15	1.00
	20	1.00	

The demand over lead time, DOLT.

12.11 to construct a frequency distribution for *demand over lead time.* You will recall that demand over lead time is the term we have given for the number of units demanded per lead time period (in our example, one week). Table 12.12 presents the frequency distribution for demand over lead time (DOLT).

Sterling's recently implemented inventory policy of ordering 140 watches results in 4.64 orders being placed per year

$$\frac{13 \text{ watches/week} \times 50 \text{ weeks}}{140} = 4.64$$

or a reorder every 350/4.64 = 75 days. At the time an order is placed, presuming that a perpetual inventory system is maintained, the number of units on hand will equal the reorder point of 13 watches. But, within the one-week period until the next shipment arrives, Sterling's is *exposed* to a stockout. If they do not maintain safety stock the risk of a stockout is greater than if an adequate safety stock level is being held.

Stockout exposure.

Suppose Mr. O'Malley has decided that one stockout every year is the maximum that he will allow. That is, he is willing to take one chance in 4.64 exposures or a 1/4.64 = 21.55 percent chance of a stockout at each exposure. Using Table 12.12, constructed from Table 12.11, we can determine the probability of a stockout for any given reorder point. The probability of a stockout is calculated as 1.00 minus the probability shown in the right-hand column of the table that demand will be less than a given demand over lead time.

These probabilities of a stockout for each reorder point are shown in Table 12.13. From this table we can see that in order to have less than a 21.55 percent chance of a stockout (that is, more than 78.45 percent chance of demand over the lead time being *less* than the reorder point, the units on hand when an order is placed) the reorder point will have to be set at 15 watches and therefore the safety stock is 15 − 13 = 2 units. With this reorder point, the probability of no stockout is 85 percent. This "probability of no

Table 12.13 Probability of a Stockout for Each Reorder Point

Reorder Point	Safety Stock	Probability of Stockout	Service Level (%)
10	−3	.90	10
11	−2	.75	25
12	−1	.60	40
13	0	.35	65
14	1	.25	75
15	2	.15	85
16	3	0	100

The service level concept.

stockout" is referred to as the **service level** for this inventory policy and is the same as the cumulative probability column of Table 12.12.*

If Mr. O'Malley were to decide that a 25 percent chance of a stockout is the maximum acceptable (that is, he wants at least a 75 percent service level), then the reorder point would be set at 14 and the safety stock would be reduced to one (14 − 13) watch.

12.9 UNCERTAINTY IN BOTH DEMAND AND LEAD TIME: THE SERVICE LEVEL CONCEPT

Analytic and simulation approaches.

In the Sterling's Jewelers example the lead time was assumed to be known. If lead time is also uncertain the problem of determining the proper amount of safety stock takes on an added dimension. We can approach this problem from two directions; attempting either to determine a solution *analytically* (as we have done in all of the previous inventory control situations discussed so far) or through **simulation**. We will use the following example to demonstrate both approaches.

Great Gusher Oil and Gas Exploration Co.

The Great Gusher Oil and Gas Exploration Co. has been drilling oil and gas wells, working at one site at a time, for the past three years. Weekly use of diamond-tipped drill bits over the past year has been between zero and three units per week, as shown in Table 12.14. The supplier is located several hundred miles from Great Gusher's primary drill site and the drilling foreman has tabulated lead times for bit delivery to the site. Based on these data he has developed the probability distribution shown in Table 12.15.

Over the past three years Great Gusher has never stocked out of the required drill bit, primarily because an excessively high inventory of the units has always been maintained. The foreman wants to reduce the invest-

---

*Frequently, a service level is stated instead (such as "95 percent") and the corresponding number of stockouts a year is found.

Table 12.14 Probability
Distribution for Weekly
Drill Bit Use

Number Required	Probability
0	0.10
1	0.40
2	0.30
3	0.20
	1.00

ment in the inventory by reducing the safety stock currently being held. He reasons that some number of stockouts is acceptable since, in an emergency, he could "borrow" a bit from any of six other drilling companies working in adjacent areas. Because of the number of personnel and the investment in equipment, shutdowns of the drilling rig must be avoided.

Analytical Approach

The foreman initially needs to know the probability distribution for demand over lead time (DOLT). Just as with Sterling's Jewelers, the distribution of DOLT is essential in determining the risk of a stockout associated with each of the various levels of safety stock that could be maintained. Because both weekly usage and lead time are uncertain, the distribution of demand (usage) over lead time is a function of the probability distributions of *both* lead time and demand. This DOLT distribution is known as a *joint probability distribution* which, for relatively simple problems like the Great Gusher example, can be computed using a simple tree diagram.

Using the joint probability distribution.

Figure 12.17 presents the tree diagram used to compute Great Gusher's drill bit DOLT distribution. To illustrate the computations involved in the tree, consider the branch "*LT* = 2 weeks." The probability that lead time will be two weeks is .3. If lead time is two weeks, then there will be two weeks during which demand can be either 0, 1, 2, or 3 units each week. Hence, there are two levels or branches after the "*LT* = 2 weeks" branch in the figure. That is, demand can be 0, 1, 2, or 3 units in week 1 and 0, 1, 2, or 3 units in week 2, each weekly demand being determined by the probability distribution shown in Table 12.14. For example, if lead time is two

Table 12.15 Probability Distribution
for Drill Bit Lead Time

Number of Weeks from Order to Delivery	Probability
0	0.20
1	0.50
2	0.30
	1.00

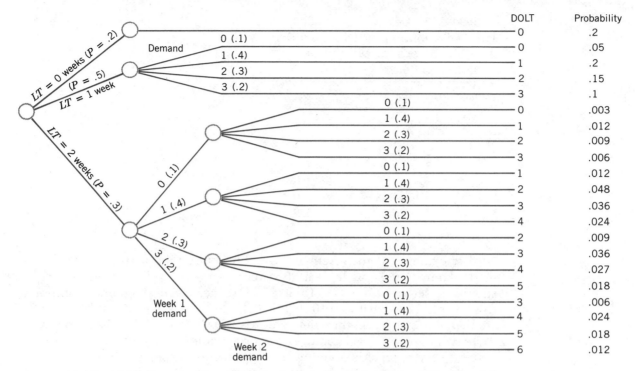

	DOLT	Probability
	0	.2
	0	.05
	1	.2
	2	.15
	3	.1
	0	.003
	1	.012
	2	.009
	3	.006
	1	.012
	2	.048
	3	.036
	4	.024
	2	.009
	3	.036
	4	.027
	5	.018
	3	.006
	4	.024
	5	.018
	6	.012

Figure 12.17   Tree diagram for drill bit demand over lead time distribution.

weeks, the probability that demand will be 3 units the first week and 1 unit the second week is $0.2 \times 0.4 = 0.08$. The probability of the *joint* occurrence of LT = 2 weeks *and* 3 units demanded in the first week *and* 1 unit demanded in the second is $0.3 \times 0.2 \times 0.4 = 0.024$. The probabilities of each of the other branches of the trees are computed in an identical manner.

The last two columns of data labeled "DOLT" and "Probability" provide the data necessary for the construction of the DOLT probability distribution. You will notice that there are several ways in which to get a total demand over lead time equal to a specific number of units. For example, to get a DOLT of 4 drill bits, lead time must be two weeks and demand for weeks 1 and 2 could be either 1 and 3, 2 and 2, or 3 and 1, respectively. Since the end result of each of these demand patterns is the same (i.e., DOLT = 4 drill bits) we simply add the probabilities for all like DOLTs to find that the probability of DOLT equaling 4 is .075 (i.e., .024 + .027 + .024). The final result of these calculations is shown in the DOLT probability distribution, Table 12.16.

We can now use this DOLT probability distribution just as we did in the earlier example with Sterling's Jewelers. First, we construct the cumulative probability distribution for demand over lead time, as shown in Table 12.17. We can now use this distribution to determine safety stocks and reorder points given the foreman's desired maximum risk of stockout, that is, his service level.

Safety stock based on desired service level.

Table 12.16 Demand over Lead Time Distribution for Diamond Drill Bits—Great Gusher Oil and Gas Exploration Co.

Demand over Lead Time	Probability
0	0.253
1	0.224
2	0.216
3	0.184
4	0.075
5	0.036
6	0.012
	1.000

For example, if the foreman wished no more than a 10 percent chance of stockout (that is, at least a 90 percent service level), the reorder point should be set at 4 units (see Table 12.17). Since *average* demand (computed from Table 12.14 as $0 \times 0.10 + 1 \times 0.40 + 2 \times 0.30 + 3 \times 0.20 = 1.6$) is 1.6 drill bits per week, the safety stock is thus 2.4 units ($4 - 1.6$). To have a 99 percent service level requires a reorder point of 6 units and if an 87.7 percent service level is acceptable (stockouts are expected to occur on 12.3 percent of exposures) the reorder point can drop to 3 units.

Simulation Approach

The second approach to inventory problems with uncertainty in both demand and lead time is simulation. Clearly, the tree diagram approach would become quite cumbersome if lead time exceeded three or four weeks (e.g., adding a lead time of three weeks to Great Gusher's problem would add 64 branches to the tree). Also, if the distributions of demand and lead time were continuous probability distributions rather than discrete distributions, as we have used here, the tree approach would be impossible and the mathematics required to form the joint distribution for DOLT quite complex. The simulation approach is illustrated in Section 12.11 (Appendix: Monte Carlo Simulation).

Table 12.17 Cumulative Probability Distribution for DOLT

Demand, D	Service Level or P $(DOLT \leq D)$
0	0.253
1	0.477
2	0.693
3	0.877
4	0.952
5	0.988
6	1.000

12.10 UNCERTAINTY AND NORMALLY DISTRIBUTED DOLT

If DOLT is normally distributed.

An assumption that is often made in determining safety stock is that demand over lead time is normally distributed. This assumption, which should always be tested before it is employed, significantly reduces the complexity of safety stock determination.

Dry Gulch Metropolitan Police Department

The Dry Gulch Metropolitan Police Department orders accident report forms from a printing company in a nearby town. Lead time has remained constant at one week and the demand per week has averaged 500 forms with a standard deviation of 250 forms. Figure 12.18 illustrates the distribution of demand over lead time for the accident report forms. The police chief has been ordering in quantities of 2600 units (two cartons). After much deliberation, the chief has decided that a policy of no more than one stockout in four years is appropriate. What reorder point (and safety stock) will satisfy the chief's policy?

Analysis

First, the annual demand is 500/week × 52 weeks = 26,000 forms/year. Ordering 2600 forms per order leads to 10 exposures per year and the chief will allow one stockout in four years, or one stockout in 40 exposures. This translates into an allowable stockout probability of 2.5 percent or, alternatively, a 97.5 percent (100 percent − 2.5 percent) *service level.*

The required safety stock can be determined by multiplying the *standard normal deviate, Z,* for a 97.5 percent service level times the standard deviation of demand over lead time.* Figure 12.19 presents the normal distribution of DOLT with the 2.5 percent probability area shaded. This shaded area represents the probability that DOLT will exceed the order point, which is the unknown in the problem. The order point is determined by finding the amount of safety stock that will have to be maintained. The value of Z for a 97.5 percent service level is, from Appendix A at the end of this text, 1.96; therefore the safety stock is

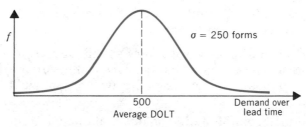

Figure 12.18   DOLT for Dry Gulch Police Dept.

*See Appendix B on probability and statistics, at the end of this text, if this procedure confuses you.

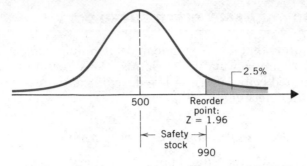

Figure 12.19 Normal distribution of DOLT.

safety stock = *Z factor* × standard deviation of DOLT   (12.13)
safety stock = 1.96 × 250
            = 490

and the reorder point is therefore

reorder point = average DOLT + safety stock   (12.14)
reorder point = 500 + 490
            = 990

If an order is placed when 990 units are on hand, the chance of running out before receiving the order is 2.5 percent.

12.11 APPENDIX: MONTE CARLO SIMULATION

Simulation by mathematical/ logical model.

Simulation is a technique for experimenting with a real situation through an artificial model that represents that situation. The three-dimensional models that architects and car designers frequently employ are forms of simulation. In these cases, the models are physical and small-scale versions of the real object. However, the simulations we are concerned with here are *mathematical/logical* models, which are usually programmed on a computer. The purpose of the simulation is to discover the "characteristics" of a particular processing design.

Simulation has a number of inherent advantages that other evaluation methods frequently do not have.

- The simulation can begin very simply and grow with the addition of more and more realistic processing complexity as the operations manager gradually understands the dynamics of what is happening in the system.
- The mathematics and logic of simulation are relatively simple.
- There are no "generalized" parts to the model; every component in the model corresponds to some real-life element.
- A considerable amount of "what if" type experimentation can be con-

ducted on the model to test new and creative designs, without altering an existing actual design.

● Considerable time compression is possible, especially if the simulation is computerized. Years of experience can be obtained in seconds of model operation.

● Simulation can handle an extremely large variety of situations and problems.

The primary disadvantage of simulation is that it takes time and money to construct the model, especially if a complex system is being simulated. Also, it will not *find* an optimal design—it will only describe the results of those designs identified by the manager.

Monte Carlo simulation.

The type of mathematical simulation we will consider here is called *Monte Carlo,* after the famous gambling kingdom. The procedure is used where events follow patterns that can be described by probability distributions. The steps for building a Monte Carlo simulation are shown in Figure 12.20. As an example we will manually simulate the Great Gusher problem for several periods.

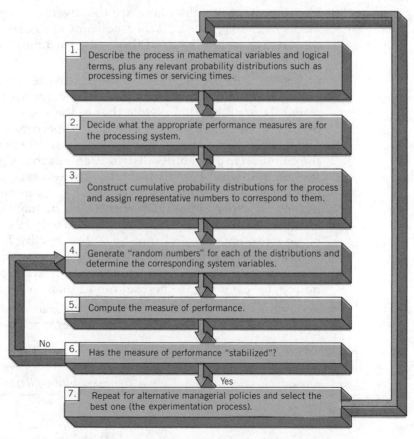

1. Describe the process in mathematical variables and logical terms, plus any relevant probability distributions such as processing times or servicing times.

2. Decide what the appropriate performance measures are for the processing system.

3. Construct cumulative probability distributions for the process and assign representative numbers to correspond to them.

4. Generate "random numbers" for each of the distributions and determine the corresponding system variables.

5. Compute the measure of performance.

6. Has the measure of performance "stabilized"?

No

Yes

7. Repeat for alternative managerial policies and select the best one (the experimentation process).

Figure 12.20 Monte Carlo simulation steps.

Table 12.18 Simulation for Weekly Demand

Demand Equals	Probability	Cumulative Probability	Representative Nos.
0	0.10	0.10	00–09
1	0.40	0.50	10–49
2	0.30	0.80	50–79
3	0.20	1.00	80–99

1. The supply and demand process for Great Gusher drill bits was described earlier in Section 12.9 by Tables 12.14 and 12.15. In addition to this information, we will now need to specify the managerial policies that describe a service level. Recall that simulation does not itself *find* optimal policies, it only *describes* the result of *given* policies. Let us assume that the economic order quantity of drill bits is 15 and that this amount is currently in inventory. In addition, let us for the moment try a policy of reordering whenever the weekly ending inventory level falls to 2 units or less. Alternative policies regarding order quantities and reorder levels may also be simulated later.

2. The important variables here are the inventory level, which the foreman wishes to reduce, and the frequency of stockouts. We will "track" the average weekly value of these two variables as our "measures of performance."

3. In Tables 12.18 and 12.19 we have constructed the cumulative probability distributions and assigned "representative numbers" to represent these probabilities. Note that of the 100 digits used (00–99), 10 percent of them represent 0 demand, 40 percent a demand of 1 unit, and so on. A simple way of assigning these 100 digits is by following the cumulative probability distribution—each assignment *begins* with the cumulative probability from the previous category. It actually does not matter *how* the digits are assigned, or even how many there are, as long as 10 percent of them represent a demand of 0, and so on. For example, we could just as easily have used only 10 digits with 0 demand being represented by 3; 1 unit by 4, 2, 0, 8; 2 by 7, 9, 1; and 3 by 5, 6. If more precise probability values had been given such as .103 for 0 demand, then 3-digit representative numbers would have been required; for example, the first set might then have run from 000 to 102.

4. To conduct the simulation, we first create a table to enter the data, Table 12.20. We will represent weekly demand by choosing two-digit

Table 12.19 Simulation for Lead Time

Lead Time Equals	Probability	Cumulative Probability	Representative Nos.
0	0.2	0.20	00–19
1	0.5	0.70	20–69
2	0.3	1.00	70–99

Table 12.20 Great Gusher Simulation

(1) Week No.	(2) Receipts	(3) Beginning Inventory	(4) Random No., RN	(5) Demand	(6) Ending Inventory	(7) Stockouts	(8) Order Placed	(9) RN	(10) Weeks to Arrive	(11) Average of (6)	(12) Average of (7)
0					15						
1	0	15	39	1	14					14.0	0
2	0	14	73	2	12					13.0	0
3	0	12	72	2	10					12.0	0
4	0	10	75	2	8					11.0	0
5	0	8	37	1	7					10.2	0
6	0	7	02	0	7					9.7	0
7	0	7	87	3	4					8.6	0
8	0	4	98	3	1		15	76	2	7.9	0
9	0	1	10	1	0					7.0	0
10	0	0	47	1	0	1				6.3	.100
11	15	15	93	3	12					6.8	.091
12	0	12	21	1	11					7.2	.083
13	0	11	95	3	8					7.2	.077
14	0	8	97	3	5					7.1	.071
15	0	5	69	2	3					6.8	.066
16	0	3	41	1	2		15	23	1	6.5	.063
17	0	2	91	3	0	1				6.1	.118
18	15	15	80	3	12					6.4	.111
19	0	12	67	2	10					6.6	.105
20	0	10	59	2	8					6.7	.100

random numbers from the random number table in Appendix A in the back of the book starting at the top left and working across the row. Generally speaking, random numbers for different paramenters should start at different places in the table and work in different directions. For example, middle of the table and working up, bottom right and working left, and so on. For lead time random numbers we will arbitrarily select a number by closing our eyes and picking from the table. As we obtain random numbers for demand we will enter Table 12.18 and see which set of representative numbers the random number falls in and then select the corresponding demand.

The first random number is 39, which falls between 10 and 49 in Table 12.18. Therefore the demand for week 1 is 1 unit. Ending inventory for the week is therefore 14 units (15 − 1), and since it is not less than or equal to the reorder point of 2, no order is placed. Demand for week 2 is 2 units, found by using the second random number. Ending inventory is 12, which is still not below the reorder point. Table 12.20 presents the results of the simulation for 20 weeks. At the end of the eighth week the ending inventory has fallen to 1 unit and, therefore, an order for 15 drill bits is placed between weeks 8 and 9. The lead time random number (column 9) of 76 generates (Table 12.19) a lead time of 2 weeks, and therefore receipt of the order is scheduled between week 10 and 11.

5. The measures of performance are listed in the last two columns of Table 12.20: the average weekly ending inventory and the average weekly number of stockouts.

6. The two measures are plotted in Figure 12.21 to determine if they have stabilized over the 20-week simulation; such simulations are typically run for a hundred or a thousand trials. From the figure it appears that neither measure has stabilized but that "inventory" is stabilizing faster than stockouts and will end up between 6 and 7 units. "Stockouts" appears that it will converge to around 0.08 or 0.09 per week (12 or 11 weeks between stockouts).

"Stabilization" is normally determined by the average absolute rate of change in the parameter and the cost to run the simulation for a longer period. If the expense represented by a weekly inventory of 6 compared to 7 units is not especially significant, then the 20 runs in Table 12.20 may be sufficient. Stabilization generally occurs faster for variables that occur often. In our example, replenishments and stockouts only occurred about every 10 weeks, so the stockout graph jumped excessively every time a stockout occurred. With 100 weeks of simulation the jumps in the graph would have been much subdued.

7. The managerial decision policy simulated of "order 15 when ending inventory reaches 2 units" resulted in a relatively poor service level—in both cases of reordering, a stockout occurred. This could possibly be avoided by ordering sooner, for example, when inventory reaches 3 or 4 units. For that matter, ordering fewer units more frequently

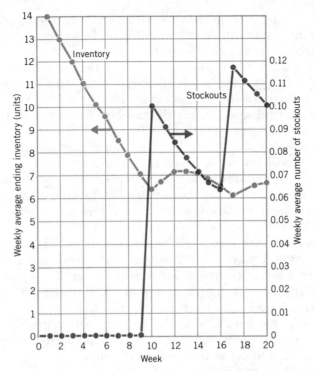

Figure 12.21   Great Gusher simulation stabilization.

may give much better service without a significant increase in cost. By varying the two decision policy parameters and simulating them in a short computer program (a minimal programming effort), the foreman could quickly find the best policy without disrupting his current inventory process.

This example has illustrated the use of simulation in analyzing inventory policy alternatives. Although the example was highly simplified, simulation can also handle exceedingly complex processes. Simulation is particularly appropriate for problems that do not satisfy the assumptions of some of the optimizing models of management science, or where human behavior is concerned. Of course, simulation is not limited to inventory analysis but has been used throughout the field of operations management for logistics analysis, quality control, maintenance, layout, scheduling, and so on. And, of course, simulation is so general and powerful that it is used in physics (to study atomic interactions), chemistry (for analyzing molecular behavior), biology (to study metabolism), and many other fields as well.

12.12 SUMMARY AND KEY LEARNING POINTS

This chapter has continued the discussion of materials management from Chapter 11 and looked in detail at the management of inventories of independently demanded materials such as supplies and raw materials. Discussion was initiated with an examination of the various costs of inventory and some of the more common systems such as reorder point or perpetual, periodic review, two-bin, just-in-time, and the Kanban system practiced in Japan. We then looked at identifying the most critical inventory items to manage in terms of the ABC concept.

Following these overview discussions we developed and illustrated a number of inventory models that tell us *when* to order and *how much* to order in various situations. First, we looked at the basic economic order quantity model for most inventory situations. We then extended this by considering the possibility of quantity discounts, by allowing for noninstantaneous production of the materials, and by considering the possibility of nonindependence between inventories in terms of their production on common facilities.

We further extended the basic model by looking at demand and lead time uncertainties. We first considered demand uncertainty in the single period situation, a common occurrence in service organizations. We then moved to the multiple period situation and brought in the concepts of safety stock and service levels. Last, we considered the situation of uncertainty in both demand and lead time in the multiple period problem. In the appendix to the chapter we described how to develop a Monte Carlo simulation model to handle this and other types of uncertainty.

The key learning points have been

- The main costs involved in inventory systems are ordering (or setup), carrying (or holding), stockout, capacity-associated cost, and the costs of the goods themselves.

- All inventory systems must tell the manager *when* to order and *how much*.

- The three major types of inventory management systems are reorder point (or perpetual, including two-bin), periodic review, and material requirements planning (including just-in-time such as Kanban) systems.

- The ABC system is to identify the approximately 15 percent of the inventory items that represent about 75 percent of the total annual inventory value, called A items, the 30 or so percent, called B items, that represent about 15 percent of the value, and the approximately 55 percent, called C items, that account for about 10 percent of the value. A items receive tight control, B items moderate control, and C minimal control.

- The EOQ model assumes constant demand, no stockouts, a nonvarying replenishment period, ordering and per-unit holding costs do not vary with order quantity, and items are ordered independently. The model identifies the best order quantity as that which minimizes the sum of those annual holding and ordering costs that vary with order quantity.

- The key to analyzing quantity discount offers is to compare total costs at EOQ points, if they fall into valid regions, with the total costs at price breaks.

- The ELS situation involves the receipt of inventory at a finite, rather than instantaneous rate, which more closely parallels the situation of internally produced items rather than purchased items. The model is developed on the same basis as the EOQ.

- When multiple items are produced on the same facilities, the ELS quantities may produce scheduling conflicts. Even though overall capacity is adequate, inventories may stockout before a replenishment batch can be scheduled. A solution to this problem is to deviate from the ELS and instead produce batches that last an equal amount of time.

- Uncertainty in demand raises the risk of either overordering or underordering, both of which bear extra costs. Underordering brings ill will and potential profit losses. Overordering requires carrying extra inventory that, on average, will not be needed or, in the single-period situation, will be wasted. The primary solution approach is to order the amount of stock that balances the expected cost of underordering with the expected cost of overordering. If the stock can be used again in a later period, the main cost of underordering is ill will, or the cost of shortages, and the approach used in this case is to let management set a desired "service level." A "safety stock" is then calculated and ordered to protect the organization up to that service level.

- There are numerous quantitative tools for handling uncertainty in inventory situations. Decision, or "payoff," tables consider every alternative for every possible state of nature and a calculation of the expected outcome with each alternative is made. Incremental analysis balances the expected cost of overordering with the expected cost of underordering. Probability trees graphically portray all possibilities at each stage and note their likelihood and outcomes, from which an expected outcome for each policy may be determined. Last, Monte Carlo simulation mathematically simulates a physical process so experimentation with managerial policies can be conducted to determine the probable outcomes.

12.13 KEY TERMS

reorder point (p. 442)

lead time (p. 442)

economic order quantity
(EOQ) (p. 442)

two-bin (p. 442)

perpetual inventory
system (p. 442)

periodic review system
  (p. 443)

independent demand (p. 444)

MRP (p. 445)

just-in-time (JIT) (p. 445)

ABC classification system
  (p. 446)

economic production lot size
(ELS) (p. 459)

payoff table (p. 466)

incremental (or marginal)
analysis (p. 468)

DOLT (p. 471)

service level (p. 473)

simulation (p. 478)

12.14 REVIEW AND DISCUSSION QUESTIONS

1. Grocery stores have traditionally operated on a periodic review basis for inventory control. What type of system can (will) be maintained with the new automatic sensing equipment being installed at checkout counters?

2. Discuss the limitations of the EOQ model. Is certainty in demand and lead time a reasonable assumption?

3. Discuss the use of EOQ-type models in such places as hospitals (blood banking, gauze, pacemakers, etc.) and pharmacies. What type of service level is appropriate?

4. If you were implementing a new inventory system on a computer and top management wanted to get the most "value" from the new system in the first week of installation, what priority would you give the order of entry of the inventory items on the master file?

5. Discuss why the reorder period will vary in a reorder point system.

6. Why is the decision tree not practical for solving inventory problems with a large number of uncertain demand and lead time possibilities?

7. With the two probability distributions of demand and lead time, how can the distribution of DOLT be found? Under what conditions can (should) each be used?

8. Why would a marketing program that would "stabilize" demands benefit inventory levels?

9. Describe what service level means from the perspectives of the marketing manager and the inventory control manager.

10. List two organizations that have high service levels and two that should probably have low service levels. Why would you expect these service levels in each case?

11. What happens to total annual inventory cost as lead time uncertainty increases? As demand uncertainty increases?

12. What other inventory situations are similar to the "newsboy" inventory situation discussed in this chapter?

13. How could simulation help a physician plan her office staff and facility requirements?

14. How would an operations manager decide in practice if a simulation was sufficiently stable to terminate the analysis?

12.15 PROBLEMS

Practice Problems

1. Categorize the following inventory items as type A, B, or C.

Unit Cost ($)	Annual Usage (units)
10,000	4
7,000	1
4,000	13
1,200	5
700	500
300	20
250	45
60	5,000
25	400
17	4,000
9	1,000
7	8,000
3	750
2	4,000
1	12,000

2. Given: annual demand of 12,000 units; monthly carrying cost of $1 per unit; ordering cost of $5.

Find the EOQ and the annual ordering cost.

3. The Frame Up, a self-service picture framing shop, orders 3000 feet of a certain molding every month. The order cost is $40 and the holding cost is $0.05 per foot per year. What is the current annual cost? What is the maximum inventory level? What is the EOQ?

4. Wing Computer Corp. uses 15,000 keyboards each year in the production of computer terminals. Order cost for the keyboards is $50.00 and holding cost for one keyboard is $1.50 per unit per year. What is the EOQ? If Wing ordered 1250 per month, what will the total annual cost be? What is the average inventory level?

5. The Quick In-Quick Out Corner Convenient Store receives orders from its distributor in three days from the time an order is placed. Lighter Than Air beer sells at the rate of 860 cans per day (they can sell 250 days of the year). A six pack of Lighter Than Air costs QIQOCCS $1.20. Annual holding cost is 10 percent of the cost of the beer. Order cost is $25.00. What is QIQOCCS's EOQ and what is the reorder point?

6. The Discount Drum Co. buys used 55-gallon drums from several chemical companies and cleans and resells them. One supplier has offered the following quantity discount schedule.

0–49	$3.00
50–99	2.75
100 and over	2.50

The order cost is $100 and holding cost is $0.50 per drum per year. If Discount can sell 8000 drums per year, what order quantity should they use?

7. If the annual demand for a $0.50 item is 2000, ordering cost is $1, and annual carrying cost is $0.10 each but a discount of $0.10 each is available for orders of at least 400, what is the best amount to order?

8. Happy Days Jacket Company manufactures 1950s vintage leather jackets. They can produce jackets at the rate of 5000 per year. Sales average 3000 per year. What production lot size should be used if setup costs are $200 and holding costs are $3 per jacket per year?

9. John operates a boring mill and Frank a hone. John's parts, when finished, are placed in crates and moved to Frank's location where they are honed to remove internal burs. Both men are on an incentive system that requires the company to pay for at least 2 hours of work for each person when a machine fails. That is, if John's boring mill were to stop, Frank would continue working until parts ran out, but would get paid for at least 2 hours even if the parts did not last that long. Frank can hone one part in 2 minutes and set up the next in a half-minute. If the company

policy is to have enough parts so that Frank must work the full 2 hours for which he will be paid, how much inventory must be maintained between the two workers?

10. Two products, W and Z, have to be produced on the same facilities. Annual demands (and production capacity) for W and Z are 1800 units (3000 units capacity) and 1000 units (2500 units capacity), respectively. Design a feasible production schedule for these products.

11. Demand for strawberries at McDonald's Berry Patch, Inc., has been recorded as follows.

Demand (quarts)	Probability
13,000	.1
15,000	.5
18,000	.3
20,000	.1

McDonald's orders berries on Monday morning from a large wholesaler and pays $0.40 per quart. Any berries not sold at the retail price of $0.95 per quart are sold for $0.30 per quart to a local family that makes strawberry jelly for sale at the flea market. How many quarts of berries should McDonald's purchase to maximize profits? Solve two different ways.

12. Mario's Pizza, across from the campus main gate, serves pizza by the slice and does a substantial lunch business. The following table provides demand information based on an analysis of the last six months' activity. Mario's direct cost in a pizza is $2.00. He sells each pizza for a total revenue of $5.00. If Mario wants to maximize profits, how many pizzas should he make each day?

Demand	Probability
45	.15
46	.15
47	.25
48	.20
49	.15
50	.10

13. Given: yearly demand = 12,000; carrying cost/unit/year = $1; ordering cost = $15; lead time = 5 days; safety stock = 200; price = $0.10 each. Find the total annual cost of the inventory system under an optimal ordering policy.

14. Given: maximum inventory = 1200 units; safety stock = 200 units; usage period = 20 days; order lead time = 10 days. Find the reorder point in units.

15. Lead time for delivery of frozen hamburgers to a fast-food restaurant is one day. Daily demand has been charted as follows.

Daily Demand	Probability
1200	.30
1300	.20
1400	.50

If a service level of at least 85 percent is desired, what safety stock should be held? What is the reorder point?

16. Resolve Problem 15 if the lead time is three days.

17. For the following distributions, determine the DOLT distribution.

Lead Time (weeks)	Probability		Demand/Week	Probability
1	.7		3	.6
2	.3		4	.4

What service level will a reorder point of 7 generate? What reorder point is needed to give an 80 percent service level?

18. Weekly demand for gasoline at a local service station is normally distributed with a mean of 6000 gallons and a standard deviation of 800 gallons. If order cost is $50 and holding cost is $0.02 per gallon per year, what order quantity and reorder point should be used to provide an 85 percent service level? Assume lead time is one week.

More Complex Problems

19. Categorize the following inventory-related expenses as to cost type and probable relevance in an inventory model to determine the best order size: postage, warehouse rent, purchase order forms, secretarial order-writing labor, warehouse guard, interest cost of money, cost of the goods, distribution cost per unit, receiving cost for raw materials, ill will for lost sales, warehouse heating, advertising, expediting costs to meet due dates, president's salary, fire insurance on finished goods.

20. It is time to consider reordering material in a periodic review inventory system. The inventory on hand is 100 units, maximum desired level of inventory is 250 units, usage rate is 10 units a day, the reorder period is every two weeks (10 working days), the lead time for resupply is 15 days, and the amount on order is 250 units. How much should be ordered?

21. The Efficiently Operating Quarry Company places orders for blasting caps once each month. The order quantity is 500 per month. The purchasing agent has just learned of the EOQ model and wants to try it out.

He determines that order costs are $1.50 and that holding cost is $8 per cap per year. What is the EOQ? Should they change their order quantity to the EOQ? Base your answer on economic and practical grounds.

22. A wholesaler purchases a million dollars worth of equipment a year. It costs $100 to place and receive an order and the annual holding cost per item is 20 percent of the item's value.
   a. What is the dollar value of the EOQ?
   b. How many months' supply is the EOQ?
   c. How often should orders be placed?
   d. How much will the annual holding cost change if the company orders monthly? How much will the annual ordering cost change?
   e. What should the dollar value of the EOQ be if the wholesaler doubles her annual purchases? What should it be if (instead) the ordering cost doubles? What should it be if the holding cost drops to 10 percent?

23. Solve Problem 2 if the holding cost is charged against the *maximum* inventory space required rather than the average. Compare the total annual costs (holding and ordering) under the two different holding cost policies.

24. A company orders the EOQ of 100 items every month at an ordering cost of $1.50 each time. The items cost $2 each.
   a. If the carrying cost is computed on the basis of an interest charge on invested capital, what is the effective simple monthly interest rate?
   b. If the holding cost is computed as the sum of a monthly warehousing charge of $0.01 per unit plus a capital interest charge, now what is the simple monthly interest rate?

25. A major equipment producer sells 4000 units of its $90 product a year. Ordering cost is $30 and holding cost is 8 percent of the product's value. Each item requires 5 square meters for storage and there is currently a room 20 meters by 40 meters available for storing the items. If additional annual storage space is available by lease at $0.10 a square meter, should the producer lease it?

26. The following price discounts are available for an item with an annual demand of 20,000, a $5 ordering cost, and a holding cost of 10 percent of the item value. What is the best ordering quantity? What discount price would be required to make it worthwhile buying 5000 at a time?

Quantity	Price
0–499	$3.00
500–999	2.85
1000–4999	2.75
5000 or over	2.70

27. AM/FM/VacM Co. produces musical vacuum cleaners to meet an annual demand of 240 units on equipment that has a production capacity of 960 units a year. Equipment setup cost is $750 and annual holding cost per cleaner is $300. Devise a production plan to optimally produce an integer number of cleaners.

a. How many units should be produced each time?

b. How many days will it take at full production? (Assume 240 working days a year.)

c. What will be the maximum inventory level?

d. Graph the inventory-production cycle.

e. How many days of no production will there be per month, on average?

f. What will be the total annual inventory cost?

28. In the multiple-product example of Table 12.6, there is some slack in the facility usage of Figure 12.15 that could be used to reduce production-inventory costs by producing A and B in batches nearer their ELSs. If the setup costs for A and B are both $150 and the holding costs are $1.50 and $1.00 a month, respectively, what is a more cost-effective, yet feasible, production schedule?

29. A book publisher prints softcover manuals for $10 each. If he stocks out and must produce extras, they will cost $30 each. If demand for the manuals is considered equally probable for all values between one and a hundred, how many should be produced? If demand is normally distributed around 100 with a standard deviation of 20, how many should be produced?

30. Kidney machines cost $100,000 apiece. The chance of needing two such machines in a large midwest city is exactly one in a hundred and of needing three is one in a thousand. If the city hospital buys three such machines what is the implied cost of ill will due to the unavailability of such a machine?

31. Storage cost for an industrial pump is $12 but *only* if it is stored for the entire six months between replenishment cycles. Shortage cost is $60 per month per pump and the company supplies an average of 50 pumps a month to customers. Find the best safety stock level from the following history of demand probabilities over the replenishment cycle.

Demand	Probability
60	.05
150	.10
240	.15
300	.40
360	.15
450	.10
540	.05

Use the following random digits in the remaining problems:

4564261074984201550147032719548.6.

32. Use simulation to solve Problem 16.

33. If, in Problem 17, a stockout costs $10 a week and holding stock costs $8/ unit a week, find the best reorder point by simulation.

34. Simulate 10 days of operation in Problem 12 with each of the following policies: (1) Make the same number as demanded the day before (48 yesterday); (2) make 48 every day; (3) make the smaller of (1) or (2). Answer the following:

    a. What was Mario's average daily pizza shortage under each policy?

    b. What was Mario's average daily overstock under each policy?

    c. What was the probability of a shortage with each policy?

    d. What was the likelihood of an overage with each policy?

    e. What was the most profitable policy in this short simulation?

12.16 CASE

VETTER CORPORATION

Vetter Corporation manufactures tables and work stations for the ever-growing computer industry. Vetter began operations three years ago with a single product, a cathode ray tube (CRT) stand which sold for $98. That product was designed by Vetter, completely subcontracted for manufacture of parts and assembled at the Vetter plant.

Since that beginning, Vetter has continually developed new products and has made efforts to vertically integrate their production and assembly operations. Currently, Vetter manufactures all of their own tops, does all laminating work and all sheet metal work with the exception of chromed tubular steel table legs. These legs are manufactured by a large company located approximately 120 miles away. Vetter's demand has been growing at such a rate that supplies of the table legs have been constantly short. Vetter's expeditors have been pressed to keep a supply of legs in stock. Vetter uses 300 sets of table legs per day in the manufacture of two different CRT stands. Because of the delays and delivery uncertainties, Vetter has been considering manufacturing these legs themselves. Vetter has been using an eco-

nomic order quantity of 6000 sets. The annual holding cost per set is $1.20. Vetter's industrial engineer estimates that with the proper equipment they can produce 800 leg sets per day. Setup costs for the equipment will be $750.

Jim Lochary, the production supervisor, is in favor of self-production by purchasing the new equipment. He argues that "being able to produce the legs ourselves will result in virtually no inventory being on hand. Our inventory holding costs will drop substantially." Peter Thomsen, the purchasing agent, argues that "if we are the only source of supply, downtime will surely kill us." Bobby Smith, the warehouse supervisor, contends that "we simply don't have space to increase inventory any more. If making them ourselves will help to solve the space problem, I'm all for it."

Questions for Discussion

1. What production lot size is justified if Vetter decides to purchase the leg manufacturing equipment?

2. How would you approach the problem of resolving these inventory level comments?

12.17 REFERENCES AND BIBLIOGRAPHY

1. Buffa, E. S., and Miller, J., *Production-Inventory Systems: Planning and Control*, 3rd ed., Homewood, IL: Irwin, 1979.
2. Graybeal, W., and Pooch, U. W., *Simulation: Principles and Methods*, Cambridge, MA: Winthrop, 1980.
3. Hadley, G., and Whitin, T. M., *Analysis of Inventory Systems*, Englewood Cliffs, NJ: Prentice-Hall, 1963.
4. Peterson, R., and Silver, E. A., *Decision Systems for Inventory Management and Production Planning*, New York: Wiley, 1979.
5. Plossl, G. W., and Wight, O. W., *Production and Inventory Control*, Englewood Cliffs, NJ: Prentice-Hall, 1967.
6. Plossl, G. W., and Welch, W. C., *The Role of Top Management in the Control of Inventory*, Reston, VA: Reston Publishing Co., 1979.
7. Tersine, R. J., *Materials Management and Inventory Systems*, New York: Elsevier North Holland, 1976.
8. Wagner, H. M., *Statistical Management of Inventory Systems*, New York: Wiley, 1962.
9. Wight, O. W., *Production and Inventory Management in the Computer Age*, Boston: Cahners, 1974.

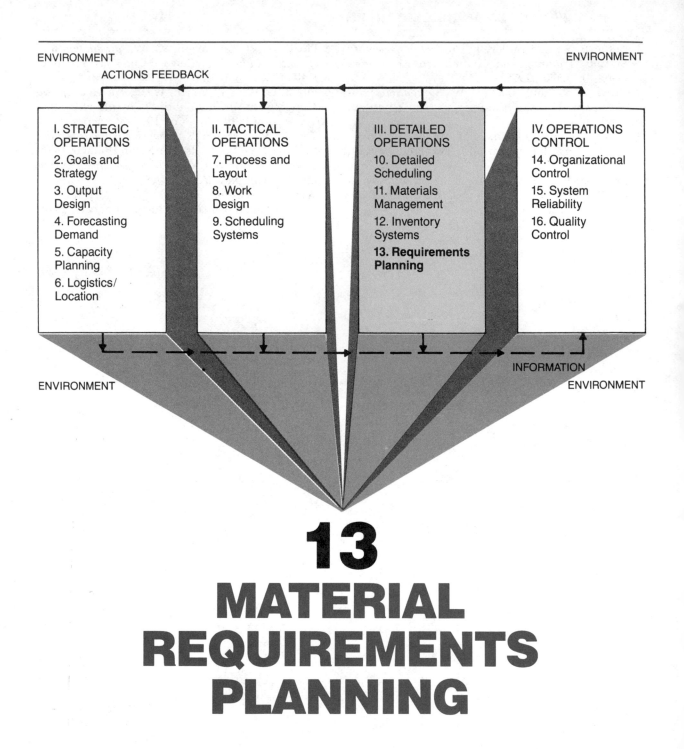

ENVIRONMENT   ENVIRONMENT

ACTIONS FEEDBACK

I. STRATEGIC OPERATIONS

2. Goals and Strategy

3. Output Design

4. Forecasting Demand

5. Capacity Planning

6. Logistics/ Location

II. TACTICAL OPERATIONS

7. Process and Layout

8. Work Design

9. Scheduling Systems

III. DETAILED OPERATIONS

10. Detailed Scheduling

11. Materials Management

12. Inventory Systems

13. Requirements Planning

IV. OPERATIONS CONTROL

14. Organizational Control

15. System Reliability

16. Quality Control

ENVIRONMENT   ENVIRONMENT

INFORMATION

13
MATERIAL REQUIREMENTS PLANNING

13

LEARNING OBJECTIVES

By the completion of this chapter the student should

- Clearly understand the difference between independent and dependent demand.
- Be familiar with the concepts of a product tree, parent items, and a bill of materials.
- Appreciate the difference between pre- and postcomputer inventory management.
- Have a feel for the inputs and outputs required for an MRP system.
- Be able to develop an MRP explosion with appropriate lead times and order releases based on a master production schedule and on-hand inventories.
- Know how to conduct a lot sizing using the part-period balancing method.

This chapter introduces a relatively new concept in inventory control, that of **dependent demand.** In the previous chapter we discussed the use of reorder point and periodic review inventory management systems. We concentrated our attention on the problems and solutions for situations with unknown periodic demand and uncertain lead times. But, as we have previously indicated, these *statistical* or *probabilistic* inventory management systems perform best for demands of finished goods inventories and for some raw materials inventories. That is, inventories such as men's slacks and shirts in a retail store, cases of cereal from a wholesale grocery, and demand for airline flights from a given city are independent of other demands. Also, some raw materials, such as nails in a modular home assembly plant or latches in a storm window manufacturing facility, can also be considered as independent because they would be used in equal quantities no matter what product is being produced. Statistical reorder systems, though, have typically proved themselves inadequate for many types of raw materials and for assemblies and subassemblies used in producing a "higher level" product.

The key to this lack of performance has been pointed out and researched by Dr. Joseph Orlicky [6,7] and has been further developed and promoted by such other noted inventory management specialists as George Plossl and Oliver Wight [7,8]. As these and other researchers and practitioners have noted, statistical methods perform well for "smooth" or "constant" demand, that is, demand with rather normal fluctuations around an average value or a trend value. But they perform poorly if demand is "lumpy," that is, if demand remains fairly constant for a period, then surges for a short duration, and then returns to its previous constant level.

Examples of constant and *lumpy demands* are shown in Figure 13.1. For the constant demand case, demand varies around the average (shown by the dashed line). A standard deviation can be calculated and a reorder point determined which will provide a specific level of assurance against a stockout. But, for the lumpy demand case, using the same statistical approach results in average inventory levels that are much too high. The example in the next section will illustrate this point. The entire focus of this chapter is material requirements planning (**MRP**), which is a system designed specifically for the lumpy demand situation when the "lumps" are known about beforehand, typically because the demands are "dependent."

Independent demand materials.

Smooth versus lumpy demand.

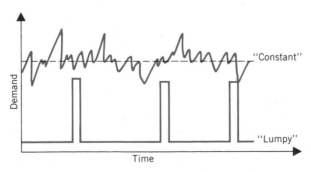

Figure 13.1 Constant and lumpy demand.

The successful implementation of an MRP system is not an easy task, taking an average of $240,000, 16 months, and 10 hours a month of a vice-president's time [5]. (Refer back to the implementation discussion in Section 9.2.) For those who are successful, however, the rewards are significant: much lower inventory investment, shorter lead times, fewer missed delivery dates, and higher productivity. Some have claimed that MRP may well be the answer to Japan's "just-in-time" production system.

13.1 INDEPENDENT VERSUS DEPENDENT DEMAND

Independent finished goods but dependent subassemblies and raw materials.

Many items, particularly *finished products* that are demanded in many small quantities by customers (e.g., General Motors auto sales to dealers, sales of ice cream at a local grocery, etc.), are said to experience "independent" demand. That is, the demand cannot easily be related to or traced to a known or predictable requirement. Demand appears to be random, or caused by chance events. But most *raw materials, components,* and *subassemblies* are "dependent" on demands for finished goods and other (sub)assemblies. This is because production is usually done in lots or batches, and when a lot is ordered for production in the factory, all materials and components needed for production are ordered at the same time, hence a "lump" in demand. For example, in a wooden door production facility, reorders of (finished) doors may be based on a reorder point system. When the number of finished doors on hand reaches the reorder point, R, then an order of quantity Q is placed into production on the shop floor. Figure 13.2a illustrates this inventory time pattern.

Lumpy demand for lumber.

If a reorder point system similar to the one used in managing the finished door inventory were used in managing the inventory of lumber used in the production of the finished doors, the inventory pattern shown in Figure 13.2b would result. Notice that in Figure 13.2b the "normal" inventory level is X units. When the finished door inventory in Figure 13.2a reaches its reorder point and a production order is released to the shop, a requisition for the required quantity of lumber is made against that inventory. The inventory level will drop by the quantity used in producing the lot, thus causing the raw materials inventory to fall below its reorder point. This triggers a reorder for a quantity of lumber resulting in replenishment of the inventory after its purchase lead time.

Order for when needed.

As you can see, the average inventory level for the lumber is quite high, and most of this inventory is being held for long periods of time without being used. A logical approach to the reduction of the inventory level is to anticipate the timing and quantities of demands on the lumber inventory and then to schedule purchases to meet this requirement. Figure 13.3 illustrates the results on the lumber inventory level of this anticipation-of-demand approach. Figure 13.3a illustrates the same finished product "inventory" pattern as Figure 13.2a. Figure 13.3b depicts the scheduling of receipt of lumber just prior to the time when it is needed. The impact on average inventory level is obvious.

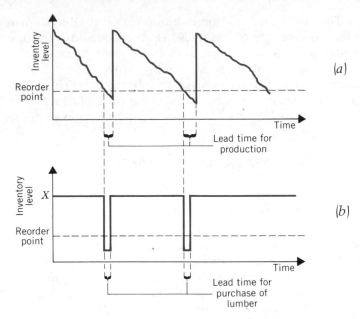

Figure 13.2 Relationship between finished item inventory and raw material/subassembly item inventory—reorder point approach (*a*) Finished doors. (*b*) Lumber.

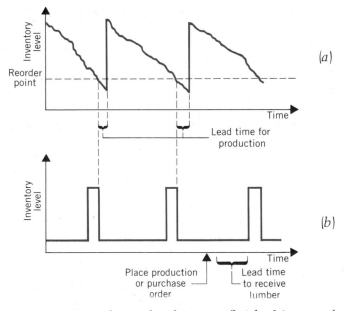

Figure 13.3 Relationship between finished item and subassembly/raw material item inventories—a requirement planning approach. (*a*) Finished doors. (*b*) Lumber.

All reorder point systems presume (even though implicitly) that demand for each item in inventory is independent of the demand for a finished item or any other items in the inventory. Reorder point approaches work well when this presumption holds but rather poorly for items whose demands are dependent on higher level items. Material requirements planning is the fundamental method used in inventory management systems for dependent inventory items.

The student should note that dependent demand is not the only cause of lumpy demand. Demand can appear in lumps if only a small number of customers exist for the item and their purchasing habits are discontinuous. MRP is not a solution to the general lumpy demand case since no basis exists for development of the materials plan unless the demand is dependent on something that a planner can either measure or forecast.

13.2 PRECOMPUTER VERSUS POSTCOMPUTER INVENTORY MANAGEMENT

The need for a computer.

The availability and practicality of MRP systems is related directly to the advent of relatively inexpensive computer power. Without the electronic computer, operations managers would simply be unable to perform all of the calculations and maintain all the schedules necessary to perform requirements planning. A simple example will illustrate this point.

The Breakneck Company

The Breakneck Company produces skateboards known as the Sidewalk Suicide Special. The Special is made up of one fiberglass board and two wheel assemblies. The lead time to assemble a special from its two major components is one week. The first component, the board, is purchased and has a three-week delivery lead time. The second major component, the wheel assembly is assembled by Breakneck. Each wheel assembly is made up (with a one-week lead time) of one wheel mounting stand (manufactured by Breakneck with a four-week lead time), two wheels (purchased with a one-week lead time), one spindle (manufactured by Breakneck with a two-week lead time), and two chrome-plated locknuts (purchased with a one-week lead time). The product structure (or **product tree**) is shown in Figure 13.4.

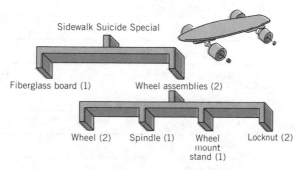

Figure 13.4 Skateboard product tree.

To produce an order for 50 Special skateboards, the materials requirements are computed as follows.

Fiberglass boards: $1 \times$ no. of specials $= 1 \times 50 = 50$

Wheel assemblies: $2 \times$ no. of specials $= 2 \times 50 = 100$

Wheels: $2 \times$ no. of wheel assemblies $= 2 \times 100 = 200$

Spindles: $1 \times$ no. of wheel assemblies $= 1 \times 100 = 100$

Wheel mount stand: $1 \times$ no. of wheel assemblies $= 1 \times 100 = 100$

Locknut: $2 \times$ no. of wheel assemblies $= 2 \times 100 = 200$

Furthermore, presume that the master schedule indicates that an order for 50 Specials is due to be delivered in 10 weeks. The calendar in Table 13.1 illustrates the timing of due dates and the necessary order dates (presuming the lead times stated earlier) that must be met in order to deliver in the tenth week.

Note that MRP is a highly *logical* system. Knowing that 50 Specials must be shipped at the end of week 10 means that 50 boards must be placed on order for outside procurement at the end of week 6, that an order for 100 mounting stands must be placed in the shop at the end of week 4, and so forth. Ordering later than these dates would result in late shipment (or working overtime and otherwise expediting the order), and ordering earlier would

Table 13.1 Suicide Specials Demand

		Week										
		1	2	3	4	5	6	7	8	9	10
Suicide Specials												50
Boards	Date needed										3 week	50
	Order date						50	lead time				
Wheel assembly	Date needed										100	
	Order date								100			
Wheels	Date needed										200	
	Order date							200				
Spindles	Date needed										100	
	Order date						100					
Mounting stands	Date needed										100	
	Order date				100							
Locknuts	Date needed										200	
	Order date							200				

Lower level items.

result in inventory being available (and occupying space, requiring paperwork and other holding costs) before it is needed. MRP looks at each end product and the dates when each is needed. From these due dates, needed dates for all lower level items are computed, and from these due dates starting or order dates are determined.

MRP not a new idea.

While the overall idea is simple, consider the extreme complexity of operating an MRP system on a manual basis. In this simple example with only one end product the calculations and record-keeping requirements are straightforward. But, for a large firm that manufactures hundreds of end items with thousands of intermediate components, only a computer can keep up with the processing volume. This is an important point, for it is not that MRP is a revolutionary idea. The basic idea has been around for quite some time. It is and has been practiced for construction projects (from a single house to a mammoth skyscraper) that are scheduled according to a "right materials to the right place at the right time" philosophy. MRP has come of age in manufacturing and assembly operations with large numbers of end and intermediate items because large-scale and relatively inexpensive computer power is available.

Precomputer Inventory Management

Precomputer inventory management was characterized by the following.

1. Concentration on order quantities.

2. Concern for "when to order."

3. Expediting of "late" orders.

4. Production control and inventory management viewed as separate functions.

Concentration on Order Quantities

The concern for order quantities stems primarily from the emphasis on ordering economic order quantities (EOQs). Numerous articles in trade and industrial magazines touted the praises of ordering in economic quantities. Claims of substantial savings in inventory cost were common. But, upon further scrutiny, it has been found that in situations where the demand for the inventory item is dependent, the EOQ methodology is less helpful. Good order quantities for "constant" demand items are not necessarily good for lumpy demand items. Getting the right quantity at the wrong time does not accomplish anything. Timing is particularly important in situations where subassemblies must be available to assemble the finished product.

Concern for "When to Order"

The concern for "when to order" was typically answered by reorder point calculations. The reorder point was calculated, as we saw in the last chapter as

reorder point = demand over lead time + safety stock

But, this "when to order" concern was typically translated into *order launching*, that is, orders were sent out into production or to a vendor or supplier simply on the basis of a reorder point. Consideration was not given to when the items were needed.

As a result, items not needed again for six months may have been ordered today if the order point had been reached. Likewise, an item needed in two weeks, but with a production lead time of eight weeks may not have been ordered until today—again, when the reorder point is reached. While logical managerial "override" should have prevailed to ensure that such ridiculous results did not occur, these possibilities are real failures of the statistical reorder point approach. And since for very large inventories, the attention necessary to ensure that such blunders do not take place was prohibitively expensive, these types of errors in fact occurred.

Expediting of "Late" Orders

Expediting of late orders also became the rule. The job of the expediter in a production system was to push jobs along in the shop which were either needed for another stage of production or to satisfy a customer's demand. All "launched" orders were presumed to be of equal priority unless they were being expedited. A common occurrence on factory floors was the RUSH ticket. Orders tagged with a RUSH ticket were to receive special treatment (e.g., moving ahead of other orders waiting to get on a particular machine, special handling from work station to work station, etc.). But, an equally common occurrence was the use of RUSH tickets on 50 to 80 percent of the jobs in the shop and also the introduction of the RUSH-RUSH and the RUSH-RUSH-RUSH ticket. Obviously, everything cannot have first priority and, thus, such methods often result in confusion for the operations manager and almost no improvement in getting jobs out the door.

Rush-rush tickets.

Production Control Separate from Inventory Management

Production control and inventory management were viewed as independent functions. Those concerned with inventory management were concerned with calculating "correct" or "scientific" order quantities and order points. But the production control personnel were concerned with moving items through the operations to produce the outputs in the right quantities and at the right time. Clearly, these two functions have an impact on one another. Without the raw materials, purchased components, work-in-process inventory, subassemblies, and so forth, the production control personnel would have nothing to schedule and control through the facility. Likewise, the inventory management personnel had no purpose except to assume that inventory was available to meet demand.

Postcomputer Inventory Management

Postcomputer inventory management, and particularly MRP, is characterized by

1. Concern for "when needed."
2. Concern for order "priorities."
3. Deexpediting as well as expediting.
4. Production control and inventory management viewed as integral functions.

Concern for "When Needed"

Once the computer was available to handle the myriad calculations and multiple data files, it was not long until the production control and inventory management functions were considered to be integral. The integration of thinking between these two functions resulted in a shift in concern to *when needed* rather than a direct concern for "when to order." If the operations manager has good information regarding the due date for an order, the ordering and scheduling of parts and components to make up that order becomes a matter of "back scheduling," as we have shown in the Breakneck Company example, from the due date for each part and operation.

Concern for Order "Priorities"

There has also been the realization that all orders on the shop floor do not have the same *priority*. Certain products are more important than others and certain customers take precedence over others. Knowing the priority of individual orders in relation to the others allows scheduling to fulfill these priorities.

Deexpediting Orders

Recognition of different priorities also results in the concept of *deexpediting*, that is, holding up production or order release for items that were scheduled earlier but are now found to be due at a later date. Expediting and deexpediting work hand in hand to maximize the throughput of operations. If an order for skateboard wheels had been assigned a high priority because they were needed in the production of a particular order of skateboards, then it should be deexpedited if the original order has been cancelled or rescheduled for later delivery. Failing to reduce the priority or to deexpedite the order provides misinformation to the production department and will perhaps cause incorrect schedules to be developed.

13.3 THE MECHANICS OF MRP

Material requirements planning is a production/inventory management system. As such, it requires both production and inventory information in order to produce its primary output—a schedule or plan for orders, both released and pending, which specifies actions to be taken now and in the future. Figure 13.5 illustrates the flows of information within an MRP system.

Figure 13.5 indicates three primary inputs to the MRP computer system.

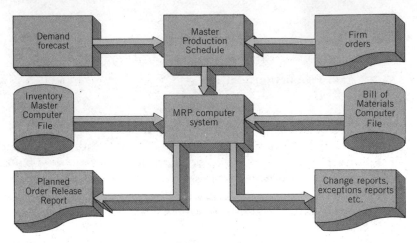

Figure 13.5   Schematic of MRP system.

MRP inputs.

1. The Master Production Schedule.

2. The Bill of Materials Computer File.

3. The Inventory Master Computer File.

MRP outputs.

A major output from the MRP computer system is the planned order release report, although there are other change reports, exceptions reports, and reports used for deexpediting orders already released.

Figure 13.5 is a detailed portion of Figure 9.1. Aggregate scheduling and the production plan are ignored here and the demand forecast is passed right through to the Master Production Schedule, which feeds the MRP system. However, MRP requires other inputs also, not related to the major scheduling functions of Figure 9.1, such as current inventories and bills of material for the products. The direct MRP output reports shown in Figure 13.5 are then the inputs to the Capacity Planning function in Figure 9.1.

The relationship between materials planning and operations scheduling is, of necessity, an intimate one. Any attempt to design these two systems so they operate independently will either fail outright or, at best, be grossly inefficient.

The MRP Inputs

As indicated, the MRP inputs are the Master Production Schedules, the Bill of Materials Computer File, and the Inventory Master Computer File.

1. The **Master Production Schedule** is prepared based on "actual" customer orders and predicted demand. This schedule indicates exactly when each ordered item will be produced to meet the firm and predicted demand; that is, it is a time-phased production plan. "Tuesday we make 100 S-3s for Smith; Wednesday 200 R-1s for Jones", and so on.

2. For each item in the Master Production Schedule, a bill of materials exists. The **Bill of Materials Computer File** indicates all of the raw materials, components, subassemblies, and assemblies required to produce an item. The MRP computer system accesses the Bill of Materials Computer Files to determine exactly what items, and in what quantities, are required to complete an order for a given item.

3. The **Inventory Master Computer File** contains detailed information regarding the number or quantity of each item on hand, on order, and committed to use in various time periods. The MRP computer system accesses the Inventory Master Computer File to determine the quantity available for use in a given time period and, if enough are available to meet the order needs, commits these for use during the time period by updating the inventory record. If sufficient items are not available, the system includes this item, with the necessary quantity for an EOQ or ELS, on the planned order release report.

Because these items are crucial to the operation of an MRP system, we will discuss each in more detail in the following sections.

The Master Production Schedule

The Master Production Schedule is a summary of planned end product needs for specific future time periods. The schedule is based on *firm customer orders* which are typically submitted by salespersons or received directly from the customer. These orders include the quantity that the customer desires and, typically, a promised delivery date. The schedule is also based on forecasts of future demand for which orders have not yet been received. These formal projected orders are summed by time period and these time-phased requirements then make up the Master Production Schedule.

It should be noted that this schedule is only a trial schedule. There is no guarantee that production capacity will be available to produce according to the schedule. Therefore, this trial schedule is used as input to the MRP computer system to produce the Planned Order Release Report. The MRP system assumes the demands listed in the Master Production Schedule are certain, even if they are only forecasts, or, more frequently, unrealistic delivery promises. The MRP will schedule the production regardless.

Based on the orders to be released in specific time periods and the total capacity available during these periods, the schedule is modified. If capacity is insufficient, the schedule is modified and tried again. When a reasonable schedule is achieved, the Planned Order Release Report will outline a detailed production schedule that is feasible for the resources and capacity available.

The Bill of Materials Computer File

Once a master schedule is available, MRP uses a *Bill of Materials Computer File* to determine all of the individual items that will be required to complete production on the product represented in the Master Production Schedule. A bill of materials is a structured parts list. The Bill of Materials

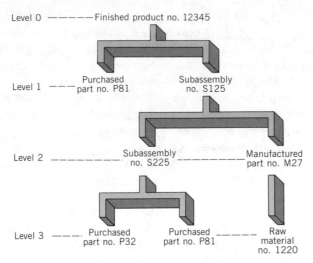

Level 0 ————Finished product no. 12345

Level 1 ——┐ Purchased   Subassembly
            part no. P81   no. S125

Level 2 ——————— Subassembly ————————— Manufactured
                no. S225   part no. M27

Level 3 ——. Purchased   Purchased ——————— Raw
            part no. P32   part no. P81   material
                                              no. 1220

Figure 13.6   Product structure tree.

Computer File is the set of all structured parts lists for all items that an organization produces. Rather than simply listing all of the parts necessary to produce one finished product, the bill of materials shows the way a finished product is put together from individual items, components, and subassemblies. For example, a product with the product structure illustrated in Figure 13.6 would generate the bill of materials illustrated in Figure 13.7.

Parent, or zero level, items.

This bill of materials shows the finished product (sometimes called the **parent item**) at the highest, or zero, level. Subassemblies and parts that go directly into the assembly of the finished product are called level 1 components, parts and subassemblies that go into level 1 components are shown as level 2, and so on. Thus, when a Master Production Schedule shows a requirement for a given quantity of finished products for a certain due date, production planners can **explode** the bill of materials for that finished product to determine the number, due dates, and necessary order dates of subcomponents that are required to meet the time and quantity requirements.

Exploding the BOM.

Level 1 Parts	Level 2 Parts	Level 3 Parts	Description	Quantity	Source
No. P81				1	Purchased
No. S125				1	Manufactured
	No. S225			1	Manufactured
		No. P32		1	Purchased
		No. P81		2	Purchased
	No. M27			1	Manufactured
		No. 1220		3 lb	Purchased

Figure 13.7   Bill of materials for a three-level product.

Exploding a BOM (bill of materials) simply means stepping down through all the levels of the bill of materials and determining the quantity and lead time for each item required to make up the item at that level. Note that if some items are manufactured internally, their lead time will be a function of the number of items to be produced rather than a fixed period as typically input. The result of exploding a bill of materials for a given item is a time-phased requirement for specific quantities of each item necessary to produce the finished product. We exploded an order for skateboards earlier in this chapter, although we had not formally introduced the notion of a bill of materials. A great deal of the time required to implement an MRP system is spent restructuring BOMs (so they can be exploded properly) and verifying their accuracy. Clearly, exploding incorrect BOMs will only cause trouble further downstream.

Note in Figures 13.6 and 13.7 that purchased part number P81 is used both as a level 1 and a level 3 component and is specifically identified in both locations in the product tree and bill of materials. Purchased part number P81 could perhaps be a stainless steel nut and bolt assembly which is used to produce subassembly number S225 as well as to complete the assembly of the finished product 12345 by assembling with subassembly number S125. We do not aggregate the number of P81s used to produce a single finished product (that is, we do not show part number P81 as requiring 3 to produce finished product number 12345) because aggregating would not allow us to identify the specific number of P81s necessary to produce a lot of S225 subassemblies. It would also preclude knowing how many P81s would be necessary to complete final assembly of S125 subassemblies into finished products.

The Inventory Master Computer File

The Inventory Master File (IMF) is made up of all the individual inventory records, one for each finished product and item in the bill of materials. Although these records can be quite lengthy and contain a significant volume of data, the primary requirements for MRP are the master data and item status segments of the record. The master data are the typically unchanging portion of the record (e.g., identification, make, description, cost, EOQ or ELS, setup time, etc.). The status segment contains information used in time-phased planning. Specifically, this segment contains the gross (actual quantity needed during the period) and net (the gross less the quantity available) requirements for each period, the planned receipts of inventory scheduled by time period, the number currently on hand, and the planned orders to be released by time period.

The Inventory Master File is kept up-to-date through periodic updates, which post the receipts of purchased and manufactured items into inventory, the release of items onto the production floor for production, the losses due to scrap, the orders that have been canceled or expedited/deexpedited, and so forth. IMFs are typically only 70 percent accurate in manual systems, but for MRP they need to be 95 to 99 percent accurate. Again, this takes much time.

MRP System Outputs

Three specific MRP system outputs constitute the plan of action for released and pending orders. These are

1. The Order Action Report.
2. The Open Orders Report.
3. The Planned Order Release Report.

The Order Action Report indicates which orders are to be released during the current time period and which orders are to be canceled. The Open Orders Report shows which orders are to be expedited or deexpedited. This report is typically an exception report listing only those open orders for which action is necessary. The Planned Order Release Report is the time-phased plan for orders to be released in future time periods. It is this report that determines whether a master production schedule is feasible or not.

MRP Computations

An order for 100 of a finished product due 12 weeks from today may or may not be cause for action in the production/inventory system. If 1000 are currently on hand and planned order deliveries for 350 are scheduled between now and 12 weeks from now, 650 will be available from which the order for 100 can be shipped. But if 400 are now available and 350 will be shipped between now and the due date for the order of 100, action is necessary.

Gross versus net requirements.   MRP computations are based, in large part, on **gross** and **net requirements.** The order for 100 to be shipped in 12 weeks is a gross requirement. Actions, though, should be based on net requirements. In the first instance, the net requirement is -550 (i.e., $100 - 650$); thus, there is no production requirement. But in the second case, the net requirement in the twelfth week is 50 (i.e., $100 - 50$). Since there is a net requirement for 50 units, at least that quantity will have to be produced to meet the shipping requirement for 50. These quantities are based on the following two formulas:

net requirements for planning period = gross requirements
for the planning period − planned on hand at planning period   (13.1)

and

planned *on-hand* at planning period = current on-hand +
scheduled receipts prior to planning period − scheduled   (13.2)
requirements prior to planning period

Backtracking through lead times.   Using the lead times that are available in the inventory file, order release dates are calculated by backscheduling or time phasing from the planning period (the due date) by the amount of the lead time. Orders are scheduled to be received when needed to meet the due date(s). If the net requirements for the planning period are positive, then an order must be scheduled to be received in time for use in the planning period. MRP answers the question of "when to order" by first determining when items are needed, and then scheduling an order release so that the items will be received just prior to the needed date. On the other hand, if the net requirements are negative or zero, no order is necessary.

Each successively lower level item that goes into production of the 100 parent items is scheduled in an analogous fashion. A planned order release at one level generates requirements at the next lower level. The differences in on-hand inventory at each level, the order quantities used at successively lower levels, and the number of different finished products that use a particular lower level component result in different order cycles for items at the various levels.

For example, suppose that in the order for 100 items in week 12, the planned on-hand quantity is 50 and the lead time for production (assembly) of level 1 items is three weeks. Then, an order for at least 50 (and possibly more, depending on the company's policy to order in economic lot sizes) would be placed in week 9. The material requirements plan at level 0 of the product is shown in Table 13.2.

At level 1, a purchased hose may be required and therefore a requirement plan must be developed for this item as well. But, the same hose may be used on another product. Therefore, the requirements plan for the hose must incorporate the requirements generated from all higher level items in which it is used. The material requirements plan for the purchased hose is shown in Table 13.3. Lead time is four weeks.

But notice the demand in week 10 for 200 of the hoses. Presume that these are required to produce subassemblies used in an entirely different end product. The requirements for both uses are aggregated and an order planned in week 10 − 4 = 6 for 250. The order, again, could have been for an EOQ.

At each level this same procedure is followed. All requirements from higher levels generate needs at lower levels. These needs are aggregated at each level for each item and a requirements plan established using the formulas and tables outlined above.

Table 13.2 Zero Level MRP

Week	1	2	3	4	5	6	7	8	9	10	11	12
Gross requirements		50			150			50	100			100
On hand 400	400	400	350	350	350	200	200	200	150	50	50	50
Net requirements	—	—	—	—	—	—	—	—	—	—	—	50
Planned order receipts												50
Planned order releases									50			
Lead time = 3 weeks												

Table 13.3 Level 1 MRP

Week	1	2	3	4	5	6	7	8	9	10	11	12
Gross requirements									50	200		
On hand 100	100	100	100	100	100	100	100	100	100	50	100	
Net requirements	—	—	—	—	—	—	—	—	—	150		
Planned order receipt										250		
Planned order releases						250						

Lead time = 4 weeks

The MRP system is not complete when a requirements plan is finally prepared. Whenever the master schedule changes or priorities on scheduled orders change, rescheduling of order releases takes place. Since the order release generates all requirements for items at lower levels, changing an order release requires the regeneration of new requirement plans. Also, released orders may be expedited or deexpedited based on schedule changes, changes in priorities, and cancellation of orders.

Daily changes affect the MRP plan.

Lot Sizing

How many to order?

In conjunction with scheduling orders to be released (i.e., the "when to order" decision), the second major inventory management question "How many to order?" must also be answered. Determining the appropriate **lot size** for the production of intermittently demanded products is more complex than using the simple EOQ or ELS models presented in Chapter 12. But, the general objective of balancing ordering or setup costs with inventory holding costs is the same.

The difficulty stems again from the lumpy nature of demand in a dependent inventory situation. Both the EOQ and ELS models assumed a constant demand. Therefore, the rate of decline of the inventory level over time could be predicted with relative certainty. Since the costs of holding and ordering inventory are related to inventory levels over time and to the rate at which inventory is consumed, logical calculations could be made on the basis of this constant rate (you might want to refer back to Chapter 12, particularly to the discussion of the number of orders placed each year and to the average inventory level). But, with lumpy demand neither the rate of use nor the average level of inventory can be easily predicted. Instead of a formal equation for determining the appropriate order quantity or lot size, several heuristics have been used.

Trial and error.

One approach is to determine, through trial and error, the best order

Optimization via Wagner-Whitin.

quantity by trying every possible order quantity that meets the master schedule requirements. This is obviously a large and tedious problem since there are so many possibilities. Another method, known as the *Wagner-Whitin algorithm* [3], systematically determines optimal lot sizes by evaluating all possible ways of ordering to meet the master schedule. Note that this procedure is an optimizing technique. The major drawback to the method is the rapid increase in computational time as the number of ordering alternatives increases.

Accumulation.

Another approach simply tries the lot sizes determined by accumulating the time-phased requirements. That is, suppose requirements of 100, 40, and 75 units were scheduled for weeks 13, 18, and 21, respectively. This approach would simply evaluate the three order quantities 100, 140 (100 + 40), and 215 (100 + 40 + 75).

The evaluation would compare the costs of ordering three times (quantities of 100, 40, 75), two times (quantities of 140, 75) and one time (quantity of 215) with the costs of holding the extra inventory above the first 100 units after weeks 13 and 18. Although this appears to be a logical approach, and is certainly better than performing no evaluation at all, it does not consider all alternatives (e.g., 100 + 75), (40 + 75) and therefore does not guarantee an optimal solution.

Part period balancing.

The *part period balancing method* provides a more systematic solution procedure which uses the same general approach. **Part period balancing** attempts to equate the cost of placing a single order with the cost of holding the inventory produced by that order. You will recall from our discussion of EOQ and ELS that the optimal order quantity was that quantity for which order cost equaled holding cost. The part period balancing method recognizes this relationship and attempts to use it to find an order quantity, from those available, for which the order and the holding cost associated with that order are approximately the same.

While this method is not guaranteed to produce optimal order quantities, it does produce satisfactory approximations and with much less computational difficulty than required of the methods that produce optimal solutions. For example, in one study [3], Berry compared the Wagner-Whitin algorithm (which does produce optimal results) with the part period balancing method and found that the cost of the optimal solution was only 7 percent lower than the solution developed with the part period balancing heuristic. We will demonstrate the approach with an example.

Limp Spring Co.

Limp Spring Company manufactures a variety of compression springs for use in automobile rocker arm assemblies. Current orders for the x-250 model used in several V6 engines are as follows.

Wcck 28	10,000
Week 31	18,000
Week 40	12,000

Setup of the spring winding equipment for a production run costs approximately $700. The cost of holding an x-250 spring in inventory for a week is considered to be $0.0025.

Under the part period balancing method, the three lot size alternatives available before week 28 are as follows:

Alternative	1	2	3
Produce in week 28	10,000	28,000	40,000

Part period balancing selects the alternative for which holding cost is closest to the order cost of $700. The three holding costs are

$$C_H(10,000) = 0$$

$$C_H(28,000) = 3 \text{ weeks} \times 18,000 \text{ excess units}$$
$$\times \$0.0025/\text{unit/week} = \$135$$

$$C_H(40,000) = 3 \times 18,000 \times 0.0025 + 12 \times 12,000$$
$$\times 0.0025 = \$495$$

Because producing all 40,000 springs in one lot results in most closely matching order cost with holding cost, the third alternative should be chosen.

To summarize, the MRP system follows these steps.

1. Determine requirements of finished products, the Master Production Schedule, from firm orders and sales forecasts.
2. Using the bill of materials, calculate the gross requirements for each item, beginning with the item at level zero.
3. Determine, using the Bill of Materials File and the Inventory Master File, the order release dates and the order quantities for each item necessary to meet the Master Production Schedule.
4. Regenerate the MRP on the basis of changes in the Master Production Schedule or in order priorities.

The complete MRP procedure is illustrated with an example in the next section of this chapter.

13.4 LEE KEY VALVE CO.

To illustrate the MRP procedure, consider the Lee Key Valve Company, which manufactures industrial valves and fittings. Lee Key has decided to implement a material requirements planning system throughout its production facilities and is planning to first test the operation of the system using one finished product, the No. 3303 check valve. Table 13.4 presents the Master Production Schedule for the No. 3303 check valve. It is based on existing orders and promised shipping dates as well as anticipated sales of the valve.

Table 13.4   No. 3303 Check Valve: Master Production Schedule

Item no.: 3303
Description: check valve
Current inventory level: 800

Week no.	Past due	18	19	20	21	22	23	24	25	26	27	28	29
Gross requirements	0	0	0	0	4000	0	0	3000	0	0	0	6000	0

This schedule indicates the number of valves required to be shipped by the end of each of the indicated weeks. The master production schedule is prepared every week for the current week and next 10 weeks. The "past due" column indicates the number of valves that are currently back ordered (in this example, none). Suppose that the current inventory of No. 3303 check valves is 800 units. Table 13.5 shows a partially completed MRP for the No. 3303 check valve. The MRP will be completed once the lot sizes are determined.

Determining Lot Size

Because this is a relatively simple situation in which only one item is being considered, all three possible order quantities can be evaluated to determine the best production lot sizes. Suppose that Lee Key's cost accounting department has determined setup cost to be $90 and holding cost per unit per week to be $0.08. If Lee Key produced one batch for each required shipment

Table 13.5   Partially Completed MRP for No. 3303 Check Valve

Week no.	Past due	18	19	20	21	22	23	24	25	26	27	28	29
Gross requirements	0	0	0	0	4000	0	0	3000	0	0	0	6000	0
On hand: 800		800	800	800	800								
Net requirement					3200								
Planned order receipts													
Planned order releases													
Lead time = 3 weeks													

there would be no excess inventory, but the total setup cost over the next 10 weeks would be $270 (3 × $90). Producing 3200 for week 21 plus the 3000 required for week 24 in one batch would result in a savings of one setup ($90) but would increase holding cost by $720 (3 weeks × 3000 units × $0.08 per unit per week). Combining all three shipping requirements results in a savings of $180 ($2 × $90) in setup costs, but additional holding costs of $4080 (3 weeks × 3000 × 0.08 + 7 × 6000 × 0.08) are incurred. Clearly, for this situation a policy of ordering in lot sizes equal to the requirements each period is the best policy since this results in the lowest total cost.

The part period balancing method, which attempts to equate the cost of placing a single order and the cost of holding the inventory produced in that order, requires the computation of the holding cost of the three lot size possibilities.

> 3,200
>
> 6,200
>
> 12,200

The part period balancing decision rule requires that Lee Key select the lot size for which holding cost is closest to the order cost, $90. The part period balancing computations are

$$C_H(3200) = 0$$

$$C_H(6200) = 3 \text{ weeks} \times 3000 \text{ excess units} \times \$0.08/\text{unit/week} = \$720$$

$$C_H(12{,}200) = 3 \times 3000 \times 0.08 + 7 \times 6000 \times 0.08 = \$4080$$

Clearly, the holding cost of zero is closest to $90 and therefore the order size of 3200 (as recommended previously) would also be selected by the part period balancing method.

Presuming a lead time for assembly of the No. 3303 check valve of 3 weeks, orders should be released in weeks 18, 21, and 25 for order quantities of 3200, 3000, and 6000, respectively. Table 13.6 illustrates the completed MRP for the No. 3303 check valve.

Parts Explosion for Scheduling

Lee Key, having determined the order quantities and release dates of finished No. 3303 valves, must now determine the quantities and timing of orders for the component parts and subassemblies that make up the No. 3303 check valve. This determination begins with a *bill of materials*, which is the structured list of all required parts needed to produce one No. 3303 valve. Table 13.7 illustrates the multilevel bill of materials (in this case there are two levels of items). Figure 13.8 shows the same bill of materials as a product tree. Note in Table 13.7 the column labeled "Quantity." The number that appears in this column indicates the number of that item required to produce one of the next higher level of items. For example, two locknuts are required to produce one poppet assembly and two poppet assemblies are necessary

Table 13.6 MRP for No. 3303 Check Valve

Week No.	Past Due	13	14	15	16	17	18	19	20	21	22	23	24	25	26	27	28	29
Gross requirements										4000			3000				6000	
On hand: 800							800	800	800	800	0	0	0	0	0	0	0	0
Net requirement										3200			3000				6000	
Planned order receipts										3200			3000				6000	
Planned order releases							3200			3000			6000					

Lead time = 3 weeks

for one No. 3303 check valve. Therefore, four locknuts are required for one No. 3303 valve. The parts in the second level are used to produce a subassembly (e.g., one valve body and one valve seat as assembled to produce one valve body assembly) and the subassemblies in turn are coupled with other first level parts to produce the finished product.

In addition to the bill of materials information, two pieces of information are required from the Inventory Master File for each item in the production of the No. 3303 check valve. This information, the quantity on hand and the lead time (for assembly, manufacture, or purchase, as appropriate), is presented in summary form in Table 13.8.

Now that the three information sources are available (i.e., Master Production Schedule, bill of materials, Inventory Master File) the MRP system can produce a requirements plan. Presume, for this example, that all order quantities will be exactly the quantity necessary to meet net requirements.

Table 13.7 Bill of Materials: No. 3303 Check Valve

First Level Part No.	Second Level Part No.	Description	Quantity	Source
79221		Valve body assembly	1	Manufacturing
	82392	Valve body	1	Manufacturing
	64103	Valve seat	2	Manufacturing
30468		Spring	2	Purchasing
84987		Poppet assembly	2	Manufacturing
	29208	Stem	1	Manufacturing
	91182	Facing	1	Purchasing
	73919	Locknut	2	Purchasing

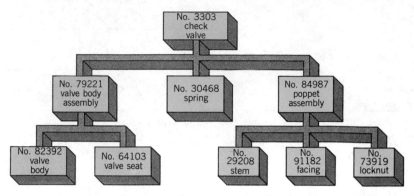

Figure 13.8   Product tree for No. 3303 check valve.

Table 13.9 shows the MRP for a complete No. 3303 check valve including all items at all levels. The entire MRP is developed by doing the following:

1. The bill of materials is referenced to determine the number of each level of item necessary to produce 3200, 3000, and 6000 check valves, respectively.

2. For each item, the inventory record is accessed and both the current inventory level and the lead time are determined.

3. Using the current inventory level, the gross and net requirements are calculated.

4. Using the lead time, the order release date is determined by back-scheduling the amount of the lead time from the needed date.

The MRP for the finished No. 3303 check valve is shown in Table 13.9a. The MRP for all items is developed from this requirement plan by first generating requirement plans for level 1 items and then, from each of these, the level 2 items are generated. Table 13.9b through i lists the requirements plans generated from this finished item plan. The arrows indicate the order and relationship of one plan to the other.

Table 13.8   Inventory Master File Information for MRP

Final Product: No. 3303	Quantity on Hand: 800
Description: Check valve	Lead Time for Assembly: 3 weeks

Item No.	Quantity on Hand	Lead Time (weeks)
79221	1000	1
82392	2200	2
64103	500	1
30468	800	2
84987	1000	3
29208	500	1
91182	1200	2
73919	2000	2

Table 13.9 Check Valve Requirements Plan

a. No. 3303 Check Valve

Week No.	Past Due	13	14	15	16	17	18	19	20	21	22	23	24	25	26	27	28	29
Gross requirement										4000			3000				6000	
On hand 800					800	800	800	800										
Net requirement										3200			3000				6000	
Planned order receipts										3200			3000				6000	
Planned order releases							3200			3000				6000				

Lead time = 3 weeks

b. No. 79221 Valve Body Assembly

Week No.	Past Due	13	14	15	16	17	18	19	20	21	22	23	24	25	26	27	28	29
Gross requirement							3200			3000				6000				
On hand 1000						1000	1000											
Net requirement							2200			3000				6000				
Planned order receipts							2200			3000				6000				
Planned order releases						2200			3000				6000					

Lead time = 1 week

c. No. 30468 Spring

Week No.	Past Due	13	14	15	16	17	18	19	20	21	22	23	24	25	26	27	28	29
Gross requirement							6400			6000				12000				
On hand 800					800	800	800											
Net requirement							5600			6000				12000				
Planned order receipts							5600			6000				12000				
Planned order releases					5600			6000				12000						

Lead time = 2 weeks

Table 13.9 (Continued)

d. No. 84787 Poppet Assembly

Week No.	Past Due	13	14	15	16	17	18	19	20	21	22	23	24	25	26	27	28	29
Gross requirement							(6400)			6000				12000				
On hand 1000				1000	1000	1000	1000											
Net requirement							5400			6000				12000				
Planned order receipts							5400			6000				12000				
Planned order releases				5400			6000				(12000)							

Lead time = 3 weeks

e. No. 82392 Valve Body

Week No.	Past Due	13	14	15	16	17	18	19	20	21	22	23	24	25	26	27	28	29
Gross requirement						(2200)			3000				6000					
On hand 2200				2200	2200	2200												
Net requirement									3000				6000					
Planned order receipts									3000				6000					
Planned order releases							3000				6000							

Lead time = 2 weeks

f. No. 64103 Valve Seat

Week No.	Past Due	13	14	15	16	17	18	19	20	21	22	23	24	25	26	27	28	29
Gross requirement						(4400)			6000				12000					
On hand 500					500	500												
Net requirement						3900			6000				12000					
Planned order receipts						3900			6000				12000					
Planned order releases					3900			6000				12000						

Lead time = 1 week

Table 13.9 (*Continued*)

g. *No. 29208 Stem*

Week No.	Past Due	13	14	15	16	17	18	19	20	21	22	23	24	25	26	27	28	29
Gross requirement				5400			6000				→(12000)							
On hand 500			500	500														
Net requirement				4900			6000				12000							
Planned order receipts				4900			6000				12000							
Planned order releases			4900				6000			12000								

Lead time = 1 week

h. *No. 91182 Facing*

Week No.	Past Due	13	14	15	16	17	18	19	20	21	22	23	24	25	26	27	28	29
Gross requirement				5400			6000				→(12000)							
On hand 1200		1200	1200	1200														
Net requirement				4200			6000				12000							
Planned order receipts				4200			6000				12000							
Planned order releases		4200			6000				12000									

Lead time = 2 weeks

i. *No. 73919 Locknut*

Week No.	Past Due	13	14	15	16	17	18	19	20	21	22	23	24	25	26	27	28	29
Gross requirement				10800			12000				→(24000)							
On hand 2000		2000	2000	2000														
Net requirement				8800			12000				24000							
Planned order receipts				8800			12000				24000							
Planned order releases		8800			12000				24000									

Lead time = 2 weeks

To clarify the development of these plans, let us consider the plan for valve seats. To meet the shipping requirements for 4000 check valves (Table 13.9a) in week 21, component parts to assemble 3200 must enter production in week 18 (a three-week lead time). In order to release an order for 3200 in week 18, 2200 *additional* valve body assemblies (Table 13.9b) must be produced by that time. To do this, an order for 2200 must be placed in week 17 (a one-week lead time). Finally, to produce 2200 additional valve body assemblies, 4400 valve seats (2 × 2200) must be available. Since 500 are currently on hand (Table 13.9f), 3900 must be produced by week 17. With a one-week lead time, this means that an order for 3900 must be released in week 16. Required order releases for each level 1 and 2 component are planned in exactly the same manner.

We began this example by assuming that Lee Key was experimenting with the use of MRP on the No. 3303 check valve. When the company decides to include all products in the system, the situation is further complicated. The major difference is that some subassemblies and components will be used in more than one end product. Therefore, for example, the MRP for an item such as the 73919 locknut would include in the "Net requirement" row all of the requirements from all final products. Orders would be scheduled simultaneously to meet all of the requirements rather than being scheduled on a product-by-product basis. The necessity of using a computer becomes obvious when one considers a situation in which there are over 1000 finished products with perhaps as many as 30,000 purchased and manufactured components. The need for rapid computation and summarization of requirements as well as handling of massive bills of materials and inventory master files is obvious.

13.5   SUMMARY AND KEY LEARNING POINTS

In this final materials chapter of Part III: Detailed Operations, we have covered the topic of planning the materials flow for lumpy, dependent demand items. We started the chapter by looking in greater detail at the difference between independent and dependent demand for items and the critical role of the computer in MRP systems for the latter. We defined product trees, bills of material, and computer files needed for MRP. We then discussed exploding the bill of materials to generate part requirements and lot sizing to set production quantities. Finally, we used an extensive example to illustrate these terms and the mechanics of MRP.

The key learning points were

- Dependent demand is based on another item whose demand is already known or predicted. Subassemblies and components of finished goods are usually dependent demand whereas finished goods are usually independent demand. Spare parts of finished goods may, however, be independently demanded also. Supplies and raw materials may be classified as either, depending on the situation.

- A parent item is the highest level of item made up of subcomponents and subassemblies. A product tree illustrates this breakdown graphically and the items are designated in the bill of materials by name, number, material, and specifications.

- Precomputer inventory management was concerned with order quantities, when to order, rushing of late orders, and segmenting of production control and inventory management. Postcomputer inventory management is concerned with when materials are needed, the priority of different orders, what orders to deexpedite as well as expedite, and integration of production control and inventory management.

- An MRP computer system needs a Master Production Schedule, Bill of Materials File, and Inventory Master File as inputs. Common outputs are a Planned Order Release Report, Order Action Report, Open Order Report, and other change and exception reports.

- The MRP explosion takes the Master Production Schedule for level 0 (parent) items, subtracts on-hand inventory and scheduled receipts to generate planned (or "needed") receipts. The planned order releases are then generated from these receipts by backing off the amount of the lead time.

  The gross requirements for level 1 items are the sum of their independent demands and the exploded order releases for level 0 items. This provides the master schedule for level 1 items and the process repeats on down through the levels.

- Part-period balancing calculates the holding costs for each alternative order size and selects that size for which the holding cost is closest to the ordering cost. The first (current) period is assumed to incur no holding cost.

13.6 KEY TERMS

dependent demand (p. 496)	**Inventory Master File** (p. 505)	**parent item** (p. 506)
MRP (p. 496)		**lot sizing** (p. 510)
Master Production Schedule (p. 504)	**net requirements** (p. 508)	**part period balancing** (p. 511)
bill of materials (p. 505)	**gross requirements** (p. 508)	
	explode (p. 506)	**product tree** (p. 499)

13.7 REVIEW AND DISCUSSION QUESTIONS

1. Why would record accuracy, particularly in bills of material and inventory records, be important in MRP?

2. What types of "demand" are considered formally in MRP?

3. In your own terms, distinguish between dependent and independent demand.

4. What is the meaning of the term "planned order release"?

5. Why has MRP taken so long to develop since it is such a logical and straightforward idea?

6. Contrast the ideas of "order launching" and "when needed."

7. Once an order is "launched" in MRP, how is it controlled?

8. Explain why the part-period balancing method will not guarantee optimal order quantities.

9. Is MRP or EOQ best for smooth, dependent demand? For lumpy, independent demand?

13.8 READINGS

PRODUCTION CONTROL: MRP ENDS GUESSING AT SOUTHWIRE

Charles H. Boyer
Assistant Editor
Industrial Engineering

When Stan Morgan, Manager of Corporate Production Control at the Southwire Company, discovered that a work-in-process inventory item had been sitting around for two long years, he knew their decision to install a computerized material requirements planning (MRP) system was the right one. A major manufacturer of utility cable and building wire, Southwire, like most larger corporations, has long utilized a computer data base to control finished goods inventory, sales order entries, and certain raw materials and parts storage. Now, they have turned their attention to controlling the critical mid-point between raw materials and final products: the manufacturing inventory (or, as they refer to it at Southwire, work-in-process inventory).

Proponents of MRP systems claim sizable potential savings in reduced inventory levels, better control, and less reliance on inherently expensive and inefficient reorder point schemes. Also, with the advent of the powerful, relatively inexpensive small computers, MRP systems now feature, as their primary function, methods for updating and revising production schedule priorities.

At Southwire, finished goods inventory and shipping allocation information was being maintained on-line with a Burroughs 3500 computer and remote terminals. And some finished goods were warehoused in a computer-controlled automated storage and retrieval system. "We had both ends of our system under control," says Morgan. "We wanted to do the same with our work-in-process inventory, and at the same time improve our production control procedures.

"Our production planners were running the show by the seat of their pants. Reordering for the manufacturing plants was being done by a mishmash of safety stock levels and gut feelings. And some of the production data, such as manufacturing specifications, had to be transferred onto production orders from hard copy. The system was slow and cumbersome."

Decisions, Decisions

The decision to go with an MRP system was not made by a strict financial comparison of alternatives. In 1973, Group VP of Operations, Gordon Johnson, appointed a special committee to study production control problems. Should the company use a computerized system, a manual system, or a combination computer/manual system? Corporate Information Systems Analyst Roger Brown co-chaired the committee with Morgan. Brown had designed the company's on-line order data entry and shipping allocation system. Corporate IE, Inventory Control, and Research and Development were represented on the committee.

The committee members decided on a computerized MRP system using Burroughs advanced PCS II (Production Control System) software as a starting point. Eventually, many of the final programs were done in-house. "It was not a pure financial choice," Morgan explains. "First, the MRP system is not an isolated, integral function. It was built upon systems that had been in use for some time, both batch and on-line. To analyze the total cost, we would have to go back and compute the cost of those systems. It would be very difficult to isolate them, both as a function and in relation to time. That is, at what point in time would you evaluate the system's economics? Six months or two years after start-up? Secondly, and most importantly, we had to consider the company and its place in the market. Starting from scratch, literally, Southwire has grown at an annualized rate of 25%, from one small plant in 1950, to nine major production facilities today, manufacturing and distributing its products all over the world. We currently supply final products to 48 distribution centers. And we are not yet a mature company. We intend to continue growing. The decision to put in a computerized MRP system was born out of business necessity—survival. Manual methods could not cope with our expanding volume and complex product mix." The target for the initial system was the company's Building Wire Plant in Carrollton, GA. John Norman, a 14-year veteran with Southwire, is Materials Manager for the plant.

Installing MRP

Three things must be known before implementing an MRP system:

1. Demand.
2. Inventory.
3. Bill of materials: Processing times, routing, and manufacturing specifications.

"At the time we first examined MRP," says Norman, "our WIP inventory accuracy was around 69%; that's not nearly good enough for MRP use."

Accuracy is vital to the success of an MRP system. Essentially, MRP compares the planned production schedule with the bill of materials needed to make the products, then examines the manufacturing inventory to see which parts and raw materials are on hand and which have to be ordered. It then time phases the necessary orders for manufacturing inventory so it is available when needed at the work center. Ideally, all manufacturing inventory would arrive no sooner than when it is needed, thus reducing the amount of work-in-process inventory. The system reexamines the production schedule, either continuously or periodically, to keep it current, thus reducing or eliminating the need to stockpile large quantities of inventory in the production area. Without accurate control of the manufacturing inventory, the system will not work.

Accuracy at Southwire's Building Wire Plant means tight control over 4900 unique stock numbers. That's 700 different final products with approximately seven components on each product's bill of materials. A tagging system was implemented to carefully track the manufacturing inventory after it entered the plant. Production, purchasing, and design specification information on 3000 of the 4900 stock items was transferred from microfiche to disk file, the necessary software modules were written, or modified, and the MRP system was "cranked up."

Stan Morgan tells what happened then: "Our first output from the system was garbage. We soon found out why. It's the computer analyst's axiom: garbage in–garbage out. The information we were feeding the system was not *accurate*. One major problem was our work-in-process tagging system. The tags were not taken seriously by the employees. Consequently, the number and type of tags turned in from the shop floor did not match the inventory consumed. We implemented an improvement program, with management emphasis, to educate everyone as to the importance of the tag system. Tags released on the shop floor are now accounted for at release, at turn in, and once during every shift. David Aber-

crombie, Systems Manager for the MRP system, reports: "Our accuracy on the WIP inventory went from 69% to 96% after we improved the tag control. We consider 96% the minimum acceptable level." A special block house was constructed on the shop floor to house an on-line terminal for recording tag information.

Getting Educated

There are many small problems encountered in the practical implementation of any idea. MRP is no exception. One problem confronted early in the year and a half required to start-up and debug Southwire's system was employee education. Several teaching aids, including videotape presentations and plant manager seminars, were used to demonstrate the advantages of MRP and gain wholehearted employee support. But it wasn't easy. After all, a conscientious foreman wants to be sure he has enough materials on hand to meet his production orders. There is a natural tendency to stockpile and hoard inventory. "It's a tough problem," says Morgan. "You don't really convince people at the front end, you convince them after you demonstrate that the system works. And you get the system working with management's help."

Roger Brown points out another problem encountered during the startup: "When the system first goes on-line, it immediately calls up inventory needed to meet the production schedule. In the first few months, this actually increases your total work-in-process inventory, because now necessary inventory is being added to the unnecessary inventory previously stockpiled. It takes a few months before the total inventory volume in the manufacturing area begins to decline. But for a while, it appears the system is not working. This is another reason it is not easy to inspire employee confidence in the early stages."

The Output

Southwire is using a "schedule regeneration" MRP system. Their key production planning document, the Planned Order Report, is updated whenever necessary, usually two or three times a week, to accommodate changes in the production schedule. The other major type of MRP system is the "net change." This type of system updates automatically with the slightest change in the production schedule. Net change was considered too sensitive for the Building Wire Plant, which is a combination continuous manufacture and job shop operation. "We thought 'net change' would be too nervous for our type of production," says Morgan. "We prefer to regenerate our key production document—the Planned Order Report—whenever *we* deem it's necessary." Old planned order reports are discarded after updated ones are generated. Production orders that have been released to the shop floor are not subject to MRP updates.

Recently, Southwire changed their on-line final products inventory and order entry systems from Burroughs 3500 computers, using disk forte storage, to Burroughs 6700 computers using integrated DMS (data management system) file structure. The heart of the MRP system, the PCS II and Southwire software, operates on a 24-hour batch system. Sometime in the next three years, as MRP is expanded to corporate-wide use, this system will be placed on-line also. Since MRP system startup began, the number of unique stock items in WIP inventory has been reduced 50%, and the better than 96% accuracy level of inventory control has eliminated the need for taking manual inventory counts in the future. Total work-in-process inventory volume is expected to be reduced by 30%.

Source. Reprinted from *Industrial Engineering*, March 1977. Copyright © 1977 by the American Institute of Industrial Engineers, Inc., Norcross, Georgia.

13.9 PROBLEMS

Practice Problems

1. Product 101 consists of three 202 subassemblies and a 204 subassembly. The 202 subassembly consists of one 617, a 324 subassembly, and a 401. A 204 subassembly consists of a 500 and a 401. The 324 subassembly consists of a 617 and a 515.

   a. Prepare a product tree.

   b. Prepare an indented bill of materials.

   c. Determine the number of each subassembly/component required to produce fifty 101s.

2. Complete the MRP for item No. 6606 below.

Week	5	6	7	8	9	10	11	12	13	14	15	16	17	18
Gross requirement				100			50	30			80			
On hand 100														
Net requirement														
Planned order receipts														
Planned order releases														
Lead time = 3 weeks														

3. Suppose that in Problem 2 the company wishes to maintain a safety stock of 50 No. 6066s. Complete the MRP.

4. Conduct a part-period lot sizing for part 1098 given the following demand schedule and the facts that holding a 1098 part in inventory for a week costs $1 and the ordering and shipment (0 lead time) costs a total of $100 for any size order.

Week	16	17	18	19	20	21	22
1098 demand	85	40	25	40	105	75	80

5. Conduct a lot sizing by part-period balancing for the following item which has a $190 ordering cost and a holding cost of $0.10 per unit per month.

Month	1	2	3	4	5	6	7	8	9	10	11	12
Demand	700	400	200	300	400	500	560	400	800	400	200	300

6. Develop the MRP for Lee Key Valve Company presuming that lead time for the assembly of valve body assemblies increases to four weeks.

More Complex Problems

7. Fractured Frame Co. sells two 8 by 10 inch picture frames complete with backs and glass. The standard model uses a thin black frame and the deluxe model uses a gold trim frame. The backs and glass are the same for both. Assembly lead time for the complete process from frame material, glass, and back is two weeks for either model. Frame material is ordered (2.5 feet for each frame) from a local supplier and has a one-week lead time. The glass is purchased, cut to size, and has a three-week lead time. Backs are purchased finished from a hardboard manufacturer with a two-week lead time. The Master Production Schedule for the two models is shown in the following table.

Week	8	9	10	11	12	13	14
Standard frame				100	150		300
Deluxe frame			200		200		150

The on-hand inventory is as follows:

Deluxe frame material	300 ft
Standard frame material	150 ft
Glass plates	150
Backs	50

Standard frames (complete)   75
Deluxe frames (complete)   100

Prepare the MRP to exactly meet the demand schedule.

8. Given the following, how many No. 1342 items should be purchased and when?

Item	Lead Times (weeks)	On Hand	Demand in Week No.				
			11	12	13	14	15
19	1	100	100	0	100	200	0
1342	2	200	0	500	0	0	0
102	1	0	50	0	0	0	0
312	2	0	5	0	0	10	0

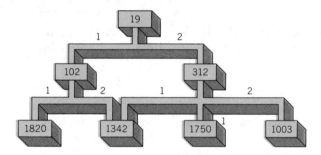

9. Solve Problem 5 by ordering in EOQ batches and compare the cost to the part-period method.

10. Another lot sizing technique is called "period order quantity" or POQ. This approach converts the EOQ into an integer number of periods and then lot sizes for whatever demand occurs in the next POQ number of periods. Solve Problem 5 by POQ and compare to the costs in Problem 9.

11. Solve Problem 5 by ordering in every period the amount needed the next period (called "lot-for-lot") and compare it to the previous costs.

12. Another lot sizing method similar to part-period balancing is called "least unit cost." In this method the part-period holding cost accumulation procedure is followed but the ordering cost is added to the total and this entire sum is divided by the total number of units ordered. The ordering policy with the smallest per-unit total cost is then ordered. Solve Problem 5 by the least unit cost method and compare the results to the previous costs.

13.10 CASE

ANDREW JACOBS & COMPANY

Andrew Jacobs & Company employs approximately 280 people in the manufacture of a number of "add-on appliances for residential heating and air-conditioning units." The company began 15 years ago producing a home humidifier and has since expanded into the dehumidifier and air purifier lines. They currently produce 30 different models but, because of heavy competition, engineering changes are constantly taking place and the product line is often changing. Each model is made up of between 40 and several hundred different parts which range from purchased nuts and bolts and prefabricated subassemblies to internally manufactured components.

Andrew Jacobs purchases over 2500 parts and manufactures over 1000 parts and assemblies of its own. Many of the parts are used on several different models and some parts such as nuts and bolts are used on over 75 percent of the finished products.

The finished goods inventory is kept relatively small. Sales are forecast on a month-to-month basis and production is scheduled according to actual sales orders and the sales forecast. For this reason, production lots placed in the final assembly line are usually for relatively small quantities.

Rather than producing manufactured parts and subcomponents and purchasing other parts according to the sales forecast, parts, subassemblies, and purchased items are ordered on a reorder point/economic order quantity basis. Since it is imperative to maintain accurate control of these raw materials and subassembly items, all parts and materials stored in the main supply area are controlled with the use of perpetual inventory cards which are maintained by the scheduling department. Each card contains the reorder point, the economic order quantity, and the lead time for outside procurement or internal manufacture. Both receipt of new inventory into the main supply room and use of items from the supply room are recorded on the inventory card.

The scheduling department is responsible for checking the availability of inventory on the inventory cards. Approximately three weeks before a final assembly order is to be placed on the floor, the scheduler checks all the cards for parts needed in that assembly to determine whether issuing the number required to complete the assembly will reduce the inventory of the subassembly or part below the reorder point. If the scheduler determines that the projected final assembly order will result in hitting the reorder point, a production order or a purchase order is issued.

Physical inventories are taken every quarter and there are usually a substantial number of small adjustments that must be made. The quarterly physical inventory was suggested after a series of major inventory shortages occurred several years ago. The company's current policy allows any worker to enter the main supply area to remove needed parts. The workers are to fill out materials requisitions and to sign for all parts removed, but they are frequently in a rush and fail to complete the inventory requisitions accurately. There have been several cases in which parts staged for final assembly of one product were removed and used on the assembly of another item.

To adjust for many of these problems, the production schedulers often add a safety factor to the reorder point when placing orders and have typically increased the order quantity from 10 to 25 percent over the economic order quantity. Their justification for this is that "it is less expensive to carry a little extra inventory than to shut down the production facility waiting for a rush order."

Questions for Discussion

1. Evaluate and critique the existing system used by Andrew Jacobs & Company.

2. How might MRP work in a situation like this?

3. Suppose that a computer is unavailable and that MRP cannot be sensibly implemented without one. What improvements can you suggest to the existing system to help alleviate Andrew Jacobs' problems?

13.11 REFERENCES AND BIBLIOGRAPHY

1. APICS Special Report, *Material Requirements Planning by Computer*, Washington, DC: APICS, 1971.
2. APICS Special Report, *Material Requirements Planning Report*, Washington, DC: APICS, 1973.
3. Berry, William L., "Lot Sizing Procedures for Requirements Planning Systems: A Framework for Analysis," *Production and Inventory Management*, 2nd Quarter 1972, pp. 19–34.
4. Davis, Edward W., *Case Studies in Materials Requirements Planning*, Washington, DC: APICS, 1978.
5. Meredith, J. R., "The Implementation of Computer Based Systems," *Journal of Operations Management*, 2:11–22 (Oct. 1981).
6. Orlicky, Joseph, *Material Requirements Planning*, New York: McGraw-Hill, 1975.
7. Orlicky, Joseph A., Plossl, George W., and Wight, Oliver W., *Material Requirements Planning*, IBM Publication No. 6320-1170, 1971.
8. Plossl, George W., and Wight, Oliver W., *Material Requirements Planning by Computer*, Washington, DC: APICS, 1971.
9. Schroeder, R. G. et al., "A Study of MRP Benefits and Costs," *Journal of Operations Management*, 2:1–10 (Oct. 1981).
10. Wacker, J., and Hills, F. S., "The Key to Success or Failure of MRP: Overcoming Human Resistance," *Production and Inventory Management*, 17:7–15 (No. 4, 1977).
11. Wight, Oliver W., *Production and Inventory Management in the Computer Age*, Boston: Cahners, 1974.

IV

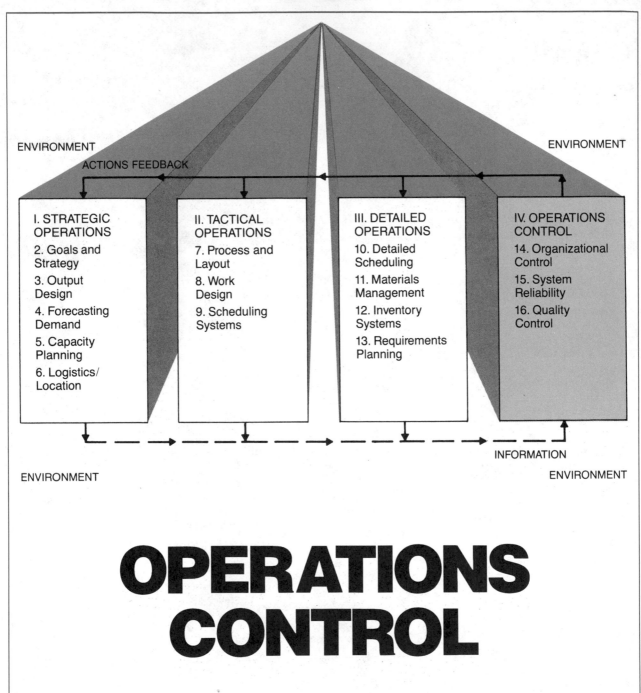

ENVIRONMENT

ENVIRONMENT

ACTIONS FEEDBACK

I. STRATEGIC OPERATIONS

2. Goals and Strategy

3. Output Design

4. Forecasting Demand

5. Capacity Planning

6. Logistics/ Location

II. TACTICAL OPERATIONS

7. Process and Layout

8. Work Design

9. Scheduling Systems

III. DETAILED OPERATIONS

10. Detailed Scheduling

11. Materials Management

12. Inventory Systems

13. Requirements Planning

IV. OPERATIONS CONTROL

14. Organizational Control

15. System Reliability

16. Quality Control

INFORMATION

ENVIRONMENT

ENVIRONMENT

OPERATIONS CONTROL

At this point in the text the discussion of the design of the organization's operations is largely complete. However, no system operates for long in the way that it was designed. Thus, it is necessary to also consider the design of *control* systems that will keep operations on course as reality deviates from expectations to ensure their efficient and effective achievement of the organization's goals. In essence, these systems monitor internal operations and the external environment through the information system, feed back this information for comparison against a master plan, note serious deviations, and apply *control* to correct for these deviations.

In Chapter 14 we initiate our discussion by looking at the overall subject of organizational control and how it is largely attained through two general control processes—preventive control and feedback control. We describe and illustrate these two control mechanisms and note the importance of budgeting's role in these systems. We next look at the monitoring function and the importance of information in monitoring. We describe the purposes of information, the different types of information and information systems, and the negative effects of a time lag in receiving information.

We then consider the comparison function where actual results are compared to plan and describe the design and use of control charts and variance analysis to tell when a system is out of control and needs corrective action. Last, we present some specific control systems that have been designed to control specific types of transformation processes and solve particular production problems.

Then in Chapter 15 we address the topic of maintaining the proper functioning of the operations system in particular. We look at two aspects of keeping this system operating properly: reliability, which concerns how long the system operates before going out of control, and maintenance, which addresses the issue of getting a system back into control once it has started going, or has gone, out of control.

We present various methods of increasing the reliability and maintainability of a system, such as building in redundancy, using preventive maintenance, and keeping standbys available. These approaches are first described and explained, then illustrated with examples. Repair crew sizing, particularly appropriate to pure service operations, is discussed in the final section. The chapter appendix describes the common financial tools used for equipment selection and replacement decisions, such as life cycle costing, net present value calculations, and the tax impacts of depreciation and leasing.

Chapter 16 closes our discussion of the control function with a detailed look at controlling the quality of the output. Following a discussion of some measures of quality and factors that affect an output's quality, we look at the role of inspection in maintaining quality. From there we move into a discussion of the tools of statistical quality control, noting the effect of type I and type II errors on quality. We return to the subject of control charts first introduced in Chapter 14 and demonstrate the derivation of means and control limits for controlling both "variables" (length, weight) and "attributes" (defective, acceptable).

We then look at the acceptance sampling process and how to design sampling plans that give the needed control without being excessive in their cost. Included in the discussion is the use of multiple sampling procedures, including double and sequential sampling. We conclude our discussion with possibly the most important element of quality control, the attitudes and behavior of the workers who produce the output. We identify some possible reasons for insufficient attention to quality and compare this with the elements of the Japanese "quality crusade" that so markedly reversed their reputation for shoddy goods.

We continue this discussion of the challenge to operations in the Epilogue: Operations Management and the Future. Here we go beyond the current problems of capital scarcity and stiff international competition for world markets. We consider the challenges and opportunities of modern technology, the increasing demand for services, and the availability of almost unlimited information, and what this means to those who must use this technology and information to produce those services—the operations manager.

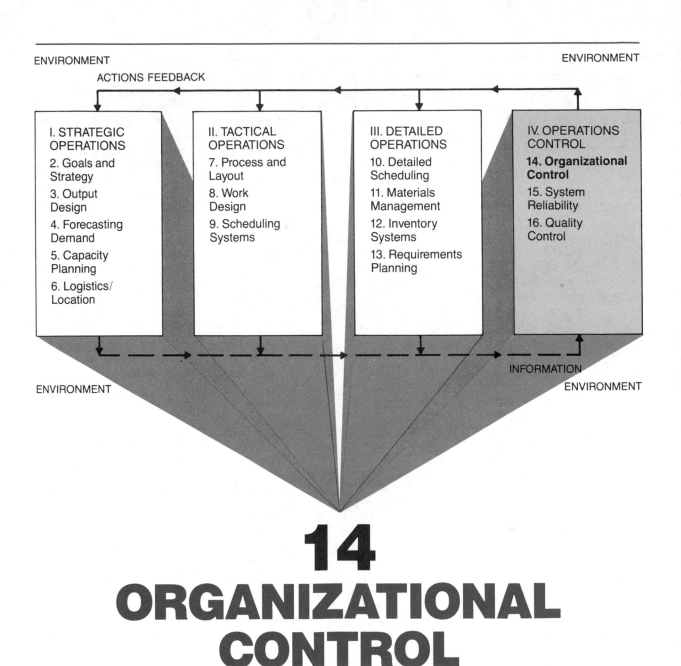

14
ORGANIZATIONAL
CONTROL

14

LEARNING OBJECTIVES

By the completion of this chapter the student should

- Have developed a feel for the operation of control systems.
- Know the different types and kinds of control systems.
- Be aware of the crucial role of information in the monitoring function, the purposes of information, and the recent types of computerized information systems.
- Appreciate the comparison function and the roles of variance analysis in making the comparisons.
- Comprehend the design and use of control charts in evaluating variances for significance.
- Know the various types of feedback control methods and when they are appropriate.

Basically the job of general manager in a small industrial organization . . . is like running a multiringed circus. Daily demands and decisions emanate from all parts of the organization. One must at one and the same time be involved in production activities, selling, personnel issues and day to day financial management. Most information gathering and decision making occurs on an interpersonal basis characterized by brevity and verbal communications. The time and information available for detailed and indepth analysis is nonexistent. One must have some basic priorities and/or strategy clearly in mind to be able to handle the constant flow of interruptions and decisions. Otherwise it is very simple for the total operation to go rapidly out of control.

—J. R. M. Gordon, in *Perspectives* (Academy of Management), 5:19 (Fall 1977).

Control: assuring desired results are attained.

In this chapter we begin our consideration of the all-important control function in organizations. So far we have discussed planning and designing the operations, but without control all this effort is virtually useless—control ensures that actual performance conforms to plan. Anthony and Reese [2] state it in even simpler terms: "Control is assuring that desired results are attained." Planned and actual results are very often not the same. Plans are based on imperfect information and on estimates about the future. Once activity begins to take place and plans are implemented, the organization may learn that original expectations were too ambitious or not ambitious enough.

Implementation is a problem.

Generally speaking, managers in the United States are very good planners. Good planning is well recognized in U.S. industry and in academe as well. But where U.S. industry seems to have endless problems is in the *implementation* of those excellent plans, controlling the materials and labor and machines so that plans yield effective results. In contrast, foreign competitors, most notably Japan, are excellent in bringing their plans to fruition.

We start this chapter by elaborating on the generic concept of control and dissecting its elements. We contrast *preventive* control with *feedback* control and give examples of each. A particularly important feedback control tool is the organization's "budget," and we spend some time discussing "zero-based budgeting" and other such concepts.

Following this we address the organization's monitoring system and discuss the concepts of information and information systems, particularly "decision support systems." We use a manufacturer-distributor-retailer distribution chain example to illustrate the deleterious effects of information lag in the control system. The next stage of control involves the comparison of performance data with plans and standards. In addition to the common tool of variance analysis, the concept of control charting is described, using project management as an example.

Last, we look at the feedback control actions themselves and describe the concepts of order, flow, block, and load control in terms of the generic types of production systems for which they are applicable.

14.1 THE CONTROL FUNCTION

The general management process, as described earlier in Chapter 1, consists of three major functions: planning, monitoring, and control. Many essays, articles, and papers on management purport to address themselves to "the planning and control function." Close scrutiny of such papers, however, usually reveals that 90 percent of the discussion is concerned with *planning*. This is no oversight on the authors' part. Many people simply do not realize that control is different from planning, and those who do often do not know what to say about control anyway.

Ninety percent planning.

It is no accident that we in the United States do extensive planning of our activities but fail miserably in their execution—we know precious little about the concept of *control*. For that matter, we do not even *like* control. We don't like to have to control others, and we especially don't like others trying to control us.

Recent research indicates that top managers feel that the worker and lower level managers have much more control over productivity and quality than they do and that they only have, at most, 15 percent control over the workplace. And a survey [11] of European industrial firms revealed *no* strategic control systems in operation. Yet the Japanese exercise excellent control—both short- and long-range, or strategic, control—in their firms. Clearly, the management function of control is worth understanding well.

No strategic control.

Let us reconstruct the general managerial process; Figure 14.1 illustrates the procedure. After environmental screening, goals are first identified and plans developed. Activities are undertaken and, according to plan, produce outputs that bring returns (such as money) to the organization. Paralleling this basic operating system, however, is the managerial control system which monitors the activities, outputs, returns, and environment; compares the data against the goals, plans, and predetermined standards; and, if necessary, effects adjustments to the goals, plans, and actions; that is, it exercises "control."

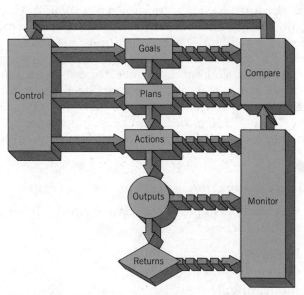

Figure 14.1 The control process.

We have already discussed in preceding chapters the basic operating system illustrated above. In the following sections we will describe each of the elements of the managerial control system. But before proceeding to these elements, we should consider what functional plans and activities we are concerned with here. Clearly, marketing, finance, engineering, personnel, and other such areas all have their own managerial control systems. We wish to focus on the *operations* control system, though in so doing we will have to interact with other areas' systems. In the operations area our control system must include raw materials, supplies, equipment, production rates, capacities, efficiencies, breakdowns, quality, facilities, schedules, and so on. All of these have been mentioned previously, but two in particular will be discussed in greater detail in the following chapters: (1) operations system reliability and maintenance, and (2) product quality.

The operations control system.

14.2 CONTROL THROUGH PLANNING

Feedback control systems.

The control process in Figure 14.1 is called a **feedback control** system. Feedback is simply information about a process that is returned to a decision maker (or controller) as input to a "control" decision. In a feedback control system a plan or standard is adopted, the actual performance of the system is monitored and measured, and the system status is fed back to a decision maker. Significant deviations from plan indicate the need for adjusting action (control) to put the system back on course. Now where in the process of Figure 14.1 is this feedback control system *designed?* In the "plans" stage. Here, too, is where standards by which performance is measured are derived and policies are chosen to correct actions deemed to be out of control. (We will delay the discussion of how to derive these standards until Section 14.4 on Comparing.)

Dynamic systems.

Feedback control systems are known as *dynamic* systems because of their constant monitoring and feedback actions. Being dynamic, feedback control systems are easy to identify in organizations: alarms on "FIRE EXIT ONLY" doors, roving managers, end-of-aisle mirrors, employee performance evaluations, report cards, votes of confidence, time clocks, complaint departments, applause, and so on. One of the primary feedback control systems in any organization is the *budget*, which, like performance standards, is derived during the "plans" stage. Because of its importance in so many organizations' control processes, this unique control system will be briefly elaborated on next.

The budget: a primary feedback control system.

Budgets and Budgeting

Four purposes of budgets.

Budgets are clearly a standard for control within the organization, but they also serve other purposes.

1. In planning.
2. In communicating.
3. In motivating.

Budgets for
planning.

In planning an organization's activities for an upcoming period, the budgeting process provides a focal point for the planning effort. Budgets present a quantitative picture of the resources to be allocated to the various divisions of an organization, and most managers seek an active role in planning their activities and acquiring resources for the upcoming period. Budgeting is often, for financial managers, just a mechanical process. It is important for budget planners to understand thoroughly how the budget relates to functional area planning or else the budget is meaningless.

Budgets for
communication.

An organization's plans, no matter how well formulated and supported by members of the organization, will not be carried out if they are not clearly understood. And, since plans are often complex, requiring the joint efforts of a large number of different departments and divisions in various geographic locations, communication and coordination are especially crucial. The budget communicates, in specific terms, the activities to be carried out, the resources available, and the timing of expenditures and expected returns. The budget specifies the amounts to be spent on materials, labor, consultant's fees, advertising, and so on and also anticipates the receipt of various returns to the organization.

Budgets for
motivation.

If the budgeting process is carried out in the proper atmosphere, the budget can be a powerful motivator within the organization. The proper atmosphere is generally created when at least the following three factors exist.

- First, individual managers must recognize the overall goals of the organization and understand how their department's activities contribute to the accomplishment of those goals.

- Second, managers must participate in the formulation of their own budget (rather than having the budget handed down from "on high") and agree (and believe) that resources are adequate to fulfill the tasks set out for the upcoming period.

- Third, managers must be rewarded (or not rewarded) according to their success in achieving the agreed upon targets.

Budgets guarantee
the uniformity
of plans.

Consider the position of a machine shop superintendent in a large manufacturing facility. The budgeting process forces the superintendent to clearly delineate the expected production for the machine shop during the budget period. To prepare the budget the performance of the department must be planned. The specification of production levels, however, is based on an overall organizational plan, and therefore the superintendent is reasonably assured that the personnel manager will have received and planned for the same activity level, and likewise the purchasing agent who must ensure that raw material is available for machining. The same is true for all other production departments in the factory as well as other organizational units such as the marketing and accounting departments.

Review and
negotiation before
finalization.

A process of review and negotiation is usually undertaken after the "first round" of budget development. Each manager prepares a budget and submits it to the next higher level of management for review and integration with other departmental and divisional budgets. Once this review has taken place, the manager and the manager's superior meet to negotiate and finalize the budget.

Not too tight, nor too loose.

Negotiation is important if a budget is to serve as a motivating device and as a proper standard for performance. If the budget is too "tight" and not attainable, the manager preparing the budget will only feel frustrated by efforts to achieve the standard and eventually will give up trying. On the other hand, if the budget is too "loose" it will most often be met, but no real effort will have been expended. A budget that is tight but attainable provides a fair standard for performance measurement and also a motivator for improved performance.

The importance of commitment.

If all parties to the budgeting process, including superiors and subordinates, are not committed to the accomplishment of the plans it represents, the budget is likely to produce as many negative results as it does positive ones. The attitude with which the parties enter into the budgeting process, and the way in which the budget is viewed as a control tool contribute largely to success or failure in achieving the desired results from operations.

After this negotiation process has been completed throughout the organization and a complete budget is prepared for the entire organization, it is submitted to top management for approval. Approval constitutes the granting of authority to act on the basis of the plans reflected in the budget and to make expenditures specified in the budget. The approved budget is communicated throughout the organization as the major guide to action in the upcoming period.

A solid basis for budgeting.

Note that the development of the forecasting system, aggregate scheduling process, and even the MRP system, all discussed previously, now provides a solid basis for the preparation of the budget. Because materials,

"Why can I sell it so cheap? I got no overhead!"

(Copyright © 1974, The Kiplinger Washington Editors, Inc.)

equipment, and labor are all scheduled through these systems, detailed expenditures can be forecast and a detailed budget drawn up.

The budget is one expression of the organizational plan, but deviations from plans are commonplace, so changes during the operating period must be viewed in their proper perspective and not disallowed simply because "the budget does not call for that."

Similarly, if a budget is found to be unrealistic during the operating cycle, changes should be made to reflect the new information. A manager who will not allow budget modifications when real changes in environmental or operating conditions have come about is not only unlikely to meet the original plan but will also promote ill will in subordinates. For example, if a purchasing manager has purchased an inferior raw material to that planned for in the budget, the production manager must recognize that deviations from the standard usage should be expected. The problem is not in production but in procurement, and to hold fast the previously determined use rates will only compound the problem by promoting unfair expectations to shop employees.

Two particular budgeting methods developed in the public sector [14] have become quite well known. These are the *planning programming budgeting system (PPBS)*, which is also extensively used by private industry for project management, and *zero-based budgeting (ZBB)*. Both of these budgeting systems are attempts to accomplish two objectives in not-for-profit budgeting.

Tying the budget
to goals with PPBS
and ZBB.

First, these methods tie the budgeted expenditures to an objective or purpose so that budget approval and modification can be based on the results desired rather than simply a type of expenditure. (It's always easier to delay construction of a structure than to lay off an employee!) Second, the budgets are not based on historical expenditures but on new justification for the function or purpose. Rather than granting blanket "across the board" budget increases, PPBS and ZBB require that each program be justified on its own continuing merits, not on previous merits or amounts expended.

Preventive Control

Feedback versus
preventive control.

There exists another type of control that operates without feedback and is also initiated in the *planning* stage of the basic operating system, called **preventive control.** Preventive control systems act as constraints, such as rules and regulations, which operate to prevent the occurrence of deviations from plan. That is, preventive controls attempt to keep deviations from happening in the first place through good system design. Since no feedback occurs in preventive control systems they are considered *static*, or motionless, systems.

Preventive control
procedures.

The preventive control systems of an organization consist, in large part, of the policies, procedures, rules, budgets, and regulations of the organization. Many of these systems are described in training and procedure manuals given out to new employees, but many more are communicated simply by word of mouth or even nonverbally (a frown) through the informal organization. ("Committee meetings are *never* set for Friday," "Where's your safety helmet, Bob?")

In addition to formal procedures, numerous other means of communicating preventive controls are employed, the most formal of which is, of course, one's immediate superior. But even the yellow lines painted on the warehouse floor, the goggles hanging near the machine's switch, the one-way theater turnstile, and the supermarket railings that are just slightly narrower than the shopping carts are preventive control systems.

Design for preventive control.

A considerable amount of thought goes into the design of such systems to make them as foolproof as possible, thus requiring minimal supervision. This, for example, is the basis for the numerous franchises in the fast-food business, the chain drugstores, and other such standardized multilocation organizations. An efficient system is developed that closely controls the activities of the employees, and, on occasion, the recipients as well, thus guaranteeing a certain quality of output. The scoop is designed to hold just enough french fries to fill a bag, the camera requires the librarian to simultaneously actuate a switch with *each* hand before it will take a picture of the borrower's library card (so that idle fingers do not cover the lens by accident).

Use of both types necessary.

Clearly, both feedback and preventive control systems will typically be used in the control of organizational activities. Although either type, by itself, *could* exercise sufficient control for most situations, if well designed, the experience of the system designer is usually too limited to design a system that is acceptable under all conditions. Preset traffic lights are a good example of preventive control systems that are typically well designed. Nevertheless, in many cities it has been found to be necessary to augment these systems with pedestrian and in-roadway switches. These switches provide *feedback* to a nearby electrical controller, which overrides the preset light sequence if traffic becomes too heavy. It should be noted that even dynamic feedback systems may not be adequate to control some activities—in these cases we may need to resort to higher levels of control (lawsuits, firing, police, army).

14.3 MONITORING

Monitor.

The **monitoring** activity in a feedback control process serves as a data collection activity. Data regarding the activity of a program, the outputs produced by the program, and the results accomplished by the production of these outputs are routinely measured and processed to provide specific reports. This monitoring activity is provided, in part, by the organization's information system, described later, and especially by the accounting information system, which captures and processes economic data about the organization's activities and outputs.

Monitoring *results* for most organizations is less routinized than for activities and outputs. Even in business organizations (wherein one of the many results is "level of profit"), the results of specific activities and outputs are very seldom systematically collected. For example, neither the pollution damage resulting from one of an organization's activities nor the societal good achieved by an equal employment opportunity program or a life-saving product are systematically measured.

Monitoring outputs instead of inputs.

For not-for-profit organizations the monitoring problem is even more acute. Taxpayers would like to know the *results* of a legal system or a mental health system, not how many assets were used or how many mental patients have been hospitalized. These measures are clearly difficult to develop, but without them the organization is less able to control operations intelligently.

The Nature of Information

Information is one of the basic inputs to organizations, along with materials, capital, staff, and so on. Information may be classified in any of a number of ways, one of which is external versus internal.

Sources of external information.

External information comes to the organization in many forms: through reports, manuals, newspapers, magazines; by way of salespeople, clients, consultants, stockholders, suppliers; and in many other forms. But probably the most important source of external information in the organization is staff, who, from their own personal external activities such as shopping,

"We've got all the "Know-How." We just don't know where it is."

(Reprinted by courtesy of Esselte Pendaflex Corporation.)

taking classes, and the thousands of normal day-to-day activities that constitute living in a modern society, bring information to the organization.

Sources of internal information.

Of equal or even greater significance to the organization is *internal information* concerning the organization and its operation. This information consists of performance reports, directives, marketing studies, research reports, phone updates, the "grapevine" (gossip), committee conferences, and all the thousands of other means by which the organization's staff come to obtain the information necessary to perform their duties.

Simon [15] comments that information is used at various levels within an organization to answer three broad types of questions:

1. Scorekeeping questions.

2. Attention-directing questions.

3. Problem-solving questions.

Scorekeeping information for reporting.

Scorekeeping information allows managers to answer questions such as "How well am I doing in meeting my budget?," "What is the currently available spare parts inventory balance?," "Which department produced this defective item?," and so on. A considerable amount of organizational information is recorded and stored simply for reporting purposes and possible later use. In some organizations this scorekeeping information is gathered and reported by an "integrated" information system. In other organizations, special information systems (accounting, operations, personnel) produce scorekeeping information relevant to particular purposes only. Recent trends in information system design are based on the latter but with additional reporting to a central source that monitors and reports selected information. These

Distributed data processing.

systems are called "distributed data processing" and are growing in popularity with the growth of functionally dedicated mini- and microcomputers.

Figure 14.2 illustrates the tracking and comparison of scorekeeping information in a project. Close control over project costs is mandatory or they quickly get out of hand. The trend projection (dashed line) of the actual (colored line) costs is compared to the planned budget and indicates a sizable

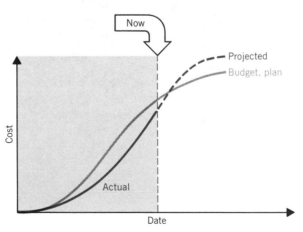

Figure 14.2   Trend projection.

cost overrun by project end. The colored line represents the scorekeeping information; the dashed line illustrates the next type of information—attention directing.

Attention-directing information helps managers to answer the general question "Are there any problems or impending problems that I should be concerned about and/or working on?" Attention-directing information is generally less widely available within organizations than is scorekeeping information and is typically derived from special formatting, or analysis, of scorekeeping information or directly from a control system. The variance reports and control charts discussed later in this chapter are examples of attention-directing information used by the operations manager.

Problem-solving information aids managers in solving specific problems, such as which machine to purchase, how many items to order in one production lot, whether to make or buy a needed subcomponent, and so on. Because of the complexity of this information, usually requiring special analyses of data, it is the least likely to be systematically collected by most organizations. Numerous examples of problem-solving information have been presented in this book. For example, in the chapters on inventory management, data on costs and volumes of use were combined to provide answers to questions of "how much" and "when" to order. The development of **information systems (IS)**, discussed next, was an outgrowth of the need for better problem-solving information.

It is the function of the organization's information system to provide the information necessary to answer each of the previous three types of questions. In actuality, this information system consists of a number of smaller information systems, each serving a specialized purpose. The accounting information system gathers and records data for financial accountability and reporting purposes. In a similar fashion, operations and marketing each have their own information systems, which may be either formalized or quite informal. Of all the information systems, perhaps the one receiving the most attention has been the *management information system (MIS)*. The intent of this formalized system is to provide the various levels of management with the information needed to perform their functions.

The formal **MIS** refers to the set of policies, procedures, people, forms, equipment, and reports required to produce information for management's needs, especially their decision-making needs. However, every manager knows that such a formal system will never provide *all* the information needed and, thus, other sources and contacts, an *informal information system*, must still be maintained. For example, rumors reaching the manager faintly implying that Joe is playing politics, or that XYZ Corp. may soon be coming out with a new soap called "SWET," are extremely valuable bits of information that will probably never be found in a formalized information system, yet may provide 80 percent of the basis for a particular management decision. Gordon [9] gives an example of this from his own experience.

A critical aspect of the (management) task is determining the nature of the invisible information system which exists in any organization. In a small organi-

Margin notes:
Attention-directing information for "management by exception."

Problem-solving information from data analysis.

The IS.

Management information system to provide timely information to management.

Formal versus informal information systems.

zation which has been staffed for many years by the same people this information system is not necessarily formalized but may be critical in sensing developments in its health. An ability to deal on a one to one basis with employees, customers, suppliers, and other contacts appears to be daily and without advance warning. Finally, the necessity of constant interaction with employees at their work stations on a personal basis is an essential form of motivating performance and at the same time gathering information.

One problem with early MISs was their data output. Managers found that voluminous amounts of data, such as in thick computer reports, effectively hid whatever value lay within. For example, it is easier to find a needle in a box of straw than it is in a box of pins. Some computerized management information systems have been corrected of their earlier "overreporting" tendencies and now print *exception reports* for managers in order to facilitate the "management by exception" concept. A production manager in a large job shop does not need a daily status report on all 300 jobs in the shop but rather a report on those jobs falling behind schedule. Still, the MIS concept has not been a success.

Overreporting and management by exception.

Decision support systems.

The explosive growth in the **decision support systems (DSS)** concept is based, in part, on the failings of the earlier MIS. The DSS concept is to provide direct, personal support for managerial decision making, as opposed to capturing information for possible later use.

More specifically, DSS aims to allow the manager to interact directly with the computer's data and model bases through data and model base management systems (DBMS and MBMS). The emphasis is on supporting rather than replacing managerial judgment and improving the effectiveness of decisions rather than their efficiency. DSS attempts to create *specialized* tools and models under the control of the decision maker in order to examine data, create unique reports, perform special analyses, simulate decisions, and ask "what-if" types of questions. The results are reported instantly back to the manager on the video screen in the form of tables, graphs, and charts. It is not clear, at this time, whether the DSS concept will be any more successful than MIS was.

DBMS, MBMS

"What-if" questions.

Although the tendency is to think of organizational information systems as computerized, because the majority of the publicity about information systems has concerned the computer and its abilities in this capacity, most information systems are manual. In fact, computer systems analysts will caution against computerizing *any* system for which an acceptable manual system has never been designed. The point is to refrain from "building in" the errors and inadequacies of previous manual systems. Rather, a computerized system should be an expansion of a successful manual system to simply handle larger volumes of data or to provide more rapid compilation of needed information, or both.

Computerizing successful systems.

There are, however, exceptions to this caution. Some systems, such as the MRP systems discussed in Chapter 13, were not feasible before the development of the computer. The sheer effort required to "explode" product profiles and to prepare capacity plans in a timely manner was beyond the capability of human "processors." Such systems as these are exceptions to the general rule that a good manual system should exist first.

Information Lag

Effects of information lag.

A critical aspect of the monitoring-feedback process is the *information lag* that is built (usually unintentionally) into a system. The effect of lag on management control can be similar to the effect of switching electric blanket controls on the occupants of a double bed. As the left occupant gets too warm and turns down the (right side's) thermostat, the right occupant gets too cold and turns *up* the (left side's) thermostat. This makes the left occupant warmer still, resulting in a further lowering of the right side thermostat, and so on.

Industrial dynamics.

To investigate the result of information lag in systems, Jay Forrester of MIT used a computer simulation technique called **industrial dynamics** [8]. He investigated the effect of a permanent 10 percent increase in retail sales on the response of a retailer-distributor-manufacturer, distribution-production system. The inventory-reordering lags between levels of the system were about 15 days each and response lags were about 5 days each. The total information lag in the distribution system from the retailer's view was thus almost two months.

The result of the 10 percent January sales increase is shown in Figure 14.3 by the curves ① through ⑤ with curve ① representing the 10 percent sales increase. The retailer's response in terms of ordering is shown by curve

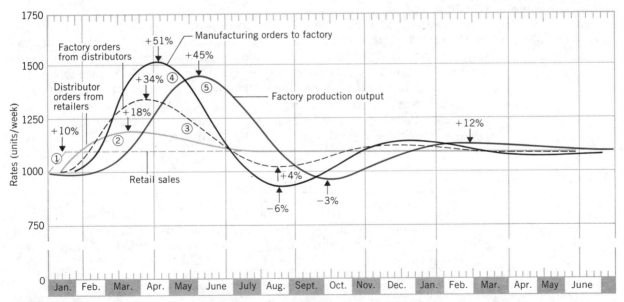

Figure 14.3 The effect of lags in the feedback control system. (*Source.* Reprinted from *Industrial Dynamics* by Jay Forrester by permission of The MIT Press, Cambridge, Massachusetts. Copyright © 1961 by the Massachusetts Institute of Technology.)

② and reaches an anticipation-of-further-sales-increases peak of 18 percent in March. The distributor, seeing an increase in orders from the retail customers, also overanticipates (curve ③) and reaches a 34 percent peak in early April. The manufacturer also overresponds (curve ④) and peaks at 51 percent in late April. By the time the factory can respond to the continuing increase, each level has started to realize their mistake and cut back their orders, resulting in a factory production peak (curve ⑤) in June of only 45 percent, less than the 51 percent originally ordered in April.

As the retailer cuts back from the 18 percent peak toward the actual 10 percent increase (curve ②, June) the distributor and manufacturer as well cut back also, again amplifying the lower level effect. The result is a 6 percent drop below the new 10 percent level (curve ③, August) for the distributor (4 percent above original level), a 16 percent drop below the new 10 percent level (curve ④, August) for the manufacturer (6 percent below original level), and a final 13 percent actual drop in production in October (curve ⑤, 3 percent below original).

By now, however, the distributor realizes she or he has cut back *too* far and starts to increase again, repeating the entire cycling process but at a much *lower* level. The oscillating cycles finally stabilize at the 10 percent level in the following June, a year and a half after the initial effect. In this particular case, the following oscillations were at lower levels than the original peaks and valleys, thus leading to what is termed *damped* oscillations or a *stable* system. In some cases, however, as with the electric blanket example, the oscillations tend to get *higher* each time and the *unstable* system becomes *explosive*.

Stable versus unstable (explosive) systems. Positive versus negative feedback.

Explosive systems usually result from *positive feedback* systems where the feedback action or adjustment increases rather than decreases the external effect (as with the electric blanket). But information lag in a *negative feedback* system can also, on occasion, result in an explosive system if the lag, and resulting adjustments, are sufficient. By reducing either the strength of the adjustment, or the length of the lag (e.g., by using a computerized real-time information system, as mentioned earlier in the text), an explosive negative feedback system can usually be dampened.

14.4 COMPARING

Comparator.

Simply knowing that activities, outputs, and results have been accomplished is still not enough for control. The organization must *compare* these accomplishments with what is intended. The following are some typical questions that need to be asked and answered:

1. Are we working as many hours as we had planned?
2. Are we producing as many services with the available resources as had been intended?
3. Are our outputs being translated into the kinds of results we want?
4. Are our costs excessive?

One of the more formal comparison systems that is common in firms is the cost accounting reporting system, which we will briefly consider next.

Cost Variance Analysis

Variance reporting for control.

One of the most widely used feedback control systems in organizations is the *standard cost variance reporting system.* A standard is a performance expectation, that is, an anticipated per-unit cost for items to be produced or for activity to be performed in an upcoming budget period. Standards are determined through engineering estimates or through analysis of past performance and are established as the cost targets to be aimed for in the upcoming operating cycle. These standards are communicated to the operating system, which, as it operates, produces an "actual" cost per unit. This actual cost is monitored by the organization's cost accounting system and *Cost standards for comparison.* compared with the cost standard. Feedback information is provided to a manager who can exert any necessary control if the difference between standard and actual (called a *variance*) is considered to be significant.

As an example, consider the cost-schedule reconciliation charts of Figure 14.4 as used in project management. In Figure 14.4*a* actual progress is plotted alongside planned progress and the "effective" progress time (TE) is noted. Because progress is less than planned, TE is less than actual time (TA). On the cost chart (Figure 14.4*b*) we see that the "total variance" from the planned cost at this time is quite small despite the lack of progress. But this is misleading; the variance should be much more given the lack of progress. The actual "spending variance" is found from the "planned amount spent" curve corresponding to point TE. Adding the two then gives the manager a "schedule variance," as shown in the figure.

These two graphs are commonly combined for project managers into an "earned value" chart, Figure 14.5, where the planned cost, actual cost, and value completed (actual earned dollars of progress) are plotted. In this sit-

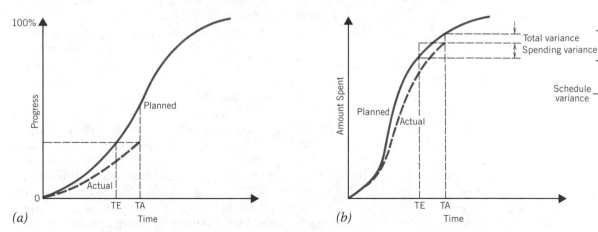

Figure 14.4 Cost-schedule reconciliation charts.

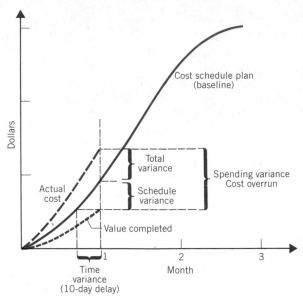

Figure 14.5 Earned value chart.

uation (a different one from that in 14.4) the actual cost is *greater* than the plan, even though *progress* lags the plan (thus the huge spending variance). Plotted in this manner only one chart is needed to monitor both progress and cost.

When these variances are significant, management must identify (or at least attempt to identify) an *assignable cause* for the variance. That is, the manager responsible for the control of the element that is at variance with the standard must study the operational process to determine why the variance occurred. This is so the proper remedy can be used to keep the variance from occurring in the next period. A corrective action is called for if some inefficiency or change in the prescribed process caused the variance.

Favorable and unfavorable variances.

Variances can be both favorable and unfavorable. A significant *favorable variance* (for example, that which might have resulted from getting a large quantity discount on material) will usually not require a corrective action. But, a change in the standard itself may be necessary if an underlying condition has changed which makes the current standard obsolete and will therefore continuously result in a large favorable variance.

The same is true for an unfavorable variance. An electric utility that has used a $10 per ton coal price as standard must change the standard in light of a $30 to $35 per ton price. There is no sense in planning a continued unfavorable variance.

Control charts for identifying significant deviations.

The last step is the reporting of these variances for proper follow-up. In some cases, specific action will be necessary to ensure that excessive variances of the same sort do not recur. In other cases, the variances are within reason and follow-up is unnecessary. One method of determining whether or not a variance is excessive is to use a "control chart," discussed further below. Upper and lower control "limits" can be established and only variances lying outside these limits are followed up.

Whether or not follow-up is required for a particular variance, the operations manager is well advised to monitor variance reports to recognize trends and recurring variances. While immediate scheduling, inventory control, or other problems appear to be more important at the time than a "history" of last period's operations, it is this historical view that senior managers with the organization are seeing and on which many of their decisions will be based.

Searching for an assignable cause is sometimes like looking for a needle in a haystack. But often the causes are straightforward. New employees are being trained and are not yet far enough along the learning curve. Material quality has declined and parts now require much rework. A machine is breaking down more often than usual. Output has increased requiring the use of more overtime. All of these and many more are the first "suspects" looked to by operations managers when variances arise.

Control Charts

In or out of control?
Library control.

One of the feedback control system elements that is the most difficult is where the manager must decide whether or not an activity is "out of control" and needs adjustment. Consider the task of managing the operations of a large city library. To manage such an organization will require monitoring and controlling the flow and inventories of library materials (books, periodicals, records, cassettes, etc.), the condition of facilities and equipment (building, chairs, shelves, tables, phonographs, utilities, duplicating machines, perhaps even a computer system for book-borrower records), the hours and performance of employees (payroll, personnel records, interview forms), user information (book requests, reference calls, monthly borrowings, returns), and so on.

What information should be monitored?

The majority of this information need not be closely controlled since it either varies slowly (condition of the building), has little to do with direct performance (personnel records), or will be brought to the attention of the staff if it becomes serious (condition of phonographs). Of more importance, however, are ongoing measures of activity that will affect budgets, personnel, scheduling, and user service. Examples of such measures are daily book checkouts, percentage of overdue books, and the number of daily requests for reference information.

Control charts to identify systems out of control.

To monitor the performance of measures similar to these at Bell Telephone Laboratories in the 1920s, Walter A. Shewhart developed the concept of statistical **control charts** to aid in distinguishing between *chance variation* in a system and variation caused by the system being "out of control," called *assignable variation*. Should a process go out of control it must first be detected, then the assignable cause located, and, finally, the appropriate control action or adjustment made. The control chart is used to detect when a process has gone out of control.

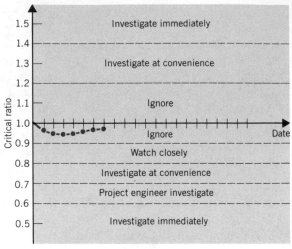

Note: ●—● = actual data.

Figure 14.6 Critical ratio control chart.

One example of a general control chart, used to detect loss of cost and schedule control in a project, is illustrated in Figure 14.6. This chart is monitoring the project's *critical ratio (CR)*, first introduced in Chapter 10, and defined here for projects as

Critical ratio.

$$\frac{\text{actual progress}}{\text{scheduled progress}} \times \frac{\text{budgeted cost}}{\text{actual cost}}$$

The standard of performance is 1.0, where everything is on schedule or else the deviation in cost exactly counterbalances the deviation in progress. Above 1.0, progress is ahead of cost for that point or cost is below progress, in either case a welcome situation unless the ratio gets very large. Then the project manager should investigate to find out why things are going so well. Are data really being reported accurately; has someone made a breakthrough the project manager has not heard about?

CR > 1.0.

CR < 1.0.

For ratios less than 1.0 trouble is indicated. As noted in the figure, slight deviations from 1.0 may be safely ignored but further deviations warrant investigation, the extent and promptness increasing with the size of the deviation. The heavy line indicates the actual plotted critical ratio values to date. The critical ratio looked as if trouble was coming but things seem to have been corrected.

Applications of ratio analysis, such as in the previous example, are particularly useful in pure service operations where control is still critical but hard, physical measurements of outputs or progress are unavailable. Many other ratios can then be monitored as well.

A repetitive process or operation will seldom produce *exactly* the same quality, size, or other measure to be controlled; rather, with each repetition the process will generate variation around some average. Because this variation is usually due to a large number of small, uncontrollable sources, the

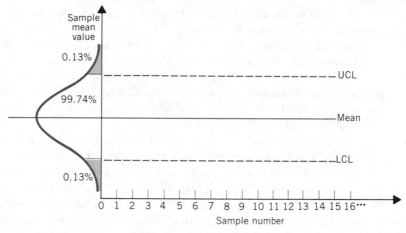

Figure 14.7 Control chart with the limits set at three standard deviations.

Normal distribution of variations.

pattern of variability is often well described by a standard frequency distribution such as the *normal distribution*, shown plotted against the vertical scale in Figure 14.7.

The succession of measures that result from the continued repetition of the process can thus be thought of as a *population* of numbers that is normally distributed with some mean and standard deviation. As long as the distribution remains the same, the process is considered to be "in control" and simply exhibiting chance variation. One way to help determine if the distribution is staying the same is to keep checking the mean of the distribution—if it changes to some other value, the process may be considered to be "out of control."

Checking the mean for control.

The problem, however, is that it is too expensive for organizations to keep constantly checking operations. Therefore, *samples* of the operation's output are checked instead. When sampling output for inspection, it is imperative that the *sample* fully *represent* the population being checked; therefore, a *random sample* should be used. A *random sample* is one taken in such a way that every item in the population has an equal chance of being included in the sample. An important caution here regards a common sampling technique known as *systematic sampling;* for example, every tenth name in a phone book is drawn at random. Although this sampling method may result in a random sample of phone listings, it may not result in a random sample of *households*, because unlisted numbers are not included in the sample, nor are households that do not have telephones.

Sampling to reduce cost.

The sample must be representative.

For example, if such an approach is used to inspect items coming off an assembly line, it may result in a *very* biased sample. It may be that in some particular plant, final assembly is conducted by five workers who sequentially place their finished work on the conveyor belt. Therefore, every fifth, tenth, fifteenth, and so on, item has been assembled by the *same worker*, and if every tenth item is inspected, then only one person's work is being checked.

Biased samples.

Risk introduced.

But when checks are only made of sample averages, rather than 100 percent of the output, there is always a chance of having selected a particular sample with an unusually high, or low, mean. The problem facing the operations manager is thus to decide what is *too high*, or *too low*, and should be considered as a process out of control. Also, the manager must consider the fact that the more samples eventually taken, the more likely that a sample will accidentally be selected that has too high (or low) a mean *when the process is actually still in control.*

Setting the values
of the UCL
and LCL.

The values of the mean selected by the manager as too high or low are called the upper **control limit (UCL)** and the lower control limit **(LCL),** respectively. These limits generally allow a *management by exception* approach to control since, theoretically, no action need be taken by the manager unless a *sample mean* exceeds the control limits. The control limits most commonly used in organizations are plus and minus three *standard deviations* (on occasion, two or even one standard deviation). We know from statistics (see Appendix A) that the chance of a simple mean exceeding three standard deviations, in either direction, due simply to chance variation, is only 0.3 percent (i.e., three times per 1000 samples). The equivalent values for two and one standard deviation are 4.55 percent and 31.73 percent, respectively. Figure 14.7 illustrates the use of control limits set at three standard deviations. Of course, using the higher limit values (three or more) increases the risk of not detecting a process that is only slightly out of control.

There are other rules, besides simply finding a data point outside the control limits, which should warn a manager of a potential "out of control" condition. These are listed in Figure 14.8, generally known as the **2-5-7 rules.** Note in the first two figures that even *improvement* in a chart should be investigated, not just loss of control. Perhaps a new method or tool has been discovered by a worker that could be applied to other, similar processes. (Or maybe the worker is throwing away defective items.) In the third figure it appears that there has been a definite, and permanent, change in the process which should clearly be investigated.

General utility of
control charts.

It should be noted that the control chart approach, although originally developed for quality control in manufacturing, is applicable to all sorts of repetitive processes in any kind of organization. Thus, it can be used for services as well as products, people or machines, cost or quality, and so on. We will look at the control chart concept, and particularly the setting of control limits, in more detail in Chapter 16.

General Variance Analysis

Control charts of selected indicator variables may help in indicating that trouble is brewing, but discovering what that trouble is may not be quite so easy. Similar to cost variance analysis, a general variance analysis may be required for uncovering a quality problem, a schedule delay, a labor difficulty, or any of a number of other such factors.

The investigation may require some statistical tests to be performed, some modeling or simulation to be conducted, or a more thorough ratio

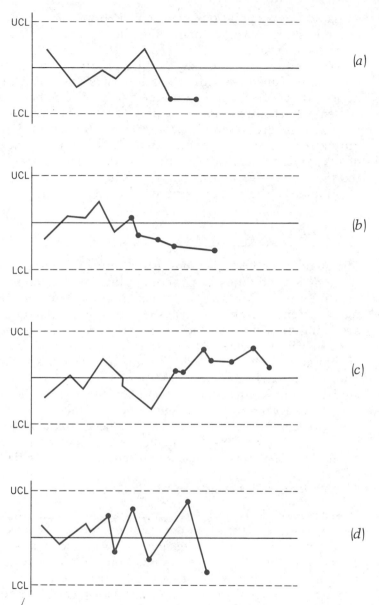

Figure 14.8   Special conditions warranting investigation.
(a) Two consecutive points, near a control limit.
(b) Five consecutively decreasing (or increasing) points.
(c) Seven consecutive points on one side of central line.
(d) Worsening erratic behavior.

analysis be completed. General ratio analysis is familiar to financial managers who daily consider debt to equity, price to earnings, and dozens of other common financial ratios. But there are also many less well known operations ratios, similar to the "critical ratio" mentioned earlier, that are

The "fat ratio."

valuable to the operations manager. Examples are the "productivity ratio" (pounds shipped/worker hour) and the "fat ratio" (indirect worker hours/ direct worker hours).

The general analysis may require plotting or otherwise comparing current data gleaned from the more intensive analysis against historical data in order to accurately ascertain the true difficulty. For example, suppose the critical ratio control chart for a project indicates serious progress problems, though costs are acceptable compared with budget. Further analysis may require mathematical programming to determine if the optimal allocation of materials to facilities has been made, linear regression to examine the relationship between order shipments and labor productivity, and a history of productivity ratios for this type of project.

14.5 FEEDBACK CONTROL

The analyses and comparisons made in the preceding step provide the basis for *feedback* and adjustment through managerial action. Both negative and positive answers to these questions are important. It could be the case that management's original plans were too conservative and that opportunities are being missed to produce more with the available resources. Also, comparison can show that, while activity levels are up to expectation, the outputs of that activity are not. Perhaps some inefficiencies have crept into the system, or the environmental conditions that existed when the program was envisioned have since changed and goals need to be adjusted.

The exact nature of the control actions taken will obviously depend on the situation at hand and cannot all be elaborated here. However, some general "categories" of the manner in which control is effected in different types of processes are defined and briefly described in the following sections.

"Order Control" for Intermittent Operations

Order control derives its name from the fact that in intermittent operations most output is "made to order." For example, in a sheet metal fabricating company each manufactured part is produced because a customer order exists for that part. Even in organizations that produce items in anticipation of demand (i.e., before an order actually is received), the product is usually produced as a result of a "shop order" for a certain amount of the item. In either instance, order control is called for.

Organization of orders.

Organizations based on order control use copies of the orders to run the organization. The accounting is based on orders, scheduling of staff and equipment is derived from the orders sitting in the "load files," financing needs are based on the orders (especially large ones), purchasing issues purchase orders based on the customer orders, and so forth. In other words, to find out almost anything in the organization requires knowledge of the appropriate order.

Preventive and feedback controls.

Order control is made up of a rather large number of specific preventive and feedback controls which attempt to ensure that the operations are coordinated to produce the desired quantity of the product, delivered to the appropriate location by the desired due date at the agree-upon price. An example of a preventive control in an order control situation is a scheduling policy which calls for establishing order dates for raw materials by back-scheduling from the due date some amount of time based on delivery time for the raw material and production time for the item. A feedback control example in an order control environment is provided by monitoring and reporting systems that "track" the order's progress through the system, comparing actual progress with planned progress, such as when using a critical ratio chart.

Order control is applicable to service delivery as well as manufacturing. For example, control of a patient's stay in the hospital (the patient being the "order") requires the same general type of control as the production of a manufacturing order. Likewise, controlling the operations of any computer center, restaurant, or university registration system requires some form of order control.

Order control systems are simple conceptually, but difficult to implement. Each order is unique and therefore requires special action to ensure its progress through the organization. For example, an order for 10 mattresses in a mattress factory will require different buying (purchasing) decisions, different production methods, different quality assurance plans, different cost control, and so on, than an order for 1000 of the same mattresses.

"Flow Control" for Continuous Operations

Flow control is used in continuous and semicontinuous operations. In semicontinuous operations the volume of production seldom changes drastically, and output is of a similar type day after day. The major control method in flow control is feedback. Actual output costs, quality, and so forth, are constantly compared with planned levels of performance and deviations reported so that corrective actions can be implemented. Much of the control in continuous operations centers on scheduling of operations so that delays in the process are avoided.

Major concerns in flow control.

The basic principal behind flow control is that jobs started into a system will progress most efficiently if work-in-process is kept low. To do this, the organization must know its capacity limitations and release jobs to the operations area on a due date priority basis. From a practical side, clear reporting of finished jobs and jobs waiting to be started, along with reports on delayed or late jobs, are necessary to keep the system moving.

Flow control by feedback and scheduling.

Many specific types of feedback controls have been devised for continuous operations, depending on the activity concerned. Inventory control is one of the major activities of this nature and was discussed at length in Chapters 12 and 13. Similarly, quality control is another such activity and will be considered in Chapter 16. The control of materials, equipment, and staff through careful scheduling to maximize their utilization was discussed in Chapters 9 and 10.

"Block Control"

Although operations frequently use both flow and order control, on occasion *block control* is more appropriate. **Block control** is a modification of flow control used in operations which produce the same output and require the same steps or processes, but which process the output in batches or "blocks." That is, for operations in which variations in the output do not cause significant variations in the transformation process, block control is used. An example of a setting in which block control is appropriate is in shoe and garment manufacturing. The processes required to produce a pair of slacks are essentially the same, no matter what the colors, sizes, or styles. Yet, any one of these variables might be used to "batch" or "block" an order and thus require that all production on the block be completed in a given department before equipment can be reset for the next block.

Output in batches.

The sizes of departments usually are manipulated so the production throughput can be continuous. That is, each department is given equal capacity so that a block requiring 3 hours in department A will require 3 hours in each of the other departments. This approach keeps production moving smoothly through the shop without major bottlenecks between departments.

"Load Control"

Load control may be necessary in intermittent, continuous, processing, or even project-type operations. It is used in any operation that requires the use of one piece of equipment or one department that essentially limits the throughput of the entire operation. This constraining factor is typically an expensive resource that cannot economically be duplicated but is necessary for all production. A good example of such a resource is the computer. The objective of load control is to maximize the throughput of the system by making the most effective use of the constraining resource. Essentially what this means is scheduling all other operations and equipment so that the limited resource never waits because of lack of work or because of a delay in some earlier stage of the operation. If an organization changes product or service mixes, the bottleneck resource may also change, thereby necessitating a dynamic load control policy.

Bottlenecks in all types of organizations.

Load control is frequently observed with printing presses, physicians, judges, presidents, surgery rooms, sauna baths, and some high-capacity construction equipment. Often, the scarce resource may be shared between many organizations so as to maximize the utility of the resource, even frequently at the expense of efficiency.

14.6 SUMMARY AND KEY LEARNING POINTS

This chapter on organizational control initiated our discussion of actual productive activity instead of just *planning* for such activity. We began by discussing the role of the control function in detail and described the different types and mechanisms of control, such as feedback control and dynamic control. We discussed some of the more common control systems such as budgets and organizational procedures.

We then moved to the monitoring function and spent some time discussing information: its purposes, the kinds of information systems that exist, and the dangers of information lag in organizations. Next, we looked at the comparison process and described variance analysis and the use of control charts to determine out-of-control conditions. Last, we looked at the common feedback control systems used for the different types of transformation processes and for various situations, noting how they worked and when to use them.

The key learning points were

- The managerial control system typically operates when information fed by the monitoring system to the comparative system indicates a significant variance from standard or out-of-control situations.
- Control systems are usually either preventive (static), feedback (dynamic), or both combined. Rules and regulations are the common examples of preventive control "systems." A budget is one example of a common feedback control system, as are yearly evaluations and product inspections.
- Accurate, timely information is crucial to good control. When information lag exists in a system it can, by itself, be a destabilizing factor. Three primary purposes of information are scorekeeping, directing attention, and solving problems. There are many information systems (IS) in organizations, such as the informal ("grapevine") IS, the management IS (MIS), and the more recent "decision support systems" (DSS).
- Variance analysis is probably most highly developed in the cost area where standard cost variance reporting systems are employed. The comparison of standard to actual yields the variance, but a determination of whether the variance is significant or not must still be made.
- Control charts can be used to monitor many variables, such as critical ratios, rates of defects, or variances. Upper and lower control limits are set to indicate whether a variable is out of control or a variance is significant and requires investigation. However, other conditions, indicated by the 2-5-7 rule, can also require investigation.
- Specific types of feedback control procedures are order control for intermittent operations, flow control for continuous operations, block control for batch operations, and load control for bottleneck operations.

14.7 KEY TERMS

feedback control (p. 536)

preventive control (p. 539)

monitoring (p. 540)

information systems (IS) (p. 543)

MIS (p. 543)

industrial dynamics (p. 545)

control chart (p. 549)

control limit (p. 552)

UCL (p. 552)

LCL (p. 552)

2-5-7 rules (p. 552)

order control (p. 554)

flow control (p. 555)

block control (p. 556)

load control (p. 556)

DSS (p. 544)

14.8 REVIEW AND DISCUSSION QUESTIONS

1. Name some external prevention and feedback control systems.

2. Which of the three functions of information do you feel is most critical in aiding operations managers?

3. How should one determine if data should be stored for later use; and how long should historical data be kept in the files of various organizations?

4. Does not the fact that "what is *information* depends on the receiver" make the idea of an *organizational* information system ridiculous?

5. What type of information systems would you expect to find in a government agency such as the Census Bureau?

6. Why is it important that managers have access to the informal organizational information system in a company?

7. The production manager is asked to produce a labor and materials budget each quarter of the year. He uses last quarter's sales volume to estimate his needs in the next quarter. What problems may arise from this procedure?

8. What type, if any, of labor cost variances are due to incentive-based pay systems?

9. Many new businesses fail within the first year of their existence due to cash budget problems. Why do you think this happens so frequently?

10. How can information lags be minimized?

11. What are some positive feedback systems?

12. What is the risk in using a computer for control?

13. What control limits should be used when x-raying for cancer?

14. How would a control chart be constructed to help control the stealing of books in a library?

15. How may information lag simulate a positive feedback process?

16. Contrast block and flow control of work-in-process inventories.

17. Where might load and order control be used simultaneously? Load and flow control?

14.9 READINGS

TEACHING TACTICS

Some School Systems Use Business Methods to Make Pupils Learn

They Set Proficiency Goals, Put Onus on Instructors; Indian Hill's Rigid Plan

'Quality Control' on the Line

William M. Bulkeley
Staff Reporter, The Wall Street Journal

Indian Hill, Ohio—If the students in Shirley Seifirth's fourth-grade class at Shawnee elementary school here don't learn to add fractions with common denominators by the time the school year ends next Tuesday, they'll have to repeat the subject in September. And Mrs. Seifirth, not the students, might be called to the principal's office.

The school system in this affluent suburb of Cincinnati has pledged to parents that it will teach students certain skills at certain times. Teachers have to quiz their students after each new area has been covered—such as adding those fractions—using standardized tests. The results are then turned over to the school administration.

Education as a Business

Indian Hill's approach to education has made it a leader in a national movement to run school systems somewhat like a business: by setting learning goals, meeting quotas of students who have mastered skills and making schools accountable for the children who pass through their classes.

Despite strong opposition from teacher organizations, teachers in school systems across the country are being evaluated partly on the basis of what their students learn. In Indian Hill, evaluations have led to several teachers being advised to leave.

This tough approach to education is the result of the national alarm over declining aptitude-test scores and over high-school graduates who can't read newspapers or fill out job applications. "Educators couldn't care less about teaching. They get paid no matter what," says E. Dennis Barnes, a realtor in

Upper Sandusky, Ohio, who is the leader of a group seeking to force the state to hand over control of education to school districts.

Will It Run Like a Car?

Thus, say advocates of making schools accountable, it simply makes sense to examine schools on the basis of what their product should be: educated students. Leon Lessinger, dean of the College of Education at the University of South Carolina, who helped formulate this idea about 10 years ago, says that accountability means "establishing quality control; we're seeing how many units at the end of the line look like a car but won't run like a car."

Five years ago, a committee of residents decided that the school system was inefficient. There wasn't, for example, a precise, sequential curriculum: Teachers taught whatever they felt appropriate, and there was no systematic evaluation of their performance.

The school board reacted by forcing out the superintendent and hiring a corporate recruiter to find a superintendent with a more businesslike approach to education. School board president Philip Casper points out that Procter & Gamble is based nearby in Cincinnati, and indeed several of its executives live in Indian Hill. The company "tests everything it puts out, and the same attitude permeates parents in this district," he says.

The school board found the man they wanted in Robert Boston, an expert in relating expenditures to academic achievement and a former researcher for the U.S. Office of Education. Mr. Boston is the sort of executive who uses phrases like "management by objective" and who takes a tough stance on how schools should work. "We know if we're failing," he says. "We can change the program, change the books or change the teachers."

Defining Goals

Mr. Boston's first task was to define general goals that could be turned into curricula. To do this he set up a committee of 50 parents, school administrators, teachers and students. For nearly a year the committee talked to parents and even polled them on what they thought their children should be learning. Teachers then turned these goals into a sequential school program for students at the elementary level.

Reading, writing and arithmetic were the first subjects to be planned in this fashion, with each subject broken down into specific objectives. For example, a second-grade teacher knows that her students must learn to recognize the main idea in a simple, four-sentence story. Fourth-grade students must be able to "interpret the basic emotions of the characters in a story." At each point along the way, teachers give students quick, four-question, multiple-choice tests.

The elementary schools soon will be teaching natural science and social studies in this fashion. Goal-setting for physical education (learning to trap a kicked ball in the second grade, for instance) already has been introduced, and programs for art and music are planned. The school system plans to use the program in the high schools so that eventually there will be goal-setting curricula from kindergarten through 12th grade.

The goal system clearly puts a good deal of pressure on the teachers. Teachers whose pupils consistently fail the skills tests are given help by the principal or even by other teachers. But those teachers who can't keep up with the new standards are asked to leave. In just the last three years, 15 Indian Hill teachers have, in Mr. Boston's words, been "counseled out."

Mr. Boston feels that the implicit threat of being fired keeps teachers on their toes. Although Indian Hill teachers are not supposed to be evaluated on the basis of test results, some teachers worry that in time the tests will become the yardstick for measuring performance. "It would be dangerous if the tests were used as a threat to the staff," says one high-school teacher. And Debra Hunter, president of the Indian Hill Classroom Teachers Association, says that "with the present changes occurring in the district, teachers are somewhat apprehensive."

But generally, the teachers and parents seem happy with the program. "One thing that's been lacking in education is defining what you're trying to do. In the past it's been kind of hit or miss. This is an effort to alleviate that problem," says David Terrel, a junior-high math teacher.

"Rather than just saying we've covered it, we're saying the kid has mastered it," says Michael Grawe, a second-grade teacher. "I feel I'm teaching more efficiently, with more direction. I have objectives just like any other job."

14.10   PROBLEMS

Practice Problems

1. A particular air quality hazard occurs on about 12 percent of the batches of paint prepared by the Mixit Chemical Company. The plant manager is considering two controls, one preventive, the other feedback. The preventive control is 90 percent effective; that is, if the problem is about to occur, it will remedy it 90 percent of the time. The feedback control will remedy the situation 98 percent of the time, after it occurs for 2 minutes. If a batch runs for 60 minutes, which of the two controls provides the least total time exposure to the air quality hazard?

2. Similar to the situation illustrated in Figure 14.4, a project at day 70 exhibits only 35 percent progress, when 40 percent was planned, for an effective date of 55. Planned cost was $17,000 at day 55 and $24,000 at day 70, and actual cost was $20,000 at day 55 and $30,000 at day 70. Find the total cost variance, the spending cost variance, and the schedule cost variance.

3. Similar to the situation shown in Figure 14.5, a project at month 2 exhibited an actual cost of $78,000, a scheduled (planned) cost of $84,000, and a value completed of $81,000. Find the spending, total, and scheduled cost variance.

4. What actions should be taken, based on Figure 14.6, for critical ratios based on the following data?

	Actual Progress (%)	Scheduled Progress (%)	Budgeted Cost ($1000)	Actual Cost ($1000)
a.	40	30	60	70
b.	30	40	60	70
c.	30	40	70	60
d.	40	30	70	60
e.	40	30	67	65

5. Where should the UCL and LCL be set for a control chart of defect rates if the mean is 18 and the standard deviation is 5? Use plus three- and minus two-sigma control limits.

6. The average cost of processing a particular computer run at a local service bureau is $38 with an upper control limit of $46 and a lower control limit of $30. Consider the following four sets of observations:
   a. $35, $42, $45, $38, $46.
   b. $39, $38, $41, $45, $31.
   c. $31, $33, $41, $45, $46.
   d. $42, $41, $40, $46, $45.

Are they all in control? On what rule would you base your decision?

More Complex Problems

7. Consider a distribution chain of firm-warehouse-wholesaler-retailer. If the links between each point require 3 days to pass information, or goods, the points themselves require 6 days to pass information or goods, and the product takes 30 days to make, when will a new order reach the retailer?

8. A distribution chain from a manufacturer consists of three warehouses, each warehouse distributes to four wholesalers, and each wholesaler distributes to five retailers. Retail sales for the firm's product are normally 100 units a day per retailer. Calculate the normal daily demand on the firm and the effect of a 10 percent increase in retail sales if each stocking point in the chain adds a 15 percent safety factor to any sales increases before passing it on to their supplier.

9. A control chart has a mean of 50 and two-sigma control limits of 40 and 60. The following data are plotted on the chart: 38, 55, 58, 42, 64, 49, 51, 58, 61, 46, 44, 50. Should action be taken?

14.11 CASE

PAINT TINT, INC.

In November of 1979, Jim Runnels, a salesman for the Paint Tint Corporation, was called to the plant of Townhouse Paint Company, one of his largest accounts. The purchasing agent for Townhouse Paint was complaining that the tubes of paint tint that had just been received were short weight by approximately 5 percent.

The lightweight tubes were not detected by Townhouse's receiving clerks and had not been weighed or otherwise checked by their quality control staff. The problem arose when Townhouse began to use the tubes of tinting agent and found that paint colors were not matching the specifications. The mixing charts used by sales people in Townhouse's retail stores were based on 5-ounce tubes of tinting agent. Overfilled or underfilled tubes would result in improper paint mixes and, thus, colors that did not meet customer's expectations.

In consequence, Townhouse had to issue special instructions to all their retail people which would allow them to compensate for the short-weight tubes. The Townhouse purchasing agent made it clear that a new supplier would be sought if this problem recurred. Paint Tint's quality control department was immediately summoned to assist in determining the cause of the problem. They speculated the problem may be the result of adding a second and third shift to the first shift operations. The first shift ran from 6 A.M. until 2 P.M. The second shift from 2 P.M. to 10

P.M. and the third shift from 10 P.M. to 6 A.M. Many of the night shift employees were new and turnover in both of the later shifts was higher than for the first shift. To help in determining the problem the quality control staff sampled 50 tubes each hour and calculated the average weight in ounces of the sample tubes. The results of that sampling are presented in the following table.

Time	Weight (oz)	Time	Weight (oz)
6:00 A.M.	4.92	12:00 midnight	4.72
7:00	4.90	1:00 A.M.	4.64
8:00	4.84	2:00	4.64
9:00	4.76	3:00	4.72
10:00	4.74	4:00	5.00
11:00	4.82	5:00	4.72
12:00 noon	4.80	6:00	4.70
1:00 P.M.	4.84	7:00	4.84
2:00	4.84	8:00	4.88
3:00	4.97	9:00	4.96
4:00	5.01	10:00	5.00
5:00	5.00	11:00	4.98
6:00	5.00	12:00 noon	4.98
7:00	5.02	1:00 P.M.	4.89
8:00	5.03	2:00	5.00
9:00	4.98	3:00	5.04
10:00	5.00	4:00	5.10
11:00	4.86	5:00	5.00

Questions for Discussion

1. Analyze the data and determine the tube weight problem.

2. What control techniques might you employ to resolve this problem?

14.12 REFERENCES AND BIBLIOGRAPHY

1. Anthony, R. N., and Herzlinger, R., *Management Control in Nonprofit Organizations*, Homewood, IL: Irwin, 1975.
2. Anthony, R. H., and Reese, J. S., *Management Accounting*, Homewood, IL: Irwin, 1975.
3. Burch, J. G., and Strater, F. R.: *Information Systems: Theory and Practice*, Santa Barbara, CA: Wiley/Hamilton, 1974.
4. Cushing, B. E., *Accounting Information Systems and Business Organizations*, 2nd ed., Reading, MA: Addison-Wesley, 1978.
5. Davis, G. B., *Management Information Systems*, New York: McGraw-Hill, 1974.
6. DeCoster, D., and Schafer, E., *Management Accounting: A Decision Emphasis*, Santa Barbara, CA: Wiley/Hamilton, 1976.
7. Duncan, A. J., *Quality Control and Industrial Statistics*, 4th ed., Homewood, IL: Irwin, 1974.
8. Forrester, J., *Industrial Dynamics*, Cambridge, MA: MIT Press, 1961.
9. Gordon, J. R. M., *Perspectives* (Academy of Management), 5:19 (Fall 1977).
10. Horngren, C. T., *Cost Accounting: A Managerial Emphasis*, 4th ed., Englewood Cliffs, NJ: Prentice-Hall, 1977.
11. Horovitz, J. H., "Strategic Control: A New Task for Top Management," *Long Range Planning*, 12:2–7 (June 1979).
12. Mock, T. J., "Concepts of Information Value and Accounting," *The Accounting Review*, 46:765–778 (1971).
13. Plossl, G. W., "Tactics for Manufacturing Control," *Production and Inventory Management*, 15:21–30 (No. 3, 1974).
14. Schick, A., "The Road to PPB: The Stages of Budget Reform," *Public Administration Review*, 20:243–258 (1966).
15. Simon, H. A., *Administrative Behavior*, 2nd ed., New York: Macmillan, 1961.

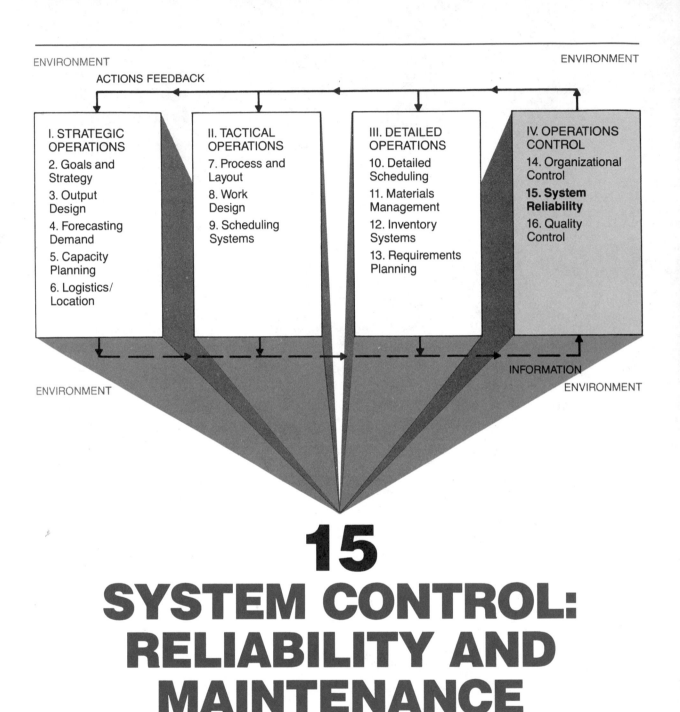

ENVIRONMENT   ENVIRONMENT

ACTIONS FEEDBACK

I. STRATEGIC OPERATIONS

2. Goals and Strategy

3. Output Design

4. Forecasting Demand

5. Capacity Planning

6. Logistics/ Location

II. TACTICAL OPERATIONS

7. Process and Layout

8. Work Design

9. Scheduling Systems

III. DETAILED OPERATIONS

10. Detailed Scheduling

11. Materials Management

12. Inventory Systems

13. Requirements Planning

IV. OPERATIONS CONTROL

14. Organizational Control

15. System Reliability

16. Quality Control

ENVIRONMENT   INFORMATION

                                                   ENVIRONMENT

15
SYSTEM CONTROL: RELIABILITY AND MAINTENANCE

15

LEARNING OBJECTIVES

By the completion of this chapter the student should

- Be familiar with the methods of enhancing a system's reliability.
- Know how to compute the reliability of elements in series and in parallel.
- Comprehend the difference between reliability, maintainability, and availability.
- Understand the difference between corrective and preventive maintenance and the advantages of each.
- Be able to determine the optimal time to replace an asset.
- Know how to use present value and other financial analysis tools to evaluate when to replace one asset with a different asset.
- Appreciate the concept of the group replacement option and be familiar with the methods of calculating its advantages over individual replacement.
- Realize the advantages of using standbys over maintenance and reliability approaches and know how to evaluate their economic impact.
- Understand the process for optimally sizing a repair crew.

In Chapter 14 we considered the general problem of organizational control from the manager's viewpoint. There we were concerned with controlling the organization and the "process" for producing the output. In this chapter we look specifically at control of the operations system. We consider the reliability of the productive system, how it can be enhanced, and ways to maintain it so it remains productive. As mentioned in Part I, organizations frequently do not maintain their operations system or do not modify it as the strategic focus of the organization changes, and their productivity suffers as a result.

Though our discussion here is oriented toward the reliability and maintenance of a *managerial* system, everything we say applies equally well to a product, since it must also be reliable and maintained. Again, the generic discussion easily lends itself to extension. Thus, the concepts in this chapter, if applied to products, could be considered an extension of the product and service design discussion of Part I.

Similar to the inventory problem.

Interestingly, many of the concepts we address here have the same nonlinear tradeoff form as the inventory problem, and some of the approaches used there will be adapted for use here.

We first address the general concept of reliability and the ways it is measured. We then discuss the maintenance function and contrast corrective maintenance with preventive maintenance. We consider the replacement problem of capital assets using examples from electronics and farming. We then look at the group versus individual replacement issue in a typing pool.

Our next major topic is a discussion of the use of standby equipment in a hair salon. We extend the discussion by using decision trees to evaluate risk and cost with standbys for a funeral home. Last, we consider the use of a repair crew for corrective maintenance in a queuing situation during the harvesting season.

Because of the importance of financial analysis in the replacement problem, we include an appendix to the chapter illustrating the financial topics of life cycle costing, leasing, payback, depreciation, taxes, and present value.

15.1 THE RELIABILITY CONCEPT

Reliability defined.

The **reliability** of a system is the probability that it will perform "properly" under certain predefined conditions. The definition of "properly" then gives rise to the consideration of the many and varied ways by which a system can fail, otherwise known as its "modes of failure."

> **Mode 1:** *Outright failure.* In this mode a key part breaks, the firm files for bankruptcy, and the tennis ball goes into the net.

> **Mode 2:** *Apparent failure.* The output enters final inspection bearing no resemblance whatever to the planned output, there is a large oil slick emerging from beneath your car, and the score is 15 to 0 in the bottom of the ninth, two out, no one on, two strikes, no balls.

Modes of failure.

Mode 3: *Insufficient performance.* "Chicago Slough" comes in fourth by a nose, highest bid is just what the product cost, Jimmy misses winning the $1,000,000 state lottery by one digit.

Mode 4: *Improper conditions.* The robbers hit the bank just *after* the armored car has taken the deposits, the dentist pulls the wrong tooth, the field goal is nullified by a flag on the play.

These modes illustrate the fact that there is usually one right way for a system to perform but many, many wrong ways. Hence, it should come as no surprise that systems consisting of many parts, each of which can fail in one or more ways, will probably be unreliable unless special precautions are taken. And, of course, this is especially true of systems composed of elements with a wide range of variability in their functioning, such as people. Since the majority of services are labor intensive, it would be expected that the reliability of services, at least in terms of a standard output, would not be as high as for machine-produced products. Although this is often the case, there are also many services in which the human element of the system can modify its performance so as to increase the reliability of the system as well. (This, for example, is the function of the staff in a final inspection operation.)

Reliability of services.

Approaches to Enhancing Reliability

Through experience, a number of ways have been developed to enhance the reliability of a system. Below are several alternatives available to management in dealing with the reliability problem.

- *Build redundant elements into the system.* (Section 15.2): This approach results in a dramatic improvement in system reliability but often significantly increases the cost of the system as well. In situations where the same element is used many times, one backup may suffice (e.g., *one* spare tire). Or, as in the human body, the system may be designed so that the backup is used in part of the normal functioning of the system as well (kidneys, eyes).

- *Increase element reliabilities.* (Section 15.2): Through special design features the reliability of the system may be enhanced. For example, special high quality materials may be used, such as self-lubricating bearings, or elements may be "overdesigned" to handle higher-than-expected loads [e.g., using thick-skinned customer relations (complaints) personnel]. Two considerations exist here: increasing the reliability of the *weakest* (most likely to fail) "link" in the system, and increasing the reliability of the *most critical* (highest expected cost) link in the system. These may well not be the same elements, and proper consideration should be given to each. In a vacuum cleaner, for example, the belt is the weakest link whereas the motor is the most critical. In some models, the vacuum cleaner will continue to draw air and dirt when the belt is broken but the brushes won't turn. With a motor failure, however, *nothing* works.

- *Improve working conditions.* (Section 15.2): On occasion, it is possible to increase the reliability of a system by improving the conditions under which it must perform. Reducing the load on a system, giving more frequent breaks, improving the quality of the environment (new oil for an engine, carpeting for an office, air conditioning for a plant), and other, similar attention may considerably extend the working life of the system's elements.

- *Conduct preventive maintenance.* (Sections 15.3 and 15.4): It may be worthwhile to plan, ahead of time, on shutting down the system at off-peak hours to conduct maintenance on elements that are at high risk (especially bottleneck machines such as computers). Such maintenance could consist of inspection, repair, or replacement. The costs of such programs vary considerably and their utility depends, in part, on the seriousness of a system breakdown.

- *Provide a standby system.* (Section 15.5): As an extreme of the redundant concept, another alternative is to make a complete replacement system available as a backup for a failed system ("pair and a spare" stockings). Many two-car families operate on this basis, using one dependable (or even new) car and a second, unreliable jalopy for transportation to and from work. If the jalopy fails, the good car is used until the old one can be fixed. To minimize the effective cost of such an expensive backup, it is typically used for other miscellaneous duties as well, such as around-town shopping, child chauffeuring, and so forth.

- *Speed the repair process.* (Section 15.6): The seriousness of a system failure may be minimized by providing sufficient facilities to repair it in case of a breakdown (extra buttons for clothes, extra needles for sewing machines). This approach is especially useful when the inherent reliability of the system is hard to increase. The repair speed can sometimes be increased by providing a larger, or higher quality, repair crew or facilities. It may also be possible to design the system for speed of repair by using, for example, modules that can be replaced quickly (television "works in a drawer") all at one time instead of having to identify the individual element that failed.

- *Isolate system elements:* At times it is possible to isolate critical or high-risk system elements from the rest of the system, at least for some period of time. In a production system, for example, it may be possible to provide storage between operations for the items being processed so that the failure of one operation in the system does not stop the functioning of all the operations downstream of it. Although it is expensive to provide such in-process storage, it may well be worthwhile from a reliability standpoint.

- *Accept the risk:* The final alternative we consider here is for the manager to simply accept the risk of failure. It may well be that all other alternatives appear too expensive in light of the effects of system failure. A particularly relevant topic in this regard concerns consumer product safety. The manager *must* decide at what point sufficient safety precautions have been taken in view of legal safety regulations and possible damage claims a consumer may bring against the organization.

15.2 INTERDEPENDENT (SERIES) VERSUS REDUNDANT (PARALLEL) ELEMENTS

If a system consists of two elements, one that works 60 percent of the time (has a "reliability" of 60 percent) and the other 40 percent of the time, then the reliability of the system is $0.60 \times 0.40 = 0.24$ or 24 percent if both elements must perform properly. Thus a system consisting of *interdependent* (or "series") elements has a combined reliability worse than any of its individual elements. Furthermore, if there are many elements, even of high reliability, the system reliability may still be poor.* Certainly, then, any common household item such as a sewing machine or radio consisting of at least 50 interdependent parts must have an extremely high part reliability, say 99.99 percent, in order for the device to operate most of the time. To an

Reliability of complex operations.

extent, the same holds true for organizations and department operations, but the situation is more complex. For instance, in an operations department, such as final assembly or check processing, there are a number of elements involved (people, machines, etc.), each with different reliabilities, and a number of ways (modes) the system can fail.

How, then, can an automobile, with many thousands of parts, function

Redundancy to increase reliability.

so reliably? There are three answers to that. For one thing, it may, indeed, not be so reliable. If you have ever owned an old car you have probably experienced the irritation of needing to fix something every time you drive it. Second, the car will "run" even if the radio does not work, or the lights, or even third gear. That is, not all the elements are in "series," per se. So the failure of one part does not necessarily lead to a failure of the whole system—just a portion of the system (perhaps critical, perhaps not).

Last, intelligent designers often build **redundancy** ("parallel" elements) into a system to *increase* its reliability. For example, our bodies contain numerous redundancies: redundant kidneys, eyes, hands, and so on. For example, with two eyes, seeing is easier, the field of vision is enlarged, and depth perception is possible. The loss of one eye reduces these advantages but does not render the system blind. The cardiovascular system of the body contains even more complex redundancy since it has the ability to rebuild substitutes for some injured and destroyed sections of the body.

Redundancy in automobiles.

Redundancy in an automobile is illustrated by multiple cylinders, dual headlights and taillights, spare tires, and dual brake systems (hydraulic and mechanical). Furthermore, in emergency situations there are usually even more backup systems available, at a cost. For example, if the brakes fail on your car while coming down a long, steep hill, the mechanical (parking) brakes can be used. If these also fail, the transmission can be shifted into

---

*For example, a seven-element system with element reliabilities of 0.9 will have a system reliability of $(0.9)^7 = 0.48$.

"low" to slow the car down. If this is insufficient, the ignition can be turned off (on some cars) to further slow the car. And if the emergency is serious enough, the car can be shifted into "reverse" or "park" to lock (and probably destroy) the transmission so the wheels will not turn. Dual circuitry in computers is another common example of redundancy.

Reliability for Elements in Series

Effect of two elements in series:

We can illustrate the effect on system reliability of multiple, interacting elements with the systems diagrammed in Figure 15.1. At the left, in Figure 15.1*a*, are two separate elements in **series**, *A* and *B*. In order for the system to work, both elements must operate properly (e.g., the car must start and the transmission must function). If the reliability (the probability of proper operation) of *A* and *B* are written as *R(A)* and *R(B)* then

$$\text{reliability of the system, } R = R(A \text{ and } B) = R(A)R(B) \tag{15.1}$$

if the operation of the two elements, *A* and *B*, are **independent** of each other. In the special case where $R(A) = R(B) = r$ the reliability of the system will be r^2.

Reliability of interdependent elements.

At the right of Figure 15.1 are shown seven identical elements in, we shall assume, a semiseries configuration. That is, *all* the elements must function properly in order for the system to function properly. In this case the reliability of the system will be r^7.

Series reliability curve.

If *r*, for example, is 90 percent, then the reliability, *R*, of the two-element system as a whole (Figure 15.1*a*) would be (0.9)(0.9) = 0.81 and the reliability of the seven-element system (Figure 15.1*b*) would be $(0.9)^7 = 0.48$, both considerably less than 0.9. Figure 15.2 illustrates this degradation in reliability, *R*, as the number of interdependent (series type) elements, *n*, increases for a number of typical values of *r*. At the top of the figure is the curve for a one-element system whose reliability *R* is equal to the reliability of the element itself, *r*. Thus, at the far right where *r* = 100 percent, *R* = 100 percent and at the far left where *r* = 80 percent, *R* also is 80 percent. The next curve down represents a 10-element (series or semiseries) system. Again at the right, if every element has a reliability *r* of 100 percent the reliability of the system *R* will also be 100 percent. But if the reliability of each element *r* is

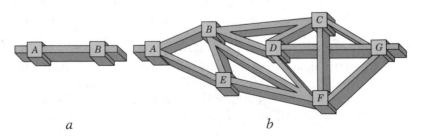

a   *b*

Figure 15.1 Multiple-element series systems. (*a*) Two elements. (*b*) Multiple, interdependent elements.

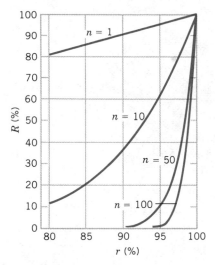

Figure 15.2 Series system reliability.

only 90 percent then R is $(0.9)^{10}$ = 35 percent. And for element reliabilities of 80 percent R is only 11 percent.

Reliability for Elements in Parallel

The effect of **parallel** elements (redundancy) on a system's reliability is illustrated in Figure 15.3. Here, if A fails to work, B can take over and vice versa. For the system as a whole to fail, both A *and* B must fail, which is unlikely. The reliability of the system, R, in this case of, again independent, elements is

$$R = R(A \text{ or } B) = R(A) + R(B) - R(A \text{ and } B) \tag{15.2}$$

Venn diagram.

Since, in calculating $R(A)$, we have included those times when B is also working [$R(A$ and $B)$] and in the calculation of $R(B)$ we have included those times when A is also working [$R(A$ and $B)$], we have therefore included those times when both are properly functioning twice. To avoid this double count, we must subtract one $R(A$ and $B)$ out. This is shown in the **Venn diagram** of Figure 15.4.

The reliability of element A is given by the left circle, $R(A)$, and for element B by the right circle $R(B)$. If, as in the last subsection, *both* A and B must operate properly for the system to work (series), this reliability is

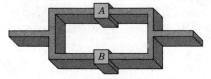

Figure 15.3 A parallel redundant system.

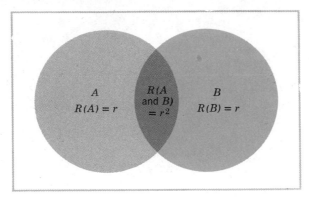

Figure 15.4 The reliability of a two-element system.

given by the cross-hatched area of overlap, $R(A$ and $B)$ or, for independent elements with identical reliabilities r, simply r^2 (as explained earlier).

But if the system will work when *either* A or B are operating properly, then $R(A$ or $B)$ is given by the total area enclosed by circles A and B. This area would normally be $R(A) + R(B)$ but, because A and B are not **mutually exclusive** (i.e., A's working does not keep B from working and vice versa) there is some overlap in their areas and this area is counted twice in the term $R(A) + R(B)$ and thus must be subtracted out once. The overall resulting reliability of the redundant, parallel system is then

Mutually exclusive elements.

$$R(A) + R(B) - R(A \text{ and } B) = r + r - r^2 = 2r - r^2 \qquad (15.3)$$

A simpler logic.

Another, easier, way to obtain this result uses the following logic: The reliability of the system is

$$1 - \text{prob}(A \text{ and } B \text{ both fail})$$

where prob means probability. The probability that A will fail is $1 - R(A)$ or $1 - r$ and the probability for B is $1 - R(B)$ or $1 - r$ again. The resulting reliability of the system is therefore

$$1 - (1 - r)^2 = 1 - 1 + 2r - r^2 = 2r - r^2$$

This simple approach can easily be extended to any number of elements. For example, with n elements in parallel, all with the same reliability r, we have

$$R = 1 - (1 - r)^n \qquad (15.4)$$

The resulting reliability figures for various values of n and r are plotted, in a fashion similar to Figure 15.2, in Figure 15.5. Note now that for three elements in parallel with reliabilities of only 0.9 each, the system reliability is enhanced to

$$R = 1 - (1 - 0.9)^3 = 1 - 0.1^3 = 1 - 0.001 = 0.999$$

or only one expected failure in a thousand trials.

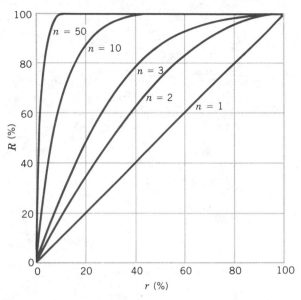

Figure 15.5 Parallel system reliability.

15.3 THE MAINTENANCE FUNCTION

Maintenance for reliability.

Although the design and installation of an organization's operating system, consisting of facilities, equipment, materials, supplies, and staff, is a large and expensive undertaking, the trouble and expense does not end there. To keep these resources productive and reliable, constant maintenance must be performed by way of repair, rest, lubrication, replacement, inspection, and so forth. Belts wear down, grease wears thin, valves tighten up, corrosion sets in, parts crack and break, people get bored and tired, paint peels, pipes leak, and on and on. All of these items must be repaired or replaced if allowed to reach a point of failure, or failure must be prevented or retarded through certain activities if the system is to remain reliable. This is the general role of maintenance.

In the factory there is usually a maintenance engineer or manager whose job it is to keep the buildings and equipment in proper working order. In other organizations the maintenance function may be performed at random (as things break down) or by contract to an external party, or in a number of other ways.

Corrective versus preventive maintenance.

Regardless of whether the maintenance task is performed formally or informally, the function is essential. The proper role of maintenance is not only to *repair* disabled resources when they fail, termed **corrective maintenance (CM),** but to prevent their breakdown or poor performance as well. This idea of prevention, similar to our notion of preventive control, is termed **preventive maintenance (PM)** and is accomplished through inspection, service, and replacement of parts before they fail (all topics to be discussed in more

"Go ahead, hate me. It's included in the bill."

(Copyright © 1978, The Kiplinger Washington Editors, Inc.)

detail later). When equipment is designed and built so that it tends to remain trouble-free and can be easily repaired when necessary, the system is said to have good **maintainability** [3].

Maintainability.

Maintainability is sometimes measured by the mean time to repair (**MTTR**) the product, where a smaller value is better. A similar measure can be defined for a product's reliability where the mean time before (or between) failures (**MTBF**) is measured rather than the probability of the product failing within a given period. By combining these measures, an overall measure of a product's **availability** for service may be obtained

"Availability."

$$availability = \frac{MTBF}{MTBF + MTTR} \qquad (15.5)$$

For example, if a computer terminal has a mean time between failures of 1000 hours and a mean time to repair of four days (96 hours), then its availability will be 1000/1096 = 91 percent. If the repair time can be cut in half (48 hours), the terminal's availability would increase to 1000/1048 = 95 percent.

The Maintenance Problem

The problem facing the operations manager concerned about maintenance is, as always, how to minimize the total costs to the organization. Idled production due to an unanticipated breakdown can be very expensive; but so can a large maintenance crew* who frequently sit idle, as well as down-

Maintenance cost.

---

*The queuing situation, to be handled later in this chapter, is clear here. A service crew (facility) waits for machines (or some sort of "customer") to break down and require servicing.

time due to extensive preventive maintenance. The general cost curves facing the manager are illustrated in Figure 15.6. The "quality of maintenance" axis refers to a combination of elements such as the size and ability of the repair crew, the frequency of inspection, and the frequency of replacing critical system elements through PM. As this quality goes up, the cost typically goes up even faster, while the cost of breakdowns, both in terms of number of failures and duration of idled equipment due to failure, decreases. At some point, as illustrated in the colored "total cost" curve, a minimum is reached. This is the point the manager is trying to locate.

Another way of interpreting the "quality of maintenance" axis is as a frequency of PM scale, with less frequent PM (annually) on the left and more frequent PM (monthly) on the right. Then the breakdown cost will be high and the PM cost low on the left and vice versa on the right. In the midrange PM periods (quarterly) the total costs may tend to be minimal.

In many cases only a subjective estimate of this point is ever attempted, and even that is typically based on having experienced, or not experienced, a recent breakdown. Of necessity, some elements of the cost of a breakdown are subjective (such as the cost of ill will), but still many other aspects of the costs can be obtained and analyzed fairly accurately.

Preventive Versus Corrective Maintenance

The expense of PM.

As noted earlier, repairing systems *before* they fail is called *preventive maintenance* (PM) and after they fail, *corrective maintenance* (CM). Performing preventive maintenance is an expensive undertaking. The commitment to regularly incurring the high costs of skilled labor, shutting down a productive system on purpose, and replacing parts that still have some life in them is not a light one to make. Besides, there will *still* be breakdowns that happen when the system is needed—in some cases possibly even due to something that was done during PM! Let us consider the advantages.

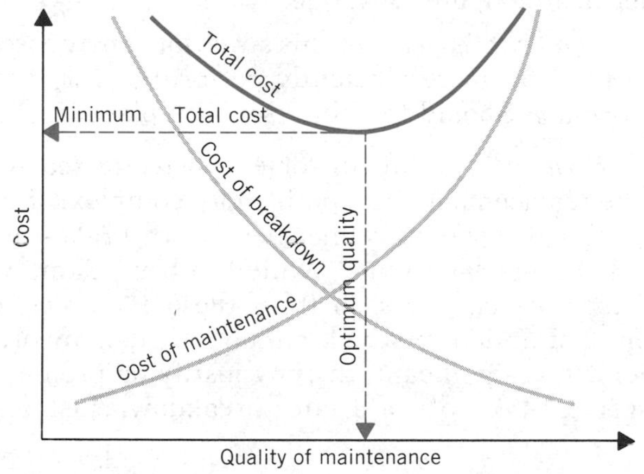

Figure 15.6 The cost factors in maintenance.

The advantage of PM.

PM repairs are typically much cheaper than breakdown repairs. When a system fails, many other elements of the system besides the failed element, if there is one, are usually damaged in the process. For example, if a $50 motor freezes up it may destroy a $1000 pump that it powers. Even if a part does not completely fail, as one element in a system begins to deteriorate it puts more of a load on other elements in the system—a load that they typically were not designed to accommodate. If alcoholism begins to affect the comptroller of a business, purchasing will start having more trouble getting materials, finance will have problems with its credit, and so forth.

Murphy's law.

In addition to the repair costs, there are often the much greater costs of idled production. In some cases this loss must be made up by overtime—perhaps at time and a half or possibly even double time. As *Murphy's law* states: "What *can* go wrong *will* go wrong." And it will go wrong in exactly the worst possible way, at the worst possible time, and in the worst possible place. PM, on the other hand, can be scheduled for a convenient time, such as at night or during lunch.

Inapplicability of PM.

PM is not, of course, always desirable. If breakdown repairs are hardly more costly, overall, than PM repairs, then there is probably not a sufficient reason for PM. Or, if other alternatives are easily available when a breakdown occurs, such as standby equipment, then PM is unnecessary from a continuity-of-production viewpoint.

15.4 THE REPLACEMENT PROBLEM*

When only an economic problem.

When a system's critical element is easily reached and a breakdown is no great inconvenience, the replacement problem is simply one of economics and usually arises in either of the following forms (both of which are discussed in more detail further on):

1. *Optimum life:* The situation here is anticipating the most economic future time to replace a current asset (typically, a machine) with another identical, but new, one.

2. *Value of a "challenger:"* In this situation a new asset has become available that can more efficiently perform a task that a current asset is performing. Should the old asset be replaced?

When inconvenience and trouble are involved.

However, when it is difficult or expensive to reach the critical system element, the replacement decision is more complex. "Since we got the tires off, lady, mebbe we should reline those worn brakes, too. Save ya a lot of trouble and expense later on." "While I'm here, Sam, why don'cha replace the filter, too." As can be seen from these examples, early replacements derive from a situation in which either the labor involved in *getting to* the critical element is significant, thereby justifying premature replacement, or the inconvenience or cost of a later breakdown justifies the early replacement.

*Much of this section is based on Terborgh [11].

A common example of this situation is when a large number of, typically, low-priced items are more and more likely to fail with age. This is called the **group replacement** decision and relies heavily on knowledge of the item's lifetime distribution. We will investigate somewhat later a number of the various possible replacement policies (such as item versus group replacement), but first let us consider the simpler economic policies.

Group replacement.

Optimal Life

Minimize the average annual cost.

The analysis to determine the optimum life of an asset is one of trying to find that replacement cycle which minimizes the average annual cost of the asset. Typically, the asset deteriorates over its life, resulting in higher operating costs and loss of resale value. The behavior of these costs with asset age is illustrated in Figure 15.7. As the age of the asset increases, the operating cost increases due to reduced efficiency, wear, and maintenance. And, for much the same reasons, the salvage value of the asset decreases, but by a steadily lessening amount, year by year. In some particular year the total annual cost of the asset will be a minimum—if possible, we would like to use the asset only for *that* particular time period, but we generally cannot. Following that year the costs start rising and after a few years we have gotten "the best years" (in terms of the average annual cost) out of the asset and it is uneconomical to hold the asset beyond that point.

Identify the best years.

The simplest way to find the optimum life is to *accumulate* the total annual costs and find that year for which the average cost (cumulative total annual cost divided by number of years) is the lowest. This calculation procedure is illustrated in the following example.

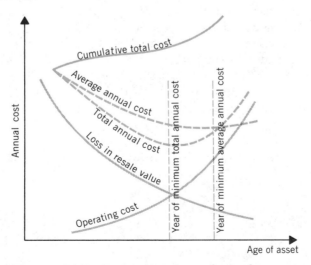

Figure 15.7 Determination of single asset optimum life.

Quadro Stereo

The costs for a particular quadraphonic stereo used for background music in retail stores are listed in Table 15.1. We see that the lowest total annual cost for the stereo, $150, occurs in year 3. However, the *average* annual cost through year 3 (years 1, 2, and 3 combined) is $176, higher than the average annual cost through year 4, $172. But by year 5 the average annual cost has again risen to $176, and since this is an increase, the stereo is not worth holding through this year.

If desired, interest and present value corrections (see 15.7 Appendix) can also be incorporated into the figures. The point also might be noted that expected future occurrences should be factored into consideration. For example, if a retailer planned to terminate business after three years and sell the stereos, then the $172 average cost would not be the appropriate figure for selecting the *most economical* stereo to purchase. Rather, a three-year horizon should be used, resulting in $176. In general, costs should be minimized only over the horizon of expected need for the asset. Similarly, if a much more efficient asset is expected to enter the market in the following year, perhaps the best strategy would be to delay the purchase one year and lease an acceptable asset in the interim.

The optimum life problem exists for all operations investments where the asset, unlike an antique, loses value with age and wear. On occasion, such assets may be replaced prematurely if a newer type of asset becomes available, as discussed in the next subsection.

Value of a Challenger

This situation deals with the arrival of a new type of asset (called a *challenger*), which could replace the existing asset (called the *defender*) with a (typically) lower operating cost. The problem is that the challenger is expensive. Also, a considerable amount may have been paid for the defender and its book value may still be high. Managers are reluctant to part with a like-new asset unless they can obtain a good resale price for it on the used asset market; to the extent that they *cannot* the difference is called a *sunk cost*. It is important to realize that sunk costs should not enter the replacement decision; only expected future costs are relevant.

New challengers and sunk costs.

Table 15.1   Establishing the Optimum Life of a Stereo

Year	0	1	2	3	4	5	6
1. Resale value	600	450	370	320	290	270	260
2. Loss in resale value	—	150	80	50	30	20	10
3. Repair cost	—	70	80	100	130	170	220
4. Total annual cost	—	220	160	150	160	190	230
5. Cumulative total cost	—	220	380	530	690	880	1110
6. Average annual cost	—	220	190	176	172	176	185

For example, suppose you bought a labor-saving machine and paid a considerable amount for it, but felt it was well worth it. Then a month later, a new type of machine becomes available that can do the same job at almost no operating cost at all and overnight makes your machine worthless. If the cost to do the job with the new machine, considering all acquisition, resale, and operating costs, is less than the operating cost alone of the old machine, then the new machine should be bought. What about the money you poured into the purchase of the original machine? That is a sunk cost and should be ignored. There is no point in using the original machine if another one will have less overall costs for the duration of need. Consider the following example.

Old Mac's Tomato Farm

Old Mac, owner and operations manager of Old Mac's Tomato Farm, is eagerly looking forward to retiring after three more years. Five years ago he purchased a mechanical tomato picker for $70,000 when they were new on the market. The machine's operating cost was $5000 last year and has steadily been increasing at the rate of $1000 each year. For a new type of harvesting machine its performance is not bad. It probably only destroys about $10,000 worth of tomatoes per year. Mac figures the machine would probably bring about $20,000 today on the used market and will bring about $4000 less each year until it is worn out (in 20,000/4000 = 5 years).

A "second-generation" tomato picker has recently appeared on the market for $50,000. It is said to be so gentle in picking tomatoes that none at all are harmed and operating costs are only $3000 per year for at least the first five years. Mac has been considering buying one of these machines and then selling it for, he estimates, perhaps $35,000, when he retires. Money is worth 10 percent to Mac.

Analysis

In this, as in probably the great majority of replacement situations, the crucial factor in the decision is the *horizon of need*. For an indefinite, continuing horizon, one decision may be best whereas for a sharply abbreviated horizon an entirely different decision may be appropriate. In this case, if Old Mac changes his retirement plans by even a year this may alter the optimal decision. For example, suppose he decides not to retire in three years after all (when he will be 62) but to wait until he is 65. The crucial question in that case would be how to replace the worn out current machine in that last, sixth year.

For the existing situation we can simply compare the present value of all costs and benefits for the three-year horizon. The analysis is given in Table 15.2. The present value calculations are conducted in the same manner as explained in Section 15.7 Appendix, using the present value table in Appendix A. The conclusion is that Old Mac should definitely buy the challenger (new tomato picking machine) for a present value savings of about $25,000 (i.e., 36 − 11 = 25).

Table 15.2 Present Value of Costs Comparison for Old Mac

Item ($1000s)			Present Value Factor	Present Value ($1000s)
Alternative 1: Keep the Defender				
Year 1	Operating cost:	−6	0.9091	−5.4546
	Tomato damage:	−10	0.9091	−9.0910
Year 2	Operating cost:	−7	0.8264	−5.7848
	Tomato damage:	−10	0.8264	−8.2640
Year 3	Operating cost:	−8	0.7513	−6.0104
	Tomato damage:	−10	0.7513	−7.5130
	Resale:	+8	0.7513	+6.0104
	Total:			−36.1074
Alternative 2: Purchase Challenger, Sell Defender				
Year 0	Purchase:	−50	1.0000	−50.0000
	Sell:	+20	1.0000	+20.0000
Year 1	Operating cost:	−3	0.9091	−2.7273
Year 2	Operating cost:	−3	0.8264	−2.4792
Year 3	Operating cost:	−3	0.7513	−2.2539
	Resale:	+35	0.7513	+26.2955
	Total:			−11.1649

Another way of calculating this present value savings is to consider only the yearly cost *savings* of the challenger over the defender. Thus, in year 2, for example, the net savings is

$$
\begin{array}{ll}
\text{Operating cost:} & 7 - 3 = 4 \\
\text{Tomato damage:} & \underline{10} \\
\text{Net savings:} & 14
\end{array}
$$

By applying the present value factors to these annual savings (year zero would still be a loss) and adding them, the same $25,000 answer would be obtained.

Another approach to the investment problem is provided by the Machinery and Allied Products Institute (**MAPI**). The MAPI system is composed of a number of worksheets, graphs, and a formula for easy application by managers. The result is an adjusted, one-year, after-tax rate of return relative to making the investment as compared to deferring the investment for one year. For further details consult Reference 12.

The MAPI system.

Group Versus Individual Replacement

The group replacement problem, one form of *preventive maintenance*, arises in situations where the cost or trouble associated with a replacement upon

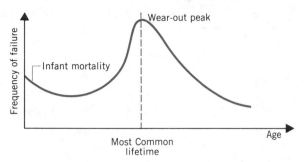

Figure 15.8 A typical failure rate distribution.

A number of policies.

failure is very high. A number of policies may be considered: replace only defective items, replace defectives plus all those exceeding x hours of service, replace all the items.

Failure rates and infant mortality.

The most important set of data needed to address the problem is the **failure rate distribution** of the item in question. A common distribution is shown in Figure 15.8. Here there is an initially high failure rate, called **infant mortality,** followed by a drop in frequency until a fairly common wear-out period is reached where the failure frequency increases again and then finally tails off. The exact nature of this curve depends on the item in question. In some cases the infant mortality peak is almost nonexistent whereas in other cases the wear-out peak is missing.

Sensitive, hard to balance.

The infant mortality peak is typified by situations in which the item is highly sensitive or very difficult to adjust or balance properly and most of the failures occur from an inaccurate previous repair. If, as time goes on, fewer and fewer items are still operating, then no wear-out peak will appear.

The wear-out peak is characterized by a few items failing before this period and a few afterward, but most of the items failing right around this period. The curve of Figure 15.8 may even be considered a human mortality graph in a society with a rather high infant mortality rate.

Nimble Fingers Typing Service

Jane Nimble operates a typing service that employs 50 typists, each using an identical typewriter. The typewriters are older models, which use loose ribbons rather than snap-in cartridges, and so the ribbon changing procedure is fairly time-consuming. Because many of the typists cannot change the ribbon, Jane, as operations manager, personally changes all of them when they run out. Jane's typists vary in typing speeds and accuracy; hence, ribbons are used up at varying rates, as shown in Table 15.3.

Jane estimates that the cost of interruption of her work and the idle time of the typist while a ribbon is being removed and replaced is $10. The ribbon cost is $2. One of Jane's typists has suggested that, rather than use only corrective maintenance and replacing the ribbons when they run out, per-

Table 15.3 Failure Rate Distribution of Typewriter Ribbons

Ribbon life, days	1[a]	2	3	4	5	6	7
Probability of "failure" during the day	.15	.05	.10	.15	.20	.30	.05

[a]Early failure due to defective ribbons.

haps preventive maintenance should also be employed, replacing all the ribbons every evening, or every other evening. Someone could be trained to do the job at a cost of $1 per change since the machines would be idle anyway. Does the additional replace-each-night or every-other-night policy make sense?

Analysis

The *cost of the current policy* can be computed by first calculating the expected life of a ribbon. This is

$$E(\text{life}) = .15(1) + .05(2) + .10(3) + .15(4) + .20(5) + .3(6) + .05(7)$$
$$= .15 + .1 + .3 + .6 + 1.0 + 1.8 + .35$$
$$= 4.3 \text{ days}$$

The current policy therefore calls for, on the average, replacement of all ribbons at $12 each ($10 + $2 ribbon cost) every 4.3 days for a cost of

$$\$12 \times 50 = \$600$$

or, on a per day basis

$$\frac{\$600}{4.3} = \underline{\$139.53} \text{ per day}$$

Replacing at the end of each day would result in costs of

$$
\begin{array}{lr}
\text{failures during day} = .15 \times 50 \times \$12 = & \$90 \\
\text{plus end of day replacement of all} = \quad 50 \times \$3 = & \underline{\$150} \\
\text{Total} & \$240
\end{array}
$$

or

$$\text{daily cost} = \underline{\$240}$$

Replacing at the end of every other day would result in costs of

$$
\begin{array}{lr}
\text{failures during day 1} = .15 \times 50 \times \$12 & = \$90.00 \\
\text{failures during day 2} = .05 \times 50 \times \$12 & = 30.00 \\
\text{day 1 replacements failing in day 2} = .15 \times (.15 \times 50) \times \$12 & = 13.50 \\
\text{end of day 2 replacement of all} = 50 \times \$3 & = \underline{150.00} \\
\text{Total} = & \$283.50
\end{array}
$$

or

$$\text{daily cost} = \frac{\$283.50}{2} = \underline{141.75} \text{ per day}$$

Therefore, for this problem, replacement every evening, or every other evening, are not better policies. (As an exercise, what would the average daily cost be of ribbon replacement every *third* night?)

The policies considered in the Nimble Fingers example were only three of several policies. Jane could also have used a policy of replacing those each night which appeared more than half used, or any other plan. Because the calculations become unmanageable very quickly, this problem is very amenable to a simulation solution. Through simulation, exact times until "failure" may be employed rather than "nearest day" times. Once a model has been developed for a replacement problem any number of potential policies can be tested.

The replacement problem occurs in a number of operations settings but always where the cost of group replacement is much less than that of individual replacement. This is usually because the items are hard to get to, require special tools or equipment, or idle other productive resources. Examples that are seen frequently are the replacement of light bulbs; supplies such as paper, ink, toner in machines; products in vending machines; fast-wearing parts in certain equipment; and so forth.

15.5 STANDBYS TO INCREASE RELIABILITY

If the investment cost is not excessive and **standby** equipment can be quickly moved in to take over for regular equipment breakdowns, then using standbys may be the most economical route for increasing system reliability. Let us demonstrate with an example.

Beauty and Beast's Hair Salon

Bill Beauty and Bob Beast own and manage a beauty salon near the upper-middle class suburb of a large city. The salon has a dozen relatively new hair "Kurl-n-Dri"ers, which provide the majority of the salon's income. Bob has kept track of the number of these curler-dryers out of order every day since the salon opened. Forty percent of the time none were out of order; 30 percent, one was out; 20 percent, two; and 10 percent, three. Considering this history, Bob has wondered if it might be worthwhile to keep one or even two or three spare curler-dryers on hand to recoup the inevitable $20 daily loss of income when a regular machine is out of order. The curler-dryers cost $5 a day, on the average, over their short lifetimes.

Analysis

By use of the following expected value formula we may analyze each of Bob's possible operations alternatives.

$$E(L) = \sum_{n=0}^{3} p_n(n - s)c \qquad (15.6)$$

where $E(L)$ = the expected loss

p_n = the probability n curler-dryers are out of order

s = the number of spares available *and used* as replacements

c = the loss per unavailable curler-dryer

Current Situation (0 spares). The current expected loss per day is

$$.4(0) + .3(1)(\$20) + .2(2)\$20 + .1(3)\$20 = \$20$$

One Spare. The expected revenue loss is

$$.4(0) + .3(1 - 1)\$20 + .2(2 - 1)\$20 + .1(3 - 1)\$20 \quad = \quad \$8$$
$$\text{the cost of the spare} \quad = \quad \underline{\$5}$$
$$\text{total daily cost} \quad \$13$$

Two Spares. The expected revenue loss is

$$.4(0) + .3(1 - 1)\$20 + .2(2 - 2)\$20 + .1(3 - 2)\$20 \quad = \quad \$2$$
$$\text{cost of spares} \quad = \underline{\$10}$$
$$\text{total daily cost} \quad \$12 \text{ (best)}$$

Three Spares. The expected revenue loss is

$$.4(0) + .3(1 - 1)\$20 + .2(2 - 2)\$20 + .1(3 - 3)\$20 \quad = \quad 0$$
$$\text{cost of spares} \quad = \underline{\$15}$$
$$\text{total daily cost} \quad \$15$$

It is clear that four or more spares would be unnecessary. Thus, the best policy is to keep two spares handy and reduce current losses from $20 a day to $12 for an $8 per day savings.

The "newsboy" problem again.

Note that this problem is very similar to the "newsboy" problem described earlier in the inventory chapter. The marginal approach used there will also solve this problem, but the variables must be redefined because the situation is not quite the same. Let p now represent the probability that *at least* one more curler-dryer will be needed. Since there is no "profit" to consider in this example, we look at the costs saved by having a unit available (or equivalently, the cost incurred by underordering spares—the $20 loss of income). The cost of overordering spares is $5. Then we add spares until the expected cost saved is equal to the expected cost incurred

$$\$20p \geq \$5(1 - p)$$

or

$$p \geq \frac{5}{25} = 0.2$$

At $N = 2$ the cumulative probability in Table 15.4 still meets the minimal value of $p = 0.2$, but at 3 the cumulative probability is now too small, thus two spares is the answer.

Importance of a spare.

This type of conclusion is typical of operations problems. Often just one spare will significantly improve the production system; the spare may be raw material, equipment, finished goods, or staff.

Table 15.4 Marginal Solution

No. Ordered, N	Probability	Cumulative Probability (of needing N or more)
0	0.4	1.0
1	0.3	0.6
2	0.2	0.3
3	0.1	0.1

Decision Trees with Standbys

Comparing reliability alternatives. Earlier, in Chapter 5, we looked at the use of *decision trees* to aid in capacity decisions with risk involved. Decision trees are also useful in many other areas and especially for reliability considerations. The following example illustrates some of the risk-cost tradeoffs available to the manager in handling system reliability problems.

The Phlashy Phuneral Home

I. M. Macabre, operations manager for Phlashy Phuneral, has total responsibility for the operation of Phlashy Phuneral's latest model Cadillac hearse, which is used in funeral processions. Being the fanciest funeral home in a small (but wealthy) town, Phlashy has need of only one hearse but it must be absolutely the latest model available or else Phlashy Phuneral's reputation is dead (so to speak). I. M. Macabre has three choices in guaranteeing the operation of the latest model hearse for a funeral.

1. He can keep the company hearse in top condition and risk about one chance in a hundred that it will be unavailable due to a breakdown just when it is needed. In such a case he feels the future lost sales to the company and other costs due to humiliation and such would amount to $1 million.

2. He can put a local garage mechanic on a personal retainer for $2000 a year and have only one chance in ten that the mechanic could not fix the hearse in time for the funeral.

3. He could buy a second, identical hearse as a standby which could find sufficient additional use to reduce the extra cost to $8000.

Analysis

I. M. Macabre's alternatives are sketched in Figure 15.9. As can be seen, with a backup system (alternatives 2 and 3) the expected cost of the potential million dollar loss is reduced to a very small amount—so small that the cost of the backup becomes the major consideration in the decision. Since the mechanic is only $2000 compared to the $8000 for the second hearse, the mechanic is the best alternative.

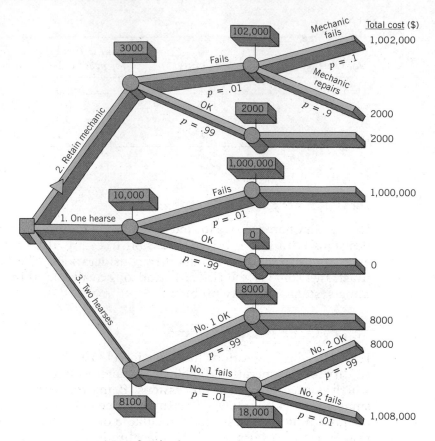

Figure 15.9 Macabre's decision alternatives.

It is instructive to also consider other values of the probability of hearse failure. The costs under the three alternatives for various probabilities of failure are given in Table 15.5. The best alternative depends on the probability of failure, alternatives 1 and 2 being equivalent at a probability of .00222. . . . In this example alternative 3 cannot be "best" irrespective of the probabilities, although it could be for lower values of hearse cost.

Table 15.5 Macabre's Expected Costs Under Various Probabilities of Failure

	P(Fail)		
Alternative	*.001*	*.01*	*.10*
1	1,000	10,000	100,000
2	2,100	3,000	12,000
3	8,001	8,100	18,000

Other uses of
decision trees.

Since the decision tree concept was specifically developed for the consideration of risk, it is particularly useful for decisions regarding the reliability of operations. It can help in the analysis of providing standby machines, carrying spare parts, using "floating" personnel (e.g., floor nurses), employing larger repair crews, and so forth.

15.6 CORRECTIVE MAINTENANCE USING A REPAIR CREW

Queuing theory to
size repair crews.

If a corrective maintenance (CM) system is adopted, one of the major issues is that of the size of the maintenance staff. When a machine or system fails, operations are generally either stopped or severely hampered. Keeping a large maintenance staff ready for repairs will reduce this idle or "downtime" but only at a rather high fixed cost of supporting that staff. *Queuing theory* represents one approach to this maintenance problem. System breakdowns can be perceived as "customers" arriving for service and the repair crew represents the servicing facility or facilities. The form of this problem differs from that presented in Chapter 10 in that the breakdowns occur in a *limited number* of items, such as machines or workers, and, hence, the queue of items waiting for service cannot grow beyond some maximum value (e.g., if you have only six typewriters it is impossible to have any more than six breakdowns at one time).

Queuing situation
and assumptions.

First, we let M denote the finite number of identical "machines," λ *each* machine's "arrival" (breakdown) rate, and μ the service rate (as in Chapter 10). The same situation and assumptions discussed in Chapter 10 apply here (no jockeying; first come, first served; random arrivals and service; etc.). The only difference in this situation is that the population of customers is not infinite but limited to M. Then the expected length of the queue of machines waiting for service is given in Figures 15.10, 15.11, and 15.12 for the situation of having $K = 1$ repairman (or crew), $K = 5$ repairmen (each of whom would work on a separate machine), and $K = 10$ repairmen, respectively.

Hayseed Harvesting

One of the more common scenes around family-sized farms in the last few years has been the arrival, somewhat before harvesting season, of an agent representing the owner of *very* large harvesting equipment—equipment whose price is in the neighborhood of $200,000 or more! This equipment can, in the course of hours, completely harvest a farmer's entire crop at the optimum harvesting time, thus sparing the farmers the risk of weather turning bad before they can finish harvesting the crop. Such large equipment is too expensive for a single farmer, but entrepreneurs invest in such machines and then contract with *many* farmers to harvest their fields, thus increasing the utilization of the equipment so as to exceed the breakeven point. Clearly, it is mandatory that equipment be available for harvesting during those periods for which contracts have been signed. This requires a repairman to

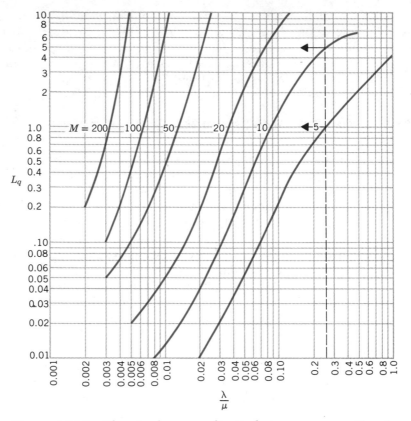

Figure 15.10 The single-server limited-source queue, $K = 1$. (*Source.* Adapted by permission from Efraim Turban and Jack R. Meredith, *Fundamentals of Management Science*, 2nd ed. (Dallas: Business Publications, 1981) p. 496.)

accompany the machines during their work since standby equipment is too expensive.

Suppose a very sensitive, specialized type of machine owned by Hayseed Harvesting is known to break down randomly but at the average rate of every 4 hours. Servicing by the repairman also varies randomly but requires an hour, on the average. For an upcoming one-day contract with Farmer Jones, the operations manager of Hayseed has decided that five of these specialized machines will be continuously required to harvest the crop. But if he sends only five, and a repairman, the machines will spend much of their time waiting for repairs and the harvest won't be finished by the end of the day. How many should the manager therefore send?

Figure 15.10 for one repairman can help here. The variables are

$\lambda = 1$ breakdown/4 hr $= 0.25$/hr
$\mu = 1$ repair/1 hr $\quad = 1$/hr

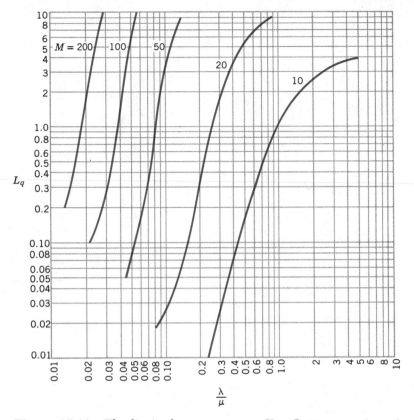

L_q

$\dfrac{\lambda}{\mu}$

Figure 15.11   The limited source queue, $K = 5$. (*Source*. Adapted by permission from Efraim Turban and Jack R. Meredith, *Fundamentals of Management Science*, 2nd ed. (Dallas: Business Publications, 1981) p. 497.)

Therefore $\lambda/\mu = 0.25$. At $\lambda/\mu = 0.25$ on the graph a dashed vertical line has been drawn. As can be seen, it intersects the curve $M = 5$ machines at a queue length of 1.0. This means that by sending five machines, one will always be in queue for service, on the average, with another *or less* being repaired, leaving three for harvesting. If two extra are also sent to make up for this slack, they too will probably break down and require repair. Thus, many more than simply *two* extra will be required. From the graph it is seen that the vertical line intersects the curve $M = 10$ machines at $L_q = 5$. This then says that even with 10 machines, on the average, 5 will be waiting in queue, and 1 in service, leaving 4 available for harvesting.

Another alternative, clearly, is to employ more repairmen. We can see, from Figure 15.11 that if $K = 5$ repairmen were to accompany the $M = 10$ machines the queue length would reduce to 0.012, but this solution is too expensive. Suppose instead an inexpensive "helper" is hired to aid the repairman, thereby reducing the average repair time to 48 minutes or 0.8

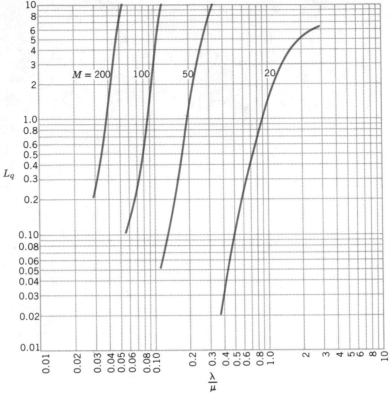

Figure 15.12   The limited-source queue, $K = 10$.

hours. Then $\mu = 1/0.8$ or 1.25/hr and $\lambda/\mu = 0.2$. From Figure 15.10 we find that $L_q = 4$ at $M = 10$ machines. The result is therefore that five or more machines, on the average, will be harvesting. For other values of M and K the tables of Peck and Hazlewood are recommended [10]. A simulation of the situation could also be conducted to gain insight into the problem.

This situation is a very common one in operations management and occurs in service, as well as product, organizations such as police and fire departments and ambulance and hospital services.

15.7 APPENDIX: FINANCIAL ASPECTS OF EQUIPMENT REPLACEMENT

Life Cycle Costing

Life cycle costing now favored over "low bid."

While it is found less often in capital procurement procedures of private organizations than it is in state and local governments and in not-for-profit organizations, the "low bid" decision rule is still widely utilized. The *low bid* rule states simply that the vendor submitting the bid with the lowest initial purchase price is awarded the order. The federal government, through the Department of Defense and other organizations (such as the Logistics

Management Institute), is now, however, encouraging the use of life cycle costing (LCC) instead.

LCC considers the lifetime cost.

Kaufman [6] describes LCC as "the total cost of ownership of a system during its operational life." LCC includes the initial purchase price of a piece of equipment but also includes the implementation, support, maintenance, operation, and training costs resulting from the acquisition of the equipment. It is thus particularly relevant to operations management. To determine the LCC of various alternative capital investments every conceivable cost must be identified and measured.

The notion of life cycle costing is of extreme importance to the operations manager. Very often in large corporate settings, capital budgeting decisions are relegated to financial analysts and planners who have a less-than-adequate understanding of many aspects of the operations function. A capital expenditure project that appears to be very sound on a financial basis may prove to be completely unworthy when such intangibles as ease of operations and maintenance, local parts inventory availability for repair of breakdowns, setup time, operation speed, and quality of the product are all considered.

There are essentially seven steps in the formulation of the LCC for a given piece of equipment.

1. Establish the operating profile.
2. Establish utilization factors.
3. Identify all cost factors.
4. Calculate all costs at current prices.
5. Escalate current labor and material costs.
6. Discount all costs to a base period.
7. Sum up all discounted and undiscounted costs.

The *operating profile* describes, in calendar form, the planned timing of equipment operations. At any given time, the equipment can be either operating or not operating. It can be in a start-up mode, in steady state, or in overhaul. The important consideration is that each machine being evaluated

Same operating profile used.

should be considered with the same *operating profile* except for those elements not planned by management but dictated by the equipment itself (e.g., preventive maintenance, expected breakdown rate).

The *utilization factor* varies with operating profile. During an operating mode a machine may run 75 percent of the time and be stopped for loading and unloading 25 percent of the time. For setup, the machine may be utilized 20 percent of the time and stopped 80 percent of the time.

Lifetime costs identified and inflated or deflated.

Next, all costs are identified and estimated at current prices. Since costs are unlikely to decrease for any of the cost elements, estimates should be made of the costs over the operating life of the equipment. Various multipliers such as specific industry price inflators might be used here.

Smoky Flats Electric Company

To illustrate these first five steps, consider the case of the Smoky Flats Electric Company, which is considering the replacement of a generator system. Two contractors have made proposals on the system based on the pre-scribed operating profile. The profile calls for continuous operation with semiannual 24-hour preventive maintenance sessions. The equipment has to be able to produce peak power at twice the rate of the called for average daily output. These peaks are expected to occur during the high use service months and especially during the early afternoon hours. When the equip-ment is "down" for maintenance, it is totally nonproductive.

The cost factors involved are as follows:

1. Initial purchase.

2. Coal consumption.

3. Labor requirements.

4. Semiannual maintenance costs.

For systems A and B these costs are estimated as follows (on an annual basis):

	A	B
Initial purchase	$165,000	$200,000
Coal consumption	30,000	26,000
Labor cost	18,500	20,100
Maintenance cost	14,000	6,500

The life of each system is estimated to be eight years and coal cost is esti-mated to increase at the rate of 8 percent per year. Labor cost is expected to increase at the rate of 10 percent per year and maintenance cost is esti-mated to grow at 5 percent per year.

Based on this information, Table 15.5 and 15.6 present the total life cycle costs of these two systems.

The time value of money recognized. The last two steps are based on the concept of the time/value of money. A banker, for example, is willing to pay interest to you for money deposited in your savings account. A dollar today is worth more than a dollar next

Table 15.5 Life Cycle Costs for System A

	Coal	Labor	Maintenance	Total
Initial purchase cost				$165,000
Year 1	$30,000	$18,500	$14,000	62,500
2	32,400	20,350	14,700	67,450
3	34,992	22,385	15,435	72,812
4	37,791	24,623	16,206	78,620
5	40,814	27,085	17,017	84,916
6	44,079	29,794	17,868	91,740
7	47,606	32,773	18,761	99,140
8	51,414	36,051	19,699	107,164

Table 15.6 Life Cycle Costs for System B

	Coal	Labor	Maintenance	Total
Initial purchase cost				$200,000
Year 1	$26,000	$20,100	$ 6,500	52,600
2	28,080	22,110	6,825	57,015
3	30,326	24,321	7,166	61,813
4	32,752	26,753	7,524	67,029
5	35,372	29,428	7,900	72,700
6	38,202	32,371	8,295	78,868
7	41,258	35,608	8,710	85,576
8	44,559	39,169	9,146	92,874

year, because (1) it can be invested today to earn a profit or return and (2) it inflates. Therefore, dollars of cost paid out in the future are less valuable dollars than current dollars. We *discount* future dollars to present terms using the appropriate *discount rate*. This discounting process results in the *present value* of the total costs. The initial purchase price (or the initial payment) is in current dollars and is, therefore, not discounted. But all future costs are discounted to the current period using the discount rate.

What discount rate?

The discount rate is usually determined judgmentally. Factors entering into the decision of the appropriate discount rate are industry rate of return estimates, inflation rates, cost of debt and equity money to the company, and the degree of risk in the investment.

Clearly, this procedure is more complicated than simply determining the lowest bid and awarding contracts on that basis. But as Kaufman points out, the costs beyond the initial purchase price are often much more important to the determination of LCC. In fact, for most industrial equipment, purchase price is normally between 20 and 60 percent of the LCC [6]. In order that the equipment selected be the least costly, in a "real" sense, a method that considers the costs of an investment over its total life should be employed rather than the "lowest bid" method.

Purchase price only 20–60 percent of total.

We will return later to the subject of present value as previously introduced and described, but first we will consider a less complicated decision rule called "payback" which has historically been used in operations management for capital investment selection and replacement decisions.

The Payback Method

Because of its simplicity, the *payback* method of investment selection has for many years been the most popular method of analyzing alternative investment possibilities. Simply put, the method computes the number of years required to recover the cost of the investment, either through increased revenues or decreased costs (savings) or a combination of the two. A company using the payback method will usually have determined a standard minimum payback period (e.g., three years) and all investment proposals will be

Payback: years to recover cost.

compared with this standard. Proposals with payback periods in excess of the standard are typically rejected, or at least are subjected to more study before adoption.

Operations managers can use this simple investment evaluation technique to "self-critique" their own proposals for new equipment. Payback provides a quick check on the financial reasonableness of an investment. For an operations manager to argue for the purchase of a new machine because it "reduces variable costs by 80 percent" is not sensible if the payback is 10 years and company policy is a 4-year maximum. Payback, however, does not recognize the timing of the payments and thus ignores the important "time value of money" as we will demonstrate later.

The Salt and Shotgun Mining Company

This company uses a payback standard of three years. Two equipment proposals, A and B, are being considered by Salt and Shotgun's management. Their net cash savings and their initial costs are shown in Table 15.7. Machine A has a payback period of 2⅓ years ($400,000 in two years + $100,000 in the first third of the third year) whereas machine B has a payback period of 3¼ years ($180,000 in three years + $20,000 in the first quarter of the fourth year). Based on this simple analysis, investment A is the only acceptable alternative (i.e., less than a three-year payback).

Three problems with payback.

But, as a wise philosopher once said, "There are no simple solutions to complex problems, only simple-minded solutions." Payback, while simple, suffers from three very real limitations. First, the method is a totally short-term approach to investment and replacement decisions. Many firms today are suffering from the short-term approach taken years ago to replacement decisions. For example, in the steel industry no one ever asked "What will become of our facilities if we *don't* replace and modernize them, even if they exceed our payback period policy?" This is another reason why life cycle costing is a better method for making investment/replacement decisions.

Second, the approach does not recognize timing of the repayment. Third,

Table 15.7 Cash Flows for Two Investments

	Equipment Proposals	
	A	B
Initial investment	$500,000	$200,000
Savings,[a] year 1	150,000	50,000
Savings, year 2	250,000	60,000
Savings, year 3	300,000	70,000
Savings, year 4	200,000	80,000
Savings, year 5	200,000	90,000

[a]Savings are due to decreased labor.

Table 15.8 Same Payback, B Preferred for Rate

	A	B
Initial investment	$100,000	$100,000
Return, year 1	25,000	75,000
Return, year 2	25,000	10,000
Return, year 3	25,000	10,000
Return, year 4	25,000	5,000

the method does not recognize differences in the total return from a project. Consider the following two examples, depicted in Tables 15.8 and 15.9.

Ignores timing of returns.

In Table 15.8 both projects have a payback period of four years and, therefore, the method indicates that the organization should be indifferent between the two alternatives. Clearly, alternative B generates the return much more rapidly than A and, because of the time value of money, should therefore be preferred.

Ignores returns beyond horizon.

In Table 15.9 both projects have two-year payback periods. But again, a rational investor would not be indifferent as the decision rule indicates, because project B returns $15,000 more than project A over its total life.

Net present value is better.

Both of these flaws in the logic of the payback method are the result of little or no consideration of time. Returns *past the payback year* and the *timing of returns* are not properly considered. However, the *net present value* method overcomes these two shortcomings of the payback method.

The Net Present Value (NPV) Method

As we discussed earlier in our presentation of the life cycle costing concept, costs and returns over the life of a system's operation should be discounted to their present values using an appropriate discount rate. We discount future costs and returns because future dollars are of less value to us than present dollars.

Table 15.9 Same Payback, B Preferred for Amount

	A	B
Initial investment	$ 50,000	$ 50,000
Return, year 1	30,000	30,000
Return, year 2	20,000	20,000
Return, year 3	10,000	10,000
Return, year 4	0	5,000
Return, year 5	0	5,000
Return, year 6	0	5,000

To illustrate, consider the investment of $1 today at an interest or inflation rate of 10 percent. The amount, A_1, at the end of one year is

$$A_1 = 1 + 0.1(1) = \$1.10$$

or, if we let A_0 equal the amount of the initial investment and i equal the interest rate, then

$$A_1 = A_0 + iA_0$$

or

$$A_1 = A_0(1 + i)$$

The amount at the end of the second year is A_2.

$$A_2 = A_1 + iA_1$$
$$= (1 + i)A_1$$

But $A_1 = A_0(1 + i)$. Therefore

$$A_2 = (1 + i)[A_0(1 + i)]$$
$$= A_0(1 + i)^2$$
$$= 1(1.1)^2$$
$$= \$1.21$$

In general, the *amount* A_n at the end of n periods is

$$A_n = A_0(1 + i)^n \tag{15.7}$$

From this example we see that receiving $1.21 at the end of two years is only worth $1.00 now (presuming an interest or an inflation rate of 10 percent), because that $1.00 invested today would grow to equal $1.21 by the end of two years.

In order to discount each annual cost or revenue back to its present value in current dollars we simply solve Equation 15.7 for A_0, the present value of the amount A_n.

$$A_0 = \frac{A_n}{(1 + i)^n}$$
$$= A_n\left(\frac{1}{(1 + i)^n}\right) \tag{15.8}$$

The discount factor.

The term $1/(1 + i)^n$ is called the "discount factor." To demonstrate, $1.00 received three years from now with an available interest rate of 5 percent is worth only

$$A_0 = \frac{1}{(1.05)^3} = \$0.86$$

in current dollars.

Rigid Box, Inc.

Rigid box is considering the purchase of a new carton folding machine which would save $10,000 per year for five years in labor costs. The machine costs $35,000 to be paid as follows.

$20,000 at time of purchase.

$10,000 at end of first year.

$5000 at end of second year.

If the company requires a 5 percent return on new equipment purchases, what is the net present value of this investment? Data for this problem are presented in Table 15.10.

The NPV for the Rigid Box Company problem is $9234.82, which is computed as the *sum* of the discounted net cash flows over the five-year useful life of the machine. Having a *positive* NPV means that the actual return on the investment is greater than the 5 percent return required by the company.

Positive versus negative NPV.

The computations become quite cumbersome for projects with longer lives. If the future cash flows are equal amounts, the flows can be considered to be an **annuity** and the determination of the present value simplifies to calculating just the following equation.

The present value of an annuity.

$$A_0 = A\left(\frac{1 - \frac{1}{(1 + i)^n}}{i}\right) \tag{15.9}$$

where A is the equal cash flows each year. Rather than computing the discount factor for each of the n years, one discount factor (the term in parentheses in Equation 15.9) is computed.

For example, the net present value at 10 percent of a project which saves $3000 per year for four years and costs $10,000 initially is computed as $-$10,000 plus

$$A_0 = 3000\left(\frac{1 - \frac{1}{(1 + 0.10)^4}}{0.10}\right)$$

$$= 3000\left(\frac{1 - 0.683}{0.10}\right)$$

$$= 3000\left(\frac{0.317}{0.10}\right)$$

$$= 3000(3.17)$$

$$= \$9510$$

or

$$-\$10,000 + 9510 = -\$490$$

This project does not earn the required 10 percent return.

Table 15.10 Folding Machine Cash Flows

(1) Year	(2) Cash Outflow	(3) Cash Inflow	(4) Net Cash Flow	(5) Discount Factor	(6) Discounted Cash Flow or NPV (4 × 5)
0	$20,000	0	−$20,000	$1/(1 + 0.05)^0$	−$20,000.00
1	10,000	10,000	0	$1/(1 + 0.05)^1$	0
2	5,000	10,000	5,000	$1/(1 + 0.05)^2$	4,535.15
3	0	10,000	10,000	$1/(1 + 0.05)^3$	8,638.38
4	0	10,000	10,000	$1/(1 + 0.05)^4$	8,226.03
5	0	10,000	10,000	$1/(1 + 0.05)^5$	7,835.26
					$ 9,234.82

Another, similar method of evaluating investment/replacement decisions is called "internal rate of return." Here the interest rate that *equates* the costs with the returns, in present value terms, is determined and called the internal rate of return or IRR. The difficulty with this method is that trial and error must frequently be used to calculate the IRR. With computer aid this problem is less serious.

Present Value Tables

Appendix tables for present values.

To even further simplify the computations of present values, two tables are available. Table A1 in Appendix A is called the "present value of $1" table. To use it we simply read the discount factor in the body of the table corresponding to an interest rate of i and number of years n and multiply this factor times the cash flow in the nth year. For example, $10 received in year 4 at 10 percent interest is worth $10 \times 0.683 = \$6.83$.

Table A2 in Appendix A is the "present value of an annuity of $1" table. From it we read the discount factor for an interest rate of i and annuity life of n.

For example, to compute the present value of a $100 annuity for 10 years at an 8 percent interest rate we find the discount factor 6.71 corresponding to the 10 year row and 8 percent column of Table A2 and multiply the factor times the amount of the annuity, $100.

$$A_0 = 6.71 \times 100 = \$671$$

Return to Smoky Flats

If the Smoky Flats Electric Company uses an 8 percent discount rate for new investment projects, which of the previously analyzed systems should be selected on a life cycle costing basis? The discount factors to be used can be found in Table A1 under the 8 percent column heading. They are as follows:

Year	Discount Factor
1	0.926
2	0.857
3	0.794
4	0.735
5	0.681
6	0.630
7	0.583
8	0.540

Applying these factors to the two project cost flows yields the following present values for systems A and B.

System A: $627,569.

System B: $595,153.

Since System B has the lowest life cycle cost, it should be selected by Smoky Flats. Notice that system A has the lowest initial cost and, according to the "low bid" rule, would have been selected.

Depreciation, Leasing, and Taxes

Depreciation.

For the most part, the major expenditures requested by the operations manager will be for capital assets. These assets cannot be expensed in the year required, but must be *depreciated* over their useful lives. This depreciation simply reflects the "using up" of the asset and matches the cost of this use with the revenue-generating, or productive, capability of the asset. The operations manager must recognize that this depreciation, while being a bona fide expense and deductible for income taxation purposes, does not result in any out-of-pocket cash flow. Understanding the effect on cash flows of depreciation and taxes will aid significantly in the preparation of capital budgeting requests and will often produce a stronger argument for the operations manager.

Effect of taxes.

In our previous examples of net present value we ignored the very real consequences of taxes and tax-deductible expenses such as depreciation. For example, if a corporation paying taxes at the rate of 50 percent of net income were to increase net income by $100,000 per year, the cash benefit would be only $50,000 since 50 percent of the additional earnings would be paid out in income taxes. Since only the actual net cash flows are relevant to a capital budgeting decision, the role of income taxes must be considered.

Effect of depreciation.

Also, since certain expenses do not result in an actual cash outflow, the tax savings generated are also important to the investment decision. Depreciation on capital items, including equipment and buildings, is a major non-cash expense, which results in a reduction in tax payments for a business. Depreciation expense is simply the accounting allocation of the initial cost

Three depreciation
methods.

of an asset over its useful life. It does not result in actual cash outflows, yet it is a deductible expense for the purposes of computing taxable income.

There are three major depreciation methods: *straight-line, sum-of-year's-digits,* and *double-declining balance.*

Straight-Line

Under the straight-line depreciation method, cost is allocated equally to every year of the asset's life. The depreciation method, D, is computed as

$$D = \frac{A - S}{L} \tag{15.10}$$

where A is the initial asset cost and S is the salvage value at the end of its life, L years from now. For a \$20,000 asset with a 10-year life and \$5000 salvage value, the annual depreciation is (\$20,000 − \$5000)/10 = \$1500 per year. This type of depreciation schedule is appropriate to an asset that is used up equally over its lifetime.

Sum-of-Year's-Digits

The sum-of-year's-digits approach is appropriate when the asset loses more value in the early years of its lifetime. The annual depreciation charge is

$$D = \frac{Y}{T}(A - S) \tag{15.11}$$

where Y is the number of years of remaining useful life in the asset, and T is the sum of all the Y values from L to 1. For the example used above, T would be $10 + 9 + 8 + 7 + 6 + 5 + 4 + 3 + 2 + 1 = 55$ and the first year's depreciation would be

$$\frac{10}{55}(\$20,000 - \$5000) = \$2727$$

whereas the second year's depreciation would be

$$\frac{9}{55}(\$20,000 - \$5000) = \$2454$$

and the last year's depreciation would be

$$\frac{1}{55}(\$20,000 - \$5000) = \$272.73$$

Double-Declining Balance

The double-declining balance approach also writes off more value in the early years but has a built-in salvage value factor and hence does not specifically include salvage in the annual depreciation formula.

$$D = \left(\frac{2}{L}\right)V \tag{15.12}$$

where V is the remaining value of the asset. Again using the previous example data, the first year's depreciation would be

$$\left(\frac{2}{10}\right)(\$20{,}000 - 0) = \$4000$$

and the second year's depreciation expense would be

$$\left(\frac{2}{10}\right)(\$20{,}000 - \$4000) = \$3200$$

Figure 15.13 indicates the relationship between the three depreciation methods for the previous example. The figure illustrates the early write-off advantage (in year 7) of the double-declining balance method. In 1981 the IRS introduced a new tabular depreciation method called ACRS, which includes built-in accelerated depreciation. Next we will consider a brief taxation-depreciation example.

Abacus Computer Services (ACS)

ACS is considering the purchase of a computer system that has an initial cost of $120,000 and a useful life of five years (no salvage value). Abacus' tax rate is 50 percent and they plan to depreciate the system using the straight-line method. The asset is assumed to have no salvage value at the end of its five-year life. The machine is expected to produce a net income before depreciation and taxes of $35,000 per year and Abacus uses a 7 percent interest rate on all investment proposals. Cash flows for each year are given in Table 15.11.

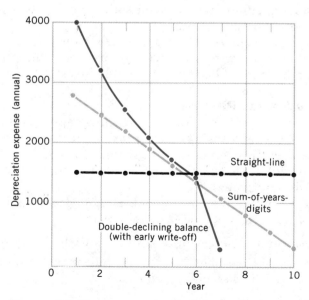

Figure 15.13 Comparison of depreciation methods.

Table 15.11 Net Present Value of Abacus' Computer Investment

(1) Year	(2) Cash Inflow	(3) Cash Outflow	(4) Net Cash Flow	(5) Discount Factor	(6) Discounted Cash Flow
0	0	$120,000	−$120,000	1	−$120,000
1	$29,500	0	29,500 ⎫		
2	29,500	0	29,500 ⎪		
3	29,500	0	29,500 ⎬	4.1[a]	120,950
4	29,500	0	29,500 ⎪		
5	29,500	0	29,500 ⎭		
				Net present value	$ 950

[a]Since all cash inflows are equal amounts, we use the present value of an annuity discount factor (Table A2, in text Appendix A).

Calculations for the first year are as follows:

Net income before depreciation and taxes	$35,000
Less: depreciation expense*	24,000
Net income before taxes	11,000
Less: taxes (50 percent)	5,500
Net income after taxes	5,500
Plus: depreciation expense	24,000
Cash inflow	$29,500

Depreciation is added back for cash flow.

Note that the depreciation expense is "added back" in our calculations. The reason for this is that depreciation is deductible as an expense for taxation purposes but actually does not result in an outflow of cash. The general rule for cash flow calculations is to begin with accounting income after taxes and add back all noncash expenses.

Since the present value is positive ($950), the project meets (even though just barely) the company's 7 percent return policy and, therefore, should be adopted, presuming other more profitable investments are not available.

Lease Versus Purchase

Purchasing is only one way of obtaining capital equipment. Another alternative is leasing. Leasing involves a series of payments made by the *lessee* (the party acquiring use of the equipment) to the *lessor* (the party who owns the leased equipment) for the *use* of the equipment rather than for the *ownership* of the equipment.

Lease, lessee, leasing, lessor.

There are both advantages and disadvantages to capital equipment leasing. The advantages include the following:

1. Low initial investment by lessee allows liquidity to be maintained.

Advantages of leasing.

2. The risk of owning obsolete equipment or equipment with too little or too much capacity is reduced.

*Computed as ($120,000)/5 = $24,000.

3. Commitment to equipment/test period before purchasing is reduced.

4. Lease rentals are expenses for income tax purposes.

The disadvantages include the following:

Disadvantages.

1. The total lease cost is likely to be higher than the total purchase cost.

2. There are usually restrictions imposed on the use of the equipment by the lessor.

The operations manager should recognize that leasing is a very reasonable alternative, particularly when company cash flows are tight or when technology advances are rapid. The computer operations manager has recognized this fact for a number of years. In less than 20 years the data processing world has seen four computer generations arrive. Managers who owned their own equipment were committed to a long-term use of the hardware. Once a new generation was announced, preceding generations became virtually worthless.

Leasing computers.

Owning equipment that has a high risk of becoming obsolete can jeopardize the operations productivity of a firm. A competitor who leases and can take advantage of the newly available technology will have a competitive advantage over the firm that owns obsolete machinery. The operations manager must recognize the tradeoff inherent here. For the reduction in risk of obsolescence, the firm must typically pay a premium price for the use of the equipment.

A tradeoff.

Consider again the Abacus Computer Services problem of the last section. Suppose that the computer manufacturer has just initiated a lease plan that will allow General to lease the same computer that it has been considering for purchase at a lease rate of $30,000 per year, payable at the end of each year. However, to obtain this rate ACS must provide its own maintenance and servicing. Table 15.12 presents the lease data for this problem; the calculations for year 1 are shown in the following.

Net income before lease payment and taxes	$35,000
Less: lease payment	30,000
Net income before taxes	5,000
Less: taxes (50 percent)	2,500
Net income after taxes (net cash flow)	$ 2,500

Table 15.12 Net Present Value of Abacus' Lease Alternative

Year	Net Cash Flow	Discount Factor	Discounted Cash Flow
0			
1	$2500 ⎫		
2	2500 ⎪		
3	2500 ⎬	4.1	$10,250
4	2500 ⎪		————
5	2500 ⎭		
		Net present value	$10,250

Clearly, in this example, leasing is the better alternative. The NPV of the lease is $10,250 compared to only $950 for the outright purchase of the machine.

15.8   SUMMARY AND KEY LEARNING POINTS

In this chapter we moved from the topic of general organizational control in Chapter 14 to strict operations control. We focused on maintaining the function of the operations system through the concepts of reliability and maintenance. Our treatment of reliability included general reliability analysis and methods for enhancing a system's reliability.

In our discussion of maintenance we first distinguished between measures of reliability, maintainability, and availability. We then went on to discuss and compare corrective maintenance and preventive maintenance. We looked at the replacement problem and how to determine the best time to replace an asset and considered group replacement instead of individual replacement. Next, we addressed the possibility of using standbys instead of providing maintenance. Finally, we considered the problem of determining the best repair crew size.

In the appendix to the chapter we looked at the financial aspects of asset replacement. We described the tools and concepts of life cycle costing, cost comparisons over time, depreciation, leasing, and tax considerations.

The key learning points have been

- Ways to increase the reliability of a system are using redundant elements, increasing the element reliabilities, improving the working conditions of the system, conducting preventive maintenance, providing standbys, speeding the repair process, and isolating high-risk elements.

- The reliability of independent elements in series is the product of their reliabilities. The reliability of independent elements in parallel is 1.0 less the product of their *failure* probabilities, where an element's failure probability is 1.0 less its reliability.

- Maintainability has to do with ease and speed of repair, reliability is concerned with time between repairs, and availability relates to total *usable* time.

- Corrective maintenance (CM) is repair upon breakdown. Preventive maintenance (PM) attempts to eliminate breakdowns ahead of time and save the cost of an expensive failure. However, PM, though it may be less expensive, must be conducted more frequently, requires scrapping parts that still have useful life in them, and may even cause a breakdown if improperly done.

- The proper time to replace an asset with an identical one is when its long-run average annual cost is at a minimum.

- Using present value analysis, horizons of need, scrap value, generated income, and expected costs, an evaluation of existing and potential replacement assets can be conducted to determine whether an asset should be replaced.

- Group replacement is a form of preventive maintenance and has the same advantages and disadvantages. The calculations become complex because the corrective maintenance replacements between PM periods must usually also be factored into the analysis.

- Standby equipment or parts offer an alternative to expensive maintenance or the high cost of enhanced reliability. Simple expected value analysis in a payoff table, decision tree, or incremental analysis approach is sufficient to determine the best number of standbys.

- The use of queuing theory can aid in optimally sizing a repair crew. The service situation can be modeled as a limited-source queue and special graphs employed to size the crew.

15.9 KEY TERMS

reliability (p. 566)
redundancy (p. 569)
series (p. 570)
independent (p. 570)
parallel (p. 571)
Venn diagram (p. 571)
mutually exclusive (p. 572)

corrective maintenance (p. 573)
preventive maintenance (p. 573)
maintainability (p. 574)
MTTR (p. 574)
MTBF (p. 574)

availability (p. 574)
group replacement (p. 577)
MAPI (p. 580)
failure rate distribution (p. 581)
infant mortality (p. 581)
standby (p. 583)

15.10 REVIEW AND DISCUSSION QUESTIONS

1. How do you think reliability is enhanced in NASA space equipment? In elevators?
2. Why do managers find it so hard to ignore sunk costs on expensive equipment?
3. How might group replacement analysis be used in personnel acquisition and promotion?
4. Do the replacement techniques of this chapter apply to public benefits? Other services?
5. Classify a number of failures you are familiar with according to the four basic failure modes.
6. Why are services so unreliable compared with products?
7. Draw a Venn diagram to help calculate the reliability of three parallel elements and compare it to Equation 15.4.
8. How do the reliability formulas change if the element reliabilities are not all identical?
9. Is it better to increase the reliability of the weakest link in a system or the most critical link?
10. Preventive maintenance is often viewed as a long-term approach to reliability. Why?
11. When should PM not be used?
12. For what kinds of situations is early replacement appropriate?

13. Why should an asset not be replaced at the end of its minimum annual cost year?

14. How does the horizon of need affect the replacement decision?

15. What are other types of capital investments besides capital assets?

16. Enumerate the reasons LCC is preferred to "low bid."

17. What is the difference between the discount factor and the interest rate?

18. What other methods besides payback and NPV exist for comparing investments?

15.11   PROBLEMS

Practice Problems

1. The Blue Grass Computer Center provides data processing services for area businesses. Blue Grass currently contracts with a computer vendor for maintenance of the equipment. The cost is $120 per day. The probability of equipment failure on any given day is .13. The computer vendor must send a repairman from a city nearly 100 miles away; consequently, the machine is typically down for 24 hours until it is repaired. The cost of the downtime is estimated to be $1000. A local computer repair company has just opened and Blue Grass has been solicited as a potential client. The local firm claims 8-hour service from machine failure to repair, but their rates are somewhat higher than the computer vendor, $160 per day. Advise Blue Grass as to the expected cost of each maintenance option.

2. For a new clock-radio that you purchased, the clock, the alarm switch, and the radio must all work in order for you to be awakened in the morning. If the reliabilities of the three independent components are 0.95, 0.90, and 0.92, respectively, what is the probability that the alarm clock will perform as expected in the morning?

3. If, in Problem 2, there is a backup switch (with the same reliability as the first) that will function if the primary switch fails, what is the chance of your being awakened in time?

4. Use Figure 15.2 to determine the requisite increase in *element* reliability of a series of 50 identical 95 percent reliable items to reach a *system* reliability of 40 percent.

5. What, according to Figure 15.5 is the increase in system reliability of a network of 10 identical and parallel 10-percent-reliable items if their element reliabilities are increased to 20 percent? What would have been the decrease in reliability if, instead, 7 items were removed from the network?

6. A machine is needed that will, on average, be available 35 hours a week, out of a 40-hour-a-week shift. Two machines are being considered. One can be repaired in 90 minutes but only has an average time between

failures of 20 hours. The other machine has an MTBF of 30 hours with an average repair time of 3 hours. Which machine, if either, will meet the need?

7. A firm has a machine with an MTBF of 100 hours and an MTTR of 10 hours. They are considering two ways of raising its availability. One way is to invest in improving the working environment. For every $10 they invest the MTBF will increase 2 hours. The second alternative is to hire a part-time helper for the repairman. Every hour of help will cost $5 but reduce the MTTR by 10 minutes. Which alternative is best for the firm?

8. The Last National Bank of Pleasantville uses a magnetic ink character reader (MICR) to process checks. The machine loses 20 percent each year in resale value (its original purchase price was $80,000) and has the following maintenance cost schedule over its 10-year useful life.

Year	1	2	3	4	5	6	7	8	9	10
Cost	$8000	$9000	$10,200	$12,000	$15,000	$16,500	$17,000	$17,400	$17,750	$18,000

When should the machine be replaced?

9. A machine costing $4000 with a five-year life loses 30 percent of its value every year. Maintenance the first year is free but increases $600 every year. When is the best time to replace the machine?

10. Compare the three following robots to determine whether to keep the present one or replace it with one of the new models. Use a four-year horizon and a 20 percent cost of capital.

	Present	Model A	Model B
Now: Value	$2,000	$20,000	$25,000
Year 1: Income	3,000	5,000	6,000
Repairs	500	0	0
Year 2: Income	3,000	5,000	6,000
Repairs	600	1,000	1,200
Year 3: Income	3,000	5,000	6,000
Repairs	800	1,500	1,600
Year 4: Income	3,000	5,000	6,000
Repairs	1,000	1,800	2,000
Value	500	12,000	14,000

11. Is corrective maintenance, at a cost of $50 each for repairing the following dozen machines whenever they fail, the best policy or is additional nightly preventive maintenance at a cost of $10 per machine better?

Days	1	2	3	4
Probability of failure	.2	.1	.3	.4

12. Evaluate the cost of additional preventive maintenance every *other* night and compare it to the answers in Problem 11.

13. Resolve Problems 11 and 12 with each of the following two lifetime distributions.

Days	1	2	3	4
(a) P(failure)	.25	.25	.25	.25
(b) P(failure)	.4	.3	.2	.1

14. Ray Gordon, owner-operator of a single "18 wheeler" tractor trailer has had trouble with flat tires over the past year. Ray is considering the possibility of using additional spare tires. His rig currently carries one spare. On any given trip, the probability of zero or more flat tires is given as follows.

Flats	Probability
0	.3
1	.5
2	.1
3	.1

If Ray has more than one flat tire, a new tire must be purchased on the road and a special "road service" fee paid to the tire company. The cost to Ray is $600. The cost per trip of each extra spare is based on the expected tire life (even if it is not used, it is subject to dry rot so its life is not indefinite) and is anticipated to be $20 per trip. How many spares would you recommend that Ray carry?

15. Solve Problem 14 with marginal analysis.

16. Solve Problem 14 as a decision tree.

17. A factory repair crew of five maintain 20 high-volume pumps which break down at an average rate of 15 per week. The pumps are repaired by a single serviceperson in half a week, on the average. What is the expected number of pumps waiting for service?

18. Find the average length of the queue for a geriatric clinic of 10 physicians who service a practice of 200 elderly patients. The patients each come to the clinic, on average, twice a week (40-hour week) and are serviced in an hour.

19. Crittenden County operates eight swimming pools, each of which is due to have the filtration system replaced. There are two filter systems that will work on these pools. Their characteristics are listed in the following table.

	Filter Systems	
Characteristics	1	2
Initial purchase price	$3000	$1800
Cost of chemicals used	$ 350	$ 500
Annual cleanings required	2	3
Cost per cleaning	$ 120	$ 90
Useful life	5 yr	3 yr

Two county council members are debating over the merits of the two filtration systems. Jones argues that cost per cleaning is higher for 1 than for 2 and also that its purchase price is higher. Smith contends that 2's life is shorter and that the chemicals used are greater, as is the "total" cleaning cost. The mayor states that he will settle this argument by invoking an age-old rule—the minimum bid gets the business. How would you advise the county council regarding this problem? What role does life cycle costing play in this analysis?

20. Two molding sanders are available to The Wooden Tree, a custom molding and trim manufacturer. Model 101 has fixed operating costs of $4500 per year and variable costs of production of $0.005 per linear foot of sanding. Model 201 has $6200 fixed costs each year but $0.0037 per linear foot of sanding. Doug Bush, the owner, has come up with the following estimates for annual sanding volume over the next 10 years.

Volume (linear ft)	Probability
200,000	.2
400,000	.5
600,000	.3

Which machine is expected to produce the lowest annual cost?

21. Standard Tool and Die, Inc., is considering the purchase of a minicomputer to maintain its accounts receivable records and to send out monthly statements. Standard is currently using a local computer service bureau for this service. The service bureau charges a flat monthly fee of $80 plus $0.10 per transaction posted to the accounts receivable file. The monthly cost of the minicomputer and the programs necessary to operate it will be $200, but the cost per posted transaction will be only $0.03 since Standard can hire a part-time key punch operator at this rate. If standard anticipates a monthly volume of transactions of 1500, should they continue with the computer service or purchase the mini? What minimum volume of transactions is required to warrant the minicomputer purchase?

22. Hiway Motel is deliberating about enclosing their outdoor swimming pool so that it can be used year-round. Hiway's manager believes that

with this change annual revenues would increase by $18,000 while pool operating expenses would rise by only $3500. The enclosure is expected to cost $30,000 and has a 10-year life. If another of Hiway's investment opportunities promises to return 12 percent, should the pool cover be constructed? What is the payback period for this investment?

23. Rat Trap Homes, Inc., has just purchased a new bulldozer for use in excavating basements for new homes. The purchase price of the dozer was $37,000. Delivery and initial setup and adjustment by a factory service person costs an additional $2200. The expected life of the dozer is eight years, and it is anticipated that its salvage value will be $5000 at the time. Compute the depreciation using (a) straight-line, (b) sum-of-year's-digits, and (c) double-declining balance. What is the difference in tax advantage between the straight-line and the double-declining balance depreciation for the first year if Rat Trap is in the 48 percent tax bracket?

More Complex Problems

24. Determine the reliability of the following system:

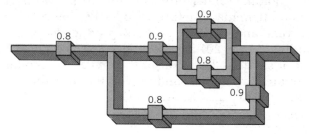

25. Use Problem 9 to investigate the effect of different cost trends and patterns on the optimal replacement period. Consider the effect of the following:
    a. The machine's initial cost.
    b. The rate of loss of value.
    c. Whether the loss of value per year is constant or decreases exponentially (as in Problem 9).
    d. The rate of maintenance cost increase.
    e. The initial maintenance cost.
    f. If the maintenance cost increase is linear or exponential.

26. Solve the Nimble Fingers group replacement problem of Section 15.4 for replacements every *third* night. Can you derive an equation for the cost of PM at any arbitrary interval?

27. Resolve the Beauty and Beast problem of Section 15.5 if
    a. the cost of one curler-dryer out of order is $20, two is $50, and three is $90.
    b. The cost of one curler-dryer out of order is $20, two is $35, and three is $45.

c. The curler-dryers cost $5 for one, $12 for two, and $20 for three.

d. The curler-dryers cost $5 for one, $8 for two, and $9 for three.

28. Solve the following decision tree where a negative sign means a loss and a plus sign means a gain.

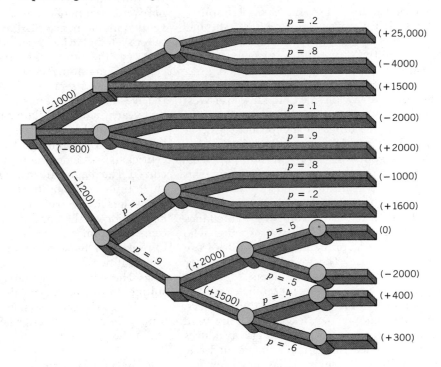

29. Intuitively explain your answer to Problem 17 when the machines are failing at a faster rate than the crew can repair them.

30. Doyle Mining Co. is about to replace several coal trucks. They have received two proposals from truck distributors. The first proposal is for the purchase of a truck with an annual hauling value of 300,000 ton-miles. The truck has a price of $100,000 and a salvage value at the end of its three-year life of $10,000. Annual operating costs are expected to be $0.10 per ton-mile and revenues are forecast to be $0.80 per ton-mile. The second proposal is for an identical truck, but for a three-year lease instead of a purchase. The lease payments are $30,000 at the beginning of each of the three years and a final payment of $35,000 at the end of year 3. With this final payment, the deed to the truck is passed to Doyle. Doyle can borrow from the local bank at a 10 percent interest rate.

a. Ignoring taxes, which proposal should be accepted?

b. Presuming that the $30,000 lease payments are tax deductible and that $25,000 of the final payment is deductible for tax purposes, which proposal is the best? Doyle is in the 50 percent bracket, uses straight-line depreciation, and has other income to offset any losses.

15.12 CASE I

MID-WEST WHOLESALE

The sales representative for Hardware Reliability, Inc., had just left Jim Dewberry's office. She had presented an hour-long sales pitch for preventive maintenance on Jim's year-old minicomputer system. The sales pitch had been quite convincing.

Jim Dewberry is the president and general manager of the Mid-West Wholesale Company. Mid-West Wholesale distributes over 300 different varieties of canned goods to 165 different independent grocery stores throughout a three-state territory. Mid-West installed a minicomputer last year to accept customer orders over touch-tone telephone systems. This system has been performing about as well as expected, but there have been five equipment failures since the hardware was installed. Maintenance services are provided by the hardware vendor, who has an office located approximately 20 miles from Mid-West's warehouse. The average downtime for the five hardware failures was 9.5 hours.

Mid-West has come to depend on the computer system. Once orders are received from customers, the computer prints picking tickets which are used to pick orders in the warehouse and also produces the customers' invoices, a summary statement at the end of the month, and various management reports. When the machine is down, the orders are taken over the telephone for distant customers whereas nearby customers hand deliver their orders. With the computer system, each order is sorted into warehouse sequence location before the picking tickets are printed. This resequencing of the order produces quite a dramatic production increase for the order pickers since they only cover each aisle once in their filling of a single order. In all, Dewberry feels that each machine failure is costing him $5000 in lost production.

Hardware Reliability, Inc. (HRI), is offering a hardware maintenance package that includes a preventive maintenance plan for Mid-West's minicomputer system. HRI will perform a series of diagnostic checks on the hardware each month and will provide corrective maintenance service for any machine failures. The sales representative has analyzed each of the five hardware failures which occurred during the first year period. She claims that the HRI diagnostic package could have detected two of those failures before they occurred and had a better than 50 percent chance of catching a third failure before it occurred. The diagnostic testing requires 1 hour of machine time each month. HRI will schedule the tests to take place at 8 o'clock in the morning, which is 1 hour prior to the time when Mid-West begins accepting customer orders. If the tests indicate the need to replace or make adjustments to any component, HRI will perform the required maintenance at that time. The sales representative indicated that the resulting downtime is typically cut in half.

Jim has asked the sales representative to call him again next week after he has had time to think about the proposal.

Questions for Discussion

1. What factors should Jim consider in evaluating this proposal?

2. What potential problems exist from switching the maintenance contract from the vendor to HRI (you might call several local computer hardware vendors to gain insight into this question)?

3. Can you determine a maximum amount that you would be willing to pay for HRI's services?

CASE II

SAVEWAY FOODSTORES

John Grashoff, president of Saveway Foodstores, has recently returned from a supermarket industry convention during which he attended a presentation on computerized energy management. John knew that energy costs for motors, compressors, conveyers, lights, heating, air conditioning, and so forth were quite high for his six stores, but he always looked on this expense as simply being a cost of doing business. John returned from the seminar convinced that a computerized energy management system would be beneficial for his stores.

Upon his return, John invited a computer sales representative to visit several of his locations and together they figured that the cost of installing an energy management system in each store would be $21,000 per store. They also estimated that energy consumption and peak loading charges could be reduced from 12 to 18 percent per month. The following table presents the average per-store energy consumption costs for the last 12 months.

John estimates that energy costs will increase at an annual rate of 7½ percent over the next seven years. His required rate of return is 2 percentage points over the prime interest rate, which is 12.5 percent. John will depreciate the assets over a seven-year life using a straight-line depreciation method and will also use seven years as the project life. His effective tax rate is 22 percent.

Month	Average Cost per Store
March	$4800
April	4100
May	3900
June	4100
July	4800
Aug.	5300
Sept.	4700
Oct.	4100
Nov.	4200
Dec.	5100
Jan.	5600
Feb.	5400

Questions for Discussion

1. How would you advise John regarding the installation of an energy management system in his stores?

2. What other factors would you consider, or what cautions would you give to John, before placing an order for six systems?

15.13 REFERENCES AND BIBLIOGRAPHY

1. Adam, E. E., Jr., and Pohlen, M. F., "A Scoring Methodology for Equipment Replacement Model Evaluation," *AIIE Transactions*, 6:308–314 (1974).
2. Barlow, R., and Hunter, L., "Optimum Preventive Maintenance Policies," *Operations Research*, 8:90–100 (1960).
3. Goldman, A. S., and Slattery, T. B., *Maintainability: A Major Element of System Effectiveness*, New York: Wiley, 1964.
4. Hardy, S. T., and Krajewski, L. J., "A Simulation of Interactive Maintenance Decisions," *Decision Sciences*, 6:92–105 (1975).
5. Jardine, A. K. S., *Maintenance, Replacement, and Reliability*, New York: Wiley, 1973.
6. Kaufman, R. J., "Life Cycle Costing: Decision Making Tool for Capital Equipment Acquisitions," *Journal of Purchasing*, 5:16–31 (Aug. 1969).
7. Landers, R. R., *Reliability and Product Assurance*, Englewood Cliffs, NJ: Prentice-Hall, 1963.
8. McClain, J. O., "Physician Confidence and Reliability in Utilization Review," *Medical Care*, 10 (No. 6, 1972).
9. Morrow, L. C., *Maintenance Engineering Handbook*, 2nd ed., New York: McGraw-Hill, 1966.
10. Peck, L. G., and Hazelwood, R. N., *Finite Queuing Tables*, New York: Wiley, 1958.
11. Terborgh, G., *Business Investment Management*, Washington, DC: Machinery and Allied Products Institute, 1967.
12. Terborgh, G., *A Practical Method of Investment Analysis: The MAPI System*, Washington, DC: Machinery and Allied Products Institute and Council for Technological Advancement, 1971.
13. Turban, E., "The Use of Mathematical Models in Plant Maintenance," *Management Science*, 13:342–358 (1967).
14. Turban, E., "The Complete Computerized Maintenance System," *Industrial Engineering*, March 1969, p. 20–27.
15. Vonalven, W. H., ed., *Reliability Engineering*, Englewood Cliffs, NJ: Prentice-Hall, 1964.
16. Weston, J. Fred, and Brigham, Eugene F., *Managerial Finance*, New York: Holt, 1972.
17. Wilkinson, J. J., "How to Manage Maintenance," *Harvard Business Review*, 46:100–111 (March–April 1968).

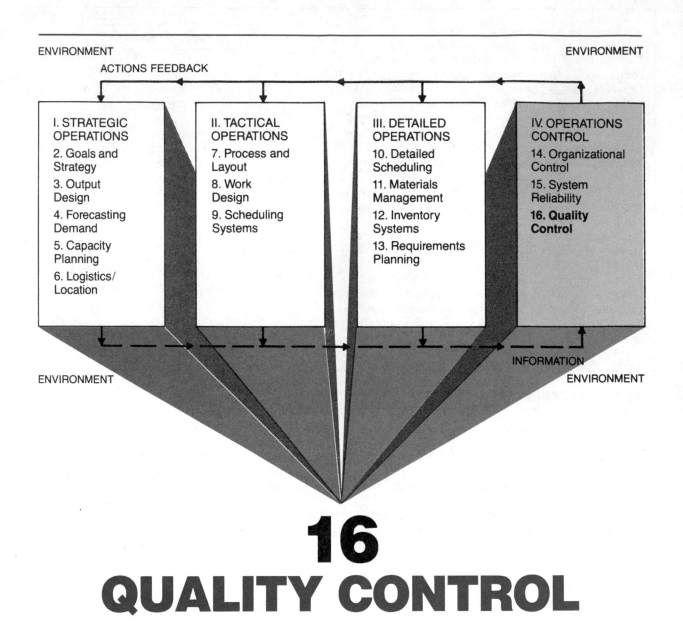

ENVIRONMENT   ENVIRONMENT

ACTIONS FEEDBACK

I. STRATEGIC OPERATIONS

2. Goals and Strategy

3. Output Design

4. Forecasting Demand

5. Capacity Planning

6. Logistics/ Location

II. TACTICAL OPERATIONS

7. Process and Layout

8. Work Design

9. Scheduling Systems

III. DETAILED OPERATIONS

10. Detailed Scheduling

11. Materials Management

12. Inventory Systems

13. Requirements Planning

IV. OPERATIONS CONTROL

14. Organizational Control

15. System Reliability

16. Quality Control

ENVIRONMENT   INFORMATION

                                                                          ENVIRONMENT

16
QUALITY CONTROL

16

LEARNING OBJECTIVES
By the conclusion of this chapter the student should

- Better understand the nature of quality, its major measures, and the cost tradeoffs in attaining output quality.

- Appreciate the role of inspection in quality control.

- Be familiar with the reasons for both sampling and complete inspection.

- Have developed a sense for the concepts of consumer's risk, producer's risk, and chance versus assignable variation.

- Understand the two major approaches to statistical quality control.

- Have a feel for the tradeoffs in setting control limits.

- Know how to set up, use, and interpret control charts for means, ranges, fraction defective, and number of defects.

- Realize the significance of the operating characteristic curve for acceptance sampling and know how to design a sampling plan.

- Be aware of the advantages of multiple sampling.

- Comprehend the importance of behavior and attitude in quality control and some of these types of reasons behind good and bad quality control situations.

We hear of "quality" everywhere these days: quality circles, zero defects, inferior quality, quality teams, and so on. Though this is the last chapter of the book, the subject of quality must be one of the first the organization considers in its operations strategy, as discussed in Part I of the text. This characteristic of the output is affected throughout the operations process from the quality of the raw materials, through the skill and capabilities of the workers and equipment, to the performance of the operations supporting systems such as the scheduling system, the inventory system, and the logistics system. In this chapter we will investigate how these functions affect output quality and the procedures that have been developed for controlling them.

Again, we will attempt to keep our discussion in the generic framework we have employed throughout the text while drawing examples from various sectors. In this chapter we employ examples from nail manufacturing, aerospace, ice cream retailing, transportation, library services, and banking.

We first address the general nature of quality, its cost, and its control. We then focus on the inspection element of quality control and employ a World War II game to illustrate some difficulties of inspection. Next, we briefly look at the theory of statistical quality control to gain understanding and direction for the application of quality control procedures. Following this short theoretical treatment we illustrate the procedure of quality control during production, called "process control," through examples of the construction of control charts for variables and attributes. Then we illustrate the control of quality for batches of material, especially receivables, called "acceptance sampling." Last, we address the issue of the application of quality control procedures in the United States and, for contrast, in Japan, which currently enjoys an excellent reputation for quality. We also consider some of the reasons for the difference in quality levels of these two countries.

16.1   THE NATURE OF QUALITY

From pride of workmanship to one cog in a system.

In the days of the craftsmen and guilds, the quality of an individual's output was that person's *advertising*, declaration of *skill level*, and source of *personal pride* of workmanship. With the coming of the Industrial Revolution and its infinite degree of specialization and interchangeability of parts (and workers), pride of workmanship became secondary to effective functioning of the individual as simply one cog in an enormous organizational "system." Quite naturally, quality deteriorated and therefore had to be specifically identified and controlled as a functional aspect of the output.

Recognition of the need to control quality.

This recognition of the need to specifically consider the quality of an output was given impetus by the adoption of statistical sampling procedures by the military in World War II through Military Standard 105. The result was a significant increase in interest in quality control in firms supplying arms and materials to the armed forces, which then spread even further into firms in the general economy.

In addition, this interest spread to Japan which, by the middle 1950s,

Shoddy goods.

had been producing cheap imitations of U.S. and foreign goods and exporting them around the world. This interest culminated in their inviting W. Edwards Deming, a U.S. quality control expert, to come to Japan and speak

Quality teams.

on his ideas about using worker teams to improve product quality.

Relativeness of quality.

Quality, however, is a relative term, meaning different things to different people at different times. Depending on the situation, an output's "quality" may refer to its *reliability* of performance, its *durability*, its *timeliness*, its *appearance*, its *integrity*, its *purity*, its *individuality*, or more likely, some combination of such factors. The problem of maintaining a product's or service's quality, then, is dependent, in part, on knowing the end-use of the output and the conditions under which it will be judged.

Top quality not always desired.

It is usually assumed that recipients desire only "top" quality products and services. To an extent this is true, but only if the price and other characteristics can be kept at appropriate levels. If not, people will usually accept a lower quality output, trading quality for improvement in another criterion. Not only may top quality be too expensive for recipient needs—it may also be too far away, too slow, too pretentious, too much trouble, or have other negative aspects associated with it. We therefore do not all buy Cadillacs, live in Beverly Hills, or shop at Nieman-Marcus.

Real versus imitation.

Furthermore, with our highly advanced technology, we often cannot even *tell* what is high quality and what is not. Plastic flowers *look*, and sometimes *feel*, real; imitation walnut furniture frequently looks *better* than the real thing; and, to some consumers, "nondairy coffee creamers" are "better" than real cream. Even the old adage "You get what you pay for" may not be true these days—many people feel they are still paying, but not getting it any more.

Where is the problem?

No one really seems to be quite sure where the trouble lies. Is the quality of what we pay for indeed lower than it used to be? Or are we getting something different now for our money from what we used to get—such as better service? Or, perhaps, we are simply more sophisticated buyers now, demanding excellence (as the advertising promotions insist we should) from our organizations and their products and services. For that matter, perhaps the sheer variety of services available is the reason for our disenchantment with quality these days, especially since it is so difficult to measure the

How is quality measured?

quality of services. Should the quality of a police department be measured by the decrease in arrests? Or the increase? Should students be graded in a class by what they know, by how much was learned, or how hard the students tried? For that matter, is the quality of an education measured by the knowledge gained, the average starting salary of the graduates, or how satisfied the students were with the experience?

Measuring the quality of a product is usually relatively straightforward. Juran [12] notes three quality measures that may be applied to products.

Design.

● *Design quality:* The quality level of the product's design relates to the inclusion of superior attributes when the product is originally envisioned. This is sometimes known as its "grade level," as with "AAA rated" bonds. In part, this reflects intensive market research to ascertain the need of the market and then to conceptually match new technologies to meet this need. As an example, microwave ovens use new technology to cook faster, better, and with less energy than conventional ovens.

Conformance.

- *Conformance quality:* The quality of conformance concerns whether the product meets its stated (or even unstated but nevertheless expected) specifications. Did the bulb last 100 hours as it was supposed to? Did the automobile get 35 miles per gallon as advertised? Did the paint last "many years," or peel after the first winter?

Availability.

Reliability.

Maintainability.

- *Availability quality:* This aspect of quality involves the product performing as specified at some *future* time, after it was initially obtained. Two factors interact here to determine "availability." The first is the reliability of the product, which relates to its mean time before or between failures, as discussed in the previous chapter. The second factor, also discussed in the previous chapter, is the product's maintainability, which refers to the ability to quickly repair or replace the product when it fails.

Service quality.

As mentioned earlier, measuring the quality of a service is more difficult, and for a variety of reasons. The thing we are trying to measure is often abstract rather than physical, transient rather than permanent, or psychological or subjective rather than objective. A hotel, for example, may be perceived as high quality because of its "class," its "superior service," and its "reputation." All of these attributes, however, may simply be reflections of its expensive decor, its speed of service, its amenities, its location, its cleanliness, its spaciousness, or its peacefulness. And these may, in turn, be measurable in terms such as

Measures of hotel service.

- Dollars spent per room.
- Overall dollars spent on the hotel.
- Ratio of employees to patrons.
- Inches of insulation between rooms.
- Square footage per room.
- Number, size, and cost of amenities.
- Location in the city.

Measures of "reputation."

Even a characteristic as subtle as "reputation" may be measured through the evaluations of groups that rate hotels and their dining facilities, regional writeups in papers and magazines, and surveys of attitudes of upper-class citizens in the region.

Zero defects.

Traditional methods for controlling quality, especially in service organizations, have been through the establishment of goals, or standards, to guide workers in their activities. These goals are then periodically reemphasized through organizational programs, contests, posters, and the annual budget. Typical of such programs is "zero defects," a 1962 aerospace quality control development. This program attempts to *prevent* errors by eliminating their cause rather than remedying them after they have been made. <u>Better training and motivation on the part of both the worker and the manager</u> are primary ingredients of such a program. Committees are formed, the union is involved, training review sessions are sponsored, posters are hung, contests are run, banners are pinned up, achievement dinners are given, and so forth.

Appropriate quality level.
This type of program, however, is much more appropriate to a field such as aerospace, where one loose solder connection can abort a $100 million moon shot, than to many other areas, such as the manufacture of nails. For such commonplace products it is clearly not cost-effective to have workers pay extreme attention to identifying potential defects.

Figure 16.1 illustrates the cost reasons behind the very different levels of quality control most appropriate for these two products. Clearly, the costs of quality control and the products themselves, plotted on the vertical scale, are magnitudes apart. But the reason for the difference in quality levels is

Same quality cost, different defects cost.
the significantly different *slopes* of the cost of defects curves, defects due to low quality levels being much more expensive in the moon rocket than in nails. This is the same effect we observed in Figure 4.2 when selecting a forecasting approach.

A number of factors impact on the overall quality of the organization's output. Generally these factors may be classified as stemming from either (1) the operational facility (physical conditions, building, utilities), (2) tools and equipment, (3) input materials, or (4) the organization's staff (workers and managers). More specifically, however, quality is frequently determined by the following kinds of factors.

- *The market:* Competition is often the final factor in determining the appropriate, and necessary, level of quality of an organization's output.

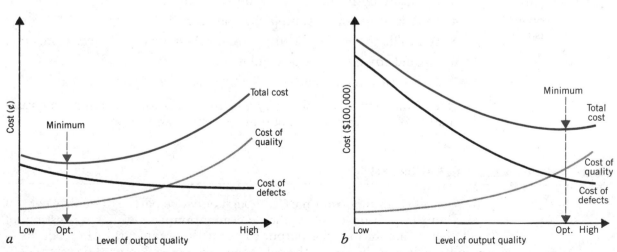

Figure 16.1 Optimum quality levels for two types of products. (*a*) Nails. (*b*) Moon rocket.

Quality impacting factors.

- *Organizational objectives:* Is the output to be a high-volume, low-priced item or an exclusive, expensive one?
- *Product testing:* Insufficient testing of the output may fail to reveal important flaws.
- *Output design:* The manner in which the output is designed may itself doom the product's or service's quality from the start.
- *Production process:* The procedure for producing the output may also adversely affect the quality.
- *Quality of inputs:* If poor materials, insufficiently trained workers, or inappropriate equipment must be used, quality will suffer.
- *Maintenance:* If equipment is not properly maintained, parts are not available in inventories, or communications not kept open within the organization, the quality of the resulting output will be less than it should be.
- *Quality standards:* If concern for quality throughout the organization is not apparent, no economically feasible amount of final testing or inspection will result in a high-quality output.
- *Customer feedback:* If the organization is insensitive to recipient complaints and requests for repairs or service, quality will not significantly improve.

Organizations, in an attempt to deal with these factors, often address the quality issue by specifically assigning responsibility for quality to someone, or a number of people, within the organization. There are a number of reasons behind the creation of a specific quality control function:

Reasons for assigning responsibility for quality.

1. To reduce mistakes and corrections.
2. To increase the average quality level of the output.
3. To ensure better interchangeability of parts.
4. To reduce customer complaints and returns.
5. To enable the *grading* of output (A, AA, AAA; prime, choice, good; etc.).
6. To abide by new laws or regulations.
7. To decrease the amount of defective incoming materials.

One of the primary methods by which organizations attempt to ensure the quality of their inputs and outputs is testing and inspection.

16.2 THE ROLE OF INSPECTION

Inspection is an important part, although only *one* part, of a quality control program. Inspection involves the determination, sometimes by testing, of whether or not an input or output conforms to organizational standards of quality. It is not, however, the role of inspection to *correct* the system defi-

SHOE

(Chicago Tribune-New York News Syndicate, 1978. Reprinted by permission of the Chicago Tribune. New York News Syndicate, Inc.)

ciencies that produced the defective items or, for that matter, even to decide *what* to inspect or *when*.

Commonness of inspection.

Inspection is a very commonplace activity. Not only is it prominent in manufacturing organizations but clearly in processing, distributing, and service organizations as well. The wine and coffee tasters inspect their outputs for many different quality criteria. Order pickers in warehouses inspect the packaging and age of the goods they send out. And bank examiners, federal Occupational Safety and Health (OSHA) inspectors, and Food and Drug Administration agents may interrupt the activities of organizations at any time to test conformance to regulations and standards. We often hear about licensing boards who have closed local businesses such as restaurants because their facilities could not pass inspection. And even at home, we regularly inspect the food we eat, the cars we drive, and the clothes we wear.

Because of the extent and difficulty of inspection, it can occupy a considerable amount of time. For simple, repetitive, automated production it may only require a small fraction of a direct worker's time. But in complex, technical, and/or manual work, such as in computer software services, it may occupy upwards of half the direct labor hours.

Ease of missing defects.

In spite of such dedication of time to the function, it is still not uncommon for inspectors to miss half of all the defects passing by them. Most commonly, about two-thirds of the defects are caught but, depending on the situation, this rate may vary from one in five to four in five. As an example, spend a minute with Figure 16.2.

Bear in mind that most inspectors are probably tired, not quite as enthusiastic about their work as they once were, nor as young as they used to be. To produce approximately the equivalent conditions, the exercise in Figure 16.2 should be completed during the last quarter or semester of your schooling, on a Friday night, and at about one o'clock in the morning. The correct number of "e"s on the pack of cigarettes is 11. The typical number reported by a class of undergraduates is from 7 to 11 with an average of 10.

"Don't look for coupons or premiums in this pack. The cost of the tabaccos blended in **HORSE** *cigarettes prohibits the use of them."*

Figure 16.2 Counting-the-defects exercise. During World War II, soldiers used to bet a new recruit $50 that he could not count all the "e"s on the back of a pack of a certain brand of cigarettes in one reading. Here is an approximate rendition of what that 1940's package back stated; try it yourself for about 15 seconds.

From this it should be clear that inserting inspectors into the end of a production process is not going to miraculously improve the quality of an organization's output.

Proper screening and training required.

Better quality will be obtained through inspection if the inspectors know what to look for, have been properly trained (including human relations), and have the physical and psychological makeup required for the job. Regardless, many organizations make use of inspectors who are not properly qualified simply because they never checked to see if they *were* qualified. Instances exist, for example, when inspection jobs demanding high visual acuity were given to workers who were partially blind.

There are a number of particularly important points in the transformation process where inspection is more valuable than at other times. Some of these are the following:

1. Upon receipt of resources: checking the quality of raw materials and purchased parts and supplies, testing equipment for ability to meet specifications, verifying the skills of staff.

2. Before transformation processes by the worker: if the process at hand is expensive, irreversible (such as mixing food ingredients), or of a concealing nature (such as assemblies, coatings, platings).

Where to inspect.

3. When the first few items come out of an automatic process.

4. After transformation processes (inspection by the worker).

5. After transformation processes (inspection by an inspector).

6. In final inspection.

7. When customers complain, return goods, or require service.

Organizations typically cannot afford to inspect at *all* of these points, but inspection at *some* of these points should be conducted. In addition to deciding *what* is to be inspected, the organization must also decide *when* to inspect (or, equivalently, how often), *where* to inspect (on the "floor" or in one specialized area), *who* should inspect, and *how* to inspect. (The topic of when to inspect will be covered later under statistical quality control.)

The location of inspection is usually either at the workplace itself (called *floor inspection*) or in a centralized inspection area. Floor inspection usually consists of approving equipment setups before runs are made, checking "first-off" items (shaving balloons at a barber school), and checking and recording semiautomatic equipment output. Frequently, floor inspectors have the authority to halt operations that are producing excessive defectives.

Floor inspection has some clear advantages to an organization. It saves the time and cost of transporting material to a central inspection area and the resultant queuing delay once there. However, if a floor inspector is unavailable, then both the worker *and* the equipment must sit idle until the inspector comes. Central inspection is typically used for tests requiring special equipment and total performance tests, such as when seniors must pass a state competency exam before graduating.

Who inspects?

The topic of *who* should inspect is important primarily in regard to who is responsible for quality control. If that person is the production manager, then an obvious conflict of interest will arise. Yet it is worthwhile to give the person who is responsible for producing the output the commensurate responsibility for the quality of that output. A common resolution to this dilemma is to have the floor inspectors report to the production manager but final inspection report at a higher level in the organization. In this manner the floor inspectors will be viewed by production as aids in getting work through the *final inspection* area.

How to inspect.

How to inspect involves the tools and equipment used by both floor and central inspection. Clearly, the more expensive, sensitive, and immobile equipment will remain at central inspection while small, lightweight, or rugged gauges and instruments will often be carried by the floor inspectors. Although inspection devices vary considerably from organization to organization, depending on the output, most of them are familiar: thermometers, questions, gauges, magnifying glasses, and so forth.

Handling of defectives.

After inspection has revealed a defective item or material, what should be done with it? Typically, it is not discarded. If it is worthwhile it may be reworked and repaired or refashioned into another output. If not, it may be sold as a "second" as is done with clothing and "second pressings" of wine. If even sale as a second is not feasible it may be recycled (e.g., shredded, remelted), if possible, and used as new raw material. Last, it may be sold as scrap.

Two bads equal a good.

In some instances it is possible to take a number of defective outputs and combine them to form an acceptable output. This "magic" is common in "processing-type" industries. Grain in silos and mined coal are both tested for a number of characteristics, any one of which may be either exceeded or insufficient. For example, the moisture content of corn in one silo may be too high to qualify as top grade corn, while the sugar content of corn in another silo may be too low. By *mixing* the contents of these two silos, however, a combined product is achieved which is now within *both* moisture and sugar requirements for classification as top grade corn, an interesting example of **synergism,** where the whole is equal to more than the sum of the parts.

16.3 STATISTICAL QUALITY CONTROL

Reasons for sampling.

To maintain the quality of their output, organizations must inspect and test* throughout their operations. In some processes 100 percent of the output is machine tested, but many others require manual inspection by a human. Fortunately, it is not usually necessary to inspect *all* the items or material during an inspection but only a *sample*. This is fortunate since there are a number of reasons for not conducting 100 percent manual inspection:

1. *Infinite population:* To inspect all the paper clips coming out of a factory, or all the oil from a refinery, would be virtually impossible. In the first situation, the inspection would fall far behind the production rate and go on forever, and in the second, the output is not in *discrete* form but infinitely divisible.

2. *Lack of time:* The time to adequately test each item may preclude inspecting *all* the items, as with the paper clips. Answers are needed very quickly for management decisions and late answers are worthless.

3. *Excessive cost:* Even if time were no problem, the cost of 100 percent inspection and testing is typically prohibitive.

4. *Destructive testing:* In some cases **destructive testing** is performed by testing the output until it fails, as is sometimes done with fuses, structural beams, and light bulbs. If this testing were applied to all of the organization's output, there would be nothing left to sell.

5. *Inaccuracy:* It was pointed out earlier that inspection does not catch all the defects. As the inspector becomes fatigued and/or bored, more defects slip by. With 100 percent inspection this would occur rather quickly. Therefore, better accuracy is usually obtained by inspecting and testing only a representative sample rather than the entire output, even with the inherent sampling error.

There are some instances, however, when 100 percent manual inspection may still be called for. These infrequent cases usually fall among the following situations:

1. *Extreme cost of defects:* If, by a failure of an output, an extreme cost is incurred, such as a loss of human life in a space shot, complete inspection is called for.

2. *High variability:* In cases where the variability of the output may be extreme (typically with human inputs such as in education) but consistency is desired (thus excluding art works, musical compositions, novels, etc.), 100 percent inspection may be desirable, if not too expensive or time-consuming.

When full inspection is needed.

3. *Operating unit assemblies:* When an assembled item is dispensed to recipients a unit at a time and is always expected to initially operate,

*The procedure is actually that of "hypothesis testing," as used in statistics.

such as a television set, automobile, or dryer, it is desirable to check the gross performance of 100 percent of the output if it can be done quickly and cheaply. For example, whether a dryer heats up and spins when turned on can be checked in seconds. But checking all the various cycles of a clothes dryer could entail a major, time-consuming test.

4. *Rejected lots:* If a *lot* (binfull, gross, filled railroad car) has been sampled and rejected it may be desirable to check the entire lot, not to determine the **defect rate** of the lot, but to locate and *remove* the defective items so that those remaining can be used or sold.

Quality control like the trial process in law.

The inspection decision is identical in concept to our society's trial procedure in law. We assume that a defendant is innocent until proven guilty. Likewise, we assume that output is of acceptable quality until proven otherwise. The sampling information then determines the evidence on which a "verdict" is reached. As in the legal process, two types of errors can be made (Figure 16.3). A **type I error** is committed when an innocent defendant (a good quality lot) is found guilty (declared "defective"). A **type II error** is made when a guilty defendant ("defective" lot) is found innocent (declared of good quality). The seriousness of these two types of errors is dependent on the organization and the type of output. Our society considers a type I error in the legal process extremely serious and goes to great lengths to prevent such a tragedy. Goods and service producing organizations, on the other hand, do not need to worry about the "rights" of their outputs and hence have more concern with the harm that may be done by passing a lot off as good when it actually is defective. This concern is thus oriented to type II errors.

Importance of type II errors.

In the medical field, where a disease has no "rights," and the patient suffers the consequences of an inspection error, type II errors are of even more concern. The result has therefore been to utilize more and more sophisticated (and expensive) testing equipment to reduce the possibility of a patient's *having* a particular disease but being diagnosed from a test as being *disease-free*, a type II error.

Risk for both producer and consumer.

In quality control terminology, the probability of making a type I error is known as the **producer's risk** since it is the chance that the producer's product or service is incorrectly declared defective or unacceptable. The probability of a type II error is known as the **consumer's risk.** Likewise, the

Lot (defendant) is actually	Inspection decision (verdict)	
	Quality (innocent)	Defective (guilty)
Quality (innocent)	Correct	Type I error
Defective (guilty)	Type II error	Correct

Figure 16.3 The inspection error possibilities.

consumer will sometimes, because of the sampling plan, accept a lot as being of acceptable quality when it is actually defective. As we will see in the next section, one objective of a sampling plan is to balance these two risks.

Every productive process generates variability in its output. One of the goals of quality control is to ensure that this variability is small enough that the output as a whole may be deemed of acceptable quality. This natural variability is seen as emanating primarily from two sources: *chance (random) variation* and *assignable (nonrandom) variation.*

Chance or assignable variation?

Built-in variation.

Chance variation is the variability that is built into (actually, allowed to remain in) the system. There is "play" between the gears and mechanical parts of machines. There is variation in the inputs. Processing conditions are variable. And human performance is particularly variable. When the productive operations are designed, the allowable chance variability (*tolerance* in engineering) is accounted for and the most economical system that can produce within those limits is constructed. If it later turns out that this chance variation is too great, the entire system may have to be reworked.

Identifying the cause of variation.

Assignable variation occurs because some system element or operating condition is out of control. A machine may be excessively worn, a part broken, a worker mistrained, faulty inspection gauges or instruments used, and so forth. It is this variation that quality control must identify so as to correct the faulty system element (or to refuse shipment of the goods).

If we consider the simplest possible model of an organization's operations—the input-process-output model (Figure 1.1 of Chapter 1)—we see that there are two elements, "inputs" and the "transformation process," that must be controlled in order to control the quality variation of the output. Two separate types of control have been developed for these two elements. Taken in "design" order, process control is for the transformation process and **acceptance sampling** for the inputs.

1. *Process control:* The control of the productive operations of the organization. Upon regular examination of an output, quality control can determine if a system element is malfunctioning. A blood test, for example, can detect many anomalies in human body performance.

2. *Acceptance sampling:* The determination of acceptable and unacceptable products and services. This function is important to the organization in its acquisition of appropriate resources, especially materials, for producing its output. Although every organization must certify the acceptability of its resources, the *quality control* area typically performs this function for physical materials (parts, raw materials), *personnel* for human resources, *engineering* for plant and equipment, and so on. Since most of the nonmaterials purchases are single unit acquisitions, sampling is not usually done but each item is inspected by itself.

Variables versus attributes.

When quality control is performing an inspection it will either *measure* something or simply determine the existence of a characteristic. The former, called inspection for *variables*, usually relates to weight, length, degree, intensity, or some other variable that can be *scaled*. The latter, called inspection of *attributes*, can also examine scaled variables but usually considers *dichotomous* variables such as right-wrong, acceptable-defective, black-white, timely-late, and other such characteristics that either cannot be measured or do not *need* to be measured with any more precision than yes-no. With scaled variables the dichotomy might be light-heavy, short-long, hot-cold, weak-strong, and so forth. Both types of inspection, either for variables or attributes, can be used for either process control or acceptance sampling. Sections 16.5—16.7 will discuss the common techniques used for process control and acceptance sampling.

16.4 SETTING OPTIMAL CONTROL LIMITS

Optimal control limits.

As mentioned in Chapter 14, control limits are usually set at either two or three standard deviations, the latter being most common in quality control settings. These control limits are essentially rule-of-thumb measures. Ideally, control limits should be set in accordance with the costs and benefits to be derived from alternative settings. Let us consider a formal analysis of the problem of determining optimal control limits.

Suppose that we have available the following information regarding control conditions and investigations for a particular situation.

1. Cost of investigation, whether the process is in or out of control, is $100. (It is assumed that investigation will always determine the cause if the process is out of control.)

Cost of control.

2. Cost of correcting the system, if it is out of control, is $300.

3. Cost of not correcting (in "present value" terms) if the system is out of control is $1500.

This problem can be formulated as a problem of decision making under uncertainty. First, define the two possible states of the system as follows:

θ_1 = system is "in control"

θ_2 = system is "out of control"

And define the two possible actions that can be taken after each sample is observed as

a_1 = investigate

a_2 = do not investigate

Based on the information listed above, a "payoff" *matrix* (Table 16.1) can be developed. Note that when the system is out of control and a decision is made to investigate, the total cost is $400 ($100 for investigation and $300 for correction).

If we let

$P(\theta_1)$ = the probability that the system is in control

Table 16.1 Payoff Matrix of Costs

Actions \ States	θ_1 In Control	θ_2 Out of Control
a_1 Investigate	$100	$100 + $300
a_2 Do Not Investigate	0	$1500

and

$P(\theta_2)$ = the *critical probability* that the system is out of control

then

$$P(\theta_1) = 1 - P(\theta_2)$$

Also, let $E(a_1)$ equal the expected value of investigation after observing a sample $\overline{X}$. Now, we can determine the critical probability for this situation and use this probability in establishing our control limits.

Essentially, what we are asking is "at what value of the *critical probability*, $P(\theta_2)$ will the manager be indifferent between the two available actions, to investigate and not to investigate?" We can find this probability by setting the expected values of these two actions equal to one another.

The expected value of the action *investigate* is

$$E(a_1) = 100 \times P(\theta_1) + 400 \times P(\theta_2)$$

or, in terms of $P(\theta_2)$

$$E(a_1) = 100 \times [1 - P(\theta_2)] + 400 \times P(\theta_2)$$

The expected value of the action *do not investigate* is

$$E(a_2) = 1500 \times P(\theta_2)$$

Now, setting these two expected values equal to one another we can solve for $P(\theta_2)$, the critical probability, as follows

$$100 \times [1 - P(\theta_2)] + 400P(\theta_2) = 1500P(\theta_2)$$

or

$$P(\theta_2) = .083$$

That is, control limits should be set so that an investigation is made if the probability of being out of control is 8.3 percent or greater, which conversely means that the probability of being in control is 91.7 percent or less. If the control limits are set at a probability exceeding 8.3 percent, the manager will be investigating, at a cost of $100 each time, more often than is worthwhile. Similarly, if the limits are set at a probability less than 8.3 percent, the manager will be risking a $1500 out-of-control situation too often.

If we consider Figure 14.7, which we used to show the relationship between $\pm 3S_{\overline{X}}$ limits and a normal distribution, what we want are control limits that cut off 8.3 percent of the area under the normal curve in the two tails combined. Conversely, 91.7 percent of the area will be between the control limits.

Referring to the table of the normal distribution in Appendix A we can find the value of Z beyond which 4.15 percent of the area under the curve lies (one-half of 8.3 percent). That is, $1 - .0415 = .9585$ gives the appropriate Z value, 1.73 standard deviations.

16.5 PROCESS CONTROL

Control charts.
The general concept of process control by the use of control charts was covered in Chapter 14. Here we will discuss the use of this concept specifically to control quality variables and attributes of the organization's output. Remember that a control chart showed an average for the variable of interest and upper and lower "control limits," usually, though not always, set at plus and minus three standard deviations.

Control of Variables

For the control of variables, two control charts are commonly employed.

Two control charts for variables.

1. A chart of the process sample *means* ($\overline{X}$).

2. A chart of the item *range* (R) in values indicated by the items in each sample (largest value of X − smallest).

It is important to use two control charts for variables because of the way in which control of process quality can be lost.

Figure 16.4 shows two patterns of change in the distribution of process values. These changes might be due to boredom, tool wear, the weather, fatigue, or any other such influence. In the top figure the variability in the process remains the same but the mean changes; this effect would be seen in the means ($\overline{X}$) chart but not in the range (R) chart. In the lower figure the mean remains the same but the variability tends to increase; this would be seen in the range (R) chart but not the means ($\overline{X}$) chart.

Two ways of going out of control.

In terms of quality of the output, either type of change could result in lower quality, depending on the situation. Regarding control limits, the lower control limit (LCL) for the means chart *may* be negative (profit, temperature, etc.) but can *never* be for the range chart (see definition of R). If calculations indicate a negative LCL for the range chart, it should simply be set to zero.

Minimum value of LCL.

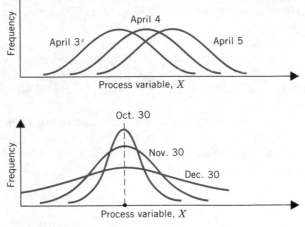

Figure 16.4 Patterns of change in process distributions.

Sweetn' Cold, Inc.

Sweetn' Cold is a chain of 10 fountain ice cream stores in southern Texas. Management is keenly concerned over the age of the ice cream being dispensed in their stores since their ads stress "jes' like home made" as compared to that of their competitors. To maintain a continuing check on this quality they have, for the last three weeks, been selecting four stores at random from their chain each day and noting the age of the ice cream being served. Management believes that, due to the trouble of sampling, a sample of 4 of the 10 stores each day will give them the best control for the trouble involved (cf. Figure 16.1).

The mean age and range in ages for each sample are presented in Table 16.2. The grand mean $(\overline{\overline{X}})$, the sample standard deviation of the means, $(S_{\overline{X}})$, the average range $(\overline{R})$, and sample standard deviation of the ranges (S_R), are also calculated and shown in Table 16.2. As an example, the calculations for June 1 were

Main St. store:	7 days
Southside store:	2 days
Bayfront store:	20 days
West Mall store:	11 days
Total	40 days

$$\text{mean, } \overline{X} = \frac{40}{4} = 10 \text{ days}$$

$$\text{range, } R = 20 - 2 = 18 \text{ days}$$

The grand mean, $\overline{\overline{X}}$ is then simply the average of all the daily means:

$$\overline{\overline{X}} = \frac{\Sigma \overline{X}}{n} \tag{16.1}$$

Table 16.2 Mean and Range of Ages of Ice Cream

Date	$\overline{X}$	R	$\overline{X} - \overline{\overline{X}}$	$(\overline{X} - \overline{\overline{X}})^2$	$(R - \overline{R})$	$(R - \overline{R})^2$
June 1	10	18	−1	1	4	16
2	13	13	2	4	−1	1
3	11	15	0	0	1	1
4	14	14	3	9	0	0
5	9	14	−2	4	0	0
6	11	10	0	0	−4	16
7	8	15	−3	9	1	1
8	12	17	1	1	3	9
9	13	9	2	4	−5	25
10	10	16	−1	1	2	4
11	13	12	2	4	−2	4
12	12	14	1	1	0	0
13	8	13	−3	9	−1	1
14	11	15	0	0	1	1
15	11	11	0	0	−3	9
16	9	14	−2	4	0	0
17	10	13	−1	1	−1	1
18	9	19	−2	4	5	25
19	12	14	1	1	0	0
20	14	14	3	9	0	0
Total	220	280		63		114

Mean, $\overline{\overline{X}} = 220/20 = 11$ days
Range, $\overline{R} = 280/20 = 14$ days
Sample standard deviation, $S_{\overline{X}} = \sqrt{63/(20-1)} = 1.82$ days
Sample standard deviation, $S_R = \sqrt{114/(20-1)} = 2.45$ days

where n here is 20 days of samples and the sample standard deviation is

$$S_{\overline{X}} = \sqrt{\frac{\Sigma(\overline{X} - \overline{\overline{X}})^2}{n-1}} \tag{16.2}$$

Similar equations hold for $\overline{R}$ and S_R

$$\overline{R} = \Sigma R/n; \quad S_R = \sqrt{\frac{\Sigma(R - \overline{R})^2}{n-1}}$$

The data in Table 16.2 can now be used to construct control charts that will indicate to management any sudden change, either for better or worse, in the quality (age) of their ice cream. Both a chart of means, to check the age of the ice cream being served, and a chart of ranges to check consistency among stores, will be used. For example, the two standard deviation control limits for means would be $\overline{\overline{X}} + 2S_{\overline{X}} = 11 \pm 2(1.82)$ or 7.36 and 14.64. These limits would only be valid, of course, for the means of samples of size 4.

The grand mean and average range will give the center line on these charts and the sample standard deviations will give the control limits. For illustration, both one and two standard deviation limits will be shown, but normally just three standard deviation limits would be used.

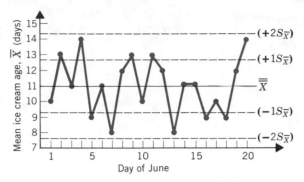

Figure 16.5 Mean ice cream age, days.

These charts are shown in Figure 16.5 and 16.6. In addition, the data in Table 16.2 are graphed on the charts. As seen in Figure 16.5, 10 of the $\overline{X}$ points exceed the $1S_{\overline{X}}$ limits, whereas only 7 would be expected to. However, none of the points exceed the $2S_{\overline{X}}$ limits and one is expected to. This indicates that there is considerable variability in the process but of limited deviation. That is, there is considerable variation within an age limit of about 6 days (from 8 to 14 days old) but not beyond that. Whether or not this is acceptable to management is a separate question.

Interpreting the control charts.

The range chart, Figure 16.6, shows six points exceeding the $1S_R$ limits and one point exceeds the $2S_R$ limits, about what should be expected. This indicates that variability between stores does not seem to be either increasing or decreasing. Again, whether or not this normal range of variability (of 10 days) is acceptable to management is another question.

Each day, as a new sample is taken, $\overline{X}$ and R are calculated and plotted on the two charts. If either $\overline{X}$ or R are outside the given (typically three sigma) LCL or UCL, management must then decide whether to wait for another day's sample or, more common, to undertake to find the assignable cause for the variation. This decision, again, depends on the output and the cost associated with continuing to sell for one more day a product of too low quality and the cost of the investigation.

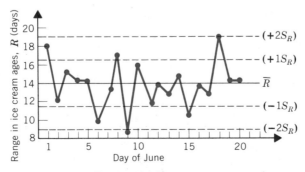

Figure 16.6 Range in ice cream ages, days.

Control charts are also used for the control of dichotomous *attributes*, as mentioned earlier. Two examples of such applications are given in the next section.

Although originally confined to the manufacturing setting, it should be clear that process control charts represent a significant tool for the control of *services* as well. Furthermore, because of their simplicity of use, workers can employ them to monitor their own performance, as in the previous example. Thus, a positive behavioral effect can also be achieved.

16.6   CONTROL CHARTS FOR ATTRIBUTES

Two types of attributes. The control chart process is also valuable for controlling attributes of the output. The most common of these charts are the "fraction defective" (*p*) chart and the "number of defects" (*c*) chart. These names were given to the charts from their emergence in a manufacturing context but they apply to a number of other situations as well. Similar to the range chart, the lower control limit for attribute charts can never be negative.

Fraction Defective (p) Charts

The fraction defective chart can be used for any two-state (*dichotomous*) process such as heavy-light or big-little. The control chart for *p* is constructed in much the same way as the control chart for $\overline{X}$. First, a large sample of historical data is gathered and the fraction having the characteristic in question (e.g., too light, defective, too old), $\overline{p}$, is computed on the entire set of data as a whole.

Large samples needed. Large samples are usually taken because the fraction of interest is typically small and the number of items in the samples should be large enough to include *some* of the defectives. For example, when talking about defectives, a fraction defective may be 3 percent or less. Therefore, a sample size of 33 would have to be taken (i.e., $\frac{1}{0.03} = 33$) to expect to include even one defective item.

Since the fraction defective follows a *binomial* distribution ("bi" means two: either an item is or it is not) rather than a normal distribution, the standard deviation may be calculated directly from $\overline{p}$ as

$$\sigma_p = \sqrt{\frac{\overline{p}(1 - \overline{p})}{n}} \qquad (16.3)$$

where *n* is the uniform sample size to be used for controlling quality. Although the fraction defective follows the binomial distribution, if $\overline{p}$ is near 0.5, or *n* is "large" (greater than 30 or so), the normal distribution is a good approximation and the 1, 2, or $3\sigma_p$ control limits will again represent 68, 95, and 99.7 percent of the sample observations. Again, the LCL cannot be negative. An example is given in the next section.

Table 16.3   Lost Book Data for p Chart

Date	Books Requested	Books That Could Not Be Located (Lost)
Feb. 7	122	15
8	91	12
9	137	13
	Total 350	40

$$\bar{p} = \frac{40}{350} = 0.114$$

$$\sigma_p = \sqrt{0.114(0.886)/50}$$
$$= 0.045$$

Downtown Library

Downtown Library has decided to monitor the number of lost books, as a fraction of those requested, by checking daily samples of 50 books requested by their patrons. Library staff have, through the procedures described previously, developed the control chart illustrated in Figure 16.7 based on three typical days of requests (Table 16.3). If the library wishes to use $\pm 2\sigma_p$ limits, then no assignable variations in lost books appear to have occurred in the four days of April plotted so far in Figure 16.7.

Note in this example that the data used to *derive* the control chart did not use the sample size of the samples used to determine $\bar{p}$. *Any* set of data could have been used to determine $\bar{p}$. In this case three samples were used from two months previously, one of size 122, one of 91, and the last of 137. Regardless, all the data were *combined* and then $\bar{p}$ was found. However, to set control limits, the actual value of the size of the sample to be monitored (n) was used in the calculation of σ_p. If, on a particular day, fewer than 50 books are requested, say 40, then a new value of σ_p, and new control limits based on the value $n = 40$, should be determined.

Sample size must stay constant.

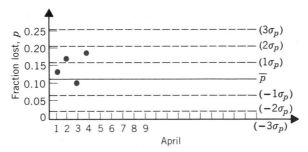

Figure 16.7   Control chart for percentage of lost books.

Number of Defects (c) Charts

The c chart is used for a single situation in which any number of incidents may occur, each with a small probability. Typical of such incidents are scratches in tables, fire alarms in a city, and typesetting errors in a newspaper. Again, an average number of incidents, $\bar{c}$, is determined from combined past data. The distribution of such incidents is known to follow the *Poisson* distribution with a standard deviation of

$$\sigma_c = \sqrt{\bar{c}} \tag{16.4}$$

Again, the normal distribution is used as an approximation to derive control limits with a minimum LCL of zero.

Stufie Bank, Ltd.

In an effort to better monitor the quality of their 24-hour teller services, Stufie Bank has instituted a charting procedure for the number of customer complaints. A quick review of the previous week's complaints gave the following information.

	Number of Complaints
Monday	5
Tuesday	0
Wednesday	3
Thursday	(data missing)
Friday	8
Total	16

$$\bar{c} = \frac{16}{4} = 4/day$$

$$\sigma_c = \sqrt{4} = 2$$

The control chart based on this one week sample of daily complaints is given in Figure 16.8. The two data points (Tuesday, Friday) out of four, on the $2\sigma_c$ limits, tend to imply the bank's quality of services is not in control. An investigation should be conducted and additional data collected.

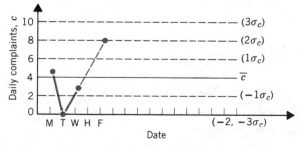

Figure 16.8 Control chart for complaints.

16.7 ACCEPTANCE SAMPLING

Static control of acceptance sampling.

Whereas process quality control is a *dynamic* quality control technique, acceptance sampling, another manufacturing development, is a *static* technique for computing incoming and outgoing quality of lots. Originally developed to provide a means whereby manufacturers could efficiently decide whether to accept or reject a shipment of incoming material, the approach has utility for services as well in checking the characteristics of large groups of services in order to classify them into, for example, grades of quality.

Again, either variables or attributes.

Sampling by variables would allow such a classification because each item is measured along a scale that can be partitioned into grades. More commonly, however, only a single bit of information is desired: whether a minimum level of quality exists or not. If not, the entire group may be returned to the

Attributes most common.

supplier or else subjected to 100 percent inspection. For such a simple purpose only *sampling by attributes* is required.

As opposed to control charts, it is not necessary for the organization to construct its own acceptance charts or tables. Two men, again from Bell Telephone Laboratories, H. F. Dodge and H. G. Romig, applied the theory of statistics to acceptance sampling and derived the necessary data in a form

Tables are available.

now known as the **Dodge-Romig** *Sampling Inspection Tables* [6].

Sampling plans from OC curves.

Given certain information, to be discussed later, these tables will provide an inspector with a **sampling plan** consisting of the size of the sample, n, and the maximum acceptable number of defectives, c (not to be confused with the c used in control charts). The ability of this plan to discriminate between "good" lots and "bad" lots is described by the curve of the chance of accepting the lot versus the percentage of defects in the lot, known as the plan's **operating characteristic** (OC) curve. Clearly, the greater the percentage of defects in the lot, the smaller the chance it will be accepted.

The ideal OC curve.

Ideally, such a plan would have the curve shown in Figure 16.9. In this case, the "stated" quality of the lot is 4 percent or less defectives. The ideal sampling plan would accept the lot if the actual percentage of defectives was 4 or less but reject it if it was more than 4. Such a result, however, could only come about by very careful inspection of the *entire lot*! Only then

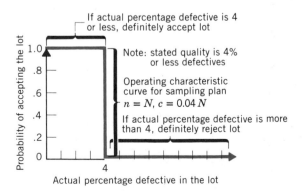

Figure 16.9   Ideal sampling plan.

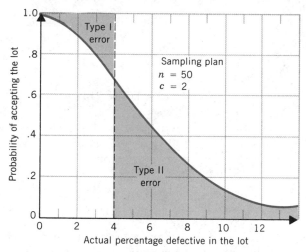

Figure 16.10 A typical operating characteristic curve.

. . . But too expensive.

could its *true* percentage of defectives be known (and quite possibly not even then) and the lot accepted or rejected according to the 4 percent figure. However, such a process would undoubtedly prove extremely expensive and very inefficient to the organization. A much better plan to minimize the total cost of both accepting defective items (cost of errors, Figure 16.1) and paying for inspection (cost of quality) would probably be to *sample* the lot and make a decision on the basis of the sample.

Trading off type I and type II errors.

The result of implementing such a strategy is to increase the chance of making type I and type II errors, as discussed earlier, especially very near the 4 percent point in the previous situation. This increased chance of error is illustrated by the shading in Figure 16.10. This figure shows a plan which rejects lots having samples with more than 4 percent defectives in them. In this case, the sampling plan is to sample 50 items ($n = 50$) and reject the lot if more than two defects ($2/50 = 4$ percent) are found ($c = 2$). The figure also illustrates what the chances of accepting the lot are, depending on the actual lot percentage of defectives. As can be seen, if the actual defect rate is 4 percent, there is about a 68 percent chance of accepting the lot. If 2 percent are actually defective the probability of acceptance is 91 percent (or a 9 percent chance of rejecting the lot even though only 2 percent are defective, a type I error called "the producer's risk") and if 6 percent are actually defective, the probability of accepting of the lot decreases to about 45 percent (a type II error called "the consumer's risk"). Note that, with this plan, if there are just *slightly* more than 4 percent defectives the chance of making a type II error is about 2 out of 3. Even so, this may be acceptable to management, considering the cost of inspection!

Effect of n and c on type I and II errors.

Figure 16.11 illustrates the effect of changing various parameters in the plan. Note that those plans based on 4 percent are either more or less discriminating (steep) than the plan in Figure 16.10, depending on whether n

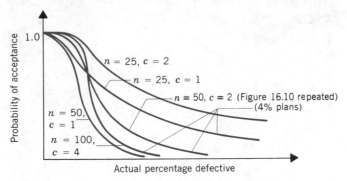

Figure 16.11   Other sampling plan's OC curves.

is greater, or less, than 50. For example, the plan $n = 100$, $c = 4$ is very discriminating but requires twice as much sampling.

For a given lot size N, the specification (by management) of the two probabilities of making a type I and type II error determines, through the use of the Dodge-Romig tables, a sampling plan. The parameters of interest are sketched in Figure 16.12. The two parameters that must be specified by management are

Sampling plan
from AQL and
LTPD.

AQL   The **acceptable quality level.** The actual percentage defective in the lot that the organization is willing to mistakenly reject (by chance) 5 percent of the time (called the producer's risk, $\alpha = 5$ percent) when the lot is *actually* "good" (of this quality or better; i.e., less percentage). For example, in a lot of 4 percent stated quality management might be willing to risk *mistakenly* returning 3 percent quality goods (5 percent of the time).

LTPD   The **lot tolerance percentage defective.** The actual lot percentage defective the organization is willing to mistakenly accept (by chance) 10 percent of the time (called the consumer's risk, $\beta = 10$ percent) when the lot is *actually* "bad." Here manage-

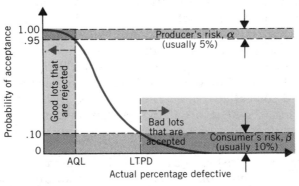

Figure 16.12   Sampling plan input parameters.

ment might only be willing to mistakenly accept 4.5 percent goods (10 percent of the time).

If the use of these numbers in the Dodge-Romig tables results in an "excessive" value of n (amount of sampling) to the organization, then they must be willing to risk either accepting worse quality lots (increase LTPD), rejecting better quality lots (decrease AQL), or both. Those are the only trade-offs possible (at this point in the discussion. We will discuss another alternative, multiple sampling, shortly.).

General Receivers and Shippers Co. (GRSC)

The receiving department of GRSC is under orders from the vice-president of receiving to carefully inspect every order received from a new supplier. For truckload-sized orders of 3 percent stated quality, top management has indicated that they would be willing to risk only a 10 percent chance (consumer's risk) of accepting an order containing 11 percent (LTPD = 11 percent) or more defectives. On the other side, they would be willing to risk a 5 percent chance (producer's risk) of rejecting an order whose quality was 1.5 percent (AQL = 1.5 percent) or less defectives.

Using this information, the acceptance sampling Table A5 in Appendix A indicates that the proper sample size, n, is 50 and the limiting acceptance value, c, is 2. This sampling plan's operating characteristic curve is that sketched in Figure 16.10. If this sample size is too expensive for top management and a smaller size, say 40, is desired, then they must be willing to accept an LTPD of about 12 percent (at the same AQL level) or an AQL of about 1.1 percent (at the same LTPD level). That is, either the defect rate at a 10 percent risk of acceptance must increase from 11 to 12 percent, or the defect rate at a 5 percent risk of incorrect rejection must decrease from 1.5 to 1.1 percent.

Multiple Sampling

All of the preceding discussion concerning acceptance sampling assumed, as is typically the case, that only *one* sample was to be selected and inspected. However, one method of reducing the expected sampling necessary but still maintaining the same confidence in the sampling process is to use a **multiple sampling** plan. The idea behind this process is that, at some increase in sampling time and complexity, a small, partial sample taken first may indicate which lots are extremely good or bad (by having very few, or many, defects in the small sample) and these lots would then not need to be sampled further. For instance, if taking a half-sized sample eliminated one-third of all the lots from further sampling, the amount of sampling saved would be $\frac{1}{2} \times \frac{1}{3} = \frac{1}{6}$, or 17 percent, a considerable saving.

The details of the *double sampling* procedure described above would be as follows:

Step 1   Take a sample n_1.

Reducing sample size by multiple sampling.

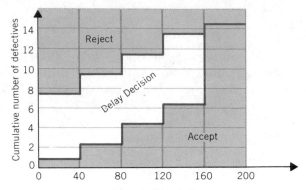

Figure 16.13 Portrayal of five-stage sequential sampling plan.

Step 2 If the number of defectives is greater than c_2, reject the entire lot. However, if it is not more than c_1 (where c_1 is less than c_2), then accept the entire lot. Otherwise, take another sample of size n_2.

Double sampling.

Step 3 Find the number of defectives in n_2. If the number of defectives in $n_1 + n_2$ (that is, in *both* samples combined) is now greater than c_2, reject the lot; otherwise accept it.

Sequential sampling.

Sequential sampling extends this notion even further, to the point where up to only half as many samples, on the average, as with single sampling need be used (at the cost, again, of increased complexity and time). The procedure is illustrated in Table 16.4 and Figure 16.13 for a five-stage sequential sampling plan centered on 7 percent defectives. The hope, of course, is that somewhere before the fifth sample, a decision can be made, thus making it unnecessary to take all five samples. Note how, in Table 16.4, the range in percent defectives over which a "delay decision" response is appropriate shrinks toward 7 percent with the increasing number of samples.

Table 16.4 Five-Stage Sequential Sampling Plan

Sample No.	Sample Size	Cumulative Size	ACCEPT if Total No. Defectives ≤:	(%)	REJECT if Total No. Defectives ≥:	(%)	Delay Region (%)
1	40	40	0	0	8	20.0	$7 \begin{array}{l} + \ 13 \\ - \ 7 \end{array}$
2	40	80	2	2.5	10	12.0	$7 \begin{array}{l} + \ 5 \\ - \ 4.5 \end{array}$
3	40	120	4	3.3	12	10.0	$7 \begin{array}{l} + \ 3 \\ - \ 3.7 \end{array}$
4	40	160	6	3.75	14	9.0	$7 \begin{array}{l} + \ 2 \\ - \ 3.25 \end{array}$
5	40	200	14	7.0	15	7.5	$7 \begin{array}{l} + \ 0.5 \\ - \ 0 \end{array}$

The "delay" range.| That is, the *"delay"* range begins at 20 percent (20 − 0 percent) for a sample size of 40 and decreases to 6.7 percent at 120 items sampled and finally to 0.5 percent at 200 items sampled.

Details regarding the construction of such plans can be found in Duncan [7]. Another approach, in lieu of using the Dodge-Romig or preceding tables, is experimenting with different sampling plans through simulation. In addition to providing time and cost data and allowing different combinations of plans, other values of producer's and consumer's risk (α and β) than 5 and 10 percent may be tested if desired.

16.8 APPLICATION

Too little use of methods.| Although currently deemed crucial to the United States' competitive ability in international markets, close attention to quality has not been a strength of U.S. products. This chapter has introduced only a few of the many techniques available for quality control. Yet too few firms actually employ them, and those that do typically use only the very well known methods: single sample fraction defective acceptance sampling (many fewer employ double or multiple sampling), and $\overline{X}$, R, p, and c charts for process control.

There are many reasons for the lack of attention to quality control in the United States. Following are the major reasons:

1. Lack of attention in U.S. organizations to the control function itself, as discussed in Chapter 14.

2. The inadequate assignment of responsibility for quality to the worker performing the task. Rarely is this responsibility specified; it is more or less "assumed" to be part of the task.

3. Lack of familiarity at the worker level with quality control methods and procedures.

Reasons for inattention to quality.| 4. The use of piece rate and other pay incentive schemes that emphasize and reward quantity rather than quality of output.

5. The use of work-in-process and buffer inventories, which bury poor quality in the system until a later time when these items are reissued for further processing.

6. Long supplier lead times, which prohibit the rejection of defective incoming materials. This is a common problem today in the United States, particularly in the case of castings. Frequently the lead times on castings are 6 to 18 months. After waiting this long, the manufacturer *cannot* wait any longer for a defective casting to be recast or to order from another foundry—the customer would cancel the order. The manufacturer must repair the casting as best they can and proceed with the job. They cannot even threaten to switch to another foundry in the future because foundries have closed up in droves over the last two decades. That is why the casting took 18 months to get in the first place and then was excessively rushed in its production to the point of being defective.

Castings—no alternative.|

The Japanese once had poor quality, too, much worse than what the United States currently has. In the 1950s, the label "Made in Japan" meant "cheap imitation goods" that invariably broke after minimal use. (It was even rumored that Japan had renamed one of its major manufacturing regions "Usa" so they could stamp "MADE IN USA" on their products.) It is doubtful if any country before, or even since, had such a worldwide reputation for bad quality. Clearly, their turnaround of this reputation, starting with the visit by W. Edwards Deming, is barely short of miraculous.

"Made in Usa."

The Japanese did this not by imitating the United States, or any other country, but by tying the concept of quality control directly into their production process, and now even their entire economy through export inspections to guarantee the quality of exports. The natural inclinations of their culture were exploited in the quality crusade that followed:

Quality integrated with their culture.

- Quality circles were based on natural teamwork procedures and individual worker responsibility for results. Behavioral and attitudinal factors were considered of primary importance in improving quality levels.

- Extensive training for all levels of workers was used to also instruct them in the use of quality control procedures.

- Cross-training and job rotation were used to demonstrate the importance of good quality.

- Lifetime employment made clear the necessity of living with your product's quality reputation.

- The natural Japanese disinclination to store unneeded materials fostered the development of "just-in-time" operations, which furthered the quality concept through immediate inspection, processing, and use. If a product was defective, it was *immediately* clear.

"Just-in-time" aids quality.

- Japanese patience was exercised to extensively test and check components before installing them in products and then take the time to check the products again before shipping them to customers.

Two decades of patience.

After nearly two decades (more patience) of such a national emphasis on quality, Japan's reputation for producing shoddy goods was totally reversed. Now, by comparison, it is the United States (and other countries, too, it might be noted) who seems to be producing the "shoddy" goods. In fact, the United States' and others' quality levels may not have actually fallen that much. Nevertheless, when high quality is combined with competitive pricing, another strength of the Japanese system, the result is extremely strong competition for existing producers.

16.9   SUMMARY AND KEY LEARNING POINTS

In this chapter we first discussed the general nature of quality, some ways by which it could be measured, and the factors that impact on it. We then looked at the role of inspection in quality control. Shifting our focus to consider some statistical aspects of quality control, we interpreted the meaning of type I and type II errors and, given the costs of each, saw how to best set upper and lower control limits to minimize these costs. We then picked up our discussion of control charts from Chapter 14 and discussed their use in monitoring variables and attributes.

Next, we looked at acceptance sampling and how to design sampling plans to minimize both risk of error and sampling at the same time. We concluded this subject by noting the cost savings available by using multiple sampling. Last, we considered possibly the most important aspect of quality control, the behavior and attitudes of the employees toward quality, and compared poor attitudes with those exhibited during the Japanese "quality crusade."

The key learning points were

- Quality is affected by a number of factors, such as competition, product testing, the quality of resource inputs, and maintenance. It can be measured along a number of dimensions, such as design quality, conformance quality, and availability quality. The best quality level for an output is not always the highest but must reflect a tradeoff of the cost of high quality with the cost of low quality (primarily defects).

- Inspection is more appropriate at certain points in the transformation process, but it must be remembered that quality cannot be inspected into the outputs and, for that matter, inspection itself is quite prone to error.

- Sampling is usually employed over complete inspection when there is an essentially infinite population, time is lacking, the cost for full inspection is excessive, destructive testing is employed, or there is a need for high accuracy the first time. Full inspection is used if there is high variability in the output, if an extreme cost for defects is incurred, for certain assemblies that are expected to always work the first time, and for rejected lots under some policies of inspection.

- Consumer's risk is the chance that an item considered good is actually bad, a type II error. Producer's risk is the chance that an item considered bad is actually good, a type I error. Variation occurs naturally in processes and is considered a chance event. Sometimes, however, a process goes out of control and variation then is considered "assignable."

- The two major approaches to statistical quality control are acceptance sampling and process control. Either approach may *measure* something, called inspection for *variables,* or attempt to determine the existence of a characteristic, called inspection of *attributes.*

- Control limits on process charts should reflect the costs of setting the limits too low and making type I errors and setting them too high and incurring type II errors.

- Historical data are used to obtain a mean for the statistic in question and its standard deviation. To control variables, both a means and range chart should be used. Appropriate equations are given by Equations 16.1 through

16.4. UCL and LCL values are usually set at three-sigma and any plotted data exceeding these limits are investigated.

● The OC curve illustrates the risks of type I and II errors for each possible sampling plan. A plan can be obtained from statistical theory or Dodge-Romig tables once an acceptable quality level and lot tolerance percentage defective are specified (at standard or otherwise stated levels of consumer's and producer's risks).

● Multiple sampling offers the potential of reduced sampling cost for the same level of accuracy (or higher accuracy for the same cost) by identifying significantly high or low quality lots early and not having to inspect them as fully.

● Some reasons for poor quality control include lack of attention to the subject, inadequate assignment of responsibility, lack of familiarity with quality control tools and methods, the use of quantity incentives, maintaining buffer inventories, and accepting long supplier lead times. Some elements behind good quality control are the use of teamwork, extensive worker training, job rotation, lifetime employment, just-in-time scheduling of work, and patience.

16.10 KEY TERMS

destructive testing (p. 624)

defect rate (p. 625)

type I error (p. 625)

type II error (p. 625)

producer's risk (p. 625)

consumer's risk (p. 625)

acceptance sampling (p. 626)

fraction defective (p) chart (p. 633)

number of defects (c) chart (p. 635)

Dodge-Romig tables (p. 636)

sampling plan (p. 636)

operating characteristic (p. 636)

acceptable quality level (AQL) (p. 638)

lot tolerance percentage defective (LTPD) (p. 638)

multiple sampling (p. 639)

sequential sampling (p. 640)

16.11 REVIEW AND DISCUSSION QUESTIONS

1. How could a college control the quality of their graduates?

2. What are the quality measures of a theatrical performance?

3. What quality control program would be appropriate for the post office? Include attributes and variables.

4. We often hear about the decreasing "quality of life." What does this mean?

5. What are the benefits of teaching workers to control their own quality through tools such as control charts and acceptance sampling?

6. What types of outputs do not require high quality?

7. How could a quality control program be used in American politics?

8. Why was the military the first to be concerned about quality?

9. If a plastic imitation cannot be distinguished from the real thing, what difference does it make?

10. Why are services of such poor quality these days?

11. Can adding poor quality lots together to form a higher resulting output be used outside the processing industry?

12. What are some situations where type I error is most important? Type II error?

13. Why is variables acceptance sampling not common?

14. Why is multiple sampling not increased even beyond five stages since it would continue to decrease the amount of sampling required?

16.12 READINGS

WHY THINGS DON'T WORK ANY MORE

John Diebold
Chairman
Diebold Group, Inc.

The need for action on today's crises of unemployment, urban decay, energy dependence, environmental pollution and . . . you name it . . . is urgent. But we had better recognize that crisis management is self-defeating when it excludes attention to what I think of as our *real* problems. These problems are part of the very machinery with which our society manages itself and the processes by which we cope with the you-name-it crises as they come along.

Energy, unemployment and welfare are real and pressing enough problems to demand our best efforts. But we need too to make the institutions of our society capable of dealing with life in the advanced industrial world in which we live, or we are going to expend increasing resources in coping with a stream of ever more demanding crises. The risk in this situation is not so much that we won't be able to make things work but that we will turn to increasingly more authoritarian governments to do so.

Things don't work any more because we rely upon brute-force solutions for crisis instead of heading off the crises by changing the *processes* with which we cope with public issues. The *processes* we use to handle problems and to make public decisions are not adequate in today's complex and demanding world.

Decline in Quality

Some examples of what I think of as our *real* problems:

• *No matter how we organize things to produce management efficiency, nothing is going to keep increasingly unproductive, labor-intensive public services in important areas of life from declining.* It is a paradox of our society that many public services were originally taken over by the government precisely because they were so important we wanted them available to as many citizens as possible at uniform quality. Yet today, the modern, broadly available and dependable items are consumer goods—portable color TV's, computer-driven sewing machines or cheap pocket calculators with the capability of yesterday's giant computers. Most of our *really* important activities—education, public transport, medical-service distribution, the running of cities—don't rely on advanced technology and therefore decline in quality and their costs spiral up.

The *real* problem here is not to try to force technology and modern management through the system—which is like trying to push a string—but to see if we can't find ways to create the kind of demand that stimulates innovation and high productivity in the private sector.

The problem is to learn how to define the results we want and then create incentives to achieve them. The natural ingenuity of our people, one of America's greatest strengths, will do the rest, just as it has in the things we are best at.

There are isolated examples—in various U.S. cities and towns—of privately run "public" services that reflect lower-cost, better service in response to competition and the incentive of profit. For example, a private, for-profit fire department in Scottsdale, Ariz., costs citizens substantially less than the nationwide average for similar communities. If such trendlets mean the creation in the public sector of the kind of demand-pull for science and technology that has produced such success in industrial and consumer products, we may have found the key to a wholly new approach to higher-quality public services.

- *We do not have "distant early warning systems" to anticipate future consequences of current and past decisions, to foresee the problems they may pose, and to identify the trade-offs in priority that we may have to make among alternatives right now.* Many problems don't lend themselves to forecasting—no mid 1950s projection would have included an overnight quadrupling of oil prices, the social divisiveness of Vietnam, or Watergate. But there is a great deal we could know that we don't really consider. We avoid that very act of consideration, otherwise known as "planning."

Priorities for Resources

While strong emotions and proper skepticism surround the term "national planning," we do need some imaginative political inventing to allow us to compare the alternative demands on our limited resources, to assign priorities to those ends and to create incentives and disincentives so that the play of forces in the marketplace occurs within a framework of politically agreed-upon direction. The recent creation of the Congressional Budget Office was a good step, but we need many more.

- *Attitudes toward work and personal value systems have changed radically, but few large organizations have altered their systems for managing, promoting and paying people.* Coupled with the alienation from authority and regimentation that characterizes current changing values, the productivity of our economy is declining. We need large organizations; we also need our creative younger people. Yet, the way we handle people in business and government agencies has not kept up with the changes in their values. Imaginative innovation in adapting job hours and pay to today's realities could go a long way toward unleashing the energies and creativity of many members of our society who are "turned off" by yesterday's organization concepts and practices.

Innovative approaches to manpower used abroad have proved highly successful. The key in these cases seems to be the effective identification of the employees' interests with that of industry. In Japan, employees see themselves as part of a vital working community. In Germany, they have and feel as great an economic stake in productivity and profitability as does "management." We should be able to combine the possibility of self-fulfillment with the fact of working in large organizations, building on our own traditions of individual initiative and the recognition of talent.

16.13 PROBLEMS

Practice Problems

1. Top Management of the Security National Bank monitors the volume of activity at their 38 branch banks with control charts. If a branch deposit volume (or any of perhaps a dozen other volume indicators) falls below the LCL, there is apparently some problem with the branch's market share. If, on the other hand, the volume exceeds the UCL, this is an indication that the branch should be considered for expansion or that a new branch might be opened in an adjacent neighborhood.

Based on the 10-day samples for each of the six months below, prepare an $\overline{X}$ chart for monthly deposit volume (in terms of hundreds of thousands of dollars) for the Transylvania branch. Use $\pm 2\sigma$ control limits.

	Average of 10-Day Deposits ($\overline{X}$) (in hundreds of thousands of dollars)
June	0.93
July	1.05
August	1.21
September	0.91
October	0.89
November	1.13

2. Based on the following weekly demand data for Heavyaslead beer (It's twice as fattening as our normal beer!), determine the upper and lower control limits that can be used in recognizing a change in demand patterns. Use $\pm 2\sigma$ control limits.

Week Number	Demand (6 packs)
1	3500
2	4100
3	3750
4	4300
5	4000
6	3650

3. A fishing weight manufacturer produces ocean weights with a mean weight of 5.0 ounces and a standard deviation of 0.3 ounces. If a customer accepts the weights that weigh between 4.8 and 5.2 ounces as "5 ounce" weights, how many will the customer consider "defective" in a shipment of 1000?

4. The average demand for a product is 38 units per week with upper and lower control limits of 46 and 30 units at the two-sigma level. Find the standard deviation and the upper and lower control limits at the three standard deviation level.

5. Output from a process contains 0.02 defectives. Defective units that go into final assemblies cost $25 to replace. An inspector, at $8 per hour, can inspect 20 units per hour and is 100 percent effective in finding defectives. What is the gain or loss from using an inspector?

6. The Environmental Protection Agency conducts studies to monitor the pollution levels in rivers. One measure concerns the amount of copper found. Between 0.0003 and 0.0006 mgs of copper per cubic foot of water is considered acceptable and normal. Given sample means in one area of 0.0004 and a standard deviation of 0.0007, what is the probability of a given sample being considered polluted?

7. Given the following data, construct a three-sigma range control chart. If Friday's results are 15, 14, and 21, is the process in control?

Day of Sample	Sample Values
Saturday	22, 19, 20
Sunday	21, 20, 17
Monday	16, 17, 18
Tuesday	20, 16, 21
Wednesday	23, 20, 20
Thursday	19, 16, 21

8. Construct a three-sigma means control chart using the data in Problem 7 and determine if the process is still in control on Friday.

9. Construct a p chart using 2σ limits based on the following results of 20 samples of size 400.

Sample Number	Number of Defects
1	2
2	0
3	8
4	5
5	8
6	4
7	4
8	2
9	9
10	2
11	3
12	0
13	5
14	6
15	7
16	1
17	5
18	8
19	2
20	1

10. Twenty samples of 100 were taken with the following number of defectives: 8, 5, 3, 9, 4, 5, 8, 5, 3, 6, 4, 3, 5, 6, 2, 5, 0 3, 4, 2. Construct a 2σ p chart and determine if the process is in control.

11. Sheets of Styrofoam are being inspected for flaws. The first day's results from a new machine that produced five sheets were 17, 28, 9, 21, 14. Design a control chart for future production.

12. The Tick & Tye Company, CPAs, is willing to accept a 10 percent chance of accepting a file of invoices as being properly paid when up to 5 percent

were not. But they do not want to reject the file (and therefore have to audit the whole file) if the actual nonpayment rate is 1 percent or less. They are willing to accept a 5 percent chance of doing this. What sample size and acceptance value should be used?

13. Management of the Midtown Garment Outlet has decided that too many truckload lots of dresses have been accepted with too low an average quality. Midtown is a discount dress shop that sells "seconds" of famous brand merchandise. Midtown recognizes that "thirds" (not suitable for sale) often are mixed with the "seconds" merchandise, but lately too many items have been thirds. A sampling plan has been adopted with an AQL of 5 percent, with a 5 percent producer's risk and an LTPD of 15 percent with a 10 percent consumer's risk. What sample size and acceptance number of defectives should be used?

More Complex Problems

14. Find the optimal level of quality, L, if the cost of quality $C_Q = 50 + 4L$ and the cost of defects $C_F = 10 + 100/L$.

15. Given the following control payoff matrix, what minimum probability of being out of control should be used in setting control limits?

Action \ States	In Control	Out of Control
Investigate	$10	$150
Do not investigate	0	$300

16. Connecting rods for large steam generators are x-ray tested for stress cracks. If a crack exists and is not detected, the rod will break within the first 100 hours of use and require a complete "teardown" of the generator. The x-ray test is accurate 95 percent of the time in rejecting a cracked connecting rod and accurate 85 percent of the time in correctly "accepting" rods with no cracks. Historical data indicate that 15 percent of the rods have stress cracks. If the x-ray test result indicates that the rod should be rejected, what is the probability that it is actually cracked?

17. In Problem 16, a complete "teardown" of a generator costs $75,000. One connecting rod costs $1500 up to the time that it is tested. Suppose that a new testing procedure is available that can improve the accuracy of accepting rods without cracks to 90 percent. How much, on a per test basis, is this procedure worth in comparison with the x-ray testing?

18. Norris Rubber Company manufactures rubber hose washers. These washers are manufactured on automatic equipment which is adjusted to produce outside diameters of 0.75 inch. Historically, the standard deviation of this diameter has been 0.01 inch. Each hour, a sample of 30 washers is selected and $\overline{X}$ is calculated and plotted on an $\overline{X}$ chart.

a. Based on this information, draw an $\overline{X}$ control chart for 95 percent confidence control limits.

b. For the first 5 hours the following average diameters were found: 0.7510, 0.7503, 0.7491, 0.7521, 0.7499. Was the process ever out of control?

19. A local beverage bottler uses equipment to fill 12-ounce soft drink bottles. State regulations require that all bottles be filled to within ± 0.3 ounce of the 12-ounce nominal volume. The machine is adjusted to fill 12 ounces with a standard deviation of 0.3 ounce. If state inspectors check the filling machine daily using a sample size of five and shut down the machines if the average fill volume of the five bottles tested is less than 11.7 ounces or greater than 12.3 ounces, on what proportion of the days will the machine be stopped due simply to random fluctuation?

20. Based on the following data, prepare a p chart for the control of picking accuracy in a wholesale food warehouse.

Day	Number of Cases Picked	Number of Incorrect Picks
1	4700	38
2	5100	49
3	3800	27
4	4100	31
5	4500	42
6	5200	48

Plot 1, 2, and $3\sigma_p$, limits assuming that the sample size will be 100 cases.

21. In Problem 20 determine if days 7, 8, and 9 are in control.

Day	No. Cases Picked	No. Incorrect
7	4600	53
8	6100	57
9	3900	48

22. A new machine for making nails produced 25 defective nails on Monday, 36 on Tuesday, and 17 on Wednesday. On Thursday 47 defectives were produced. Construct an $\overline{X}$ chart, p chart, and c chart based on Monday–Wednesday results and determine if Thursday's production was in control. The machine produces a million or so nails a day. Which is the proper chart to use?

23. Midtown is unhappy about the amount of sampling required in Problem 13. Recommend two alternative single sampling plans that will reduce the amount of sampling by a third.

24. Design a double sampling plan for Midtown and describe your confidence associated with the first sample.

16.14 CASE

THE WESTERN HILLS DISPATCH

In April 1979 the Western Hills Dispatch was born. The objective of the newspaper was to provide an outlet for news, advertising, and community information for a rapidly growing section of a large midwestern city. The population of this western section had been growing at the rate of about 8 percent per year for the last five years. Current population is approximately 85,000. The dispatch brought together a good staff and immediately attracted a substantial readership. The current circulation now exceeds 22,000 homes. Mick Pates, editor of the Dispatch, bases the success of his newspaper on the accuracy and timeliness of his news coverage, his strong proactive editorial policy, and the focus on local news with analysis of regional and national items as they impact on the locality. Many others attribute the newspaper's success to Mr. Pates' own personal dedication, his ability to sell to advertisers, and his professional staff. He is widely recognized in the business as one of the best developers of newspaper talent.

One of Pates' recent brainstorms has been his "Scientific Quality Control Program." He controls the quality of the typesetting output by actively monitoring the performance of three other weekly newspapers, which are distributed in adjoining communities, and basing his upper and lower error control limits on the results of his samples of these newspapers' quality.

Each Friday morning, as a paper is coming off the press, Mr. Pates randomly selects a hundred letters and counts the number of typesetting errors in the newsprint. The following table shows the results of the samples over the previous quarter.

Sample	Typesetting Errors
1	9
2	11
3	0
4	13
5	1
6	2
7	4
8	4
9	10
10	1
11	4
12	3

Questions for Discussion

1. What assumptions are necessary using the upper and lower control limits established by reviewing other weekly newspapers?

2. Suppose that the control limits established by reviewing other news weeklies are 0.08 and 0.035, respectively. Plot last quarter's data on this control chart.

3. Compare the upper and lower control limits above with the upper control limit and lower control limit calculated from the 12 samples presented in the table.

16.15 REFERENCES AND BIBLIOGRAPHY

1. Adam, E. E. et al., *Productivity and Quality*, Englewood Cliffs, NJ: Prentice-Hall, 1981.

2. American Management Association, *Zero Defects: Doing It Right the First Time*, New York: AMA, 1965.

3. American Society for Quality Control, *Quality Motivation Workbook*, Milwaukee: ASQC, 1967.

4. Armstrong, W. H., *Mechanical Inspection*, New York: McGraw-Hill, 1953.

5. Crosby, P. B., *Quality Is Free*, New York: McGraw-Hill, 1979.

6. Dodge, H. F. and Romig, H. G., *Sampling Inspection Tables*, New York: Wiley, 1959.

7. Duncan, A. J., *Quality Control and Industrial Statistics*, 4th ed., Homewood, IL: Irwin, 1974.

8. Grant, E. L. and Leavenworth, R. S., *Statistical Quality Control*, 4th ed., New York: McGraw-Hill, 1974.

9. Hayes, G. E. and Romig, H. G., *Modern Quality Control*, Encino, CA: Bruce, 1977.

10. Hostage, G. M., "Quality Control in a Service Business," *Harvard Business Review*, 53:98–106 (July–Aug. 1975).

11. Juran, J. M., "Japanese and Western Quality—A Contrast," *Quality Progress*, Dec. 1978.

12. Juran, J. M. et al., eds., *Quality Control Handbook*, 3rd ed., New York: McGraw-Hill, 1974.

13. Konz, S., "Quality Circles: Japanese Success Story," *Industrial Engineering*, 11:24–27 (Oct. 1979).

14. Saniga, E. M. et al., "Quality Control in Practice—A Survey," *Quality Progress*, 10:30–33 (May 1977).

15. Swartz, G. E. et al., "One Firm's Experience with Quality Circles," *Quality Progress*, 12:14–16 (Sept. 1979).

16. U.S. Department of Defense, *A Guide to Zero Defects; Quality and Reliability Assurance Handbook*, Public. 4115.12, Washington, DC, 1965.

EPILOGUE
OPERATIONS MANAGEMENT AND THE FUTURE

The future holds tremendous opportunities and challenges for the field of operations. The nature of these expected developments and their implications for operations managers are briefly described here.

INCREASED INTERNATIONAL COMPETITION

Competition for both worldwide and domestic markets will continue to intensify. Operations managers will see increased pressure on a number of fronts:

Broader points of competition.

- *Productivity:* More output per unit of resource used (labor, capital, facilities, materials) will continue to be important.
- *Cost:* Competition on price will continue to increase and overhead, distribution, and marketing costs will be increasingly scrutinized for ineffective expenditures.
- *Quality:* Quality performance will become increasingly used to segment and capture markets. Public expectations of acceptable quality will rise significantly.
- *Variety:* Options, variants, and customization will become increasingly available and used as a competitive weapon after standard cost and quality levels have been reached in the industry.
- *New outputs:* New offerings will probably become the major point of competition in the future. Higher profits and less threat of competition are available in products and services that, when offered, largely make obsolete the existing offerings (e.g., digital watches, electronic games, word processing, television). Clearly, research and development (R&D) will play a major role here.

CAPITAL SCARCITY

Capital availability will continue to decrease with increasing federal budget deficits, high inflation, and high interest rates. Yet capital will become more

Unprecedented need for capital.

important than ever to remain competitive in the future: for funding new technological production processes, for increased levels of R&D, for modernizing obsolete facilities, and so on. Internally generated working capital will thus become much more important to organizations and purchasing, scrap reduction, and the elimination of all types of waste will receive significantly increased attention.

NEW TECHNOLOGY

The automated office.

New technology will revolutionize organizations. Office automation, word processing, computerized data handling and report generation, and other such technologies will become commonplace in offices and service facilities. In the factory we will find automated facilities, group technology, AS/RS, robots, computer-aided design and manufacturing, MRP, computerized manufacturing information systems, and similar innovations raising quality, increasing productivity, and eliminating scrap and waste. The challenge to operations managers is to learn how to profitably employ these technologies, and at the same time profitably employ the skills of the workforce. Immense retraining will be called for as needs shift between skill categories.

SERVICES

Challenge: service productivity.

The growth of services will continue to gain strength and importance. The need to improve the productivity of these services will pose a major challenge to operations management. Techniques and approaches will have to be developed to handle scheduling problems, quality control, cost constraints, and the myriad of other issues typically faced by operations managers. In some cases, adaptations of manufacturing techniques will suffice; in other situations totally new approaches must be conceived.

INFORMATION

Challenge: reacting quickly to recent events.

The world has grown considerably "smaller" in the last 30 years with the advent of jet travel, telecommunications, satellite relayed telephones, computerized monitoring and information systems, microwave transmission, and so forth. The net effect of this "future shock" on operations management is an increased need for fast responses, on the one hand, and an accelerated rate of impact of distant events on the other. Due to modern technology, as illustrated above, word of increased prices for energy, Supreme Court decisions on hiring, embargoing of scarce materials, increases in the prime interest rate, passage of bills in Congress, or a fall of the dollar against the franc is instantly relayed to operations managers and requires immediate decisions to find alternative sources of supplies, to divert shipments, sell off inventories, and change product mixes.

The result will be a greater need for contingency planning in operations, and an increased importance placed on operations flexibility as compared with efficiency, effectiveness, and capacity. Flexibility will also be an aid in offering output variety to consumers and recipients as the public becomes more educated and selective in the satisfaction of its needs.

COMPUTERS

Computers for rote, massive, and complex tasks.

It is clear that the use of computers will continue to permeate all areas of the organization, especially with the much lower cost of mini- and micro-computers. In general, the computer will continue to take over the rote, clerical tasks; the massive information tasks, and the complex mathematical-statistical tasks that were formerly done poorly, by intuition, or not at all.

Yet, beyond this there will lie a bigger challenge in the use of computers. In addition to the use of minicomputers in organizations for the planning, monitoring, and control of operations within departments, the use of integrated information systems is also expected to increase. The challenge of coordinated planning of outputs by tying together output rates, mixes, quality, costs, materials requirements, workforce needs, and so on demands a *systems* view of the entire organization. Only by tying together multiple data bases within and external to the organization can such an all-encompassing systems view be provided.

Challenge: coordination of large systems.

The continuing role of management.

Such systems will then allow the organization-wide coordination of purchasing, marketing, finance, operations, and personnel, and handling of the repetitive, clerical tasks and the massive data manipulation tasks (such as in accounting). This facilitates coordination, thereby increasing efficiency, but makes little provision for effectiveness. That is, the *management* tasks of goal setting, assessing returns to the organization, evaluating information, and making decisions will not be solved simply through better coordination and more timely information. These will always remain the challenge to management.

APPENDIX A

TABLES

Table A1 Present Value of $1

Period	1%	2%	3%	4%	5%	6%	7%	8%	9%	10%	12%	14%	15%	16%	18%	20%	24%	28%	30%	32%	36%	40%	50%	60%	70%	80%	90%
1	0.990	0.980	0.971	0.962	0.952	0.943	0.935	0.926	0.917	0.909	0.893	0.877	0.870	0.862	0.847	0.833	0.806	0.781	0.769	0.758	0.735	0.714	0.667	0.625	0.588	0.556	0.526
2	0.980	0.961	0.943	0.925	0.907	0.890	0.873	0.857	0.842	0.826	0.797	0.769	0.756	0.743	0.718	0.694	0.650	0.610	0.592	0.574	0.541	0.510	0.444	0.391	0.346	0.309	0.277
3	0.971	0.942	0.915	0.889	0.864	0.840	0.816	0.794	0.772	0.751	0.712	0.675	0.658	0.641	0.609	0.579	0.524	0.477	0.455	0.435	0.398	0.364	0.296	0.244	0.204	0.171	0.146
4	0.961	0.924	0.889	0.855	0.823	0.792	0.763	0.735	0.708	0.683	0.636	0.592	0.572	0.552	0.516	0.482	0.423	0.373	0.350	0.329	0.292	0.260	0.198	0.153	0.120	0.095	0.077
5	0.951	0.906	0.863	0.822	0.784	0.747	0.713	0.681	0.650	0.621	0.567	0.519	0.497	0.476	0.437	0.402	0.341	0.291	0.269	0.250	0.215	0.186	0.132	0.095	0.070	0.053	0.040
6	0.942	0.888	0.838	0.790	0.746	0.705	0.666	0.630	0.596	0.564	0.507	0.456	0.432	0.410	0.370	0.335	0.275	0.227	0.207	0.189	0.158	0.133	0.088	0.060	0.041	0.029	0.021
7	0.933	0.871	0.813	0.760	0.711	0.665	0.623	0.583	0.547	0.513	0.452	0.400	0.376	0.354	0.314	0.279	0.222	0.178	0.159	0.143	0.116	0.095	0.059	0.037	0.024	0.016	0.011
8	0.923	0.853	0.789	0.731	0.677	0.627	0.582	0.540	0.502	0.467	0.404	0.351	0.327	0.305	0.266	0.233	0.179	0.139	0.123	0.108	0.085	0.068	0.039	0.023	0.014	0.009	0.006
9	0.914	0.837	0.766	0.703	0.645	0.592	0.544	0.500	0.460	0.424	0.361	0.308	0.284	0.263	0.226	0.194	0.144	0.108	0.094	0.082	0.063	0.048	0.026	0.015	0.008	0.005	0.003
10	0.905	0.820	0.744	0.676	0.614	0.558	0.508	0.463	0.422	0.386	0.322	0.270	0.247	0.227	0.191	0.162	0.116	0.085	0.073	0.062	0.046	0.035	0.017	0.009	0.005	0.003	0.002
11	0.896	0.804	0.722	0.650	0.585	0.527	0.475	0.429	0.388	0.350	0.287	0.237	0.215	0.195	0.162	0.135	0.094	0.066	0.056	0.047	0.034	0.025	0.012	0.006	0.003	0.002	0.001
12	0.887	0.788	0.701	0.625	0.557	0.497	0.444	0.397	0.356	0.319	0.257	0.208	0.187	0.168	0.137	0.112	0.076	0.052	0.043	0.036	0.025	0.018	0.008	0.004	0.002	0.001	0.001
13	0.879	0.773	0.681	0.601	0.530	0.469	0.415	0.368	0.326	0.290	0.229	0.182	0.163	0.145	0.116	0.093	0.061	0.040	0.033	0.027	0.018	0.013	0.005	0.002	0.001	0.001	0.000
14	0.870	0.758	0.661	0.577	0.505	0.442	0.388	0.340	0.299	0.263	0.205	0.160	0.141	0.125	0.099	0.078	0.049	0.032	0.025	0.021	0.014	0.009	0.003	0.001	0.001	0.000	0.000
15	0.861	0.743	0.642	0.555	0.481	0.417	0.362	0.315	0.275	0.239	0.183	0.140	0.123	0.108	0.084	0.065	0.040	0.025	0.020	0.016	0.010	0.006	0.002	0.001	0.000	0.000	0.000
16	0.853	0.728	0.623	0.534	0.458	0.394	0.339	0.292	0.252	0.218	0.163	0.123	0.107	0.093	0.071	0.054	0.032	0.019	0.015	0.012	0.007	0.005	0.002	0.001	0.000		
17	0.844	0.714	0.605	0.513	0.436	0.371	0.317	0.270	0.231	0.198	0.146	0.108	0.093	0.080	0.060	0.045	0.026	0.015	0.012	0.009	0.005	0.003	0.001	0.000	0.000		
18	0.836	0.700	0.587	0.494	0.416	0.350	0.296	0.250	0.212	0.180	0.130	0.095	0.081	0.069	0.051	0.038	0.021	0.012	0.009	0.007	0.004	0.002	0.001	0.000			
19	0.828	0.686	0.570	0.475	0.396	0.331	0.276	0.232	0.194	0.164	0.116	0.083	0.070	0.060	0.043	0.031	0.017	0.009	0.007	0.005	0.003	0.002	0.000	0.000			
20	0.820	0.673	0.554	0.456	0.377	0.312	0.258	0.215	0.178	0.149	0.104	0.073	0.061	0.051	0.037	0.026	0.014	0.007	0.005	0.004	0.002	0.001	0.000	0.000			
25	0.780	0.610	0.478	0.375	0.295	0.233	0.184	0.146	0.116	0.092	0.059	0.038	0.030	0.024	0.016	0.010	0.005	0.002	0.001	0.001	0.000	0.000					
30	0.742	0.552	0.412	0.308	0.231	0.174	0.131	0.099	0.075	0.057	0.033	0.020	0.015	0.012	0.007	0.004	0.002	0.001	0.000	0.000							
40	0.672	0.453	0.307	0.208	0.142	0.097	0.067	0.046	0.032	0.022	0.011	0.005	0.004	0.003	0.001	0.001	0.000										
50	0.608	0.372	0.228	0.141	0.087	0.054	0.034	0.021	0.013	0.009	0.003	0.001	0.001	0.001	0.000												

Table A2 Present Value of an Annuity of $1

Period	1%	2%	3%	4%	5%	6%	8%	10%	12%	14%	15%	16%	18%	20%	24%	30%	40%	50%
1	0.990	0.980	0.971	0.962	0.952	0.943	0.926	0.909	0.893	0.877	0.870	0.862	0.847	0.833	0.806	0.769	0.714	0.667
2	1.970	1.942	1.914	1.886	1.859	1.833	1.783	1.736	1.690	1.647	1.626	1.605	1.566	1.528	1.457	1.361	1.224	1.111
3	2.941	2.884	2.829	2.775	2.723	2.673	2.577	2.487	2.402	2.322	2.283	2.246	2.174	2.106	1.981	1.816	1.589	1.407
4	3.902	3.808	3.717	3.630	3.546	3.465	3.312	3.170	3.037	2.914	2.855	2.798	2.690	2.589	2.404	2.166	1.849	1.605
5	4.853	4.713	4.580	4.452	4.330	4.212	3.993	3.791	3.605	3.433	3.352	3.274	3.127	2.991	2.745	2.436	2.035	1.737
6	5.795	5.601	5.417	5.242	5.076	4.917	4.623	4.355	4.111	3.889	3.784	3.685	3.498	3.326	3.020	2.643	2.168	1.824
7	6.728	6.472	6.230	6.002	5.786	5.582	5.206	4.868	4.564	4.288	4.160	4.039	3.812	3.605	3.242	2.802	2.263	1.883
8	7.652	7.325	7.020	6.733	6.463	6.210	5.747	5.335	4.968	4.639	4.487	4.344	4.078	3.837	3.421	2.925	2.331	1.922
9	8.566	8.162	7.786	7.435	7.108	6.802	6.247	5.759	5.328	4.946	4.772	4.607	4.303	4.031	3.566	3.019	2.379	1.948
10	9.741	8.983	8.530	8.111	7.722	7.360	6.710	6.145	5.650	5.216	5.019	4.833	4.494	4.192	3.682	3.092	2.414	1.965
11	10.368	9.787	9.253	8.760	8.306	7.887	7.139	6.495	5.938	5.453	5.234	5.029	4.656	4.327	3.776	3.147	2.438	1.977
12	11.255	10.575	9.954	9.385	8.863	8.384	7.536	6.814	6.194	5.660	5.421	5.197	4.793	4.439	3.851	3.190	2.456	1.985
13	12.134	11.348	10.635	9.986	9.394	8.853	7.904	7.103	6.424	5.842	5.583	5.342	4.910	4.533	3.912	3.223	2.468	1.990
14	13.004	12.106	11.296	10.563	9.899	9.295	8.244	7.367	6.628	6.002	5.724	5.468	5.008	4.611	3.962	3.249	2.478	1.993
15	13.865	12.849	11.938	11.118	10.380	9.712	8.559	7.606	6.811	6.142	5.847	5.576	5.092	4.676	4.001	3.268	2.484	1.995
16	14.718	13.578	12.561	11.652	10.838	10.106	8.851	7.824	6.974	6.265	5.954	5.668	5.162	4.730	4.033	3.283	2.488	1.997
17	15.562	14.292	13.166	12.166	11.274	10.477	9.122	8.022	7.120	6.373	6.047	5.749	5.222	4.775	4.059	3.295	2.492	1.998
18	16.398	14.992	13.754	12.659	11.690	10.828	9.372	8.201	7.250	6.467	6.128	5.818	5.273	4.812	4.080	3.304	2.494	1.999
19	17.226	15.678	14.324	13.134	12.085	11.158	9.604	8.365	7.366	6.550	6.198	5.878	5.316	4.844	4.097	3.311	2.496	1.999
20	18.046	16.351	14.877	13.590	12.462	11.470	9.818	8.514	7.469	6.623	6.259	5.929	5.353	4.870	4.110	3.316	2.497	1.999
21	18.857	17.011	15.415	14.029	12.821	11.764	10.017	8.649	7.562	6.687	6.312	5.973	5.384	4.891	4.121	3.320	2.498	2.000
22	19.660	17.658	15.937	14.451	13.163	12.042	10.201	8.772	7.645	6.743	6.359	6.011	5.410	4.909	4.130	3.323	2.498	2.000
23	20.456	18.292	16.444	14.857	13.489	12.303	10.371	8.883	7.718	6.792	6.399	6.044	5.432	4.924	4.137	3.325	2.499	2.000
24	21.213	18.914	16.936	15.247	13.799	12.550	10.529	8.985	7.784	6.835	6.434	6.073	5.451	4.937	4.143	3.327	2.499	2.000
25	22.023	19.523	17.413	15.622	14.094	12.783	10.675	9.077	7.843	6.873	6.464	6.097	5.467	4.918	4.147	3.329	2.499	2.000
26	22.795	20.121	17.877	15.933	14.375	13.003	10.810	9.161	7.896	6.906	6.491	6.118	5.480	4.956	4.151	3.330	2.500	2.000
27	23.560	20.707	18.327	16.330	14.643	13.211	10.935	9.237	7.943	6.935	6.514	6.136	5.492	4.964	4.154	3.331	2.500	2.000
28	24.316	21.281	18.764	16.663	14.898	13.406	11.051	9.307	7.984	6.961	6.534	6.152	5.502	4.970	4.157	3.331	2.500	2.000
29	25.066	21.814	19.188	16.984	15.141	13.591	11.158	9.370	8.022	6.983	6.551	6.166	5.510	4.975	4.159	3.332	2.500	2.000
30	25.808	22.396	19.600	17.292	15.372	13.765	11.258	9.427	8.055	7.003	6.566	6.177	5.517	4.979	4.160	3.332	2.500	2.000
40	32.835	27.355	23.115	19.793	17.159	15.046	11.925	9.779	8.244	7.105	6.642	6.234	5.548	4.997	4.166	3.333	2.500	2.000
50	39.196	31.424	25.730	21.482	18.256	15.762	12.233	9.915	8.304	7.133	6.660	6.246	5.554	4.999	4.167	3.333	2.500	2.000

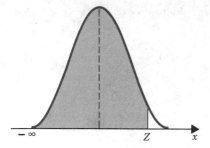

Table A3 Area Under the Normal Distribution

Z	0.00	0.01	0.02	0.03	0.04	0.05	0.06	0.07	0.08	0.09
0.0	0.5000	0.5040	0.5080	0.5120	0.5160	0.5199	0.5239	0.5279	0.5319	0.5359
0.1	0.5398	0.5438	0.5478	0.5517	0.5557	0.5596	0.5636	0.5675	0.5714	0.5753
0.2	0.5793	0.5832	0.5871	0.5910	0.5948	0.5987	0.6026	0.6064	0.6103	0.6141
0.3	0.6179	0.6217	0.6255	0.6293	0.6331	0.6368	0.6406	0.6443	0.6480	0.6517
0.4	0.6554	0.6591	0.6628	0.6664	0.6700	0.6736	0.6772	0.6808	0.6844	0.6879
0.5	0.6915	0.6950	0.6985	0.7019	0.7054	0.7088	0.7123	0.7157	0.7190	0.7224
0.6	0.7257	0.7291	0.7324	0.7357	0.7389	0.7422	0.7454	0.7486	0.7517	0.7549
0.7	0.7580	0.7611	0.7642	0.7673	0.7704	0.7734	0.7764	0.7794	0.7823	0.7852
0.8	0.7881	0.7910	0.7939	0.7967	0.7995	0.8023	0.8051	0.8078	0.8106	0.8133
0.9	0.8159	0.8186	0.8212	0.8238	0.8264	0.8289	0.8315	0.8340	0.8365	0.8389
1.0	0.8413	0.8438	0.8461	0.8485	0.8508	0.8531	0.8554	0.8577	0.8599	0.8621
1.1	0.8643	0.8665	0.8686	0.8708	0.8729	0.8749	0.8770	0.8790	0.8810	0.8830
1.2	0.8849	0.8869	0.8888	0.8907	0.8925	0.8944	0.8962	0.8980	0.8997	0.9015
1.3	0.9032	0.9049	0.9066	0.9082	0.9099	0.9115	0.9131	0.9147	0.9162	0.9177
1.4	0.9192	0.9207	0.9222	0.9236	0.9251	0.9265	0.9279	0.9292	0.9306	0.9319
1.5	0.9332	0.9345	0.9357	0.9370	0.9382	0.9394	0.9406	0.9418	0.9429	0.9441
1.6	0.9452	0.9463	0.9474	0.9484	0.9495	0.9505	0.9515	0.9525	0.9535	0.9545
1.7	0.9554	0.9564	0.9573	0.9582	0.9591	0.9599	0.9608	0.9616	0.9625	0.9633
1.8	0.9641	0.9649	0.9656	0.9664	0.9671	0.9678	0.9686	0.9693	0.9699	0.9706
1.9	0.9713	0.9719	0.9726	0.9732	0.9738	0.9744	0.9750	0.9756	0.9761	0.9767
2.0	0.9772	0.9778	0.9783	0.9788	0.9793	0.9798	0.9803	0.9808	0.9812	0.9817
2.1	0.9821	0.9826	0.9830	0.9834	0.9838	0.9842	0.9846	0.9850	0.9854	0.9857
2.2	0.9861	0.9864	0.9868	0.9871	0.9875	0.9878	0.9881	0.9884	0.9887	0.9890
2.3	0.9893	0.9896	0.9898	0.9901	0.9904	0.9906	0.9909	0.9911	0.9913	0.9916
2.4	0.9918	0.9920	0.9922	0.9925	0.9927	0.9929	0.9931	0.9932	0.9934	0.9936
2.5	0.9938	0.9940	0.9941	0.9943	0.9945	0.9946	0.9948	0.9949	0.9951	0.9952
2.6	0.9953	0.9955	0.9956	0.9957	0.9959	0.9960	0.9961	0.9962	0.9963	0.9964
2.7	0.9965	0.9966	0.9967	0.9968	0.9969	0.9970	0.9971	0.9972	0.9973	0.9974
2.8	0.9974	0.9975	0.9976	0.9977	0.9977	0.9978	0.9979	0.9979	0.9980	0.9981
2.9	0.9981	0.9982	0.9982	0.9983	0.9984	0.9984	0.9985	0.9985	0.9986	0.9986
3.0	0.9987	0.9987	0.9987	0.9988	0.9988	0.9989	0.9989	0.9989	0.9990	0.9990
3.1	0.9990	0.9991	0.9991	0.9991	0.9992	0.9992	0.9992	0.9992	0.9993	0.9993
3.2	0.9993	0.9993	0.9994	0.9994	0.9994	0.9994	0.9994	0.9995	0.9995	0.9995
3.3	0.9995	0.9995	0.9995	0.9996	0.9996	0.9996	0.9996	0.9996	0.9996	0.9997
3.4	0.9997	0.9997	0.9997	0.9997	0.9997	0.9997	0.9997	0.9997	0.9997	0.9998

Table A4 Random Numbers

39	73	72	75	37		02	87	98	10	47		93	21	95	97	69		41	91	80	67	59		34	18	04	52	35
79	57	92	36	59		89	74	39	82	15		08	58	94	34	74		21	89	11	47	99		11	20	99	45	18

Table A4 Random Numbers

```
39 73 72 75 37   02 87 98 10 47   93 21 95 97 69   41 91 80 67 59   34 18 04 52 35
79 57 92 36 59   89 74 39 82 15   08 58 94 34 74   21 89 11 47 99   11 20 99 45 18
22 45 44 84 11   87 80 61 65 31   09 71 91 74 25   95 18 94 06 97   27 37 83 28 71
80 45 67 93 82   59 73 19 85 23   53 33 65 97 21   97 08 31 55 73   10 65 81 92 59
53 58 47 70 93   66 56 45 65 79   45 56 20 19 47   69 26 88 86 13   59 71 74 17 32

26 72 39 27 67   53 77 57 68 93   60 61 97 22 61   41 47 10 25 03   87 63 93 95 17
43 00 65 98 50   45 60 33 01 07   98 99 46 50 47   91 94 14 63 62   08 61 74 51 69
52 70 05 48 34   56 65 05 61 86   90 92 10 70 80   80 06 54 18 47   08 52 85 08 40
15 33 59 05 28   22 87 26 07 47   86 96 98 29 06   67 72 77 63 99   89 85 84 46 06
85 13 99 24 44   49 18 09 79 49   74 16 32 23 02   59 40 24 13 75   42 29 72 23 19

87 03 04 79 88   08 13 13 85 51   55 34 57 72 69   02 89 08 16 94   85 53 83 29 95
52 06 79 79 45   82 63 18 27 44   69 66 92 19 09   87 18 15 70 07   37 79 49 12 38
46 72 60 18 77   55 66 12 62 11   08 99 55 64 57   98 83 71 70 15   89 09 39 59 24
47 21 61 88 32   27 80 30 21 60   10 92 35 36 12   10 08 58 07 04   76 62 16 48 68
12 73 73 99 12   49 99 57 94 82   96 88 57 17 91   47 90 56 37 31   71 82 13 50 41

63 62 06 34 41   79 53 36 02 95   20 26 36 31 62   58 24 97 14 97   95 06 70 99 00
78 47 23 53 90   79 93 96 38 63   31 56 34 19 19   47 83 75 51 33   30 62 38 20 46
87 68 62 15 43   97 48 72 66 48   98 40 07 17 66   23 05 09 51 80   59 78 11 52 49
47 60 92 10 77   26 97 05 73 51   24 33 45 77 48   69 81 84 09 29   93 22 70 45 80
56 88 87 59 41   06 87 37 78 48   01 31 60 10 27   35 07 79 71 53   28 99 52 01 41

22 17 68 65 84   87 02 22 57 51   56 27 09 24 43   21 78 55 09 82   72 61 88 73 61
19 36 27 59 46   39 77 32 77 09   48 13 93 55 96   41 92 45 71 51   09 18 25 58 94
16 77 23 02 77   28 06 24 25 93   00 06 41 41 20   14 36 59 25 47   54 45 17 24 89
78 43 76 71 61   97 67 63 99 61   58 76 17 14 86   59 53 11 52 21   66 04 18 72 87
03 28 28 26 08   69 30 16 09 05   27 55 10 24 92   28 04 67 53 44   95 23 00 84 47

04 31 17 21 56   33 73 99 19 87   74 13 39 35 22   68 95 23 92 35   36 63 70 35 33
61 06 98 03 91   87 14 77 43 96   76 51 94 84 86   13 79 93 37 55   98 16 04 41 67
23 68 35 26 00   99 53 93 61 28   79 57 95 13 91   09 61 87 25 21   56 20 11 32 44
15 39 25 70 99   93 86 52 77 65   77 31 61 95 46   20 44 90 32 64   26 99 76 75 63
58 71 96 30 24   18 46 23 34 27   48 38 75 93 29   73 37 32 04 05   60 82 29 20 25

93 22 53 64 39   07 10 63 76 35   81 83 83 04 49   77 45 85 50 51   79 88 01 97 30
78 76 58 54 74   92 38 70 96 92   92 79 43 89 79   29 18 94 51 23   14 85 11 47 23
61 81 31 96 82   00 57 25 60 59   48 40 35 94 22   72 65 71 08 86   50 03 42 99 36
42 88 07 10 05   24 98 65 63 21   64 71 06 21 66   89 37 20 70 01   61 65 70 22 12
77 94 30 05 39   28 10 99 00 27   06 94 76 10 08   81 30 15 39 14   81 83 17 16 33

39 65 76 45 45   19 90 69 64 61   94 61 09 43 62   20 21 14 68 86   84 95 48 46 45
73 71 23 70 90   65 97 60 12 11   34 85 52 05 09   21 43 01 72 73   14 93 87 81 40
72 20 47 33 84   51 67 47 97 19   53 16 71 13 81   59 97 50 99 52   24 62 20 42 31
75 17 25 69 17   17 95 21 78 58   88 46 38 03 58   72 68 49 29 31   75 70 16 08 24
37 48 79 88 74   63 52 06 34 30   65 88 69 58 39   07 29 73 72 38   51 28 84 89 47
```

Table A5 Acceptance Sampling Table*

AQL / LTPD	4.51 to 5.60	5.61 to 7.10	7.11 to 9.00	9.01 to 11.2	11.3 to 14.0	14.1 to 18.0	18.1 to 22.4
0.451 to 0.560	80	60	60	50	15	15	10
	1	1	1	1	0	0	0
0.561 to 0.710	100	80	50	50	40	10	10
	2	1	1	1	1	0	0
0.711 to 0.900	100	80	50	40	40	30	7
	2	2	1	1	1	1	0
0.901 to 1.12	120	80	60	40	30	30	25
	3	2	2	1	1	1	1
1.13 to 1.40	150	100	60	50	30	25	25
	4	3	2	2	1	1	1
1.41 to 1.80	200	120	80	50	40	25	20
	6	4	3	2	1	1	1
1.81 to 2.24	300	150	100	60	40	30	20
	10	6	4	3	2	2	1
2.25 to 2.80	n	250	120	70	50	30	25
	c	10	6	4	3	2	2
2.81 to 3.55	n	n	200	100	60	40	25
	c	c	10	6	4	3	2
3.56 to 4.50	n	n	n	150	80	50	30
	c	c	c	10	6	4	3
4.51 to 5.60	n	n	n	n	120	60	40
	c	c	c	c	10	6	4

*Entries are $\frac{n}{c}$ and assume $\alpha = 0.05$ and $\beta = 0.10$. (*Source:* J. L. Riggs, *Production Systems: Planning, Analysis, and Control,* 2nd ed., New York: Wiley, 1976. Reproduced by permission.)

APPENDIX B

PROBABILITY AND STATISTICS

This appendix is intended to serve as a brief review of the probability and statistics concepts which are used in this text. Students who require more review than is available in this appendix should consult one of the texts listed in the bibliography.

Probability

Uncertainty in organizational decision making is a fact of life. Demand for an organization's output is uncertain. The number of employees who will be absent from work on any given day is uncertain. The price of a stock tomorrow is uncertain. Whether it will snow or not tomorrow is uncertain. Each of these *events* is more or less uncertain. We do not know exactly whether the event will occur or not, nor do we know the value that a particular *random variable* (e.g., price of stock, demand for output, number of absent employees) will assume.

In common terminology we reflect our uncertainty with such phrases as "not very likely," "not a chance," "for sure," "hasn't got a snowball's chance in hell." But, while these descriptive terms communicate one's feeling regarding the chances of a particular event's occurrence, they simply are not precise enough to allow analysis of chances and odds.

Simply put, *probability* is a number on a scale used to measure uncertainty. The range of the probability scale is from 0 to 1, with a 0 probability indicating that an event has no chance of occurring and a probability of 1 indicating that an event is absolutely sure to occur. The more likely an event is to occur, the closer its probability is to 1. This probability definition, which is general, needs to be further augmented to illustrate the various types of probability that decision makers can assess. There are three types of probability that the operations manager should be aware of:

- Subjective probability.
- Logical probability.
- Experimental probability.

Subjective Probability

Subjective probability is based on individual information and belief. Different individuals will assess the chances of a particular event in different ways, and the same individual may assess different probabilities for the same event at different points in time. For example, one need only watch the blackjack players in Las Vegas to see that different people assess probabilities in different ways. Also, daily trading in the stock market is the result of different probability assessments by those trading. The sellers sell because it is their belief that the probability of appreciation is low and the buyers buy because they believe that the probability of appreciation is high. Clearly, these different probability assessments are about the same events.

Logical Probability

Logical probability is based on physical phenomena and on symmetry of events. For example, the probability of drawing a three of hearts from a standard 52-card playing deck is 1/52. Each card has an equal likelihood of being drawn. In flipping a coin, the chance of "heads" is .50. That is, since there are only two possible outcomes from one flip of a coin, each event has one-half the total probability, or .50. A final example is the roll of a single die. Since each of the six sides are identical, the chance of any one event occurring (i.e., a 6, a 3, etc.) is 1/6.

Experimental Probability

Experimental probability is based on frequency of occurrence of events in trial situations. For example, in determining the appropriate inventory level to maintain in the raw material inventory, we might measure and record the demand each day from that inventory. If, in 100 days, demand was 20 units on 16 days, the probability of demand equaling 20 units is said to be .16 (i.e., 16/100). In general, experimental probability of an event is given by

$$\text{probability of event} = \frac{\text{number of times event occurred}}{\text{total number of trials}}$$

Both logical and experimental probability are referred to as *objective* probability in contrast to the individually assessed subjective probability. Each of these are based on, and directly *computed* from, hard facts.

Event Relationships and Probability Laws

Events are classified in a number of ways that allow us to further state rules for probability computations. Some of these classifications and definitions follow.

1. *Independent events:* events are independent if the occurrence of one does not affect the probability of occurrence of the others.
2. *Dependent events:* events are termed dependent if the occurrence of one does affect the probability of occurrence of others.
3. *Mutually exclusive events:* two events are termed mutually exclusive if the occurrence of one precludes the occurrence of the other. For example, in the birth of a child, the events "It's a boy!" and "It's a girl!" are mutually exclusive.
4. *Collectively exhaustive events:* a set of events is termed collectively exhaustive if on any one trial at least one of them must occur. For example, in rolling a die, one of the events 1, 2, 3, 4, 5, or 6 must occur and therefore these six events are collectively exhaustive.

We can also define the union and intersection of two events. Consider two events A and B. The *union* of A and B includes all outcomes in A or B or in both A and B. For example, in a card game you will win if you draw a diamond or a jack. The union of these two events includes all diamonds (including the jack of diamonds) and the remaining three jacks (hearts, clubs, spades). The *or* in the union is the inclusive

or. That is, in our example you will win with a jack or a diamond or a jack of diamonds (i.e., both events).

The *intersection* of two events includes all outcomes that are members of *both* events. For example, in our previous example of jacks and diamonds, the jack of diamonds is the only outcome contained in both events and is therefore the only member of the intersection of the two events.

Let us now consider the relevant probability laws based on our understanding of the above definitions and concepts. For ease of exposition let us define the following notation:

$P(A)$ = probability that event A will occur

$P(B)$ = probability that event B will occur

If two events are mutually exclusive, then their joint occurrence is impossible. Hence, $P(A \text{ and } B) = 0$ for mutually exclusive events. If the events are not mutually exclusive $P(A \text{ and } B)$ can be computed (as we will see in the next section) and this probability is termed the *joint* probability of A and B. Also, if A and B are not mutually exclusive, then we can also define the *conditional* probability of A *given that B* has already occurred or the conditional probability of B given that A has already occurred. These probabilities are written as $P(A \mid B)$ and $P(B \mid A)$, respectively.

The Multiplication Rule

The joint probability of two events that are not mutually exclusive is found by using the multiplication rule. If the events are independent events the joint probability is given by

$$P(A \text{ and } B) = P(A) \times P(B \mid A) \text{ or } P(B) \times P(A \mid B)$$

If the events are independent, the $P(B \mid A)$ and $P(A \mid B)$ are equal to $P(B)$ and $P(A)$, respectively, and therefore the joint probability is given by

$$P(A \text{ and } B) = P(A) \times P(B)$$

From these two relationships we can find the conditional probability for two dependent events from

$$P(A \mid B) = \frac{P(A \text{ and } B)}{P(B)}$$

and

$$P(B \mid A) = \frac{P(A \text{ and } B)}{P(A)}$$

Also, the $P(A)$ and $P(B)$ can be computed if the events are independent, as

$$P(A) = \frac{P(A \text{ and } B)}{P(B)}$$

and

$$P(B) = \frac{P(A \text{ and } B)}{P(A)}$$

The Addition Rule

The addition rule is used to compute the probability of the union of two events. If two events are mutually exclusive, then $P(A \text{ and } B) = 0$ as we indicated previously. Therefore, the probability of either A or B or both is simply the probability of A or B. This is given by

$$P(A \text{ or } B) = P(A) + P(B)$$

But, if the events are not mutually exclusive, then the probability of A or B is given by

$$P(A \text{ or } B) = P(A) + P(B) - P(A \text{ and } B)$$

We can denote the reasonableness of this expression by looking at the following Venn diagram.

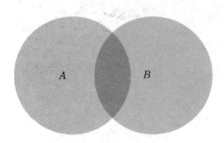

The two circles represent the probabilities of the events A and B, respectively. The shaded area represents the overlap in the events; that is, the intersection of A and B. If we add the area of A and the area of B, we have included the shaded area twice and, therefore, to get the total area of A or B we must subtract one of the areas of the intersection that we have added.

If two events are collectively exhaustive, then the probability of A or B is equal to 1. That is, for two collectively exhaustive events, one or the other or both must occur and therefore the probability of A or B must be 1.

Statistics

Because events are uncertain we must employ special analyses in organizations to ensure that our decisions recognize the chance nature of outcomes. We employ statistics and statistical analysis to

1. Concisely express the tendency and the relative uncertainty of a particular situation.
2. Develop inferences or understanding about a situation.

"Statistics" is an elusive and often misused term. Batting averages, birth weights, student grade points are all statistics. They are *descriptive* statistics. That is, they are quantitative measures of some entity and, for our purposes, can be considered as data about the entity. The second use of the term "statistics" is in relation to the body of theory and methodology used to analyze available evidence (typically quantitative) and to develop inferences from the evidence.

Two descriptive statistics that are often used in presenting information about a population of items (and consequently in inferring some conclusions about the population) are the *mean* and the *variance*. The mean in a population (denoted as μ) can be computed in two ways, each of which gives identical results.

$$\mu = \sum_{j=1}^{k} X_j P(X_j)$$

where k = the number of discrete values that the random variable X_j may assume

X_j = the value of the random variable

$P(X_j)$ is the probability (or relative frequency) of X_j in the population

Also the mean can be computed as

$$\mu = \sum_{i=1}^{N} X_i / N$$

where N = the size of the population (the number of different items in the population)

X_i = the value of the ith item in the population

The mean is also termed the *expected value* of the population and is written as $E(X)$.

The variance of the items in the population measures the dispersion of the items about their mean. It is computed in one of the following two ways.

$$\sigma^2 = \sum_{j=1}^{k} (X_j - \mu)^2 P(X_j)$$

or

$$\sigma^2 = \sum_{i=1}^{N} \frac{(X_i - \mu)^2}{N}$$

The standard deviation, another measure of dispersion, is simply the square root of the variance or

$$\sigma = \sqrt{\sigma^2}$$

Descriptive Versus Inferential Statistics

Organizations are typically faced with decisions for which a large portion of the relevant information is uncertain. In hiring graduates of your university, the "best" prospective employee is unknown to the organization. Also, in introducing a new product, proposing a tax law change to boost employment, drilling an oil well, and so on, the outcomes are always uncertain.

Statistics can often aid management in reducing this uncertainty. This is accomplished through the use of one or the other, or both, of the purposes of statistics. That is, statistics is divided according to its two major purposes: *describing* the major characteristics of a large mass of data and *inferring* something about a large mass of data from a smaller sample drawn from that mass. One methodology summarizes all of the data; the other reasons from a small set of the data to the larger total.

Descriptive statistics uses such measures as the mean, median, mode, range, variance, standard deviation, and such graphical devices as the bar chart and the histogram. When an entire population (a complete set of objects or entities with a common characteristic of interest) of data is summarized by computing such measures as the mean and the variance of a single characteristic, the measure is referred to as a *parameter* of that population. For example, if the population of interest is all female freshmen at your university and all of their ages were used to compute an arithmetic average of 19.2 years, this measure is called a parameter of that population.

Inferential statistics also uses means and variances, but in a different manner. The objective of inferential statistics is to infer the value of a population parameter through the study of a small sample (a portion of a population) from that population. For example, a random sample of 30 freshmen females could produce the information that there is 90 percent certainty that the average age of all freshmen women is between 18.9 and 19.3 years. We do not have as much information as if we had used the entire population, but then we did not have to spend the time to find and determine the age of each member of the population either.

Before considering the logic behind inferential statistics, let us define the primary measures of central tendency and dispersion used in both descriptive and inferential statistics.

Measures of Central Tendency

The central tendency of a group of data represents the average, middle, or "normal" value of the data. The most frequently used measures of central tendency are the *mean*, the *median*, and the *mode*.

The mean of a population of values was given earlier as

$$\mu = \sum_{i=1}^{N} \frac{X_i}{N}$$

where μ = the mean (μ pronounced mu)
X_i = the value of the ith data item
N = the number of data items in the population

The mean of a *sample* of items from a population is given by

$$\overline{X} = \sum_{i=1}^{n} \frac{X_i}{n}$$

where $\overline{X}$ = the sample mean (pronounced X bar)
X_i = the value of ith data item in the sample
n = the number of data items selected in the sample

The *median* is the middle value of a population of data (or sample) where the data are ordered by value. That is, in the following data set

3, 2, 9, 6, 1, 5, 7, 3, 4

4 is the median since (as you can see when we order the data)

1, 2, 3, 3, 4, 5, 6, 7, 9

50 percent of the data values are above 4 and 50 percent below 4. If there are an even number of data items, then the mean of the middle two is the median. For example, if there had also been an 8 in the above data set, the median would be 4.5 [(4 + 5)/2].

The *mode* of a population (or sample) of data items is the value that most frequently occurs. In the above data set, 3 is the mode of the set. A distribution can have more than one mode if there are two or more values that appear with equal frequency.

Measures of Dispersion

Dispersion refers to the scatter around the mean of a distribution of values. Three measures of dispersion are the range, the variance, and the standard deviation.

The *range* is the difference between the highest and the lowest value in the data set, that is, $X_{high} - X_{low}$.

The *variance of a population* of items is given by

$$\sigma^2 = \sum_{i=1}^{N} \frac{(X_i - \mu)^2}{N}$$

where σ^2 = the population variance (pronounced sigma squared)

The *variance of a sample* of items is given by

$$S^2 = \sum_{i=1}^{n} \frac{(X_i - \overline{X})^2}{n}$$

where S^2 = the sample variance

The *standard deviation* is simply the square root of the variance. That is

$$\sigma = \sqrt{\sum_{i=1}^{N} \frac{(X_i - \mu)^2}{N}}$$

and

$$S = \sqrt{\sum_{i=1}^{n} \frac{(X_i - \overline{X})^2}{n}}$$

σ and S are the population and sample standard deviations, respectively.

Inferential Statistics

A basis of inferential statistics is the *interval estimate*. Whenever we infer from partial data to an entire population, we are doing so with some uncertainty in our inference. Specifying an interval estimate (e.g., the average weight is between 10 and 12 pounds) rather than a *point estimate* (e.g., the average weight is 11.3 pounds) simply helps to relate that uncertainty. The interval estimate is not as *precise* as the point estimate.

Inferential statistics uses probability samples where the chance of selection of each item is known. A random sample is one in which each item in the population has an equal chance of selection.

The procedure used to estimate a population mean from a sample is to

1. Select a sample of size n from the population.
2. Compute $\overline{X}$ the mean and S the standard deviation.
3. Compute the precision of the estimate (i.e., the $\pm$ limits around $\overline{X}$ within which the mean μ is believed to exist).

Steps 1 and 2 are straightforward, relying on the equations we have presented in earlier sections. Step 3 deserves elaboration.

The precision of an estimate for a population parameter depends on two things: the standard deviation of the *sampling distribution*, and the confidence you desire to have in the final estimate. Two statistical laws provide the logic behind Step 3.

First, the law of large numbers states that as the size of a sample increases toward infinity, the difference between the estimate of the mean and the true population mean tends toward zero. For practical purposes, a sample of size 30 is assumed to be "large enough" for the sample estimate to be a good estimate of the population mean.

Second, the central limit theorem states that if all possible samples of size n were taken from a population with any distribution, the distribution of the means of those samples would be normally distributed with a mean equal to the population mean and a standard deviation equal to the standard deviation of the population divided by the square root of the sample size. That is, if we took all of the samples of size 100 from the population shown in Figure B1, the sampling distribution would be as shown in Figure B2. The logic behind Step 3 is that

1. Any sample of size n from the population can be considered to be one observation from the sampling distribution with mean $\mu_{\overline{X}} = \mu$ and standard deviation

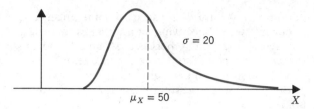

Figure B1 Population distribution.

$$\sigma_{\bar{X}} = \frac{\sigma}{\sqrt{n}}$$

2. From our knowledge of the normal distribution we know that there is a number (see Table A3, Appendix A) associated with each probability value of a normal distribution (e.g., the probability that an item will be within ± 2 standard deviations of the mean of a normal distribution is 95.45 percent. $Z = 2$ in this case).

3. The value of the number Z is simply the number of standard deviations away from the mean that a given point lies. That is, $Z = \frac{(X - \mu)}{\sigma}$, or in the case of Step 3

$$Z = \frac{(\bar{X} - \mu_{\bar{X}})}{\sigma_{\bar{X}}}$$

4. The precision of a sample estimate is given by $Z\sigma_{\bar{X}}$.

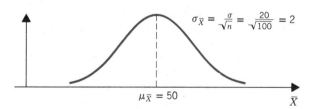

$$\sigma_{\bar{X}} = \frac{\sigma}{\sqrt{n}} = \frac{20}{\sqrt{100}} = 2$$

Figure B2 Sampling distribution.

5. The interval estimate is given by the point estimate $\bar{X}$ plus or minus the precision, or $\bar{X} \pm Z\sigma_{\bar{X}}$.

In the previous example shown in Figures B1 and B2, suppose that the sample estimate $\bar{X}$ was 306 and the population standard deviation σ was 20. Also, suppose that the desired confidence was 90 percent. Since the associated Z value is 1.645, the interval estimate for μ is

$$306 \pm 1.645\left(\frac{20}{\sqrt{100}}\right)$$

or

$$306 \pm 3.29 \quad \text{or} \quad 302.71 \text{ to } 309.29$$

This interval estimate of the population mean is based solely on information derived from a sample and states that the estimator is 90 percent confident that the true mean is between 302.71 and 309.29. There are numerous other sampling methods and other parameters that can be estimated; the student is referred to one of the references for further discussion.

Bibliography

Boot, John C. G., and Cox, Edwin B., *Statistical Analysis for Managerial Decisions*, New York: McGraw-Hill, 1974.

Dixon, W. J., and Massey, F. J., Jr., *Introduction to Statistical Analysis*, 3rd ed., New York: McGraw-Hill, 1969.

Parsons, Robert, *Statistical Analysis: A Decision-Making Approach*, New York: Harper & Row, 1974.

Schlaifer, R., *Introduction to Statistics for Business Decisions*, New York: McGraw-Hill, 1961.

Glossary

ABC (80-20) categorization of elements into three levels of importance.

acceptable quality level (AQL) that percent defective that corresponds to the producer's risk.

activity chart a time-scaled chart showing the activity of an operator and his or her equipment.

aggregate combined into one measure.

ALDEP automated layout design. Program for layout planning.

algorithm a set of logical steps that lead to a solution.

allowance a proportion of normal time allowed for fatigue, maintenance, and so on.

anthropometric human body measurements.

assembly chart a chart showing how parts go together and in what order.

assignment method a specialized type of linear program particularly suitable for allocation on a one-to-one basis.

attributes nonmeasurable characteristics such as number of defects.

automation replacing human sensing with machines.

backordering ordering an item for a customer when a shortage has occurred.

balance delay 1.0 − efficiency.

balanced line a production line whose task times in each station conform to the overall cycle time.

bill of materials the list of materials.

block control a control system for batch production.

brainstorming a process for improving creativity by building new ideas on previous thoughts without evaluation.

breakeven the point of no profit or loss beyond which a profit will accrue.

buffer safety amount.

capital intensive large investment in machinery and equipment as opposed to labor.

causal identifying events which cause other events.

challenger a new item that can do a task economically.

chase demand a policy of producing only the amount demanded in each period.

comfort zone a temperature-humidity zone comfortable to humans.

comparator an element that compares actual performance with expected.

COMSOAL a computerized technique for line balancing.

constraint limitation or restriction on actions.

consumer's risk the chance that a bad lot will be accepted.

containerization use of standard-sized containers for ease in transporting.

control limit the boundary on a control chart beyond which variation is considered to be assignable.

CORELAP computerized relationship layout planning.

corrective maintenance repairing an item when it fails.

correlation the amount of relationship between two variables.

CPM critical path method for project scheduling and control.

CRAFT computerized relative allocation of facilities technique for layout planning.

crashing expediting a project activity.

criteria measures of performance.

critical if delayed, it will delay the project.

critical ratio a method to determine what item to run next on a facility.

CRP capacity requirements planning; also, cash requirements planning.

cycle time the uniform time intervals at which output emerges from the facility.

cyclic a long-term variation about the trend.

dB decibels of noise.

dead load file the file of jobs to be done that are not yet dispatched.

decision tree a set of nodes and branches representing a decision or chance situation.

decouple disengage, isolate.

defender an old item that does a task.

delphi a special form of nominal group analysis.

deviation a difference between two points.

dispatching releasing work orders.

DOLT demand over lead time.

double-declining balance a depreciation method.

DS dynamic slack priority rule.

DSS decision support system.

dummy not real but shows precedence.

duty tours extra long work shifts.

econometric a quantitative approach used in economics.

economies of scale the reduction in unit cost with increasing size.

effectiveness ratio of actual to potential or desired attainment.

effector an element that takes action to modify a system.

efficiency output per unit input.

ELS economic lot size for least cost production runs.

EOQ economic order quantity for least cost purchases.

ergonomics the study of work.

expected value the average or mean.

expediting rushing a job through operations.

exploding detailing each part of a system so its relationship to the other parts can be seen.

exponential smoothing weighting a set of data with exponentially decreasing coefficients.

FCFS first come, first served priority rule.

feedback information returned to an effector for control purposes.

firm order an actual customer order.

fixed position large production operations that are usually treated as projects.

flow process chart (see **operations process chart**).

flow shop a continuous production operation.

FORTRAN a computer language.

Gantt chart a chart with time along the horizontal axis used to display the status of multiple jobs, machines, and so on.

generic generalizable to all such functions.

grapevine the informal communication channel.

heuristic a logically or experimentally derived procedure or rule of thumb.

hierarchy consisting of a set of ordered levels.

holistic considering all of the effects of each part on the whole.

hot jobs rush jobs.

incremental analysis making small changes in each direction to ascertain the effect.

index method an approach for allocating jobs to work centers.

infant mortality early, premature failures.

infinite loading adding work to a resource without regard for its capacity.

interface the region where two elements or functions meet.

intermittent in a stop-and-go fashion, as with customized work.

internal rate of return the rate of interest that makes a future or past return worth the present value.

iterative repetitive, with an improvement each cycle.

job shop an intermittent production operation.

Johnson's rule a technique for sequencing jobs.

kanban a Japanese form of "just-in-time" production.

lead time the delay in obtaining something.

lessee one who leases.

level production a policy of producing the same amount each period.

level zero final products.

life cycle a generalized, four-stage life model.

line the workers who produce the output.

linear straight line.

linear decision rule (LDR) a solution approach to the aggregate scheduling problem that approximates costs with quadratic functions.

load control a control system for careful scheduling of bottleneck resources to maximize their utilization.

load matrix a matrix showing the work between elements.

logistics supplying and maintaining material resources.

lot sizing determining production lot size.

lot tolerance percentage defective (LTPD) that percent defective corresponding to the consumer's risk.

MTM methods time measurement for constructing time standards for jobs.

MAD the mean absolute deviation equal to $\Sigma \,|\, x - \bar{x} \,|\, /n$.

maintainability designing equipment to be easily kept in operating condition.

MALB a computerized technique for line balancing.

management coefficients an aggregate scheduling approach that imitates manager's behavior.

man-machine chart (see **activity chart**).

margin the increase or decrease from one more unit.

master schedule the actual production schedule for items.

mechanization replacing human labor with machines.

memomotion use of a slow-speed camera akin to "time lapse" photography.

MICR magnetic ink character recognition.

microchronometer a high-speed clock.

MIS management information system.

mode common method; most common value.

modularization using standardized components in different combinations to achieve variety in outputs.

monitor sample or tap performance.

Monte Carlo a simulation process using random numbers.

mortality curve a curve on a graph showing the number still alive (working) or the number dead.

motion study analyzing the motions involved in a job in order to simplify and improve it.

MRP material requirements planning for dependent demand inventory.

multiple sampling using more than a single sample in order to reduce sampling costs.

Murphy's law "What can go wrong, will go wrong."

net change calculating only the effect of changes on the master schedule.

net requirement gross requirement less on-hand stock.

nominal group a group in name only which may not meet face to face.

normal time the time an average worker takes when performing normally.

numerical control (NC)   machine processing by coded numerical instructions.

objective function   the criterion in a programming problem.

OCR   optical character recognition.

on-line   connected directly to the computer.

open-loop   no feedback control is used.

operating characteristic   the relationship between percentage defective and probability of acceptance.

operations process chart   a chart showing part specifications and production requirements and times.

organizational fit   a matching against the characteristics of the organization.

OSHA   Occupational Safety and Health Act.

output mix   the proportion of items output in each category.

paced line   a production line where every item must be completed in the same amount of time.

pallet   a platform for stacking materials.

parent item   (see **level zero**).

part-period balancing   a method for lot sizing which attempts to balance holding and setup costs.

payback   a method of evaluating projects.

performance rating   a factor in work measurement indicating how fast the worker performed in comparison with an average worker.

PERT   program evaluation review technique for project scheduling and control.

PICS   IBM's Production-Inventory Control System.

piggyback   truckload trailers hauled on railroad flatcars.

pipelining   sending materials through a pipe.

PPBS   program planning budgeting system.

precedence   the order in which tasks must be completed.

present value   the worth today of something in the future or past.

preventive control   controlling by anticipation rather than by feedback.

preventive maintenance   repairing an item before it fails.

priority rules   policies designed to give good sequences.

producer's risk   the chance that a good lot will be rejected.

product tree   the detailing of assemblies and subassemblies for parent items.

productivity   output per worker-hour.

programming   formulating and/or solving a problem by use of an algorithm.

quadratic   of second degree.

qualitative   not defined by numbers (frequently subjective).

queue   waiting line.

R & D   research and development.

RAND   random priority rule.

random   unpredictable, occurring by chance.

random number   a number occurring purely by chance.

random sample   a sample in which every element has an equal chance of being selected.

regeneration   recalculating the entire master schedule on a regular basis.

regression   a mathematical equation fit to a set of data.

reliability   the chance that an item will work over a given period of time.

representative number   a number corresponding to a point in a distribution.

route sheet   a chart describing each operation, the responsible department, the equipment needed, and the setup and running times.

routing   finding a best route between stops.

safety stock inventory stock to protect against a shortage.

Scanlon plan a group incentive plan.

seasonal a regular variation during the period.

sequencing determining the best sequence for work orders.

service level fraction of time demand can be filled from stock.

setup the process of preparing for an action.

shrink wrap a plastic film for holding and protecting pallet loads.

simplification attempting to eliminate portions of elements.

simulation an imitation of reality with a model.

Simo chart a time-scaled chart showing the simultaneous activities of each of a worker's hands.

slack unutilized.

slurry a liquefied mixture.

smoothing constant alpha, a value between 0 and 1 which weights the importance of the last datum in exponential smoothing.

snap-back timing resetting the stopwatch to zero after each work element is measured.

software computer programs.

sole source using only one supplier.

SOT shortest operation time priority rule.

SS static slack priority rule.

staff the workers who support the line workers.

staging areas places for accumulating materials and resources around a fixed position project.

standard time normal time plus allowances.

standardization making every output or element the same so as to improve efficiency and reduce costs.

stockout running out of material, a shortage.

stretched-S (see **life cycle**).

suboptimize to optimize one part of a system but not, perhaps, the entire system.

sum-of-year's digits a depreciation method.

sunk cost a past cost that cannot be recovered.

surrogate an element used in place of another.

synergism parts working together to form more than the sum of each independently.

synthesis putting together or combining.

tactical midlevel operations, not strategic or global, which is typically a policy level.

therblig a small motion.

throughput time the amount of time to go through an operation.

time-phasing listing the actions to be taken at the times that are required when considering their lead times.

time study analyzing a job to determine performance standards for it.

TMU time measurement units of 0.00001 hour.

TPOP time-phased order points for statistical inventory control.

transient not yet in steady-state motion.

transportation method a special type of linear program particularly useful in analyzing distribution problems.

trend the average long-run change.

two-bin a simple perceptual inventory system based on TPOP.

unit load items combined into one standard size.

unitization applying the unit load principle.

UPC Universal Product Code to identify the producer and product.

value analysis analysis of an output's function to find a less expensive alternative.

variance   deviation from standard.

Venn diagram   a pictorial schematic of event probabilities.

weighted average   the average of a set of data in which some elements are treated as more important than other elements.

work sampling   a random sampling approach to time study.

ZBB   Zero-based budgeting.

INDEX